Centre for Mediterranean and Near East
Trinity College Dublin

Ancient Rome: The Archaeology of the Eternal City

edited by
Jon Coulston and Hazel Dodge

Oxford University School of Archaeology
Monograph 54

Published by
Oxford University School of Archaeology
Institute of Archaeology
Beaumont Street
Oxford OX1 2PG

Typeset by
M.C. Bishop

Distributed by
Oxbow Books
Park End Place, Oxford OX1 1HN

ISBN 0 947816 54 2 Hb
0 947816 55 0 Pb

A CIP record for this book is available from the British Library

Printed in Great Britain at the Alden Press, Oxford

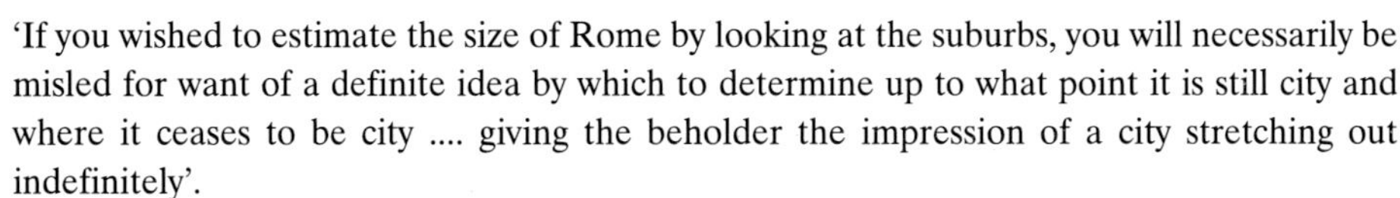

'If you wished to estimate the size of Rome by looking at the suburbs, you will necessarily be misled for want of a definite idea by which to determine up to what point it is still city and where it ceases to be city .... giving the beholder the impression of a city stretching out indefinitely'.

Dionysius of Harlicarnassus, *Roman Antiquities* 4.13-15

'The barbarians....can be left in peace, their part in the destruction of Rome being hardly worth considering when compared with the guilt of others. By "others" I mean the Romans themselves, of the Imperial, Byzantine, Mediaeval, and Renaissance periods.'

R. Lanciani, *The Destruction of Ancient Rome*, London, 1899, 9.

'Yet at the centre of the metropolis, hemmed in by an ever-expanding ring of gruesome suburban estates, the dream of a grand and tranquil civilisation could still become fleeting reality. There are capitals more efficient, more cosmopolitan than Rome; there are cities with brighter nightlife, better bookstores, superior theatres, more efficient telephones, more industrious bank clerks, less traffic and fewer thieves of all kinds. None, however, can ever grant the human heart the subtle and infusing pleasure that you find here.'

M. Sheridan, *Romans. Their Lives and Times*, London, 1994, 243.

List of Contributors

Greg Aldrete
Department of History, University of Wisconsin-Green Bay

Neil Christie
School of Archaeological Studies, University of Leicester

Kathleen Coleman
Department of the Classics, Harvard University

Tim Cornell
School of History, Manchester University

Jon Coulston
School of Greek, Latin and Ancient History, University of St Andrews

Janet DeLaine
Department of Archaeology, University of Reading

Hazel Dodge
School of Classics, Trinity College Dublin

David Mattingly
School of Archaeological Studies, University of Leicester

John Patterson
Magdalene College Cambridge

Hugh Petter
Robert Adam Architects, London

Simon Price
Lady Margaret Hall Oxford

Christopher Smith
School of Greek, Latin and Ancient History, University of St Andrews

Susan Walker
Department of Greek and Roman Antiquities, The British Museum

Peter Wiseman
Department of Classics, University of Exeter

Contents

Editors' Preface

This book comprises chapters on different aspects of the city's development and history and is based on the most up-to-date original research by leading experts in the field. The idea for the volume originated in a conference on the City of Rome, held at Rewley House in Oxford (November 1993). However, the object of the exercise was never to produce mere conference proceedings, but to assemble a series of chronological and thematic studies which together provide an integrated view of Rome's archaeology. The project has taken many years to mature, but as a result it has been possible to coincide both with celebration of the millennium and the completion of the *Lexicon Topographicum Urbis Romae*. The former has led to a massive amount of new archaeological work in the city, which in due course will create a wave of new publications. The *Lexicon* is a truly monumental achievement of Margareta Steinby and her collaborators which permeates this volume.

As with any project of this kind, debts are owed to many. We would like to thank the contributors, most of who spoke at the original conference, for their patience and cheerful co-operation in the production of this book. Help, support and advice was freely given by both our Departments and we would particularly like to thank Brian McGing and Christine Morris (Trinity College Dublin), and Christopher Smith and Greg Woolf (St Andrews). Thanks are due to Maggie Herdman and the Department for Continuing Education, Oxford University, for hosting the original conference. Barry Cunliffe has been very supportive on behalf of the Committee for Archaeology, Oxford University.

Emma Saunders and Stuart Gallagher provided major editorial assistance, and their enthusiasm and good-natured willingness to work long hours contributed immeasurably to the final result. Some referencing work was also carried out by Con Murphy. Compilation and checking for the research bibliography was helped by Catherine Bruen, Stuart Gallagher and Sian McGirven. We are particularly grateful to Hugh Petter for providing the '*Roma Capitale*' section. The cheerful involvement of all these people made the overall task much lighter.

We owe a major debt of gratitude to Mike Bishop for his preparation of the book for publication; as well as providing much valuable, general advice, he produced the camera-ready copy, finessed the illustrations, and was responsible for the computer-generation of many of the maps. David Brown of Oxbow Books ensured the swift turnaround between final submission and publication.

Trinity College Dublin has aided the project in many ways. The Centre for Mediterranean and Near Eastern Studies made a major contribution by very generously providing funds for editorial support as did the Arts and Social Sciences Benefactions Fund, the latter allowing the transfer of funds from another award. The Provost of Trinity College, Professor Tom Mitchell, gave financial support from the Provost's Fund for the production of illustrations.

The following institutions kindly granted permission for the reproduction of illustrations from their publications: Cambridge University Press, Michigan University Press, Yale University Press.

Last but by no means least, Peter Wiseman read and commented on the overall manuscript at a late stage and contributed his delightful introduction to the book.

Jon Coulston *Hazel Dodge*

September 2000

Preface: A Bird's-Eye View

T. P. Wiseman

'How great Rome was, her very ruins tell.' *Roma quanta fuit ipsa ruina docet* – but the medieval proverb no longer applies. Rome has become great again, or at least big, in the modern style of urban sprawl and air pollution. That, however, in the time-scale of the proverbially eternal city, is a very recent phenomenon. The thirteen centuries of papal Rome, which fall between the last two chapters in this book, saw a city which never outgrew, or even filled, the space enclosed by Aurelian's wall. The wall was last used for defence, and last breached by an invader, on 20 September 1870, only five generations ago.

A remarkable photograph taken about 1910 (Fig. 1) preserves the moment when the impact of modernisation was just beginning to be visible; the quintessentially modern medium of air photography shows us the Rome of Henry James. It is an image which neatly encapsulates the chronological span of this book. To the north-west **[1]**, development of the Prati – the meadows between the Vatican and the Tiber – is proceeding behind the great square bulk of the Palazzo di Giustizia, completed in 1910 (*Petter 346, Fig. 13.20*). About four miles upstream **[2]**, the point where the meanders of the Tiber turn south-west marks the site of 'fortified Antemnae' (fig. 2; Virgil *Aeneid* 7.631), Rome's nearest Iron-Age neighbour, supposedly conquered and colonised by Romulus.

Let us explore this Rome of 1910. Coming, like good Anglo-Saxons, from the north, we cross the river at Ponte Molle **[3]**, the Milvian Bridge where Constantine defeated Maxentius and his praetorians (*Coulston 99*) in 312 and saw the fateful sign in the sky. The road that leads to the city in that bold straight line is the Via Flaminia, built in 220 BC, and rebuilt by Augustus, to take Rome's armies to the Adriatic and the north. At the time of the photograph, it was

> a tramwayed suburban street delightfully encumbered with wide-horned oxen drawing heavy wagon-loads of grain, donkeys pulling carts laden with vegetables, and children and hens and dogs playing their several parts in a perspective through which one would like to continue indefinitely. (Howells 1908, 147)

The moment is precisely defined: modernity is the tramway, and the immemorial ox-carts (*compare Delaine Fig. 6.11*) are not yet motorised.

The first bridge, the new Ponte Margherita (named for Italy's first queen), marks the line of Aurelian's wall. Inside the gate, at Piazza del Popolo (*Coleman 214, Fig. 9.4*), Flaminius' road becomes the Via del Corso. It continues dead straight to Piazza Venezia, identifiable by the bright new General Insurance Building, completed in 1907. The Monument to Vittorio Emanuele (*Petter 344, Fig. 13.17*) is still mostly under scaffolding and therefore mercifully unobtrusive. The dark foliage below to the left is the garden of Palazzo Caffarelli, on the site of the Capitoline temple of Jupiter Optimus Maximus (*Smith 27*). Directly to the east, at the edge of the photograph **[4]**, is the Roman Forum.

Fig. 1: 'Rome and the Tiber: from an airship'. Cervesato 1913, 258. The numbers are keyed in the text, emboldened in square brackets.

More clearly visible **[5]** is the Quirinal Palace, seat of the popes until 1870 and thereafter of the kings, and then presidents, of united Italy. It is named after the hill of Quirinus, god of the Quirites, the Roman citizen body. Above that **[6]**, more new development: the smart hotels of Via Veneto on what used to be the Villa Ludovisi, and before that the imperial Horti Sallustiani (*Patterson 263*). Aurelian's wall still defines the city. The Porta Pinciana, vainly attacked by Vitigis' Goths in AD 537 (*Christie 323*), is where the ancient Via Salaria, the 'salt way' older than Rome itself, came up from the Tiber flood-plain to cross the high ground before descending to the Anio valley at Antemnae (Fig. 2). Conspicuous to the left, in splendid isolation, stands the Villa Medici, on the site of Lucullus' gardens (*Patterson 263*), where the empress Messallina met her wretched end in AD 48.

Now let us take another walk, this time from the south. At the bottom left **[7]**, the street grid for the Testaccio district is being laid out. The second line of blocks in from the river marks the site of the Porticus Aemilia (*Cornell 51, Figs. 3.8, 3.9*). To the right, the Aventine cliff is shaded by the morning sun, making invisible one of the surviving stretches of the fourth-century BC republican city wall (Fig. 2; *Cornell 45, Fig. 3.1*). A minor gate led to a street that has never gone

Fig. 2: Map of the environs of Rome with the 'Servian Wall' indicated.

out of use **[8]**, called Via del Priorato at the time the photograph was taken. Going up past the new Benedictine seminary of S. Anselmo, built in 1900, we turn right on to another Roman-medieval-modern street, Via di S. Sabina. The fifth-century church itself (*Christie 320, and Fig. 12.3*) is on the left, by a little piazza with a park beyond. Then we go down to the right on the line of the Clivus Publicius, built by the plebeian aediles in 241 BC, to where the starting-gates of the Circus Maximus stood (*Coleman 211*). In 1910, the site is occupied by the Rome gasworks. Just beyond **[9]**, the trees and the new path for tourists mark the western corner of the Palatine, site of the eighth-century BC hut village (*Smith 23, Fig. 2.5*), and also of the Lupercal, where the flooded Tiber deposited the twins for the she-wolf to suckle. The house of Augustus and his temple of Apollo (*Walker 62–63, Fig. 4.1*) are just beyond the edge of the picture.

Now look left, at this level, to the bridge below the island (Ponte Rotto, replacing the Roman Pons Aemilius). The riverside buildings have been cleared for the new *lungotevere* embankment, which enables us to see the rectangular second-century BC temple of Portunus (*Cornell 49, and Fig. 3.3*). Now up to the left along the embankment: opposite the island, just a little away from the river, are the trees of the garden of Palazzo Corsini, built into the Theatre of Marcellus (*Walker 63, Fig. 4.3; Coleman 223, Figs. 9.6, 9.7*). To the left again, the new Synagogue (1874) stands out, and beyond it the redevelopment of the demolished Ghetto. Due north from that, in the middle of the medieval Campo Marzio – and probably used by the photographer as his central focus – is the great dome of Hadrian's Pantheon. Due north again, at the narrowest point between the Tiber and the Corso, is what looks like another, smaller, dome. In fact, it is the roof of the concert hall that was built in 1907 on top of Augustus' Mausoleum (*Walker 69, Figs. 4.8, 4.9*).

One last item may be pointed out. It is due west of the Pantheon, but easiest to find by crossing the river from the Palazzo di Giustizia. The bridge – named after King Umberto I, assassinated in July 1900 – leads via a broad new street to the top end of Piazza Navona, that jewel of Baroque Rome which preserves the shape of Domitian's stadium (*Coleman 241–242, Fig. 9.18*). The Borromini church of S. Agnese in Agone stands where the virgin Agnes was martyred in the great persecution of AD 303, while Bernini's fountain of the rivers, visible on the photograph, features an obelisk transferred by Pope Innocent X from the Circus of Maxentius (*Coleman 99*), but originally brought to Rome by Domitian himself for the Isis sanctuary in the Campus Martius (*Price 298, Figs. 11.5 and 11.7*).

Wherever you look, the palimpsest shows through. Rome is a marvel, and the expert authors of this book have vividly illuminated the life of the city in the first thirteen hundred years of its history. Read carefully, and you will find the seven million man-days it took to build the Baths of Caracalla, the nine million porter-loads per year of grain, oil and wine to feed the city, the forty or fifty metric tons of human waste sent down the Cloaca Maxima every day. How great Rome was, not ruins only but statistics tell.

August 2000

BIBLIOGRAPHY

CERVESATO, A. 1913: *The Roman Campagna,* London and Leipsic, 1913 (first published as *Latina Tellus: la Campagna Romana,* Roma 1911).

HOWELLS, W.D. 1908: *Roman Holidays and others,* London and New York, 1908.

VILLARI, L. (ed.) 1990: *Roma. Una Capitale in Europe, 1870–1911*. Firenze, 1990.

1. Introduction: the archaeology and topography of Rome

Jon Coulston and Hazel Dodge

Throughout her history Rome has been a centre of power, on a small scale initially, but steadily growing to form an empire which, for the first and last time, unified the Mediterranean world. In economic terms the influence of Rome eventually encompassed the whole of Eurasia and northern Africa. The city as consumer of mass imports (foods, water, luxuries, slaves, animals, building materials and people) grew physically in both extent and architectural complexity. Evolving building materials and techniques acted as a barometer of wealth and territorial power. The earliest structures, the huts on the Palatine (Figs. 1.1, 2.5), left only the negative imprint of sunken floors and post-holes, but requirement for larger sacred and public buildings led to the use of less perishable inorganic materials, terracotta and local tufa stones (Smith, Cornell in this volume). These began to seriously impact the archaeological record, and an increasing range of stones reflected spreading control of the Tevere (Tiber) valley and Latium (Gabian, Alban and Veian tufas; DeLaine in this volume). Hellenising cultural influences from southern Italy and further east placed a premium on hard, white stones for buildings with fine sculptural detail (white-plastered tufa, travertine, eventually marble). Finally, under the emperors, the stone resources of the whole Mediterranean and its hinterlands were organised for exploitation in a polychrome display, which consciously emphasised territorial power and technical achievement.[1] There was inflationary competition between emperors and their predecessors in the provision of public amenities, such as baths or games, on an ever-increasing scale and level of luxury (Dodge, Coleman in this volume). Hand in hand with the need for buildings of increasing size to serve an ever-growing population was the development of concrete *(opus caementicium)* as a building material. This employed economic, mass-producible local resources in efficient, durable, vaulted structures (DeLaine in this volume).

Ancient Rome was certainly a huge urban development for any pre-industrial society to maintain, and modern scholars have tried every means to quantify her scale. Population has been calculated using overall area, built up and open space hectarage, funerary inscription statistics, and comparative modern population densities. Ancient figures for numbers of domestic dwellings by type (*domus* and *insula*), corn-dole recipients, and quantities of corn imports have all been pressed into service. Thus it has been postulated that up to 1,200,000 people lived in Rome at her 1st–2nd century AD height.[2] However, every method of calculation and set of statistics runs into problems. The most fundamental is that the modern desire to quantify Rome's scale uses evidence provided by an ancient society which had no real necessity for, nor ability to achieve, exactitude. Figures were quoted in the sources precisely to express magnitude, to reflect glory on the metropolis, or to laud the beneficent patron. Thus, the 4th century AD Regionary Catalogues presented statistics, which appear authoritative through their very detail (see Appendix). Nevertheless, close examination reveals them to have been unusable for any 'official', administrative purpose, such as feeding or policing the city, or maintaining the urban fabric. The arithmetic is sloppy, with numbers spelt out in detail not tallying with quoted totals.[3] Rather, these figures reflect the scale of Rome taking on a life of its own, drawing in the wonder and awe of observers by its sheer quantity of statues, temples, basilicas, theatres, amphitheatres, circuses, streets, houses, mansions, military bases, aqueducts, baths, fountains, warehouses, bakers, cemeteries, and even public lavatories, churches, and brothels.[4]

When the economic tide receded from the 3rd century AD onwards, the urban fabric remained for future generations to live in, adapt, and continue to marvel at. The skeletons of massive buildings, their original functions often forgotten, remained to constantly remind of past glories and to provide a language for expressing present and future aspirations. The transformation of Rome into a christian capital during the 4th century ensured her a continuing central place in medieval and modern history, and continuing patronage by a series of rulers concerned with a world stage.[5] The 'idea' of Rome has been employed through epigraphy, numismatics, art and architecture to strengthen and project the successive regimes of Late Roman and Byzantine emperors, popes, Holy Roman Emperors and other western monarchs, secular local governments, Italian kings, a fascist dictator, and the post-war Italian republic.[6] Rome, like an animal in hibernation living on stored resources, has always fed on herself for inspiration and physical means. The millions of tons of stone imported by the ancient emperors were thereafter available for recycling into churches, *palazzi* and other monuments. The thousands of inscriptions and artworks were there to be collected and emulated.[7]

Underlying and channelling this urban development are the fundamentals of geology, geomorphology and topography that are now rather difficult to envisage in the presence of the modern city. Much work has been done on hilltop and valley geology, dominated by volcanic deposits and fluvial erosion (Fig. 1.2).[8] Indeed, the action of the Tiber and its tributary streams is critical to the city's location (Dodge in this volume). Erosion of the Esquiline plateau created a series of peninsulas and linked or isolated hills, divided by steep-sided valleys, which open out onto the flood plain. The Palatine Hill was small enough to be defended at an early date but large enough for a growing community (Smith in this volume). The Capitoline Hill was suitably small and defensible for it to subsequently become the acropolis of the expanded regal city. The Tiber Island provided the lowest fording-point above the mouth of the river and an overland line of communication between Etruria to the north-west and Latium and Hellenized Campania to the south-east. The river valley facilitated movement up into the Apennines, particularly commerce in salt from the coastal pans.[9] Thus the city was locally well placed with regard to communications and trade. It was also on a cultural frontier between Etruscans, Faliscans and Latins. The local geology provided soft tufas for building and volcanic sands for mortars (DeLaine in this volume). The geologically ancient volcanoes close by in South Etruria and the Colli Albani, and the more recent eruptions further afield in Campania, ensure that not only the past but the present city is periodically rocked by earthquakes, as in AD 1980 (Fig. 1.2).[10]

Until the late 19th and early 20th century canalisation of the Tevere, the river dominated the life of the city, not least because of perennial flooding of the low-lying areas.[11] The Campo Marzio (Campus Martius, *Mezza Luna*) was particularly vulnerable when the Apennine snows melted (Fig. 1.2). At this time the river increased its rate of flow in a comparatively straight stretch to the north, then turned virtually ninety degrees to the west to pass round the meander core. The weight of water would burst over the bank flooding the flat area south of the turn. These inundations caused destruction of buildings and the spread of

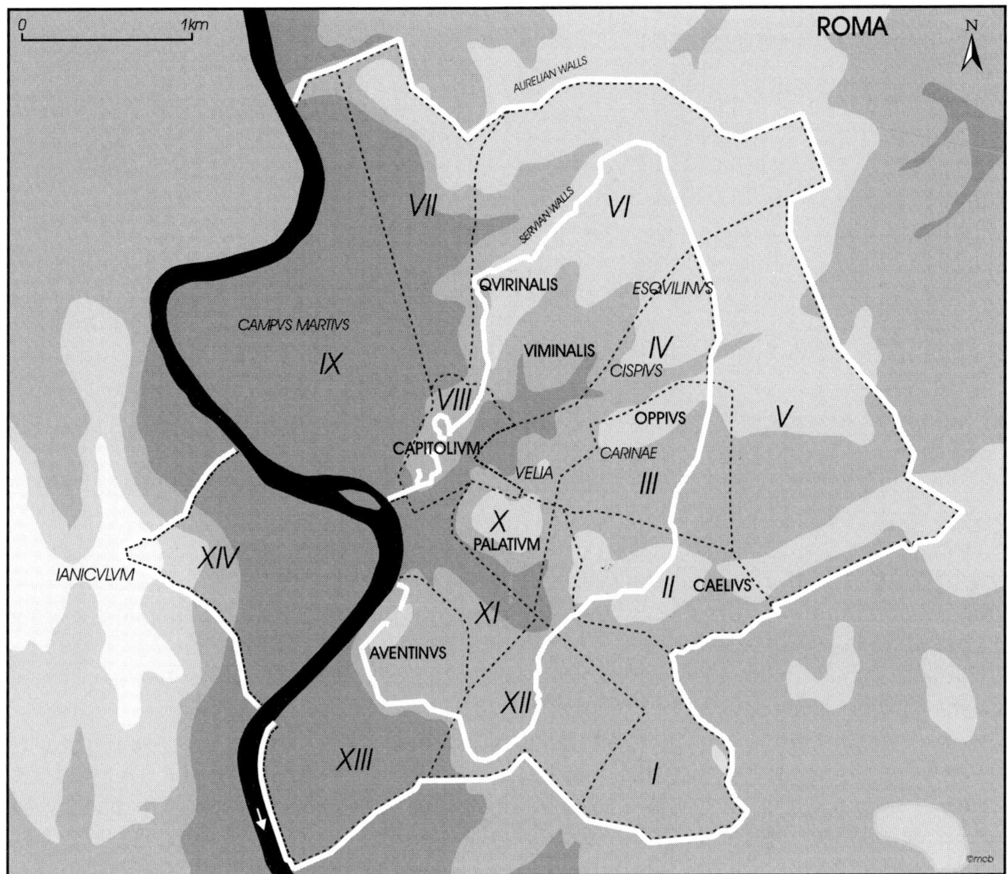

Figure 1.1: Map of Rome showing topography and main toponyms. The names of the Regiones *are I Porta Capena, II Caelimontium, III Isis et Serapis, IV Templum Pacis, V Esquiliae, VI Alta Semita, VII Via Lata, VIII Forum Romanum, IX Circus Flaminius, X Palatium, XI Circus Maximus, XII Piscina Publica, XIII Aventinus, XIV Trans Tiberim.*

disease. They also resulted in a steady deposition of riverine silt which, together with erosion from the hillsides and deposition in the valleys, raised the ground-level steadily over the city's history. This continuous depositional process is especially obvious in the Campo Marzio and is reflected in the observable depth of archaeological excavations. For example, the temples in the Largo Argentina were steadily overtaken by successive levels of paving from the early 3rd century BC to the later 1st century AD (Fig. 1.3). By the Hadrianic period the Augustan Ara Pacis sat in a pit, whilst the Augustan Horologium meridian paving required a 'facelift' around the same time.[12] The post-Roman build-up of material is extraordinary, comparing, for example, the modern ground level with the ancient surface around the Tomb of Hirtius under the Palazzo della Cancelleria.[13]

Elsewhere a combination of hill-wash and successive building activities has buried successive generations of building on the same site, as at S. Clemente in the valley south-east of the Colosseum.[14] Continuous building and levelling of sites, especially work on a large engineering scale under the emperors, often modified the morphology of hills and valleys,

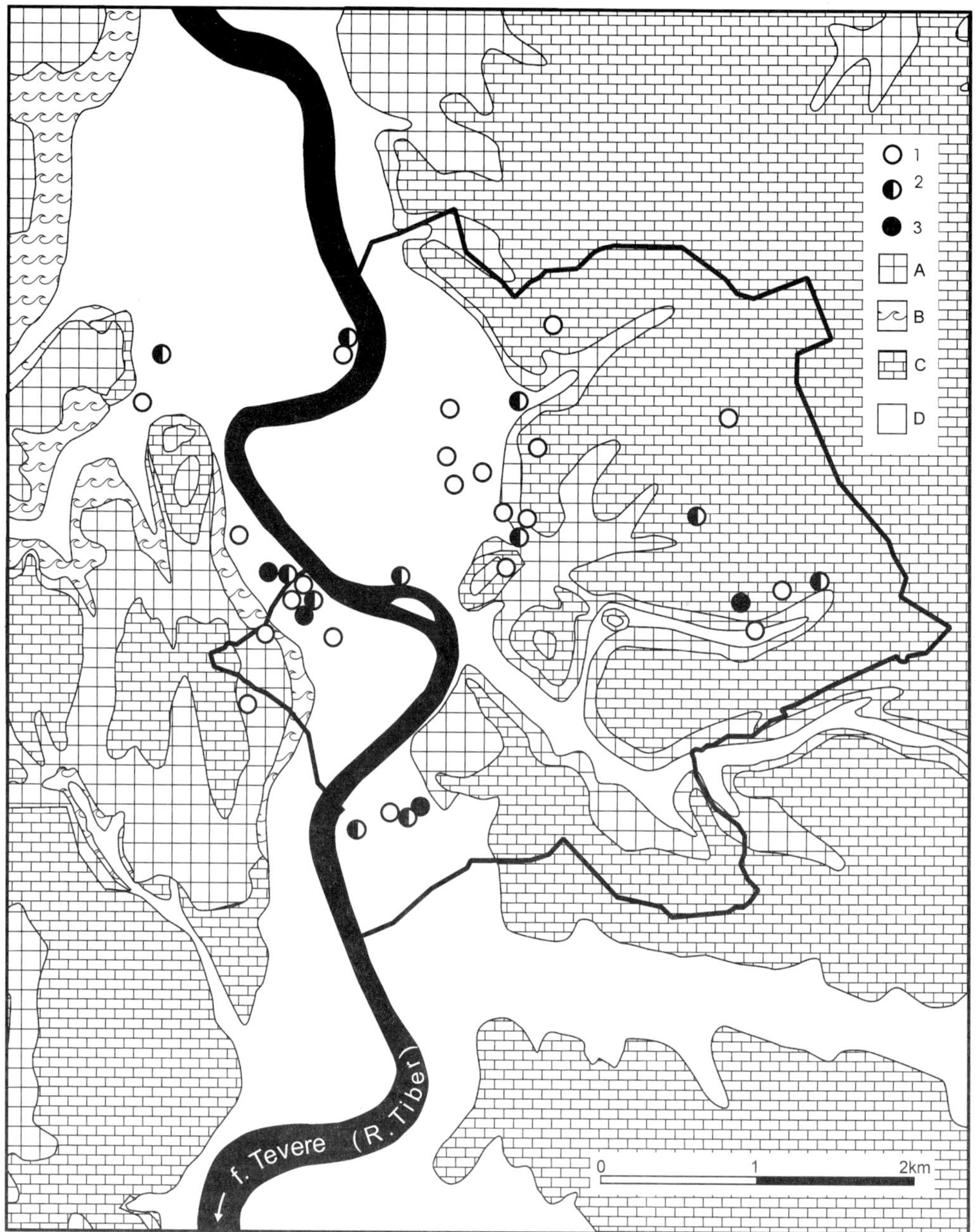

Figure 1.2: Map of Rome showing geological features and AD 1980 earthquake damage (after Benevolo and Scoppola 1988). Key: 1 light earthquake damage, 2 intermediate damage, 3 heavy damage; A volcanic material, B blue clay, C continental and transitional facies comprising the 'fluvio-lacustrine' and 'marshy' formations, and the 'complex of clays, sands, and gravels', D alluvium.

Figure 1.3: Largo Argentina Temple C. Successive periods of paving levels looking SW (Photo: authors).

flattening hilltops and terracing out over their sides to increase horizontal building space. In the process earlier structures were incorporated as revetting and thus preserved, as in the cases of the republican buildings under the Palatine palaces, the Domus Aurea under the Baths of Trajan, and the Hadrianic house under the Baths of Caracalla, all with surviving wall-paintings.[15] In places this has created veritable man-made cliffs, as on the north-east side of the Palatine.[16] One particularly famous and graphic example of human geomorphing is the cutting back of the Quirinal Hill to form a site for the Forum and Markets of Trajan, as celebrated in the inscription on Trajan's Column (*CIL* 6.960; Fig. 1.4). Elsewhere, the effect has been to smooth out and soften the topography, a process greatly accelerated by the development of open areas within the walls after 1870. The combination of fluvial deposition and human building activity has created an 'underground' Rome (*Roma Sotterranea*) of deep, excavated sites. Added to these are the ancient structures that were originally subterranean, such as cisterns, sewers, *mithraea* (Price in this volume), and of course catacombs.[17] Thus a uniquely deep, rich and well preserved structural record exists in Rome.

Another agent of destruction, but also of renewal, was fire in the ancient city. The great fire of AD 64 was only the most famous and most destructive of many. For example, fires swept through the central Campo Marzio in AD 80 and the Forum Romanum area in AD 191 and 283.[18] Most were accidental and were followed by major rebuilding activities. On a few occasions there was deliberate destruction, as when the Curia formed the funeral pyre of P. Clodius Pulcher in 52 BC, or when buildings on the Capitol were burnt during the Civil War fighting of AD 69. There were few actual sackings of Rome by external enemies during her long history that potentially damaged the whole city: by the Gauls in *c.*390 BC, by Visigoths in AD 410, and by Vandals in 455 (Cornell, Christie in this volume).[19] Saracen destruction in 846 only really affected areas outside the walls, such as the Vatican and S. Paolo. Norman damage in 1084 was inflicted chiefly on outlying churches within the walls (e.g. SS. Quattro Coronati, S. Clemente). In 1527 Imperial troops concentrated on churches and *palazzi*, leaving the ancient buildings relatively untouched.[20]

Notwithstanding these sacks, Rome's security was generally successfully ensured throughout her history by a strongly constructed series of defences. Circuits first enclosed the

Figure 1.4: View of Trajan's Column and the Basilica Ulpia, looking WNW (Photo: authors).

Palatine, and later included the Capitoline, Esquiline and Caelian Hills.[21] This latter enclosed the city sacked by the Gauls. Following this event, the new 'Servian Wall' perhaps followed the same line as before and reusing earlier defences, but further enclosed the Aventine Hill (11 km, 6.5 mls; 400 ha, 1000 ac). It was built of tufa ashlar in Hellenistic style (Cornell in this volume). This circuit saw off Hannibal and remained in use until defences were no long required in the 1st century BC. Thereafter Rome's shield was her provincial armies. However, in the AD 270s it was judged that the city again required defences, particularly because of barbarian pressures on the northern frontiers. The new 'Aurelianic Wall' was constructed of brick-faced concrete in metropolitan style, reusing and incidentally preserving earlier structures along its line and recycling large quantities of brick. It was required to enclose the much expanded imperial city (19 km, 11 mls; 375 ha, 3393 ac) and represented the single largest building project ever undertaken in the city's history (see Christie in this volume). It also enclosed considerable areas of gardens (*horti*) which forever after remained open space, or at least until the period 1870–1900.[22]

The main problem in the medieval period was that a shrinking population without a standing defence force had difficulty in manning the immense Aurelianic Wall circuit.[23] With the development of gunpowder artillery, an attacker's most efficient approach was to assault the papal defences to the west on the Gianicolo (ancient Janiculum Hill) front and then dominate the city with his guns. This is what happened in 1527 and when the French attacked in support of the pope in 1849.[24] The last time the Aurelianic Wall was defended was by papal troops in 1870; there was some bombardment damage inflicted by the Italian royal army but only a token resistance at *La Breccia* beside Porta Pia (Petter in this volume).

Through the medieval period the population and its area of habitation contracted into the Campo Marzio and a few other centres (the *abitato*), leaving a zone of gardens, orchards and ruins within the walls (the *disabitato*).[25] Yet the city was a great pilgrimage centre with perennial influxes of people. The diplomatic, territorial and spiritual importance of the papacy, and the concentration of saints' shrines ensured major patronage of new building construction. This resulted in waves of church-building and decoration, notably in the Carolingian and 12th century renaissances.[26] Through much of the period local élite families and the papacy struggled over papal elections, city government and the interventions of European monarchs. Many of the larger ancient buildings still stood as concrete skeletons, stripped of their marble decoration (and often even their facings of reusable brick). Some were preserved by conversion into churches, some through their value as fortresses in the embattled city,[27] and a few because of their revenue potential.[28] Their marble went into churches, tombs, *palazzi* and other monuments. Alternatively it was burnt for lime and huge amounts of limestone and geologically 'true' marbles disappeared in this way to make mortar for medieval constructions. This has meant that other stones, principally breccias, granites and porphyries, have an artificially high profile in the surviving corpus of ancient imports.[29]

Like the building of churches in the city, study of Rome's past has gone in waves of endeavour and wider European interest. Excavation through the medieval and early modern periods was rather haphazard.[30] However, the acquisition and preservation of ancient artworks (albeit often with confusing 'restorations') by renaissance popes, cardinals, monarchs and aristocrats, established collections in the 15th–17th centuries which have acted as foci for subsequent research.[31] The rise of encyclopedism and categorisation in the 18th century led to typological study and wider publication for a readership that was increasingly mobile, made up partly as it was of Grand Tourists. This rationalism of the European Enlightenment was rather bluntly expressed in the excavation and recording of buildings during the Napoleonic regime in Rome (1809–14).[32] The 19th century saw the formalisation of antiquities institutions under papal rule and the flowering of studies in *Roma Sotteranea*, particularly with regard to the christian catacombs.[33]

Roman urban archaeology was transformed by the establishment of the city as the capital of a 'unified' Italy in 1870 (Petter in this volume). The growth in population expanded the *abitato* out to, and beyond, the Aurelianic Wall. Some areas of the *disabitato* were built over for the very first time.[34] The need for grandiose new government buildings and planned infrastructure combined with the relative speed of construction resulted in a major impact on archaeological resources, an acceleration of archaeological 'rescue' work, and a proliferation of new artefacts and data.[35] To this period belong some of the great finds of bronze statuary, such as the seated boxer, found on the Teatro Drammatico site (Via Nazionale, 1885).[36] Technology, resources and political will came together in the late 19th and early 20th centuries to solve at last the age-old problem of seasonal Tevere flooding. The new travertine embankments both killed off river traffic (in common with earlier developments in London and Paris) and revealed the archaeology of ancient river-front wharves, warehouses and imperishable imports (Mattingly and Aldrete in this volume).[37] Development of the Stazione di Termini revealed a large area of housing and one of the best preserved sections of the 'Servian Wall'.[38] The large-scale excavation of set-piece sites, such as the Forum Romanum, coupled with legislation to protect the ancient urbanscape, resulted in the creation of a great archaeological park (*passeggiato archeologico*) stretching from the city centre out into the Campagna along the Via Appia.[39] Although the area excavated in the Forum was large, there was a diachronic approach to recording and some developing appreciation of stratigraphic study. Both were perhaps not again attained until the 1970s.

Extremely fortuitously, the development of photography occurred just early enough specifically to record the events of 1849, but more generally to preserve the appearance of Rome before 1870. The gradual unveiling of the ancient city may be followed in sepia tone through the work of such early observers as Gioacchino Altobelli, Robert MacPherson and John Henry Parker.[40] Aerial photographs, first from balloons, later from early aeroplanes, can be studied both for the whole city and for the small detail of individual sites, such as the

Forum Romanum excavations. These follow closely on from the age-old tradition of maps and views (*vedute*) of Rome.[41]

The Rome which people have experienced since the Second World War is very much a product of fascist government planning. Indeed, the impact of Mussolini's regime may be directly compared with the period 1870-1914 and the establishment of *Roma Capitale*. Fascist obsession with the ancient city affected the archaeology in many ways. On one hand old, long-known sites, such as the Imperial Fora and the Mausoleum of Augustus were cleared, the latter having passed through the various guises of imperial burial vault, medieval fortress, garden complex, bull-ring and music hall.[42] On the other hand new sites were discovered, such as the S. Omobono temples in the Forum Holitorium.[43] There was a great emphasis on linking fascist urban renewal with the activities of Augustus, even down to the plentiful use of travertine in new buildings. The newly excavated sites were all tidied up with a surround of travertine bollards, visually marking them out as regime achievements. Monumental fascist inscriptions were set up not just on the new edifices which replaced medieval structures that had been torn down (e.g. on the office-block in the Forum Holitorium), but also on ancient constructions, such as those still extant on the Theatre of Marcellus and the Markets of Trajan.

An enlarged Piazza Venezia was created by removal of the Palazzetto Venezia. This formed a hub of fascist spectacle extending ceremonial already focussed on the Vittoriano. It also allowed large public rallies to hear Il Duce's speeches, which were delivered from the Palazzo Venezia balcony in a conscious emulation of papal presentation.[44] For the review of parades a new, fascist 'Via Triumphalis' was laid out between the Piazza Venezia and the Colosseum (Via del Impero/Via dei Fori Imperiali). This echoed the ancient triumphal route but could not follow the traditional line over the saddle between Velia and Palatine, under the Arch of Titus and down the Via Sacra, without remodelling and partly destroying the *zona archeologica*.[45] Thus an ambitious plan was formulated to cut an approximately parallel route through, and largely remove, the Velian Hill. In the process of execution (completed 1932) republican and imperial period houses were revealed, hastily recorded in plans and photographs, and destroyed. All evidence of a hilltop 'village', similar to that known on the western corner of the Palatine, was lost forever. The back of the Basilica of Maxentius, the platform of the Temple of Venus and Rome and the foundations of Neronian Domus Aurea buildings were isolated. To facilitate the marching of troops up the Via di S. Gregorio and past, or under, the Arch of Constantine, the Meta Sudans was demolished (1936).[46] North-west of the Velia the flat area of the Imperial Fora (the medieval Campo Torreggiato[47]) was cleared of churches and houses to form the main avenue and parks on either side. This 'landscaping' went hand-in-hand with archaeological work, principally the rapid clearance of parts of the Fora of Caesar, Augustus, Nerva and Trajan, and the 'disengagement' of the Curia Iulia from its guise as S. Adriano.[48]

Another road-clearance project extending out from the Piazza Venezia involved opening up the present Piazza Aracoeli and driving through a line south to join up with the Lungotevere. The resultant Via del Teatro di Marcello cut a swathe through crowded medieval buildings and opened up the Forum Holitorium and Forum Boarium. In the process various ancient sites were excavated and/or 'isolated', including the Theatre of Marcellus, the Forum Boarium and Forum Holitorium temples, and the S. Omobono precinct.[49]

Elsewhere in the city fascist planners and archaeologists carried out smaller-scale projects, such as the excavation of the curved end of the Stadium of Domitian and the clearance and restoration of part of a temple in the Via delle Bottege Oscure. Monastic and other medieval buildings were swept away to reveal the four temples of the Largo Argentina.[50] More ambitiously, the Mausoleum of Augustus was cleared and patched up with the important discovery of imperial funerary inscriptions, but this was still deemed insufficient to link regime, monument and Augustan identity. The whole area was therefore turned into a fascist square (Piazza di Augusto Imperatore) and surrounded on two sides with colonnaded buildings in monumental fascist style with dedicatory inscriptions. The Ara Pacis, apogee of Augustan commemoration, was rebuilt using the original fragments in its present position on the west side of the piazza.[51]

Clearance of buildings to make way for public spaces and for broad, straight new roads was not a new experience in the city. Popes Julius II and Sixtus V had similarly left their marks on the south-west Campo Marzio and the *disabitato* respectively.[52] Royal Rome saw the removal and even movement of buildings in the layout of roads, notably along the Corso Vittorio Emanuele II, and massive destruction of ancient, medieval and renaissance buildings on the site of the Vittorio Emanuele Monument (Petter in this volume). However, it was the far more grandiloquent scale of fascist clearance, and the motives behind it, which distinguished it from earlier activities. Fascist archaeology was carried out in great haste with concern only for the final presentation of the monument. This had various results. Firstly, only one main period was investigated with evidence for subsequent occupation being destroyed and ignored unless it was very substantial. Thus the post-imperial structural history of the Fora of Augustus and Trajan is largely lost. Elsewhere, the *campaniletto* and frescoed apse of S. Biagio al Mercato/S. Rita were retained after clearance of the *insula* building below the Aracoeli steps. However, much might have been learned about how a 2nd century AD residential block evolved structurally into a Romanesque church complex.[53] As a result of such disdain for post-imperial evidence, the study of early medieval Rome is still in its infancy, despite major leaps forward in the 1980s and 1990s.[54] The speed of fascist work also went naturally with poor recording, and many sites were never published. It has been left to recent scholars to attempt coherent publication from fragmentary archives, for example, of the Largo Argentina temples and the Forum of Trajan.[55]

The post-war renaissance of Rome as a centre of European culture and world heritage has seen many changes in the archaeology of the city and in the methodologies applied by archaeologists, both native and foreign. The spread of the Metropolitana has affected individual sites (Coulston Fig. 5.9). Construction of the outer ring-road (Grande Raccordo Anulare) has transformed the field of prehistoric archaeology (Smith in this volume).[56] In the early 1980s a new concern for reform galvanized the study and treatment of Rome's past, commencing with the plan for excavation, renovation and museum renewal advocated by the Sopprintendente, Adriano La Regina. The effects of acid rain pollution on marble monuments became a prime focus.[57] Thus the 1980s will be remembered as the decade of monuments shrouded in scaffolding and green netting. This period had a revolutionary impact on the understanding of ancient art and architecture because scholars were able to study monuments nose-to-nose, rather than just through engravings, photographs and binoculars.[58] The removal and cleaning of the equestrian statue of Marcus Aurelius symbolised the new methods. There has been a wave of exemplary new publications that primarily study ancient technique based on a philosophy of detailed data recording.[59] Whilst the full import of this work is still being digested, a new impetus (and a new generation of scaffolding) is being felt in Rome, largely as a result of both state and church taking the millennium (*Giubileo*) year seriously. Major new excavations have been undertaken, notably in the Imperial Fora on either side of the Via dei Fori Imperiali (Fig. 1.5).[60]

Figure 1.5: View over excavation of Trajan's Forum, November 1998, looking south-south-west (Photo: authors).

The city of Rome has always been a rich and inspirational field of academic endeavour. That it continues to be so into the third millennium is amply demonstrated by the vibrancy and originality of research that has created the chapters of this volume.

NOTES

1 DODGE and WARD-PERKINS 1992; GNOLI 1988; BORGHINI 1989; MAISCHBERGER 1997; CLARIDGE 1998, 38–42.

2 The more recent estimates have decreased overall numbers, *c*.800,000 under Augustus, rising to 1,000,000, and by the Severan period falling back again after 2nd century plagues. See BELOCH 1886, 392–412; OATES 1934; MAIER 1953–54; BRUNT 1971, 376–88; HERMANSEN 1978; HOPKINS 1978, 96–8; JONGMANN 1991, 73–5; ROBINSON 1992, 8–9; KOLB 1995, 451–53; MORLEY 1996, 2–3, 33–46; LO CASCIO 1997, 24; PURCELL 1999, 135–50; NOY 2000, 15–29.

3 As is also the case in Frontinus, *On Aqueducts*; see Dodge in this volume.

4 For ancient laudatory descriptions of Rome see LUGLI 1952–62, I, 109–12. Epithets for the city used in the Roman period speak for themselves: Aeterna, Alta, Augusta, Aurea, Caput, Decus, Domina, Felix, Genetrix, Iclita, Immensa, Invicta, Magna, Maxima, Martia, Mater, Prima, Potens, Regia, Regina, Sacra, Sacratissima, Venerabilis, Victrix etc.

5 KRAUTHEIMER 1980; 1983, 7–40, 93–121; HARRIS 1999.

6 THOMPSON 1971; KRAUTHEIMER 1983, 93–121; STINGER 1985; ANDREOTTI 1990; MANACORDA and TAMASSIA 1985; Petter in this volume.

7 WARD-PERKINS 1984, 214–18; GREENHALGH 1989.

8 E.g. VENTRIGLIA 1971; BENEVOLO and SCOPPOLA 1988, Fig. 81; TORTORICI 1991, Fig. 6; PANELLA 1996, 9–25; *Lexicon* IV, Fig. 2–4; V, Fig. 16.

9 LUGLI 1952–62, I, 3–7; CORNELL 1995, 48; SMITH 1996, 179–80.

10 LUGLI 1952–62, I, 46, 50–2, 65–7, 69; BENEVOLO and SCOPPOLA 1988, Fig. 81.

11 LUGLI 1952–62, II, 13–123; LE GALL 1953; D'ONOFRIO 1970; ARCHEOLOGIA A ROMA 1989, 143–53. In March 1997 a new programme was launched to study the whole Tiber valley, intended to put the city into its broader riverine context (Tiber Valley Project). See PATTERSON and MILLETT 1998.

12 *Lexicon* IV, *s.v.* 'Pax Augusta, Ara', 70–4; III. *s.v.* 'Horologium Augusti', 35–7.

13 *Lexicon* IV, *s.v.* 'Sepulcrum: A. Hirtius', 290–1. There is some evidence that the northern margin of the Campus Martius was raised artificially as a flood counter-measure under Hadrian. Two *pomerium cippi* were found *in situ*, one superimposed above the other, on the corner of Viccola della Torretta and Via di Campo Marzio. The lower Vespasianic *cippus* indicated a street level of 7.1 m below the modern street , whilst the upper Hadrianic

stone indicated a level of 4.1 m below modern street level. The 3 m difference is too great for natural build-up alone. See BOATWRIGHT 1987, 64–6.

14 It is very noticeable that long-established churches form a preservation mechanism, and to an extent a traditional window of opportunity for examination, e.g. S. Anastasia, S. Carlo ai Catinari, S. Cecilia, S. Clemente, S. Crisogono, S. Giovanni in Laterano, SS. Giovanni e Paolo, S. Lorenzo in Lucina, S. Maria in Via Lata, S. Martino ai Monti, S. Pietro in Montorio, S. Pietro in Vaticano, S. Pietro in Vincoli, S. Prisca, S. Rufina, S. Saba, S. Sabina, S. Salvatore in Onda, S. Stefano Rotondo.

15 *Lexicon* II, *s.v.* 'Domus Transitoria', 199–202; 'Domus Aurea: il palazzo sull'Esquilino', 56–64; IV, *s.v.* 'Palatium, Palatinus Mons', 14–28; V, 44; IACOPI 1985; 1997; DELAINE 1997, 227–28; PINOT DE VILLECHENON 1998; SEGALA and SCIORTINO 1999.

16 *Lexicon* II, Fig. 53, 59. See also the terrace walls of the Horti Sallustiani, the Muro Torto, and later, on a smaller scale, SS. Quattro Coronati.

17 PAVIA 1998; PORTELLA 2000.

18 For urban fires see LUGLI 1952–62, I, 42–6, 49–59, 62–6; SABLAYROLLES 1996, 771–802.

19 LUGLI 1952–62, I, 67–71; SABLAYROLLES 1996, 772, 779, 793–4, 802.

20 FRUTAZ 1962, Pl. 171–73; KRAUTHEIMER 1980, 117, 149–50; CHASTEL 1983; GUICCIARDINI 1993.

21 *Lexicon* III, *s.v.* "Murus Romuli", 318–9; CRISTOFANI 1990, Fig.4: CORNELL 1995, 198–204; SMITH 1996, 151–55.

22 RICHMOND 1930; *Lexicon* III, *s.v.* 'Muri Aureliani', 290–314; WISEMAN 1998.

23 Constantinople experienced a similar problem but the city was only taken twice in its history from AD 330 to the present. In 1204 the Fourth Crusade 'cheated' by scrambling over the Golden Horn wall from ships. Only in 1453 was the Theodosian Land Wall breached, and then by gunpowder artillery (RUNCIMAN 1965; MÜLLER-WIENER 1977, *s.v.* 'Landmauer', 286–307 and 308).

24 CHASTEL 1983, Map 1; FRUTAZ 1962, Pl. 513; HIBBERT 1985, 248–69. See ROME 1977, No. 165.

25 FRUTAZ 1962, Pl. 533–34, 536–64; BRIZZI 1975, 88–9. 92–3, 100–5, 188–89, 192–96, 201; ROME 1977, No. 53, 56, 182, 185, 189, 193A; KRAUTHEIMER 1980, 271–88, 311–22, Fig.20, 52, 59–61, 193a, 199, 249, 255; BECCHETTI 1993, No. 74.

26 Main waves of churches: Constantinian; Theodosian; 5th century 'Sistine Renaissance'; Gregorian; Carolingian; Romanesque; Early Renaissance; Counter-Reformation; Baroque (MALE 1960; KRAUTHEIMER 1937–77; 1980; 1985; BRENTANO 1990; PARTRIDGE 1996, 43–69). Pilgrims: BIRCH 1998.

27 Like other medieval Italian cities, Rome bristled with fortress towers (*torre*), many of the smaller examples perching on ancient monuments (KRAUTHEIMER 1980, 289–310, 317–22, Fig.256; BIANCHI 1998).

28 Churches: S. Nicolas ad Columnam against Trajan's Column; S. Adriano in the Curia; SS. Cosma e Damiano in Forum Pacis buildings; S. Lorenzo in Miranda, in Temple of Pius and Faustina; S. Maria Antiqua in Palatine palace atrium; S. Maria in Egiziaca, in Temple of Portunus; S. Maria ad Martyres in Pantheon; S. Maria Nova in Temple of Venus and Rome; S. Nicola in Carcere, in Forum Holitorium temples; S. Stefano delle Carrozze in Forum Boarium round temple. Fortresses: Arches of Constantine, 'Janus', Severus and Titus, Colosseum, Mausolea of Augustus, Hadrian, and Caecilia Metella, Septizodium (subsequently demolished), Tabularium, Theatre of Marcellus. Revenues: Columns of Trajan and Marcus.

29 WARD-PERKINS 1984, 214–18.

30 Very usefully collected in LANCIANI 1902–94, each volume of which covers a specific period: I, AD 1000–1530; II, 1531–49; III, 1550–65; IV, 1566–1605; V, 1605–1700. See also RIDLEY 1992, 9–46; MOATTI 1993, 13–99.

31 Notably, establishment in 1471 of the sculpture collection on the Campidoglio by Sixtus IV, which included the Capitoline wolf, 'Lo Spinario' and the Ara Maxima Hercules (CAMPIDOGLIO 1984, 23–6, No. 2, 4, 12). Thereafter, papal collection was centred on the Vatican Belvedere, hence the display there of the Laocoön, discovered in 1506. This was a signal year which also saw the creation of the Guarda Svizzera and the laying of the foundation stone of S. Pietro by Julius II. The preservation of the '*statue parlante*' and the use of these antique artworks was a mechanism of preservation and the maintainance of public interest: 'Il Marforio' on the Campidoglio; 'Madama Lucrezia' by the Palazzo S. Marco; 'Il Babuino' in Via Babuino; 'Abate Luigi' beside S. Andrea della Valle; 'Il Pasquino' behind Palazzo Brasci (DICKINSON 1960, 155–63; VIRGILI 1993).

32 GROSS 1990, especially 310–30; RIDLEY 1992.

33 An area very conveniently summarised in MANCINELLI 1981. Awakening interest in early christian buildings also resulted in the 'disengagement' of baroque facades and interiors from some churches (e.g. S. Sabina, S. Maria in Cosmedin).

34 FRUTAZ 1962, Pl. 533–34, 536–64; BENEVOLO 1985, Fig. 39–41.

35 BUONOCORE 1997. Ancient buildings were hastily excavated and recorded under virtually all the new government buildings, for example under the Ministero d'Interno (CAPRARIIS 1987–88). For a photograph of all the assembled sculpture finds of 1874 see BRIZZI 1975, 203.

36 MANACORDA and TAMASSIA 1985, 124. Cf. ROME 1977, No. 116.

37 See BRIZZI 1975, 131; ROME 1977, No. 134; HIBBERT 1985, Fig. 87; BECCHETTI 1993, No. 152–56.

38 BRIZZI 1975, 85; ROME 1977, No. 57; *BullCom* 90, 1985, 323; BARBERA and PARIS 1996, 192–210; WISEMAN 1998.

39 In February to April 1882 an area in the Forum of 2800 m^2 was excavated with the removal of 10,200 m^3 of spoil. The park was legislated for in 1887 and inaugurated in 1911. A royal decree of 8th November 1870 established the Soprintendenza for the excavation and preservation of monuments in Rome (BRIZZI 1975, 156–73; ROMA 1977, No. 28–40; BULL-SIMONSEN EINAUDI 1978, No. 19–30; FORI 1981, Pl. 24, 88; BECCHETTI 1993, No. 8–22.

40 This was a truly international endeavour. See, for example, BRIZZI 1975; ROME 1977; ; BULL-SIMONSEN EINAUDI 1978; CAMPAGNA 1986; ARCHEOLOGIA A ROMA 1989; ANDREOTTI 1990; BECCHETTI 1993.

41 Maps of Rome from the 3rd century AD onwards are indispensably collected in FRUTAZ 1962. For aerial photographs see FRUTAZ 1962, Pl. 578–82; FORI 1981, Pl. 25–6, 40, 76, 78.

42 MANACORDA and TAMASSIA 1985, 198–9; MOATTI 1993, 42–5; *Lexicon* III, *s.v.* 'Mausoleum Augusti', 234–39.

43 *Lexicon* II, *s.v.* 'Fortuna et Mater Matuta, Aedes', 281–85. At least one of the Largo Argentina temples was known before their fascist clearance (Temple B: BRIZZI 1975, 64; ROME 1977, No. 115; COARELLI 1981).

44 The papal *urbi et orbi* addresses were delivered initially from the Lateran, latterly from the facade overlooking Piazza S. Pietro (KRAUTHEIMER 1980, 209, 227, 326).

45 Ancient route: KÜNZL 1988, 14–44, 141–50; FAVRO 1994. This was consciously followed for the triumphal entry into Rome of Charles V on April 5th, 1536, which passed under the Arches of Constantine, Titus and Severus, up over the Campidoglio, thence to S. Pietro (CHASTEL 1983, 207–14; PARTRIDGE 1996, 26–31). A papal 'Via Triumphalis' might be taken as the Via del Corso, followed after a triumphal entry into the city through the Porta Flaminia, as when Marcantonio Colonna returned to Rome after the Battle of Lepanto (1571), or when Pius VII returned the city in 1814 after captivity in Napoleonic France. Veladier redesigned an enlarged Piazza del Popolo for the latter occasion (HIBBERT 1985, Fig. 68–9). For papal ceremonial and topography see STINGER 1985, 46–59.

46 Via del Impero: CEDERNA 1980, Fig. 48–60, Map; BARROERO 1983, 62–100, 117–55, 167–224, Pl. 1–10, 13; MANNACORDA and TAMASSIA 1985, 181–94; MORSELLI 1985; TORTORICI 1985; 1991, Fig. 5; BENEVOLO and SCOPPOLA 1988, 67–94, Fig. 50, 67, 78–80, 85–97; TELLINI SANTONI 1998, No. 51–6, 62–6. Losses: *Lexicon* II, Fig. 52; CEDERNA 1980, Fig. 43–6; PISANI SARTORIO 1983; BUZZETTI 1985, Fig. 13; BENEVOLO and SCOPPOLA 1988, Fig. 71–2. Meta Sudans: TELLINI SANTONI 1998, No. 1–3, 7–10, 15, 122; PANELLA 1996.

47 KRAUTHEIMER 1980, 319, Fig.255.

48 CEDERNA 1980, Fig. 61–2; MORSELLI and TORTORICI 1989; TORTORICI 1991. Some parts of this work have proved to be less destructive than was once feared. For example, the footings and basements of early modern houses survive over the area of the Imperial Fora and no more material was removed along the course of the Via dei Fori Imperiale than was necessary to make a flat road-bed. Buildings elsewhere in Rome were certainly completely destroyed, even ancient ones such as the Basilica of Iunius Bassus from which the *opus sectile* was rescued (in 1930: NASH 1961–62, I, 190–95; *Lexicon* II, *s.v.* 'Domus: Iunius Bassus', 69–70).

49 CEDERNA 1980, Fig. 17–20, 35–6, Map; MANACORDA and TAMASSIA 1985, 13–4; CIANFA 1985; BENEVOLO 1985, Fig. 59–60. For a consolidated map of buildings demolished for projects in the centre of Rome between 1873 and 1940 see BARROERO 1983, Pl. 16.

50 COARELLI 1981.

51 The Ara Pacis is now some distance from its original position alongside the Via Lata. See MANACORDA and TAMASSIA 1985, 195–205. Fragments of the altar have turned up since the 16th century (*Lexicon* IV, *s.v.* 'Pax Augusta, Ara', 70–4).

52 FRUTAZ 1962, Pl. 189.17–18, 257–59, 261; STINGER 1985, 14–31. See also WESTFALL 1974.

53 CLARIDGE 1998, 232–34; CONNOLLY and DODGE 1998, 141–44.

54 See now for example AUGENTI 1996; COATES-STEPHENS 1996; 1997; 1998; HARRIS 1999; MANACORDA 2000.

55 COARELLI 1981; AMICI 1982; PACKER 1997; MENEGHINI 1998.

56 See also BIETTI SESTIERI and SANTIS 2000; CARANDINI and CAPPELLI 2000.

57 New projects: FORI 1981; PROGETTO 1983;WHITEHOUSE 1983; MANACORDA and TAMASSIA 1985, 53–8; PANELLA 1989. Acid rain and other damage: MASSA and PARIBENI 1984; ROME EN PÉRIL 1984; ROSSVALL 1986: COULSTON 1990, 303–6; CONTI 2000.

58 Notably on the Columns of Trajan, Marcus Aurelius and Phocas; Arches of Severus and Constantine; Forum of Augustus, Hadrianeum, Temple of Saturn.

59 MELUCCO VACCARO and MURA SOMMELLA 1989; PATTERSON 1992; ARCHEOLOGIA NEL CENTRO 1985.

60 For an overview see WALLACE-HADRILL 2000. Rome's history has been marked by self-reflective anniversary celebrations, such as the great festival in April AD 247 for the first urban millennium (SHA, *Three Gordians* 33.3).

BIBLIOGRAPHY

AMICI, C.M. 1982: *Foro di Traiano: Basilica Ulpia e Biblioteche*, Roman, 1982.

ANDREOTTI, G. ROLANDO, S. and VILLARI, L. 1990: *Roma. Un Capitale in Europa, 1870–1911*, Firenze, 1990.

ARCHEOLOGIA NEL CENTRO 1985: *Roma: archeologia nel centro I, l'area archeologica centrale; II, La 'Città Murata'*, Roma, 1985.

ARCHEOLOGIA A ROMA 1989: *Archeologia a Roma nelle fotografie di Thomas Ashby, 1891–1930*, British School at Rome Archive 2, Napoli, 1989.

AUGENTI, A. 1996: *Il Palatino nel Medioevo: archeologia e topografia (secoli VI–XIII)*, BullCom Supplementi 4, Roma, 1996.

BARBERA, M. and PARIS, R. 1996: *Antiche Stanze: un quartiere di Roma imperiale nella zona di Termini, Roma dicembre 1996–giugno 1997*, Catalogo della mostra, Roma, 1996.

BARROERO, L., CONTI, A., RACHELI, A.M. and SERIO, M. 1983: *Via dei Fori Imperiali: la zona archeologica di Roma*, Roma/Venezia, 1983.

BECCHETTI, P. 1993: *Roma nelle fotografie della Fondazione Marco Besso 1850–1920*, Roma, 1993.

BELOCH, J. 1886: *Die Bevölkerung der griechisch-römischen Welt*, Leipzig, 1886.

BENEVOLO, L. 1985: *Roma. Studio per la sistemazione dell'area archeologica centrale*, LSA 7, Roma 1985.

BENEVOLO, L. and SCOPPOLA, F. (ed.) 1988: *L'Area Archeologia Centrale e la Città Moderna*, LSA 10, Roma, 1988.

BIANCHI, L. (ed.) 1998: *Case e torre medioevali a Roma. Documentazione, storia e sopravvivenza di edifici medioevali nel tessuto urbano di Roma*, Roma, 1988.

BIETTI SESTIERI, A.M. and SANTIS, A. de 2000: *Protostoria dei Popoli Latini. Museo Nazionale Romano, Terme di Diocleziano*, Milano, 2000.

BIRCH , D.J. 1998: *Pilgrimage to Rome in the Middle Ages*, Woodbridge, 1998.

BOATWRIGHT, M.T. 1987: *Hadrian and the City of Rome*, Princeton, 1987.

BORGHINI, G. (ed.) 1989: *Marmi Antichi*, Roma, 1989.

BUONOCORE, M. 1997: *Appunti di topografia Romana nei codici Lanciani nella Biblioteca Apostolica Vaticana*, Roma, 1997.

BRENTANO, R. 1990: *Rome Before Avignon*, London, 1990.

BRIZZI, B. 1975: *Roma cento anni fa nelle fotografie della raccoltà Parker*, Roma, 1975.

BRUNT, P.A. 1971: *Italian Manpower, 225 BC–AD 14*, Oxford, 1971.

BULL-SIMONSEN EINAUDI, K. (ed.) 1978: *Fotografia archeologica 1865–1914*, Roma, 1978.

BUZZETTI, C. 1985: 'Velia', *BullCom* 90, 1985, 314–20.

CAMPAGNA 1986: *Thomas Ashby. Un archeologo fotografa la Campagna romana tra ' 800 e '900*, British School at Rome Archive 1, Roma, 1986.

CAMPIDOGLIO 1984: *Il Campidoglio all'epoca di Raffaello*, Roma 1984.

CAPRARIIS, F. de 1987–88: 'Topografia archeologica dell'area del Palazzo del Viminale', *BullCom* 92, 1987–88, 109–126.

CARANDINI, A. and CAPPELLI, R. (ed.) 2000: *Roma, Romolo, Remo e la fondazione della città*, Milano, 2000.

CEDERNA, A. 1980: *Mussolini urbanista. Lo sventramento di Roma negli anni del consenso*, Roma, 1980.

CHASTEL, A. 1983: *The Sack of Rome, 1527*, Princeton, 1983.

CIANFA, T., CUSANNO, A.M., LABIANCA, L., PAPARATTI, E. and PETSECCA, M. 1985: 'Area Archeologica del Teatro di Marcello e del Portico d'Ottavia', in *Roma: archeologia nel centro* II, *La 'Città Murata'*, Roma, 1985, 533–45.

CLARIDGE, A. 1998: *Rome: an Archaeological Guide*, Oxford, 1998.

COARELLI, F., KAJANTO, I. and NYBERG, U. 1981: *L'area sacra di Largo Argentina* I: *topografia e storia*, Roma, 1981.

COATES-STEPHENS, R. 1996: 'Housing in early Medieval Rome', *PBSR* 64, 1996, 239–59.

COATES-STEPHENS, R. 1997: 'Dark Age Architecture in Rome', *PBSR* 65, 1997, 177–232.

COATES-STEPHENS, R. 1998: 'The Walls and Aqueducts of Rome in the Early Middle Ages, A.D. 500–1000', *JRS* 88, 1998, 166–178.

CONNOLLY, P. and DODGE, H. 1998: *The Ancient City*, Oxford, 1998.

CONTI, C. 2000: 'The restoration of Trajan's Column', in F. Coarelli, *The Column of Trajan*, Roma, 2000, 245–49.

CORNELL, T.J. 1995: *The Beginnings of Rome: Italy and Rome from the Bronze Age to the Punic Wars (c. 1000–264 BC)*, London, 1995.

COULSTON, J.C.N. 1990: 'Three New Books on Trajan's Column', *JRA* 3, 1990, 290–309.

CRISTOFANI, M. (ed.) 1990: *La grande Roma dei Tarquini: Roma, Palazzo delle Esposizioni, 12 giugno–30 settembre 1990*, Catalogo della mostra, Roma, 1990.

DICKINSON, G. 1960: *Du Bellay in Rome*, Leiden, 1960.
DODGE, H. and WARD-PERKINS B. 1992: *Marble in Antiquity, Collected Papers and lectures of J.B. Ward-Perkins*, British School at Rome Archaeological Monograph 6, London, 1992.
DELAINE, J. 1997: *The Baths of Caracalla: a study in the design, construction, and economics of large-scale building projects in imperial Rome*, JRA Supplementary Series 25, Portsmouth RI, 1997.
D'ONOFRIO, C. 1970: *Il Tevere e Roma*, Roma, 1970.
FAVRO, D. 1994: 'The Street Triumphant: the urban impact of Roman triumphal parades', in Z. Çelik, D. Favro and R. Ingersoll (ed.), *Streets of the World: Critical Perspectives on Public Space*, Berkeley, 1994, 151–64.
FORI 1981: *Roma: continuità dell'antico. I Fori Imperiali nel progetto della città*, Roma, 1981.
FRUTAZ, A.P. (ed.) 1962: *Le Piante di Roma*, I–III, Roma, 1962.
GUICCIARDINI, L. 1993: *The Sack of Rome*, translated by J.H. McGregor, New York, 1993.
GNOLI, R. 1988: *Marmora Romana*, ed. 2, Roma, 1988.
GREENHALGH, M. 1989: *The Survival of Roman Antiquities in the Middle Ages*, London, 1989.
GROSS, H. 1990: *Rome in the Age of Enlightenment*, Cambridge, 1990.
HARRIS, W.V. (ed.) 1999: *The Transformations of Urbs Roma in Late Antiquity*, JRA Supplementary Series 33, Portsmouth RI, 1999.
HERMANSEN, G. 1978: 'The population of imperial Rome: the Regionaries', *Historia* 27, 1978, 129–68.
HIBBERT, C. 1985: *Rome: the biography of a city*, London, 1985.
HOPKINS, K. 1978: *Conquerors and Slaves*, Cambridge, 1978.
IACOPI, I. 1985: 'Esempi di stratificazione pittorica dalla domus sotto le terme', in *Roma: archeologia nel centro II, La 'Città Murata'*, Roma, 1985, 605–22.
IACOPI, I. 1997: *La decorazione pittorica dell'Aula Isiaca*, Milano, 1997.
JONGMANN, W. 1991: *The Economy and Society of Pompeii*, Amsterdam, 1991.
KOLB, F. 1995: *Rom. Die Geschichte der Stadt in der Antike*, München, 1995.
KRAUTHEIMER, R. *et al.* 1937–77: *Corpus Basilicarum Christianarum Romae* I–V, Città di Vaticano, 1937–77.
KRAUTHEIMER, R. 1980: *Rome: Profile of a City, 312–1308*, Princeton, 1980.
KRAUTHEIMER, R. 1983: *Three Christian Capitals. Topography and Politics*, Berkeley, 1983.
KRAUTHEIMER, R. 1985: *The Rome of Alexander VII: 1655–1667*, Princeton, 1985.
KÜNZL, E. 1988: *Der römische Triumph. Siegesfeiern im antiken Rom*, München, 1988.
LANCIANI, R. 1899: *The Destruction of Ancient Rome, London, 1899.*
LANCIANI, R. 1902–94: *Storia degli scavi di Roma*, I–V, Roma, 1902–94.
LE GALL, I. 1953: *Le Tibre, fleuve de Rome dans l'antiquité*, Paris, 1953.
LLEWELYN, P. 1971: *Rome in the Dark Ages*, repr. 1993, London, 1971.
LO CASCIO, E. 1997: 'Le procedure di *recensus* dalla tarda repubblica al tardoantico e il calcolo della popolazione di Roma', in *La Rome impériale. Démographie et logistique. Actes de la table ronde (Rome, 25 mars 1994)*, Roma, 1997, 3–76.
LUGLI, G. 1952–62: *Fontes ad Topographiam veteris urbis Romae pertinentes* I–VIII, Roma, 1952–62.
MANACORDA, D. and TAMASSIA, R. 1985: *Il piccone del Regime*, Roma, 1985.
MANACORDA, D. *et al* 2000: *Crypta Balbi*, Milano, 2000.
MANCINELLI, F. 1981: *Catacombs and basilicas. The Early Christians in Rome,* Firenze, 1981.
MAIER, F.G. 1953–54: 'Römische Bevölkerungsgeschichte und Inschriftenstatistik', *Historia* 2, 1953–54, 318–51.
MAISCHBERGER, M. 1997: *Marmor in Rom*, Wiesbaden, 1997.
MÂLE, E. 1960: *The Early Churches of Rome*, London 1960.
MASSA, S. and PARIBENI, M. 1982: 'Il deperimento delle opere d'arte: cause, evoluzione, possibilità di valutazioni qualitativi', *Recerche di Storia dell' arte* 16, 1982, 11–18.
MENEGHINI, R. 1998 'L'architettura del Foro di Traiano attraverso i ritrovamenti archeologici piu' recenti', *RM* 105, 1998, 127–48.
MOATTI, C. 1993: *In Search of Ancient Rome*, London, 1993.
MORLEY, N. 1996: *Metropolis and Hinterland: The city of Rome and the Italian economy, 200 BC – AD 200*, Cambridge, 1996.
MORSELLI, C. 1985: 'Ricostruzione delle principali vicende urbanistiche fino allo suentramento di Via dei Fori Imperiali', in *Roma: archeologia nel centro* I, *l'area archeologica centrale*, Roma, 1985, 250–57.
MORSELLI, C. and TORTORICI, E. (ed.) 1989: *Curia Forum Iulium. Forum Transitorium* I–II, Roma, 1989.
MÜLLER-WIENER, W. 1977: *Bildlexikon zur Topographie Istanbuls: Byzantion-Konstantinupolis-Istanbul bis zum Beginn des 17. Jahrhunderts*, Tübingen. 1977.
NASH, E. 1961–62: *A Pictorial Dictionary of Ancient Rome*, Roma, 1961–62.

NOY, D. 2000: *Foreigners at Rome. Citizens and Strangers*, London, 2000.
OATES, W.J. 1934: 'The Population of Rome', *CP* 29, 1934, 101–16.
PACKER, J.E. 1997: *The Forum of Trajan: a study of the monuments* I–II, Berkeley, 1997.
PANELLA, R. 1989: *Roma Città e Foro. Questioni di progettazione del Centro archeologico monumentale della capitale*, Roma, 1989.
PANELLA, C. 1996: *Meta Sudans* I*: Un'area sacra in Palatino e le valle del Colosseo primo e dopo Nerone*, Roma, 1996.
PARTRIDGE, L. 1996: *The Renaissance in Rome*, London, 1996.
PATTERSON, H. and MILLETT, M. 1998: 'The Tiber Valley Project', *PBSR* 66, 1998, 1–20.
PATTERSON, J.R. 1992: 'The City of Rome: from Republic to Empire', *JRS* 82, 1992, 186–215.
PAVIA, C. 1998: *Guida di Roma sotterranea*, Roma, 1998.
PINOT DE VILLECHENON, M.N. 1998: *Domus Aurea. La decorazione pittorica del palazzo neroniano nell'album delle 'Terme di Tito' conservato al Louvre*, Milano, 1998.
PISANI SARTORIO, G. 1983: 'Una domus sotto il giardino del Pio Istituto Rivaldi sulla Velia', in K. de Fine Licht (ed.), *Città e Architettura nella Roma Imperiale. Atti del seminario del 27 ottobre 1981*, Analecta Romana Instituti Danici Supplement 10, Odense, 1983, 147–68.
PROGETTO 1983: *Roma Archeologia e Progetto*, Roma, 1983.
PURCELL, N. 1999: 'The populace of Rome in Late Antiquity: problems of classification and historical description', in W.V. Harris (ed.), *The Transformations of* Urbs Roma *in Late Antiquity*, JRA Supplementary Series 33, 1999, 135–62.
RICHMOND, I. 1930: *The City Walls of Imperial Rome*, Oxford, 1930.
RIDLEY, R.T. 1992: *The Eagle and the Spade. The Archaeology of Rome during the Napoleonic Era 1809–1814*, Cambridge, 1992.
ROBINSON, O.F. 1992: *Ancient Rome: City Planning and Administration*, London, 1992.
ROME 1977: *Rome in Early Photographs. The Age of Pius IX. Photographs 1847–78 from Roman and Danish Collections*, Copenhagen, 1977.
ROME EN PÉRIL 1984: *Rome en Péril*, Les Dossiers Histoire et Archéologie 82, 1984.
ROSSVALL, J. 1986: *Air Pollution. Safeguarding our architectural heritage*, Interdisciplinary Symposium in Rome, October 15–17, 1986, Introductory Information, Gothenburg, 1986.
RUNCIMAN, S. 1965: *The Fall of Constantinople 1453*, Cambridge 1965.
SABLAYROLLES, R. 1996: *Libertinus Miles. Les cohortes de vigiles*, Collection de l'Ecole Française de Rome 224, Roma, 1996.
SEGALA, E. and SCIORTINO, I. 1999: *Domus Aurea*, Milano, 1999.
SMITH, C.J. 1996: *Early Rome and Latium. Economy and Society c.1000–500 BC*, Oxford, 1996.
STINGER, C.L. 1985: *The Renaissance in Rome*, Bloomington, 1985.
TELLINI SANTONI, B., MANABONI, A., CAPODIFERRO, A. and PIRANOMONTE, M. 1998: *Archeologia in Posa. Dal Colosseo a Cecilia Metella nell'antica documentazione fotografica*, Milano, 1998.
THOMPSON, D. 1971: *The Idea of Rome from Antiquity to the Renaissance*, Albuquerque, 1971.
TORTORICI, E. 1985: 'Le demolizioni per l'apertura di Via dei Fori Imperiali', in *Roma: archeologia nel centro* I, *l'area archeologica centrale*, Roma, 1985, 258–67.
TORTORICI, E. 1991: *Argiletum. Commercio speculazione edilizia e lotta politica dall'analisi topografica di un quartieri di Roma di età repubblicana*, Roma, 1991
VENTRIGLIA, U. 1971: *La geologia della città di Roma*, Roma, 1971.
VIRGILI, P. 1993: 'Statue Parlante', *BullCom* 95.2, 1993, 121–128.
WALLACE-HADRILL, A. 2000 : 'Letter from Rome', *Times Literary Supplement* April 28, 2000, 15.
WARD-PERKINS, B. 1984: *From Classical Antiquity to the Middle Ages*, Oxford, 1984.
WESTFALL, C.W. 1974: *In This Most Perfect Paradise. Alberti, Nicholas V, and the Invention of Conscious Urban Planning in Rome, 1447–55,* University Park Pennsylvania, 1974.
WHITEHOUSE, D. 1983: 'The future of Ancient Rome', *Antiquity* 57, 1983, 38–44.
WISEMAN, T.P. 1998: 'A walk along the rampart', in *Horti Romani*, Bullettino della Commissione Archeologica Comunale di Roma, Supplementi 6, Roma, 1998, 13–22.

2. Early and Archaic Rome

Christopher Smith

INTRODUCTION

In Book 8 of Virgil's *Aeneid*, Aeneas arrives in the nascent city of Rome, ruled by the kindly Arcadian exile Evander.[1] He is given a brief guided tour of the settlement, having come ashore in the Forum Boarium. Evander points to the fissure in the Aventine Hill which Heracles had created in an angry fight with the monster Cacus over the cattle of Geryon, and invites Aeneas to join the 'Romans' in a sacrifice at the Ara Maxima in honour of the great hero.

After the sacrifice the two wander through the Porta Carmentalis where a temple of Apollo would one day be built, and rebuilt by Augustus,[2] into the Forum, with Evander pointing out the Asylum near the Arx and the Capitoline Hill, before they walk together up the Via Sacra towards Evander's hut, identified as on or near the site of Augustus' house (Fig. 2.1).[3] It is a poetic tour de force, a journey through time as well as space, since the Romulean sites of the Asylum and Lupercal give way to the Capitol and the Forum, the heart of Republican Rome, before the two ascend onto the Palatine, which was to become the imperial centre of Rome.

This is how the educated Roman might have seen his city at the end of the 1st century BC, a settlement which had far surpassed its humble origins in the days of Saturn and Evander when woods covered the hills and cattle lowed in the Forum and Forum Boarium. Part of the charm of Virgil's account is that one can try to match up a picture based on literary imagination and a modicum of unreliable tradition or historical guesswork with the actual city in the period from the 10th to the 6th centuries BC as revealed to us by archaeology and antiquarian research.[4] At the time of writing, with new discoveries in the Forum and on the Palatine and a wealth of information which has accumulated over more than a century of at times painstaking and at times woefully destructive excavation and urban redevelopment, we are in a better position than ever before to reassess the Rome of the kings.[5]

THE LITERARY SOURCES

Virgil is not the only author to have commented on the early city. In fact, the history of regal Rome was a subject of great fascination to many writers from various different traditions of thought. Livy, for instance, gives us a sober and unspectacular account, but behind Livy stand a number of annalists who seem to have had their own opinions about the development of the settlement.

It is not the Livian tradition, however, that helps us most, but a tradition of antiquarian rather than annalistic research which is represented in the work of Varro and in countless fragments and quotations in grammarians, encyclopaedists and interested scholars, such as

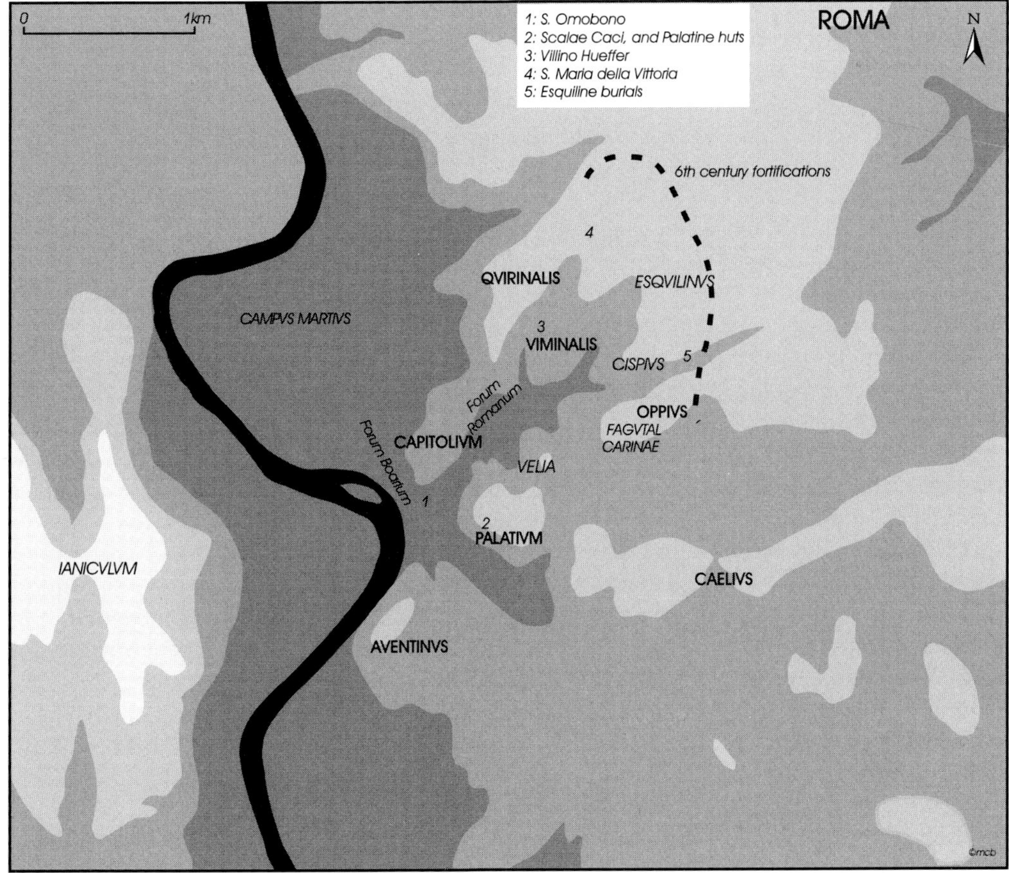

Figure 2.1: Map of the site of Early Rome.

Plutarch in his *Roman Questions*, or Festus in his mutilated dictionary. Trawling through the byways of ancient literature has yielded a rich trove of abstruse knowledge which has been used to reconstruct everything from the history of the early Roman calendar to the topography of the Roman Forum.[6] Monuments now lost have been restored to our imagination; monuments long known have been identified and re-identified.

The sources which our sources had available are a matter of dispute. If one could know that Livy and his annalistic predecessors had reliable information about the regal period, numerous inconclusive debates would never have taken place. The Livian accounts of portents, triumphs and disasters owes much to the yearly record which is supposed to have existed from the beginning of the Republic, but there is no evidence that anything similar existed for the regal period. Yet Livy preserves a coherent and credible account of Roman expansion, particularly under the later kings. This may simply be an invention, celebrating Rome's steady march to power, but we shall see some hints in the archaeological record to bear out the general pattern.

For festivals and ceremonies, the continued observation of certain rituals for centuries, not perhaps unchanged but recognizably the same, permits us to make some general remarks about early Roman religion. Certain dates or associations may also have been preserved, especially with regard to temples. It may be that the sources are right to attribute the temples of Fortuna and Diana to Servius Tullius, and that their evidence came from the local knowledge of those responsible for those temples. A good deal of intelligent guesswork may also have occurred. Presumably this is why the 4th century wall in Grotta Oscura tufa is attributed to Servius Tullius, because it had an elderly appearance in the later Republic.[7]

Cornell has argued that we perhaps underestimate the amount of information that may have been written down on perishable material, but survived long enough to enter the historical accounts.[8] We should also not exclude the possibility of there being heroic songs about the great exploits of the past; we hear of *carmina convivalia* to be sung at a *symposium* (Cicero, *Brutus* 7; Cato, *Origines* fr. 118 Peter).[9] The reliability of the sources for early Rome is limited, and the real difference between the history of archaic Rome and the history of archaic Greece is that the first was written with full knowledge of the second and at a much greater temporal distance from the events – Fabius Pictor, the first Roman historian, was not working before the end of the 3rd century BC. It is unsurprising that we should find structural similarities between accounts of Greek tyrants and accounts of the last kings of Rome. On the other hand, Rome was part of Mediterranean society, and we should not be surprised to see certain patterns occurring in Rome that look familiar from Athens or Sparta.[10]

The surest guide to the topography and the socio-economic conditions of early Rome before the 6th century remains the archaeological material. Nothing in the literary evidence is secure before that date, and much is evident make-believe. The amount of faith which one has in the sources thereafter varies according to taste, but the recent discoveries seem to indicate that the sources are more credible rather than less.

THE EARLIEST SETTLEMENT

As for most of Latium, evidence for the Bronze Age period at Rome is scattered and scanty, though according to Peroni some kind of continuous presence may be dated from the 14th century BC, at which period the Capitoline hill seems to have been used or visited.[11] It is not until the 10th century, however, that the evidence is of sufficient quantity to allow us to say anything significant about the nature of the community. Peroni has suggested a profound restructuring of society in this period, between Recent and Final Bronze Ages, using the increased amounts of weaponry as a guide.[12]

Once Rome begins to be used as a settled base early in the 1st millennium BC, it remains inhabited without a break. It is worth at this point reflecting on what the earliest 'Romans' might have seen in their home. Beyond doubt, Rome's hills must have been much more thickly wooded than they are today; modern Veii with its dense cover of trees and undergrowth over the hills bears a closer resemblance to the early site than anything in Rome itself (Fig. 2.2). The hills would have stood out more prominently; subsequent centuries have seen them flattened, quarried and transformed repeatedly, whilst the ground level has risen substantially. The low-lying ground will have been marshy and prone to flooding as the Tiber with its minor tributaries spread out through the south-west Forum and Campus Martius, making them dank and gloomy places, long afterwards associated with the Underworld.[13]

For the first settlers, Rome had no single identity, only the small hills on which they based their settlements. The earliest evidence for settlement may come from beneath the Regia in the Forum Romanum and the Domus Augustana on the Palatine, though it is possible that the Velia, which was cut away to make room for the Via dei Fori Imperiali in the 1930s, might

Figure 2.2: General view over the site of Veii (Photo: author).

have added to our knowledge.[14] There is no mystery as to why the Palatine was chosen; high and naturally defended, it was close to water supplies from the Tiber and afforded clear views in all directions, besides providing a larger area than the Capitoline.

Rome's natural features are often praised and cited as reasons for her later greatness, in particular the proximity of the Tiber River leading up into the heart of Italy and Sabine country.[15] It is hard to tell if the Tiber was used in this early period for trade, but in the 11th century the generalized Subappennine culture makes it difficult to trace trading links. Almost certainly it would have been used for fishing, and the countryside around Rome exploited for hunting. Alongside the Tiber ran the Via Salaria from the salt pans at the mouth of the Tiber; salt is such a vital product for preservation of food that it may well have been exchanged from an early period.[16]

Virgil, like Dionysius of Halicarnassus, believed that Rome had a Greek foundation, and some scholars have sought to find a material analogue to this story[17]. There is none so far, and it seems unlikely that one will ever be found. The few rather wretched sherds of Mycenaean pottery in Central Italy have all been found in Etruria, and at the time of writing amount, in total, to five.[18] The major concentration is to be found in Southern Italy, where some Mycenaeans appear to have explored towards the end of the Bronze Age and just before the cataclysm which ended their civilization.[19] It seems rather more likely that some Mycenaean pieces will have found their way up through Italy with traders or shepherds on Italy's transhumance routes.[20]

Another part of the myth, that Rome had close links with Alba Longa, some fifteen miles away in the heart of Latium (and was in fact a colony of that settlement) has a more reputable basis, since the material culture of Rome and the Alban Hills in the 10th century are closely linked typologically, and can be separated from other regional groups within the Latin area by those with a sharp eye. The Rome-Colli Albani group has close links also with an iron-producing area of Etruria, the Tolfa-Allumiere Hills, and we may perhaps see here the beginnings of Rome's role as an entrepôt for the Latin plain.[21] Nothing in the material record, however, would justify us in seeing Rome as dominant in any sense at this stage. Rome is no larger or more culturally advanced than its neighbours, such as Ardea and Lavinium.

THE FIRST PHASES OF LATIN CIVILIZATION

It is in the 10th century that we begin to be able to examine burial evidence for Rome and other sites in Latium, and with the appearance of burials with goods deposited in them comes the possibility of seriation and chronology, and also the comparison of grave goods from one settlement to another. This is not the place to engage in a lengthy discussion of the value and the precariousness of inferences about a living society drawn from the way it treats its dead, but a methodological statement is perhaps in order.[22]

It is impossible to map mortuary evidence onto a living society and to expect to trace in one the exact contours of the other. Such positivism is nowadays swiftly discounted. As Morris has rightly said, burial ritual tells us about the way in which a society treats its dead, not about the way a society engages in daily life. That said, it would be astonishing if in the broad sense, major structural features of the settlements in Latium in the 10th to the 6th centuries did not find some sort of reflection in the burials which they produced. At a very general level, the presence of weapons in graves should be taken to indicate some form of military activity; the presence of spinning equipment indicates the task of weaving clothes, rugs and so forth; and the presence of luxury items of intrinsic value and/or the extra value of having been produced outside Italy in some but not all graves suggests the existence of a stratified society.

We can probably go further. I have sought to argue that nothing in the evidence would seem to show with any degree of certainty that the graves which we find in Latium represent a cross-section of society at any time.[23] The argument that they do has led directly to the assumption that Latium in the 10th and 9th centuries was an egalitarian society, because the grave goods are to a large extent similar in nature and in number from one grave to another. This is not a necessary conclusion, but the premise is also faulty. The early burials in Rome, as at Osteria dell'Osa (now the best known necropolis, and perhaps the most carefully excavated and published one in Central Italy beside Pithecusa) are cremations, and on the whole, male cremations.[24] The grave goods which are found with the burials tend to be metal goods such as weaponry and the so-called razors, as well as typical hand-made pottery, mostly reduced in size, presumably as part of the economy of the ritual. The ashes are placed in a hut-urn and the whole group enclosed in a large jar or *dolium* (Fig. 2.3).

Cremation is not the easiest option for disposing of a body; it is a labour intensive practice requiring much wood to be found and a pyre to be built and stoked so that it reaches and retains a high temperature for some considerable time. In Osteria dell'Osa, where the burial evidence has been less destroyed by later building than in Rome, the concentration on males is very noticeable when the necropolis is established. It is at least arguable that in the early period, burial in a designated necropolis, with prestige goods (metal has to be imported into Latium, since there are no mineral resources in the region) and a particular form of burial which has not been so visible in the record before, is itself a mark of status.

This practice of exclusive burial continues in all Latin sites from the 10th century to the 6th century, when burial evidence ceases for a couple of hundred years, with only a handful of exceptions. Any objection that rests on the question of what happened to the rest of the bodies falters on this striking void.

If this line of argument is correct, it has serious implications for our understanding of the nature of the early Latin settlements and of Rome itself. In the 10th century, Latium like other regions of Central Italy (Etruria, Umbria, Campania) moves away from the undifferentiated Subappennine culture to find a local regional identity. In Etruria we find Proto-Villanovan culture moving into Villanovan culture; in Latium, Latial Phase I and IIA

Figure 2.3: Hut-urn from the Forum necropolis (Photo: editors).

Figure 2.4: The Forum necropolis during Boni's excavations 1902–1911 (Photo: Soprintendenza Archeologica di Roma).

represent an increasingly distinct Latin material culture.[25] Some sites which have not been occupied previously are now founded (Satricum appears to be an example); others continue more visibly than before. In Rome itself, even if we assume there to have been a stable population in the 11th century, which the exiguous remains scarcely justify, we cannot but notice the difference by the 10th century with the beginning of the Forum necropolis, apparently serving the community on the Palatine Hill (Fig. 2.4). There are also some cremations and associated huts near the later Temple of Divus Julius.[26]

All across Latium in the 10th century, for reasons that are now hard to specify, material culture and the forms of social life seem to have moved on to a higher level of sophistication. No such move can be wholly unconscious, or can happen without some degree of greater control of labour. The existence of specific places for burials marks a community that has decided to stay, and with stability comes a crystallization of certain forms of dominance and dependence that are not so rigid in a mobile group. In short, the evidence leads one to exactly the opposite conclusion from that of an egalitarian society in the 10th century. Rather we should see a society in the process of developing those structures which will provide an increasing surplus from the many to the few.

If we look at this crucial phase of Latin civilization from the other chronological end, from what is known as Latial Phase II (*c*. 900–770 BC), the results of this change are quite visible. The numbers of burials go up across the region, and the quantity of grave goods per burial also increases. Contacts across the region may be more visible in the record as each site develops its own pottery style. Burials which themselves stand out from the rest are to be found, marking individuals who had a prominence within the leading elite that I have identified as constituting the mortuary population. Settlements appear to grow, presumably as a result of expanding populations. Designs of pottery decoration become more sophisticated and elaborate. There is even a piece of gold jewellery in a IIA tomb in the Forum, matched by another single example in the Alban hills (Villa Cavaletti VIII).[27]

In Rome, a very interesting change has been thought to accompany the uniform transition from cremation to inhumation as the form of burial which occurred at the transition between Latial Phase I and IIA (i.e. towards the end of the 10th century). The Forum necropolis gradually goes out of use, and a new larger area is exploited on the Esquiline Hill.[28] There are various suggestions for the motives for this shift. One is that the upper stretch of the Forum, out of the way of all but the worst flooding, was becoming the focus of attention for settlement and daily use. The Forum necropolis was never destroyed, and remained for Boni to excavate alongside the Temple of Antoninus and Faustina. The more central areas of the Forum like the areas near the Regia and the 'Equus Domitiani' received very few burials and these ceased long before the first visible building work, though arguably not before the first social use. There are some huts underneath the Regia which have been associated with animal pens,[29] and some remains perhaps of huts under the Tabularium on the Capitoline Hill; it is not unreasonable to associate these with the later religious use of the site.[30] Burial and settlement evidence for the same period has been found on the Quirinal (Villa Spithöver).[31]

It should be noted that a major challenge has recently been made to the traditional chronology of this shift, which is largely based on Müller-Karpe's work.[32] Holloway has criticized the suggested move from the Forum to the Esquiline, citing two cremations on the Esquiline which ought to be early, and suggesting that we simply do not know enough about the Forum necropolis to be sure that it did not continue longer than is usually suggested. He would prefer to see the two necropoleis as contemporary, and the differences in pottery styles between the two areas as reflecting local tradition. This would be a perfect analogy with the situation at Osteria dell'Osa, where Bietti-Sestieri has identified two different pottery styles in two different burial groups, which may thus be distinguished within the necropolis.[33]

This is an extremely important suggestion, and certainly makes us more aware of the possibility that we are dealing with a period of gradual change, though it appears that we must still accept some kind of change until we find clear evidence that the Forum necropolis was not abandoned around 900 BC. The comparison with Osteria dell'Osa here also raises other issues about the nature of material record. Decoration and motif need not be regarded, as has been traditional, in a purely temporal framework. It seems very likely that in the production of an object as important as a grave-good, little would be random. The nature of decoration and shape would have been traditionally determined, and would have represented part of the self-identification of the group. Thus the place of the artisan is illuminated by this new interpretation; the artisan was as much a religious figure as a menial drudge, whose skills were called upon in very special occasions, and who would have been expected to conform to, and to remember, inherited patterns. He would therefore have been an integral part of any community.[34] It is worth noting that specifically Latin pottery was used in Latin graves beyond the 8th century, and it was only ousted from graves by imported material at a period when burials had ceased to have any real significance as a communal act and had become exclusively a matter of conspicuous consumption.

Whilst the burial evidence cannot now be taken straightforwardly as evidence for a move to a larger necropolis, it does seem to be the case that Rome's population was increasing, and that during the 9th century more of Rome's territory was being exploited, both within the future city and in the countryside. This is matched by the expansion of other Latin sites, as well as the consolidation of the Etruscan settlements which moved towards synoecism at around 900. For Etruria in particular, this growth was fortunate, for by the 8th century the Etruscan settlements were in an excellent position to profit from the new opportunities which the Greeks and Phoenicians brought with them to Central Italy.[35]

THE ORIENTALIZING PERIOD

Rome's development in the 8th century is if anything more obscure than that in previous periods, and the evidence has clearly been decimated by later building.[36] For the period described as Latial III (770–730 BC), we have only about 40 tombs surviving, the majority coming from the Esquiline burials, though there are two children's burials along the Via Sacra. There are a further four there in Period IVA (730–630 BC).[37] If we assume that these tombs were associated with houses, as I think is legitimate given evidence of intra-mural burials of children elsewhere in Latium, and in Rome itself a little later, we have an important change in burial customs, one which has an interesting analogue in Greece. The suggestion would be that children were more appropriately buried outside the necropolis, perhaps because they had not properly joined the citizen body. There is no shortage of wealth involved, since some of these burials are marked by the quantity and quality of the burial goods.[38]

It has been suggested that this is also the period at which close contacts with the Greek world began, since there have been found some fragments of Greek pottery at S. Omobono in the Forum Boarium, though it is not at all clear that there was a community of resident Greek artisans as has sometimes been envisaged.[39] It is far more likely that these pieces arrived in Rome from Etruria, possibly as part of a local trade, for we begin to find in the city from this time on larger and larger quantities of *bucchero* ware, the classic Etruscan export. Nevertheless, it may be that Rome is already challenging Veii's position as the major port on the Tiber; Bartoloni has suggested that around this time, Veii's hitherto extensive influence began to fade.[40]

The most important indication for Rome's development is a literary one: Varro's testimony for an earthen wall at the Carinae between the Oppian and the Velian hills, to which we may now add the important discovery of an 8th century wall around the Palatine Hill (Varro, *On the Latin Language* 5.48).[41] The latter has dubious qualifications as a defensive wall, but would work quite well as part of a system of defences of the Palatine, and we should perhaps imagine something similar for the Velia. The earthen wall would be a further indication that the inhabitants were protecting themselves against incursions, and that they regarded the Forum, the Palatine and the Velia as important areas which needed protection. The Tigillum Sororium, the yoke under which Horatius was forced to enter Rome after killing his sister, which appears to be some sort of ceremonial entrance with a combination of martial and religious connotations, is situated here, and may belong to the 8th century (Livy 1.26.13). The famous Palatine huts (Fig. 2.5) date to early in this period.[42]

The scarcity of burials in Rome, which is partly a product of the destruction of large parts of the material remains rather than a reflection of Roman society, makes it difficult to place Rome in context in the 7th century. If we look outside Rome, this is the period of the amazingly wealthy burials at Praeneste, burials which indicate a close link with Etruria, and thereby a link with the eastern Mediterranean.[43] The IVA burials at Rome, with quantities of beads and grape pips, indicate at a lower level the same kind of associations.[44]

Elsewhere in Latium, burials are also few in number, reflecting a deliberate depositional practice. In general, in Periods IVA and IVB, burials become fewer in number but much

Figure 2.5: A Palatine hut (Photo: author).

wealthier, until around 600 BC when they cease to be a part of the record except in isolated instances.[45] If we extrapolate from the rest of Latium to Rome, we should be thinking of an elite with access to extremely valuable luxury items from all over the Mediterranean, though seemingly channelled through Etruria, and to the kinds of surplus necessary to participate in such exchanges. It is quite possible that we have forms of peer polity interaction and gift exchange taking place, but the elite of Latium must somehow have been able to offer something in return. The most obvious item would be agricultural wealth in terms of grain and market garden vegetables for short distance contacts, and textiles as a less degradable object for more long distance contacts. Spinning equipment is common in female graves throughout Latium in this early period.[46]

The extent to which Latium could play an equal role in such exchanges is debatable, sandwiched as it is between the tremendous potential of the Campanian land, later to be so important for Rome's grain supply, and Etruria with its own agricultural strength and the added bonus of mineral resources on a large scale. Modern scholars may have underestimated the importance of Latium as an agricultural region, but it remains true that we do not find in Latium the quantities of imported Greek pottery or luxury goods that have come from Etruria and Campania, the latter of course being integrated into the Greek world through the colony at Cumae. It is a point of general validity that Rome does not grow great on its own, or on Latium's assets, but through the control of the assets of others.[47]

THE 7TH AND 6TH CENTURIES[48]

In the later part of the 7th century, Rome undergoes some major changes which indicate the development of a new and different kind of settlement. As we have seen, up until this period the lower Forum valley would have been marshy and under constant threat from flooding. If recent research is correct, a major landfill was attempted at this period to remedy the problem, raising the level of the ground by as much as two metres in places, and involving some ten to twenty thousand cubic metres of soil.[49] Subsequently pavements were built across the landfill, and the political space began to be marked out; there is a votive deposit at the Lapis Niger site and a stone building underneath the Curia. The first Regia follows not

Figure 2.6: General view of the Roman Forum from the Palatine (Photo: editors).

Figure 2.7: The Regia during excavation (Photo: Soprintendenza Archeologica di Roma).

long afterwards, and a number of votive deposits can be traced to roughly this period, including ones under the S. Omobono complex, and the Atrium Vestae.[50]

This is matched by the development of other sites in Latium, where we find votive deposits, huts of a more elaborate design, evolving towards the first stone built residences, and most importantly, clear evidence of the synoecism of various settlements, most significantly of the scattered communities around the Lago di Castiglione into the single site of Gabii around 600 BC.[51] Similar developments are attested for Etruria as well.[52]

Such trends indicate that Latin society was becoming more centred around the idea of community. If we take the example of Rome, the development of the Forum must be considered in the light of the political importance of the site at a later stage (Fig. 2.6). There were one or two new attempts to pave the Forum before the end of the 6th century, and the construction of the Cloaca Maxima at the same time must have eased flooding problems considerably.[53] This is the area where the Senate House stood, where the people met at the Comitium, where speeches were made and elections held.[54] The first Roman assembly, the

Figure 2.8: Part of the 6th century BC wall on the Arx (Photo: editors).

Figure 2.9: The S. Omobono complex (Photo: editors).

Comitia Calata, met outside the Forum at the *Curia Calabra* on the Capitoline, and may represent the thirty *curiae* of the city.[55] It was summoned by a *kalator*, this office being attested on the 6th century inscription which stood at the Lapis Niger. This inscription, apparently some kind of declaration of religious law, also contains a reference to the king. A piece of pottery with the word REX inscribed upon it has been found underneath the Regia (Fig. 2.7).[56]

Crucially, the growing visibility of the Roman king goes hand in hand with the development of the political space of Rome. At some stage, a much larger area of the site must have become designated as 'Roman', as the extension of the *pomerium* or sacred boundary of the city shows. According to Tacitus (*Annals* 12.24), the first *pomerium*, instituted by Romulus, circled the Palatine; at some stage it was extended to include a number of the other hills, and the *Comitia Calata* itself suggests an identification of a political citizen body on a much larger scale. This was the assembly which ratified wills and adoptions, as well as being involved in the selection or acclamation of the king.

The motives for these developments probably include two factors which are visible in the material record. First, the population of Latium was growing, as one would expect with the stable occupancy of a relatively well-watered and fertile area. Secondly, and not unrelated, competition for resources was increasing. From the 8th century onwards, we find increasing evidence of warrior equipment in male graves, including the accoutrements for cavalry and chariots. Furthermore, fortifications sprang up all across Latium, and the synoecism of a site like Gabii may well reflect a recognition of the need to defend territory. The development of fortifications is itself a strong impetus to the definition of a citizen body, and the development of an assembly may also reflect the need to make decisions concerning united action on the military front. The literary sources are unanimous in seeing the 7th and 6th centuries as periods of warfare; Ancus Marcius, Tullus Hostilius, Servius Tullius and both the Tarquins are all characterized by their military endeavours.[57]

Once the new definition of the settlement had been made, the monumentalization of the central areas proceeded apace. The first major stone temples and houses are found in Rome and elsewhere in Latium at precisely the same time as the burial evidence begins to dry up, indicating a redirection of wealth by an elite from personal memorialization in burial to permanent and public displays of magnificence. The motives for the elaboration of the Roman landscape will be precisely those which operate throughout Roman history – the desire to appear as a benefactor, and to leave permanent record of one's achievements.

The sources (e.g. Livy) attribute a great enceinte wall around the city to Servius Tullius in the 6th century.[58] This is almost certainly an error; the wall to which they referred was

Figure 2.10: Terracotta statue group of Athena and Heracles from the sanctuary of S. Omobono (after Holloway 1994).

constructed after the Gallic Sack of 390 BC, but traces of what may well be a 6th century fortification may be found here and there in the city, for instance, on the Capitol at the base of the Temple of Jupiter Optimus Maximus (Fig. 2.8).[59] Certainly, Rome would be extremely unusual in not having some kind of wall at this date, since all other Latin sites seem to have expanded their fortifications.[60]

This raises the question of the size of Rome, on which much has been written. General estimates, based on the idea of the four Servian regions with some form of defence around them, put the area of the city at around 285 hectares. Comparisons with other sites at the same time reveal that Rome was considerably larger than most central Italian states, though still smaller than some of the major Greek settlements in the south such as Metapontum and Gela. Ampolo estimates a population of twenty to thirty thousand for the 6th century BC. These estimates are valuable not for their accuracy but for the idea which they give of the comparative scale of Rome at this time, and as a helpful clue to the power of Rome in the later 6th century before the Battle of Lake Regillus in the 490s. If one adds in the extension of the territory of Rome through the creation of rural tribes, one has a picture of a city which, whilst its cultural forms may be to a large extent derivative, commanded an enormous source of labour and troops. The military strength of Rome was a factor from the beginning.[61]

Many of the votive deposits which have already been mentioned are covered with temples dated to the 6th century.[62] One example is the site at S. Omobono, where there is at least one temple at this time (Fig. 2.9). Coarelli has identified the site as that of Fortuna and Mater Matuta, and elaborated a series of close parallels with Pyrgi and Gravisca in Etruria, both also sites with a commercial significance. The S. Omobono area in the Forum Boarium, which was Rome's port, is indeed the site one would most expect to be in contact with influences at least from Etruria, and perhaps by this period from Greece and Carthage as well.[63] There are over 500 pieces of allegedly Greek pottery in Rome from the 7th and 6th centuries, though many of them are alas now out of context.

Another aspect of these buildings which has been alleged to be Greek in inspiration is the use of architectural terracottas, and in the context of a chapter on archaic Rome, some consideration of the work on the surviving fragments of such decoration is necessary.[64] The pioneer of such studies, Arvid Andrén, set the study on a proper footing with his attempts to create a relative chronology, and further discoveries have allowed us to progress to the point where the arguments are only over details, and not over the whole system. Creating an absolute chronology is a great deal more difficult, and to an extent works by attaching some fragments to a building whose foundation date is supposedly known from the literary sources and then calibrating the chronology for all the other pieces in the series.

That aside, we must marvel at the considerable workmanship of these early friezes with their various depictions of processions and animals. Nothing indicates the nature of early trade and artisan activity in Central Italy better than the friezes found at the Regia. These seem to be from the same matrix as others found at Velletri near the Alban Hills, both examples having a very close affinity with fragments found at Veii, which, together with Cerveteri, has been suggested as the original point of manufacture. We can imagine a few highly skilled artists whose work was distributed by others or by themselves throughout the region. Their innovations in style, design and technical boldness, particularly in the field of the great acroterial sculptures, must have been followed with the same eagerness as innovations in church architecture and ornamentation in the Middle Ages and Renaissance.[65]

One of the most important contributions which the study of the architectural terracottas can make is to clarify the building history of the Roman Forum, where most have been found. From this evidence, it appears that the Forum was seriously damaged by fire and flood some time before the middle of the 6th century, when the second Regia was destroyed, and again in the third quarter of the same century. Fire must have been a common threat due to the frequency of sacrifice followed by immolation of the offerings, and also because the roofs of buildings, though covered in terracotta decorations and tiles, were largely constructed of wood. Rebuilding can be found at the Temple of Vesta, the Comitium and even the Forum Boarium at similar times.

What did the terracottas mean? Some of the statues are evidently celebratory, for instance the marvellous group of Athena and Heracles, now thought once more after Cristofani's doubts, to have stood on the roof of the temple near S. Omobono (Fig. 2.10).[66] What of the animal terracottas? If Heracles was a popular deity in Rome, it may have been because of his exploits in defeating monsters, a set of stories which in some form or other might easily have reached Rome by the 6th century, either through Etruria or from Magna Graecia. Whatever their meaning, and indeed whether or not they had a meaning, the figures stand so firmly in a tradition of representations of hybrid creatures, lions and panthers that the fact that we have the adoption of decorative schemes from another culture can hardly be denied. At this time, Etruria was producing its own copies of the Corinthian pottery which had been imported, and which was decorated with precisely the same kinds of figures. Similarly, the popularity of scenes of procession and the hunt, also to be found on the Syrian gilt silver bowls found at Praeneste and Cerveteri, have associations both with the east, and with ideas of kingship and aristocracy.

In this context, we must mention Christer Bruun's brilliant reinterpretation of the frieze from Velletri which has been taken to represent Heracles' introduction to heaven as

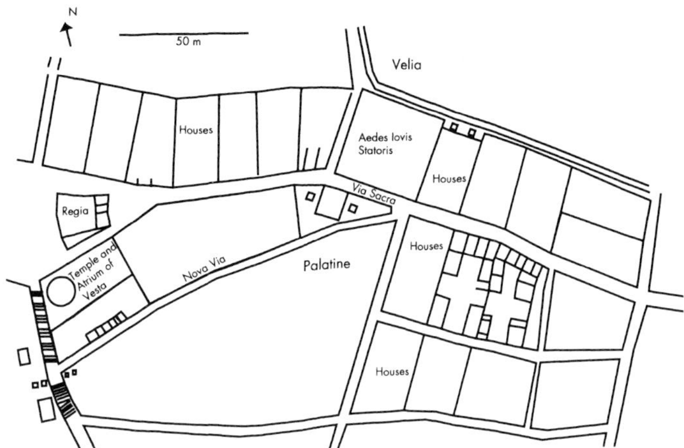

Figure 2.11: 6th century BC Rome: houses and temples along the Via Sacra (Drawing: author).

> "a group of seated figures holding various power attributes ... A common denominator for all of them can be said to be that they all depict aspects of aristocratic life; the Chariot Race, the Riding Warriors, the Banquet, and two Processions."[67]

It is very significant that the frieze contains activities which can readily be fitted into the importance of games in the ancient world, since recent work has shown the extent to which political power can be expressed in many ways at sporting spectacles.[68] The presence of a large circus in Rome at the Circus Maximus site from the archaic period is thus perfectly explicable as part of elite behaviour.

Dating other temples often relies upon the literary tradition,[69] but there is no reason to doubt the very important belief that the Temple of Jupiter Optimus Maximus, a massive structure with a podium about 61 × 55 m in size, was begun in the later 6th century, and dedicated at the beginning of the Republic. The Temple of Diana on the Aventine is also to be dated to the 6th century if we accept the association with Servius Tullius.[70] Associated finds seem to confirm an early 5th century date for the Temple of Castor and Pollux in the Forum.[71] Other votive deposits remain uncovered; there is a suggestion of a 6th century ritual deposit between the Temple of Concordia and that of Vespasian and Titus.[72] Another is on the Oppian Hill between the Palazzo Brancaccio and the Baths of Trajan.[73]

Thanks to the excavations on the slopes of the Palatine beside the Via Sacra, we now have evidence of 6th century houses as well as public buildings, and these appear to be large in size (Fig. 2.11).[74] There were probably houses on the lower slopes of the Velia on the opposite side of the Via Sacra. Apart from being on the important augural line from the Arx to the Alban Hills, the Via Sacra was also the road by which the triumphal procession of a victorious general approached the Capitoline Hill. The triumph has been identified fairly clearly as an Etruscan festival, and since the 6th century is traditionally the period of the Etruscan domination of Rome, as well as a period in which Etruscan imports are most prevalent, this would seem the appropriate context for its adoption at Rome.[75] The houses therefore flank this vital processional route, and some of their first owners may have participated in the earliest triumphs. Again this fits with the development of a site like Satricum for instance, where we find a number of large stone-built houses from the 6th century, and a clear connection with an important road through the settlement.[76]

The issue of the Etruscan presence in Rome may be combined with some comments on indications of literacy within the city. A number of the inscriptions which survive record Etruscan personal names. Very few are lengthy, though, as has been indicated above, it is arguable that we have lost a great deal. Many are to be found on votive offerings and record either maker or owner, or some kind of prayer. The habit of inscribing objects may well have been learnt from the Greeks, and particularly the Athenians whose pottery flooded into Etruria and Southern Greece in the later 6th century, taking over from Corinthian ceramics in popularity. Literacy cannot have been widespread, in the sense of an ability to read and write, but it may have been a required attribute of the elite.[77]

The sources tell us that two of the last three kings of Rome came from Etruria. The archaeological evidence also indicates an Etruscan presence; *bucchero* is found everywhere, and Rome borrows much of its religious life from Etruria, including its temple shape, the triumph, and techniques of divination; some elite clothing and marks of office such as the *lituus* may also have been adopted. There was even a part of Rome known as the Vicus Tuscus.

All of this evidence shows that the Etruscan presence in Rome was important, but it does not allow us to come to an easy conclusion about the quantity or social status of the Etruscans at Rome. If some were artisans, others were clearly more powerful and important, but it is interesting that the Etruscans are not predominant in the Republic.[78]

Two models of the ways in which foreigners may have interacted with Romans in this period may be mentioned. For the artisans, we might note that according to Pliny the Elder (*Natural History* 35.157), an Etruscan called Vulca was invited to Rome to assist with the terracottas of the Temple of Jupiter Optimus Maximus. As Bonghi Jovino has shown, it is not practical for an artisan of this kind to move his workshop from one area to another, but we might think in terms of temporary hospitality offered by one workshop to the master of another, thus allowing for the transmission of ideas across a large area.[79] At a more privileged level of society, Ampolo has developed a model of the horizontal mobility of the elite of Central Italy – individuals could easily move from one centre to another in a friendly manner, or with a certain degree of charisma and military force.[80] It may make sense to see the Etruscan impact on Rome at three different levels: a rather transient political level, with opportunist aristocrats taking the chance of power in a foreign town; a more lasting religious level, where customs and practices which the political elite employed as part of the legitimation of their power remained as part of the legitimation of a rather different elite in the Republic; and a material level, with certain Etruscan goods, or certain goods which were brought into Rome via Etruria, being desirable, encouraging the presence in Rome of merchants and artisans on a permanent or temporary but frequent basis. Their presence and their enthusiasm will have been dependent on political factors, both in Rome and in Etruria. This remains, however, one of the more difficult aspects of the 6th century at Rome, and only the continuing combination of archaeology, epigraphy and historical research will shed new light.[81]

What is less contentious is that in Rome and across Latium we can see the visible signs of an elite conspicuously consuming its wealth in the monumental development of public architecture, and attendant services like drains and cisterns (Fig. 2.12). Where does their wealth come from? If we accept the general tradition of Rome's expansion in the 6th century under strong military kings like Servius Tullius and Tarquinius Superbus, we can envisage a Rome whose territory had already extended to the 5-mile boundary which is enshrined in so many rituals dating to the 6th century, such as the Robigalia, the Amburbium, the festival of Terminalia.[82] Further support for this view is given by Livy's notice of the extent of the rural tribes by the beginning of the 5th century (Livy 2.21.7).[83] With the absorption of some small

Figure 2.12: 6th century BC cistern on the Palatine (Photo: author).

communities within the Roman system (Ficana and Castel di Decima may be examples), Rome's population was growing, and thereby Rome's army. This sets the trend for the next centuries; with each military victory, Rome begins the process of absorbing the resources of the new territory, and using its population to strengthen the army for the next objective.

THE CITY OF ROME

What does it mean to call archaic Rome a city, and when does it become appropriate to do so? These questions take us to the heart of a number of arguments about the ancient world, and are not peculiar to the Roman experience. De Polignac's influential book *La Naissance de la cité grecque* (1984, translated de Polignac 1995) contains in its very title a metaphor about the emergence of the *polis*; there is a gestation and then a moment of appearance. We may compare Müller-Karpe's idea of *Stadtwerdung*. The traditional Roman account, borrowing heavily from Greek descriptions of the act of foundation, has Romulus build a tiny wall around his small community, an act which is marked by, and incites, the first fratricide; it could be dated precisely to 21st April 753 BC. Myths of Rome's foundation are all characterized by issues of the bloodshed and horror which beset the Roman world in its later years.[84]

The Roman accounts show that by the 1st century BC at the latest, topographical and historical guesses were being made to justify various preconceived ideas of the development of the city, and that it is now rather difficult to disentangle any grains of truth which might in fact have existed. Grandazzi has recently focused on the complex web of ideas concerning the idea of *Roma quadrata*, both in the sense of a Rome laid out like an Etruscan city with an augural division of sky and land into four quarters, and also in the sense of the four regions of Rome which Servius Tullius was supposed to have instituted in place of the three tribes of Romulus. As Grandazzi shows, there is a strong tradition which would place the point from which this augury was taken on the Palatine itself, thereby making a link with the Casa Romuli and also the House of Augustus, but there was another tradition which emphasized the importance of the Aventine Hill. It is facile to regard this dispute as an indication of ignorance by the Romans, or to dismiss as pure coincidence the 8th century wall on the Palatine and the clear traces of early settlement there. The Romans seem to have known quite clearly that the Palatine was a central part of the earliest history of Rome. One of the ways of indicating this centrality was by giving the hill a sacred and symbolic topography, which was open to constant reinterpretation. This was central to a proper explanation of the nature of early Rome, and it recalls the shift of emphasis from the Palatine to the political centre of the Comitium in the Forum (whilst the area of the Mundus is itself transformed by the Augustan Umbilicus Urbis). The Mundus is a sort of parallel to the other notable cutting of the earth, the *sulcus primigenius* or first ditch which Romulus drew around the Palatine.[85]

Modern scholars tend to answer questions about the early history of Rome in terms of actual function of particular buildings and landscapes. In an important collection of material, Guidi followed various attempts to find quantifiable indicators of urban development. He suggested that Rome had a proto-urban phase in the 8th century, with population increase, the development of a central area around the Forum-Palatine and a secondary centre by the Quirinal, and evidence of trading connections with Etruria and Latium, with Rome acting as a 'central-place'. The 7th century was the period of the complete institutionalization of urban structures.[86] His article, very much in the tradition of New Archaeology, must be incorporated into more recent post-processualist approaches which would question the validity of the approach of quantifying the remains, in favour of a more experiential methodology.

Such an account has not to my knowledge been written for archaic Rome, though I suspect any conclusions which might be drawn would differ little from those of Guidi. The crucial aspects of a post-processualist account would focus on such issues as the increasingly visible reflection of hierarchical structures in the art of the 7th and 6th centuries, together with the evolution of ritual and the monumentalization of temple structures as an index of the control of the patriciate. One might also hope that such an account would explore aspects of the experience of the lower classes through the examination of the changing function of artisan activity and the expression of religious belief outside the structures of the state religion. For instance, it may be noted that the experience of placing an object in a votive deposit is likely to be significantly different from that of worshipping at a temple.

Whilst not strictly an archaeological discussion, another aspect of the arguments about early Rome needs to be raised here, and that is the exact nature of the social groupings which are attested in the sources for archaic Rome. By the 6th century there would seem to be four major groupings within the Roman state. One is the family, and the power of the Roman *paterfamilias* would appear to date back to the beginnings of Roman culture. There are three further groups which seem to have a geographical basis: the *curia*, the *tribus* and the *gens*. The *curia* is a group of men within districts of the city who come together at various occasions in order to discuss the affairs of the city and in particular the composition of the citizen body, hence their concern with adoptions and wills. The second group is the *tribus*, which has its origins in the gradual expansion of Rome into the Latin countryside. The last is the *gens*, or clan as it is sometimes translated, a body which survives in an attenuated form down into the late Republic, but which has by then lost much of its purpose and remains only to baffle the Roman jurists of the imperial period. The *gens* has been most eagerly sought for in the archaeological record; Bietti-Sestieri believes she has found a group of burials from the 8th century that might represent a *gens* at Osteria dell'Osa.[87]

One thing is very clear: the *gens* has no part as a primitive group underpinning the beginnings of the Roman state. It is far more likely to be a product of the changes of the 8th century than a component in them. If there is archaeological evidence for the *gens*, one interesting site to consider is Tor de' Cenci, just on the outskirts of Rome and within the extent of the tribal area by the end of the 6th century BC.[88] At this site burials have been found from the 7th to 6th century which were later venerated alongside a crossroads or *compitum*. According to Dionysius of Halicarnassus (4.14.3) Servius Tullius instituted the worship of ancestors at *compita* in the 6th century (another custom revived by Augustus, incidentally). If this was a site where ancestors were worshipped in the 6th century BC, we might very well have the focus here of one of the important *gentes* at Rome, many of which gave their names to tribes in this area like the Tribus Veturia and the Tribus Aemilia. Here we would have evidence also for the extension of the Roman tribal area and the exploitation of the farmland around Rome to create a surplus which supports conspicuous consumption at the centre. Here, however, we are thoroughly in the realms of the hypothetical and it is unlikely that archaeology alone will get us any closer to the realities of the time.

Another approach to the problem is through the religious festivals which have been mentioned. The October Horse (*equus October*) is a fascinating ceremony which united two parts of the city, the Forum and the Campus Martius.[89] Every year one of the two horses in a successful chariot team was sacrificed and the inhabitants of the suburbs (the *Suburranenses*) and those of the Via Sacra (the *Sacravienses*) fought for its head; if the former were successful, it was nailed to the Turris Mamilia in the Subura, and if the latter, to the Regia. The horse's tail or genitals were rushed to the Regia where they bled over the shrine of Ops Consiva, goddess (we think) of plenty.[90] The Lupercalia was originally perhaps just a race around the Palatine, indicating the importance of the settlement of that hill.[91]

A number of festivals and customs reveal a basic duality. There were two augural places in Rome; the Arx looking down the line of the Via Sacra to the Alban Hills is the most usual, but there was another on the Aventine (Varro, *On the Latin Language* 5.50). This has been explained as a lingering remembrance of a time when the communities in Rome were separate, a situation which fits with the archaeological evidence up to the 8th century. Such dualities have also been attributed to the account in the sources of Rome's dual identity, half Roman, half Sabine, after Romulus inspired the Rape of the Sabine Women. Hence there is a festival of the Quirinalia, about which little is known, which took place two days after the Lupercalia and also as part of the Parentalia festivals. We hear of Salii Palatini and Salii Collini, again reflecting the same division of Palatine and Quirinal (Dionysius of Halicarnassus 2.70.1–5). The Sabine element in Rome's history has been dismissed by some scholars for various reasons, and there is no doubt that it was overplayed in antiquity.[92] There is no clear archaeological evidence for a Sabine element in the population, though the change from cremation to inhumation and the shift of burial grounds have been taken as its effects. Rome was not unconnected to the Sabina – the Via Salaria leads directly up the river Tiber into the hinterland – but the idea of the Sabines as a distinct ethnic group in Rome from the 8th century is difficult to sustain.[93]

There were local divisions of the city as well. The shrines of the Argei *(Argeorum Sacraria)* numbered 27 and were dotted all around the city. Once a year the representatives of these shrines gathered together to throw 27 straw figures (called Argei) off the Pons Sublicius; unfortunately this festival is completely obscure (Varro, *On the Latin Language* 5.45–54).[94] The Amburbium festival was celebrated in February by a circuit of the *pomerium*, the Ambarvalia in May by a circuit of the Roman fields (though later by sacrifice at certain points).[95] The latter may have been one of the tasks of the Arval Brethren, whose grove for the goddess Dea Dia just outside the city has been explored.[96]

There is no single moment at which Rome can be called a city, or indeed a *polis*. There is a sense, however, in which the beliefs which we attribute to the *polis* mentality find an archaeological reflection in the later 7th and 6th centuries BC, just a few decades after the same developments can be seen in Greece – the creation of fortifications around synoecized sites, the emergence of a clearly defined citizen population, the abandonment of funerary display for monumental public architecture, the increased importance of sanctuary sites. We

Figure 2.13: The Lapis Niger inscription (Photo: Soprintendenza Archeologica di Roma).

do not need to assume that the Romans learnt the concept of the *polis* from the Greeks, however. I would prefer to say that in two different parts of the Mediterranean a combination of internal developments and external dynamics brought about a similar kind of response.[97]

LOOKING FORWARD

The history of early and archaic Rome as revealed by the archaeological remains is in no sense a prolegomenon to later developments, but an integral part of our understanding of why Rome comes to develop as it does. This is due to the veneration in which Rome's earliest foundations are held throughout the Republic and more particularly during the deliberate recreation of Rome's early history during the reign of Augustus. Augustus developed his own house next to the Casa Romuli on the Palatine. The Temple of Jupiter Optimus Maximus remained a focus for Roman religion for centuries. The Forum area was the scene of major reconstructions by Julius Caesar and Augustus, even though they both to some extent relocated the centre of Roman politics away from its regal and Republican home as a reflection of the changed circumstances.

Much of what we know about early Rome was in some way preserved deliberately by later generations. The Regia for instance remains frozen in the peculiar shape which it had attained by 509 BC, even though it is often rebuilt; the same was true of the Temple of Jupiter Optimus Maximus, according to the sources, and the Temple of Vesta. If Carandini is correct, the 6th century houses along the Via Sacra were inhabited by such figures as Cicero, Metellus Celer and Publius Clodius in the last century of the Republic. Even the Circus Maximus seems to be on the site of an archaic area for games and spectators. Varro could see the earthen wall which we date to the 8th century and the great *agger* of Servius Tullius near the Esquiline, and Romans knew that they trod on ancient ground by the Comitium, since the Lapis Niger was set in the floor to mark the site of the votive deposit and inscription which were later associated with the grave of a mysterious archaic personality (sometimes Romulus, sometimes another figure) (Fig. 2.13). Similarly, archaic rituals and festivals were still celebrated and recorded for centuries after their institution. The fundamental Mediterranean concerns of patronage, benefaction, honour and monumentality which link Rome with any number of sites like Athens, Pergamum and Carthage emerge in Central Italy in the 7th and 6th centuries, but the social structures which permitted such display go back further into the economic opportunities and drives which took Latium into the larger world of the 8th century, when Greeks and Phoenicians were exploring the western seas.

If the ghosts of Aeneas and Evander had repeated their walk at the end of the regal period, they would have been proud and perhaps a little amazed at how far the city had come. In the Forum Boarium, they could have met crowds of traders, most but not all from Etruria, bringing pottery containers for olive oil, perfume and wine, and precious metals in the form of brooches and vessels for the great and the good. If there were cattle in the Forum Boarium, they would now be penned, and kept away from the temples of Fortune and of Heracles. These had been built, not it is true in glistening marble, but in the malleable local tufa which could be cut into finely dressed stone, with highly painted terracotta figures on the roofs and antefixes, showing the hierarchy of the gods from the great acroterial groups like that of Athena and Heracles down to gorgons and satyrs and strange hybrid animals. They might well hear a mixture of Latin, Etruscan, Greek and Phoenician in the bustle of the market.

The tremendous Temple of Jupiter Optimus Maximus would dominate wherever they stood, high on its enormous podium. An augur might be standing on the Arx looking out towards the Alban Hills to take the augury, his eye moving along the Sacred Way. Down in the Forum, the two heroes would find themselves not in the muddy marshy emptiness they would remember, but in a wide open paved space where a crowd might be gathered to hear the proclamations of the magistrates, and near the Veteres Tabernae selling food and vegetables brought in by the farmers from the outskirts of the city.[98] As they wandered up the Via Sacra, they would see enormous houses with decoration on the outside flanking the paved path, just beyond the trapezoidal Regia and the Temple of Vesta where the sacred flame would be burning. As they climbed the Palatine they would be able to see in the distance the beginnings of fields under cultivation, and they could look down on the first Circus, where they might see races and dances. Already looking rather out of place would be the Casa Romuli, now scarcely different from one of the peasant's huts in the fields.[99] If Aeneas were to be reminded of anything, it might be the scene in Book 1 of the *Aeneid* where Aeneas and Achates look down on the new town of Carthage (Virgil, *Aeneid* 1.419–26):

> "Now they climbed the hill which most dominated the city, and looked across at the high towers opposite. Aeneas marvelled at the solid bulk of houses which were once shepherds' huts, at the gates and the noise and the paved streets. The Tyrians are busy at work there; some are building walls, labouring at constructing a citadel, and manhandling blocks of stone; others are choosing the place for a home and putting in the trench for foundations; and they choose their laws and magistrates and a reverend senate…"

ACKNOWLEDGEMENTS

I am very grateful to the editors for their comments on the text and for supplying illustrations, and to Peter Wiseman for making some valuable corrections.

NOTES

1. See GRANSDEN 1976, 29–36 and commentary.
2. The temple was vowed in 433/2 BC in response to a plague; the present remains near the Theatre of Marcellus are the work of C. Sosius, consul in 32 BC.
3. See now however REES 1996 for a powerful argument in favour of identifying Evander's Regia with the Regia in the Forum.
4. See GABBA 1991 and AMPOLO 1983 for discussions of rival accounts of early Rome, especially in the context of Augustan Rome; cf. POUCET 1985 for a sceptical account.
5. The basic description of the finds remains GJERSTAD 1953–73, though see now ANZIDEI 1985; MEYER 1983; HOLLOWAY 1994; SMITH 1994; 1996 for more recent general accounts. A great deal of information has been presented in catalogues of exhibitions; see ENEA 1981; CIVILTÀ 1976; CRISTOFANI 1990; VIVER 1989.
6. See MICHELS 1967 for the calendar; COARELLI 1986 for the Forum; CORNELL 1995, 1–30 for the sources in general.
7. *Lexicon* III, *s.v.* '"Murus Servii Tullii"; Mura repubblicane', 319–24.
8. CORNELL 1991.
9. ZORZETTI 1990.
10. On the value of the comparative approach to early Roman history, see RAAFLAUB 1986 and SMITH 1997.
11. PERONI 1988, 7; SOMELLA MURA 1978; BEDINI and BERGONZI 1979; CARDARELLI 1979. See BARKER 1981 for a general account.
12. PERONI 1979.
13. AMMERMAN 1990; COARELLI 1986, 227–98.
14. LAZIO 1980, 48; BROWN 1967; GJERSTAD 1953–73, III, 63–71; *Lexicon* V, *s.v.* 'Velia', 109–12.
15. For example, Cicero, *On the Republic* 2.3.5, 5.10, 6.11; Vitruvius, *On Architecture* 6.1.2; Livy 5.54.4; Strabo 5.3.7. See also TEVERE 1986; LE GALL 1953.
16. GIOVANNINI 1985; *Lexicon* V, *s.v.* 'Tiberis', 69–73; 'Via Salaria', 144–45.
17. Virgil, *Aeneid* 8.102 for Evander the Arcadian king; Dionysius of Halicarnassus 1.5.1 for the Greek origin of the founders of Rome.
18. PERUZZI 1980, with speculative analysis.
19. WHITEHOUSE 1973; VAGNETTI 1983.
20. See BARKER 1989 for the importance of transhumance.
21. For the Alban hills, see GIEROW 1964–66; 1983.
22. See MORRIS 1992, 1–30 for a summary of different approaches.
23. SMITH 1996.
24. BIETTI-SESTIERI 1992a; 1992b.
25. RITTATORE VONWILLER 1975; RIDGWAY 1988, 40–50; LAZIO 1980, 65–78.
26. GJERSTAD 1953–73, III, 265–94.
27. LAZIO 1980, 47–64.
28. HOLLOWAY 1994, 20–50; compare BETELLI 1997.
29. BROWN 1976.
30. SOMELLA MURA 1978.
31. GUIDI 1982, 282 with references.
32. MÜLLER-KARPE 1959; 1962.
33. HOLLOWAY 34–6; BIETTI-SESTIERI 1992a, 141–98; 1992b.
34. COLONNA 1988; SMITH 1998.
35. RIDGWAY 1992.
36. BIETTI-SESTIERI and DE SANTIS 1985 for some general discussion.
37. MEYER 1983, 49–58.
38. GJERSTAD 1954b; cf. SOURVINOU-INWOOD 1983 for the Greek parallel.
39. COARELLI 1988a; LA ROCCA 1977; CIVILTÂ 1976, 367–71.

40. BARTOLONI 1991.
41. CRISTOFANI 1990, 79–85; CARANDINI 1992; *Lexicon* III, *s.v.* '"Murus Romuli"', 315–17.
42. *Lexicon* V, *s.v.* 'Tigillum Sororium', 74–5; SMITH 1996, 81; *Lexicon* I, *s.v.* 'Casa Romuli (cermalis)', 241–42.
43. CANCIANI and VON HASE 1979.
44. GRAS 1985, 367 with refs.
45. COLONNA 1977; AMPOLO 1984b.
46. BIETTI-SESTIERI 1992a; BARBER 1991.
47. LAZIO 1980, 15–46 for the most detailed account of Latium as an agricultural region.
48. AMPOLO 1986.
49. AMMERMAN 1990
50. COARELLI 1986, 119–226; CARAFA 1998; BARTOLONI 1987; *Lexicon* II, *s.v.* 'Forum Romanum (fino alla prima età repubblicana)', 313–25; CLARIDGE 1998, 61–100 (the Roman Forum).
51. BIETTI-SESTIERI 1992a.
52. RENDELI 1991;1993.
53. *Lexicon* I, *s.v.* 'Cloaca, Cloaca Maxima', 288–90.
54. CLARIDGE 1998, 70–2 (Senate House); *Lexicon* I, *s.v.* 'Comitium', 309–14; CLARIDGE 1998, 72–4.
55. *Lexicon* I, *s.v.* 'Curia Calabra', 330.
56. COARELLI 1986; CRISTOFANI 1990, 22–3.
57. CORNELL 1995, 198–214.
58. THOMSON 1980 for all aspects of the reign of Servius Tullius; GJERSTAD 1954.
59. See RUGGIERO 1990 for the identification of 6th century *capellaccio* behind S. Omobono.
60. GUAITOLI 1984.
61. AMPOLO 1988; cf. COARELLI 1988b; CORNELL 1995, 202–10.
62. BARTOLONI 1989–90.
63. COARELLI 1988a; *Lexicon* II, *s.v.* 'Fortuna et Mater Matuta, Aedes', 281–85; cf. CRISTOFANI 1990, 111–30; VIVER 1989; *Lexicon* II, *s.v.* 'Forum Boarium', 295–97.
64. The Greek and eastern background is heavily stressed in TORELLI 1983; TORELLI also suggests that the architectural form of the buildings owes much to Greece and the Near East.
65. See now RYSTEDT 1993 for a magnificent collection of essays on the subject and a full bibliography of Andrén's writing; cf. SMITH 1998.
66. See SOMELLA 1978.
67. BRUUN 1993.
68. See THUILLIER 1993 for several essays on the centrality of games in the Etrusco-Latin world, and on the Circus Maximus, see HUMPHREY 1986, 60–7.
69. COLONNA 1984 for a summary; cf. RENDELI 1989.
70. *Lexicon* III, *s.v.* 'Iuppiter Optimus Maximus Capitolinus, Aedes, Templum (fino all'a 83 a.C)', 144–48; *Lexicon* II, *s.v.* 'Diana Aventina, Aedes', 11–3; CASSATELLA and VENDITELLI 1985; VENDITELLI 1987 and 1988 for a possible identification on the Via S. Alberto Magno.
71. NIELSEN and ZAHLE 1985; *Lexicon* I, *s.v.* 'Castor, Aedes, Templum', 242–45; CLARIDGE 1998, 91–2.
72. SCIORTINA and SEGALA 1990.
73. CORDISCHI 1993.
74. CRISTOFANI 1990, 97–9; cf. TORELLI 1983 for Etruscan parallels; *Lexicon* IV, *s.v.* 'Via Sacra', 223–28.
75. VERSNEL 1970.
76. SMITH 1994 and 1999 for further bibliography.
77. CORNELL 1991.
78. CORNELL 1995, 151–72.
79. BONGHI JOVINO 1990.
80. AMPOLO 1970–71; 1976–77.
81. For a general account, see AMPOLO 1981a; COLONNA 1981a.
82. SCULLARD 1981.
83. HUMBERT 1978.
84. For important contributions to these subjects, see now FOX 1996; GRANDAZZI 1997.
85. GRANDAZZI 1993; MAGDELAIN 1990, 188; cf. RYKWERT 1976; CASTAGNOLI 1951. Another issue which has been explored in a similar way is that of the development of a canonical Septimontium, usually attributed to Varro (*On the Latin Language* 5.41). AMPOLO has suggested that the presence of Querquetulani and Velienses in the list of those peoples who shared in the *Feriae Latinae* recalls a time when the Caelian and Velian Hills were not fully absorbed into the Roman settlement but preserved an independent existence (in

MOMIGLIANO and SCHIAVONE 1988, 167). Certainly the importance of the union of the hills for the development of early Rome was appreciated by Varro; see GELSOMINO 1975; 1976.

86. The later 7th century is taken by AMPOLO 1980–82 to be the proper date for the origin of a community, a *koinonia* or *societas*, without which the concept of the city has no meaning; cf. discussion in DREWS 1981.
87. DRUMMOND 1989, 143–54; FRANCIOSI 1984; 1988; BIETTI-SESTIERI 1992a, 199–220.
88. BEDINI 1988–89; 1990.
89. AMPOLO 1981b.
90. SCULLARD 1981, 193–94; BEARD 1998, 47–8.
91. MICHELS 1953; ULF 1982; SCULLARD 1981, 76–8.
92. For a discussion of Sabine-Roman duality, see CORNELL 1995, 75–7. For the Quirinalia festival, see SCULLARD 1981, 78–9.
93. POUCET 1967; CORNELL 1995, 29–30 and n. 70.
94. SCULLARD 1981, 90–1 and 120–21; RICHARDSON 1992, 37–9; *Lexicon* I, *s.v.* 'Argei, Sacraria', 120–25.
95. Amburbium: SCULLARD 1981, 82–4; Ambarvalia: SCULLARD 1981, 124–25; Strabo 5.3.2.
96. BROISE and SCHEID 1993.
97. SMITH 1997.
98. See FRAYN 1993, 12–37.
99. The cisterns of the 6th century on the Palatine suggest habitation; see PENSABENE 1993.

BIBLIOGRAPHY

AMMERMAN, A. 1990: 'On the Origins of the Forum Romanum', *AJA* 94, 1990, 627–45.

AMPOLO, C. 1970–71: 'Su alcuni mutamenti sociali nel Lazio tra l'VIII sec. e il IV sec.', *DialArch* 4–5, 1970–71, 37–99.

AMPOLO, C. 1976–77: 'Demarato. Osservazioni sulla mobilità sociale arcaica', *DialArch* 9–10, 1976–77, 333–45.

AMPOLO, C. 1980–82: 'Le origini di Roma e la "Cité Antique"', *MEFRA* 92, 1980, 567–76.

AMPOLO, C. 1981a: 'I gruppi etnici in Roma arcaica: posizione del problema e fonti,' in *Gli Etruschi in Roma. Atti dell'Incontro di studio in onore di M. Pallotino, Roma 11–13 dicembre 1979*, Roma, 1981, 45–70.

AMPOLO, C. 1981b: 'La città arcaica e le sue feste: due ricerche sul Septimontium e sull'Equus October', *AL* 4, 1981, 233–40.

AMPOLO, C. 1981c: 'Il gruppo acroteriale di S. Omobono', *La parola del passato* 36, 1981, 32–5.

AMPOLO, C. 1983: 'La storiografia su Roma arcaica e i documenti', in E. Gabba (ed.), *Tria Corda: Scritti in onore di Arnaldo Momigliano*, Como, 1983, 9–26.

AMPOLO, C. 1984a: 'Il lusso nelle società arcaiche', *Opus* 3/2, 1984, 469–76.

AMPOLO, C. 1984b: 'Il lusso funerario e la città arcaica', *Annali dell'Istituto Orientale di Napoli: Archeologia Storia Antropologia* 6, 1984, 71–102.

AMPOLO, C. 1986: 'Roma ed il Latium Vetus nel VI e V sec. a.C.', POPOLI VIII 1986.

AMPOLO, C. 1988: 'La città riformata e l'organizzazione centuriata. Lo spazio, il tempo, il sacro nella nuova realtà urbana', in MOMIGLIANO and SCHIAVONE 1988, 203–40.

ANZIDEI, A.P. and BIETTI-SESTIERI, A.M. 1985: *Roma e il Lazio dall'età della pietra alla formazione della città*, Roma, 1985.

BARBER, E.J.W. 1991: *Prehistoric Textiles: The Development of Cloth in the Neolithic and Bronze Ages with Special Reference to the Aegean*, Princeton, 1991.

BARKER, G. 1981: *Landscape and society: Prehistoric Central Italy*, London, 1981.

BARKER, G. 1989: 'The archaeology of the Italian shepherd', *Proceedings of the Cambridge Philological Society* 35, 1989, 1–19.

BARTOLONI, G. 1987: 'Esibizione di richezza a Roma nel VI e V secolo: Doni votivi e corredi funerari', *Scienze dell'Antichità: storia archeologia antropologia* 1, 1987, 143–59.

BARTOLONI, G. 1989–90: 'I depositivi votivi di Roma arcaica: Alcune considerazioni', *Scienze dell'Antichità: storia archeologia antropologia* 3–4, 1989–90, 747–59.

BARTOLONI, G. 1991: 'Veio e il Tevere. Considerazioni sul ruolo della comunità tiberina negli scambi tra nord e sud italia durante la prima età del ferro', *DialArch* 9.1–2, 1991, 35–48.

BEARD, M., NORTH, J. and PRICE, S. 1998: *Religions of Rome, Vol. I: A History*, Cambridge, 1998.

BEDINI, A. 1988–89: 'Tor de' Cenci (Roma) – Tombe protostoriche', *Notizie degli Scavi* 42–43, 1988–89, 221–82.

BEDINI, A. 1990: 'Un compitum dell'origine protostorica a Tor de Cenci', *AL* 10, 1990, 121–33.

BEDINI, A. and BERGONZI, G. 1979: 'La fase più antica della cultura laziale', in *Il Bronzo Finale: Atti della XXI Riunione Scientifica, Istituto Italiano di Preistoria e Protostoria,* Firenze, 1979, 399–423.

BETELLI, M. 1997: *Roma: La città prima della città: i tempi di una nascita. La cronologia delle sepolture ad inumazione di Roma e del Lazio nella prima età del ferro*, Roma, 1997.

BIETTI-SESTIERI, A.M. 1992a: *The Iron Age Community of Osteria dell'Osa: A study of socio-political development on central Tyrrhenian Italy*, Cambridge, 1992.

BIETTI-SESTIERI, A.M. (ed.) 1992b: *La necropoli laziale di Osteria dell'Osa*, Roma, 1992.

BIETTI-SESTIERI, A.M. and DE SANTIS, A. 1985: 'Indicatori archeologici di cambiamento nella struttura delle comunità laziali nell'VIII secolo a.C.', *DialArch* 3, 1985, 34–45.

BONGHI JOVINO, M. 1990: 'Artigiani e botteghe nell'Italia preromana. Appunti e riflessioni per un sistema di analisi', in M. Bonghi Jovino (ed.), *Artigiani e Botteghe nell'Italia preromana: Studi sulla coroplastica di area Etrusco-Laziale-Campana*, Roma, 19–59.

BROISE, H. and SCHIED, J. 1993: 'Étude d'un cas: Le lucus Deae Diaea á Rome,' in O. Le Cazanove and J. Scheid (ed.), *Les Bois Sacrés*, Napoli, 1993, 145–57.

BROWN, F.E. 1967: 'New Soundings in the Regia: the evidence for the early Republic', in *Les Origines de la République Romaine,* Fondation Hardt Entretiens sur l'Antiquité Classique 13, Geneva 1967, 45–64.

BROWN, F.E. 1974–75: 'La Protostoria della Regia', *RendPontAcc* 47, 1974–75, 15–36.

BROWN, F.E. 1976: 'Of Huts and Houses', in L. Bonfante and H. Von Heintze (ed.), *In Memoriam Otto. J. Brendel*, Mainz, 1976, 5–12.

BRUUN, C. 1993: 'Herakles and the tyrants: An archaic frieze from Velletri', in RYSTEDT *et al.* 1993, 267–75.

CANCIANI, F. and HASE, F-W. von 1979: *La Tomba Bernardini di Palestrina*, Roma, 1979.

CARAFA, P. 1985: *Officine ceramiche di età regia*, Roma, 1995.

CARAFA, P. 1998: *Il Comizio di Roma dalle origini all'età di Augusto*, BullCom Supplementi 5, Roma, 1998.

CARANDINI, A. 1992: 'La Mura del Palatino: nuove fonte sulla Roma di età regia', *BA* 16–18, 1992, 1–18.

CARDARELLI, A. 1979: 'Siti del passagio alla media età del Bronzo nel Lazio', *AL* 2, 1979, 139–47.

CASSATELLA, A. and VENDITELLI, L. 1985: 'Santuario di Diana sull' Aventino: Il problema della localizzazione', in *Roma: Archeologia nel Centro II; La 'Città Murata'*, Roma, 1985, 442–51.

CASTAGNOLI, F. 1951: 'Roma Quadrata', in *Studies Presented to David Moore Robinson on his seventieth birthday* I, Saint-Louis, 1951, 388–99.

CIVILTÀ 1976: *Civiltà del Lazio primitivo, Palazzo delle Esposizioni*, Roma, 1976.

CLARIDGE, A. 1998: *Rome: An Oxford Archaeological Guide*, Oxford, 1998.

COARELLI, F. 1986: *Il Foro Romano: Periodo Arcaico*, Roma, 1986.

COARELLI, F. 1988a: *Il Foro Boario dalle origini alla fine della repubblica*, Roma, 1988.

COARELLI, F. 1988b: 'Demografia e territorio', in MOMIGLIANO and SCHIAVONE 1988, 318–39.

COLONNA, G. 1977: 'Un aspetto oscuro del Lazio antico: Le tombe del Vi–V sec. a.C.', *La parola del passato* 32, 1977, 131–65.

COLONNA, G. 1981a: 'Quali Etruschi a Roma', in *Gli Etruschi in Roma: Incontro di studio in onore di M. Pallotino, Roma 11–13 dicembre 1979*, Roma, 1981, 159–72.

COLONNA, G. 1984: 'I tempii del Lazio fino al V secolo compreso', *AL* 6, 1984, 396–411.

COLONNA, G. 1988: 'La produzione artigianale', in MOMIGLIANO and SCHIAVONE 1988, 292–316.

CORDISCHI, L. 1993: 'Nuove acquisizioni su un'area di culto al Colle Oppio', *AL* 11.2, 1993, 39–44.

CORNELL, T. 1991: 'The tyranny of the evidence: A discussion of the possible uses of literacy in Etruria and Latium in the archaic age', in J. Humphrey (ed.), *Literacy in the Roman World*, JRA Supplementary Series 3, Ann Arbor, 1991, 7–34.

CORNELL, T. 1995: *The Beginnings of Rome: Italy and Rome from the Bronze Age to the Punic Wars c. 1000–264 BC*, London, 1995.

CRISTOFANI, M. (ed.) 1990: *La Grande Roma dei Tarquini: Palazzo delle esposizioni, Roma 12 giugno – 30 settembre 1990*, Catalogo della mostra, Roma, 1990.

DREWS, R. 1981: 'The Coming of the City to Central Italy', *AJAH* 6, 1981, 133–65.

DRUMMOND, A. 1989: 'Rome in the fifth century: I: The social and economic framework', in CAH2 VII.2, 113–71.

ENEA 1981: *Enea nel Lazio: Archeologia e mito – Bimillenario virgiliano. Palazzo dei Conservatori, Campidoglio, Roma, 22 settembre – 31 dicembre 1981*, Roma, 1981.

FOX, M. 1996: *Roman Historical Myths: The Regal Period in Augustan Literature*, Oxford, 1996.

FRANCIOSI, G. (ed.) 1984–88: *Ricerche sulla organizzazione gentilizia romana* I–II, Napoli, 1984–88.

FRAYN, J. 1993: *Markets and Fairs in Roman Italy: Their Social and Economic Importance from the Second Century BC to the Third Century AD*, Oxford, 1993.

GABBA, E. 1991: *Dionysius and the History of Archaic Rome*, California, 1991.
GELSOMINO, R. 1975: *Varrone e i sette colli di Roma*, Roma, 1975.
GELSOMINO, R. 1976: 'Varrone e i sette colli di Roma,' in *Atti del Congresso Internazionale di Studi Varroniani 2: Rieti, settembre 1974*, Rieti, 1976, 379–89.
GIEROW, P.G. 1964–66: *The Iron Age Culture of Latium* I–II.1, Lund, 1964–66.
GIEROW, P.G. 1983: 'I Colli Albani nel quadro archeologico della civiltà laziale', *Opuscula romana* 14, 1983, 7–18.
GIOVANNI, A. 1985: 'Le sel et la fortune de Rome', *Athenaeum* 63, 1985, 373–86.
GJERSTAD, E. 1951: 'The Agger of Servius Tullius', *Studies Presented to David Moore Robinson on his seventieth birthday* I, Saint Louis, 1951, 413–22.
GJERSTAD, E. 1953–73: *Early Rome* I–VI, Lund, 1953–73.
GJERSTAD, E. 1954a: 'The Fortifications of early Rome', *Opuscula Romana* 1, 1954, 50–65.
GJERSTAD, E. 1954b: 'Sugrundaria', in *Neue Beitrage zur klassischen Altertumswissenschaft Festschrift zum 60 Geburtstag von B. Schweitzer*, Stuttgart, 1954, 291–96.
GRANDAZZI, A. 1993: 'La Roma Quadrata: Mythe ou realité?', *MEFRA* 105.2, 1993, 493–541.
GRANDAZZI, A. 1997: *The Foundation of Rome: Myth and History*, Cornell, 1997.
GRANSDEN, K. W. 1976: *Virgil, Aeneid Book VIII*, Cambridge, 1976.
GRAS, M. 1985: *Trafics Tyrrhéniens Archaques*, Roma, 1985.
GUAITOLI, M. 1984: 'Urbanistica', *AL* 6, 1984, 364–81.
GUIDI, A. 1982: 'Sulle prime fasi dell'urbanizzazione nel Lazio protostorico', *Opus* 1/2, 1982, 279–90.
HOLLOWAY, R.R. 1994: *The Archaeology of Early Rome and Latium*, London, 1994.
HUMBERT, M. 1978: *Municipium et Civitas Sine Sugffragio: L'Organisation de la conquête jusqu'à la guerre sociale,* Collection de école français de Rome 36, Roma, 1978.
HUMPHREY, J. 1986: *Roman Circuses: Arenas for Chariot-Racing*, London, 1986.
LA ROCCA, E. 1974–75: 'Due tombe dell'Esquilino: Alcune novità sul commercio euboico in Italia centrale nell'VIII sec. a.C.', *DialArch* 8, 1974–75, 86–103.
LA ROCCA, E. 1977: 'Note sulle importazioni greche in territorie laziale nell'VIII sec a.C.', *La parola del passato* 32, 1977, 375–97.
LAZIO 1980: *La formazione della città nel Lazio*, DialArch 2, 1980.
LE GALL, J. 1953: *Le Tibre, Fleuve de Rome dans l'Antiquité*, Paris, 1953.
MAGDELAIN, A. 1990: *Ius, Imperium, Auctoritas*, Roma, 1990.
MEYER, J. 1983: *Pre-Republican Rome,* Analecta Romana Instituti Danici, Supplementi 11, Roma, 1983.
MICHELS, A.K. 1953: 'The Topography and Interpretation of the Lupercalia', *TAPhA* 84, 1953, 35–59.
MICHELS, A.K. 1967: *The Calendar of the Roman Republic*, Princeton, 1967.
MOMIGLIANO, A. and SCHIAVONE, A. (ed.) 1988: *Storia di Roma I: Roma in Italia*, Torino, 1988.
MORRIS, I. 1992: *Death Ritual and Social Structure in Classical Antiquity*, Cambridge, 1992.
MÜLLER-KARPE, H. 1959: *Vom Anfang Roms*, Heidelberg, 1959.
MÜLLER-KARPE, H. 1962: *Zur Stadtwerdung Roms*, Heidelberg, 1962.
NIELSEN, I. and ZAHLE, J. 1985: 'The Temple of Castor and Pollux on the Forum Romanum. A preliminary report on the Scandinavian excavations 1983–85, I', *Acta Archaeologica* 56, 1985, 1–29.
PENSABENE, P., RIZZO, M.A., ROGHI, M. and TALAMO, E. 1993: 'Campagne di scavo 1988–1991 nell'area sud-ovest del Palatino', *AL* 11.2, 1993, 19–36.
PERONI, R. 1979: 'L'insediamento subappeninico della Valle del Foro e il problema della continuità di insediamento tra l'età del Bronzo Recente e quella Finale nel Lazio', *AL* 2, 1979, 171–76.
PERONI, R. 1988: 'Comunità e insediamento in Italia fra Età del Bronzo e prima Età del Ferro', in MOMIGLIANO, A. and SCHIAVONE 1988, 7–38.
PERUZZI, E. 1980: *Mycenaeans in Early Latium*, Roma, 1980.
POLIGNAC, F. de 1995: *Cults, Territory, and the Origins of the Greek City-State*, Chicago, 1995.
POPOLI 1974–86: *Popoli e Civiltà dell'Italia Antica* I–IX, Roma, 1974–86.
POUCET, J. 1967: *Recherches sur la legende sabine des origines de Rome*, Louvin, 1967.
POUCET, J. 1985: *Les origines de Rome*, Bruxelles, 1985.
QUILICI GIGLI, S. (ed.) 1986: *Il Tevere e le altre vie d'acqua nel Lazio antico: settimo Incontro di studio del Comitato per l'archeologia laziale*, AL 12, Roma, 1986.
RAAFLAUB, K.A. 1986: 'The conflict of the orders in archaic Rome: A comprehensive and comparative approach', in K.A. Raaflaub (ed.), *Social Struggles in Archaic Rome: New Perspectives on the Struggle of the Orders*, California, 1986, 1–51.
REES, R. 1996: 'Revisiting Evander at *Aeneid* 8.363', *CQ* 46, 1996, 583–86.

RENDELI, M. 1989: '"Muratori, ho fretta di erigere questa casa" (Ant. Pal. 14.136): Concorrenza fra formazioni urbane dell'Italia centrale tirrenica nella costruzione di edifici di culto arcaico', *Rivista dell'Istituto Nazionale di Archeologia e Storia dell'Arte* 10, 1989, 49–68.

RENDELI, M. 1991: 'Sulla nascita delle comunità urbane in Etruria meridionale', *Annali dell'Istituto Orientale di Napoli: Archeologia Storia Antropologia* 13, 1991, 9–45.

RENDELI, M. 1993: *Città aperte: Ambiente e paesaggio rurale organizzato nell'Etruria meridionale costiera durante l'età orientalizzante e arcaica*, Roma, 1993.

RIDGWAY, D. 1988: 'The Etruscans', in CAH[2] IV, 634–75.

RIDGWAY, D. 1992: *The First Western Greeks*, Cambridge, 1992.

RITTATORE VONWILLER, F. 1975: 'La Cultura Protovillanoviana with Ripostigli "Protovillanoviani" dell'Italia Peninsulare (M.A. Fugazzola Delpino)', POPOLI IV 1975, 11–41.

RUGGIERO, I. 1990: 'La cinta muraria presso il Foro Boario in età arcaica e medio Repubblicana', *AL* 10, 1990, 23–30.

RYKWERT, J. 1976: *The Idea of a Town: The Anthropology of Urban Form in Rome, Italy and the Ancient World*, London, 1976.

RYSTEDT, E., WIKANDER, C. and WIKANDER, O. (ed.) 1993: *Deliciae Fictiles: Proceedings of the First International Conference on Architectural Terracottas at the Swedish institute at Rome, 10–12 December 1990. Acta instittuti romani regni sueciae* I–IV, Stockholm, 1993.

SCIORTINO, I. and SEGALA, E. 1990: 'Rinvenimento di un deposito votivo presso il Clivo capitolino', *AL* 10, 1990, 17–22.

SCULLARD, H.H. 1981: *Festivals and Ceremonies of the Roman Republic*, London, 1981.

SMITH, C.J. 1994: 'A review of archaeological studies on Iron Age and Archaic Latium', *JRA* 7, 1994, 285–302.

SMITH, C.J. 1996: *Early Rome and Latium: Economy and Society c. 1000–500 BC*, Oxford, 1996.

SMITH, C.J. 1997: 'Servius Tullius, Cleisthenes, and the emergence of the *polis* in Central Italy', in L. Mitchell and P.J. Rhodes (ed.), *The Development of the Polis in Archaic Greece*, London, 1997, 208–16.

SMITH, C.J. 1998: 'Traders and artisans in archaic Central Italy', in H. Parkins and C. Smith (ed.), *Trade, Traders and the Ancient City*, London, 1998, 31–56.

SMITH, C.J. 1999: 'Reviewing archaic Latium: settlement, burials, and religion at Satricium', *JRA* 12, 453–75.

SOMELLA MURA, A. 1978: 'Roma: Campidoglio e Esquilino', *AL* 1, 1978, 28–9.

SOURVINOU-INWOOD, C. 1983: 'A trauma in flux: Death in the 8th century and after', in R. Hägg (ed.), *The Greek Renaissance of the 8th Century BC: Tradition and Innovation*, Lund, 1983, 33–48.

THOMSEN, R. 1980: *King Servius Tullius: A Historical Synthesis*, Copenhagen, 1980.

THUILLIER, J.-P. (ed.) 1993: *Spectacles Sportifs et Scéniques dans le Monde Étrusco-Italique*, Roma, 1993.

TORELLI, M. 1983: 'Polis e Palazzo: Architettura, ideologia e artigianato greco in Etruria tra VII e VI sec. a.C.', in *Architecture et Société de l'archaisme grec à la fin de la république romaine. Actes du colloque international, Rome 2–4 decembre 1980*, Collection de l'école française de Rome 66, Roma, 1983, 471–500.

ULF, C. 1982: *Das römische Lupercalienfest: Ein Modellfall fuer Methodenprobleme in der Altertumwissenschaft*, Darmstadt, 1982.

VAGNETTI, L. 1983: 'I Micenei in Occidente: Dati acquisiti e prospettive future', in *Modes du contact et processus de transformation dans les sociétés anciennes: forme di contatto e processi di transformazione nelle società antiche. Actes du colloque de Cortone, 24–30 mai 1981*, Collection de l'école française de Rome 67, Roma, 1983, 165–85.

VENDITELLI, L. 1987: 'Aventino: La localizzazione del tempio di Diana: Saggi di scavo nell'area tra v. S. Alberto Magno e Largo Arrigo VII', *AL* 8, 1987, 33–8.

VENDITELLI, L. 1988: 'Prosecuzione delle indagini topografiche sull'Aventino: La localizzazione del Tempio di Diana', *AL* 9, 1988, 105–10.

VERSNEL, H.S. 1970: *Triumphus: An inquiry into the origin, development and meaning of the Roman triumph*, Leiden, 1970.

VIVER 1989: *Il Viver Quotidiano in Roma arcaica: materiali dagli scavi del tempio arcaico nell'area sacra di S. Omobono*, Roma, 1989.

WHITEHOUSE, R. 1973: 'The earliest towns in peninsular Italy', in C. Renfrew (ed.), *The Explanation of Cultural Change: Models in Prehistory*, London, 1973, 617–24.

ZORZETTI, N. 1990: 'The *Carmina Convivalia*,' in O. Murray (ed.), *Sympotica: A symposium on the Symposion*, Oxford, 1990, 289–307.

3. The City of Rome in the Middle Republic (*c*. 400–100 BC)

T. J. Cornell

The paradoxical mixture of traditionalism and innovation that is so characteristic of the Roman outlook at all periods is nowhere more evident than in the development of the city of Rome. Alongside their reverence for ancient buildings and monuments, we can detect a willingness on the part of the Romans to experiment and to introduce new types of building, new techniques of construction, and new architectural forms. On the other hand the rapid development of the city and the phenomenal growth of its population in the Republican period did not efface all traces of its ancient past. On the contrary, many relics of the archaic period survived, their form and often their actual fabric being lovingly preserved, so that even in the late Republic the city, enormous and cosmopolitan as it was, still retained the appearance of an archaic town.

Livy (40.5.7 [182 BC]) tells an interesting story about the 2nd-century BC Macedonian prince Demetrius, who was well disposed to the Romans. His enemies at the Macedonian court, who formed an anti-Roman faction, taunted him by continually aiming insults at Rome and the Romans; in particular, says Livy, "they poked fun at the appearance of the city itself, which had not yet been beautified in either its public or its private spaces". Even at the start of the 1st century BC there was little sign of rational planning, and the few marble, Greek-style buildings stood out in stark isolation. It is often, and rightly, argued that the grandiose building projects of the dynasts in the later 1st century BC were long overdue. Pompey, Caesar and Augustus were, for the first time, giving Rome the monumental appearance it deserved as the centre of a world empire.

The period covered in this chapter, from *c*. 400 to *c*. 100 BC, witnessed a dramatic transformation in the physical appearance of the city and a phenomenal increase in the size of its population. These changes occurred as a result of the Roman conquest of Italy, an extraordinary explosion of violent energy in the period from around 340 to 270 BC, and the even more remarkable series of conquests that followed the Roman victories against Carthage in the First and Second Punic Wars (264–241 and 218–202 BC), which made Rome the dominant power in the Mediterranean. Before we consider the impact of these changes, however, it will be well to define briefly what we know about the size and character of the city at the beginning of the 4th century BC.

The story of the growth of Rome in the archaic period is described in this volume by Smith. Here it is sufficient to remind ourselves that by 500 BC the site of Rome was occupied by a substantial urban settlement forming the centre of a powerful city-state. Recent discoveries have shown that 'the Great Rome of the Tarquins' ('*la grande Roma dei Tarquini*'), as it has been called, was not the product of wishful thinking on the part of the Roman annalists, but was a genuine reality of the archaic period.[1]

By contrast, the first century or so of the Republic (which traditionally began around 500 BC) was a period of decline and recession. Recent research has drawn attention to a '5th-century crisis', which affected not only Rome, but much of Italy and other areas of the Western Mediterranean, including Carthage.[2] The archaeological record of sites in Magna Graecia, Campania, Latium and Etruria during the middle years of the 5th century is extremely meagre: imports of Attic pottery virtually cease, craft production stagnates, and the artistic quality of prestige artefacts declines.[3] This bleak archaeological picture is consistent with what the literary sources tell us about Rome at this period; it was an age of military reverses and political turmoil caused by poverty and social discontent.[4]

Especially interesting is the fact that the literary sources, which record the construction of numerous public buildings during the late 6th and early 5th centuries (e.g. the temples of Jupiter Optimus Maximus, Castor and Pollux, and Saturn[5]), contain no mention of any such constructions after 484 BC. This is consistent with the archaeological record, which provides evidence of extensive building activity during the 6th century, but nothing for the succeeding period down to the early 4th century. The two sets of data fit together, which is to my mind the strongest single argument for treating the written sources with respect, and for adopting a generally conservative approach to the traditional story of early Rome.[6]

Taken together, the two bodies of evidence suggest a picture of Rome at the start of the 4th-century as a once-great city, now fallen on hard times and displaying only the faded grandeur of a glorious past. On this view it might seem that the city reached its lowest ebb in 390 BC when it was sacked by the Gauls.

That the sack was a real historical event cannot be seriously doubted (it was referred to by a number of 4th-century Greek writers, including Aristotle[7]), but the conventional view of it as a total disaster may perhaps be questioned. There are good reasons for thinking that both ancient and modern writers have exaggerated its effects. Livy (5.42–43.1 and 5.55) suggests that the city was completely destroyed and had to be rebuilt from scratch, but in this he was demonstrably mistaken.

This conclusion is based partly on the fact that the sack has left no trace whatever in the archaeological record, which is extremely surprising (note that the burnt layer in the Comitium, which Gjerstad connected with the sack, is now dated to around 500 BC and is most probably to be linked to the upheaval that accompanied the overthrow of the kings).[8] But the main reason for doubt arises from general historical considerations. It is clear that the Gauls who sacked the city were a warrior band bent on plunder and adventure, and had no particular interest in Rome as such. After ransacking the city they moved south and enlisted as mercenaries under Dionysius of Syracuse before returning home to northern Italy. It had never been their intention to occupy Rome permanently, or to destroy it in a systematic fashion, and there may well be some truth in the story that the Romans bought them off with a large payment of gold, which is unlikely to have been invented.[9]

Livy (and the many modern scholars who follow him without thinking[10]) was quite wrong to suggest that Rome was obliterated and had to be completely rebuilt. The haphazard and unplanned character of the later city centre was not the result of hasty rebuilding, as Livy thought, but rather of its gradual development from its beginnings at a very remote period. Much of the archaic city remained standing, as the archaeological evidence confirms. Many important buildings and monuments that have been excavated down to the earliest levels can be shown to have survived the Gallic attack unharmed. They include the Regia, the Comitium, the Temple of Castor, and above all the great Temple of Jupiter Optimus Maximus on the Capitol.[11] The archaic houses that Professor Andrea Carandini and his team have unearthed on the northern slopes of the Palatine[12] were also unharmed by the sack. The 6th century structures were preserved unchanged until the later 2nd century BC. Incidentally this suggests that the aristocratic families that lived in them derived much prestige from the fact that their houses were centuries old.

Finally we should note that the Gallic raid did not seriously interrupt what seems to have been a resurgence of Roman power at the turn of the 5th and 4th centuries BC. Six years earlier the Romans had conquered Veii and annexed its territory; this was part of a concerted programme of expansion which continued during the following decades, Gauls notwithstanding. The main stages in this programme include the conquest of Tusculum (381), the foundation of colonies in Southern Etruria and Latium, the annexation of the Pomptine Plain (started in 383, completed in 358), and the beginnings of an interest in maritime affairs. The evidence for the latter includes an alliance with Massalia (389), colonial expeditions to Corsica and Sardinia, and the foundation of a fortified settlement at Ostia, dated on archaeological grounds to between 380 and 350 BC.[13]

It is arguable that the main consequence of the Gallic raid was political rather than material or economic. The conflict between patricians and plebeians seems to have intensified after the departure of the Gauls (indeed it is possible that internal divisions in Rome contributed to the disaster); but these years also witnessed the beginnings of a resolution, partly resulting from the extensive resettlement of poor citizens on conquered land, and partly through the admission of plebeians to the chief magistracies under the Licinio-Sextian Laws of 367 BC (Livy 6.35–42).[14] Tradition records that this famous agreement was marked by the dedication of a Temple to Concordia in the Forum Romanum, one of a number of new constructions attributed to Marcus Furius Camillus, the semi-legendary hero who had conquered Veii and defeated the Gauls after the capture of the city (Plutarch, *Camillus* 42.4–6). Camillus is also said to have built temples to Juno Regina (the protective goddess of Veii) on the Aventine, and to Fortuna and Mater Matuta in the Forum Boarium (Livy 5.31.3 and 5.23.7).[15]

Camillus' Temple of Concord has been questioned by some scholars, but there is some archaeological evidence in its favour. Investigations of the later Temple of Concord, built in 121 BC after the murder of Gaius Gracchus, have revealed that the concrete platform on which it stood contained fragments of stone taken from a 4th century building, which could therefore have been Camillus' temple.[16] The Temple of Juno has not yet been identified, but the twin temples of Fortuna and Mater Matuta have been located at the foot of the Capitol near the Church of Sant'Omobono, built on a vast platform with a pavement in [17]*cappellaccio* tufa. This platform covered (to a depth of about 6 m) the earlier level together with the ruins of the celebrated archaic temple (see Smith in this volume), which had been destroyed and abandoned at the end of the monarchy.[18] Other temples belonging to this period include those of Mars outside the Porta Capena (388 BC) and Juno Lucina on the Cispius (375 BC).

Taken together this evidence indicates that in the early 4th century the Romans had embarked on a new programme of monumental building, after an interval of around a hundred years. This must be seen as a sign of increasing prosperity, and can be related directly to successful military conquests, since the great majority of Republican temples were built in fulfilment of vows to the gods in wartime, and were paid for out of spoils – *ex manubiis*.[19] There is therefore a correlation between the general historical picture recorded in our sources and the evidence for developments in the city itself – a fact that serves to confirm the authenticity of both.

Fig. 3.1: Surviving stretch of the Republican city-wall (378 BC), outside the Termini Station (Photo: author).

But the most significant sign of the revival of Rome's fortunes at this time is the construction of a defensive wall around the city. This is the gigantic fortification of which substantial traces remain, notably on the south side of the Aventine and in the Piazza dei Cinquecento outside the Termini station (Fig. 3.1). Although conventionally known (in modern times) as the 'Servian Wall', its connection with Servius Tullius is doubtful to say the least, and is not supported by any ancient source. The theory that it followed the line of an earlier defensive wall dating from the time of the kings is unlikely; the Gauls would never have been able to take the city in 390 if it had had all-round defences.

The construction of the wall began in 378 BC, according to Livy (6.32.1).[20] It was made of tufa from the Grotta Oscura quarries near Veii, which symbolized Rome's recent conquest of the area and incidentally confirms the date of the wall. The squared blocks were laid as headers and stretchers in a regular fashion for the whole length of the wall, which extends to some 11 km (6.5 miles) in all. Masons' marks, in the form of Greek letters, are visible on many of the surviving blocks, and suggest that the Romans brought in specialist Greek contractors, perhaps from Syracuse, which was at that time the leading centre in fortification technology.

The construction of the wall was an immense undertaking. The ashlar blocks were of irregular size, but on average measuring around 1.5 × 0.5 × 0.6 m. The millions of blocks needed for a construction over 10 m high and 4 m thick had to be quarried, shaped, transported (over a distance of more than 12 km), and laid in place; this represents a huge investment of resources by the Roman state. A reference in Livy (7.20.9) implies that the construction of the city's defences was still not complete in 353 BC, and it is not at all unbelievable that it took over thirty years to build.

When complete the wall enclosed an area of *c*. 426 hectares (about 1000 acres), including all of the famous seven hills. Although this area was probably not yet densely inhabited, the extent of the fortified area is noteworthy, and places Rome on a par with the largest urban settlements in the western Mediterranean at this date (e.g. Agrigentum 450 ha., Syracuse 315 ha., Tarentum 510 ha., Croton 615 ha.).[21] Its population was undoubtedly considerable, probably not less than 50,000 persons (see further below). Everything suggests that by the middle of the 4th century Rome was a large, dynamic centre with resources that few, if any, other states in Italy could match.

This conclusion is unlikely to convince those scholars who are inclined to minimize the significance of Rome at this date, and to dismiss as unhistorical and anachronistic any suggestion that she could have been a major player in the age before the Punic Wars. Holloway, for instance, is inclined to lower the date of the 'Servian' Wall to the later 3rd century, largely on the grounds that Rome could not have occupied an area of 426 hectares before the time of Hannibal.[22] But it is only by assuming that already by 350 BC Rome was the largest and most powerful city in central Italy that one can make any sense of the astonishing developments of the succeeding period.

In the second half of the 4th century Rome embarked on a programme of conquest and imperialism that continued without a break down to the late Republican period.[23] The rise of the Roman empire was the product of centuries of continuous and successful warfare, first in peninsular Italy, which was conquered by 272 BC, and subsequently overseas, leading to the acquisition of provinces in the Mediterranean islands, continental Italy, eastern and southern Spain, Macedonia and Greece, parts of North Africa and the South of France. By the end of the 2nd century Rome completely dominated the Mediterranean basin.

These developments had a profound impact on the social and economic life of Italy, and particularly on the city of Rome itself. Most obviously, there was a vast and continuing influx of public and private wealth, deriving from war booty, taxation and the exploitation of the natural and human resources of the empire. The city grew in size, and became not only a centre of trade and production but also more particularly a centre of consumption, as the ruling elite sought to spend the profits of empire on extravagant living and competitive display.[24] A vast service sector developed in order to support the luxurious lifestyle of the aristocracy, and to procure and supply the necessities of life for an ever-growing population.[25]

The first signs of this transformation are evident already at the end of the 4th century BC. [26] By then the Roman state was producing coined money, craft production had reached new levels, and a flourishing maritime trade had grown up, centred on the river harbour (*Portus*) which appears to have been substantially redeveloped at this time. This latter conclusion is based largely on indications in the literary sources, but there is archaeological confirmation in the fact that the earliest phases of the Temple of Portunus, the god of the harbour, go back to this period.[27]

A further sign of the change in the nature of Roman society at this time is the increasing use of slave labour, which by the end of the 4th century was already having a marked influence on the rural economy and on the structure of the urban population. The use of slaves in urban production and in domestic service was one of the principal causes of the rise in the population of the city, and can itself be illustrated by the growing number of manumissions. The act of manumission (the granting of freedom to a slave by a formal legal procedure) was made subject to a tax in 357 BC (Livy 7.16.7), and by the end of the century freedmen had become a significant group within the urban *plebs*.

The forced immigration (and subsequent manumission) of slaves was the single most important cause of the rapid increase of the city's population at this time. Voluntary immigration from the countryside was no doubt also a factor. In any case, the fact of population growth cannot be doubted. According to one estimate the city had a population of *c.* 30,000 in the mid-4th century, rising to 60,000 by 300 and exceeding 90,000 by 270.[28] If anything these figures are too cautious; others have argued for a population of *c.* 190,000 in 270, rising to 375,000 by the 120s.[29] My own opinion is that a figure of 150,000 is possible for 270, and I accept the widely held view that the city had at least 200,000 people by 200 BC.[30]

Confirmation that this was happening is provided by evidence of measures to increase Rome's water supply. The first major public aqueduct, the Aqua Appia, was built in 312 BC on the orders of the censor Appius Claudius Caecus, from whom it took its name. The capacity of the Appia (73,000 m^3 per day) was exceeded by that of its successor, the Anio Vetus, built by Manius Curius Dentatus in 272 (176,000 m^3 per day). These were among the most significant public works to be constructed during the entire Republican period.[31]

In the nature of things it would seem inevitable that the growth in population was accompanied by changes in the appearance and spatial organization of the urban area, but of these presumed changes during the middle Republic we know little. Of domestic architecture at this time we know nothing whatever, beyond what can be inferred from developments at sites such as Pompeii – on the assumption, which seems reasonable, that similar things were happening at Rome. The earliest substantial traces of domestic architecture at Pompeii date from the 3rd century, and include three early *atrium*-style houses (those of the Surgeon, of Pansa and of Sallust); as we now know, houses of this type had existed at Rome since the 6th century (see n. 12), and it is reasonable to postulate the continuing development and proliferation of a type of house that served so well the social needs of a wealthy, competitive and self-conscious elite.[32] The *atrium*-house provided space in which a wealthy *paterfamilias* could perform the rituals and functions of patronage; it was equally able to accommodate the slaves who had become essential to the running of a well-to-do household.

The dwellings of the free poor, however, are entirely beyond our knowledge in the period before the late Republic. It is worth noting, however, that a curious story in Livy (21.62.3 [218 BC]) about a cow climbing to the third storey of a building in the Forum Boarium indicates the existence of high-rise blocks (which were later the principal slum dwellings of the poor) already at the start of the Hannibalic War.

Our knowledge of public buildings in the city is not much better, but something can be done with references in literary sources and a small but significant body of archaeological material. Combining these two types of evidence can produce interesting results, even if the process is sometimes speculative. An example is provided by the case of the Comitium, the meeting place for assemblies of the people in the Roman Forum, the political and commercial centre of the city. The area was enlarged and remodelled in the second half of the 4th century, a development that is perhaps to be connected with the consulship of C. Maenius (338 BC), who decorated the speakers' platform with the beaks of the ships he had taken from Antium (338 BC). The platform was henceforth known as the *rostra* ('the Beaks'), a word that has passed into modern usage (Livy 8.14.12). He also set up a column as a monument to his victory.[33]

Victory monuments of this type became increasingly common in Rome during the course of the following centuries, as one would expect in a period of triumphant military conquest. Notable examples include the column of C. Duilius, consul in 260 BC, to commemorate a naval victory over the Carthaginians in the First Punic War, and the two arches of L. Stertinius, erected after his victories as proconsul in Spain in 196 BC (Livy 33.27.4). Another arch was erected by Scipio Africanus in 190 BC at the entrance to the precinct of Jupiter on the Capitol. These are the first known examples of the triumphal arch, a characteristic Roman structure that was to have an important place in the western tradition of monumental architecture.[34]

By far the most common type of victory monument, however, was the votive temple, vowed to a deity during a campaign, often in the heat of battle, and subsequently constructed as a thank-offering for the victory and financed from the spoils. The series of mid-Republican temples begins around 300 BC and continues through the 3rd century and into the 2nd. After around 180 BC they are recorded less frequently, and in the 1st century BC temple construction virtually ceased until the accession of Augustus.[35] At first sight this seems a strange pattern, and scholars have sought either to explain it as a symptom of a decline in traditional Roman religious beliefs and practices, or to explain it away as the product of gaps in the record.[36]

Neither of these explanations is convincing. The argument from the sources is not valid, and the suggestion that fewer temples were built because the Romans were becoming less devout is unacceptable, if only because we know that the repair and reconstruction of existing temples went on unceasingly throughout the later 2nd and early 1st centuries BC. In any case, piety was never the principal motive behind the earlier temples. Their main function was to commemorate the achievements of victorious Roman generals and to confer prestige on them and their descendants. Generals were free to dispose of the spoils of war in any way they chose, and the dedication of a temple was therefore seen as equivalent to an act of private munificence. The temples themselves were associated directly in the public mind with the men who built them, and in some cases even bore their names, at least informally, so that titles like 'Temple of Metellan Jupiter' became common. The Temple of Honour and Virtue (*Honos et Virtus*) built by Gaius Marius after his victory over the Germans in 101 BC became known simply as the 'Monument of Marius'.[37]

It is important to remember that the great majority of Republican temples were victory monuments paid for out of spoils (at least 85%, as far as our record goes[38]). Many of them were dedicated to gods of victory – Victoria, Victoria Virgo, Venus Victrix, Hercules Victor, Hercules Invictus, etc[39] – and were situated along the triumphal route from the Campus Martius to the Capitol, along which victorious generals rode in triumph.[40] Temple dedications and triumphs were closely linked, and it is to be noted that the frequency of triumphs is exactly parallel to the pattern of temple dedications: extremely frequent in the 3rd and early 2nd centuries, with peaks in the periods from 300 to 250, and 200 to 160, and with a sharp decline in the second half of the 2nd century BC.[41] This decline, which is matched in the record of temple dedications, reflects the changing character of Roman warfare in the last century of the Republic.[42]

The great majority of mid-Republican temples are known only from literary sources, and only then because of the dramatic circumstances in which they were vowed, or the fame of the persons who vowed them, rather than because of their importance as buildings or their contribution to the urban landscape. We should be careful not to exaggerate the significance of buildings that happen to have been recorded in annalistic sources whose principal purpose was to register the activities of aristocratic politicians and generals.

As far as we can tell, most of the mid-Republican victory temples were small isolated shrines in the old 'Etrusco-Italic' style, built of wood and tufa and with terracotta decorations.[43] The primitive state of Roman temple architecture at this time is illustrated by the story of Q. Fulvius Flaccus, who as censor in 173 BC began the construction of a temple to Fortuna Equestris which he had vowed during his campaign against the Celtiberians seven years earlier. In his effort to make it the largest and most magnificent temple in Rome, he could think of no better plan than to strip the marble roof-tiles from a Greek temple in southern Italy.[44]

Fig. 3.2: Round temple in the Forum Boarium, probably to be identified with the Temple of Hercules Victor (c. 120 BC) (Photo: editors).

The earliest marble temples in Rome made their appearance only in the second half of the 2nd century. The first was the Temple of Jupiter Stator (otherwise known as the Temple of Metellan Jupiter), vowed by Metellus Macedonicus in 146 BC, shortly followed by the Temple of Mars, vowed by D. Junius Brutus Callaicus (132 BC). Both were the work of a Greek architect, Hermodorus of Salamis, and were built of white marble transported from Greece.[45] Another early marble temple, the round temple in the Forum Boarium, is still partly preserved; the original roof and marble entablature are missing, but the columns and part of the *cella* still survive, to make this one of the oldest standing structures in the city of Rome (Fig. 3.2). It is most probably to be identified with the Temple of Hercules Victor, and dates from around 120 BC. It is made of Greek (Pentelic) marble, and was almost certainly the work of a Greek architect, perhaps none other than Hermodorus of Salamis himself.[46]

Standing remains of Republican buildings are extremely rare in Rome, but another temple, not far from the round temple and dating probably from a few decades later, is preserved almost intact. This is the Temple of Portunus (Fig. 3.3), built around 100 BC to replace the original structure of the late 4th or early 3rd century, of which traces have been uncovered by excavation (see above). Built largely of travertine, it is a classic example of a hellenized Etrusco-Italic temple, on a high podium with frontal steps, enclosed on three sides and with a deep porch supported by six Ionic columns in pure Greek style.[47]

Other Republican temples of which traces survive include the Temple of Victory on the Palatine, dedicated by Lucius Postumius Megellus in 294 BC, but completely restored in the early 1st century, and three adjacent temples in the Forum Holitorium, once again represented by standing remains of 1st-century BC restorations (Fig. 3.4). They can be identified as the temples of Spes (Hope) and Janus (both originally built in the mid-3rd century), and Juno Sospita (early 2nd century).[48] Finally, a group of four Republican victory temples was unearthed in the 1920s in the Largo Argentina (Figs. 3.5 & 3.6). These too were modified and restored in the 1st century BC, but traces of earlier structures remain. Identification is controversial, although the latest of them, Temple B, is almost certainly to be identified with the Temple to Fortuna huiusce dei, vowed by Quintus Lutatius Catulus during a battle

Fig. 3.3: Temple of Portunus in the Forum Boarium (c. 100 BC) (Photo: author).

Fig. 3.4: Columns of the Temple of Spes in the Forum Holitorium: early imperial reconstruction of an original building dating from the 3rd century BC (Photo: author).

against the Cimbri in 102 BC. The others date from the early and mid-3rd century (Temples C and A respectively), and the early 2nd (Temple D).[49]

The archaeological evidence makes it quite clear that most of the victory temples of the 3rd and early 2nd centuries were systematically repaired and frequently rebuilt during the last century of the Republic; when Augustus proudly claimed that in his sixth consulship (28 BC) he repaired 82 temples in the city (*Res Gestae* 20.4), he was doing no more than observing traditional practice after what if anything was only a fairly short period of neglect. But the resources and efforts expended on the task of restoration in the 2nd and 1st centuries BC were relatively small by comparison with what was spent on public works of other kinds.

In the 2nd century there was a shift from victory monuments, dedicated by generals and financed from the booty of one-off campaigns, towards civic buildings and public amenities constructed at public expense and funded from regular taxation and exploitation of permanent provinces. This shift reflects a change in the military policy and financial structures of the state. The magistrates who were at the center of this system were the censors, who held office every five years and supervised the system of public contracts, whereby private individuals and companies undertook to provide goods and services for the state. The importance of this system is beyond doubt; Polybius (6.17.2–7) tells us that the whole population had an interest in the contracts, and that this dependence made the people subservient to the senate, which provided the funds that were administered by its representatives, the censors.

The regular contracts for the construction and repair of public buildings let out by the censors are recorded in our sources (especially Livy), and included an increasing volume and range of activities as the empire grew and the state's revenues increased. The works in question included bridges across the Tiber, such as the Pons Aemilius, constructed in 179 BC on the foundations of an earlier bridge of (probably) 3rd-century date. The existing remains, the Ponte Rottoth (the 'broken bridge'), are of a reconstruction by Augustus (Fig. 3.7).[50] The city's drains, perhaps including the Cloaca Maxima, were refashioned in 184, and in 174 a systematic programme of street paving was undertaken.[51]

These improvements to what would now be called the infrastructure were extremely significant in terms of the amount of money invested and the levels of employment created. Probably the most important of all was the Aqua Marcia, the aqueduct constructed in the years 144–40, the single most expensive building undertaken during the Republic.[52] Its capacity was 187,000 m^3 per day, and it virtually doubled the city's water supply. The need for it was apparently urgent, a piece of information that tends to confirm that the population of the city had doubled since the mid-3rd century and was now well in excess of 300,000.

The water supply was only one of the basic needs that had to be met if a city of such gigantic size was to survive. It could not have been sustained solely by the produce of its own agricultural hinterland, and we know that Rome had regularly been importing part of its food supply since the 4th century.[53] By 200 BC most of its basic needs were being imported, which necessitated the development of new port facilities on the banks of the Tiber. The old river harbour at the foot of the Capitol was no longer adequate, and a new commercial area with port facilities, the Emporium, was developed downstream in the area to the south west of the Aventine.

The Severan Marble Plan indicates that around AD 200 this whole area was taken up with warehouses and granaries. We know from literary sources that the earliest store buildings in this area were erected in the 2nd century BC, and the substantial surviving traces of the Horrea Galbana can be attributed to Ser. Sulpicius Galba, the consul of 108 BC.[54] Of particular historical significance were the Horrea Sempronia, built by the tribune Gaius Gracchus in 122 BC after his epoch-making law which for the first time made the food supply of the city a responsibility of the state.[55] Under this measure grain was to be procured in bulk from the provinces, stored in purpose-built granaries, and sold at a fixed price to the citizens, who were each entitled to a monthly ration. By the end of the Republic the rations were being given out free, and the number of adult male citizens entitled to receive them had reached 320,000 (Suetonius, *Julius Caesar* 41). This figure has allowed scholars to calculate that the total population of the city, including women, children and slaves, must by then have been of the order of one million persons.[56]

Along the river in front of the granaries ran a huge roofed structure, the Porticus Aemilia, first erected in 193 BC by the curule aediles M. Aemilius Lepidus and L. Aemilius Paullus, but rebuilt in concrete by the censors of 174 BC. Measuring 487 × 60 m, with a barrel-vaulted concrete roof supported by 294 internal pillars, it represents a vast covered space into which goods could be offloaded directly from the quayside. Parts of this remarkable building are still standing (Figs. 3.8 & 3.9), and provide evidence of the large-scale use of concrete at the start of the 2nd century BC.[57]

This was a revolutionary development in building technology that must have been developed during the course of the 3rd century. The earliest attested use of masonry work consisting of rubble bound by mortar in Rome is in the substructure of the first Temple of Magna Mater on the Palatine, dedicated in 191 BC.[58] This and other early concrete structures (like the Porticus Aemilia) were faced with small irregularly shaped pieces of stone (*opus incertum*). In the course of the 2nd century concrete facings gradually became more regular, until 100 BC, a facing known as *opus reticulatum,* consisting of a network of pyramidal-shaped pieces of stone, with their bases set diagonally and forming a diamond pattern, became standard (Fig. 3.10).[59]

The reasons for this change are not clear. The later method was no stronger than the earlier irregular one, and an aesthetic motive can be ruled out because the finished surface was rendered with plaster.[60] The most plausible explanation is that the rapid growth of the

Fig. 3.5: Largo Argentina, Temple A (mid-3rd century BC, restored in the 1st century BC) (Photo: author).

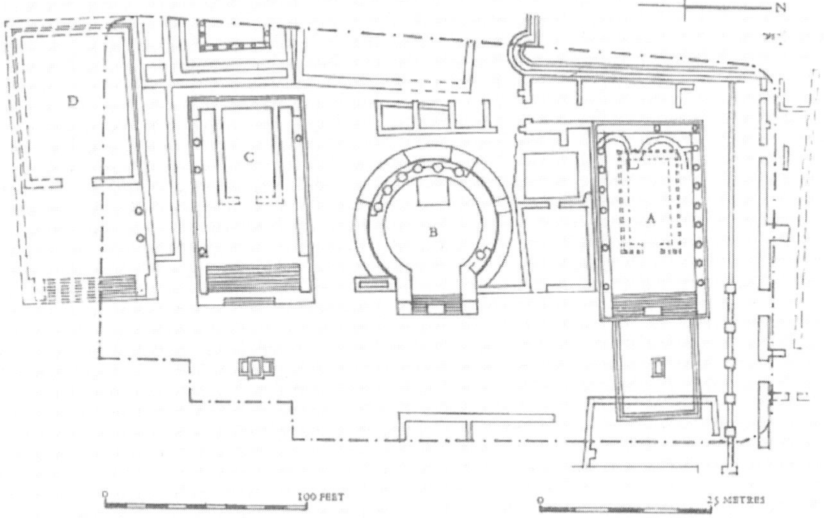

Fig. 3.6: Republican Victory temples in the Largo Argentina: plan (after Boethius 1978).

Fig. 3.7: Remains of the Pons Aemilius (179 BC), now known as the Ponte Rotto (the 'Broken Bridge'). The stone facing belongs to a reconstruction of the Augustan age. (Photo: editors).

city in the later 2nd century necessitated the introduction of 'industrialized' building techniques, using regular standardized components suitable for a mass labour force, perhaps largely consisting of slaves.[61]

It was also during the 2nd century that the first attempts were made to introduce monumental planning and the systematic organization of urban space. In particular we may observe efforts to surround public squares with porticoes and colonnades to create an appearance of symmetry or axiality. The earliest building to be referred to as a *porticus* (the Porticus Aemilia, described above) was, for all its impressive dimensions, a utilitarian structure, but it was followed by others which were designed on the model of a Greek stoa, to enclose a temple precinct or to run along opposing sides of a forum or street. At least twelve of these monumental porticoes were constructed in the course of the 2nd century BC. Important examples include the Porticus Octavia built by Gnaeus Octavius (168 BC), the Porticus Metelli (147 BC) and the Porticus Minucia Vetus (110 BC), all of them in the Campus Martius.[62] The precise location of these structures is still unclear, however, and few remains are preserved; some details are known from the *FUR*.[63]

Similar to the porticoes both in function and design were the earliest basilicas. A basilica was a large rectangular building in the form of a covered hall resting on rows of pillars, and its original purpose seems to have been to provide shelter from rain or sun for activities that would otherwise have been conducted in the open. Its name suggests a Greek origin, although curiously no Greek precedents have been identified for the distinctive Roman basilicas that were constructed around the Roman Forum in the 2nd-century BC, and are found reproduced at Pompeii and many other Roman towns.[64] The first was the Basilica Porcia, built by the censor M. Porcius Cato in 184 BC, followed by the Fulvia (179BC), the Sempronia (169), and the Opimia (121). Nothing survives of these 2nd century examples, which were replaced in the 1st century BC by the Basilica Paulli (Aemilia) and Basilica Julia, which flanked the northern and southern sides of the Forum (respectively) and of which substantial traces remain.[65]

In spite of these efforts to give the city of Rome a coherent monumental appearance, there can be no doubt that at the end of the 2nd century it was still a largely haphazard and disorganized place. It would have seemed unsophisticated and backward by comparison not only with contemporary Greek cities, but even with the increasingly hellenized towns of central and southern Italy, of which Pompeii is only the best-known example. These Italian towns not only possessed a degree of formal monumentality that was far in advance of Rome (one only has to think of the elaborate hellenistic sanctuaries at nearby Praeneste and Tibur);[66] they were also served with comforts and amenities that the people of Rome were denied. In the first half of the 1st century BC Rome still possessed no permanent stone theatre, no amphitheatre, and no monumental complex of public baths, even though such facilities were well established at Pompeii and elsewhere.

The explanation for this deliberate self-denial (for such it surely was) must be political. It is to be noted that many of the innovations described above (such as the first basilica, built by Cato the Censor) were introduced against strong senatorial opposition. Attempts to construct a stone theatre were frustrated by conservative reactionaries in 154, and again in 106 BC.[67] The ostensible reason given by the sources is that a Greek-style theatre would demoralize the people, which seems hardly plausible (Tacitus, *Annals* 14.20). A more persuasive suggestion is that the senatorial oligarchy was alarmed by the fact that theatres in Greek cities were used for popular gatherings, and were associated with democracy.[68] There may be something in this, but it is not likely to be the whole answer since the phenomenon extends to other institutions, such as baths, which are less obviously political in the same sense.

More probably it has to do with the fact that public building in Rome was always the object of competitive display among the aristocracy, and that buildings of all types, not just victory monuments, conferred prestige on the men who built them. The most obvious sign of this is the fact that all public works – roads, aqueducts and granaries no less than porticoes and basilicas – bore the family names of their authors and were regarded as in some sense family monuments. They stood, isolated from one another, as reminders of individual achievement, with little or no attempt to contribute to a wider overall plan. The Republican city was no more than the sum of its parts. In this it precisely reflected the social and political system. In Rome there was no concept of a collective abstraction such as 'the government' or 'the state' that could take action independently of the individual magistrates holding office at any one time.

The ruling senatorial nobility was a group of fiercely competing individuals, each fired by two countervailing ambitions: to be the first among equals by doing everything possible to outmatch his fellows, and to prevent at all costs any of his rivals from doing the same thing. The characteristic feature of the political system was the diffusion of official roles and the fragmentation of political authority. Official power was shared, and limited, by the joint principles of collegiality and annual tenure. Whatever a man achieved in any one year could in theory be matched or outdone by colleagues or successors. A military victory in one area did not preclude successful campaigns in other theatres or in future wars. A triumph elevated the general to the highest level – indeed to the status of a god – but lasted only for a day.[69]

The dedication of a victory monument was a way of creating a permanent reminder of one's achievement, but others could do the same. Major civic buildings and public works were rather more sensitive, and it is not an accident that this was an area of activity left to the censors, the highest magistrates in the state appointed only at five-year intervals from the most distinguished ex-consuls. Even so, the more ambitious works promoted by the censors aroused suspicion and often outright opposition. Individual civic buildings and public works were permitted, but within limited bounds, and there was no chance that any one individual would be able to make radical changes to the appearance of the city by imposing an integrated plan.

Above all, it seems, the oligarchy were suspicious of any permanent institutions or structures that would provide tangible benefits for the mass of the people. To give only one example that has already been mentioned, Gaius Gracchus' grain law was bitterly resented, and was one of the acts that caused the nobility to murder him.[70] Public benefactions that were permitted included entertainments and shows, and these were the object of intense rivalry between office-holders and their colleagues and successors. But in the nature of things the effects of a public show, however spectacular and expensive, lasted only for the duration of people's memories and were rapidly superseded. It is symptomatic of this state of affairs that the spectacles were held in public open spaces and that temporary structures were erected to stage the performance and to provide seating for the crowd (see Coleman in this volume).

Gladiatorial combats, for instance, were staged in the Forum, and the people watched from wooden seating and the balconies and upper storeys of the basilicas and other surrounding buildings.[71] The temporary structures could themselves be extremely elaborate. The Elder Pliny (*Natural History* 36.113–15) gives a remarkable description of the temporary theatre erected by M. Aemilius Scaurus, *aedile* in 58 BC, which supposedly held 80,000 spectators and had a stage consisting of marble columns interspersed with bronze statues.[72] This was permitted only because the theatre was a temporary structure that was removed after the shows ended. The absurdity of this is noted by Tacitus (*Annals* 14.21), who observed that a

Fig. 3.8: Part of the Porticus Aemilia (174 BC), faced in opus incertum *(Photo: author).*

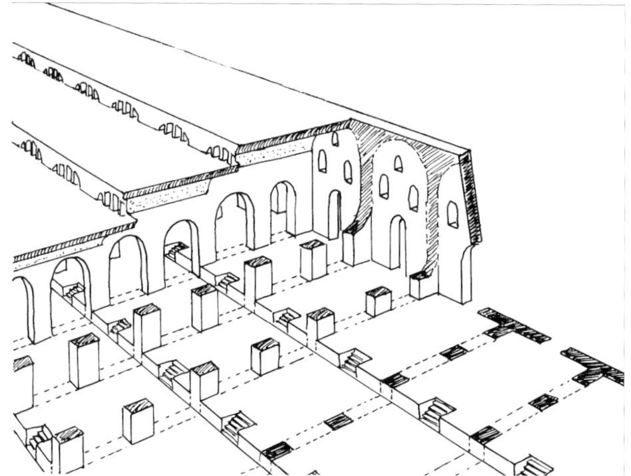

Fig. 3.9: Porticus Aemilia: axonometric reconstruction (after Boethius 1978).

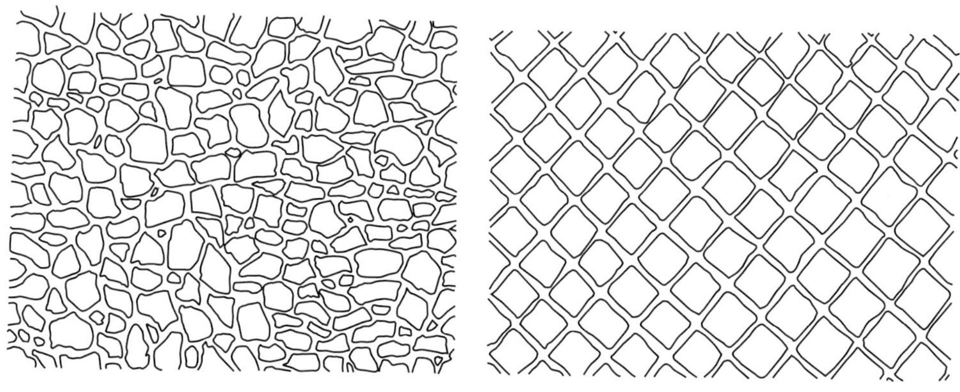

a. *Opus incertum* b. *Opus reticulatum*

Fig. 3.10: Facing techniques for Roman concrete in the later Republic.

permanent theatre would be less costly than elaborate edifices that were put up and razed to the ground year after year at immense cost.

It follows that the crude, backward and unplanned character of the city of Rome and its buildings in the middle Republic was not an accident or the product of backward technology or lack of sophistication; on the contrary, it was the result of artificial factors sustained by social, political and institutional pressures. Things eventually changed in the 1st century BC when political power became concentrated in the hands of the great military dynasts. The first permanent stone theatre was begun by Pompey in 61 BC and completed in 55. Caesar started a second theatre which was finished by Augustus and named after his nephew Marcellus. Caesar also initiated a grandiose plan to rebuild the city centre, including an additional forum and a new Senate House.[73] This scheme was completed and extended by Augustus, who added a new forum of his own and carried out a systematic reconstruction of all the major buildings in the city, allowing him to make the famous claim that he found a city of brick and left it a city of marble (Suetonius, *Augustus* 28; see Walker in this volume). His aide T. Statilius Taurus built the first permanent amphitheatre in 30 BC, and his son-in-law Agrippa was responsible, among other initiatives, for the first of the great public bath complexes in Rome.[74]

The transformation of the city under Pompey, Caesar and Augustus was, as noted at the start of this chapter, long overdue. But it was only possible because of the change in the political situation. By the end of Augustus' reign the city had been transformed in accordance with some semblance of an integrated urban plan. The buildings and monuments that bore his name or those of his relatives and associates were evident on every side, as he himself was able to boast in the *Res Gestae*. To anyone observing this at the time, as Millar has pointed out, it would have been obvious that Rome was now under the rule of a monarchy.[75]

NOTES

1 PASQUALI 1936; CRISTOFANI 1990; CORNELL 1995, 198–214; SMITH 1996. For a different view of the period see HOLLOWAY 1994.
2 COLONNA 1990; CORNELL 1995, 225.
3 GJERSTAD 1966, 514–18; MEDIO REPUBBLICANA 1973, 96–9.
4 On the difficulties faced by Rome in the 5th century see CORNELL 1995, 265–71, 304–9.
5 *Lexicon* I, *s.v.* 'Castor, Aedes, Templum', 242–45; *Lexicon* III, *s.v.* 'Iuppiter Optimus Maximus Capitolinus, Aedes, Templum (fino all'a 83 a.C.)', 144–48; *Lexicon* IV, *s.v.* 'Saturnus, Aedes', 234–36.
6 CORNELL 1995, especially 28, 198–214.
7 Plutarch, *Camillus* 22, citing Heraclides Ponticus as well as Aristotle; other Greek writers who mentioned the sack include the 4th century historian Theopompus (fr. 317 Jac. = Pliny, *Natural History* 3.57).
8 GJERSTAD 1941, 148–50, revised by COARELLI 1983, 129–30.
9 See further CORNELL 1989, 302–8.
10 For example, GJERSTAD 1960, 220; for an opposing view see CASTAGNOLI 1974, 425–27.
11 *Lexicon* I, *s.v.* 'Comitium', 309–14; 'Castor, Aedes, Templum', 242–45; *Lexicon* III, *s.v.* 'Iuppiter Optimus Maximus Capitolinus, Aedes, Templum (fino all'a 83 a.C.)', 242–45; *Lexicon* IV, *s.v.* 'Regia', 189–92.
12 CRISTOFANI 1990, 97–9; CORNELL 1995, 96–9; CLARIDGE 1998, 111–12.
13 CORNELL 1989, 309–15.
14 BRUNT 1971b, 55–6.
15 *Lexicon* III, *s.v.* 'Iuno Regina', 125–26; II, *s.v.* 'Fortuna et Mater Mutata, Aedes', 281–85.
16 *Lexicon* I, *s.v.* 'Concordia, Aedes', 316–20, especially 317.
17 SMITH 1996, 159–60.
18 *Lexicon* II, *s.v.* 'Fortuna et Mater Matuta, Aedes', 281–85.
19 PAIS 1920, 489–506; AMPOLO 1990, 482–89; FAVRO 1994, 159.

20 On the Servian Wall, see SÄFLUND 1930; MEDIO REPUBBLICANA 1973, 7–31; TODD 1978, 13–20; *Lexicon* III, *s.v.* '"Murus Servii Tullii"; Mura repubblicane', 319–24.
21 CORNELL 1995, 204. The walls excluded the Campus Martius and the Transtiber region.
22 HOLLOWAY 1994, 100; the figures he gives need to be corrected.
23 HARRIS 1979, 9–10, and *passim*.
24 HOPKINS 1978, 38–40.
25 For a general discussion, see ROBINSON 1992, 130–59.
26 MEDIO REPUBBLICANA 1973; STARR 1980; CORNELL 1995, 380–98.
27 COLINI and BUZZETTI 1986; ADAM 1994b.
28 STARR 1980, 11–26.
29 BRUNT 1971a, 376.
30 MORLEY 1996, 39.
31 On aqueducts, see ASHBY 1935, especially 49 (Aqua Appia) and 54 (Anio Vetus); HODGE 1992; AICHER 1995. See Dodge in this volume for aqueducts and delivery capacities.
32 WALLACE-HADRILL 1988, particularly 43–7; CLARKE 1991, 2–12; PATTERSON 2000, 38–43.
33 *Lexicon* I, *s.v.* 'Comitium', 309–14; 'Columna Maenia', 301–2; *Lexicon* IV, *s.v.* 'Rostra (età repubblicana)', 212–14. A generation later the Comitium was again restructured as a circular space, perhaps on a Greek model, a form that was to be reproduced in Roman colonies, which were also equipped with circular spaces for political assemblies (BOËTHIUS 1978, 112, 133; COARELLI 1983, 138–49; BALTY 1991).
34 VERSNEL 1970, 134–37; see also KÜNZL 1988, 45–64; 101–3 (column of C. Duilius) and 50 (triumphal arches). On victory monuments in general see also HARRIS 1979, 261–62; PIETILÄ-CASTREN 1987; ABERSON 1994; FAVRO 1994; COARELLI 1996, 26–34; PATTERSON 2000, 31–8.
35 Data in WISSOWA 1912, 594–95; PAIS 1920, 489–506; ZIOLKOWSKI 1992, 187–88.
36 Thus, for example, BEARD 1994, 736–38. The argument is paradoxical, given the vast increase in source material of all kinds for the last generation of the Republic. Beard claims that our knowledge of temple construction derives principally from Livy, whose surviving text ceases in 167 BC. In fact Livy is not the only source to provide information on 3rd and 2nd century temples; even without him the pattern would still be quite clear, though less pronounced. It should be noted that Livy is not available for most of the 3rd century (the period 292–218), but we know of at least 25 temples that date from that period!
37 *Lexicon* III, *s.v.* 'Honos et Virtus, Aedes Mariana', 33–5.
38 PAIS 1920, 489–506; AMPOLO 1990, 482–89.
39 These victory cults were based on contemporary hellenistic models, and their appearance in Rome at the beginning of the 3rd century is a clear sign of Greek cultural influence (WEINSTOCK 1957). Other recipients of temples included warlike deities – Bellona, Mars, Honos, Virtus – and gods whose favour and protection was needed in war, such as Fortuna (fortune), Salus (safety), Spes (hope), Felicitas (good luck), and Fortuna huiusce dei (the fortune of this day).
40 PIETILÄ-CASTREN 1987, 154–58; FAVRO 1994.
41 RICH 1993, 50.
42 RICH 1993, 44–55; CORNELL 1993, 156–60.
43 For a general discussion of the 'Etrusco-Italic' style, see BOËTHIUS 1978, 35–64.
44 Livy 42.3; for the general point, see GROS 1978, 11–2.
45 GROS 1978, 37–9; BOYD 1953, 152–59; MORGAN 1971, 480–505; OLINDER 1974, 83–124; *Lexicon* III, *s.v.* 'Iuppiter Stator, Aedes ad Circum', 157–59 and 'Mars in Circo', 226–29.
46 *Lexicon* II, *s.v.* 'Forum Boarium', 295–97; COARELLI 1988, 180–204; ZIOLKOWSKI 1988 (identifying the round temple with the victory temple of L. Mummius Achaicus, constructed during his censorship in 142 BC).
47 ADAM 1994b; *Lexicon* IV, *s.v.* 'Portunus, Aedes', 153–54.
48 *Lexicon* IV, *s.v.* 'Palatium (età repubblicana – 64 D.C.)', 22–8, especially 23; *Lexicon* II, *s.v.* 'Forum Holitorium', 299; CLARIDGE 1998, 247–50.
49 COARELLI 1981; CLARIDGE 1998, 215–19.
50 *Lexicon* IV, *s.v.* 'Pons Aemilius', 106–7.
51 *Lexicon* I, *s.v.* 'Cloaca, Cloaca Maxima', 288–90.
52 Frontinus, *On Aqueducts* 1.7, giving the figure of 180 million sesterces; see Dodge in this volume for discussion and bibliography, particularly on the problems of discussing aqueduct capacities.
53 CORNELL 1989, 409; RICKMAN 1980, 94–119; GARNSEY 1983, 119–20; 1988, 178–81.
54 *Lexicon* III, *s.v.* 'Horrea Galbana', 40–2; COARELLI 1977, 15. On granaries in general, see RICKMAN 1971.
55 *Lexicon* III. *s.v.* 'Horrea Sempronia', 47.
56 BRUNT 1971a, 376–88; HOPKINS 1978, 96–8; MORLEY 1996, 33–9. STOREY 1997 argues for a much lower total figure (around 450,000), but does not convince.

57 The identification of the surviving physical remains as the Porticus Aemilia has now been seriously questioned by Stephen Tuck, see *Lexicon* IV, *s.v.* 'Porticus Aemilia', 116–17; *Lexicon* V, *s.v.* '(Horrea Corn)elia', 263.
58 *Lexicon* III, *s.v.* 'Magna Mater, Aedes', 206–8.
59 BLAKE 1947, 227–75 (with dates that need modification); COARELLI 1977, 9–19; ADAM 1994a, 125–34.
60 Vitruvius actually thought it was weaker (*On Architecture* 2.8.1), but in this he was possibly mistaken (CARTER 1989, 39–40). There is some controversy regarding the use of a plaster rendering on concrete facings: see ADAM 1994a, 133, who suggests that plaster might have been added at a later date when architectural practices and fashions were different. See MACDONALD 1982, 85 and 114–15 for this practice in the imperial period.
61 COARELLI 1977, 9–19; TORELLI 1995, 212–45.
62 Full list in BLAKE 1947, 130 n. 1; *Lexicon* IV, *s.v.* 'Porticus Octavia', 139–41; 'Porticus Metelli', 130–32; 'Porticus Minucia Vetus', 137–38; OLINDER 1974; MORGAN 1971; BOYD 1953.
63 WISEMAN 1974.
64 See BOËTHIUS 1978, 149–56; Vitruvius, *On Architecture* 5.1.4–10.
65 *Lexicon* I, *s.v.* 'Basilica Porcia', 187; 'Basilica Fulvia', 173–75; 'Basilica Sempronia', 187–88; 'Basilica Opimia', 183;'Basilica Paul(l)i', 183–87 and 'Basilica Iulii, Iuliae', 179–80.
66 The classic study is still that of DELBRÜCK 1907–12. See also BOËTHIUS 1978, 166–69 (Sanctuary of Hercules Victor at Tibur), 169–74 (Sanctuary of Fortuna Primigenia at Praeneste), although his dates are around 50 years too low.
67 Livy, *Periochae* 48 (154 BC); Appian, *Civil Wars* 1.28 (106 BC); Valerius Maximus 2.4.2. Discussion in NORTH 1992.
68 Cicero, *Speech for Flaccus* 16; RUMPF 1950; FRÉZOULS 1983, 193–96.
69 VERSNEL 1970, 56–93; KÜNZL 1988; for aristocratic competition see PATTERSON 2000, 29–52.
70 See, for example, Appian, *Civil Wars* 1.21; Cicero, *Speech for Sestius* 103.
71 WELCH 1994, 69–78.
72 *Lexicon* V, *s.v.* 'Theatrum Scauri', 38–9.
73 Theatre of Pompey: CLARIDGE 1998, 214; *Lexicon* V, *s.v.* 'Theatrum Pompei', 35–8; Theatre of Marcellus: CLARIDGE 1998, 243–45; *Lexicon* V, *s.v.* 'Theatrum Marcelli', 31–5. See also FAVRO 1996, 57–60 (Pompey), 60–78 (Julius Caesar) and *Lexicon* I, *s.v.* 'Curia Iulia', 332–34.
74 *Lexicon* I, *s.v.* 'Amphitheatrum Statilii Tauri', 36–7; FAVRO 1996, 164. For Agrippa's building activities, see SHIPLEY 1933; FAVRO 1996 and *Lexicon* V, *s.v.* 'Thermae Agrippae', 40–2.
75 MILLAR 1984, 56–8.

BIBLIOGRAPHY

ABERSON, M. 1994: *Temples votifs et butin de guerre dans la Rome republicaine*, Biblioteca Helvetica Romana 26, Roma, 1994.
ADAM, J.-P. 1994a: *Roman Building: Materials and Techniques*, London, 1994.
ADAM, J.-P. 1994b: *Le temple de Portunus à Rome*, Roma, 1994.
AICHER, P.J. 1995: *Guide to the Aqueducts of Ancient Rome*, Wauconda, 1995.
AMPOLO, C. 1990: 'Aspetti dello sviluppo economico agl'inizi della repubblica romana', in W. Eder (ed.), *Staat und Staatlichkeit in der frühen römischen Republik*, Stuttgart, 1990, 482–93.
ASHBY, T. 1935: *The Aqueducts of Ancient Rome*, Oxford, 1935.
BALTY, J.-C. 1991: *Curia ordinis*, Bruxelles, 1991.
BEARD, M. 1994: 'Religion', in *CAH* 9, 1994, 729–68.
BEARD, M., NORTH, J. and PRICE, S. 1998: *Religions of Rome, Vol. I: A History*, Cambridge, 1998.
BLAKE, M.E. 1947: *Ancient Roman Construction in Italy from the Prehistoric Period to Augustus*, Washington DC, 1947.
BOËTHIUS, A. 1978: *Etruscan and Early Roman Architecture*, Harmondsworth, 1978.
BOYD, M.J. 1953: 'The Porticoes of Metellus and Octavia and their Two Temples', *PBSR* 21, 1953, 152–59.
BRUNT, P.A. 1971a: *Italian Manpower, 225 BC – AD 14*, Oxford, 1971.
BRUNT, P.A. 1971b: *Social Conflicts in the Roman Republic*, London, 1971.
CARTER, J.M. 1989: 'Civic and Other Buildings', in I.M. Barton (ed.), *Roman Public Buildings*, Exeter, 1989, 31–65.
CASTAGNOLI, F. 1974: 'Topografia e urbanistica di Roma nel IV secolo a.C.', *Studi Romani* 22, 1974, 425–27.
CLARIDGE, A. 1998: *Rome: An Oxford Archaeological Guide*, Oxford, 1998.
CLARKE, J.R. 1991: *The Houses of Roman Italy, 100 BC – AD 250*, Berkeley, 1991.
COARELLI, F. 1996: *Revixit ars: arte e ideologia a Roma. Dai modelli ellenistici alla tradizione repubblicana*, Roma, 1996.
COARELLI, C., KAJANTO, I. and NYBERG, U. 1981: *L'Area Sacra di Largo Argentina: Topografia e Storia*, Roma, 1981.

COARELLI, F. 1977: 'Public Building in Rome between the Second Punic War and Sulla', *PBSR* 45, 1977, 1–23.
COARELLI, F. 1983: *Il Foro Romano 1. Periodo arcaico*, Roma, 1983.
COARELLI, F. 1988: *Il Foro Boario dalle origini alla fine della repubblica*, Roma, 1988.
COLINI, A.M. and BUZZETTI, C. 1986: 'Aedes Portuni in Portu Tiberino', *BullCom* 90, 1986, 7–30.
COLONNA, G. 1990: 'Città e territorio nell'Etruria meridionale del V secolo', in *Crise et transformation des sociétés archaïques de l'Italie antique au Ve siècle av. J.C. Actes de la table ronde, Rome 19–21 novembre 1987*, Collection de l'École Française de Rome 137, Roma, 1990, 7–21.
CORNELL, T.J. 1989: 'The Recovery of Rome' and 'The Conquest of Italy', in *CAH* 7, 2, 1989, 309–419.
CORNELL, T.J. 1993: 'The End of Roman Imperial Expansion', in J.W. Rich and G. Shipley (ed.), *War and Society in the Roman World*, London, 1993, 139–70.
CORNELL, T.J. 1995: *The Beginnings of Rome*, London, 1995.
CRISTOFANI, M. (ed.) 1990: *La grande Roma dei Tarquini: Palazzo delle esposizioni, Roma 12 giugno – 30 settembre 1990*, Catalogo della mostra, Roma, 1990.
DELBRÜCK, R. 1907–12: *Hellenistische Bauten in Latium*, Strasbourg, 1907–12.
FAVRO, D. 1996: *The Urban Image of Augustan Rome*, Cambridge, 1996.
FAVRO, D. 1994: 'Rome. The Street Triumphant: The Urban Impact of Roman Triumphal Parades', in Z. Çelik, D. Favro and R. Ingersoll (ed.), *Streets of the World, Critical Perspectives on Public Space*, Berkeley, 1994, 151–64.
FRÉZOULS, E. 1983: 'La construction du theatrum lapideum et son contexte politique', in *Théâtre et spectacles dans l'antiquité, Actes du colloque de Strasbourg*, Strasbourg, 1983, 193–214.
GARNSEY, P. 1983: 'Grain for Rome', in P. Garnsey, K. Hopkins and C.R. Whittaker (ed.), *Trade in the Ancient Economy*, London, 1983, 118–30.
GARNSEY, P. 1988: *Famine and Food Supply in the Graeco-Roman World: Responses to Risk and Crisis*, Cambridge, 1988.
GJERSTAD, E. 1941: 'Il comizio romano dell'età repubblicana', *Opuscula Romana* 2, 1941, 97–158.
GJERSTAD, E. 1960: *Early Rome III*, Lund, 1960.
GJERSTAD, E. 1966: *Early Rome IV*, Lund, 1966.
GROS, P. 1978: *Architecture et société à Rome*, Bruxelles, 1978.
HARRIS, W.V. 1979: *War and Imperialism in Republican Rome, 327–70 BC*, Oxford, 1979.
HODGE, A.T. 1992: *Roman Aqueducts and Water Supply*, London, 1992.
HOLLOWAY, R.R. 1994: *The Archaeology of Early Rome and Latium*, London 1994.
HOPKINS, K. 1978: *Conquerors and Slaves*, Cambridge, 1978.
KÜNZL, E. 1988: *Der römische Triumphe*, München, 1988.
MEDIO REPUBBLICANA 1973: *Roma medio-repubblicana: aspetti culturali di Roma e del Lazio nei secoli IV e III a.C.*, Catalogo della mostra, Roma, 1973.
MILLAR, F.G.B. 1984: 'State and Subject: The Impact of Monarchy', in F. Millar and E. Segal (ed.), *Caesar Augustus: Seven Aspects*, Oxford, 1984, 37–60.
MORGAN, M.G. 1971: 'The Porticus of Metellus: A Reconsideration', *Hermes* 99, 1971, 480–505.
MORLEY, N. 1996: *Metropolis and Hinterland: The city of Rome and the Italian economy, 200 BC – AD 200*, Cambridge, 1996.
NORTH, J.A. 1992: 'Deconstructing Stone Theatres', in *Apodosis: Essays in honour of Dr W.W. Cruickshank to mark his eightieth birthday*, London, 1992, 75–83.
OLINDER, B. 1974: *Porticus Octavia in Circo Flaminio*, Stockholm, 1974.
PAIS, E. 1920: *Fasti Triumphales Populi Romani*, Roma, 1920.
PASQUALI, G. 1936: 'La grande Roma dei Tarquini', *La Nuova Antologia*, 16 August 1936, 405–16 (= Pasquali, G. 1942: *Terze pagine stravaganti*, Firenze, 1942, 1–24).
PATTERSON, J.R. 2000: *Political Life in the City of Rome*, London, 2000.
PIETILÄ-CASTREN, L. 1987: *Magnificentia Publica: The Victory Monuments of Roman Generals in the Era of the Punic Wars*, Commentationes Humanarum Litterarum 84, Helsinki, 1987.
RICH, J.W. 1993: 'Fear, Greed and Glory: the causes of Roman war-making in the middle Republic', in J.W. Rich and G. Shipley (ed.), *War and Society in the Roman World*, London, 1993, 38–68.
RICHMOND, I.A. 1930: *The City Walls of Imperial Rome*, Oxford, 1930.
RICKMAN, G.E. 1971: *Roman Granaries and Store Buildings*, Oxford, 1971.
RICKMAN, G.E. 1980: *The Corn Supply of Ancient Rome*, Oxford, 1980.
ROBINSON, O.F. 1992: *Ancient Rome. City Planning and Administration*, London, 1992.
RUMPF, A. 1950: 'Die Entstehung des römischen Theaters', *Römische Mitteilungen* 3, 1950, 40–50.
SÄFLUND, G. 1930: *Le mura di Roma repubblicana*, Lund, 1930.

SHIPLEY, F.W. 1933: *Agrippa's Building Activities in Rome*, Washington, 1933.
SMITH, C. 1996: *Early Rome and Latium. Economy and Society c. 1000 BC to 500 BC*, Oxford, 1996.
STARR, C.G. 1980: *The Beginnings of Imperial Rome: Rome in the mid-Republic*, Ann Arbor, 1980.
STOREY, G.R. 1997: 'The population of ancient Rome', *Antiquity* 71, 1997, 966–78.
TODD, M. 1978: *The Walls of Rome*, London, 1978.
TORELLI, M. 1995: *Studies in the Romanization of Italy*, (edited and translated by H. Fracchia and M. Gualtieri), Alberta, 1995.
VERSNEL, H. 1970: Triumphus. *An inquiry into the origin, development and meaning of the Roman triumph*, Leiden, 1970.
WALLACE-HADRILL, A. 1988: 'The Social Structure of the Roman House', *PBSR* 56, 1988, 43–97.
WEINSTOCK, S. 1957: 'Victor and Invictus', *Harvard Theological Review* 50, 1957, 211–47.
WELCH, K. 1994: 'The Roman arena in late-Republican Italy: a new interpretation', *JRA* 7, 1994, 59–81.
WISEMAN, T.P. 1974: 'The Circus Flaminius', *PBSR* 42, 1974, 3–26.
WISSOWA, G. 1912: *Religion und Kultus der Römer*, ed. 2, München, 1912.
ZIOLKOWSKI, A. 1988: 'Mummius' Temple of Hercules Victor and the Round Temple on the Tiber', *Phoenix* 42, 1988, 309–33.
ZIOLKOWSKI, A. 1992: *The Templės of Mid-Republican Rome*, London, 1992.

4. The Moral Museum: Augustus and the City of Rome

Susan Walker

"You ask why I am late in coming to you. The golden porticoes of Phoebus Apollo were opened by mighty Caesar; so vast was it to view, arranged with Punic columns, between which stood a group of the daughters of old Danaus. Next in the centre rose the temple of gleaming marble, more dear to Phoebus than his Phrygian home; and above the pediment were two chariots of the sun, and the doors, magnificent work in Libyan ivory, told on the one side the story of the Gauls thrown down from Parnassus' peak, while the other mourned the death of the daughter of Tantalus. Finally between his mother and sister the Pythian god himself in long tunic raises his voice in song. I for my part found this marble figure, with silent lyre and lips parted in song, a finer sight than Phoebus himself; and around the altar stood Myron's herd, four skilfully made oxen, statues that seemed alive."

Thus Propertius celebrated in one of two poems on this theme (*Elegies* 2.31) the opening of the Temple of Actian Apollo on the Palatine Hill at Rome, the ceremony conducted by Octavian (as he then was) on October 9th, 28 BC.[1] The expected references to the emergence of empire are there: the exotic building materials, reminders of Rome's sovereignty over distant lands, the columns called 'Punic' rather than Numidian to reflect Rome's defeat of Carthage;[2] the singing statue better than the real god; the tales of Rome's enemies vanquished by natural forces; the old myths; even the unlikely notion that Phoebus might feel more at home in Rome than in his native Phrygia. The ode closes with an interesting museological note, that around the altar of Apollo grazed four life-like oxen, the work of the classical Greek sculptor Myron; indeed, earlier comes a reference to a set of sculptures representing the daughters of Danaus.[3] From other accounts we learn that the statues within the temple representing Apollo with his mother Artemis and sister Leto were the work, respectively, of the later classical masters Scopas and Timotheos, both of whom collaborated in the mid-4th century BC on the Mausoleum at Halicarnassus, and of Cephisodotus; a fragmentary head thought to belong to the cult statue was excavated in the foundations of the temple.[4] Timotheus' statue of Artemis was restored by the distinguished sculptor Evander, who no doubt in common with other artists moved to Rome following Octavian's capture of Alexandria in 30 BC.[5] According to Pliny (*Natural History* 36.11–4), the pediments contained works by the archaic masters Bupalis and Athenis, sons of Archermos of Chios. Pliny noted that nearly all the temples restored in Rome by Augustus contained archaic Greek originals by these sculptors.

It is the purpose of this chapter to ask what Octavian (from 27 BC renamed Augustus) may have had in mind in creating within the city of Rome a museum of Greek sculpture; what visual impact his work may have had; and how he even addressed the question of the personal appearance of residents and visitors to Rome. The surviving evidence is a mixture of literary and archaeological scraps; aspects of the subject have been well studied in recent years.[6]

THE HOUSE OF AUGUSTUS ON THE PALATINE

One of the more remarkable archaeological features of the Temple of Actian Apollo, as it has been excavated, is the direct link between the sacred building and Augustus' private house, offering the emperor the facility of private use of the temple (Fig. 4.1).[7] It is a feature of later commentaries on the first emperor of Rome that he lived very modestly, a view that finds some support from a retrospective comparison of Augustus' personal lifestyle with those of his successors. However not every modest Roman had his front door on the coinage, where the door to Augustus' house appears flanked by two laurel trees (sacred to Apollo and an acceptably non-regal sign of victory), and the connection with the Temple of Actian Apollo speaks of the unique status of its owner (Fig. 4.2).

Suetonius (*Augustus* 72), writing early in the 2nd century AD, noted that Augustus' house was not very large and had no marble veneer or fine pavements. The emperor slept in the same bedroom for forty years, while other rich Romans changed rooms (and indeed houses) with the seasons. Archaeological evidence offered by the so-called Room of the Masks, while confirming the impression of imperial restraint in the choice of decor, has revealed in the central panel of one of its walls a theme which is also used in the adjacent temple: the *betylos*, an aniconic idol used in the worship of Apollo, a quaintly archaizing motif also represented on terracotta panels found in the excavation of the temple.[8]

With regard to the site of his house, as early as 36 BC Octavian had set about buying property in a particularly sacred corner of the Palatine Hill, the lower slopes of which were by that time well established as a desirable residential quarter.[9] The acquisition was made in response to an omen, when a bolt of lightning struck the future site of the Temple of Apollo, and the soothsayers interpreted this as an indication that the god required a temple within the walls of Rome (Dio 49.15.5). Instead of making a palace, Octavian bought separate lots for members of his family; hence the 'House of Augustus', 'House of Livia' and so on.[10] The 'House of Augustus' was not only connected by a ramp to the Temple of Apollo but also lay adjacent to a precinct containing a Temple of Victory and a Temple of Cybele or the Great Mother (Magna Mater), another Phrygian deity adapted to Roman sensibilities (Fig. 4.1).[11] The hut supposed to be the residence of Romulus was located nearby.[12] Directly below these structures stood the ancient walls of Rome, attributed to Romulus and marking the 'Roma Quadrata', famed as the seat of empire.[13] Who needs a palace when he can sleep every night at the historic centre of his world, protected on every side by patron gods?

If the Temple of Apollo Palatinus may be regarded as Augustus' private shrine, the portico of the Danaids with its Numidian columns was perhaps the equivalent space to that part of the Roman house used for receiving guests on official business. Here Augustus met with foreign ambassadors and called meetings of the Roman senate.[14] There were also two fine libraries of Greek and Latin literature, which no doubt attracted the poets of Augustus' court; perhaps this, and the feeling the site must have engendered of intimacy with the emperor – not to speak of Ovid's claim (*The Art of Love* 1.74) that it was a fine place to pick up a pretty girl – is why so many poets wrote of the Sanctuary of Apollo Palatinus.

The temple, however, had another, less celebratory aspect. It may be seen as one of the last examples of competitive public building within the city of Rome, which during the reign of Augustus became the preserve of the emperor alone, in the sense that, by the later years of his reign, no other individual or body was permitted to erect public monuments other than those honouring the emperor and his family.[15] The Temple of Apollo Palatinus was built at about the same time as the Temple of Apollo Medicus, more widely known as Apollo

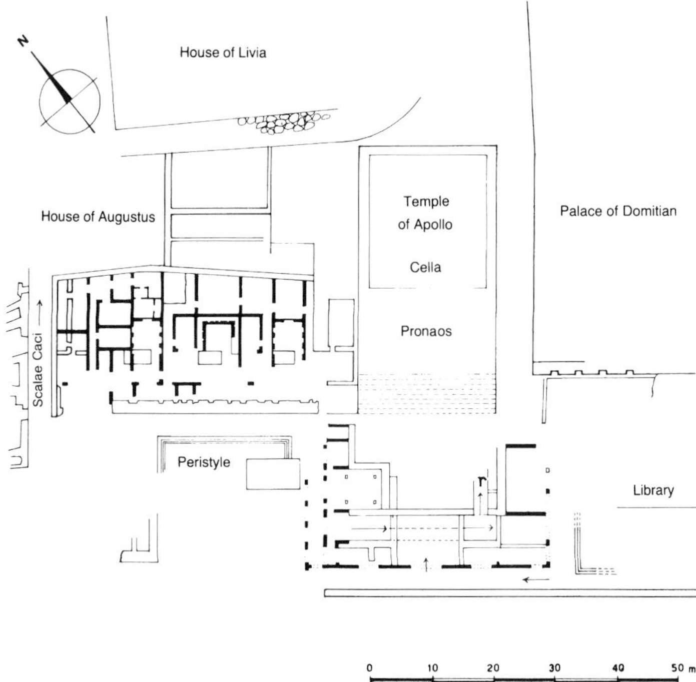

Fig. 4.1: Plan of the area surrounding the House of Augustus on the Palatine (after Zanker 1988).

Sosianus after its patron builder Gaius Sosius, a supporter of Octavian's rival Antony who was later reconciled to Augustus (it is also sometimes referred to as Apollo in Circo). Sosius paid for the temple with the spoils of his victory in Judaea in 34 BC; the date of completion of the temple is controversial. It is interesting to note that although the subject matter of the internal frieze is triumphal in nature, it in fact celebrates Octavian's triple triumph of 29 BC, not his own. The interior of the building was richly decorated with imported marbles, perhaps indicating that the building was finished by Augustus.[16] The three standing columns that mark the site today were re-erected, in too much haste and in the wrong position, to celebrate Rome's birthday in 1940.[17] The Temple of Apollo Sosianus stood outside the sacred boundary of the city in a district traditionally used for the display of spoils of war; it appears that, as emperor, Augustus tried to minimize the visual impact of the temple by having the Theatre of Marcellus constructed directly in front of it, thereby even today blocking the view of the temple's façade (Fig. 4.3).[18] He also rebuilt the adjacent Portico of Octavia, named after his sister, who had been deserted by her then husband Antony for Cleopatra of Egypt.[19]

THE DISPLAY OF ORIGINAL GREEK SCULPTURES IN AUGUSTAN ROME

It was in the course of excavation of the Theatre of Marcellus that several sculptures of alien appearance were uncovered; after much study they have been attributed to the pediments of the Temple of Apollo Sosianus.[20] The sculptures are original Greek works in Parian marble, rehung to fit the Roman building. They represent the battle between the Greeks, led by

Fig. 4.2: Coin of Augustus showing the laurel trees flanking the door of his house, with laurel crown above (Photo: British Museum).

Heracles under the protection of Athena, and the Amazons, led by their queen Hippolyta. It is thought that the sculptures were taken by the Romans from the Temple of Apollo Daphnophorus at Eretria; indeed, many Greek cities and sanctuaries were plundered in the course of the Roman conquest and its aftermath, most notably by the general (later dictator) Sulla in the mid-80s BC.[21] The reconstructed pediments of the Temple of Apollo offer a rare surviving illustration of the visual appearance of classical Greek masterpieces at Rome.

It should be borne in mind that the Greek originals were displayed against a backdrop of architecture in a radically new style (the Temple of Apollo Sosianus is widely considered even now a masterpiece of Augustan architecture). The gleaming columns of the Temple of Actian Apollo celebrated by Propertius were most likely of Carrara (or Luna) marble from the Tuscan quarries opened for use at Rome less than two decades previously.[22] As Propertius observed in his elegy on the temple, and is reflected in other literature of the period, Augustus used many different marbles to express Roman control of distant territories and to furnish Rome as capital of empire.[23] He also popularized the Corinthian order, which achieved for the first time under Augustus a widely used canonical form.[24] In modern times overwhelmingly associated with Roman architecture, Corinthian had its roots in classical Greece, where the order was used in the interior of temples (most famously, that of Apollo at Bassae), not merely for its expensive prettiness but to mark the most sacred spot within the temple behind the cult statue.[25] By widely employing Corinthian as an external order in marble, Augustus effectively made the city of Rome a sacred space in which masterpieces from classical Greek sanctuaries were displayed to great effect. He was thus able to expand significantly the Republican practice (not always observed) of dedicating the booty paraded in military triumphs in the temples of the gods. Now many more saw the works of art so exposed in public spaces.[26]

THE ROMAN FORUM AND SURROUNDING AREA

Much of the centre of the city was transformed, not least the Roman Forum, where a series of structures was restored and new buildings arose, but also where monuments critical to the identity of Rome were preserved (Fig. 4.4). Thus the marble halls of the newly restored Basilica Aemilia could be admired, but the sites of such ancient curiosities as the Lapis Niger (Volcanal, site of the levitation of Romulus), the Lacus Curtius, the shrine of Venus Cloacina, patron goddess of Tarquin's main drain, and the Pool of Juturna, sister-nymph of

Fig. 4.3: Façade of the Theatre of Marcellus (left) up close to the Temple of Apollo Sosianus (Photo: editors).

Turnus, were preserved.[27] Indeed, all these sites are familiar to the modern visitor to Rome because Augustus chose to preserve them.[28]

Like Sosius' temple, the basilica built by the Aemilii came to be obscured, in this case by a monumental portico dedicated to Augustus' adopted sons and favoured successors, Gaius and Lucius Caesar (Fig. 4.5).[29] On the other side of the Forum, the Basilica Julia, built by Julius Caesar and restored after a fire, was named after them.[30] The neighbouring Temple of Castor and Pollux was perhaps destined to honour them, but both princes had died before its completion in AD 6.[31] At the eastern end the Forum was closed by the temple of the Deified Julius Caesar, which was flanked by the Arch of Augustus.[32] Inside the arch was a list of the triumphs celebrated at Rome; no provision was made for additions after 19 BC, when Lucius Cornelius Balbus celebrated his triumph from Africa; thereafter, the honour was the emperor's alone.[33]

The extent of imperial appropriation of public space may be seen when the Forum is shown with adjacent recent developments, the Forum of Caesar and that of Augustus himself, the latter not completed until 2 BC and making the former effectively a vestibule (Fig. 4.4).[34] The Forum of Augustus was dominated by the temple of Augustus' patron god, Mars Ultor. Here Augustus was able to plan without regard for venerable antiquities, and he slowly evolved an impressive (and surely also oppressive) architectural and sculptural programme.[35] As has recently been observed, if in the Forum Romanum the family of Augustus formed a protective ring around the ancient monuments, in the Forum of Augustus ancient Romans formed a protective ring around the emperor.[36] And while the Roman Forum was a through route and a meeting point, the Forum of Augustus was a more enclosed space, in which a marble pageant was played out against a theatrical backdrop, in the form of the great wall, 30 metres in height, which protected the monumental centre of Rome from the risk of fire in the slums beyond (Fig. 4.6).

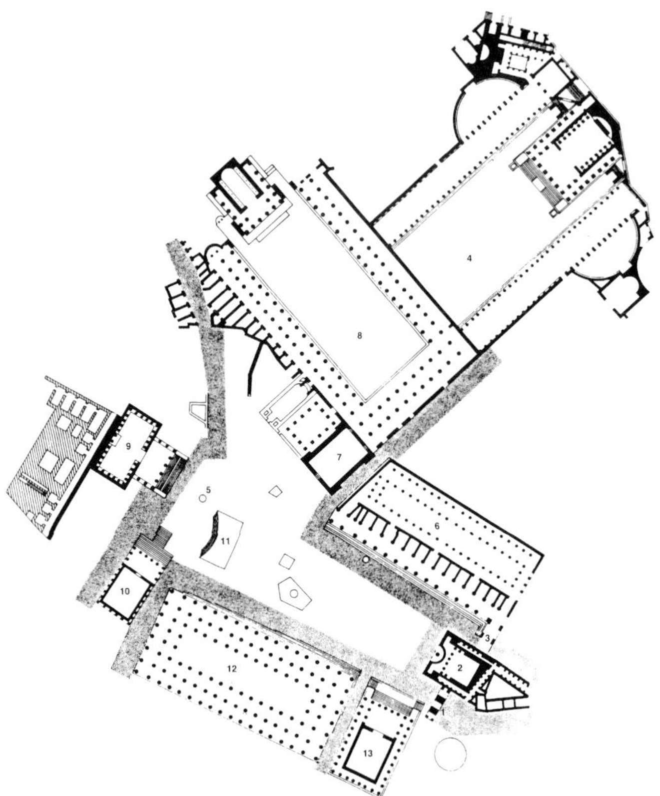

Fig. 4.4: Plan of the Roman Forum, the Forum of Caesar and the Forum of Augustus (after Favro 1996). 1. Arch of Augustus 2. Temple of the Deified Julius Caesar 3. Portico of Gaius and Lucius 4. Forum of Augustus 5. Milliarium Aureum 6. Basilica Aemilia 7. Curia Julia 8. Forum of Julius Caesar 9. Temple of Concord 10. Temple of Saturn 11. Rostra 12. Basilica Julia 13. Temple of Castor and Pollux.

Within his Forum, Augustus stood in a chariot at the centre, the Father of his Country, while respectful files of the most distinguished heroes of the Republic lined the porticoes on either side, leading up to the great exedrae in which the family of Augustus was equated with Aeneas, Romulus and the kings of Alba Longa. The emperor himself is thought to have composed the elegies inscribed on the statue bases. In this remarkable visual and verbal orchestration, Augustus' rise to supreme power was presented as the inevitable outcome of the Republic, thereby ignoring the thirteen years of bloody civil war that accompanied his rise, and at the same time legitimizing the imperial use of former public space.

Architecturally, the Forum of Augustus is a fine reflection of the contemporary taste for the Corinthian order, for the use of precious coloured stones from distant quarries (the *summi viri* are carved of *pavonazzetto* from Phrygia), and for classical borrowings – here taking the form of caryatids which were replicas of the classical figures of the Erechtheion on the Acropolis of Athens (Fig. 4.7).[37]

Fig. 4.5: Inscription from the Portico of Gaius and Lucius in the Forum Romanum (Photo: editors).

Fig. 4.6: View of the Temple of Mars Ultor in the Forum of Augustus (Photo: editors).

Fig. 4.7: Caryatid order from the flanking colonnades of the Forum of Augustus (after Ward-Perkins 1981).

Fig. 4.8: View of the Mausoleum of Augustus (photo: editors).

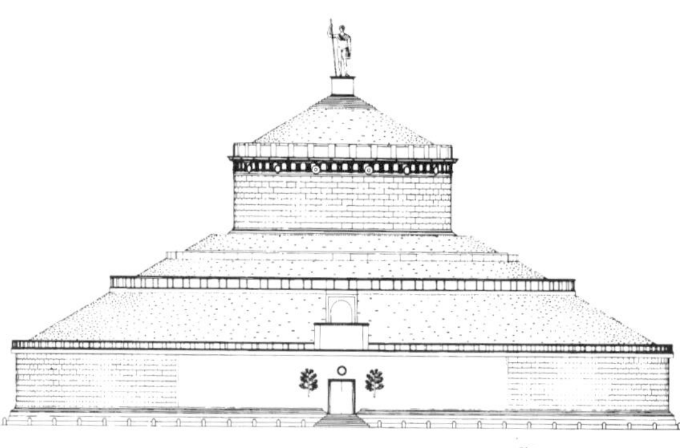

Fig. 4.9: Reconstruction of the Mausoleum of Augustus (Zanker 1988 after von Hesberg).

Fig. 4.10: Obelisk of the Horologium of Augustus which now stands in the Piazza di Montecitorio (Photo: editors).

ECHOES ABROAD

Such classical allusions at Rome were echoed in the architecture of Augustan Athens, the source of inspiration; in the order of the round temple dedicated to Rome and Augustus on the Athenian Acropolis, the distinctive necking ornament of the columns of the nearby Erechtheion were imitated.[38] Like the Roman Forum, the Athenian Agora was invaded by temples; indeed, like the sculptures adorning contemporary Rome, the temples were classical Greek originals, transplanted into the centre of Athens from the rural sanctuaries of Attica, so eager were the Athenians to mimic and no doubt profit from Rome's new interest in their classical heritage.[39]

A well-documented imitation of Augustan Rome is offered by Iol Caesarea, now Cherchel in Algeria, in Augustan times the capital of Juba II, client-king of Augustus and himself raised within the imperial family at Rome.[40] Juba had Italian masons copy in Carrara marble the capitals of the Temple of Mars Ultor in the Forum of Augustus.[41] Several classicizing statues have been found at Cherchel, including the torso of a caryatid and another of Kore (Persephone), copied from an original of 440 BC by an artist conversant with contemporary work on the Parthenon.[42] Caesarea was of course renamed (from Iol) in honour of Augustus, as was the capital of another client-king, Herod of Judaea. The eastern Caesarea, Caesarea Maritima, boasted a temple in which Augustus was portrayed as Olympian Jupiter as originally conceived by the 5th century artist Pheidias.[43]

If the client-kings had correctly followed the Augustan reverence for Greek art, such extravagant presentations of Augustus as that proposed by Herod were not permitted at Rome, where the emperor had eighty silver portraits of himself removed, remarking that the medium was inappropriate for statues of mortals (*Res Gestae* 24). However, there were some early monuments more redolent of monarchy than of the restored Republic. One survivor was the Mausoleum of Augustus, built in the northern part of the Campus Martius in 28 BC (Fig. 4.8). Over 40 m high, with a colossal bronze statue of Augustus on the top of it, the Mausoleum dominated the flat land of the Campus Martius, and formed the first of an interlinked series of monuments in this area, all personally associated with the emperor (Fig. 4.9).[44] To the south-east lay the Altar of Augustan Peace, completed in 9 BC, and originally sited on the edge of a vast piazza marked with the lines of a huge sundial, of which the pointer was an Egyptian obelisk, whose transfer to Rome also recalled the capitulation to Octavian of Cleopatra.[45] The inscription on the obelisk dates the sundial to the same year (10–9 BC) in which the Ara Pacis was completed (Fig. 4.10).[46]

THE MORAL MUSEUM: MONUMENTAL ART AND SOCIAL BEHAVIOUR

The figures on the outer walls of the Ara Pacis represent members of the imperial family and of the leading families of Rome in a procession recalling the dedication of the altar (Fig. 4.11). The frieze is a remarkable display of familial piety, with children appearing for the first time in Roman monumental art in a context other than funerary.[47] Their prominence is a reflection of the dominance of the imperial family in contemporary political life, and of the introduction of laws favouring, politically and financially, married men with children.[48] The children are portrayed in sympathetic fashion, tugging on togas or hushed by nurses. The processions illustrate another striking feature of Augustan Rome, the modesty of dress encouraged and indeed imposed on Romans resident or visiting the city. Said to be enraged at the sight of Romans dressed in dark (i.e. Greek) cloaks in the centre of Rome (Suetonius, *Augustus* 40), Augustus required all adult males of free Roman birth to wear the toga, which henceforth became an enduring symbol of Roman identity.[49] To mark its rise in status, the toga was redesigned. Thus the Republican *toga exigua* (short toga) was replaced by a much grander affair, draped over the left shoulder with a swooping train of cloth (the *sinus*) and tucked at the waist (the *umbo*) (Fig. 4.12). This form of toga became as it were the Roman equivalent of the pin-striped suit, the *vestis forensis* to be worn on business but also mandatory at ceremonial occasions such as visits to the theatre. Many portraits of Augustus show him veiled with the *sinus*, a convenient gesture permitting the wearer to perform religious sacrifice without extra clothing, though it is more likely that the statues representing the emperor in this way allude to his sense of duty (*pietas*) rather than to a specific role as priest.[50] Other surviving statues of Julio-Claudian notables reveal both sexes imitating imperial hairstyles and even physiognomies, their torsos modestly, even excessively wrapped.[51] This fashion stands in profound contrast to the few surviving statues of notables of the late Republic, which show the men in heroic semi-nudity, their hellenizing torsoes quite at odds with the veristic style then favoured for Roman portrait heads.[52] For women, too, Augustus revived a long-lost fashion for the *stola*, a tube-like garment worn over the

Fig. 4.11: Ara Pacis. Procession of figures identified as members of the imperial family (Photo: editors).

tunic but under the cloak. According to poets, the *stola* was intended to advertise the chastity of well-born Roman matrons; not even a pretty ankle showed beneath the tube, but surviving representations of *feminae stolatae* suggest that some women managed to make an attraction of restriction (Fig. 4.13).[53]

For his own image, Augustus drew upon classical Greek representations of the human form, particularly the notion of perfection evolved in the canon of the 5th century Argive sculptor Polycleitus and embodied in that sculptor's spear-carrier (*doryphorus*).[54] Thus was the emperor personally associated with the acme of classical Greek perfection, though his body was more often clothed in the Roman toga.

In his personal appearance Augustus served as a model for his subjects, and his influence may be discerned not only amongst the rich but most notably amongst those former slaves of alien origin who, through new legislation allowing legitimate marriage, acquired the right to Roman citizenship. Hundreds of surviving reliefs illustrate their desire to celebrate the new legitimacy of their families and their Roman identity.[55] From Rome itself there is very little trace of monuments honouring the wealthy. Although the rich were encouraged to give buildings to the city, at least in the early years of Augustus' reign (Suetonius, *Augustus* 29), in practice much of this activity was assumed by the emperor. Thus in the Forum the Basilica Aemilia, though still known by the name of the nobles who had first commissioned it in 179 BC, was rebuilt after a fire in 14 BC by Augustus, using his own funds (Dio 54.24). The glories of the Aemilii gave way to the celebration of the emperor's Parthian victories, realised in *pavonnazzetto* marble statues of the defeated foe. A final phase of building under Tiberius had the shield-portraits of the Aemilii replaced by images of members of the imperial family.[56] The rich are much more visible in commemorative statues set up in provincial towns, where they were permitted to act as benefactors as the emperor did in Rome, and where they posed no threat to his authority.[57]

Augustan Rome was a compelling sight for those who flocked to the city as capital of empire. Signs of imperial planning began very early, significantly, before Octavian took the name Augustus, and by the end of his long regime any sacred element in his early intentions had been overtaken by the development of much of the centre of Rome and the northern Campus Martius as a dynastic monument to the first imperial family. Against a radically changed architecture (from brick to marble, as recorded by Suetonius [*Augustus* 28]),[58]

Fig. 4.12: Augustus togatus. *Statue from the Via Labicana (Photo: editors).*

Fig. 4.13: Femina stolata*: statue in the Museo Nazionale, Parma. (Photo: Zanker 1988).*

appropriately dressed Romans and visitors played their role as applauding spectators of sacred and secular events engineered and dominated by the emperor and his court. In this well-contrived arena classical Greek works of art served not merely to raise the artistic tone of Rome nor to remind natives and visitors of the spoils of imperial conquest. It is, perhaps, unlikely that Augustus had it in mind to compete with Pericles or Mausolus, though competition with Sosius may have been an element influencing the decoration of the Temple of Apollo Palatinus. Beyond serving individual Roman aggression, the classical originals had their own moral message, a status given to Greek artists by Roman theorists, who saw the 5th and 4th-century masters as capable of expressing in art a moral authority equivalent to that of their peers in oratory and philosophy.[59] Indeed, the moral message of classical Athenian art could be specifically related to the social problems of Augustan Rome. The caryatids of Augustus' Forum remind the viewer of a city (Athens) and of an age (the classical) in which citizenship was a restricted privilege and thus legitimate birth amongst the existing citizen body was a matter of significance, safeguarded by strict rules controlling sexual and social behaviour.[60] Classical art in a sacred setting served as a visual reminder of those qualities Augustus tried to instil by other means in his subjects: modesty in dress, personal behaviour and in private surroundings, all these contrasted with a public life conducted in settings of unprecedented opulence, the whole invested with a strongly signalled sense of Roman identity. In this wide sense, and following the take-over by imperial authority of spoils that had in the late Republic become the property of private individuals, the public display of classical works of art at Rome formed a moral museum, which residents and visitors were obliged to admire and respect.

NOTES

1 *Lexicon* I, *s.v.* 'Apollo Palatinus', 54–7; *Lexicon* V, 225; CLARIDGE 1998, 131–34.

2 This is the attractive yellow stone, *giallo antico*, quarried at Simitthus in Numidia (modern Chimtou in northern Tunisia). It figured largely in Augustus' building programme in both the Forum Romanum and the Forum of Augustus as well as elsewhere in the city (FAVRO 1996, 184–85). It was one of the earliest of the decorative stones to be imported into Rome; Pliny (*Natural History* 36.49) records its use by Marcus Lepidus as door sills in his house in the 70s BC. The use of *giallo antico* for the Temple of Apollo Palatinus is the earliest archaeological evidence for the appearance of this stone in Rome (WARD-PERKINS 1981, 36). See also DODGE and WARD-PERKINS 1992, 157.

3 See CANDILIO 1989 and TOMEI 1997, 56–7, for *nero antico* herms of the Danaids excavated on the Palatine.

4 MARTIN 1988, 262–63, no. 118. For the collaborators at Halicarnassus, see WAYWELL 1978.

5 Pliny, *Natural History* 36.32. POLLITT (1992, 89–90) notes that Timotheus' statue of Artemis was only one of several important Greek cult statues which were transferred to Rome during the 1st century BC.

6 Rome: WALLACE-HADRILL 1993; FAVRO 1992; 1993; 1996; art: ZANKER 1988; HÖFTER 1988.

7 CARETTONI 1984, 48, fig. 6, 51; 1988, 263–65; TOMEI 1997, 49–53. For the House of Augustus, see *Lexicon* II, *s.v.* 'Domus: Augustus (Palatium)', 46–8; CLARIDGE 1998, 130. For architectural decoration in the House of Augustus, see PENSABENE 1997.

8 CARETTONI 1984, 27, pl.6, colour pls. E and F; 1988, 270, no. 123; ZANKER 1988, 89–90, fig. 73; TOMEI 1997, 61–2.

9 WALLACE-HADRILL 1993, 26–8.

10 *Lexicon* II, *s.v.* 'Domus: Livia', 130–32; CLARIDGE 1998, 128–30.

11 PENSABENE 1991. For the Precinct of Victory, see CLARIDGE 1998, 123–28; *Lexicon* IV, *s.v.* 'Palatium (età repubblicana – 64 d.C.)', 22–8, particularly 23; *Lexicon* III, *s.v.* 'Magna Mater, Aedes', 206–8.

12 WISEMAN 1984, 26; PENSABENE 1991; CLARIDGE 1998, 125–26; *Lexicon* I, *s.v.* 'Casa Romuli (Cermalis)', 241–42.

13 CARANDINI 1992.

14 WALLACE-HADRILL 1993, 28.

15 WALLACE-HADRILL 1993, 53.

16 ZANKER 1988, 66–9; CLARIDGE 1998, 245–47; *Lexicon* I, *s.v.* 'Apollo, Aedes in Circo', 49–54; *Lexicon* V, 224–25; LA ROCCA 1988 (site and sculpture); VISCOGLIOSI 1988 (architectural decoration).

17 LA ROCCA 1985, 21.

18 KUNZL 1988, 123; CLARIDGE 1998, 243–45; *Lexicon* V, *s.v.* 'Theatrum Marcelli', 31–5.

19 ZANKER 1988, 65–71 and 153, fig. 122. The Portico of Octavia was originally the Portico of Metellus, built by Q. Caecilius Metellus after his victory in Greece in 146 BC; it enclosed the Temples of Jupiter Stator and of Juno Regina, see CLARIDGE 1998, 224–26; *Lexicon* IV, *s.v.* 'Porticus Octaviae', 141–45.

20 LA ROCCA 1985; 1988.

21 WAURICK 1975. Sulla brought back columns from the unfinished Temple of Olympian Zeus in Athens for use in the reconstruction of the Temple of Jupiter on the Capitoline (Pliny, *Natural History* 36.45)

22 DOLCI 1980, 33–5. There is in fact no archaeological or literary evidence for Julius Caesar being responsible: see DODGE and WARD-PERKINS 1992, 21, n. 27.

23 FANT 1993.

24 HEILMEYER 1970, 25–32 (Forum of Augustus); 33–51 (Rome from the Republic until the mid-Augustan period); CLARIDGE 1998, 51 (Corinthian order).

25 ONIANS 1988, 18, fig. 9 and 19–22; LAWRENCE 1983, 231–34.

26 WALKER 1991, 8–14.

27 For the Roman Forum, see CLARIDGE 1998, 61–99; *Lexicon* II, *s.v.* 'Forum Romanum (The Republican Period)', 325–36; 'Forum Romanum (The Imperial Period)', 336–42.

28 WALLACE-HADRILL 1993, 51.

29 BAUER 1988; CLARIDGE 1998, 68; *Lexicon* IV, *s.v.* 'Porticus Gai et Luci', 122–23. For the tripod monument with *pavanazzetto* barbarians, see SCHNEIDER 1986, 120–25.

30 CLARIDGE 1998, 89–90; *Lexicon* I, *s.v.* 'Basilica Iulia', 177–79. For the rededication of the Basilica Julia and for the promotion of Gaius and Lucius as 'descendants of Venus', see ZANKER 1988, 215–23.

31 SANDE and ZAHLE 1988; *Lexicon* I, *s.v.* 'Castor, Aedes, Templum', 242–45; CLARIDGE 1998, 91–2. For the Augustan paving in the Forum Romanum, see *CIL* 6.1468, 31662; GIULIANI and VERDUCHI 1987; *Lexicon* II, *s.v.* 'Forum Romanum (Lastricati)', 343–45; CLARIDGE 1998, 85.

32 For the Temple of the Deified Julius Caesar, see CLARIDGE 1998, 97–9; *Lexicon* III, *s.v.* 'Iulius, Divus, Aedes', 116–19. For the Arch of Augustus, see CLARIDGE 1998, 99; *Lexicon* I, *s.v.* 'Arcus Augusti (a. 19 aC)', 81–5.

33 NEDERGAARD 1988; KÜNZL 1988, 51–60; WALLACE-HADRILL 1993, 54, fig. 17.

34 For the Forum of Caesar, see CLARIDGE 1998, 148–53; *Lexicon* II, *s.v.* 'Forum Iulium', 299–306. For the Forum of Augustus, see CLARIDGE 1998, 99; *Lexicon* II, *s.v.* 'Forum Augustum', 289–95.

35 GANZERT and KOCKEL 1988, 179–99; LA ROCCA 1995, 20–93.

36 WALLACE-HADRILL 1993, 56.
37 GANZERT and KOCKEL 1988, 190–91, figs. 82–5. For the Forum of Augutus and marble in other Augustan buildings, see DODGE and WARD-PERKINS 1992, 24, n. 9. For caryatids and Pegasus capitals, see WARD-PERKINS 1981, 33.
38 TRAVLOS 1971, 497, fig. 627.
39 CAMP 1986, 184–87.
40 FITTSCHEN 1979, 227–42.
41 PENSABENE 1982, 69–73.
42 HORN and RÜGER 1979, 534–37.
43 ZANKER 1988, 250; for Herod's foundation of Caesarea at the site of Strato's Tower, see Josephus, *Jewish Antiquities* 15.331–41. For Herod's building programme in general, see HORNUM 1988; ROLLER 1998.
44 VON HESBERG and PANCIERA 1994. For the Mausoleum of Augustus, see CLARIDGE 1998, 181–81; *Lexicon* III, *s.v.* 'Mausoleum Augusti: Das Monument', 234–37; 'Mausoleum Augusti: Le Sepoltre', 237–39; *Lexicon* V, *s.v.* 'Mausoleum Augusti', 275–76; Strabo 5.3.9 and ZANKER 1988, 75–6 (bronze statue). For the Campus Martius, see CLARIDGE 1998, 177–72; *Lexicon* I, *s.v.* 'Campus Martius', 220–24.
45 BUCHNER 1982; 1988, 240–45; WALLACE-HADRILL 1993, 93–6. For the Ara Pacis, see CLARIDGE 1998, 184–90; *Lexicon* IV, *s.v.* 'Pax Augusta, Ara', 70–4; *Lexicon* V, *s.v.* 'Ara Pacis', 285–86. For the Augustan sundial, see CLARIDGE 1998, 190–93; *Lexicon* III, *s.v.* 'Horologium Augusti', 35–7.
46 Buchner's assertion that the shadow of the obelisk fell onto the Ara Pacis on Augustus' birthday has been demonstrated to be incorrect by SCHUTZ 1990; GRATWICK forthcoming. The shadow would not have reached the Altar and BUCHNER confused the date. The shadow obviously would have pointed to the Ara Pacis on the birthday of Augustus as the shadow moved around every day.
47 KLEINER 1978; WALLACE-HADRILL 1993, 70–4.
48 KLEINER 1978. On family and marital laws, see for example FRANK 1976; DIXON 1992, particularly 61–71 and 98–119.
49 GOETTE 1990; ZANKER 1988, 162–66.
50 ZANKER 1988, 127–29.
51 HÖFTER 1988, 291–343; ZANKER 1988, 291–95; WALKER 1995, 81–2.
52 ZANKER 1988, 4–8; WALKER 1995, 79.
53 ZANKER 1988, 165–66 and figs. 131 and 253.
54 ZANKER 1988, 98–100; WALKER 1995, 61–71.
55 KLEINER 1978.
56 On the dedicatory inscriptions and their location, see PANCIERA 1969; see also COARELLI 1985, 296 and, on the Augustan reconstruction and coloured marble decoration of the basilica, BAUER 1988.
57 ZANKER 1983; 1988, 316–23.
58 "Augustus beautified the city, whose appearance had in no way reflected its greatness and glory and was besides constantly plagued by floods and fires, and so utterly remade it, that he could justly boast that he found Rome a city of brick and left it a city of marble". DODGE and WARD-PERKINS 1992, 21–4 and references. Much of public Rome was built of materials such as tufa, concrete and travertine, but many of the high-rise residential blocks were still of far less durable materials. Although from the archaeological and literary evidence it is quite clear that a large number of different exotic stones were being employed, they were still used in small amounts, for the most part, apart from monolithic columns, for veneering; a little could go a long way. It is only remarked upon because it is so unusual.
59 ZANKER 1988, 248–52.
60 OSBORNE 1997.

BIBLIOGRAPHY

BAUER, H. 1988: 'Basilica Aemilia', in HÖFTER 1988, 200–12.
BUCHNER, E. 1982: *Die Sonnenuhr des Augustus*, Mainz, 1982.
BUCHNER, E. 1988: 'Horologium solarium Augusti', in HÖFTER 1988, 240–45.
CAMP, J.M. 1986: *The Athenian Agora: excavations in the heart of classical Athens*, London, 1986.
CANDILIO, D. 1989: 'Nero Antico', in M.L. Anderson and L. Nista (ed.), *Radiance in Stone*, Roma, 1989, 85–90.
CARANDINI, A. 1992: 'Le Mura del Palatino', *BA* 16–8, 1992, 1–18.
CARETTONI, G. 1984: *Das Haus von Augustus auf dem Palatin*, Mainz, 1984.
CARETTONI, G. 1988: 'Die Bauten des Augustus auf dem Palatin', in HÖFTER 1988, 263–72.
CLARIDGE, A. 1998: *Rome: An Oxford Archaeological Guide*, Oxford, 1998.

COARELLI, F. 1985: *Foro Romano*, Rome, 1985.
DIXON, S. 1992: *The Roman Family*, Maryland, 1992.
DODGE, H. and WARD-PERKINS, B. 1992: *Marble in Antiquity*, London, 1992.
DOLCI, E. 1980: *Carrara Cave Antiche. Materiali Archeologici,* Carrara, 1980.
FANT, J.C. 1993: 'Ideology, gift, and trade: a distribution model for the Roman imperial marbles', in W.V. Harris (ed.), *The Inscribed Economy. Production and Distribution in the Roman Empire in the light of instrumentum domesticum*, JRA Supplement 6, 1993, 145–70.
FAVRO, D. 1992: 'Pater Urbis: Augustus as city Father of Rome', *JSAH* 61, 1992, 61–84.
FAVRO, D. 1993: 'Reading the Augustan City', in P.J. Holliday, *Narrative and Event in Ancient Art*, Cambridge, 1993.
FAVRO, D. 1996: *The Urban Image of Augustan Rome*, Cambridge, 1996.
FITTSCHEN, K. 1979: 'Juba II und seine Residenz Jol/Caesarea (Cherchel)', in HORN and RÜGER 1979, 227–42.
FRANK, R.I. 1976: 'Augustus' Legislation on Marriage and Children', *California Studies in Classical Antiquity* 8, 41–52.
GANZERT, J. and KOCKEL, V. 1988: 'Augustusforum und Mars-Ultor-Tempel', in HÖFTER 1988, 149–99.
GIULIANI, C. F. and VERDUCHI, P. (ed.) 1987: *L'area centrale del foro romano*, Firenze, 1987.
GOETTE, H.-R. 1990: *Studien zu römische Togadarstellungen*, Mainz, 1990.
GRATWICK, A. forthcoming: 'Pliny, The Obelisk, and Novius Facundus', *JRS*, forthcoming.
HEILMEYER, W.-D. 1970: *Korinthische Normalkapitelle: Studien z. Geschichte d. rom. Architekturdekoration* 16, Ergänzungsheft des DAI Mitt.Röm., Heidelberg, 1970.
HESBERG, H. von and PANCIERA, S. 1994: *Das Mausoleum des Augustus. Der Bau und seine Inschriften*, München, 1994.
HÖFTER, M. *et al.* (ed.) 1988: *Kaiser Augustus und die verlorene Republik. Eine Ausstellung im Martin-Gropius-Bau, Berlin 7 Juni–14 August 1988*, Ausstellung und Katalog, Mainz, 1988.
HORN, H.-G. and RÜGER, C.B. 1979: *Die Numider: Reiter und Könige nördlich der Sahara*, Köln/Bonn, 1979.
HORNUM, K.G., HOHLFELDER, R.L., BULL R.J. and RABAN A. 1988: *King Herod's Dream. Caesarea on the Sea*, New York, 1988.
KLEINER, D.E.E. 1978: 'The Great Friezes of the Ara Pacis Augustae – Greek Sources, Roman Derivatives and Augustan Social Policy', *MEFRA* 90, 1978, 753–85.
KÜNZL, E. 1988: *Der römische Triumph: Siegesfeiern im antiken Rom*, München, 1988.
LA ROCCA, E. 1985: *Amazonomachia. Le Sculture Frontonale del tempio di Apollo Sosiano*, Roma, 1985.
LA ROCCA, E., 1988: 'Der Apollo-Sosianus-Tempel', in HÖFTER 1988, 121–36.
LA ROCCA, E., UNGARO, L. and MENEGHINI, R. 1995: *I Luoghi del Consenso Imperiale*, Roma, 1995.
LAWRENCE, A.W. 1983: *Greek Architecture*, ed. 4, Harmondsworth, 1983.
MARTIN, H.G. 1988: 'Die Tempelkultbilder', in HÖFTER 1988, 251–63.
NEDERGAARD, E. 1988: 'Zur Problematik der Augustusbögen auf dem Forum Romanum', in HÖFTER 1988, 224–39.
ONIANS, J. 1988: *Bearers of Meaning: the Classical Orders in Antiquity, the Middle Ages and the Renaissance*, Princeton, 1988.
OSBORNE, R. 1997: 'Law, the Democratic Citizen and the representation of women in Classical Athens', *P&P* 155, 1997, 3–33.
PANCIERA, S. 1969: 'Miscellanea Epigrafica IV', *Epigrafica* 31, 104–20.
PENSABENE, P. 1982: *Les Chapiteaux de Cherchel. Étude de la Décoration Architectonique*, Algiers, 1982.
PENSABENE, P. 1991: 'Il Tempio della Vittoria sul Palatino', *BA* 11–2, 1991, 11–54.
PENSABENE, P. 1995: 'Casa Romuli sul Palatino', *RendPontAcc*, 1995, 115–62.
PENSABENE, P. 1997: 'Elementi architettonici della Casa di Augusto sul Palatino', *RM* 104, 1997, 149–92.
POLLITT, J. J. 1992: *The Art of Rome c. 753 BC–AD 337: Sources and Documents*, Cambridge, 1992.
ROLLER, D. 1998: *The Building Program of Herod the Great*, Berkeley 1998.
SANDE, S. and ZAHLE, J. 1988: 'Der Tempel der Dioskuren auf dem Forum Romanum', in HÖFTER 1988, 213–24.
SCHNEIDER, R.M. 1986: *Bunte Barbaren*, Worms, 1986.
SCHUTZ, M. 1990: 'Zur Sonnenuhr des Augustus auf dem Marsfeld: Eine Auseinandersetzung mit E. Buchners Rekonstruktion und seiner Deutung der Ausgrabungsergebnisse, aus der Sicht eines Physikers', *Gymnasium* 97, 1990, 432–57.
TOMEI, M.A. 1997: *Museo Palatino*, Roma, 1997.
TRAVLOS, J. 1971: *Pictorial Dictionary of Ancient Athens*, London, 1971.

VISCOGLIOSI, A. 1988: 'Die Architektur-Dekoration der Cella des Apollo-Sosianus-Tempels', in HÖFTER 1988, 136–48.
WALKER, S. 1991: *Roman Art*, London, 1991.
WALKER, S. 1995: *Greek and Roman Portraits*, London, 1995.
WALLACE-HADRILL, A. 1993: *Augustan Rome*, Bristol, 1993.
WARD-PERKINS J.B. 1981, *Roman Imperial Architecture*, Harmondsworth, 1981.
WAURICK, G. 1975: 'Kunstraub der Römer: Untersuchungen zu seinen Anfängen anhand der Inscriften', *Jahrbuch des Römisch-Germanischen Zentralmuseums Mainz* 22.2, 1975, 1–46.
WAYWELL, G.B. 1978: *The Free-Standing Sculptures of the Mausoleum at Halicarnassus,* London, 1978.
WISEMAN, T.P. 1984: *Poetry and Politics in the Age of Augustus*, Cambridge, 1984.
ZANKER, P. 1983: 'Zur Bildnisrepräsentation führender Männer in mittelitalischen und campanischen Städten zur Zeit der späten Republik und der julisch-claudischen Kaiser', in *'Les Bourgeoises' municipales italiennes aux IIe et IIer siècles av. J.-C. Int. Colloquium Centre Bérard Naples 1983,* Napoli and Paris, 1983, 251–56.
ZANKER, P. 1988: *The Power of Images in the Age of Augustus,* (translated by A. Shapiro), Ann Arbor, 1988.

5. 'Armed and belted men': the soldiery in imperial Rome

J. C. N. Coulston

Scholars interested in the Roman army of the Principate have traditionally been drawn to the study of Rome's imperial frontiers, to areas on the periphery where military forces and their installations clustered. The perception is one of a dichotomy between militarized frontier zones and rich, inner provinces. Rome, the populous *caput mundi*, stood at the centre, and from the 50s BC to the 270s AD she was virtually an open city. During this period the 'Servian Wall' had lost its military relevance, and the Aurelianic Wall had still to be built.[1] Yet, in fact, a larger concentration of troops was present in Rome than in any other city or fortress of the empire (Fig. 5.1).[2]

From the time of Augustus to that of Maxentius (30 BC–AD 306) the number of soldiers fluctuated, but it tended to increase steadily, reaching its peak under the Severi. Emperors required bodyguards and escorts, the city needed protection from fire and disorder, and the provincial armies had a floating population of administrators at the centre of government. All of these men, even the firemen, may be considered as soldiers (*milites*) in the modern sense, and they cannot but have influenced the life of the city on many levels. Rome was surrounded by fortified *castra*. Its streets were thronged with soldiers distinguished by their dress and weapons, the 'armed and belted men' of this chapter's title.[3] No public event involving the emperor lacked soldiers in attendance. Soldiers patronised artists and craftsmen and other service professions; soldiers owned property and had a satellite community of families, servants and slaves. They kept order, and they themselves occasionally rioted.

The purpose of this chapter is to explore a number of aspects of Rome as a 'military' city. In turn it will investigate the organisation, installations, functions and impact of the troops, both in formations and as individual soldiers. Then it will examine the influence their presence bore on metropolitan art, principally on the composition of state sculptural works, but also on classes of private commission. Lastly, these areas of study will be brought together to clarify the political implications of such a concentration of soldiers in the imperial capital.

1. A "THRONG OF MOTLEY SOLDIERS":[4] NUMBERS AND ORGANISATION

The administrative innovations enacted by Augustus included the permanent establishment of the traditional general's bodyguard.[5] The Praetorian Guard was recruited predominantly, but not exclusively, from Italian citizens, largely infantry but with a significant cavalry element (Fig. 5.2). There is some modern controversy about the organisation and strength of the Guard throughout its history, based upon the evidence of Tacitus, 'Hyginus' and Dio, and upon the epigraphic record.[6] Originally, there were nine Augustan units (*cohortes*), probably each *c*.500 strong, numbered I–IX, three of which attended the emperor. These were

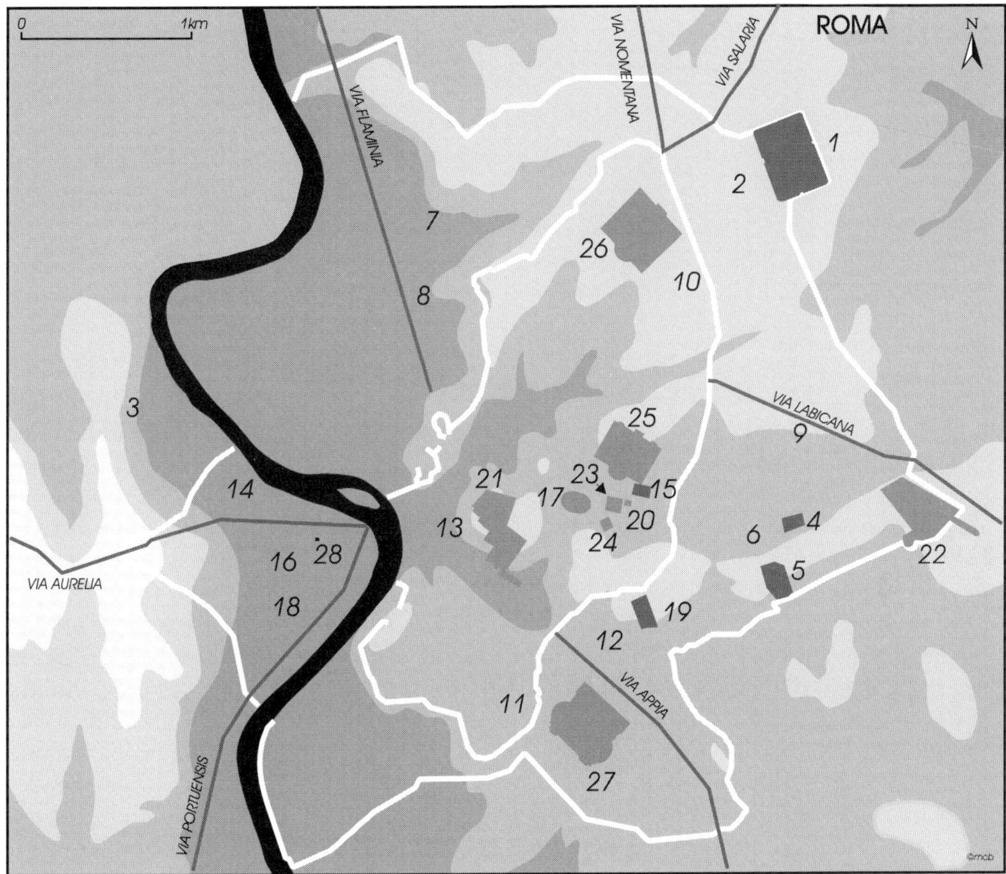

Fig. 5.1: Map of Rome. Military installations and other sites mentioned in the text. 1 Castra Praetoria, 2 Campus Praetorianus, 3 Horti Dollabellae, 4 Castra Priora Equitum Singularium, 5 Castra Nova Equitum Singularium, 6 Campus Martius Caelimontanus, 7 Castra Urbana, 8 –14 Castra Cohortium I–VII Vigilum, 15 Castra Misenatium, 16 Castra Ravennatium, 17 Amphitheatrum Flavium, 18 Naumachia Augusti, 19 Castra Peregrinorum, 20 Armamentarium, 21 Palatium, 22 Palatium Sessorianum, 23 Ludus Magnus, 24 Ludus Dacicus, 25 Thermae Traianae, 26 Thermae Diocletianae, 27 Thermae Antoninianae, 28 Excubitorium

increased to twelve before AD 47. During the Civil War (AD 68–69), Vitellius dismissed the Italian Guard which had fought for Otho, and recruited 16 *cohortes*, each *c*.1,000 strong. These latter were raised in part at least from loyal German frontier legionary manpower. Vespasian reverted to nine *cohortes* and Italian recruitment, Domitian restored a tenth *cohors*, all still possibly at the Vitellian strength (if not, then back up to 1,000 by the Antonine period). Whilst the number of units remained constant until the end of the Guard's history, the effective strength of each *cohors* may have been further raised to c.1,500 by Commodus or Septimius Severus. After Severus' reforms recruits were drawn principally, but not exclusively, from the frontier legions, especially those of the Danubian provinces.[7] The full ten *cohortes praetoriae* were still in existance in AD 306.[8]

Fig. 5.2: Trajan's Column, Rome, Scene LXXXVI. Praetorian infantry travelling with the emperor (Photo: author).

Each *cohors* had a detachment of cavalry (*equites praetoriani*, Fig. 5.3). 'Hyginus' allotted space in his encampment layout for 300 cavalry accompanying four *cohortes praetoriae* so it might be that there were *c*.1,200 horseman for the whole Guard.[9] It is likely that they were included in the strength of the infantry centuries, as with legionary cavalry, rather than organised as a separate body, as in auxiliary *cohortes equitatae*.[10] As the size of the Guard increased so too would have the numbers of cavalry, but the latter would not have affected the overall strengths. In addition, there were infantry and mounted administrative ranks (*speculatores*), and soldiers singled out for promotion by the emperor (*evocati*), in unknown numbers who may have been a separate formation.[11]

Emperors from Augustus to Galba also had another bodyguard, the *Germani corporis custodes*, or '*Batavi*'.[12] These were Rhenish cavalry, essentially German barbarians personally attached to the Julio-Claudians, some 500 strong (Fig. 5.4). Presumably because of their direct links with the frontier tribes, they were temporarily banished from Rome by Augustus after the massacre of Varus' army by the Free German tribes in AD 9.[13] This was perhaps more of a public relations exercise than reaction to any real security threat in the capital. The *corporis custodes* were dissolved by Galba in the context of confused loyalties after the death of Nero.[14] The Flavian emperors thereafter went without a mounted bodyguard, but a new one was probably raised by Trajan. Its men were drawn from the frontier auxiliary regiments, at first with a German frontier bias. There were 1000 *equites singulares Augusti*, literally 'the picked cavalry of the emperor' (Fig. 5.5).[15] Like the earlier Germanic cavalry, they were less formally known as '*Batavi*'.[16] Their number was raised to 1,500 or 2,000 by Severus.[17]

To maintain public order Augustus established three *cohortes urbanae*, perhaps each 500 strong, numbered X–XII following sequentially on from the *cohortes praetoriae*, and made up of soldiers with rank structure, standards, trumpets and weapons (Fig. 5.6). These seem to have been doubled in size under Vitellius and a fourth *cohors* added in the Flavian period. At some stage numbers were again increased to 1,500 per unit.[18] To combat fire, Augustus instituted seven *cohortes* of fire watchmen (*vigiles*), each probably 500 strong and each assigned two *regiones* of the city (Fig. 5.7). It has been suggested that these too may later have been increased in size to 1,000 men.[19] Detachments of the Mediterranean fleets based at Misenum and Ravenna were also permanently present in Rome, although the numbers of men involved is unknown.[20] There is evidence for other troops employed in the capital,

Fig. 5.3: Gravestone of Aurelius Saturninus, eques cohortis VIII praetoria, *3rd c. AD. Vatican Galleria Lapidaria (Photo: author, with permission).*

Fig. 5.4: Gravestones of corporis custodes, *Julio-Claudian. Cinquecento Garden, Museo Nazionale delle Terme, Rome (Photo: author).*

Fig. 5.5: *Gravestone of Ulpius Victorinus,* eques singularis, *3rd c. AD. Vatican Lateran Magazzini (Photo: Musei Vaticani Neg.IV.30.1).*

Fig. 5.6: Funerary altar of Q. Flavius Crito and Q. Flavius Proculus, miles cohortis XII urbana, *1st–2nd c. D. Vatican Museo Gregoriano Profano (Photo: author, with permission).*

Fig. 5.7: Gravestone of Q. Iulius Galatus, miles cohortis VI vigilum, *1st c. AD. Vatican Galleria Lapidaria (Photo: author, with permission).*

	Augustus	Tiberius	Claudius	Trajan	Marcus Aurelius	Septimius Severus
Praetoriani	1500	4500	6000	5000/10000	5000/10000	10000/15000
Horseguards	500	500	500	1000	1000	2000
Cohortes urbanae	1500	1500	1500	2000/4000 ?	4000 ?	6000
Cohortes vigilum	3500	3500	3500	3500	3500	7000 ?
Sub-total	7000	10000	11500	11500/18500	13500/18500	25000/30000
Classiarii	500 ?	500 ?	500 ?	1000 ?	1000 ?	1000 ?
Peregrini	500 ?	500 ?	500 ?	500 ?	500 ?	500 ?
Total	8000	11000	12500	13000/20000	15000/20000	26500/31500
Rome Total Population	1000000 (800000)	1000000 (800000)	1200000 (800000)	1200000 (1000000)	1200000 (1000000)	1200000 (800000)
Proportion soldier:civilian	1:125 (1:100)	1:91 (1:73)	1:96 (1:64)	1:92/60 (1:77/50)	1:80/60 (1:67/50)	1:45/38 (1:30/25)

Fig. 5.8: Types and numbers of troops stationed in Rome related to total population. Lower estimates for population, and the corresponding ratio and percentage calculations, are expressed in brackets.

notably Moors and archers attached to the guard units during the reign of Caracalla.[21] In addition, administrative troops, collectively known as 'foreigners' (*peregrini*, including *frumentarii* and *speculatores*) were detached from their parent formations in the provinces and represented a varying population of soldiers visiting Rome on official business. They were present frequently enough and/or for long enough periods of time to be organised under specially appointed centurions and to have an established series of cults. However, there is no evidence for their overall numbers which presumably fluctuated with different principates and frontier policies.[22]

Thus there are uncertainties about the exact strength of the military personnel in Rome, even relating to the *cohortes praetoriae*. Nevertheless, the estimates which may be made (Fig. 5.8) are rather more reliable than those traditionally calculated for other Rome 'statistics' (such as overall population, imported corn and water quantities). These suggest a minimum of 7,000 soldiers under Augustus, plus fleet troops and *peregrini* (total 1,000?), a total of *c*.8,000.[23] By the time of Claudius this had risen to 12,500, the equivalent of two and a half *legiones*. In the principate of Trajan there were 13,000 or 20,000 troops; 15,000 or 20,000 under Marcus. Lastly, in the Severan period, the numbers may be put as high as 26,500 or 31,500 (five to six *legiones*). To put these totals into a city-wide perspective one can compare them with modern estimates of Rome's total population.[24] If one takes a high calculation of one million people in the Augustan period, that gives a proportion of soldiers to others of 1:125. Using minima for soldiers under Trajan and Severus with a maximum total population of 1,200,000, this gives proportions of 1:92 and 1:45 respectively. The high military numbers give 1:63 and 1:38. Even when the figures are 'stacked' against the soldiers, the proportions are extraordinarily high. Results drawn from lower modern population estimates speak for themselves. Compared with the high public profile of ceremonial troops in modern mass-population cities, soldiers in ancient Rome must have been very 'visible' indeed.[25]

2. 'COHORTS AND CAVALRY ON CALL':[26] MILITARY INSTALLATIONS IN ROME

At first troops were billeted at scattered locations around Rome and in surrounding towns.[27] However, in AD 23 the Guard commander, Aelius Seianus, persuaded Tiberius to concentrate the praetorian and urban *cohortes* in a new, custom-built fortress on a level site north-east of the city (*regio* VI, Figs 5.1 and 5.9).[28] Three sides of this Castra Praetoria survive with the Tiberian gates, towers, walls and parapets topped, blocked and preserved by later defensive structures (Fig. 5.10). Measuring 440 by 380 m. (16.67 ha., 41.2 acres), it is significant as the first known large-scale 'public' building in Rome to employ concrete (*opus caementicium*) with a fired brick facing.[29] Internally there were barracks, stores, armouries, administrative buildings and shrines, but the plan so far elucidated through excavation is fragmentary and puzzling. The south-east wall is not parallel to the north-west line, and perhaps this represents an expansion of the fortress south-eastwards at some point in its history subsequent to an original square layout of 380 m. each side.

Two internal streets formed a cross plan and aligned with the two known main gates (north-west and north-east), but were blocked by buildings at various points and direct access through to a southwest gate was denied. The entire circuit of the wall seems to have been internally lined with one-room *tabernae* fronted by a paved road. There were two rows of buildings with up to sixteen pairs of rooms each set end-on to a road running north-west/south-east. A series of buildings traced along Viale Castro Pretorio had large back-to-back *tabernae* and internal staircases. A line of especially large chambers in the east corner most likely represent granaries (*horrea,* cf. Mattingly and Aldrete in this volume).[30] Various parts of the interior were probably rebuilt at different times, particularly if road-lines were blocked and the walled enclosure was extended.

The Castra Praetoria was perhaps a little tight for the *c.*6,000 soldiers and *c.*1,200 horses of the Tiberian establishment, as compared with 1st century legionary fortresses designed to hold 5,000 troops in single-storey barracks (*c.*20 ha.).[31] When numbers increased, pressure on accommodation would have been relieved by the use of multi-storey barracks, effectively military *insulae* built in metropolitan style.[32] This complicates any attempt to reconstruct layout and to calculate troop accommodation using the usual methods employed for provincial fortresses (counting rooms in barracks and numbers of barracks).[33] Civilian *insulae* often had *tabernae* on the ground floor and upper storeys on a different plan (see Patterson, DeLaine in this volume). Thus the ground-plans of potential barracks in the Castra Praetoria may actually be made up of the store-rooms found in legionary fortresses, with the upper floors given over to rooms for centuries divided up into eight-man squads (*contubernia*).[34] Additionally, barracks in Rome may not have conformed to the perceived provincial pattern of a pair of rooms for each *contubernium*, one room for the men's equipment, the other for sleeping. Certain seldom-used campaign equipment items could have been stored centrally and not held by the men in barracks (tents, entrenching tools), thus only one room was required. The buildings in rows in the central part of the *castra* were narrower than those in Viale Castro Pretorio, perhaps suggesting that the former were barracks and the latter were stores. Alternatively, they are all barracks but were built at different periods, the Viale buildings being later additions because they block the main north-east/south-west road access to the south-east gate. A third possibility is that the wider buildings were 'stable-barracks' (see below), although the rooms may have been too deep.

The barrel-vaulted, wall-back *tabernae* might at first glance appear to be a late feature such as those seen in 3rd–4th century military installations elsewhere. However, they were

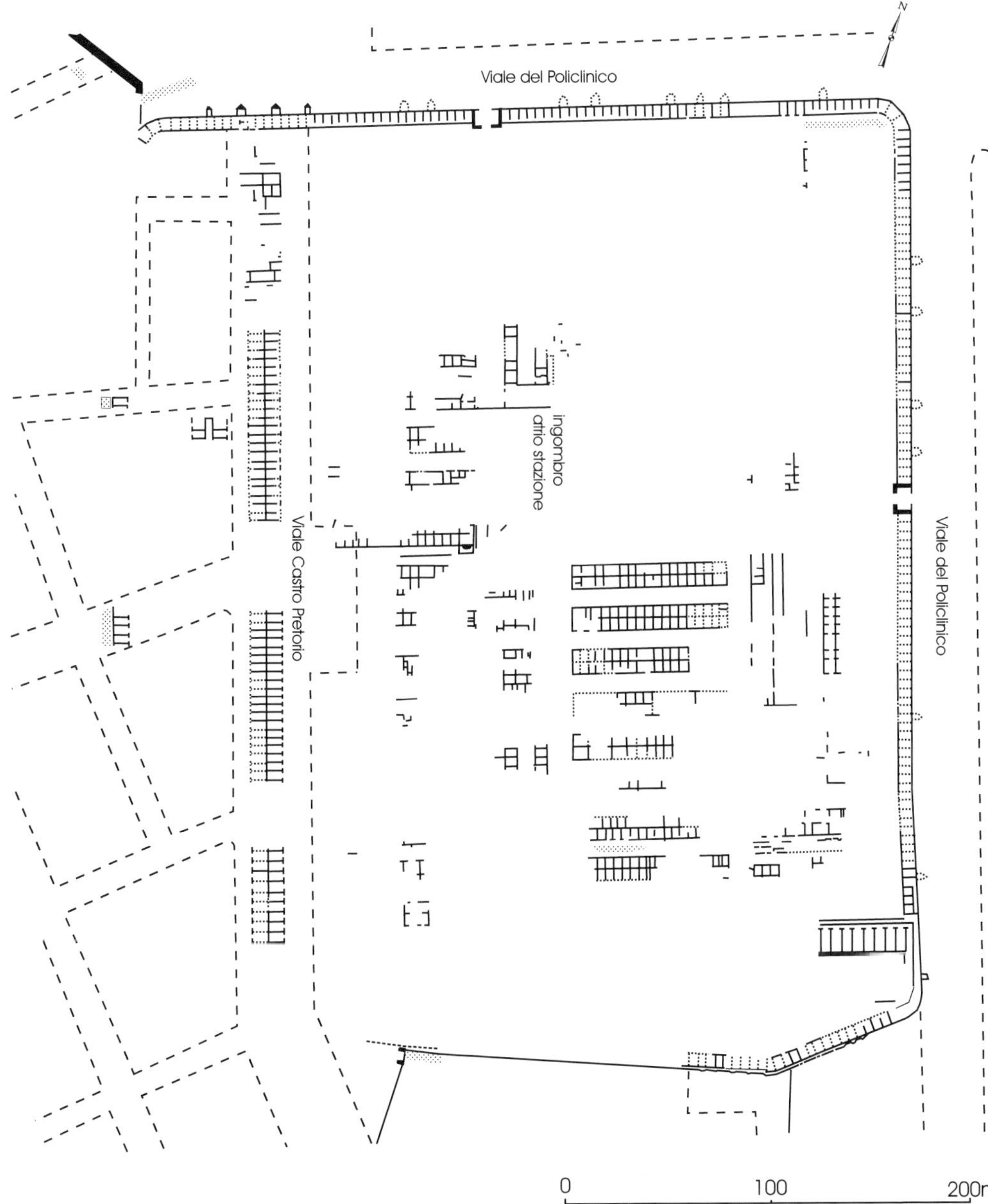

Fig. 5.9: Plan of the Castra Praetoria (Modified from Lexicon I).

constructed in *opus reticulatum*, suggesting a Tiberian date.[35] They may have been barracks rather than stores and indeed the troops stationed in Rome may have had less need than frontier forces to store transport vehicles and accommodate pack-animals. The headquarters building (*principia*) is unlocated and there were no obvious high-status houses for officers, but large areas of the north-west are virtually unexplored. The absence of élite accommodation in 'predictable' positions is inconclusive in an installation designed originally to house multiple formations, and one which was probably internally replanned

Fig. 5.10: Castra Praetoria, exterior view of west corner looking east (Photo: author).

during its life. Between the Castra and the city lay a great parade-ground, the Campus Praetorianus (*c.*440 by 280 m), surrounded by *rostra*, shrines, honorific and triumphal monuments, and wine-shops.[36]

The Julio-Claudian *Batavi* were stationed in Transtiberim (*regio* XIV) near the gardens of P. Cornelius Dolabella, a location across the river perhaps chosen for its political acceptability (Fig. 5.1).[37] The *equites singulares Augusti* occupied two fortresses on the east side of town, the Castra Priora and Castra Nova Equitum Singularium (*regiones* II and V). The former lay west of the modern Villa Wolkonsky, whilst the latter has been partially excavated nearby under S. Giovanni in Laterano. Inscriptions from both *castra* make it clear that Severus' doubling of cavalry numbers resulted in a second camp being built and used contemporaneously with the first, not one *castra* succeeding the other.[38]

Little sense can be made of the Castra Priora plan as so far recovered, other than to note the excavation of a shrine and associated imperial dedications within it. Work in the Castra Nova, on the other hand, revealed a rectangular *schola* building aligned with two long, narrow, parallel structures (the ends of which were not explored, Fig. 5.11). The latter have paired rooms; the western building may have been a storebuilding whilst the eastern was probably a barrack. Its rooms were back-to-back and each had a single, off-centre door communicating out to paved streets. The rooms were not interconnected. Two possible interpretations are that each room housed an urban *contubernium* with restricted equipment, as posited above for the Castra Praetoria, or that the building was a 'stable-barrack'. In frontier forts such as Dormagen in Germany and Wallsend in Britain, this class of building consisted of paired, unconnected rooms, one range for cavalry trooper accommodation with hearths, the other with soakways for their horses.[39]

The Campus (Martialis) Caelimontanus in the area of Piazza S. Giovanni in Laterano served the *equites singulares Augusti*, and it is probable that the famous equestrian statue of Marcus Aurelius which is now on the Campidoglio was first specifically positioned beside it.[40] The Castra Priora and Nova fronted onto its east and south sides respectively and to an extent they were unified by it despite roads and aqueduct arcades running between them.

It may appear strange that a second *castra* was constructed some 100 m apart from the first, rather than the Castra Priora being extended or its buildings built upwards, but a number of practical factors probably governed the decision. There were serious space restrictions for expansion on the Priora site. The *castra* are divided off by the Rivus Herculaneus (see Dodge in this volume) and the Via Asinaria, and both camps perch, with their *campus*, on the steep-sided Caelian saddle.[41] The latter's configuration rather dictated a diagonal placing of the Castra Nova, and there would have been reluctance to build on the Campus Caelimontanus, crucial as it was for *equites singulares* training. Another issue may have been the availability of a specific, already imperially-owned site for the Castra Nova. Moreover, vertical extension of the Castra Priora buildings was probably impractical precisely because, unlike in the Castra Praetoria, Severan reform involved doubling the number of horses to be accommodated, and thus twice the area of stabling. Whether or not upper storeys were added for human barracks, horses had to be kept on the ground floor.[42]

The urban *cohortes* lived in the Castra Praetoria until a new Castra Urbana was built for them in *regio* VII (Via Lata), perhaps during the Severan period (Fig. 5.1).[43] Each *cohors vigilum* had a *castra* and two *excubitoria* or sub-stations, the latter in each of the cohort's two *regiones*. Some are attested epigraphically but only one *castra* and one *excubitorium* have been archaeologically explored, on the Caelian Hill (*regio* II, Fig. 5.12) and in Transtiberim (XIV) respectively.[44] Fleet troops were present in the Castra Praetoria when Claudius was acclaimed.[45] However, a Castra Misenatium was located close to the Flavian Amphitheatre in *regio* II, and a Castra Ravennatium lay across the river in Transtiberim.[46] The former was probably later Flavian, built in association with development of the Amphitheatre district; the latter presumably went with the Augustan Naumachia (see Coleman in this volume). Like the Castra Urbana, nothing is known of their internal layouts. Urban, *vigil* and fleet *castra* would presumably have had their own parade-grounds.

For visiting provincial troops there was a Castra Peregrinorum on the Caelian in the area now occupied by S. Stefano Rotondo and its grounds (Fig. 5.12). Here shrines (notably a fine *mithraeum*) are known epigraphically or have been revealed by excavation. Four narrow, parallel buildings were divided off by one major and two narrower east-west roads.[47] As in other *castra*, series of single room units were laid out either back-to-back in double rows, or in single lines. They may be interpreted as barracks or store-buildings, or a combination of the two. The east ends of all of them have been examined and it appears that they were not perpendicular to a north-south road but engaged to other buildings on an angled alignment.

There seems to have been a centralised weapons store (*armamentarium*) for various troop formations, perhaps located in the Castra Praetoria. In AD 69 Otho's rebellious soldiers opened it up, indiscriminately grabbing weapons and armour without regard for praetorian, legionary or auxiliary distinctions.[48] Whilst this may have been hyperbole employed in Tacitus' account for dramatic effect to emphasise the collapse of military order, it suggests that equipment was held not just for the normal Castra occupants, but also for *peregrini* (legionaries), and perhaps *corporis custodes* and *classiarii* ('auxiliaries'). Storage of artillery in the *armamentarium* is suggested by a pedestal inscription which records one C. Vedennius Moderatus as an *architectus* at the armoury. On one side of the pedestal is a fine representation of a bolt-shooting catapult.[49]

The overall location of *castra* around the city was in part functional (Fig. 5.1). The distribution of *vigiles* installations was dictated by the layout of *regiones*, and the fleet bases were positioned first to be near Augustus' Naumachia, second by the Flavian Amphitheatre (Coleman in this volume). However, political factors influenced the main concentrations of troops. The base of the barbarian *corporis custodes* on the right bank of the Tiber was far removed from the centre of town.[50] The Castra Praetoria was right out on the Esquiline plateau to the north-east, beyond the old walls and the *pomerium* to prevent it seeming as a tyrant's citadel.[51] In accordance with Trajan's public line on despotic government, an analogous position on the Caelian to the south-east was chosen for the first Castra Equitum Singularium.[52] The Castra Nova was located nearby under Severus, as has already been discussed. Whilst being somewhat nearer to the Palatine palaces than the Castra Praetoria, these cavalry bases were very convenient for the 3rd century imperial residence at the Palatium Sessorianum (on the east edge of *regio* V).[53] In the same neighbourhood as the Castra Equitum Singularium were to be found the Castra Peregrinorum and the *statio* of *cohors V vigilum*, and all these installations over time developed into something of a Caelian military quarter.[54]

In considering these fortresses and other structures associated with troops in the city mention should be made of the military cemeteries which were associated with specific formations. For example, praetorian cemeteries were located beside the Via Salaria and the Via Nomentana. On the Via Cassia just across the Pons Mulvius and on the Tiber right bank there was a concentration of praetorian monuments with an admixture of some *urbaniciani* and *veterani*. Many of the surviving *corporis custodes* gravestones were found along the Via Portuensis and the Via Aurelia. The cemetery on the Via Labicana in the area of SS. Marcellino e Pietro yielded many *stelae* commemorating *equites singulares Augusti*, some preserved by reuse in the christian catacombs below. The Ravenna marines had a *columbarium* on the Via Aurelia and the *Misenati* occupied one on the Via Appia.[55]

3.“BODYGUARDS AND PUBLIC EXECUTIONERS”:[56] THE FUNCTIONS OF TROOPS IN ROME

The soldiers in Rome fulfilled a range of duties. The Praetorian Guard and Horseguard units escorted and protected the emperor (and his family) in all circumstances, whether in residence on the Palatine, at the many imperial villas, on journeys, or in battle. To quote Fergus Millar: “no conception of the emperor's relation to his subjects would be complete without taking into account the fact that he was almost always escorted by armed soldiers”.[57]

The task of ensuring the emperor's safety involved a range of challenges. When he was ‘static’, the residence could have been given an overall security perimeter to prevent outsiders from entering. Within the residence the emperor's person could have been closely escorted, especially in the more formal situations. His private rooms would also have been guarded with an inner perimeter. When the emperor was ‘mobile’ in a far less controllable environment, then as now, there would have been a tension between security dictates and praiseworthy, approachable informality (the bodyguard's ‘walkabout’ nightmare).

The Palatine palaces were rambling and extensive, but, as imperial building expanded, security must have been a design requirement.[58] In the early stages Gaius could be cut down in a narrow alley between houses, separated from his guards, and his assassins make their escape.[59] This was not repeated. A full *cohors praetoria* was always on duty on the Palatine with all the military attention to passwords and vigilance. Its personnel would have been distributed on all the major and minor entrances (with a set circuit for inspecting officers), around the imperial apartments, and in direct personal attendance alongside Horseguards (especially during meals).[60] Attempts have been made to identify guard stations and accommodation, for example in the rooms and corridors around the great atrium fronting onto the Forum Romanum.[61]

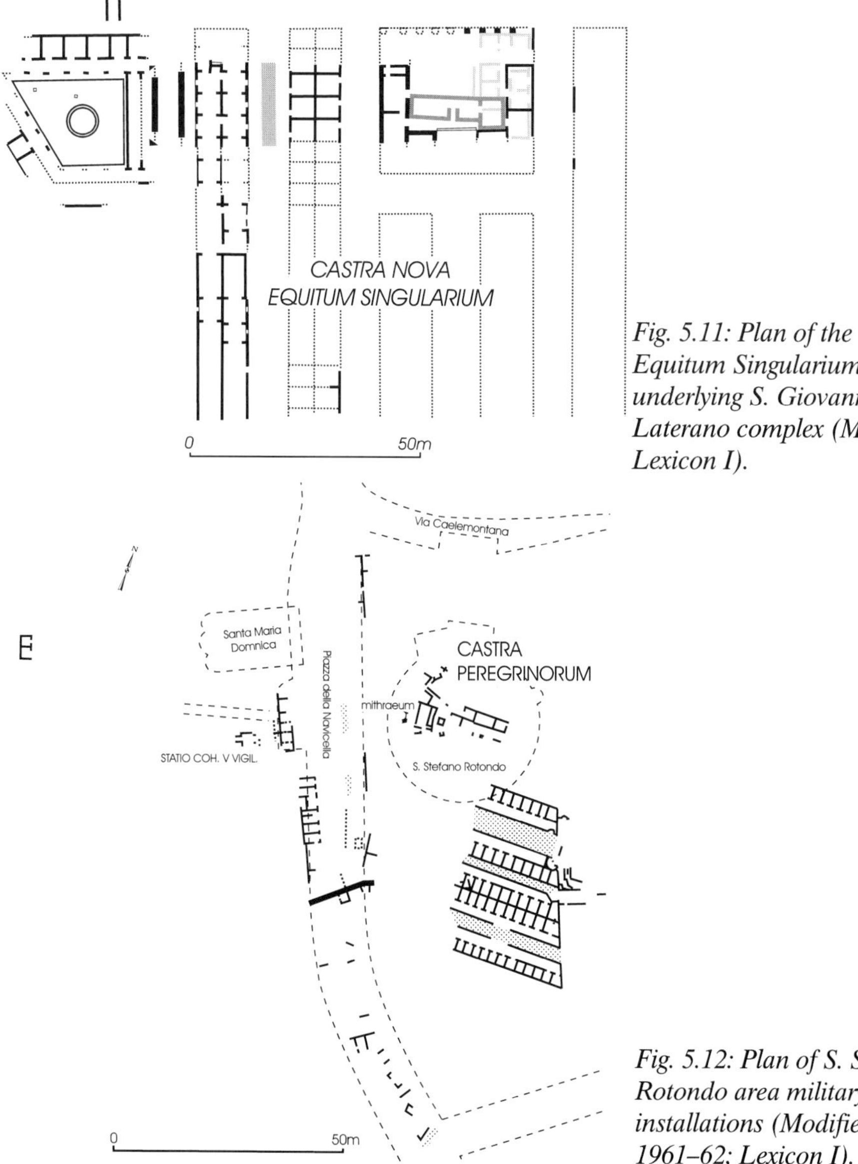

Fig. 5.11: Plan of the Castra Nova Equitum Singularium buildings, underlying S. Giovanni in Laterano complex (Modified from Lexicon I).

Fig. 5.12: Plan of S. Stefano Rotondo area military installations (Modified from Nash 1961–62; Lexicon I).

Imperial villas around the outskirts of Rome, and beyond, would perhaps have been easier to secure. The literary sources provide anecdotes about praetorians in Roman gardens, as on Capri (Tiberius brutally 'rewarding' a fisherman for bringing an unsolicited mullet).[62] At first sight Hadrian's Villa near Tivoli seems to be a sprawl of buildings and a security impossibility. In fact it is built largely on a promontory, and recent analysis has demonstrated how access to most of the area could have been controlled by a small number of entrances. Various more or less convincing identifications of guard accommodation have also been made here.[63]

The guard units would have escorted the emperor in triumphs, on arrival at Rome, on departure from the city, and on journeys through Italy and the provinces (Figs 5.2, 5.13). In the streets of Rome the emperor required not just burly *lictores* to clear a way through crowds, but also bodyguards.[64] When he appeared in public to make speeches and hear legal cases, to officiate in religious ritual and at the games, silent, vigilant men would have stood observing the audience, not the man himself – the equivalent of the men in dark suits and 'shades' who stand out today because, unlike everybody else, they are watching the crowd, not the U.S. President. Sometimes they wore togas with swords concealed, as in the Palatine palaces, but usually they were in military dress with their weapons on display (see section 5, below).[65] The security nightmare, then as now, was the lone assassin striking without care for his own life, and this danger would keep the bodyguards jumpy.[66] On one occasion a senator was almost cut down by Tiberius' guards because he unexpectedly and precipitately advanced, grasped the emperor's knees in supplication, and tripped him over! Audience with the emperor under the scrutiny of soldiers could be, and was often intended to be, a very intimidating experience. Famously, the orator Heraklides of Lycia was quite put off his stride by the presence of guards attending Severus. Conversely, home-visits by an unescorted emperor (e.g. those recorded of Tiberius, Nero and Trajan) were a special honour paid to the recipient because they expressed exceptional trust.[67]

Soldiers were useful to the emperor in performing a number of special duties such as running security for the more spectacular *munera* and being unleashed to quell public disorders. Groups of soldiers or individuals were sent on imperial missions and errands, to carry messages, to make arrests, to administer punishment, to enforce suicide and to execute traitors.[68] More pleasantly, soldiers carried out the burning of public debt records under the orders of Trajan and Hadrian, as depicted on the 'Anaglypha Traiani' and the 'Chatsworth Relief'.[69]

The guard infantry and cavalry mounted public military displays, as shown for example on the base of the Column of Antoninus Pius (Fig. 5.14).[70] They would also have been involved in triumphal processions, marching in them especially if they had been directly involved in the campaign being celebrated. Additionally, this would have been an opportunity for the city population to view provincial troops and their military standards, but the praetorians may have enjoyed pride of place.[71]

The Praetorian Guard in particular was a repository of military, architectural and engineering skills allowing, for example, Gaius to cross the Bay of Pozzuoli on a pontoon bridge, and Claudius to have artillery present during his great Fucine Lake spectacles.[72] Military formations in Rome were not just ornamental or divorced from military reality, not least because of the exchange of personnel between the Praetorian Guard and frontier legions, and between the *equites singulares Augusti* and provincial *auxilia*. Specialist skills were exercised within them, and, especially after the Severan reforms, theoretically the best men were picked from the frontier armies to serve as guards.[73] In war they marched, fought, were rewarded, and died on the battlefield with campaigning emperors such as Domitian, Trajan, Marcus Aurelius, Septimius Severus and Maximinus Thrax.[74]

The *cohortes urbanae* were principally concerned with policing the city and maintaining public order under the command of the city prefect (*praefectus urbi*). Presumably they also provided crowd-control during triumphs and other displays. It may have been *urbaniciani* who were posted by Augustus in the streets when games were held, specifically to prevent criminal activity in near-deserted areas.[75] They also occasionally took part in military campaigns.[76]

The *vigiles* functioned as a fire-fighting force and they were fully equipped with water-pumps, buckets and other material, including axes (*dolabra*) for breaking down the doors of houses on fire or suspected of harbouring a fire-risk. Artillery was used for projecting dampening materials and creating fire breaks by levelling buildings.[77] However, the *cohortes vigilum* were primarily a preventative fire-watch because once a serious fire had taken hold there was little that could be done except to stop it spreading. Night patrolling and the right of entry into private properties may also have made the *vigiles* a local police-force in a city with endemic nocturnal crime, such as mugging and burglary.[78] They were not merely organised on military lines, in the manner of modern fire-brigades, but constituted a truly military force with personal weapons and military dress, officers, standard-bearers and musicians.[79]

Fleet personnel were generally valued for their technical skills and the *classiarii* in Rome managed the awnings (*velaria*) erected to shade audiences in the Flavian Amphitheatre. Other establishments also required such services (Theatres of Pompey, Balbus, Marcellus; Stadium and Odeum of Domitian; Circus Maximus).[80] Marines would have contributed to the presentation of naval displays at the *naumachiae*, and both functions presumably dictated the location of fleet *castra*.[81] Warships could be rowed right up the Tiber to the centre of Rome, and naval vessels would have transported emperors and their entourages, and conveyed government messengers.[82] Fleet troops also operated in the field, notably during the Civil War, and alongside praetorians in AD 246 against brigands in Umbria. They were greatly valued for their engineering skills.[83] Troops in the Castra Peregrinorum will have been involved in a variety of duties connected with the musters, pay, corn-supply, appointments, promotions, discharges, movements and war-preparations of the provincial armies.[84]

4. 'WITH BRAWLING, FISTS AND SWORDS'?:[85] THE IMPACT OF SOLDIERS ON ROME

Such a major concentration of military personnel must have made soldiers a very familiar sight for the non-military inhabitants of Rome: off-duty, visiting friends and relations, conducting business, sitting together in auditoria,[86] relaxing in bars, and frequenting baths and brothels. The impact soldiers had on the city was both positive and negative. The praetorians were the most highly paid troops in the empire; the *urbaniciani* were only one level below them and still making more than *legionarii*. The scales of cash gifts (*donativa*) from the emperor were also higher for troops in Rome.[87] There would have been great economic benefits for those sections of the population which provided goods and services to the troops: builders, sculptors, letter-cutters, metal and textile workers, prostitutes, purveyors of wine and other luxuries.[88] Close links between soldiers and civilians existed, despite official attempts to keep them separate. Wives and families (tolerated before the Severan period, legal thereafter), slaves, freedmen and women, servants and grooms formed a dependant community (Fig. 5.15).[89] However, little of this appears in the literary sources which concentrate on military-civilian strife, not on harmonious relations.

Particular eating and drinking places near *castra* and *excubitoria* may have been favoured by military personnel, perhaps with territoriality exclusively exercised by specific formations.[90] Specific baths may have been popular with soldiers. For instance, the Baths of Trajan were the most convenient amongst the great *thermae* for the *equites singulares*, and the Baths of Diocletian, located just inside the 'Servian Wall', were available to the praetorians for a short period (AD 306–12).[91] Like other professions, soldiers had their own *collegia* for

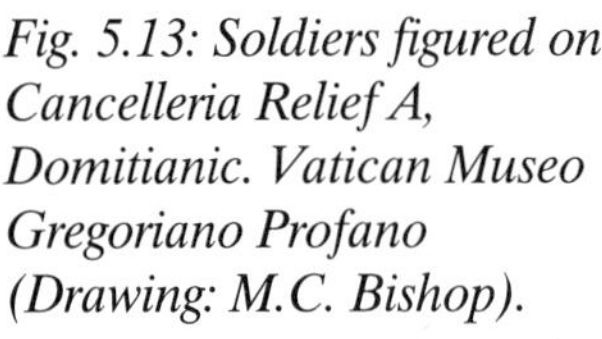

Fig. 5.13: Soldiers figured on Cancelleria Relief A, Domitianic. Vatican Museo Gregoriano Profano (Drawing: M.C. Bishop).

Fig. 5.14: Column of Antoninus Pius, sinister decursio *face, c. AD161. Musei Vaticani (Photo: author, with permission).*

dining, burial provision and religious observance (see Patterson in this volume). They also favoured particular tutelary deities associated with military service, the *castra* and the *campus*, such as Hercules, Epona, Mithras and specific Genii, bringing provincial cults with them to Rome (Fig. 5.16).[92]

Certainly there was periodic unrest in Rome and the troops had to be prepared to follow often draconian orders which must have created ill-feeling towards them from the wider metropolitan population.[93] Senators were often intimidated and affronted when emperors threatened even them with troops. This could be very personal, as in the case of Sabinus whose death was deferred because Elagabalus whispered the order of execution into the ear of a deaf centurion![94] Legal texts and gravestone representations provide evidence for the use of heavy, knobbed sticks (*fustes*) on malefactors by *praetoriani*, *urbaniciani* and *vigiles* (Fig. 5.17).[95] Impromptu thrashings could legally be administered to criminals, including people creating fire hazards. When Gaius became angry with a crowd which had burst into the circus after midnight in order to secure free seats, he had people driven out by soldiers with *fustes*. Twenty *equites*, as many matrons and numerous other people were killed in the ensuing panic.[96]

There was also plenty of scope for Roman soldiers to abuse their power and status. Uncompensated requisition of property, physical violence to civilians and general military arrogance are commonly attested in the provincial evidence.[97] However, it is not easy to determine how characteristic these were of soldier/civilian relations. Adverse behaviour was commented on in the hope of redress whilst 'good' behaviour would have passed unremarked. Juvenal painted a characteristically dark picture of relations in Rome. If a civilian was beaten up by a soldier he was best to forget about it because if he complained there would be a 'fair' trial in the Castra Praetoria under the eye of a centurion and in front of a jury of fellow-soldiers. No witnesses would dare support the plaintiff, so having made his accusation he would have all the other soldiers after him. It was stupidity beyond belief "to provoke all those boots and all those thousands of hobnails (*clavi*)".[98] This accords well with the advice of Epictetus that if a soldier wanted your mule it was best to give it to him, because, if you did not, you would have lost it anyway and received a beating into the bargain![99] Violence inflicted by troops in civil warfare of course affected the capital in AD 69.[100]

The violent actions of soldiers formed a literary *topos* because élite writers strongly resented the power allowed by indulgent emperors to these armed plebs. Accordingly, Herodian praised Pertinax for his disciplining of the troops in Rome and says that he forbade the soldiers "to insult the people, to carry axes (*dolabra*), or to strike at passers-by".[101] The striking would have been unprovoked use of the *fustis*, and the axes were employed by *vigiles* and other troops to break down doors, suggesting that the soldiers were abusing people both in the street and in their own houses. Unfortunately for Pertinax, his martinet stance made him an unpopular commander before becoming emperor, and afterwards it contributed to his death at the hands of the praetorians.[102]

Relations between soldiers and civilians in the capital probably worsened after Severus cashiered the old Praetorian Guard and replaced it with the larger force drawn principally from the Danubian legions. Dio was typically superior about the "throng of motley soldiers, most savage in appearance, most terrifying in speech and most boorish in conversation".[103] Like Tacitus, he hated the soldiery rising above what he thought their proper (lowly) station. As to his specific comments, Danubian dress and equipment may have differed from that of troops long stationed in Rome, and frontier Latin would certainly have seemed rough and 'provincial' to an élite listener. In AD 238 disagreements escalated into days of fighting between populace and praetorians, with the former assaulting the Castra Praetoria, and the latter torching parts of the city.[104]

A certain level of brutality is to be expected of all soldiers in all historical periods, especially those with the institutional structure of a regular army to support them, with compliant or corrupt officers, and in times of weak central government.[105] The society of soldiers is characteristically inward-looking and tends to distinguish itself from the non-military population through the development of jargon and unit loyalties, and by the wearing of distinctive insignia, dress and hairstyle. A Roman identified himself as a soldier by carrying arms and wearing military belts (*baltei*), rather than by being clad in 'uniform' clothing in the modern sense. The legal right to bear a sword in public was a key military privilege, indeed one which defined the military estate.[106] This is graphically emphasised on private funerary representations (see below). The belts evolved with a range of plates, buckles, strap-end pendents and other attachments which were designed primarily for ornament and to make a noise (Figs 5.2, 5.5, 5.13, 5.17).[107] Jingling metallic fittings combined with the crunch of hobnailed boots (*caligae*) to heighten the soldiers' 'presence'.[108] To strip a soldier of his belt was to humiliate him, in effect to militarily emasculate him, and even to eject him from the army altogether.

5. 'ARMED AND BELTED MEN' IN METROPOLITAN ART

It comes as no surprise, given the large numbers of troops in Rome and the constant attendance of soldiers on the emperor in public, that these men appear in imperial iconography. They also formed a significant proportion, of perhaps above average literacy, of the viewing public walking around, past and under imperial monuments. Soldiers would have seen themselves frequently rendered in painted marble.

Praetorians are first represented as audiences listening to emperors' speeches (*adlocutiones*) on Julio-Claudian coins, notably those of Gaius and Nero. They are shown armed but usually bare-headed and unarmoured. *Paenulae* are worn, a type of cloak chiefly associated with infantry and characterised by a 'W'-shaped profile at the front (Figs 5.2, 5.13, 5.18).[109] This combination of clothing and equipment seems to have been normal for duties in Rome, as the 'Anaglypha Traiani' and the 'Chatsworth' reliefs suggest. Unarmoured praetorians also appear in state sculpture carrying curved oval shields, notably on Cancelleria Relief A where four soldiers attend Domitian's departure (*profectio*) from the city (Fig. 5.13).[110] The oval shield was a feature of praetorian equipment and it is also seen on a guard's gravestone at Aquileia (Italy), although it was not a form of board used exclusively by them (Figs 5.2, 5.14).[111]

Soldiers with oval shields are figured on panels from a demolished monument of Trajan at Pozzuoli and there is a small scorpion blazon on one board.[112] It is interesting to observe that on Trajan's Column *paenulae* and oval shields (as opposed to the curved rectangular boards of all the other citizen troops) only appear in a couple of scenes where the emperor is travelling with a military escort between the Dacian Wars (Fig. 5.2).[113] The soldiers are identifiable as praetorians by their standards, which are comparable with labelled ('COH III PR') *signa* depicted on the Domitianic funerary panel of M. Pompeius Asper from Tuscolo near Rome (Fig. 5.19).[114] The latter standards also bear scorpions. This creature was used as a praetorian badge probably because concentration of the praetorians in the Castra Praetoria under Tiberius was seen as a re-foundation of the bodyguard. *Legiones* raised by Caesar and Augustus adopted as badges their founder's zodiac birth-sign, the bull and capricorn respectively. Thus the praetorians sported Tiberius' scorpion on their standards, helmets, shields and other equipment (Fig. 5.20).[115]

Some military *adlocutio* audiences depicted on coins are armoured, as on an issue of Galba which shows a scorpion shield blazon.[116] In sculpture there are few surviving parallels before Trajan's Column. One of the Column's many innovative features is its depiction of large numbers of soldiers with contemporary rather than hellenizing military equipment. The latter does have stylising elements, not least in its uniformity, and it is overtly employed to distinguish citizen from non-citizen soldiers as part of the overall message programme.[117] Citizen soldiers wear articulated plate armour ('*lorica segmentata*') and auxiliaries have mail shirts. Two variants make up the vast majority of Roman figures, thus the sculptors only had to observe one *praetorianus* and one *eques singularis* as models. Such empirical study was also evidently made of the unarmoured, *paenula*-clad praetorians prominent in the streets of Rome.

Variants of military standards were not employed by the Column sculptors to distinguish praetorians from legionaries within the citizen body. However, analysis of the types does actually reveal a preponderance of praetorian over legionary *signa* (59%), whereas the reverse would have been the reality of a campaigning army.[118] This bias is what might be expected from sculptors most familiar with the standards carried by troops in Rome, and it is these which are depicted with a marked verisimilitude and variety of detail (Fig. 5.2).

The sculptors had a wealth of readily available models in the capital on which to base Roman soldiers and their equipment, including the artillery used by praetorians and *vigiles* in the city. Artists would also have drawn upon the soldiery as a great source of information about the camps and forts used as contextual scenery. They would not have had direct experience of contemporary turf, timber and earth built campaign architecture. The resulting representations are a blend of frontier reality, the artists' own Hellenistic traditions for architectural composition, and observations of building materials and

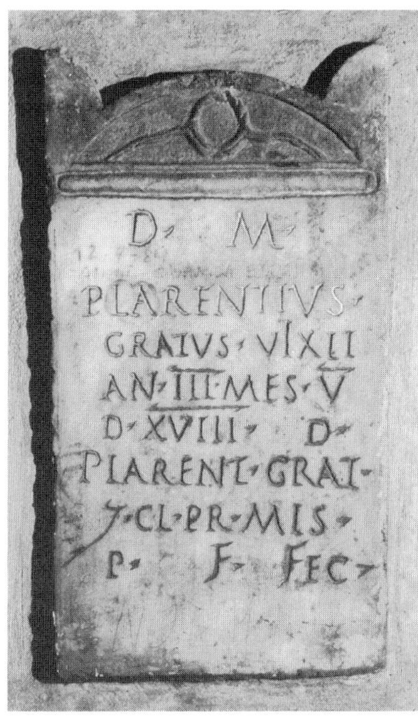

*Fig. 5.16: Pedimental inscription (*CIL 6.212*) from the Castra Praetoria recording the dediction of a marble shrine, statue and altar to the Spirit in the Century (Genius Centuriae) by a centurion,* evocati*, soldiers and a* medicus *of a* cohors praetoria *in AD 181. Vatican Galleria Lapidaria (Photo: author, with permission).*

Fig. 5.15: Gravestone of Gratus, three-year-old son of a centurion of the classis praetoria Misenensis*. S. Paolo fuori le mura (Photo: author).*

techniques applied contemporaneously in Rome. Richmond's belief that the artists had of necessity to base their work on 'campaign sketches' because the information was not available in Rome cannot be sustained.[119]

Trajan's Column had a profound influence on all subsequent sculptural monuments in Rome. An astoundingly high level of carved detail was applied, much of it invisible to the audience below. Later artists were far more practical and such small details as belt-buckles, shield-blazons and eyebrows were omitted. More use was made of compositional devices such as patterned stances for added clarity. This is particularly clear on the Column of Marcus Aurelius which in some respects plagiarised Trajan's Column, but in others learnt from earlier mistakes. The end result is a more visually effective monument. This of course makes the Marcus Column a much less useful source for Roman army studies.[120]

The Arch of Septimius Severus in the Forum Romanum (AD 203) simplifies the depictions of soldiers further whilst continuing to use armour to define the status of troops. The great siege panels are bordering on the crude even in comparison with the Marcus Column, but, in stark contrast, the pedestal reliefs are finely executed and the soldiers on them are 'conservative' in terms of their equipment.[121] Similar figures are to be seen on the contemporary Arcus Argentariorum nearby in the Velabrum (AD 204).[122] The question is whether these figures are conservative because old style equipment continued to be used by troops in Rome and to be empirically observed by sculptors, or the latter were using anachronistic models based on earlier monumental sculpture.

Looking at the evidence of imperial art, it is legitimate to ask when people did see soldiers wearing armour in Rome. Funeral games and other displays by troops involved armoured infantry and cavalry, and armour protection would have given soldiers a great advantage over rioters. There will certainly have been fully armed and armoured training exercises and reviews on the Campus Praetorianus, and other training grounds, especially when the

Fig. 5.17: Gravestone of M. Aurelius Lucianus, miles cohortis VI praetoria, *3rd c. AD. Museo Capitolino (Photo: Musei Capitolini Neg.MC131093).*

Fig. 5.18: Funerary altar of an unknown praetorian, 2nd c. AD. Vatican Galleria Lapidaria. (Photo: author, with permission).

emperor was present (as shown on the coins). However, not all parades were so equipped (as shown on other coins), and, albeit for a specific reason, the praetorians were ordered by Severus to parade without armour or weapons in AD 193 (see below).[123] Moreover, armour is generally absent from representations of triumphal processions, so troops may have marched in their best clothes, but not cuirasses and helmets.[124]

The impression that troops usually wore no armour in the city is reinforced by another rich field of military depiction: private iconographic commissions (Figs 5.3, 5.5–7, 5.17–8, 5.21). Gravestones were erected in Rome's military cemeteries for deceased soldiers throughout the imperial period but some caution must be exercised in making generalisations about them because an immense number have been lost into lime-kilns or been reused for paving post-classical buildings[125] However, a proportion of the surviving *stelae* bear pictorial representations. This is an invaluable source for the study of military equipment, not least because in the capital figural *stelae* were executed in white marbles which could sustain finely carved detail.

The erection of figural gravestones was a fashion which waxed and waned in the provinces and went through phases of popularity in Rome. Whilst the Rhineland had a good number of these figural works in the early to mid 1st century AD, trailing off in the second half of the century, only a small number of full-figure infantry representations are attested for the 1st to 2nd centuries in Rome (Fig. 5.7).[126] These include *praetoriani*, *urbaniciani*, and one *vigil*. There are no *classiarii* figured, although a few men are shown on gravestones at Ravenna and elsewhere.[127] In the 3rd century there was a great renaissance of figural *stela* erection in the

*Fig. 5.19: Funerary panel of M. Pompeius Asper from Tuscolo, detail of praetorian standard (*cohors III praetoria*), Domitianic. Palazzo Albani (Photo: DAI Neg.68.2788).*

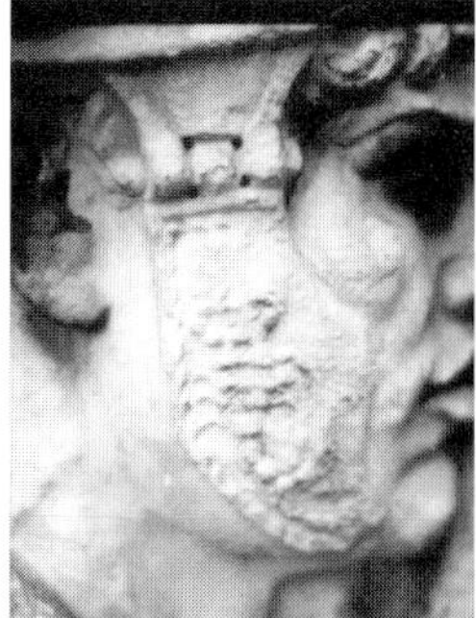

Fig. 5.20: 'Great Trajanic Frieze', detail of scorpion cheek-piece. East attic section, Arch of Constantine (Photo: author).

Fig. 5.21: Danubian rider style gravestone of M. Aurelius Bitho, eques singularis*, 3rd c. AD. Museo Capitolino (Photo: Musei Capitolini Neg.d637).*

provinces, perhaps eminating from Illyricum, and the practice spread to Rome where there is a sizeable body of praetorian representations (Figs 5.3, 5.17).[128] These include many superb pieces which accurately depict the military equipment of the period, despite the variety of local stones employed in the provinces. Ring-buckles, belt-terminals, sword and scabbard-fittings are faithfully reproduced by sculptors who were familiar with soldiers in detail.[129] This care with equipment characterises the Danubian examples, and the many stylistic links make it clear that provincial funerary practices were introduced into the capital through Severus' reform of praetorian recruitment patterns.

Similar developments may be seen with the *stelae* of *equites singulares*. Starting with Trajan's bias towards men drawn from the Rhenish *auxilia*, there are 2nd century scenes of groom (*calo*) and horse on 'long reins'. This motif is common on 1st century Lower Rhineland cavalry gravestones and constitutes a direct iconographic link.[130] The *equites singulares* were established just early enough to catch the tail-end of the Rhenish tradition. From the beginning there were also significant numbers of Illyrian soldiers in the Horseguards and the iconography of Danubian rider deities was employed for *stelae* in Rome (Fig. 5.21). The deceased, sometimes with a 3rd century ring-buckle and eagle-crested helmet, and accompanied by a *calo*, is shown hunting with a hound. A wild boar emerges from behind a tree on the right.[131] Unfortunately the *stelae* of *Germani corporis custodes* are non-figural partly because they date to the first half of the 1st century and follow contemporary praetorian fashions (Fig. 5.4).[132]

During the 2nd to 3rd centuries there was also a penchant for scenes showing a groom (*calo*) holding one or two horses by the bridle, and again this motif can be closely paralleled in the Danubian provinces.[133] Likewise, in the iconography of 3rd century Rome, the deceased soldier is shown standing in front of his horse, and, in the manner of the full-figure infantry representations, there is great attention to authentic military equipment detail (Fig. 5.5).[134]

In the 1st to 3rd centuries some funerary altars bore the depictions of deceased soldiers (Figs 5.6, 5.18).[135] Figural sarcophagi first show troops in the Antonine period ('Battle Sarcophagi'). The equipment represented on these is very stylised, but it does include some realistic detail, such as the 'wind-sock' type of wolf or snake standard (*draco*).[136] Third century 'Lionhunt Sarcophagi' sometimes depict soldiers with ring-buckle belts and the same eagle-head helmets which appear on contemporary gravestones.[137]

The 3rd century funerary figures entered into currency precisely at the time when state monuments become increasingly rare. From the Severan arches until the Tetrarchic edifices there was a great hiatus in imperial figural sculpture projects in the traditional 'Grand Style'.[138] Individual soldiers on the other hand, were patronising sculptors in ways that expressed their culture, wealth, status and unit *élan*. Collective funerary practices combined with the horror of post-mortem oblivion and the struggle against anonymity, not just within the huge population of the city, but also within an increasingly large body of soldiery. The verisimilitude of 3rd century depictions, in contrast to the blandness of earlier gravestones, may also hint at a special assertion of identity by provincial soldiers in the (hostile?) metropolis. All these factors combined to create vivid memorials to the rising military class.[139]

There were presumably many occasions when armour was socially or politically inappropriate. In any case soldiers wore armour for only a small proportion of the time when they were not actively on campaign.[140] However, swords, belts, shields and shafted weapons were often worn and carried in Rome. During the 1st to 2nd centuries praetorian, urban cohort and legionary infantry equipment differed little in form. Scorpion badges were used to distinguish the Guard and perhaps their helmets were more ornate and hellenizing in design than those employed on the frontiers, to judge from The Great Trajanic Frieze and other monuments.[141]

With respect to shafted weapons, heavy javelins (*pila*) were used by *praetoriani*, *urbaniciani*, and presumably by the *peregrini* in the 1st and 2nd centuries (Fig. 5.6).[142] Indeed, the most detailed and credible depiction of a *pilum* from anywhere in the Roman empire is on Cancelleria Relief A (Fig. 5.13).[143] This source also shows a spear with an ornate head, a badge of office borne by *beneficiarii* and other special ranks.[144] During the 3rd century equipment such as belt and sword forms continued in common currency. However, the *pilum*

Fig. 5.22: 'Great Trajanic Frieze', detail of Trajan and soldier holding up the emperor's helmet. Central passage, west section, Arch of Constantine (Photo: author).

only very rarely appears in contemporary provincial iconography, being replaced by spears and lighter javelins, whereas the praetorians continued to use it in increasingly heavy and ornate versions (Fig. 5.17).[145] Exceptionally, a *beneficiarius* of *legio II Parthica* is shown on his gravestone at Apamea (Syria) with a beribboned *pilum* but it seems likely that this served as a badge of office, rather than primarily as a javelin.[146] In Rome *pila* may similarly have become the symbol of praetorian infantry, vestigial like halberds in the pope's Guarda Svizzera, or in the Lord Mayor of London's parade. In the manner of such tasselled Renaissance halberds, sergeants' spontoons and Indian police staves, *pila* held horizontally would have been well suited to crowd control.[147] Spears (*hastae*) are depicted on fleet gravestones, and it may be assumed that these were also used with lighter javelins (*lanceae*) by *Germani corporis custodes* and *equites singulares Augusti* in common with other auxiliary cavalry (Fig. 5.3).[148] The *vigiles* may not have carried shafted weapons.[149]

6. *SENATUS MILESQUE ET POPULUS*:[150] THE SOLDIERY IN IMPERIAL POLITICS

Successful imperial rule was characterised as dependant on the maintenance of the checks and balances between the three elements of the Roman polity: senators, urban plebs and army.[151] Emperors had to observe traditional senatorial sensibilities in their treatment of the élite. Plebeian unrest had to be prevented by safeguarding food supplies to the city and by entertaining the people with public baths and games (Coleman, Dodge, Mattingly and Aldrete, in this volume). The army required regular pay, donatives and rewards, and an emperor who was seen to be safeguarding the soldiers' interests. The 'bad' emperors of the 1st to 2nd centuries fell foul of senatorial opinion, but they were often popular with the army.[152] In the 3rd century rulers came to rely increasingly on military support whilst ignoring other considerations, a course which led directly to a cycle of civil war and usurpation.[153]

In actual fact, the military forces in Rome, belying the proverbial reputation of 'Praetorian Guards' in modern politics, were generally loyal to reigning emperors and established dynasties. The troops had immediate influence in Rome, but they seldom acted without first being motivated by their officers. When their power was exercised they seldom had the political awareness to exploit and sustain it, and the praetorians were unable to maintain a usurper in the face of serious opposition from the frontier armies (e.g. Otho, Didius

Iulianus). A signally successful praetorian proclamation, albeit unplanned and opportunistic, was that of Claudius. He was snatched up and taken to the Castra Praetoria after Gaius' murder. Meanwhile the senate, meeting in the Temple of Jupiter Capitolinus under the protection of the *cohortes urbanae*, vacillated in its discussion of the future.[154] Following this model, when Galba wished to publically declare Piso as his heir, he had three choices of venue: in the Curia to the senate, from the Rostra to the people, or in the Castra to the troops. He chose the latter.[155] Thus the emperors' dealings with their armies, metropolitan and provincial, have been characterised as "holding the wolf by the ears".[156] In other words, a tight grip would ensure safety, but to relax was to be savaged!

In Rome the tight grip took a variety of forms. Praetorian Guard commanders (*praefecti praetorio*) were drawn from the equestrian class, not the politically more dangerous senate. At times a further safeguard was their appointment in pairs.[157] The emperors took great care to present themselves to the troops not just as a caring patron but as a fellow-soldier (*comilito*) sharing their toils, aspirations and interests.[158] The harmonious juxtaposition of emperor and military audience in *adlocutio* scenes made the point graphically.[159] More practically, reliance on just one bodyguard force was best avoided. Formations were established in order to counter-balance each other, and even to operate with a degree of rivalry, so that it was difficult for a military conspiracy to be organised without opposition.[160]

Generally this was a successful strategy. The praetorians were balanced by the *Germani corporis custodes*, barbarians fiercely loyal to their war leader. It was the German guard who were so violently incensed by the murder of Gaius and furiously threatened a massacre of bystanders.[161] However, having dismissed the *corporis custodes*, Galba had no defence against the praetorians when the latter were whipped up by Otho.[162] Other troops were available to support the regime in a crisis, as when the *vigiles* protected the senate and backed Macro's arrest of the praetorian prefect Seianus. They supported Claudius in AD 41 and were involved in the AD 69 fighting.[163]

The *vigiles* occasionally had an active political role, but their creation by Augustus and integration within military structures was actually designed to control the political liability of having organized fire-fighters in the city, in addition to providing efficient fire-fighting. Mobilization of firemen as political muscle and the deleterious ramifications for urban order were fresh in people's minds from the Late Republic.[164] Emperors remained suspicious of local, 'private' fire-brigades, as was demonstrated in a letter from Trajan to Pliny the Younger.[165]

Throughout the Flavian period there was still no Horseguard. Thus, when the praetorians were roused by their prefect Casperius Aelianus, burst into the palace, threatened Nerva, and demanded the surrender of Domitian's assassins, the emperor had no choice but to submit.[166] This indignity could not be allowed to go unpunished. On his accession, Nerva's successor and adoptive son, Trajan, summoned the same prefect and the praetorian ring-leaders to the German frontier. Assuming they were to be rewarded with the usual accession donative, they went willingly, and were executed on arrival.[167] For an emperor like Trajan who would already have been planning to spend much of his time away from the capital, it was a courageous act to potentially alienate the praetorians at the outset. However, Trajan took measures to safeguard his position. It is likely that it was precisely at this time that he created the *equites singulares Augusti*, drawn initially and specifically from Rhenish auxiliaries in the army group that first acclaimed him.[168]

Of course Trajan also set out to woo the praetorians, partly by using them in his wars, binding them to him by leading the armies to victory, and by exerting his propaganda in

Rome to the full. The set of reliefs reused on the Arch of Constantine, collectively making up The Great Trajanic Frieze, may be interpreted in this light. Trajan is depicted engaged in battle at the head of a body of cavalry and backed by infantry in segmental plate armour.[169] The identity of these troops is much discussed, but the infantry standards grouped behind the mounted emperor are indubitably praetorian. Both infantry and cavalry wear helmets decorated with scorpions (Fig. 5.20) and one horseman displays a quadruple scorpion shield-blazon.[170] Thus it would appear that on The Great Trajanic Frieze Trajan is depicted with *pedites* and *equites praetoriani*. Moreover, the horsemen wear very distinctive helmet plumes and crests, and one man is holding up a helmet with this crest-type for the emperor (Fig. 5.22).[171] This gesture is totally unparalleled in imperial art and may be interpreted as a graphic identification of Trajan as a praetorian *comilito*.[172] Indeed, the Frieze may have been specifically aimed at the praetorians in Rome and intended to convey the message that relations between emperor and Guard were harmonious, despite the earlier executions.

In AD 193 the praetorians again burst into the inner palace, but this time they killed the emperor Pertinax. His successor, unlike Trajan, did not employ artistic subtleties. Like Trajan, Septimius Severus duped the praetorians into thinking he was about to make the usual accession inducements, but this time in Rome, not on the frontier. He paraded the Guard on the Campus Praetorianus, surrounded it with his loyal Danubian forces, disarmed the men and cashiered the lot of them.[173] Pertinax had been Severus' friend, and was later honoured with a splendid funeral. A new, expanded Guard was then recruited from the Severan Danubian power-base, thus rewarding with promotion and higher pay soldiers who had first proclaimed Severus in Pannonia, and who eventually fought two rounds of civil war on his behalf. Destitute Italian praetorians plagued the roads of Italy as brigands for years afterwards.[174]

As an additional political control Severus created a new legion of 5000 loyal troops, the *legio II Parthica*, and stationed it in a custom-built legionary fortress located at Albano, only 22.2 km (13.7 mls) from Rome.[175] The chosen site was part of Domitian's Alban Villa complex and thus already imperial property. In the manner of provincial legionary installations, it was furnished with an extramural amphitheatre. It still has the best preserved, unmodified set of fortifications of any legionary fortress in the empire, employing stone block construction (*opus quadratum*) in the local *peperino* tufa, rather than *opus caementicium*.[176] High in the Colli Albani, it would also have been pleasantly cool for Danubians not acclimatised to the Italian summer.[177]

During the third century the Rome formations continued to play a prominent part in war, politics, and in changes of emperor.[178] The last time they did so was when they backed Maxentius in the early 4th century. Just as in the Civil War of 69, they were loyal to a Rome-based contender, and, again, they were on the losing side in 312. However, this time the victor, Constantinus I, went the logical next stage on from Severus and abolished the Guard in Rome altogether.[179] If the *equites singulares Augusti* were still in existence at this time, then they may be the cavalry that are depicted on the Arch of Constantine being hurled into the Tiber to drown with Maxentius.[180] A sort of *damnatio memoriae* was served on the Rome guard formations through their now redundant installations, all of which constituted imperial property. The Castra Praetoria was demolished except for the three walls incorporated in Aurelian's city defences.[181] The Castra Nova Equitum Singularium was made the site of Constantine's new cathedral church, S. Giovanni in Laterano.[182] Even the graves of Maxentius' supporters were defiled by christian buildings with the construction of SS. Marcellino e Pietro and the Mausoleum of Helena (Tor Pignattura) over the *equites singulares* cemetery on the Via Casilina.[183]

Thus ended the history of the imperial guards in Rome who had, with occasional lapses, served and preserved emperors loyally since the time of Augustus.[184] During that epoch the 'armed and belted men' were much more than bodyguards and public executioners. Every aspect of the city's political, economic, social and cultural life was immensely enriched by the presence of a throng of motley soldiers.

ACKNOWLEDGEMENTS

The author is very grateful to a large number of people and organisations for their generous help with research for this chapter. The directors and staffs of the Musei Capitolini, Museo della Civiltà Romana, Museo Nazionale delle Terme and Musei Vaticani extended every facility for study and photography, and kindly provided photographs on request. The British School at Rome financially supported much of the work in Rome. Individuals owed a great debt of gratitude include the following: Colin Adams, Mike Bishop, Amanda Claridge, Lucos Cozza, Charles Daniels†, Hazel Dodge, James Dodge, Bill Griffiths, Lawrence Keppie, Paolo Liverani, Adriano La Regina, Eugenio La Rocca, Maria Pia Malvezzi, Valerie Scott, Michael Speidel, Christopher Smith, Peter Wiseman and Greg Woolf. Mike Bishop, Hazel Dodge and Greg Woolf very kindly read the manuscript and made many helpful suggestions and corrections. Opinions and any errors within the finished chapter are the responsibility of the author alone.

NOTES

1 RICHMOND 1930; PLATNER and ASHBY 1929, 348–55, 402–19; NASH 1961–62, II, 86–316, 198–234; RICHARDSON 1992, 260–63; *Lexicon* III, *s.v.* 'Muri Aureliani', 290–314; '"'Murus Servii Tullii"; Mura Repubblicane', 319–34; V, *s.v.* 'Muri', 277–78. For the use of the 'Servian Wall' as a promenade, particularly the sections facing towards the Castra Praetoria, see WISEMAN 1998.

2 Overviews in DURRY 1938, 9–40; MAXFIELD 1981, 36–8; LIEB 1986; KEPPIE 1984, 186–89; STAMBAUGH 1988, 124–28; RICHARDSON 1992, 76–7; ROBINSON 1992, 181–88; PANCIERA 1993; BOHEC 1994, 20–4, 34; NOY 2000, 19–22. *Legiones* of *c.*4,800–5,300 men (ROTH 1994) were sometimes stationed in a pair in a single fortress, perhaps with the odd auxiliary regiment, but this was the maximum concentration in a permanent installation (e.g. Vetera I, Neuss, Köln, Mainz (Germany), Nicopolis (Egypt): PETRIKOVITS 1975, 153–55; JOHNSON, A. 1983, 31). After the revolt of L. Antonius Saturninus (AD 89), according to Suetonius, *Domitian* 7.3, this practice was discontinued by Domitian for reasons of political security (KEPPIE 1984, 193–96).

3 Juvenal, *Satires* 16.48: *ast illis quos arma tegunt et balteus ambit*. Throughout this chapter the word 'Guard(s)', with a capital, refers to the Praetorian Guard and its members; 'Horseguard(s)', with a capital, is employed for the *Germani corporis custodes* and the *equites singulares Augusti*.

4 Dio 75.2.6.

5 DURRY 1938, 10–1; PASSERINI 1939, 4–40; MILLAR 1977, 61; KEPPIE 1984, 84, 153–54; 1996. The key change was the ability of emperors to have a permanant military escort within the *pomerium* of the city, the way for which had been paved by the use of soldiers in the city from the 50s BC (RÜPKE 1990, 56–7; NIPPEL 1995, 78–84, 90–1; BEARD 1998, 179–80).

6 Tacitus, *Annals* 4.2, 5; *Histories* 2.93; 'Hyginus' 30; Dio 55.24.6. For discussions of the organisation and strength of the Praetorian Guard see DURRY 1938, 77–89; PASSERINI 1939, 46–70, 208; DOMASZEWSKI 1967, 20–6; KENNEDY 1978, 275–88; KEPPIE 1984, 153–54, 187–88; 1996, 109–12; RANKOV 1994, 7–8. Figures employed here for *cohors* strengths have all been rounded, as in the ancient sources and many other modern discussions (thus 500 not 480, 1000 not 960).

7 DURRY 1938, 87; PASSERINI 1939, 57, 59, 171–74; FREIS 1967, 16–7; BIRLEY, 1969, 64–6; SMITH 1972, 487–88, 494–99; KENNEDY 1978, 290–301; CAMPBELL 1984, 10–1; BIRLEY 1988, 103, 196; SPEIDEL 1994b, 57–8; NOY 2000, 20–1.

8 FORNI 1960.

9 'Hyginus' 7–8, 30 (various dates have been suggested for this work, Flavian to Antonine). See Tacitus, *Annals* 1.24, 12.56; *Histories* 2.24–5, 33; Suetonius, *Gaius* 45.1; DURRY 1938, 99–100; PASSERINI 1939, 69–70; DOMASZEWSKI 1967, 23–4; SPEIDEL 1994b, 31–3.

10 Legionary: BREEZE 1969, 53–5; DAVISON 1989, 133–34; PITTS and ST JOSEPH 1985, 169–71; PAVKOVIC 1991, 36–45; ROTH 1994, 353. Auxiliary: DAVIES 1971; HASSALL 1983, 97–8; JOHNSON, A. 1983, 23–5.

11 Dio 55.24.8. See Suetonius, *Gaius* 44.2; *Claudius* 35; *Galba* 18.1; Tacitus, *Histories* 2.11, 33; 'Hyginus' 6; DURRY 1938, 108–10; PASSERINI 1939, 70–3, 76–8; DOMASZEWSKI 1967, 20; CLAUSS 1973, 46–58; LIEB 1986, 336–37; SPEIDEL 1994b, 33–5. For the *beneficiarii* of the Rome formations see OTT 1995, 15–24.

12 BELLEN 1981; KEPPIE 1984, 154; GIULIANO 1984, 112–13; SPEIDEL 1984; 1994b, 15–31; RANKOV 1994, 11–2.

13 Suetonius, *Augustus* 49; BELLEN 1981, 40–1; SPEIDEL 1984, 40–2; 1994b, 18. One major site of the Varian defeat has now been identified archaeologically (SCHLÜTER 1993).

14 Suetonius, *Galba* 12.2; SPEIDEL 1984, 42–3; BELLEN 1981, 96–9. Nero supposedly trusted the *Batavi* because they were politically independent foreigners (Tacitus, *Annals* 15.58).

15 DURRY 1938, 29–34; GROSSO 1966; DOMASZEWSKI 1967, 51–2; SPEIDEL 1965; 1994a; 1994b.

16 SPEIDEL 1994a, No.688; 1994b, 39, 62.

17 SPEIDEL 1965, 14–5; 1994a, 24; 1994b, 57–60 (*contra* KENNEDY 1978, 299).

18 Dio 55.24.6; DURRY 1938, 12–6; DOMASZEWSKI 1967, 18; FREIS 1967, 16–7, 38–42; KENNEDY 1978, 286; BÉRARD 1988.

19 Dio 55.26.4; *Digest* 1.15.3; BAILLIE REYNOLDS 1926, 23–4, 71; DURRY 1938, 16–20; KENNEDY 1978, 299–300; RAINBIRD 1986, 150–51; NIPPEL 1995, 96–7; SABLAYROLLES 1996, 27–55.

20 DURRY 1938, 23–5; STARR 1941, 20, 23. See Josephus, *Jewish Antiquities* 253; Hyginus 30.

21 Martial, *Epigrams* 10.6.7–8; Herodian 1.15.2; Lactantius, *On the Deaths of the Persecutors* 44; *ILS* 1356; KENNEDY 1978, 299–300; SPEIDEL 1975, 226–28; 1994b,, 41, 53, 66, 105; LIEB 1986, 339–40; WELWEI 1992. For archers integral to the *equites singulares* see SPEIDEL 1994a, No.501, 684.

22 BAILLIE REYNOLDS 1923; RICKMAN 1971, 275–77; CLAUSS 1973, 90–1, 114–15; GIULIANO 1984, V.29; NIPPEL 1995, 100–1.

23 The figures in Fig. 5.8 take into account the minimum numbers for *praetoriani* advocated by DURRY 1938, 84–9, and the higher numbers for which a strong case was made by PASSERINI 1939, 58–67; KENNEDY 1978, 275–88. These assume times when the emperor was in residence at Rome with the whole guard (three *cohortes praetoriae* with Augustus, all present from Tiberius onwards). The higher figures have been generally accepted by scholars, but the lower ones are still quoted here for an unbiased picture. A figure of 500 *peregrini* is purely notional. An early 500 for *classiarii* is raised to 1,000 to reflect the increased number of entertainment buildings from the Flavian period onwards (see below, and Coleman in this volume).

24 The calculation of ancient population numbers is notoriously fraught with problems and qualifications. Even for Rome, the ancient city for which there is most evidence, modern figures are only broad approximations. The more recent estimates have decreased overall numbers, *c.*800,000 under Augustus, rising to 1,000,000, and by the Severan period falling back again after 2nd century plagues (Cf. BELOCH 1886, 392–412; OATES 1934; MAIER 1953–54; CARCOPINO 1956, 31; DUDLEY 1967, 158; BRUNT 1971, 376–88; HERMANSEN 1978; HOPKINS 1978, 96–8; FINLEY 1985, 63–4; JONGMANN 1991, 73–5; ROBINSON 1992, 8–9; KARDULIAS 1993; KOLB 1995, 451–53; MORLEY 1996, 2–3, 33–46; LO CASCIO 1997, 24; NOY 2000, 15–29). For military demographics in the city see SCHEIDEL 1996, 111–16, 124–32; NOY 2000, 63–4. Soldiers in barracks, like the civilian occupants of *insulae*, were particularly vulnerable to contagious diseases (GILLIAM 1961, 232–33; see Patterson in this volume).

25 For example in London (Buckingham Palace, 'Trooping of the Colour', Lord Mayor's parade, the Tower etc.), the Vatican City (Guarda Svizzera), Rome (Vittorio Emanuele Monument ceremonies) and København (Royal Guard).

26 Juvenal, *Satires* 10.94–5: *vis certe pila cohortes egregios equites et castra domestica*.

27 Suetonius, *Augustus* 49; Tacitus, *Annals* 4.2; Dio 57.19.6; DURRY 1938, 43–5; PASSERINI 1939, 49; MILLAR 1977, 61; KEPPIE 1996, 114–16.

28 Tacitus, *Annals* 4.2; Suetonius, *Tiberius* 37.1; Juvenal, *Satires* 10.94–5; *Histories* 3.84; DURRY 1938, 45–6; PASSERINI 1939, 49–51. For Seianus see ABSIL 1997, 100, 124–26. Was this really his idea, carried through for the reasons posited in the hostile ancient sources, or a ploy to distance the emperor from a potentially unpopular innovation?

29 RICHMOND 1927; 1930, 14–5, 55, 251; PLATNER and ASHBY 1929, 106–8; DURRY 1938, 45–54, 57–8; LUGLI 1957, 242–62; NASH 1961–62, I, 221–24; CECILIA 1986; RICHARDSON 1992, 78–9; COARELLI 1995, 282–84; KEPPIE 1996, 111–12; *Lexicon* I, *s.v.* 'Castra Praetoria', 251–54; V, *s.v.* 'Vivarium Cohortium Praetoriarum et Urbanarum', 209 (Cf. LANCIANI 1989, Pl.XI). For the most complete plan see CECILIA 1986, Fig.57; COARELLI 1995, 283; *Lexicon* I, Fig.145. *Opus caementicium*: BLAKE 1959, 14–5; WARD-PERKINS 1981, 46–8.

30 RICKMAN 1971, 108, Pl.48, built with wall-facings of *opus reticulatum* with brick bands.

31 Cf. PETRIKOVITS 1975, 116; JOHNSON, A. 1983, 31; PITTS and ST JOSEPH 1985, 57; KEPPIE 1996, 111–12. There was some crowding in the Castra Praetoria in AD 41when *praetoriani*, *classiarii* and gladiators, plus *calones*, servants etc. were all present with Claudius (Josephus, *Jewish Antiquities* 19.253).

32 RICHMOND 1927, 12; BLAKE 1959, 15; KENNEDY 1978, 287; see Patterson in this volume. Cf. Ostia *insulae* and *vigiles* installation (PACKER 1971; MEIGGS 1973, 235–62, 305–8; RAINBIRD 1986, 158–64; RAMIERI 1990, 27–9; SABLAYROLLES 1996, 289–313, Fig.3); Albano legionary barracks (TORTORICI 1975, 94–5, Fig.135; HASSALL 1983, 122, Fig.13).

33 PETRIKOVITS 1975, 36–67, 108–17; JOHNSON, A. 1983, 166–76; HASSALL 1983; PITTS and ST JOSEPH 1985, 159–77; DAVISON 1989, 164–208.

34 PETRIKOVITS 1975, 51–4, Fig.6; PITTS and ST JOSEPH 1985, 179–82.

35 E.g. JOHNSON, S. 1983, Fig.12, 57, 67. From the photograph in RICHMOND 1927, Fig.1 there appear to be no brick bands or details so a Tiberian date is most likely. With brick, as in the *horrea* discussed above, a Flavian to Hadrianic date would be possible (BLAKE 1959, 15; 1973, Pl.19–22, 25, 32, 35–6; ADAM 1994, Fig.313, 426; MACDONALD and PINTO 1995, 57–8). Thus, the Castra Praetoria plan recovered through piecemeal excavation is most likely a palimpsest of periods.

36 Tacitus, *Annals* 12.36 (*stetere in armis praetoriae cohortes campo, qui castra praeiacet*); Pliny, *Natural History* 3.67; Juvenal *Satires* 16.25–6; PLATNER and ASHBY 1929, 90; DURRY 1938, 54–6; *Lexicon* I, 254; V, Fig.89. For extramural military 'parade grounds' see JOHNSON, A. 1983, 215–19; BIDWELL and SPEAK 1994, 14, Fig.2.3. This open area was used to great advantage by the praetorians during running battles with civilian mobs in AD 238 (Herodian 7.11.9). The Castra Praetoria was supplied with water by pipes (*fistulae*) crossing the Campus Praetorianus from the Aqua Marcia-Tepula-Iulia (see Dodge in this volume). It was these pipes which were cut in AD 238 to reduce resistance through thirst, and the soldiers were particularly vulnerable to this measure because of their concentrated numbers and position on the waterless Esquiline plateau (Herodian 7.12.3–4; SHA, *Maximus and Balbinus* 10.6). For water supply to the city's *castra* in general see Frontinus, *On Aqueducts* 79–86; BRUUN 1987; EVANS 1997, 126.

37 Suetonius, *Galba* 12.2; BELLEN 1981, 56–7, 94; RANKOV 1994, 12; SPEIDEL 1994, 17–8, 29; *Lexicon* III, *s.v.* 'Horti: P. Cornelius Dolabella', 58.

38 PLATNER and ASHBY 1929, 105; COLINI 1944, 314–17; LUGLI 1957, 50–65; NASH 1961–62, I, 214–18; RICHARDSON 1992, 77; SPEIDEL 1994a, 28–9, 413; 1994b, 126–29, Pl.13; CONSALVI 1997; LIVERANI 1998, 6–16; *Lexicon* I, *s.v.* 'Castra Equitum Singularium, Singulariorum', 246–48; IV, *s.v.* 'Schola Collegii Curatorum Equitum Singularium', 246–47; V, *s.v.* 'Castra Nova Equitum Singularium', 235. It is unclear if the trapezoidal, courtyard building aligned along the Via Tusculana, excavated in 1876 behind the apse of S. Giovanni, was within the Castra Nova. It may have been excluded by one of the walls found to the east, under the apse, and running parallel with the military buildings. Unfortunately very little is known about the nature of the enclosures of either Castra Equitum Singularium.

39 JOHNSON, A. 1983, 176–82, Fig.134; HORN 1987, Fig.335, 337; CONNOLLY 1988, 16–7; DAVISON 1989, 148–68; SOMMER 1999, 175, Fig.6.6; BIDWELL 1999, 86–8, Fig.15.

40 PLATNER and ASHBY 1929, 90, 94; SPEIDEL 1994b, 114, 128; CONSALVI 1997, 117–18; *Lexicon* I, *s.v.* 'Campus Caelemontanus', 218. Equus Marci: NASH 1961–62, I, 391–92, Fig.478 (du Pérac); MELUCCI VACCARO and MURA SOMMELLA 1989, Fig.97. Reasonably enough, a civilian who allowed himself to be hit with a javelin whilst crossing a *campus* had no redress in law (*Code of Justinian* 4.3.4; SPEIDEL 1994b, 114). Despite its name, the 'Amphitheatrum Castrense' was not associated with either Castra Equitum Singularium (PLATNER and ASHBY 1929, 5–6; DURRY 1938, 57–9; NASH 1961–62, I, 13–6; GOLVIN 1988, No.189; *Lexicon* I, *s.v.* 'Amphitheatrum Castrense', 35–6; Coleman in this volume). Its title actually associated it with the nearby imperial villa complex (*Lexicon* IV, *s.v.* 'Sessorium', 304–8, Fig.158). There were small, 'private' amphitheatres in imperial complexes, notably in the Palatine 'hippodrome' garden, in Hadrian's Villa at Tivoli (MACDONALD 1982, Pl.41, 72; FRANCESCHINI 1991, Plan 15) and at the Villa of the Quintilii on the Via Appia. Whilst military bases did have extramural amphitheatres, the latter were positioned just outside the defences (TORTORICI 1975, 112–16; GOLVIN 1988, 154–56, No.17–8, 28, 37, 48, 60, 107, 111, 122, 124, 129, 190; ROUX 1990, 203–6; COULSTON forthcoming b). The Amphitheatrum Castrense is more than 600m. away from the nearest cavalry installation.

41 See *Lexicon* I, Fig.115–16, 140. A Severan parallel for two *castra* close together is provided by Ain Sinu in Iraq. Here too there were barracks with back-to-back, non-connecting paired rooms (OATES 1959; HASSALL 1983, 121, Fig.12). The larger enclosure was occupied solely by barracks, the administrative buildings being retained in the smaller *castra*. Perhaps the main *principia* for the *equites singulares Augusti* remained in the Castra Priora.

42 Ramps might have been included in building design, as with (stepped) examples in *horrea* at Rome, Ostia and Portus, but upper storey stabling would have required planning on a much larger scale to avoid hairpins awkward for turning horses (RICKMAN 1971, 22, 82, 86, Pl.3). A modern solution to this problem may be seen in the Knightbridge Barracks in London. The 1966 Basil Spence design incorporates accommodation for 514 soldiers and 273 horses of the Household Cavalry with stabling and walking space on the upper floor overlooking the city with a southern aspect (WEINREB and HIBBERT 1983, *s.v.* 'Knightsbridge Barracks', 440; *pers. obs.*).

43 PLATNER and ASHBY 1929, 108; FREIS 1967, 16–8; RICHARDSON 1992, 79; *Lexicon* I, *s.v.* 'Castra Urbana', 255.

44 The Caelian *castra* buildings were excavated along Piazza della Navicella but little was learnt beyond their alignment. There was a fountain decorated with the boat (*navicella*) sculpture. The Trastevere *excubitorium* has only been partially explored, revealing a courtyard with fountain, *aedicula* and graffitied plaster which identified the building. See BAILLIE REYNOLDS 1926, 23–4, 43–63; PLATNER and ASHBY 1929, 128–30; NASH 1961–62, I, 264–67; RAINBIRD 1986; RAMIERI 1990, 18–26; RICHARDSON 1992, 92–3; COARELLI 1995, 410–12; SABLAYROLLES 1996, 245–89, Fig.1; *Lexicon* I, *s.v.* 'Cohortium Vigilum Stationes', 292–94. Cf. Ostia MEIGGS 1973, 305–8; RAINBIRD 1986, 158–64, Fig.3–4; RAMIERI 1990, 27–9; SABLAYROLLES 1996, 289–313, Fig.3. There are difficulties with the strightforward attribution of two *regiones* per *cohors* because of *cohors VII* in Transtiberim (NORDH 1949, 75.6, 80.3, 81.16, 82.1, 15, 84.16, 93.3, 96.2, 4; RAINBIRD 1986, 153–54; SABLAYROLLES 1996, 278–89, Fig.1).

45 Josephus, *Jewish Antiquities* 19.253.

46 CARETTONI 1960, Pl.XVII.6a (*Forma Urbis*); PLATNER and ASHBY 1929, 105, 108, 603; STARR 1941, 20, 23; KIENAST 1966, 74–5; REDDÉ 1986, 452–53; RICHARDSON 1992, 77–9; COARELLI 1995, 194, 393; *Lexicon* I, *s.v.* 'Castra Misenatium', 248–9; 'Castra Ravennatium', 254–55; V, *s.v.* 'Castra Ravennatium', 235.

47 BAILLIE REYNOLDS and ASHBY 1923; PLATNER and ASHBY 1929, 105–6; DURRY 1938, 25–9; COLINI 1944, 237–53; LUGLI 1955, 92–4; NASH 1961–62, I, 219–10; CLAUSS 1973, 84–5; LISSI CARONNA 1986; RICHARDSON 1992, 78; *Lexicon* I, *s.v.* 'Castra Peregrina', 249–51.

48 Tacitus, *Histories* 1.38.

49 *CIL* 6.2725 = *ILS* 2034; AMELUNG 1903, No.128, Pl.26; DURRY 1938, 243; MARSDEN 1969, 185, Pl.1; KENNEDY 1978, 289–90; BISHOP and COULSTON 1993, Fig.45.1; BAATZ 1994, 130. This is distinct from the *armamentaria* for gladiatorial equipment shown on the *Forma Urbis*, listed in the *Regionary Catalogues*, and broken into by rioting civilians to collect arms with which to attack the Castra Praetoria in AD 238 (CARETTONI 1960, Pl.XVII.6a; NORDH 1949, 75.15; Herodian, 7.11.7).

50 BELLEN 1981, 56–7, 94.

51 *Lexicon* V, Fig.89. The Castra lay approximately 430 m beyond the 'Servian Wall' and was aligned approximately parallel with the Republican *agger* between the Porta Collina and the Porta Viminalis.

52 *Lexicon* I, Fig.115–16. Trajan ordering the praetorian prefect Suburanus to turn his sword on the emperor if the latter ruled despotically (Pliny, *Panegyric* 67.8; Dio 68.16.1; Aurelius Victor, *On the Caesars* 13.8–9) was surely not merely a private interview, but a set-piece designed for public consumption. The action was charged with political meanings in the light of Domitian's favour to, and popularity with the armies, both exciting élite disapprobation. The choice of Suburanus (ABSIL 1997, No.29) may also have played well with the Guard because of Trajan's initial problems following on from turmoil under Nerva (see section 6 in this chapter).

53 *Lexicon* IV, *s.v.* 'Sessorium', 304–8.

54 *Lexicon* I, Fig.116; DURRY 1938, 58; COARELLI 1987, 432; 1995, 246. Walled military installations within an urban context have parallels elsewhere in the empire. The Cripplegate Fort at London combined elements of Rome's Castra Praetoria and Peregrinorum, whilst, like the Castra Praetoria, it was incorporated in secondary urban defences (MILNE 1995, 58–9, 77–8, Fig.1, 33). For other military-urban parallels see COLLINGWOOD BRUCE and DANIELS 1978, 95 (Corbridge, England); PERKINS 1973, 25–8, Fig.6 (Dura-Europos, Syria); DE VRIES 1986, 231–2 (Umm el-Jimal, Jordan). Some similar arrangements must have been made to accommodate military formations in Pozzuoli, Lyon and Carthage (PASSERINI 1939, 208; FREIS 1967, 28–36; MEIGGS 1973, 75, 81, 305–8; LIEB 1986, 333–34; BÉRARD 1988, 173–79; SABLAYROLLES 1996, 45–6; NIPPEL 1995, 103–4). The *vigiles* base at Ostia was not separately walled as such, but, unlike civilian *insulae* in the town it had blind walls with slit windows, not outwardly-facing shops (MEIGGS 1973, 235–62, 305–8; RAINBIRD 1986, 158–64; RAMIERI 1990, 27–9; SABLAYROLLES 1996, 289–313, Fig.3).

55 Praetorian cemeteries: DURRY 1938, 60–3; GIULIANO 1984, No.I.6–7, IV.29a–d, V.28a–w; BRUTO 1987–88; LANCIANI 1988, 175. Cavalry cemeteries: BELLEN 1981, 62–3; GIULIANO 1984, 111–13, No.IV.29; *BullCom* 90, 1985, 413–20; SPEIDEL 1994a, 2–3; 1994b, 25, 114, 157, Fig.8; RASCH 1998, 5–6; *Lexicon* I, 247. Fleet *columbaria*: PLATNER and ASHBY 1929, 603; STARR 1941, 20, 23; BOLLINI 1968, 134.

56 A pejorative phrase put into the mouth of Cassius Chaerea by Josephus, *Jewish Antiquities* 19.42.

57 MILLAR. 1977, 61. Some distinction has been drawn in the modern literature between praetorians as military escort and Horseguards as bodyguards proper. This is an unnecessary dichotomy which has led to distortion (e.g. FRANK 1969, 24–30). Detachments of praetorians and Horseguards with other members of the imperial family: Tacitus, *Annals* 1.24 (Drusus), 15.58; Suetonius, *Nero* 34.1 (Agrippina).

58 TAMM 1968; MILLAR 1977, 19–24; MACDONALD 1982, 47–74; DARWELL-SMITH 1996, 179–215; ROYO 1999, 209–368; *Lexicon* II, *s.v.* 'Domus Augustana, Augustiana', 40–45; 'Domus Augustus (Palatium), 46–8; IV, *s.v.* 'Palatium', 22–38.

59 Suetonius, *Gaius* 58; Dio 59.29.6–7; Josephus, *Jewish Antiquities* 19.75–113; BARRETT 1989, 163–66; LEVICK 1990, 29–31; WISEMAN 1987; 1991, esp. 105–10; ROYO 1999, 275–88.

60 Togate *cohors*: Tacitus, *Annals* 12.69, 16.27; *Histories*, 1.38. See also *Annals* 1.13.6, 12.69.1; *Histories* 1.24; Suetonius, *Otho* 4.2. Passwords: Josephus, *Jewish Antiquities* 19.29, 31, 53, 85, 105; Suetonius, *Gaius* 56.2 ('Venus', 'Priapus'); *Claudius* 42.1; Dio 60.16.7; SHA, *Marcus* 7.3; *Severus* 23.4. Meals: Suetonius, *Claudius* 35.1; *Otho* 4.2; Tacitus, *Histories* 1.25, 38; Dio 60.3.3. Relaxed, reclining, perhaps inebriated, the emperor was particularly vulnerable whilst dining, whether at a formal banquet or an intimate supper (not to mention the danger of poisoning!).

61 BELLWALD 1985, Fig.83, 104, 133, 135; DARWELL-SMITH 1996, 184–85, 211, Pl.XL–III; *Lexicon* II, Fig.35–6, 60. Was there stable accommodation for guard cavalry horses on the Palatine and at other residences, or did the troopers march over from their *castra* on foot? Public access for business, amenities and festivals (dependant on calendar and time of day) caused particular security problems on the Julio-Claudian Palatine. For Nero's Domus Aurea there is the question of public access to the gardens, overall security, supervision of the formal Via Sacra entrance, and coverage for the scattered Palatine and Esquiline residences (MACDONALD 1982, 20–41; *Lexicon* II, *s.v.* 'Domus Aurea', 49–64).

62 Suetonius, *Tiberius* 60. Gardens: MILLAR 1977, 22–3; BIANCHI 1993; *Lexicon* III, *s.v.* 'Horti', 51–88; V, *s.v.* 'Horti', 263–68.

63 DURRY 1938, 59; FRANCESCHINI 1991, 635, Map 101; MACDONALD and PINTO 1995, 184.

64 Pliny, *Panegyric* 76.8. For *lictores* see Millar 1977, 67–8; SCHÄFER 1989, PL.68–74, 104–8, 112–16; NIPPEL 1995, 12–5.

65 Tacitus, *Annals* 16.27. Herodian 1.10.5–7 reports a conspiracy to kill Commodus planned by one Maternus, to be carried out by him and his fellow army deserters. They were to dress as praetorians and infiltrate the escort troops at the Megalensia. Some years ago the author with camera inadvertantly penetrated the security cordon for Italian Presidente Scalfaro at the Vittoriano by coincidentally being dressed identically to the technicians working on media installations. The resultant close-up photographs of escort troops were good and the secret service personnel moderately gentle. Even when ancient guards wore togas there would have been no doubt as to who they were, just as smart civilian suits have become a 'uniform' for American security men, and indeed have entered the public perception, notably in film (e.g. *The Bodyguard* (USA 1992), *In The Line of Fire* (USA 1993), *Guarding Tess* (USA 1994), *The Jackal* (USA 1997)).

66 One Quintianus hid in an entrance to the Flavian Amphitheatre and wasted time prosing and flourishing his weapon instead of directly stabbing Commodus, thus was overpowered by bodyguards (Herodian, 1.8.6. Cf. SHA, *Hadrian* 12.5). This is of course a familiar problem in the modern world. Recall the deaths of Henri IV, Abraham Lincoln and Archduke Franz-Ferdinand, the woundings of Ronald Reagan and John Paul II, multiple attempts on Queen Victoria, and a number of threats involving Queen Elizabeth II. John F. Kennedy was fatalistic on the subject: "If the assasin is willing to die it couldn't be simpler" (VIDAL 1995, 364). The problem is made far more difficult than in the ancient period because the assassin has the longer range and potentially greater effectiveness of firearms. Secret service bodyguards are colloquially known as 'the bullet-catchers', and there is emphasis on their shielding the 'subject' with their own bodies in the immediate crisis, then hurrying him/her away from the scene to avoid further danger.

67 Tacitus, *Annals* 1.13 (Tiberius); Philostratos, *Lives of the Sophists* 2.26 (Heraklides); Dio 57.11.7; 68.7.3, 15.5; Tacitus, *Annals* 15.52.1; MILLAR 1977, 92, 113; NIPPEL 1995, 93 (trust).

68 In entertainment buildings: Josephus, *Jewish Antiquities* 19.26; Tacitus, *Annals* 13.24–5, 14.15, 15.33; Suetonius, *Tiberius* 37.2; *Vitellius* 14.3; *Domitian* 10.1; SHA, *Commodus* 15.6; Herodian 4.6.4–5. Quelling disorder: Tacitus, *Annals* 12.43, 13.48, 14.45, 61, 15.46. Missions and errands: Josephus, *Jewish Antiquities* 19.28–9, 34, 125, 257, 270; Suetonius, *Tiberius* 53.2; Tacitus, *Annals* 1.53, 3.2, 11.1, 14.64, 15.55, 60–4, 69, 16.9, 15; Juvenal, *Satires* 10.15–8. See also Tacitus, *Annals* 4.41; Epictetus, *Discourses* 4.13.5; SHA, *Caracalla* 4.1.6. On duties in general see DURRY 1938, 274–80; PASSERINI 1939, 211–12; SPEIDEL 1965, 87–92; 1994b, 129–32; MILLAR 1977, 61–4; CAMPBELL 1984, 111–13; PANCIERA 1993, 275; NIPPEL 1995, 91–4. Domitianic development of the area south-east of the Flavian Amphitheatre had security implications with up to 1,000 gladiators housed in the new *ludi* (ROUX 1990, 210; Coleman in this volume. Cf. Josephus, *Jewish Antiquities* 19.253; Tacitus, *Annals* 15.46). Criminals and prisoners of war required escort to the arena. There was a centralised *armamentarium* by the Castra Misenatium according to the *Forma Urbis* (CARETTONI 1960, Pl.XVII.6a; *Lexicon* I, *s.v.* 'Armamentaria', 126, Fig.69), presumably for storing gladiatorial equipment, which would have needed guards (Cf. Plutarch, *Crassus* 8.2).

69 SHA, *Hadrian* 7.6; KOEPPEL 1985, No.8; 1986, No.1; KLEINER 1992, Fig.217–18.

70 NASH 1961–62, I, Fig.321, 323; VOGEL 1973, Pl.9, 15; ANDREAE 1977, Pl.489; KOEPPEL 1989, No.14; KLEINER 1992, Fig.254 (soldiers identifiable by their armour and standards). Cf. Suetonius, *Domitian* 4.1; Dio 67.8; Dio 75.4.6. For *ludi scaenici* involving *vigiles* see *CIL* 6.1063–64.

71 The triumph was the only time a general could legally enter the city with his troops during the Republican period. After 19 BC only emperors and their immediate family were allowed to be *triumphatores*. The triumph's route became formalised as a ritual corridor attracting appropriate triumphal buildings and taking advantage of congregational structures (Cf. the route between Buckingham Palace and Horseguards Parade in London). However, its exact course is problematic in places: starting perhaps near the victory temples of the Largo Argentina, moving south into the Circus Flaminius and past ranked temples, through(?) the Theatre of

Marcellus, past the ranked temples of the Forum Holitorium and through the Forum Boarium, along the length of the Circus Maximus and under the Arch of Vespasian and Titus, up the road between the Palatine and Caelian hills, under the Arches of Constantine and Titus, down the Via Sacra and presumably under the Fornix Fabianus and the Arch of Augustus, then through the Forum Romanum past the basilical viewing galleries and under the Arch of Septimius Severus. Bleachers, crowds and perhaps soldiers lined the route. See VERSNEL 1970; MAXFIELD 1981, 101–9; TALBERT 1984, 362–64; KÜNZL 1988, 14–44, 141–50; CAMPBELL 1984, 133–42; FAVRO 1994; 1996, 82–8, 236–43.

72 Gaius: Suetonius, *Gaius* 19.1; Dio 59.17.1; Josephus, *Jewish Antiquities* 19.5. Claudius: Tacitus, *Annals* 12.56 (*catapultae ballistaeque*). See also Suetonius, *Nero* 19. For specialists such as *architecti*, *mensores*, *campidoctores* etc. see DURRY 1938, 114–17; PASSERINI 1939, 74; DOMASZEWSKI 1967, 25–6; SPEIDEL 1968, 55–60; 1994b, 109–16; BAATZ 1994, 130.

73 DURRY 1938, 249–56; PASSERINI 1939, 173–84, 189; SPEIDEL 1965, 55–60; 1994b, 123–24, 148–51; DOBSON and BREEZE 1969; KENNEDY 1978, 288–96. The 'élite' nature of Rome's troops can certainly be exaggerated in terms of functional military quality (as opposed to cultural and social cachet), not least because patronage more than merit most likely played a major part in transfers (OTT 1995, 55–9).

74 PASSERINI 1939, 125, 191–96; KENNEDY 1978, 282–83; MAXFIELD 1981, 121, 132, 136, 219; STROBEL 1984, 103–4; RICCI 1994; RANKOV 1994, 11–8; SPEIDEL 1994b, 116–25. Indeed, escort of the emperor in battle was the traditional function of the *cohortes praetoriae* (KEPPIE 1996, 119–20).

75 Suetonius, *Augustus* 43 (see also 32 for the countryside); FREIS 1967, 44–6; NIPPEL 1995, 92–4. 'Policing' may normally be understood on the macro level of major public events and disorders, rather than at the level of local crime and investigation. For the latter the city policed itself as in earlier periods (NIPPEL 1995, 16–26, 30–46, 95–7. See also 113–19).

76 BÉRARD 1988.

77 Functions, tools and artillery: Petronius, *Satyricon* 78; BAILLIE REYNOLDS 1926, 97–8; DOMASZEWSKI 1967, 10; MARSDEN 1969, 193–94; ROBINSON 1977; RAINBIRD 1986, 151–53; RAMIERI 1990, 14–7; SABLAYROLLES 1995, 133; 1996, 354–69. For swords see *CIL* 6.2987; AMELUNG 1903, No.128d, Pl.29; BAILLIE REYNOLDS 1926, 98, Pl.VI; SPEIDEL 1993, Fig.6.

78 Fires: RAMAGE 1983, 74–9, Map 3; SABLAYROLLES 1996, 409–30, 771–802. For prisons administered by the *vigiles* see SABLAYROLLES 1995, 130–31. Crime and policing: ECHOLS 1967–68; RAMAGE 1983, 68; ROBINSON 1992, 191–95; NIPPEL 1995, 95–7. There is some discussion, however, about the relative importance of the fire-fighting and policing roles. With good reason some scholars are less than convinced about the latter (RAINBIRD, 1986, 145; NIPPEL 1995, 96–7, 121).

79 Ulpian, *Digest* 37.13.1: *item vigiles milites sunt et iure militari eos testari posse nulla dubitatio est*. See BAILLIE REYNOLDS 1926, 74–88; DOMASZEWSKI 1967, 9–14; SABLAYROLLES 1995; 1996, 623–72; SPEIDEL 1995. Presumably *vigiles* wore helmets based on military designs, as did Early Modern Japanese fire-fighters and as do modern fire-brigades. It is not known whether they wore cuirasses and carried shields.

80 SHA, *Commodus* 15.6; Lucretius 4.74–84; DURRY 1938, 23–5; STARR 1941, 20–21; KIENAST 1966, 75; GRAEFE 1979, 55–61; REDDÉ 1986, 451; Coleman in this volume.

81 STARR 1941, 23–4; PLATNER and ASHBY 1929, 357–58; REDDÉ 1986, 451–51; *Lexicon* III, *s.v.* 'Naumachia', 337–339; Coleman in this volume. See Suetonius, *Vespasian* 8.3 for *classiarii* at Ostia and Pozzuoli.

82 Dionysius of Halicarnassus 3.44.3; Virgil, *Aeneid* 8.81–93; Suetonius, *Gaius* 15.1; STARR 1941, 17–8, 20–1; CASSON 1965, 32; MEIGGS 1973, 291; REDDÉ 1986, 445–51. For the military port of Rome (*navalia*) see PLATNER and ASHBY 1929, 358–60; NASH 1961–62, II, 117–19; *Lexicon* III, *s.v.* 'Navalia', 339–40.

83 In the field: 'Hyginus' 24, 30; STARR 1941, 180–85; KIENAST 1966, 62–70; REDDÉ 1995, 151, 154. Umbria: *ILS* 509. Engineering and building: *RIB* 1340 (Benwell granary construction, Hadrian's Wall); CLEERE 1974 (ironworking, southeast England); STARR 1941, 149 (Brohl quarries, Germany); *ILS* 5795 (Lambaesis, Algeria, aqueduct building).

84 Little is known about necessary central planning for the frontier armies (AUSTIN and RANKOV 1995, 109–41) but there is some direct evidence for government overview of legionary dispositions (Tacitus, *Annals* 4.5; Dio 55.23.2–7). Lists of legionary titles were found in Rome inscribed on two column shafts (*CIL* 6.3492 = *ILS* 2288 = CAMPBELL 1994, No.144). Their purpose is unknown, but the arrangement, in clockwise geographical order from Britain round to Spain, probably reflects official records. According to their own formulae, copies of bronze discharge diplomas issued to soldiers (see below) were displayed in Rome either on the Capitol (*in Capitolio*) or on a wall behind the Temple of Augustus by a statue of Minerva (*in muro post templum divi Augusti ad Minervam*). See MAXFIELD 1981, 227; LIEB 1996, 329–30; *Lexicon* I, *s.v.* 'Augustus, Divus, Templum (Novum); Aedes', 145–46. This was a major exercise in record-keeping and the transmission of information between provinces and capital. For *diplomata* found in Rome see ROXAN 1981, Table 1, No.25, 140; 3a, No.118.

85 Tacitus, *Histories* 2.88: *ad iurgium, mox ad manus et ferrum transirent*.

86 Suetonius, *Augustus* 44.

87 DURRY 1938, 366–83; PASSERINI 1939, 100–23; FREIS 1967, 48–9; WATSON 1971; CAMPBELL 1984, 161–76; SPEIDEL 1992, 1995. *Praetoriani*, *urbaniciani*, *statores*, *classiarii*, *equites singulares Augusti* and

provincial *auxiliarii*, but not *legionarii* or *vigiles*, received bronze discharge diplomas (DURRY 1938, 291–301, Pl.XI–II; PASSERINI 1939, 130–41; FORNI 1960; MAXFIELD 1981, 227; ROXAN 1981; CAMPBELL 1984, 439–45; LIEB 1986; SPEIDEL 1994a, No.76–9). See ROXAN 1981, 273 for the importance of *diplomata* for 'provincial' praetorians. To some extent this higher income may have served as 'weighting' to compensate for high prices in the capital. Pay and privileges of Rome troops caused resentment in the legions whose men felt the praetorians to have a comparatively easy life (Suetonius, *Augustus* 101.3; *Tiberius* 25; Tacitus, *Annals* 1.17; *Histories* 2.93–4. See DURRY 1938, 362–63; KEPPIE 1996, 95). This is a feature of army life in many periods whereby combat soldiers direct hostility at rear echelon troops ('REMFs': HOLMES 1994, 77–9). The temptation to calculate the 'cost' of the Rome formations to the emperor's purse per annum is resisted here for two reasons. One is that to arrive at a meaningful figure separate calculations for all the pay grades would have to be made based on a variety of assumptions concerning pay structures and numbers of troops. The second is that in practical terms the emperor never parted with the annual pay in anything like full. Most of the money due was probably only ever transferred on paper.

88 For camp suppliers see *CIL* 6.9277, 9661, 9992 (LUGLI 1957, 251). For expenditure by soldiers on monuments see *CIL* 6.207, 212–14, 30881 (LUGLI 1957, 253–54). The numbers and economic importance of troops in Rome may be compared with the large section of the city population involved in the building industry (DELAINE 1997, 201; DeLaine in this volume). Troops were apparently supplied with grain from the state *horrea* (RICKMAN 1971, 277–78. See Suetonius, *Galba* 20).

89 PETRIKOVITS 1975, 168; CAMPBELL 1978; 1984, 301–3, 439–45; SALLER and SHAW 1984; WIERSCHOWSKI 1984, 65–71; SPEIDEL 1985; 1989; PANCIERA 1993, 263–64, 267–73, 275; ROTH 1994, 354–58; GILLIVER 1999, 29–31; NOY 2000, 70–4.

90 A phenomenon of 'garrison towns' the world over, e.g. 'navy' pubs in Portsmouth and 'para' pubs in Colchester, England. Bars clustered in Roman towns to the best economic advantage, for example around the theatres at Pompeii. Temporary food and drink stalls were set up for festivals and other public events, as shown on the Pompeii amphitheatre riot fresco (GREAFE 1979, Pl.113; LAURENCE 1994, 81–4).

91 See *Lexicon* I, Fig.116; V, Fig.89. The Baths of Caracalla were not much further away from the Castra Nova Equitum Singularium than the Baths of Trajan were from the Castra Priora. Did the intention to serve military clienteles partly influence the provision and location of new *thermae* built by emperors who particularly favoured the soldiery (Trajan, Caracalla, Diocletian)? Some of the sculptural decoration of the Baths of Caracalla might be taken to suggest a military interest (DELAINE 1997, Fig.50).

92 DURRY 1938, 307–48; STARR 1941, 35–6, 86–8; LUGLI 1957, 51–60, 64–5, 69–77; BOLLINI 1963, 128; SPEIDEL 1965, 68–78; 1978; 1994a, 28–93; 1994b, 139–44; LISSI CARONNA 1986; COARELLI 1995, 227; SABLAYROLLES 1996, 385–91; NOY 2000, 184; *Lexicon* I, *s.v.* 'Castra Peregrina: Mithraeum, 251; IV, *s.v.* 'Schola Collegii Curatorum Equitum Singularium', 246–47.

93 As when the *praefectus praetorio* Cleander (ABSIL 1997, 226–31) unleashed cavalry against crowds on the Via Appia (Herodian 1.12.6–9. Cf. Dio 73.13.4–5). An alternative view, suggested to the author by Greg Woolf, is that the emperors and their soldiers were actually very lenient with the *plebs urbana*, and that it is very surprising that more atrocities were not visited by soldiers on civilians in the city.

94 SHA, *Elagabalus* 16.2–3. See also Josephus, *Jewish Antiquities* 263–64; Tacitus, *Annals* 16.27; SHA, *Caracalla* 2.9, 4.6; Dio 78.17.4.

95 SPEIDEL 1993. See also AMELUNG 1903, No.163, Pl.30; BANDINELLI 1971, Fig.65; KLEINER 1987, No.120, 125; BISHOP and COULSTON 1993, Fig.101.2. Use by *beneficiarii* in the provinces: SPEIDEL 1993, 144–49.

96 Suetonius, *Gaius* 26.4. Cf. Dio 59.28.11. See Josephus, *Jewish Antiquities* 19.24–6.

97 CAMPBELL 1984, 246–54; ISAAC 1992, 282–304. Rome: Appian, *Civil Wars* 5.18.72–3, 34,.138; Dio 62.17.1; Tacitus, *Annals* 15.38.7; Josephus, *Jewish Antiquities* 19.160, 266. See Petronius, *Satyricon* 62 for an extreme case of military beastliness – a werewolf soldier!

98 Juvenal, *Satires* 16.25: *offendere tot caligas, tot milia clavorum* (Cf. 3.248). Soldiers alienated both city-dwellers (*togati*, 16.8) and country people (*pagani*, 16.33) by their behaviour. For commentary see DURRY 1935; COURTNEY 1980, 613–22.

99 Epictetus, *Discourses* 4.1.79. See 3.24.117; MILLAR 1965, 143.

100 Tacitus, *Histories* 71–2; DARWELL-SMITH 1996, 41–3.

101 Herodian 1.17.2; 2.4.1–4; Dio 74.8.1.

102 SHA, *Pertinax* 10.8–11.13; Dio 74.9.2; Herodian 2.5; BIRLEY 1988, 94–5.

103 Dio 75.2.6. Cf. Tacitus, *Histories* 2.88 for a similar description of Vitellius' Rhenish troops.

104 Herodian, 7.11–2; SHA, *Maximus and Balbinus* 10.4–8. Cf. Dio 73.13; 74.16.2; Herodian 1.12.5–9; Zosimus, *New History* 2.13. When Romans rioted, as at Pompeii in AD 59, this was a deadly business because of what would now be termed their 'sword culture' (Tacitus, *Annals* 14.17; MOELLER 1970; NIPPEL 89–90; Coulston forthcoming b). Soldiers' 'provincial' culture: PASSERINI 1939, 189–90. Provincial Latin could be a social disadvantage, as with the North African accent (BIRLEY 1988, 19–20, 35; NOY 2000, 157).

105 See the civilian being lashed by a soldier on a mosaic from Piazza Armerina, Sicily (CARANDINI 1982, Fig.12). Even in modern, 'peaceful' societies soldiers can excite civilian anger by their actions, for example the periodic rape cases brought against Légion Étrangère soldiers on Corsica and British soldiers on Cyprus.

106 Belts: Pliny, *Natural History* 33.152; Suetonius, *Augustus* 24.2; Juvenal, *Satires* 16.48; Petronius, *Satyricon* 83; Tacitus, *Histories* 1.57, 2.88; Herodian 2.13.10. Military identity: BISHOP & COULSTON 1993, 196; COULSTON 1998, 183–84. Cf. HOLMES 1994, 35. Bearing arms: NIPPEL 1995, 38–9, 51, 55, 58. In the provinces the situation was more complicated (BRUNT 1975).

107 A gravestone at Strasbourg depicts a soldier from the hips upwards standing in a niche. His 'apron' hangs out of the recess and down over the inscribed panel below. The sculptor's clear intention was to emphasise the belt-fittings (ESPÉRANDIEU 1907–81, No.5495). Similarly, weapons and belts shown on funerary altars at Pula (Croatia) proclaim military identity (STARAC 1995, Pl.4.2, 6.1–2. See also FRANZONI 1987, No.1–3, 6–7, 27, 56, Pl.XXI.2). Belt and apron development: BISHOP 1992; BISHOP & COULSTON 1993, 61–2, 96–99, 152–53, 173–79.

108 For hobnails see Juvenal, *Satires* 3.248, 16.25. Of course soldiers wearing hobnailed boots would have had some difficulty of footing on the *selce* block-paved roads of the capital and other Italian towns (ADAM 1994, 230–31, 277–81). During fighting around the Temple of Herod in Jerusalem (AD 70) the centurion Iulianus was killed after his hob-nailed boots skated out from under him on the precinct paving (Josephus, *Jewish War* 6.85). Vitellius' troops in Rome, unused to urban life and crowds, became fractious when they fell over in the slippery streets (*lubrico viae*: Tacitus, *Histories* 2.88). For *caligae* see MAGI 1945, Fig.23–5; BISHOP and COULSTON 1993, 100, Fig.61. Usually cavalrymen wore the square or rectangular cloak (*sagum*), but see SPEIDEL 1994a, No.90, 114, 509.

109 Well reproduced by BREGLIA 1968, No.19; BELLEN 1981, Fig.19–20, 22; SPEIDEL 1984, Fig.1; HANNESTAD 1986, Fig.73; BISHOP and COULSTON 1993, Fig.8.1. For *paenulae* see BISHOP and COULSTON 1993, 23, 100, 119.

110 MAGI 1945, Pl.III; ANDREAE 1977, Pl.389; KOEPPEL 1984, No.7.14–7; KLEINER 1992, Fig.159; BISHOP and COULSTON 1993, Fig.2. Praetorian identification is permissable based on the type of shield and proximity to the emperor (MAGI 1945, 81–90; GHEDINI 1986, 293–94). For general discussions of military equipment in Roman iconography see WAURICK 1983; 1989; BISHOP and COULSTON 1993, 19–28.

111 FRANZONI 1983, No.7. Praetorian shields with curved sides and straight top and bottom, or rectangular boards: KÄHLER 1951, Pl.28; KLEINER 1992, Fig.195; BISHOP and COULSTON 1993, Fig.8.1. Oval legionary shields: ESPÉRANDIEU 1907–81, No.5835; BISHOP and COULSTON 1993, 81–2, Fig.3.2, 143.1. A relief from Rome, now in the Louvre, depicting soldiers wearing muscled cuirasses and carrying oval shields, has often been interpreted as depicting praetorians (e.g. ROBINSON 1975, Pl.423; KEPPIE 1984, Pl.20). The presence of a legionary eagle standard makes this identification questionable. Koeppel has demonstrated that the piece came from the Arch of Claudius on the Via Lata and it may be that legionary troops are represented in classicising fashion (KOEPPEL 1983; 1989, No.6. Cf. No.8; DUDLEY 1967, Pl.58).

112 CAGIANO DE AZEVEDO 1939, Fig.3; KAHLER 1951, Pl.28; VERMEULE 1981, No.192, Pl.19; KLEINER 1992, Fig.195.

113 CICHORIUS 1896–1900, Scenes LXXXVI–II.

114 *CIL* 14.2523 = *ILS* 2662; DOMASZEWSKI 1885, Fig.5; RENEL 1903, Fig.52; DURRY 1938, Pl.IV; MAXFIELD 1981, Pl.12a; RANKOV 1994, 24–5. In general see DOMASZEWSKI 1885, 56–69; RENEL 1903, 363–64.

115 DURRY 1938, 205, 213; 1954, 1625; MAGI 1945, 81–2; PALLOTTINO 1938, 47–8; PASSERINI 1939, 51; KOEPPEL 1985, 152; RANKOV 1994, 6, 26–7; KEPPIE 1996, 122–23; COULSTON forthcoming a. Bulls and capricorns: DOMASZEWSKI 1885, 54–6; RENEL 1903, 199–206, 212–18; KEPPIE 1984, 134, 139–40, 142–3, 205–11; WEISS 1994; BARTON 1995.

116 Well reproduced in DURRY 1938, Pl.III.A; BREGLIA 1968, No.26, 36, 50; BELLEN 1981, Fig.21; SPEIDEL 1984, Fig.2; HANNESTAD 1986, Fig.61. Scorpion: BREGLIA 1968, No.26.

117 COULSTON 1989; forthcoming a; BISHOP and COULSTON 1993, 21–2.

118 73 praetorian; 49 legionary. Cf. STROBEL 1984, 85–104; COULSTON forthcoming a.

119 RICHMOND 1935, 3; COULSTON 1989; 1990.

120 BISHOP and COULSTON 1993, 23; *Lexicon* I, *s.v.* 'Columna Marci Aurelii Antonini', 302–5.

121 BRILLIANT 1967, Pl.49–59; *Lexicon* I, *s.v.* 'Arcus: Septimius Severus (Forum)', 103–5.

122 HAYNES and HIRST 1939, Fig.14; BRILLIANT 1967, Fig.61; KLEINER 1992, Pl.300–1; *Lexicon* I, *s.v.* 'Arcus Septimii Severi (Forum Boarium); Arcus Argentariorum; Monumentum Argentariorum', 105–6. The south side bears praetorian *signa*.

123 Herodian 2.13.2; SHA, *Severus* 6.11; Dio 75.1.1. For armoured troops in the city see Tacitus, *Annals* 12.36; 16.27; Dio 67.8.2.

124 RYBERG 1955, Pl.LIV–V, LVII; HASSEL 1966, Pl.18–22; ANDREAE 1977, Fig.426–29; 1979, Pl.80–2; PFANNER 1983, Pl.45, 54, 80–87; KOEPPEL 1984, No.3; KÜNZL 1988, Fig.8–11. An exception is the triumphal frieze on the Arch of Septimius Severus in the Forum Romanum (BRILLIANT 1967, Pl.44–8). Tacitus, *Histories*

2.68 mentions the white tunics worn by Vitellius' officers during his army's triumphal entrance into Rome. It is unlikely, therefore, that the men were wearing the usual centurial mail or scale armour with skirts of *pteryges* which would have completely obscured the under-garment (see ROBINSON 1975, Pl.442, 465). Contrast the entrance of Constantius II in AD357 where armour is a major part of Ammianus Marcellinus' description (16.10.8).

125 LANCIANI 1899, 181: "They (medieval *marmorarii*) were especially fond of epitaphs – whether pagan or Christian it mattered not – because the thin slabs of marble on which the epitaphs were inscribed could easily be adapted to their purpose, being almost ready for use in borders and panels of mosaics, *ambones* and decorative patterns." Nevertheless, there is a bias towards military subjects in the overall epigraphic record, as Noy succinctly puts it: "More significant is the over-representation of serving soldiers. The lack of epitaphs for veterans and *evocati* in comparison suggests that soldiers usually went home after discharge, but if they died at Rome they were more likely than anyone else to be commemorated with an epitaph, often under the terms of their will. The institutional nature of military life and the occupational hazard of death on active service clearly encouraged serving soldiers to make arrangements for their own commemoration and to commemorate their friends; recording the place of origin became a common feature of their epitaphs" (NOY 2000, 8–9. See PANCIERA 1993).

126 These are dateable by inscription, style, clothing, and sword and belt-fittings, e.g. *CIL* 9.4397; AMELUNG 1903, No.128d, 137o–p, Pl.28–9; OHL 1931, No.29; DURRY 1938, 208–11; GUILIANO 1984, No.V.28t; SPEIDEL 1993, Fig.2, 6; 1994a, No.90, 114, 509; 1994b, Pl.11. City soldiers outside Rome: FRANZONI 1987, No.7, 9, 38, 61, Pl.XI.3, XXI.2, XXII.2–3. Julio-Claudian praetorian *stelae* were mostly aniconic and carved from travertine (e.g. GIULIANO 1984, No.I.6–7, IV.29a–d, V.28b–c, f–i, l, n, p, s–t; BRUTO 1987–88, Fig.199, 202). The move towards figural monuments (including funerary altars, see below) was undoubtedly influenced by trends in non-military funerary iconography in Rome, which were in turn based upon the increasing availability and cheapness of imported marble for private commissions. A full corpus of praetorian funerary monuments is desperately needed to accompany SPEIDEL 1994a. A *vigil*: *CIL* 6.2987; AMELUNG 1903, No.128d, Pl.29; BAILLIE REYNOLDS 1926, 98, Pl.VI; SPEIDEL 1993, Fig.6.

127 Wearing tunic, cloak (*paenula* or *sagum*), belt-apron, short sword and dagger, and carrying *fustis* or spear and oval shield: MANSUELI 1967, No.38, 109; BOLLINI 1968, Fig.23–4; FRANZONI 1987, No.44; PFERDEHIRT 1995, Fig.36–7. See SABLAYROLLES 1996, 354 for the comparative lack of *vigil* iconography.

128 Provinces: UBL 1969; SPEIDEL 1976; NOELKE 1986; COULSTON 1987; BISHOP and COULSTON 1993, 26, Fig.85.3, 101. Rome formations: BIENKOWSKI 1919, Fig.117–19; DURRY 1939, Pl.X.B; SUSINI and PINCELLI 1960, Pl.XIX; ROCCHETTI, 1967–68, Fig.1–2, 5–7; PANCIERI 1987, Pl.XVIII–XIX; GASCOU 1988, No.2; BISHOP and COULSTON 1993, Fig.85.2, 4; SPEIDEL 1990, Pl.22, 24; 1993, Fig.1. See also PICOZZI 1979, Pl.LXIV–VI; TORTORICI 1975, Fig.303, 314 (Albano). For a lost half-figure family group from Rome which included an *evocatus* with military equipment see CASAMASSIMA and RUBINSTEIN 1993, No.37a.

129 UBL 1969, 227–39, 277–82, 291–325; OLDENSTEIN 1976; COULSTON 1987; BISHOP and COULSTON 1993, 123–59. There seems to have been a particular 3rd century penchant for eagle-head sword pommels amongst the praetorians and eagle-helmets amongst the *equites singulares*. Compare the thunderbolt and eagle wing blazons on 1st to 2nd century praetorian shields, and the eagles on Cancelleria Relief A *pilum* weights. These closely associate the guard troops with Jupiter.

130 Rheinland: ESPÉRANDIEU 1907–81, No.5838, 6448, 6454–55, 6460, 6463, 6465, 6589. Rome: SPEIDEL 1994a, No. 110–13, 127, 133–34, 137–38, 157–58, 164, 170, 189–91, 193, 201–2, 205–8, 211, 214, 216, 218, 254, 256, 265, 270–71, 368, 396, 400, 404–5, 497, 500–9, 511–15, 517–23, 542, 551, 554, 563, 569, 574, 576, 586–87; 1994b, Pl.2. The horse leads the groom (*calo*) in a manner similar to exercises carried out in displays by the Spanish Riding School at Wien (BISHOP 1988, 67). Representations of a cavalryman riding down a barbarian, especially common in the Rheinland and Britain (SCHLEIERMACHER 1984), are virtually absent from Rome. One exception is so closely linked in style to figures on the Marcus Column (SPEIDEL 1994b, No.540; PETERSEN 1896, Scene CIX) that it was probably carved by a sculptor who worked on that imperial project. A fragmentary horsearcher on a Rome gravestone finds a Rheinland *eques singularis Augusti* parallel (SPEIDEL 1994a, No.501, 684. See also PETERSEN 1896, Scene LVII).

131 Danubian riders: TUDOR 1969. Cf. SCHOBER 1923, No.120, 138. Rome: SPEIDEL 1994b, No.109, 136, 258, 363, 525, 541, 543–44, 568?, 577?, 579, 584?, 591–600, 604, 682. See NOY 2000, 190–91. For artefactual parallels for eagle-crested helmets see ROBINSON 1975, Pl.376–80, 384–86; BISHOP and COULSTON 1993, Fig.104.3–4.

132 SPEIDEL 1965, 79–83; BELLEN 1981, 62–3, Pl.IV–X; GIULIANO 1984, No.IV.29a–d.

133 Rome: SPEIDEL 1994a, No. 114, 165, 356, 400, 401?, 516, 524, 558, 565, 567, 570–71, 580, 614; 1994b, Pl.7 (plus *BullCom* 90, 1985, Fig.191). See also No.683 (Macedonia). Danube: HOFMANN 1905, Fig.25, 43–4, 62–3; SCHOBER 1923, No.259; FERRI 1933, Fig.133; BARKÓCZI 1954, No.2, 5, 181. Cf. ESPÉRANDIEU 1907–81, No.5795; BALTY and RENGEN 1993, Pl.21, 24.

134 BISHOP and COULSTON 1993, Fig.85.1; SPEIDEL 1994a, No.528–37; 1994b, Pl.9–10, 12, 14, 16. See AMELUNG 1903, No.137a, Pl.28 for a similarly depicted *eques praetorianus*. Cf. BARKÓCZI 1954, No.32 (Intercisa, Hungary).

135 GIULIANO 1983, Fig.23 = CASAMASSIMA and RUBINSTEIN 1993, No.56; GIULIANO 1984, No.V.20; KLEINER 1987, No.115, 120, 122, 125; 1992, Fig.534; SINN 1991, No.39; SPEIDEL 1994a, No.80, 83–6, 90; 1994b, Pl.11.

136 ROBINSON 1975, 65, 83, 111, 161, 184; ANDREAE 1977, Pl.504; SCHÄFER 1979; KOCH and SICHTERMANN 1982, Pl.76, 78; KLEINER 1992, Pl.228, 269–71; COULSTON 1991, 102, Fig.5–6.

137 ANDREAE 1977, Pl.587, 590, 593; KOCH and SICHTERMANN 1982, Pl.82, 84; GIULIANO 1983, NO.23; GALLOTTINO 1998, Fig.38; KLEINER 1992, Fig.360–61. Eagle-helmets Fig.359–61; KOCH and SICHTERMANN 1982, Pl.78, 82, 84; SPEIDEL 1994a, No.544, 596, 598, 682.

138 HAMBERG 1945; KOEPPEL 1982.

139 HOPKINS 1983, 213–14; NOY 2000, 218–20. See Patterson in this volume. Funerary inscriptions of *equites singulares Augusti* are disproportionally highly represented. This becomes evident when comparison is made both with the praetorian epigraphic record and with the relative numbers of troops present (Fig. 5.8; following PANCIERA 1993, Table 1). For the 2nd century this is particularly marked: 1,000 *equites* and 10,000 *praetoriani* produced 94 and 234 surviving dateable inscriptions respectively. Perhaps this too reflects the concerns of provincial soldiers in the metropolis. In the 3rd century there was also an imbalance (2,000 *equites* to 15,000 *praetoriani*; 114 and 220 inscriptions), despite the fact that now the *praetoriani* were also provincials. Perhaps the Trajanic Horseguard of provincial *peregrini* was established with such a strong concern for self-affirmation that a unit tradition of metropolitan commemoration continued thereafter.

140 See Tacitus, *Annals* 12.36, 16.27; *Histories* 1.38; Herodian 7.11.12.

141 ROBINSON 1975, Fig.152–57, Pl.423–24, 494, 498–500; LEANDER TOUATI 1987, Pl.26–30; KOEPPEL 1983, No.6–7, 33; 1984, No.12–4, 25–6, 28–30; 1985, No.9–12, 15–6; 1986, No.17, 23, 26–9, 31; 1989, No.6, 8. Cf. ROBINSON 1975, 62, 65–7; WAURICK 1983, 265–74; RANKOV 1994, 19–21. A couple of actual helmets from the western Roman provinces echo this form (ROBINSON 1975, Pl.391–96), but an example now at Toledo, Ohio (USA), is a certain forgery (VERMEULE 1960). Distinctions in types of dress, between 'camp', active service and 'parade' usages can be exaggerated. Equipment and dress would have been the same in all contexts (BISHOP 1990) except perhaps the presence or absence of armour, use of a 'best' tunic in unarmoured parades, and togate order for the Palatine. For general treatments of Rome troops' equipment see DURRY 1938, 195–236; 1954, 1625–26; SPEIDEL 1965, 84–6; 1994a, 8–10; BOLLINI 1968, 86–96; RANKOV 1994, 18–62; SABLAYROLLES 1996, 354–56.

142 E.g. OHL 1931, No.29; FRANZONI 1987, No.7, 9, 38, 47–8, 61; SINN 1991, No.39; SPEIDEL 1993, Fig.2. Provincial legionary *pila*: BISHOP and COULSTON 1993, 65–7, 109, 123, Fig.2, 5, 50, 69, 85.4, 143.1–2.

143 MAGI 1945, Fig.26–7; BISHOP and COULSTON 1993, Fig.2. A damaged *pilum* also appears on one Pozzuoli panel (CAGIANO DE AZEVEDO 1939, Fig.3; KAHLER 1951, Pl.28; VERMEULE 1981, No.192, Pl.19; KLEINER 1992, Fig.195).

144 MAGI 1945, 88–9, Fig.28. Form very closely paralleled by a head from Caerleon, Wales (BOON 1972, Fig.38). For '*beneficiarius*' spear-heads in other artworks and as artefacts see EIBL 1994. The Cancelleria soldier also carries a small, round shield, as seen on one Pozzuoli panel (Cf. KÄHLER 1951, Pl.29; KLEINER 1992, Fig.194; BISHOP and COULSTON 1993, Fig.47.2).

145 COULSTON 1987, 141, 148; BISHOP and COULSTON 1993, 123–26. See SUSINI and PINCELLI 1960, Pl.XIX; ROCCHETTI 1967–68, Fig.1–2, 4; PANCIERI 1987, Pl.XVIII–XIX; GASCOU 1988, No.2; SPEIDEL 1990, Pl.22, 24; 1993, Fig.1; BISHOP and COULSTON 1993, Fig.85.4.

146 BALTY 1988, Pl.XIV.1. Other gravestones at Apamea and elsewhere show legionaries with *lanceae* (Pl.XIV.2; BALTY and RENGEN 1993, Pl.3–5), or one or two *hastae* (PL.9; BALTY 1988, Pl.XIII.2–3; TORTORICI 1975, Fig.314; COULSTON 1987, Fig.1–2; BISHOP and COULSTON 1993, Fig.85.3).

147 STONE 1934, 275–76, 580–81.

148 Fleet: MANSUELLI 1967, No38, 109; BOLLINI 1968, Fig.23–4; PFERDEHIRT 1995, Fig.36–7. Cavalry: SPEIDEL 1994a, No.83, 355a, 535, 558, 565, 567, 580, 672, 677, plus the *calo* and horse, and rider scenes on gravestones. *Speculatores* with *lanceae*: Suetonius, *Claudius* 35.1; *Galba* 18.1.

149 There is in fact very little actual artefactual evidence from Rome for soldiers' military equipment with which to compare the iconography. Finds from excavations within the installations have seldom been reported, and indeed this is not really a context from which much might be expected in the normal course of deposition (BISHOP and COULSTON 1993, 33–8). There have been unconfirmed rumours of equipment coming up during dredging of the Tevere and later appearing in the Porta Portese market. Riverine ritual deposit of swords, shields and helmets in particular would come as no surprise. A presumably early section of mail armour was found in the Tomb of the Scipios (LIBERATI 1997, 29). Some pieces occur in antiquarian collections, as for example in the Vatican Museums where there is a fine *pelta*-decorated 3rd century baldric *phalera* (*pers. obs*). For the type see OLDENSTEIN 1976, Pl.83–6; BISHOP and COULSTON 1993, Fig.85.2, 491.1–3, 6, 92.4, 94. There is apparently a 'Montefortino' type helmet in the Vatican collections bearing a *cohors XII urbana* inscription (CONNOLLY 1981, 225; RANKOV 1994, 20. Cf. ROBINSON 1975, 13–25; BISHOP and COULSTON 1993, 60–1). The forms of some 2nd and 3rd century military fittings have been preserved by the artefacts having been pressed into bricks during manufacture as a type of stamp. These include nails, studs, belt appliques and horse-harness items (BROISE and SCHEID 1987, 130–46. Cf. OLDENSTEIN 1976, Pl.29–30,

33, 46–50, 53–4, 62–5, 70, 72, 75, 80–2). The discovery of an 'armed and belted man' on the beach at Herculaneum (Italy) is of direct relevance to equipment used in Rome. He died during the AD 79 eruption of Vesuvius whilst wearing two plated belts and an apron of studded leather strips with lunate terminals, and carrying a short infantry sword (FRAIA and D'ORIANO 1982, 20–1; JUDGE 1982, 691; GORE 1982, 20–1). The belts preclude identification as a gladiator or as an armed civilian. The most likely explanation is that he was a *classiarius* from Pliny the Elder's Misenum fleet helping to ferry off fleeing civilians (Pliny, *Letters* 6.16. See ROXAN 1981, Table 4.11 for a fleet diploma from Herculaneum). His equipment is fully paralleled by Roman frontier artefacts and iconography, and its forms would have been current in Flavian Rome (BISHOP 1992; BISHOP and COULSTON 1993, 69–74, 96–9). Two spear-heads were found in the Castra Peregrinorum excavations along with christian lamps, so probably these are late (BAILLIE REYNOLDS and ASHBY 1923, 158). A long-sword (*spatha*) found in a 6th century AD tomb at the foot of the Oppian Hill is more relevant to Christie's chapter in this volume (PANELLA 1987, 625, Fig.20).

150 Tacitus, *Annals* 1.7.

151 Clearly stated by Tacitus, *Annals* 1.7, 11.30, 14.11; *Histories* 1.4. In general see PASSERINI 1938, 207–14; MILLAR 1977, 341–55; TALBERT 1984, 425–30, 488–91; CAMPBELL 1984, 365–414; NIPPEL 1995, 85–93. A panel relief depicts an *adlocutio* of Hadrian with the emperor addressing an audience which includes the Genius Populus Romanus, whilst he is backed by the Genius Senatus and a soldier (ANDREAE 1977, Pl.486; KOEPPEL 1986, No.19; KLEINER 1992, Fig.221). Cancelleria Relief A has Domitian symbolically backed by the Genius Senatus, the Genius Populus Romanus, and the group of soldiers discussed above.

152 MAXFIELD 1981; CAMPBELL 1994, 44–5. 'Bad' emperors: Josephus, *Jewish Antiquities* 19.129, 215 (Gaius); Tacitus, *Histories* 1.4–5 (Nero); *Domitian* 23 (Domitian); SHA, *Caracalla* 11.5; Herodian 4.13.7 (Caracalla); 8.7.3, 8.8.1–2 (Maximinus Thrax).

153 Infamously, Dio 77.15.2.

154 Josephus, *Jewish Antiquities* 19.188, 212–66; *Jewish War* 2.205; Dio 58.9, 12.2; Suetonius, *Claudius* 10; FREIS 1967, 7; BELLEN 1981, 95–7; BARRETT 1989, 172–76; LEVICK 1990, 31–6; WISEMAN 1991; FLAIG 1992, 224–28. Gaius fell to a conspiracy of a few praetorian officers whose position gave them access to the emperor. There may have been centurions involved (Suetonius, *Gaius* 58.2) but the rank and file present were completly surprised and bemused by events until Claudius was found.

155 Tacitus, *Histories* 1.17.

156 Based on Suetonius, *Tiberius* 25.1. See CAMPBELL 1984, 110–17; NIPPEL 1995, 93.

157 PASSERINI 1939, 214–220; HOWE 1942; KEPPIE 1996, 113; ABSIL 1997, 83–111.

158 Pliny, *Panegyric* 13.1–3, 15.5, 19.3; CAMPBELL 1984, 32–59; COULSTON forthcoming a. CAMPBELL 1984, 57 makes the point that "on the imperial coinage virtually every emperor after Gaius is portrayed in some context with the soldiers", even those few such as Nerva and Antoninus Pius who never campaigned in person or visited the frontier armies.

159 HAMBERG 1945, 135–49; CAMPBELL 1984, 69–88.

160 Opposition between formations sometimes came into the open. In AD 41 the praetorians backed Claudius against the senate which was protected by the *cohortes urbanae* (Josephus, *Jewish Antiquities* 19.188, 236). In AD 189 Cleander unleashed the *equites singulares Augusti* on a mob which was supported by the praetorians and/ or the urban *cohortes* (Herodian 1.12.6–9. Cf. Dio 73.13.4–5. See SPEIDEL 1994b, 52).

161 Josephus, *Jewish Antiquities* 19.149–52; Suetonius, *Gaius* 58.3; Dio 30.1.1; BELLEN 1981, 95–6.

162 Tacitus, *Histories* 1.38.

163 Dio 58.9.3–6, 12.2; Josephus, *Jewish Antiquities* 19.253; Tacitus, *Histories* 3.64, 69; VISSCHER 1966; FREIS 1967, 6–7; SABLAYROLLES 1996, 42–4. For the political role of *classiarii* see REDDÉ 1986, 502–10.

164 Like *collegia* (Patterson in this volume) and the retainers of wealthy individuals, these could pose a threat to public order and to political stability (NIPPEL 1995, 37, 51–2, 71–3, 96, 104–5).

165 Pliny, *Letters* 10.34.

166 Dio 68.3.3–5; Aurelius Victor, *On the Caesars* 11; DURRY 1938, 378; SYME 1958, 10; RANKOV 1994, 12–3; CAMPBELL 1994, 45; ABSIL 1997, 106–7. Casperius Aelianus: ABSIL 1997, 156.

167 Dio 68.14.4; Pliny, *Panegyric* 6.1–2; DURRY 1938, 379; SYME 1958, 10; SPEIDEL 1994b, 43; ABSIL 1997, 107; COULSTON forthcoming a.

168 SPEIDEL 1994a, 24, 416–17; 1994b, 38–45; RANKOV 1994, 13.

169 PALLOTTINO 1938; KOEPPEL 1985, No.9; LEANDER TOUATI 1987. For *praetoriani* decorated by Trajan see MAXFIELD 1981, 214.

170 LEANDER TOUATI 1987, 45–6, Pl.55, No.25, 32, 41, 64, 70–1, 75, 77; Pl.17.3, 26.3, 32, 28.1, 29.2, 5, 7–8; 44.1. See DURRY 1938, Pl.I. Other infantry and cavalry on the Frieze carry a thunderbolt (*fulmen*) and wings-decorated shield and have *fulmen* helmet cheek-piece decoration (LEANDER TOUATI 1978, Pl.55, No.22, 30, 80, Pl.7.1, 8, 16, 21.2, 29.1, 4, 30.3, 9). This imagery of Jupiter and his eagle is associated with Roman citizen troops on other monuments (FLORESCU 1965, Fig.200, 210; 1969, 81–4; BISHOP and COULSTON 1993, Fig.2, 3.2, 5) and thus excludes the *equites singulares Augusti* (*contra* SPEIDEL 1994a, 418). A tendril-and-rosette decorated shield

(LEANDER TOUATI 1987, Pl.55, No.70, Pl.24.1) finds a parallel in the Pozzuoli praetorian reliefs (KAHLER 1951, Pl.28; KLEINER 1992, Fig.195).

171 LEANDER TOUATI 1987, 21, 60–1, Pl.55, No.52; COULSTON forthcoming a.

172 Compare Galba's fatally unsuccessful appeal: "Fellow soldiers, what's up? I am yours and you are mine" (Suetonius, *Galba* 20.1: *Quid agitis commilitones? Ego vester sum et vos meis*).

173 Herodian 2.13.10–12; SHA, *Severus* 6.11–7.1; Dio 75.1.1–2; DURRY 1938, 384; PASSERINI 1939, 171; BIRLEY 1988, 103; CAMPBELL 1984, 118–20.

174 Dio 75.2.5.

175 PASSERINI 1939, 227–28, 231–32; BIRLEY 1968, 65; SMITH 1972, 485–88; BIRLEY 1988, 129; BALTY and RENGEN 1993; BRUUN 1995. For figural *II Parthica* gravestones see TORTORICI 1975, Fig.303, 314 (Albano Laziale); BALTY 1988; BALTY and RENGEN 1993 (Apamea, Syria).

176 BENARIO 1972; PETRIKOVITS 1975, 160; TORTORICI 1975, 12–94; HASSALL 1983, 121–22, Fig.13; GOLVIN 1988, No.190. At 10.4 ha. this was a remarkably small fortress for 5,000 *legionarii*, hence the modern insistance that there were multi-storey barracks. Substantial extramural baths were built as an additional amenity under Caracalla (TORTORICI 1975, 94–110), perhaps as a *douceur* (see n.91). *Legio II* had closed the gates of the fortress on Caracalla in protest at the murder of Geta in 212 (SHA, *Caracalla* 2.7–8; DURRY 1938, 386).

177 Compare Tacitus, *Histories* 2.93–4 for the difficulties with Italian heat and sickness suffered by Vitellius' Rheinland troops in Rome.

178 E.g. SHA, *Caracalla* 4.5–7; *Geta* 6.1; *Two Maximi* 20.6; *Maximus and Balbinus* 10.4; *The Three Gordians* 22.7–8; Herodian 5.8.8, 7.11, 8.7.7; 8.8. *Legio II Parthica* activities: Dio 79.34.2, 5, 80.2.3, 4.6; SHA, *Caracalla* 2.7–8; *Elagabalus* 10.1, 14.–5, 16.5–17.1; *Two Maximi* 23.6; Herodian 8.5.8–9.

179 Zosimus, *New History* 2.9, 16; Aurelius Victor, *On the Caesars* 40.25; Eusebius, *History of the Church* 9.9.5; Lactantius, *On the Deaths of the Persecutors* 44; GROSSE 1920, 58–61; DURRY 1938, 393–94; PASSERINI 1939, 202; L'ORANGE and GERKAN 1939, 48, 70; FORNI 1960, 23; FRANK 1969, 47; MILLAR 1977, 128; SPEIDEL 1994b, 152–55; RANKOV 1994, 18; LIVERANI 1998, 15; NICASIE 1998, 45–6. Maxentius supplemented the Guard with a *cohors palatina* which appears on inscriptions in the Forum of Trajan (SPEIDEL 1988).

180 L'ORANGE and GERKAN 1939, 65–71, Pl.4b, 10–1; ANDREAE 1977, Pl.627; KLEINER 1992, Fig.410; SPEIDEL 1994b, 154. For an excellent pictorial reconstruction of the bridge battle by Peter Connolly, see HACKETT 1989, 230–31.

181 Zosimus, *New History* 2.17; PLATNER and Ashby 1929, 107; SPEIDEL 1994b, 156; RANKOV 1994, 18; *Lexicon* I, 252.

182 SPEIDEL 1994b, 156; COARELLI 1995, 259–60; CLARIDGE 1998, 346–50; *Lexicon* II, *s.v.* 'Domus: Laterani', 127; IV, *s.v.* 'S. Salvator, basilica', 230–33; V, *s.v.* 'Domus: Laterani', 248–49.

183 COARELLI 1981, 176–79; SPEIDEL 1994b, 157.

184 The military presence in the city was not quite ended. For how long after this the *cohortes urbanae* and *vigilum* survived is not at all clear. The *praefectus urbi* would still have required forces to control continuing public entertainments, and fire-risks only diminished with declining population. It seems that fire-fighting duties devolved to *collegia* and that the Late Roman city was plagued by public disturbances (FREIS 1967, 18; NIPPEL 1995, 98–100; SABLAYROLLES 1996, 59–65; Christie in this volume). *Castra* were retained in the Regionary Catalogues well into the 4th century, certainly after they had been demolished. Presumably the picture of Rome ringed with *castra* well suited the cataloguers' intention of emphasising Rome's grandeur (NORDH 1949, 75.7, 77.2, 81.7, 106.1–3, 6; HERMANSEN 1978, 136–40. Cf. Zachariah of Mytilene, *Syriac Chronicle* 10.16 = MAAS 2000, No.1.5.3). The ten *cohortes praetoriae*, four *cohortes urbanae* and seven *cohortes vigilum* also continued to be listed (NORDH 1949, 105.13–6) in an outdated manner reminiscent of parts of the *Notitia Dignitatum*. Meanwhile, the survivors of Maxentius' Guard and Horseguard were presumably absorbed into other units and new bodyguard formations developed for Constantine and his successors (FRANK 1969; SPEIDEL 1987; 1994b, 75–6; NICASIE 1998, 45–8). Guardsmen continued to be prominently figured in imperial iconography (MACCORMACK 1981, 216–17).

BIBLIOGRAPHY

ABSIL, M. 1997: *Les préfets du prétoire d'Auguste à Commode, 2 avant Jésus-Christ – 192 après Jésus-Christ*, Paris,1997.

ADAM, J.P. 1994: *Roman Building Materials and Techniques*, London, 1994.

AMELUNG, W. 1903: *Die Sculpturen des Vatikanischen Museums* I, Berlin, 1903.

ANDREAE, B. 1977: *The Art of Rome*, London, 1977.

ANDREAE, B. 1979: 'Zum Triumphfries des Trajansbogens von Benevent', *RM* 86, 1979, 325–29.

AUSTIN, N.J.E. and RANKOV, N.B. 1995: *Exploratio: Military and Political Intelligence in the Roman World from the Second Punic War to the Battle of Adrianople*, London, 1995.

BAATZ, D. 1994: 'Katapultenbewaffnung und- Produktion des römischen Heeres in der frühen und mittleren Kaiserzeit', in D. Baatz, *Bauten und Katapultes römischen Heeres*, MAVORS. Roman Army Researches 11, Stuttgart, 1994, 127–35.

BAILLIE REYNOLDS, P.K. 1923: 'Troops quartered in the Castra Peregrinorum', *JRS* 13, 1923, 168–89.

BAILLIE REYNOLDS, P.K. and ASHBY, T. 1923: 'The Castra Peregrinorum', *JRS* 13, 1923, 152–67.

BAILLIE REYNOLDS, P.K. 1926: *The Vigiles of Imperial Rome*, Oxford, 1926.

BALTY, J.C. 1988: 'Apamea in Syria in the second and third centuries AD', *JRS* 78, 1988, 91–104.

BALTY, J.C. and RENGEN, W. van 1993: *Apamea in Syria. The Winter Quarters of Legio II Parthica*, Bruxelles, 1993.

BANDINELLI, R.B. 1971: *Rome. The Late Empire*, London, 1971.

BARKÓCZI, L., ERDÉLYI, G., FERENCSZY, E., FÜLEP, F., NEMERSKÉRI, J., ALFÖLDI, M.R. and SAGI, K. 1954: *Intercisa* I *(Dunapentele-Sztalinvaros). Geschichte der Stadt in der Römerzeit*, Budapest, 1954.

BARRETT, A.A. 1989: *Caligula: the Corruption of Power*, London, 1989.

BARTON, T. 1995: 'Augustus and capricorn: astrological polyvalency and imperial rhetoric', *JRS* 85, 1995, 33–51.

BEARD, M., NORTH, J. and PRICE, S. 1998: *Religions of Rome*, 1–2, Cambridge, 1998.

BELLEN, H. 1981: *Die Liebwache der römischen Kaiser des julisch-claudischen Hauses*, Wiesbaden, 1981.

BELLWALD, U., CASSATELLI, A., GLUTZ, R., HUGI, H., KRAUSE, C., LOCHER, R., MÖRSCH, G., MONACO, E., SIGEL, B. and STUDER, E. 1985: *Domus Tiberiana. Nuove richerche – studi di restauro*, Zürich, 1985.

BELOCH, J. 1886: *Die Bevölkerung der griechisch-römischen Welt*, Leipzig, 1886.

BENARIO, H.W. 1972: 'Albano and the Second Parthian Legion', *Archaeology* 25, 1972, 257–63.

BÉRARD, F. 1988: 'Le rôle militaire des cohortes urbaines', *MEFRA* 100, 1988, 159–82.

BIANCHI, L. 1993: '*Palatiolum* e *palatium Neronis*: topografia antica del Monte di Santo Spiritu in Roma', *BullCom* 95.2, 1993, 25–46.

BIDWELL, P.T. 1999: *Hadrian's Wall 1989–1999*, Newcastle upon Tyne, 1999.

BIDWELL, P. and SPEAK, S. 1994: *Excavations at South Shields Roman Fort*, I, Newcastle upon Tyne, 1994.

BIENKOWSKI, P. von 1919: 'Zur Tracht des römischen Heeres in der spätrömischen Kaiserzeit', *Jahrbuch des Österreichischen Archäologischen Instituts* 19–20, 260–79.

BIRLEY, E. 1969: 'Septimius Severus and the Roman army', *Epigraphische Studien* 8, 1969, 63–82.

BIRLEY, A.R. 1988: *The African Emperor, Septimius Severus*, London, 1988.

BISHOP, M.C. 1988: 'Cavalry equipment of the Roman army in the first century AD', in J.C. Coulston (ed.), *Military Equipment and the Identity of Roman Soldiers. Proceedings of the Fourth Roman Military Conference*, BAR International Series 394, Oxford, 1988, 67–195.

BISHOP, M.C. 1990: 'On parade: status, display and morale in the Roman army', in H. Vetters and M. Kandler (ed.), *Akten des 14. internationalen Limeskongresses 1986 in Carnuntum*, Wien, 1990, 21–30.

BISHOP, M.C. 1992: 'The early imperial "apron"', *Journal of Roman Military Equipment Studies* 3, 1992, 81–104.

BISHOP, M.C. & COULSTON, J.C.N. 1993: *Roman Military Equipment from the Punic Wars to the Fall of Rome*, 1993, London.

BLAKE, M.E. 1959: *Roman Construction in Italy from Tiberius through the Flavians*, Washington, 1959.

BLAKE, M.E. 1973: *Roman Construction in Italy from Nerva through the Antonines*, Philadelphia, 1973.

BOHEC, Y. le 1994: *The Imperial Roman Army*, London, 1994.

BOHEC, Y. le (ed.) 1995: *La hiérarchie (Rangordnung) de l'armée romaine sous le Haut-Empire*, Paris, 1995.

BOLLINI, M. 1968: *Antichità Classiarie*, Ravenna, 1968.

BOON, G.C. 1972: *Isca. The Roman Legionary Fortress at Caerleon, Mon.*, Cardiff, 1972.

BREGLIA, L. 1968: *Roman Imperial Coins, Their Art and Technique*, London, 1968.

BREEZE, D.J. 1969: 'The organisation of the legion: the first cohort and the *equites legionis*', *JRS* 59, 1969, 50–5.

BRILLIANT, R. 1967: *The Arch of Septimius Severus in the Roman Forum*, MAAR 29, Roma, 1967.

BROISE, H. and SCHEID, J. 1987: *Le* balneum *des frères arvales*, Roma, 1987.

BRUNT, P.A. 1971: *Italian Manpower, 225 BC – AD 14*, Oxford, 1971.

BRUNT, P.A. 1975: 'Did imperial Rome disarm her subjects?', *Phoenix* 29, 1975, 260–70.

BRUTO, M.L., MESSINEO, G. and FRIGGERI, R. 1987–88: 'Tor di Quinto', *BullCom* 92, 1987–88, 477–89.

BRUUN, C. 1987: 'Water for the Castra Praetoria', *Arctos* 21, 1987, 7–18.

BRUUN, C. 1995: '*Pericula Alexandrina*: the adventures of a recently discovered centurion of the *legio II Parthica*', *Arctos* 29, 1995, 9–27.

CAGIANO DE AZEVEDO, M. 1939: 'Una dedica abrasa e i rilievi puteolani dei musei di Filadelfia e Berlino', *BullCom* 67, 1939, 45–56.

CAMPBELL, J.B. 1978: 'The marriage of soldiers under the empire', *JRS* 68, 1978, 153–66.

CAMPBELL, J.B. 1984: *The Emperor and the Roman Army, 31 BC–AD 235*, Oxford, 1984.

CAMPBELL, B. 1994: *The Roman Army 31 BC – AD 337. A Sourcebook*, London, 1994.
CARANDINI, A., RICCI, A. and VOS, M. de 1982: *Filosofiana. The Villa of Piazza Armerina. The Image of a Roman Aristocrat at the Time of Constantine*, Palermo, 1982.
CARCOPINO, J. 1956: *Daily Life in Ancient Rome*, Harmondsworth, 1956.
CARETTONI, G., COLINI, A.M., COZZA, L. and GATTI, G. 1960: *La Pianta Marmorea di Roma Antica*, Roma, 1960.
CASAMASSIMA, E. and RUBINSTEIN, R. 1993: *Antiquarian Drawings from Dosio's Roman Workshop. Biblioteca Nazionale Centrale di Firenze, N.A.1159*, Milano, 1993.
CASSON, L. 1965: 'Harbour and river boats of ancient Rome', *JRS* 55, 1965, 31–9.
CECILIA, L. 1986: 'Castra Praetoria', *BullCom* 91, 1986, 366–68.
CICHORIUS, C. 1896–1900: *Die Traianssäule*, Berlin, I–III, Berlin, 1896–1900.
CLARIDGE, A. 1998: *Rome*, Oxford Archaeological Guide, Oxford, 1998.
CLAUSS, M. 1973: *Untersuchungen zu den Principales des römischen Heeres von Augustus bis Diokletian: cornicularii, speculatores, frumentarii*, Bochum, 1973.
CLEERE, H. 1974: 'The Roman iron industry of the Weald and its connections with the *Classis Britannica*', *Antiquaries Journal* 131, 1974, 171–99.
COARELLI, F. 1981: *Dintorni di Roma*, Guide Archeologiche Laterza, Roma-Bari, 1981.
COARELLI, F. 1987: 'La situazione edilizia di Roma sotto Severo Alessandro', in PIETRI 1987, 429–56.
COARELLI, F. 1995: *Roma*, Guide Archeologiche Laterza, Roma-Bari, 1995.
COLINI, A.M. 1944: *Storia e topografia del Celio nell'antichità*, MemPontAcc 7, Roma, 1944.
COLLI, D. 1997: 'Le campagne de scavo nell'anfiteatro castrense a Roma: nuovi acquisizioni', *BullCom* 98, 1997, 242–82.
COLLINGWOOD BRUCE, J. and DANIELS, C. 1978: *Handbook to the Roman Wall*, ed. 13, Newcastle upon Tyne, 1978.
CONNOLLY, P. 1981: *Greece and Rome at War*, London, 1981.
CONNOLLY, P. 1988: *Tiberius Claudius Maximus. The Cavalryman*, Oxford, 1988.
CONSALVI, F. 1997: 'Problemi di topografia lateranense', *BullCom* 98, 1997, 111–28.
COULSTON, J.C. 1987: 'Roman military equipment of 3rd century AD tombstones', in M. Dawson (ed.), *Roman Military Equipment: the Accoutrements of War. Proceedings of the Third Roman Military Equipment Research Seminar,* BAR International Series 336, Oxford, 1987, 141–56.
COULSTON, J.C.N. 1989: 'The value of Trajan's Column as a source for Roman military equipment', in DRIEL-MURRAY 1989, 31–44.
COULSTON, J.C.N. 1990: 'The architecture and construction scenes on Trajan's Column', in Henig, M. (ed.), *Architecture and Architectural Sculpture in the Roman Empire*, Oxford, 1990, 39–50.
COULSTON, J.C.N. 1991: 'The '*draco*' standard', *Journal of Roman Military Equipment Studies* 2, 1991, 101–14.
COULSTON, J.C.N. 1998: 'How to arm a Roman soldier', in M. Austin, J. Harries and C. Smith (ed.), *Modus Operandi. Essays in Honour of Geoffrey Rickman*, London, 1998, 167–90.
COULSTON, J.C.N. forthcoming a: 'Emperor and army on Trajan's Column: a study in composition and propaganda', in A.M. Liberati (ed.), *Traiano. Optimus Princeps*, Roma, forthcoming.
COULSTON, J.C.N. forthcoming b: 'Gladiators and soldiers: personnel and equipment in *ludus* and *castra*', *Journal of Roman Military Equipment Studies* 9, forthcoming.
COURTNEY, E. 1980: *A Commentary on the Satires of Juvenal*, London, 1980.
DARWALL-SMITH, R.H. 1996: *Emperors and Architecture: a Study of Flavian Rome*, Bruxelles, 1996.
DAVIES, R.W. 1971: 'Cohortes equitatae', *Historia* 20, 1971, 751–63 = R. Davies, *Service in the Roman Army*, Edinburgh, 1989, 141–51.
DAVISON, D.P. 1989: *The Barracks of the Roman Army from the 1st to 3rd Centuries AD*, BAR International Series 472, Oxford, 1989.
DELAINE, J. 1997: *The Baths of Caracalla. A study in the design, construction, and economics of large-scale building projects in imperial Rome*, JRA Supplementary Series 25, Portsmouth RI, 1997.
DE VRIES, B. 1986: 'Umm el-Jimal in the first three centuries AD' in P. Freeman and D. Kennedy (ed.), *The Defence of the Roman and Byzantine East. Proceedings of a Colloquium Held at the University of Sheffield in April 1986*, BAR International Series 297, Oxford, 1986, 227–41.
DOBSON, B. and BREEZE, D.J. 1969: 'The Rome cohorts and the legionary centurionate', *Epigraphische Studien* 8, 1969, 100–24.
DOMASZEWSKI, A. von 1885: *Die Fahnen im römischen Heere*, Archäologisch-Epigraphischen Seminares der Universität Wien 5, Wien, 1885.

DRIEL-MURRAY, C. van (ed.), *Roman Military Equipment: the Sources of Evidence. Proceedings of the Fifth Roman Military Equipment Conference*, BAR International Series 476, Oxford, 1989.

DUDLEY, D. 1967: *Urbs Roma. A Source Book of Classical Texts on the City of Rome and its Monuments*, Aberdeen, 1967.

DURRY, M. 1935: 'Juvénal et les prétoriens', *Révue des Études Latines* 13, 1935, 95–106.

DURRY, M. 1938: *Les cohortes prétoriennes*, Paris, 1938.

DURRY, M. 1954: *'Praetoriae cohortes*', *RE* XXII.2, 1954, 1607–34.

ECHOLS, E. 1967–68: 'The Roman city police: origin and development', *CJ* 53, 1967–68, 377–85.

EIBL, K. 1994: 'Gibt es eine specifische Ausrüstung der Beneficiarier?', in *Der römische Weihebezirk von Osterburken*, Stuttgart, 1994, 273–95.

ESPÉRANDIEU, E. 1907–81 *Recueil général des bas-reliefs, statues et bustes de la Gaule romaine*, Paris, 1907–81.

EVANS, H.B. 1997: *Water Distribution in Ancient Rome. The Evidence of Frontinus*, Ann Arbor, 1997.

FAVRO, D. 1994: 'Rome. The street triumphant: the urban impact of Roman triumphal parades', in Z. Çelik, D. Favro and R. Ingersoll (ed.), *Streets of the World, Critical Perspectives on Public Space*, Berkeley, 1994, 151–64.

FAVRO, D. 1996: *The Urban Image of Augustan Rome*, Cambridge, 1996.

FERRI, S. 1933: *Arte romana sul Danubio*, Milano, 1933.

FINLEY, M.I. 1985: *Ancient History. Evidence and Models*, London, 1985.

FLORESCU, F.B. 1965: *Das Siegesdenkmal von Adamklissi: Tropaeum Traiani*, ed.3, Bucarest, 1965.

FLORESCU, F.B. 1969: *Die Traianssäule*, Bucarest & Bonn, 1969.

FLAIG, E. 1992: *Den Kaiser herausfordern: die Usurpationen im römischen Reich*, Frankfurt, 1992.

FORNI, G. 1960: 'Diploma militare del 306 d.C. rilasciato a un pretorio di origine Italiana', *Athenaeum* 38, 1960, 3–25 = G. Forni, *Esercito e marina di Roma antica. Raccolta di contributi*, MAVORS. Roman Army Researches, Stuttgart, 1992, 392–418.

FRAIA, G. di and D'ORIANO, M.R. 1982: 'Scheletri sulla battiglia', *Archeologia Viva* 1.9, 1982, 18–25.

FRANCESCHINI, M. de 1991: *Villa Adriana: mosaici – pavimenti – edifici*, Roma, 1991.

FRANK, R.I. 1969: *Scholae Palatinae. Palace Guards of the Late Roman Empire*, Papers and Monographs of the American Academy in Rome 23, Roma, 1969.

FRANZONI, C. 1987: *Habitus atque habitudo militis. Monumenti funerari di militari nella Cisalpina Romana*, Roma, 1987.

FREIS, H. 1967: *Die Cohortes Urbanae*, Epigraphische Studien 2, Köln, 1967.

GALLOTTINI, A. 1998: *Le Sculture della Collezione Giustiniani*, I. *Documenti*, Xenia Antiqua 5, Roma, 1998.

GASCOU, G. 1988: 'Inscriptions de la ville de Rome et autres inscriptions Italiennes conservées aux musées d'Aix-en-Provence, Carpentras, Avignon et Marseilles', *MEFRA* 1988, 187–243.

GHEDINI, f. 1986: 'Riflessi della politica domizianea nel rilievi flavi di Palazzo della Cancelleria', *BullCom* 91, 1986, 291–309.

GILLIAM, J.F. 1961: 'The plague under Marcus Aurelius', *AJP* 82, 1961, 225–51.

GIULIANO, A. (ed.) 1983: *Museo Nazionale Romano. Le Sculture* I.5. *I marmi Ludovisi nel Museo Nazionale Romano*, Roma, 1983.

GIULIANO, A. (ed.) 1984: *Museo Nazionale Romano. Le Sculture* I.7.i. *Catalogo delle sculture esposte nel giardino cinquecento*, Roma, 1984.

GOLVIN, J.C. 1988: *L'amphithéâtre romain. Essai sur la théorisation de sa forme et de ses fonctions*, Paris, 1988.

GORE, R. 1984: 'The dead do tell tales at Vesuvius', *National Geographic* 165.5, 1984, 557–613.

GRAEFE, R. 1979: *Vela Erunt. Die Zeltdächer der römischen Theater und ähnlicher Anlagen*, Mainz, 1979.

GROSSE, R. 1920: *Römische Militärgeschichte von Gallienus bis zum Beginn der byzantinischen Themenverfassung*, Berlin, 1920.

GROSSO, F. 1966: 'Equites singulares Augusti', *Historia* 25, 1966, 900–9.

HACKETT, J. (ed.) 1989: *Warfare in the Ancient World*, London, 1989.

HAMBERG, P.G. 1945: *Studies in Roman Imperial Art, with Special Reference to the State Reliefs of the 2nd Century*, København, 1945.

HANNESTAD, N. 1986: *Roman Art and Imperial Policy*, Aarhus, 1986.

HASSALL, M. 1983: 'The internal planning of Roman auxiliary forts', in B.R. Hartley and J. Wacher (ed.), *Rome and Her Northern Provinces*, Gloucester, 1983, 96–131.

HASSEL, F.J. 1966: *Der Traiansbogen in Benevent: ein Bauwerk des römischen Senates*, Mainz, 1966.

HAYNES, D.E.L. and HIRST, P.E.D. 1939: *Porta Argentariorum*, London, 1939.

HERMANSEN, G. 1978: 'The population of imperial Rome: the Regionaries', *Historia* 27, 1978, 129–67.

HOFMANN, A. 1905: *Römische Militärgrabsteine der Donauländer*, Sonderschriften des Österreichischen Archäologischen Instituts in Wien 5, Wien, 1905.

HOLMES, R. 1994: *Firing Line*, London, 1994.
HÖLSCHER, T. 1980: 'Die Geschichtsanfassung in der römischen Repräsentationskunst', *Jahrbuch des deutschen archäologischen Instituts* 95, 1980, 265–321.
HOPKINS, K. 1978: *Conquerors and Slaves*, Cambridge, 1978.
HOPKINS, K. 1983: *Death and Renewal*, Cambridge, 1983.
HORN, H.G. 1987: *Die Römer in Nordrhein-Westfalen*, Stuttgart, 1987.
HOWE, L.L. 1942: *The Praetorian Prefect from Commodus to Diocletian*, Chicago, 1942.
ISAAC, B. 1992: *The Limits of Empire. The Roman Army in the East*, Oxford, 1992.
JOHNSON, A. 1983: *Roman Forts of the 1st and 2nd Centuries AD in Britain and the German Provinces*, London, 1983.
JOHNSON, S. 1983: *Late Roman Fortifications*, London, 1983.
JONGMANN, W. 1991: *The Economy and Society of Pompeii*, Amsterdam, 1991.
JUDGE, J. 1982: 'A buried Roman town gives up its dead', *National Geographic* 162, 1982, 686–93.
KÄHLER, H. 1951: 'Der Trajansbogen in Puteoli', in G.E. Mylonas (ed.), *Studies Presented to David Moore Robinson on his Seventieth Birthday*, 1, St Louis, 1951, 430–39.
KARDULIAS, P.N. 1993: 'Anthropology and population estimates for the Byzantine fortress at Isthmia', in T.E. Gregory (ed.), *The Corinthia in the Roman Period*, JRA Supplementary Series 8, Ann Arbor, 1993, 139–48.
KENNEDY, D.L. 1978: 'Some observations on the praetorian guard', *Ancient Society* 9, 1978, 275–301.
KEPPIE, L. 1984: *The Making of the Roman Army from Republic to Empire*, London, 1984.
KEPPIE, L. 1996: 'The Praetorian Guard before Sejanus', *Athenaeum* 84, 1996, 101–24.
KIENAST, D. 1966: *Untersuchungen zu den Kriegsflotten der römischen Kaiserzeit*, Bonn, 1966.
KLEINER, D.E.E. 1987: *Roman Imperial Funerary Altars with Portraits*, Roma, 1987.
KLEINER, D.E.E. 1992: *Roman Sculpture*, New Haven, 1992.
KOCH, G. and SICHTERMANN, H. 1982: *Römische Sarcophage*, München, 1982.
KOEPPEL, G. 1982: 'The Grand Pictorial Tradition of Roman Historical Representation during the Early Empire', *ANRW* II, *Kunste* 12.1, 1982, 507–35.
KOEPPEL, G.M. 1983: 'Two reliefs from the Arch of Claudius in Rome', *RM* 90, 1983, 103–9.
KOEPPEL, G.M. 1984: 'Die historisches Reliefs der römischen Kaiserzeit II, Stadtrömischer Denkmäler unbekannter Bauzugehörigkeit aus flavischer Zeit', *Bonner Jahrbücher* 184, 1984, 1–65.
KOEPPEL, G.M. 1985: 'Die historisches Reliefs der römischen Kaiserzeit III, Stadtrömischer Denkmäler unbekannter Bauzugehörigkeit aus trajanischer Zeit', *Bonner Jahrbücher* 185, 1985, 143–213.
KOEPPEL, G.M. 1986: 'Die historisches Reliefs der römischen Kaiserzeit IV, Stadtrömischer Denkmäler unbekannter Bauzugehörigkeit aus hadrianischer bis konstantinischer Zeit', *Bonner Jahrbücher* 186, 1986, 1–90.
KOEPPEL, G.M. 1989: 'Die historisches Reliefs der römischen Kaiserzeit VI. Reliefs von bekannten Bauten der augusteischen bis antoninischen Zeit', *Bonner Jahrbücher* 189, 1989, 17–71.
KOLB, F. 1995: *Rom. Die Geschichte der Stadt in der Antike*, München, 1995.
KÜNZL, E. 1988: *Der römische Triumph. Siegesfeiern im antiken Rom*, München, 1988.
LANCIANI, R. 1899: *The Destruction of Ancient Rome*, New York, 1899.
LANCIANI, R. 1988: *Notes from Rome*, London, 1988.
LANCIANI, R. 1989: *Forma Urbis Romae*, Roma, 1989.
LAURENCE, R. 1994: *Pompeii. Space and Society*, London, 1994.
LEANDER TOUATI, A.M. 1987: *The Great Trajanic Frieze. The Study of a Monument and of the Mechanisms of Message Transmission in Roman Art*, Stockholm, 1987.
LEPPER, F. & FRERE, S. 1988: *Trajan's Column*, Gloucester, 1988.
LEVICK, B. 1990: *Claudius*, London, 1990.
LIBERATI, A.M. 1997: 'L'esercito di Roma nell'età delle guerre puniche. Recostruzioni e plastici del Museo della Civiltà Romana', *Journal of Roman Military Equipment Studies* 8, 1997, 25–40.
LIEB, H. 1986: 'Die constitutiones für die stadtrömischen Truppen', in W. Eck and H. Wolff (ed.), *Heer und Integrationspolitik. Die römischen Militärdiplome als historische Quelle*, Köln, 1986, 322–46.
LISSI CARONNA, E. 1986: *Il Mitreo dei Castra Peregrinorum*, Leiden, 1986.
LIVERANI, P. (ed.) 1998: *Laterano* I. *Scavi sotto la Basilica di S. Giovanni*, Vaticano, 1998.
LO CASCIO, E. 1997: 'Le procedure di *recensus* dalla tarda repubblica al tardoantico e il calcolo della populazione di Roma', in *La Rome impériale. Démographie et logistique. Actes de la table ronde (Rome, 25 mars 1994)*, Roma, 1997, 3–76.
L'ORANGE, H.P. and GERKAN, A. von 1939: *Der spätantike Bildschmuck des Konstantinsbogens*, Berlin, 1939.
LUGLI, G. 1955: *Fontes ad Topographium Veteris Urbis Romae Pertinentes*, III, Roma, 1955.
LUGLI, G. 1957: *Fontes ad Topographium Veteris Urbis Romae Pertinentes*, IV, Roma, 1957.

MAAS, M. 2000: *Readings in Late Antiquity. A Sourcebook*, London, 2000.

MACCORMACK, S.G. 1981: *Art and Ceremony in Late Antiquity*, Berkeley, 1981.

MACDONALD, W.L. 1982: *The Architecture of the Roman Empire*, New Haven, 1982.

MACDONALD, W.L. and PINTO, J.A. 1995: *Hadrian's Villa and its Legacy*, New Haven, 1995.

MAGI, F. 1945: *I rilievi flavi del Palazzo della Cancelleria*, Roma, 1945.

MAIER, F.G. 1953–54: 'Römische Bevölkerungsgeschichte und Inschriftenstatistik', *Historia* 2, 1953–54, 318–51.

MANSUELLI, G.A. 1967: *Le stele romane del territorio Ravennate e del Basso Po*, Ravenna, 1967.

MARSDEN, E.W. 1969: *Greek and Roman Artillery. Historical Developments*, Oxford, 1969.

MAXFIELD, V.A. 1981: *The Military Decorations of the Roman Army*, London, 1981.

MEIGGS, R. 1973: *Roman Ostia*, Oxford, 1973.

MELUCCI VACCARO, A. and MURA SOMMELLA, A. (ed.) 1989: *Marco Aurelio. Storia di un monumento e del suo restauro*, Milano, 1989.

MILLAR, F. 1965: 'Epictetus and the imperial court', *JRS* 55, 1965, 141–48.

MILLAR, F. 1977: *The Emperor in the Roman World (31 BC – AD 337)*, London, 1977.

MILNE, G. 1995: *Roman London. Urban Archaeology in the Nation's Capital*, London, 1995.

MOELLER, W.O. 1970: 'The riot of AD 59 at Pompeii', *Historia* 19, 1970, 84–95.

MORLEY, N. 1996: *Metropolis and Hinterland. The City of Rome and the Italian Economy, 200 BC – AD 200*, Cambridge, 1996.

NASH, E. 1961–62: *Pictorial Dictionary of Ancient Rome*, I–II, London, 1961–62.

NICASIE, M.J. 1998: *Twilight of Empire. The Roman Army from the Reign of Diocletian until the Battle of Adrianople*, Dutch Monographs in Ancient History and Archaeology 19, Amsterdam, 1998.

NIPPEL, W. 1995: *Public Order in Ancient Rome*, Cambridge, 1995.

NOELKE, P. 1986: 'Ein neuer Soldatengrabsteine aus Köln', in C. Unz (ed.), *Studien zu den Militärgrenzen Roms* III, Stuttgart, 1986, 213–25.

NORDH, A. 1949: *Libellis de regionibus urbis Romae*, Lund, 1949.

NOY, D. 2000: *Foreigners at Rome. Citizens and Strangers*, London, 2000.

OATES, D. and OATES, J. 1959: 'Ain Sinu: a Roman frontier post in northern Iraq', *Iraq* 21, 207–42.

OATES, W.J. 1934: 'The population of Rome', *Classical Philology* 29, 1934, 101–16.

OHL, R.T. 1931: 'The inscriptions in the American Academy in Rome', *MAAR* 9, 1931, 89–133.

OLDENSTEIN, J. 1976: 'Zur Ausrüstung römischer Auxiliareinheiten. Studien zu Beschlägen und Zierat an der Ausrüstung der römischen Auxiliareinheiten des obergermanisch-raetischen Limesgebietes aus dem zweiten und dritten Jahrhundert n. Chr.', *Bericht der römisch-germanischen Kommission* 57, 1976, 49–284.

OTT, J. 1995: *Die Benefiziarier. Untersuchungen zu ihrer Stellung innerhalb der Rangordnung des römischen Heeres und zu ihrer Funktion*, Historia Einzelschriften 92, Stuttgart, 1995.

PACKER, J. 1971: *The insulae of Imperial Ostia*, MAAR 31, Roma, 1971.

PALLOTTINO, W. 1938: 'Il grande fregio di Traiano', *BullCom* 66, 1938, 17–56.

PANCIERA, S. (ed.) 1987: *Le Collezione Epigrafica dei Musei Capitolini. Inediti, rivisioni, contributi al riordino*, Tituli 6, Roma, 1987.

PANCIERA, S. 1993: 'Soldati e civili a Roma nei primi tre secoli dell'impero', in W. Eck (ed.), *Prosopographie und Sozialgeschichte*, Köln, 1993, 261–76.

PANELLA, C. 1987: 'Gli spazi sulle pendici settentrionali del Colle Oppio tra Augusto e i Severi', in PIETRI 1987, 611–51.

PASSERINI, A. 1939: *Le coorti pretorie*, Roma, 1939.

PAVKOVIC, M.F. 1991: *The Legionary Horsemen: an essay on the* equites legionis *and* equites promoti, unpublished PhD dissertation, University of Hawai'i, 1991.

PERKINS, A. 1973: *The Art of Dura Europos*, Oxford, 1973.

PETERSEN, E., DOMASZEWSKI, A. von and CALDERINI, G. 1896: *Die Marcus-Säule auf der Piazza Colonna in Rom*, Monaco, 1896.

PETRIKOVITS, A. von 1975: *Die Innenbauten römischer Legionslager während der Prinzipatzeit*, Opladen, 1975.

PFANNER, M. 1983: *Der Titusbogen*, Mainz, 1983.

PFERDEHIRT, B. 1995: *Das Museum für Antike Schiffahrt* I, Mainz, 1995.

PICOZZI, M.G. 1979: 'Una stela di legionario ad Albano Laziale', *Archeologia Classica* 31, 1979, 167–84.

PIETRI, C. (ed.) 1987: *L'Urbs. Espace urbain et histoire*, Collection de l'École Française de Rome 98, Roma, 1987.

PITTS, L. and ST JOSEPH, J.K. 1985: *Inchtuthil: the Roman Legionary Fortress Excavations, 1952–65*, London, 1985.

PLATNER, S.B. and ASHBY, T. 1929: *A Topographical Dictionary of Ancient Rome*, Oxford, 1929.

RAINBIRD, J.S. 1986: 'The fire stations of imperial Rome', *PBSR* 54, 1986, 147–69.

RAMAGE, E.S. 1983: 'Urban problems in ancient Rome', in R.T. Marchese (ed.), *Aspects of Greco-Roman Urbanisation*, BAR International Series 188, Oxford, 1983, 61–92.
RAMIERI, A.M. 1990: *I Vigili del Fuoco nella Roma Antica*, Roma, 1990.
RANKOV, B. 1994: *The Praetorian Guard*, London, 1994.
RASCH, J.J. 1998: *Das Mausoleum der Kaiserin Helena in Rom und der 'Tempio della Tosse' in Tivoli*, Spätantike Zentralbauten in Rom und Latium 3, Mainz, 1998.
REDDÉ, M. 1986: *Mare Nostrum. Les infrastructures, le dispositif et l'histoire de la marine militaire sous l'empire romaine*, Rome, 1986.
REDDÉ, M. 1995: 'La Rangordnung des marins', in BOHEC 1995, 151–54.
RENEL, C. 1903: *Cultes militaires de Rome. Les enseignes*, Annales de l'Université de Lyon 12, Lyon, 1903.
RICCI, C. 1994: *Soldati della milizie urbane fuori di Roma. La documentazione epigrafica*, Opuscula Epigraphica 5, Roma, 1994.
RICHARDSON, L. 1992: *A New Topographical Dictionary of Ancient Rome*, Baltimore, 1992.
RICHMOND, I.A. 1927: 'The relation of the Praetorian Camp to Aurelian's Wall of Rome', *PBSR* 10, 1927, 12–22.
RICHMOND, I.A. 1930: *The City Wall of Imperial Rome*, Oxford, 1930.
RICHMOND, I.A. 1935: 'Trajan's army on Trajan's Column', *PBSR* 13, 1935, 1–40 = I.A. Richmond, *Trajan's Army on Trajan's Column*, London, 1982.
RICKMAN, G. 1971: *Roman Granaries and Store Buildings*, Cambridge, 1971.
ROBINSON, H.R. 1975: *The Armour of Imperial Rome*, London, 1975.
ROBINSON, O.F. 1977: 'Fire prevention at Rome', *Revue Internationale des Droits de l'Antiquité* 24, 1977, 377–88.
ROBINSON, O.F. 1992: *Ancient Rome. City Planning and Administration*, London, 1992.
ROCCHETTI, L. 1967–68: 'Su una stela del periodo tetrarchico', *Annuario Scuola Archeologia di Atene* 29–30, 1967–68, 487–98.
ROTH, J. 1994: 'The size and organization of the Roman imperial legion', *Historia* 43, 1994, 346–62.
ROUX, P. la 1990: 'L'amphithéâtre et le soldat sous l'empire romain', in C. Domergue, C. Landes and J.C. Pailler (ed.), *Spectacula* I. *Gladiateurs et amphithéâtres*, Lattes, 1990, 203–15.
ROXAN, M. 1981: 'The distribution of Roman military diplomas', *Epigraphische Studien* 12, 1981, 265–86.
ROYO, M. 1999: *Domus Imperatoriae. Topographie, formation et imaginaire des palais impériaux du Palatin (IIe siècle av. J.-C. – Ier siècle av. J.-C.)*, Roma, 1999.
RÜPKE, J. 1990: *Domi Militiae. Die religiöse Konstruktion des Krieges in Rom*, Stuttgart, 1990.
RYBERG, S. 1955: *Rites of the State Religion in Roman Art*, MAAR 22, Rome, 1955.
SABLAYROLLES, R. 1995: 'La hiérarchie inférieure des vigiles: entre traditions et originalité', in BOHEC 1995, 127–37.
SABLAYROLLES, R. 1996: *Libertinus Miles. Les cohortes de vigiles*, Collection de l'Ecole Française de Rome 224, Roma, 1996.
SALLER, R.P. and SHAW, B.D. 1984: 'Tombstones and Roman family relations in the principate: civilians, soldiers and slaves', *JRS* 74, 1984, 124–56.
SCHÄFER, T. 1979: 'Zum Schlachtsarkophag Borghese', *MEFRA* 91, 355–82.
SCHÄFER, T. 1989: *Imperii Insignia: sella curulis und fasces. Zur Repräsentation römischer Magistrate*, RM Supplement 29, Mainz, 1989.
SCHEIDEL, W. 1996: *Measuring Sex, Age and Death in the Roman Empire. Explorations in Ancient Demography*, JRA Supplementary Series 21, Ann Arbor, 1996.
SCHLEIERMACHER, M. 1984: *Römische Reitergrabsteine. Die kaiserzeitlichen Reliefs der triumphierenden Reiters*, Bonn, 1984.
SCHLÜTER, W. 1993: *Kalkriese – Römer im Osnabrücker Land. Archäologische Forschungen zur Varusschlacht*, Bramsche, 1993.
SCHOBER, A. 1923: *Die römischen Grabsteine von Noricum und Pannonien*, Sonderschriften der Österreichischen Archäologischen Instituts in Wien 10, Wien, 1923.
SINN, F. 1991: *Museo Gregoriano Profano ex Lateranense, Katalog der Skulpturen*, I.1, *Die Grabdenkmäler* 1, *Reliefs Altäre Urnen*, Mainz, 1991.
SMITH, R.E. 1972: 'The army reforms of Septimius Severus', *Historia* 21, 1972, 481–99.
SOMMER, C.S. 1999: 'From conquered territory to Roman province: recent discoveries and debate on the Roman occupation of SW Germany', in J.D. Creighton and R.J.A. Wilson (ed.), *Roman Germany. Studies in Cultural Interaction*, JRA Supplementary Series 32, Portsmouth RI, 1999, 161–98.
SPEIDEL, M.A 1992: 'Roman army pay scales', *JRS* 82, 1992, 87–106.
SPEIDEL, M.A 1995: 'Rang und Sold im römischen Heer und die Bezahlung der vigiles', in BOHEC 1995, 299–309.

SPEIDEL, M. 1965: *Die Equites Singulares Augusti. Begleittruppe der römischen Kaiser des zweiten und dritten Jahrhunderts*, Bonn, 1965.
SPEIDEL, M.P. 1975: 'The rise of ethnic units in the Roman imperial army', *ANRW* 11.3, 1975, 202–31.
SPEIDEL, M.P. 1976: 'Eagle-bearer and trumpeter: the eagle-standard and trumpets of the Roman legions illustrated by three tombstones recently found at Byzantium', *Bonner Jahrbucher* 176, 1976, 125–63.
SPEIDEL, M.P. 1978: 'The cult of the Genii in the Roman army and a new military deity', *ANRW* II.16.2, 1542–55.
SPEIDEL, M.P. 1984: 'Germani corporis custodes', *Germania* 62, 1984, 31–45.
SPEIDEL, M.P. 1985: 'A Marsacus as a Horseguard's boy in Rome', *Helinium* 25, 1985, 254–57.
SPEIDEL, M.P. 1987: 'The Late Roman Field Army and the Guard of the High Empire', *Latomus* 46, 1987, 375–79.
SPEIDEL, M.P. 1988: 'Les prétoriens de Maxence. Les cohortes palatines romaines', *MEFRA* 100, 1988, 183–86.
SPEIDEL, M.P. 1989: 'The soldiers' servants', *Ancient Society* 20, 1989, 239–47.
SPEIDEL, M.P. 1990: 'Neckarschwarben (Suebi Nigrenses)', *Archäologisches Korrespondenzblatt* 20, 1990, 201–7.
SPEIDEL, M.P. 1993: 'The *fustis* as a soldier's weapon', *Antiquités Africaines* 29, 1993, 137–49.
SPEIDEL, M.P. 1994a: *Denkmäler der Kaiserreiter, Equites Singulares Augusti*, Köln, 1994.
SPEIDEL, M.P. 1994b: *Riding for Caesar. The Roman Emperors' Horse Guards*, London, 1994.
STAMBAUGH, J.E. 1988: *The Ancient Roman City*, Baltimore, 1988.
STARAC, A. 1995: 'Rimske nadgrobne are u Puli i u Istri', *Opuscula Archaeologica* 19, 1995, 69–95.
STARR, C.G. 1941: *The Roman Imperial Navy, 31 BC–AD 324*, Chicago, 1941.
STONE, G.C. 1934: *A Glossary of the Construction, Decoration and Use of Arms and Armor*, New York, 1934.
STROBEL, K. 1984: *Untersuchungen zu den Dakerkriegen Trajans. Studien zur Geschichte des mittleren und unteren Donauraumes in der Hohen Kaiserzeit*, Bonn, 1984.
SUSINI, G. and PINCELLI, R. 1960: *Le Collezioni del Museo Civico di Bologna. Il Lapidario*, Bologna, 1960.
SYME, R. 1958: *Tacitus* I, Oxford, 1958.
TALBERT, R.J.A. 1984: *The Senate of Imperial Rome*, Princeton, 1984.
TAMM, B. 1968: 'Das Gebiet vor dem Repräsentationspalast des Domitian auf dem Palatin in forschungsgeschichtlicher Beleuchtung', *Opuscula Romana* 6, 1968, 145–91.
TORTORICI, E. 1975: *Castra Albana*, Forma Italiae 1.2, Roma, 1975.
TUDOR, D. 1969: *Corpus Monumentorum Religionis Equitum Danuviorum* I, *The Monuments*, Leiden, 1969.
UBL. H. 1969: *Waffen und Uniform des römischen Heeres der Prinzipatsepoche nach den Grabreliefs Noricums und Pannoniens*, unpublished PhD thesis, Wien, 1969.
VERSNEL, H.S. 1970: *Triumphus. An Inquiry into the Origin, Development and Meaning of the Roman Triumph*, Leiden, 1970.
VERMEULE, C.C. 1960: 'A Roman silver helmet in the Toledo (Ohio) Museum of Art', *JRS* 50, 1960, 8–11.
VERMEULE, C.C. 1981: *Greek and Roman Sculpture in America*, Berkeley, 1981.
VIDAL, G. 1995: *Palimpsest. A Memoir*, London, 1995.
VISSCHER, F. de 1966: 'Macro, Préfet des Vigiles et ses cohortes contra le tyrannie de Séjan', in *Mélanges A. Piganiol*, Paris, 1966, 761–68.
VOGEL, L. 1973: *The Column of Antoninus Pius*, Cambridge Mass., 1973.
WARD-PERKINS, J.B. 1981: *Roman Imperial Architecture*, Harmondsworth, 1981.
WATSON, G.R. 1969: *The Roman Soldier*, London, 1969.
WATSON, G.R. 1971: 'The pay of the urban forces', in *Acta of the Fifth International Congress of Greek and Latin Epigraphy, Cambridge 1967*, Oxford, 1971, 413–16.
WAURICK, G. 1983: 'Untersuchungen zur historisierenden Rüstung in der römischen Kunst', *Jahrbuch des Römisch-Germanischen Zentralmuseums Mainz* 30, 1983, 265–301.
WAURICK, G. 1989: 'Die militärische Rüstung in der römischen Kunst: Fragen zur antiquarischen Genauigkeit am Beispiel der Schwerter des 2. Jahrhunderts n. Chr.', in DRIEL-MURRAY 1989, 45–60.
WEINREB, B. and HIBBERT, C. 1983: *The London Encyclopaedia*, London, 1983.
WEISS, C. 1994: 'Virgo, Capricorn und Taurus. Zur deutung augusteischer Symbolgemmen', *Jahrbuch des Deutschen Archäologischen Instituts* 109, 1994, 353–69.
WELWEI, K.W. 1992: 'Die 'Löwen Caracallas', *Bonner Jahrbucher* 192, 1992, 231–39.
WIERSCHOWSKI, L. 1984: *Heer und Wirtschaft. Das römische Heer der Prinzipatzeit als Wirtschaftsfaktor*, Bonn, 1984.
WISEMAN, T.P. 1987: 'Josephus on the Palatine', in *Roman Studies Literary and Historical*, Liverpool, 1987, 167–75.
WISEMAN, T.P. 1991: *Flavius Josephus. Death of an Emperor*, Exeter Studies in History 30, Exeter, 1991.
WISEMAN, T.P. 1998: 'A walk along the rampart', in *Horti Romani*, Bullettino della Commissione Archeologica Comunale di Roma, Supplementi 6, Roma, 1998, 13–22.

6. Building the Eternal City: the construction industry of imperial Rome

Janet DeLaine

The city of Rome has never failed to impress visitors by its great public monuments. Even the emperor Constantius II, visiting Rome for the first and last time in AD 357, was amazed:

> "....whatever he saw first, it seemed to stand out from all the rest: the shrines of Tarpeian Jove (how far the things of the gods surpass those of the earth!); the baths built like provinces; the great solid mass of the amphitheatre, built of travertine and so tall that human sight can scarcely reach the top; the Pantheon like a city district, well-rounded and beautiful in its lofty vault; the elevated spirals which can be climbed to a platform and support statues of former emperors; the Temple of Roma and the Forum of Peace, the Theatre of Pompey, the Odeon and the Stadium, and among these other ornaments of the Eternal City. But when he came to the Forum of Trajan, unparalleled anywhere on earth, I believe, and which even the gods agree is a marvel, he stopped, thunderstruck, looking attentively around the gigantic complex, beyond description and beyond the power of mortal men to do again." (Ammianus Marcellinus 16.10.14–5)

Such reactions strike a chord with many of us, so that we also subscribe to this natural and instinctive connection between Rome the eternal city, the symbol of enduring civilization, and the permanence of its great public monuments. But there is another city, the densely inhabited city of the Subura with its teeming tenements, or the crowded warehouses and narrow streets of the Emporium, preserved only in fragments such as the Markets of Trajan or as a pale reflection in the marble plan of Rome, but familiar from the writing of Horace, Martial and Juvenal.[1] This too is an eternal city, eternal in its problems of supplying even the basic needs of food and shelter for its unprecedentedly large population, the largest city in the western world before late 18th century London and Paris.

Both of these impressions see the city in terms of constants, whether of the finished buildings or the continual problems. The city is a given; even if the tenements are crumbling and collapsing, the attention focuses on the underlying permanent problem of shelter. What we often forget is that even an eternal city is the result of a continuing process. The permanent monuments have to be built and maintained, if not repaired or rebuilt after fire or flood, while the collapsing tenements must be replaced, and these can only be achieved by human activity and by a very large amount of it at that. It is this construction process which is the focus of this paper. Other studies have been made about the buildings as architecture, and about Roman construction methods in general,[2] but here my interest is in the individuals concerned and the overall structure of the building industry, together with the mechanics of small-scale and large-scale construction projects and the supply of building materials.[3] In order to understand the role of building within the city more fully, we also need some estimate of the number of people involved. Altogether, this will allow us to look finally at the broader social and economic implications of building the eternal city.

ARCHITECTS, CONTRACTORS AND BUILDERS

It should be made clear at the outset that our written evidence – literary and epigraphic – for the building industry is limited. The best-represented group are not in fact the builders but the architects, and even here the evidence would be scanty were it not for the treatise on architecture written during the reign of the emperor Augustus by Vitruvius, himself a practising engineer and architect. Vitruvius gives us a valuable insight into the training and practices of architects of his period and earlier, while other literary and epigraphic sources reveal the names of some individuals who worked at Rome plus indications of their legal and social status. These named individuals are, however, relatively few, and only a tiny handful can be associated with known buildings within the city; Rabirius, who designed the imperial palace on the Palatine for the emperor Domitian and was known to Martial, and Trajan's architect Apollodorus of Damascus, are the only ones who are more than just a name.[4] These men, clearly of outstanding ability, who worked directly for the emperors themselves and who may have changed the face of Roman architecture, were exceptions. The remaining individuals appear to be mainly freed slaves, or free citizens of moderate social status such as Vitruvius himself. This raises the question of the training of architects. Vitruvius outlines an ideal education covering both practical and theoretical aspects of building, expecting the architect

> "to be literate, a skilled draughtsman, and good at geometry; to be well-versed in history, a diligent student of philosophy, with a knowledge of music, and not ignorant of medicine; to know law and have experience in astronomy and astronomical calculations." (*On Architecture* 1.3)

Economically this would seem feasible only for the relatively well-to-do free citizen, while a good education could also be supplied to a promising slave by a wealthy owner or patron. At the same time, anecdotal evidence from literary sources suggests that well-trained architects were not unusual and had sufficient standing to argue the toss with their clients. The criticisms of Hadrian's architectural efforts by Apollodorus are well-known (Dio 69.4), but Cicero too had to endure a lecture on optics in Greek from the architect Cyrus when he dared to criticize the size of some windows (*Letters to Atticus* 2.3.2).

For domestic construction in particular, it was always possible that the builder, or even the client, could be his own architect. Vitruvius (*On Architecture* 6 praef.6) is in favour of property owners who build for themselves in order to spend their money as they would wish rather than handing it over to untrained speculators posing as architects. This may well be the situation underlying Cicero's letter to his brother Quintus concerning his Manilius estate (*Letters to Quintus* 3.1.1–2). The builder here is the unfortunate Diphilus, who Cicero castigates for being both slow and incompetent, failing to set some columns up either straight or on the right alignment. Cicero was closely involved in deciding many of the architectural details, ordering changes to be made and criticizing some of Quintus' suggestions. Either Cicero had drawn up the original plans, and Diphilus is only the builder, or Diphilus as architect was very much at the command of his client; it has been suggested that Diphilus was Cicero's slave or freedman, but there is no clear proof. The difficulty of distinguishing between architects who supervised their own building and master-builders is met again on some funerary monuments, where the profession of the deceased is only indicated by plumb-bob and square, compasses, level and measuring rules. As on the relief of the Aebutii (Fig. 6.1),[5] there is no way of telling whether these were architects or builders – the tools could belong to either.

In many cases, particularly for public works, the control and organisation of the construction process might be in other hands than those of the architect or individual builder; these are the *redemptores* or contractors.[6] Under the Roman Republic, for which our literary evidence is best, public building works were normally let out to contract by the state, and it is probable that this continued to be the case for the emperors' building projects although the direct evidence is lacking.[7] Certainly Frontinus (*On Aqueducts* 2.119), writing about AD 100 from his position as water commissioner (*curator aquarum*), assumes that while routine repair work to the aqueducts was carried out by a permanent body of public slaves, new constructions were let out to contract. Under the Antonines, *a curator operum publicorum* – the imperial official in charge of public buildings equivalent to the *curator aquarum* – is noted as being in charge of paying the *redemptores*.[8] The legal sources show the contract system also operative in late Republican and early imperial Rome for small private building projects such as houses and villas.[9] Some of these *redemptores* are known to us by name. One possibly associated with imperial projects is Quintus Haterius Tychicus, who Coarelli has argued is to be associated with the very elaborate funerary monument to the freed family of the Haterii, from which come the well-known set of reliefs featuring a large crane (Fig. 6.2) and several public buildings of Flavian date, including the Colosseum.[10] The number and quality of the reliefs from this tomb suggest a fairly elevated degree of wealth and status, a point it will be worth bearing in mind. Another contractor known from inscriptions is Tiberius Claudius Onesimus, a freed slave of the emperor, who was not only *redemptor operum caesaris* – a contractor for the emperor's building projects – but also the chief official of that other group known from inscriptions which we can associate with the building industry: the *collegium* of the *fabri tignarii*, the association of builders.[11]

This is the largest known *collegium* in Rome, with some 1330 members in the late 2nd century AD divided into 60 *decuriae* (sub-sections), and there was another large one at Ostia with perhaps 350 members.[12] The function of the association is much debated, but it is clear from the lists of members that have survived that these were all freedmen or free born, not slaves. Since they also needed an entrance fee to join, the members appear to be of moderately good socio-economic status, perhaps the heads of small building 'firms', for want of a better word. The chief magistrates even at Ostia must have been of some considerable wealth and standing, to judge by the fine sarcophagus of Iunius Evhodus now in the Vatican, or by the public statue set up in honour of Iulius Tyrannus, both men at one time *magistri quinquennales* (chief five-yearly magistrates) of the guild.[13] Much harder to find is epigraphic evidence for the ordinary skilled builder or *faber*, and literary mentions are also relatively rare. Most of what we have suggests that some at least of the basic building workers were slaves; for example, Crassus is said to have owned 500 slave architects and builders whom he employed to redevelop buildings bought up at very low cost (Plutarch, *Crassus* 2.4–5).

A group of dedications to slave building workers, including a marble worker, and a freed *faber structor parietarius*, perhaps the Roman equivalent to a master builder, are known from the great household *columbarium* of the Statilii Tauri (the family which produced the consuls of 26 BC, AD 11, 16, 44 and 45).[14] The family interest in construction is shown by the very realistic depiction of builders at work on the city of Lavinium from the same tomb.[15] This suggests the training of skilled builders through the aristocratic household, or at second

Fig. 6.1: Tombstone of the Aebutii. Rome, Museo Capitolino (Photo: author).

Fig. 6.2: Relief from the Tomb of the Haterii. Rome, Vatican Museum (Photo: author).

remove through slaves of builders who were themselves freed slaves, as a type of apprenticeship; one of the cases discussed in the legal codes concerns a *faber* who bought and trained a slave acting on the express instructions of a friend (*Digest* 17.1.26.8). Indeed, several probable freed slaves with the name Titus Statilius are recorded in the *fabri tignarii* of Rome for the later 1st century AD, one of whom rose to be a magistrate of the *collegium* around the middle of the century.[16] The relationship with this family of Titus Statilius Aper, a *mensor aedificarum* or building surveyor, who died at the age of 22 and was given a fine tombstone by his parents (Fig. 6.3), is uncertain, but the clan name (*nomen*) is sufficiently unusual to include him in this group.[17]

Not surprisingly, the ordinary free poor working as casual day labourers on building sites are missing from the epigraphic picture entirely. One legal text, however, gives evidence, if in a rather negative way, of the common use of unskilled day-labourers on building sites:

> "...if someone has contracted to build an *insula*, he should certainly not rush the work by gathering *fabri* from all over the place and bringing in a large number of day labourers, nor should he be content with one or two, but should conduct himself like a careful builder, taking proper account of the weather and the location." (*Digest* 45.1.137.3)

Brunt has argued that free labour was used extensively on public works as well in Rome, where the need for unskilled labour would have been great (see below), although as we have seen this could also cover those with more skills.[18] The anecdote related by Suetonius about Vespasian, who, when an engineer offered him a way of moving large columns to the Capitol at little expense, dismissed him with a suitable reward saying that he should be allowed to feed the people (*Vespasian* 18.13–7), hints at the not insignificant numbers which might be involved in public building works.

ROLES AND RESPONSIBILITIES

At the professional level of architects and building surveyors, the written sources and the epigraphic record allow us to build up a picture of the individual protagonists in the Roman building trade, as they do also for some of the skilled builders trained in aristocratic households and the heads of building 'firms' training their own slaves in turn. Less clear is the evidence for the organization of labour, and the roles and responsibilities of the different individuals in the building industry, but some basic observations can be made. In general, Roman architects had responsibility for design, costing, and overall supervision of a building project, including liaison with the client. It is likely that they were engaged by a form of contract called a mandate, in which they were paid an honorarium rather than a wage and had their expenses reimbursed; the distinction was based on their higher level of expertise and the fact that the employer was paying for technical skill and/or advice rather than manual labour. An early stage in the architect-client relationship is portrayed by Aulus Gellius when describing a visit to Cornelius Fronto:

> "Several builders were present, summoned to construct some new baths, and they were showing him different plans of baths drawn on pieces of parchment. When he had selected one plan and type of work from them, he asked what the cost would be of finishing the whole project. The architect replied..." (*Attic Nights* 19.10.2–4)

Here it is obvious that in some cases architects competed for commissions, producing preliminary plans and proposals, while Vitruvius (*On Architecture* 1.2) makes it clear that some kind of elevations and three dimensional views were also used, as were models.[19] No architects' drawings on papyrus or canvas survive from Italy, but representations of plans in marble and mosaic are known, some of which show dimensions even if these do not seem to correspond to the plan as shown.[20]

That plans could be and were drawn to scale is however demonstrated by the great Marble Plan of Rome, dating to the reign of Septimius Severus, parts of which can be checked against surviving buildings. The scale is 1:240, which may have been conceived of as 1 foot representing 2 *actus* (240 Roman feet) or 1 *uncia* ($\frac{1}{12}$ Roman foot) representing 20 feet, with a general accuracy of 99% – a remarkable feat considering both the difficulties of surveying over the hilly terrain of Rome and the technical limitations of transcribing the plan onto marble.[21]

The degree to which plans and elevations were also used as a means of instructing the builders (as opposed to the clients) is unclear, but there is growing evidence to suggest that they were. Several examples have come to light of full-scale drawings of masonry and architectural ornament incised into pavements which must have served as templates for masons; the most complex example from Rome is still to be seen on the travertine forecourt of the Mausoleum of Augustus and has recently been identified as relating to the Hadrianic Pantheon.[22] Other evidence is less direct. In the Baths of Caracalla, a mistake was made in setting out the foundations for the area of the *natatio* (swimming pool), which was corrected as far as possible when construction reached the level of the *natatio* floor.[23] The error is relatively minor, a simple matter of making the diameter of one semi-circular apse 3 Roman

Fig. 6.3: Tombstone of T. Statilius Aper. Rome, Museo Capitolino (Photo: author).

feet (*c.* 1 m) too small. Even today this is hard to detect without taking measurements, suggesting that the structure was checked against a dimensioned plan rather than one which just gave the general impression of what it looked like. The correction also indicates that the architect had overall supervision of the construction process, and could order changes to be made if he or his client felt it necessary.

If the architect or client was supervising the work directly, the simplest way of ensuring that the work was done was for the client to hire the labourers individually for a daily wage, a system of direct labour which was used in ancient Greece even for large public building contracts, for example at Athens for the 5th century Erechtheum.[24] While there is no direct evidence that this system was used in the Roman period, it perhaps can be inferred from the passage in Vitruvius cited above (*On Architecture* 6. praef.6) in which landowners are commended for building for themselves in order to have control over how their money is spent, a simple process in the direct labour system. An alternative approach was for the client to pay an agreed fee for a set amount of work or for a given task, which could range from a single element, such as digging foundations or carving a marble capital, to the whole building. More commonly, the work was entrusted to a contractor or to a master-builder. Under these conditions a building contract was advisable if not essential, its purpose being first and foremost to ensure that the builder fulfilled the expectations of the client in completing the work as required. The complexity of drawing up building contracts was appreciated by Vitruvius, who recommended that architects be trained in law to help their clients in these matters and avoid unnecessary disputes (*On Architecture* 1.1.10).

The Roman legal codes relating to building, which deal mainly with private contracts between client and builder, provide much fascinating information about the working of this system and the duties of the individuals within it.[25] The codes deal with two types of building contract: a simple verbal promise by a builder to a client to do the specified work, and a more complex written contract (*locatio-conductio*) in which the client and the builder entered into a mutual agreement concerning the work to be done, the remuneration for it, and any conditions which had to be met, frequently including a fixed time limit for completion. In the second case it is clear that the client furnished the land and hired the builder as a skilled craftsman with control over construction, and that the builder produced the building for pay. Sometimes the client provided the materials, but if they were supplied by the builder they then became the property of the client in the finished building. In order to avoid problems if any dispute arose, the contract had also to state the location of the work, the nature of the building, and a time limit for completion, although this could be simply stated as 'a reasonable time'. When the work was finished, it had to be approved for the contract to be fulfilled and the builder paid; while the generally accepted standard where the matter was in dispute appears to have been the opinion of 'a good man', it was often the task of the building surveyor (*mensor aedificarum*) to make the assessment.

The three areas which obviously caused most dispute between client and builder and are dealt with most frequently in the legal codes are time, cost, and the quality of the work. Clients, naturally enough, usually wanted the work done in the minimum time to the highest standard but at the lowest cost. While most of the bargaining presumably went on before the contract was entered into, it is interesting to see what kind of problems arose where conditions were not met and the clients contemplated or took legal action against the builders. Many of the cases appear surprisingly familiar to modern ears. If the contract had a fixed time clause, and the builders were being dilatory, could the client bring a case against them before the expiry of the contract time? The answer was no (*Digest* 45.1.124). Interestingly, the same principle is extended to cases where there was no set time limit, and clients were expected to wait for a reasonable time in which the project might have been completed before taking action. The exception, or perhaps the limiting case, is the propping-up of a collapsing *insula* (itself a useful reminder of the realities of life in Rome), where no delay could be accepted since its result would be the destruction of the client's property (*Digest* 45.1.72.2 and 98.1). Another area of dispute was over damage or delay caused by events which were not the fault of either party but were liable to cause added expense. While the normal practice was for builders to be responsible for the care of the structure until approval, provided this followed close on completion, the client had to bear the cost if the damage was caused by natural forces such as earthquake, landslide or storm, provided that the work was of satisfactory standard in the first place.[26] Such accidents were not the only reason that costs might rise, and it seems that architects and builders were no better in antiquity at completing work within the original contract price than they are today. The passage from Aulus Gellius cited above concludes with the architect quoting 300,000 sesterces for the bath building, to which one of Fronto's friends interjects "And another fifty thousand!" (*Attic Nights* 19.10.2–4). Once a contract had been entered into, the client may have been willing to cover a small rise in cost, but the builder could not assume this and sometimes one side or the other opted to withdraw from the contract before incurring too great a loss.[27]

PRIVATE BUILDING IN PRACTICE

Informative as the legal codes are, the cases they deal with are either hypothetical or not fixed in time or place, just as the epigraphic evidence for builders tells us nothing about who worked on specific projects or under what conditions; nor, as has already been mentioned, can we identify the architects of more than a handful of buildings. In order to go beyond the limitations of the written sources, we need to look at the products of the construction industry – the buildings themselves – which have on the whole fared rather better than the written accounts of their builders. In Rome the survival is mainly of large-scale public buildings like the Pantheon, whereas for domestic and commercial architecture we need to look to Rome's port of Ostia. Here the overall scale is smaller than at Rome, but even so the vast rebuilding of the town in the first half of the 2nd century AD gives us some idea of the periods of extensive and intensive rebuilding of the basic fabric of Rome which inevitably followed the numerous fires and floods which plagued the city. In Ostia, perhaps two thirds of the town was rebuilt in a little over thirty years, most of it residential apartment blocks and warehouses.[28] These buildings generally had between three and five storeys, and were built of Roman concrete, a material comprising rubble bonded with a very strong mortar of lime and pozzolana and faced with brick or brick and reticulate, with vaulted ceilings at the first floor level, and probably timber floors above and a tiled roof, and often with wooden mezzanines dividing the first floor into two.

All the available evidence suggests that this type of structure could be and often was built in as little as two to four years. The legal codes make two years the construction time in hypothetical cases of building an *insula*, while the dates stamped on many of the bricks used at Ostia during this period bunch together, as with the shrine of Serapis, dedicated in January AD 127, and its associated apartment block, both containing stamps of the years AD 123–126.[29] It might be just this type of building project which is shown on one of the very few surviving scenes of Roman builders at work – the 4th century AD wall painting from the Tomb of Trebius Iustus from Rome (Fig. 6.4).[30] Notice the size and organization of the workforce (all wearing the short tunic of the slave or labourer): two men laying bricks stand on scaffolding on either side of the wall, while two other men bring up a load of mortar, carried in a half *amphora*, and a load of bricks or rubble for the wall in a basket, while a third is shown mixing the mortar or slaking lime, using a long-handled hoe. This basic organization of labour can still be observed today where brick walls are under construction, although usually the baskets are replaced by wheelbarrows and hods and the hoe by a concrete mixer; even so, on small jobs mortar is still mixed by hand.

We can put this general knowledge about the nature and length of these small-scale construction projects into a much clearer context by conducting a detailed quantitative analysis of a specific example. Since any building is the result of the application of a particular number and type of human actions to a particular quantity of materials, it should be possible to perform a type of quantity survey in reverse, that is to work back from a complete building to the quantities of materials and manpower required. In any society which uses non-mechanized modes of construction – and that means almost any western society before the start of this century – the construction of any building can be expressed as a specific number of man-days of different types of labour. By using labour constants which tell us how long it takes a man to do a given task, taken from societies which used similar building materials and methods of construction to the Romans, including Renaissance, Baroque and mid-19th century Italy, and 19th century England, we can thus begin to get some idea of the size and nature of the workforce required for these projects.[31]

Fig. 6.4: Scene of builders at work. Rome, Tomb of Trebius Justus (after Marucchi 1911).

Let us take the specific example of the Insula of the Paintings at Ostia (Figs 6.5 and 6.6), divided into two virtually identical apartments (the House of the Paintings and the House of the Infant Bacchus) flanking a garden and a larger residence (the House of Jove and Ganymede) with two shops on its main street facade.[32] The tall ground floor had mezzanines installed in many rooms, and there were at least two floors above. Building joins visible in the garden facade tell us that the block was built in three parts, starting with the larger more imposing House of Jove and Ganymede on the main street and finishing with the House of the Paintings. In keeping with the *Digest* figures for the building of an *insula*, we might allow two years to build the first section, and one year each for the other two (giving four years in all). If we accept that at the most the builders worked a twelve-hour day and for 300 days of the year, then we can calculate the size of the workforce involved. On average it would have needed a team of 16 or 17 men, of whom five must have been masons and another six or seven their labourers, to which we can add a carpenter, a roof tiler, a plasterer and a floorer, with their assistants, and the master-builder acting as general overseer.

As a rough rule of thumb, the *insula* required just over 30 mandays/m^2, if we add the extra labour needed for bringing building materials to the site but omit that required for their production. This is a convenient way to think about the cost of building; the same principle was used by Cato (*On Agriculture* 14.4–5) in calculating the cost of building a villa according to a fixed price per roof tile, clearly a measure of area, while the minimum value of the urban residence for members of the town council of Tarentum was also expressed as a number of roof-tiles.[33] If this figure of 30 mandays/m^2 is extrapolated to the rest of the Hadrianic building programme at Ostia, a rough idea of the total workforce involved can be calculated. The distribution of the dates on the bricks suggest that the building went on at a relatively uniform pace over twenty to thirty years, throughout which at the very least a thousand men must have been at work on building sites somewhere in the town at any time. This is of course a rough approximation, but the actual figures are likely to have been higher, not lower.

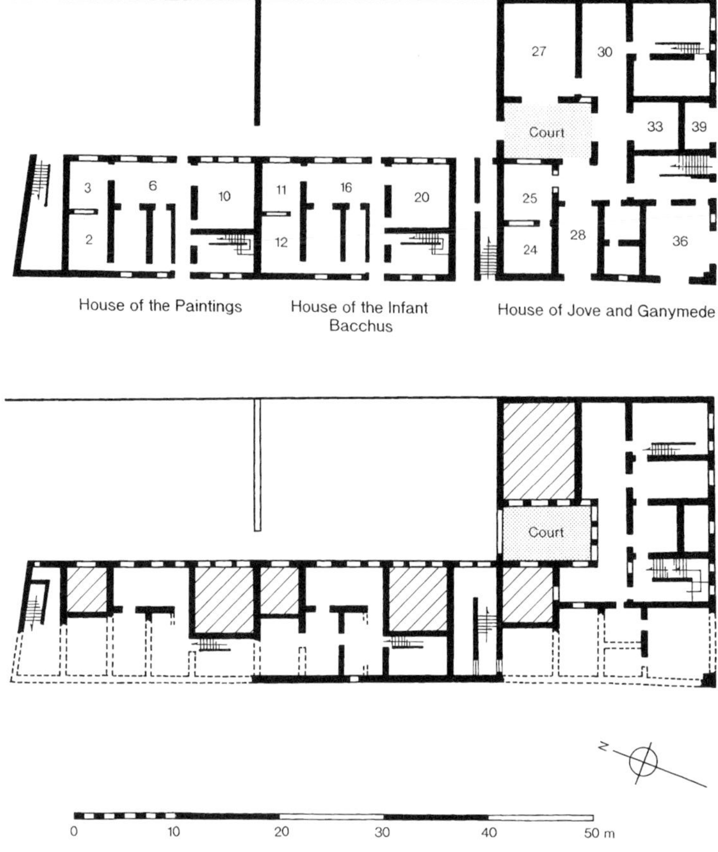

Fig. 6.5: Ostia: Insula of the Paintings, restored plan of the original structure (Drawing: author).

Fig. 6.6: Ostia: Insula of the Paintings, facade on the Via di Diana (Photo: author).

Fig. 6.7: Rome: Baths of Caracalla, south facade of central block (Photo: author).

PUBLIC BUILDING IN PRACTICE

Let us leave Ostia for a while and return to Rome, and to projects on quite a different scale.[34] The Baths of Caracalla in Rome (Fig. 6.7) are one of the three great imperial *thermae* which form the largest single building projects the Romans ever undertook in the city.[35] As far as we can tell from our written sources this remarkable building was erected in just six years, and the shortness of the construction period is confirmed by the five years it took to build the slightly smaller Baths of Trajan, and the seven or eight years required for the Baths of Diocletian despite the troubled times of the late 3rd century AD.[36] This clearly demanded a more structured building industry than the small individual teams working on the apartment blocks and warehouses of Ostia. In fact, it would have taken the team working on the Insula of the Paintings roughly a thousand years to build the Baths of Caracalla!

The Baths are composed of two major elements, a central bathing block roughly 218 × 112 m set in an artificially terraced precinct over 300 m square. At the front of the complex towards the Via Appia, the ancient road lies some 10 m below the level of the precinct, while at the rear it is only just above the natural ground level. Geological cores put down through the precinct have allowed us to reconstruct the nature of the terracing of the natural surface which was carried out as the first step in preparing the site for construction.[37] A schematic section with an exaggerated vertical scale shows how the ground was cut into a series of steps (Fig. 6.8). Into the resultant terraces were cut the foundations proper – some 6.5 m deep under the central block. Altogether half a million cubic metres of clay had to be removed,[38] and all of that, as far as we know without the aid of any machines. The soldiers who appear on Trajan's column building their earthworks show how this was done, using picks, shovels and the inevitable basket for removing the spoil – there is to my knowledge no evidence that the Romans ever used the wheelbarrow.[39]

Once the foundations had been laid, construction continued above ground, for 10 m in the case of the retaining structures facing the Via Appia, and for 8 m under the central block. Part of these can still be seen in the side of an excavation which uncovered an earlier building on the site, systematically demolished to just below the final level of the precinct at the time of construction of the Baths. Above the foundations were solid brick-faced concrete walls which supported the superstructure, pierced through and connected by maintenance passages and drains, while in the area of the open precinct service galleries wide enough to

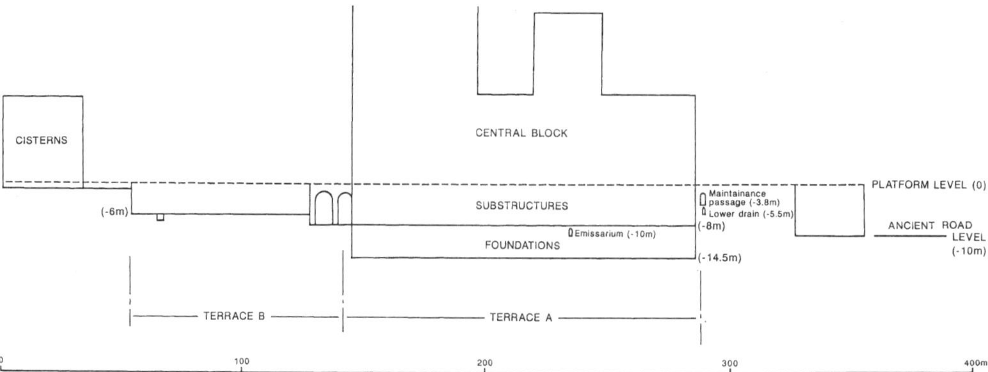

Fig. 6.8: Rome: Baths of Caracalla, section through site, exaggerated vertical scale (Drawing: author).

take two carts side by side were built – some six or seven kilometres of tunnels and passages altogether.[40] All of this had to be built up by hand and all the voids filled with inert materials, so that only in the third year after construction started and the expenditure of over two million man-days of labour, work could commence on the baths proper, which had all to rise to a height of 22 m at least, the main cold *frigidarium* and the hot *caldarium* reaching nearer 40 m.[41] Clearly, although the basic techniques of construction were the same as those used in building the apartment blocks of Ostia, the scale of the building presented very different problems of organization. In order for the building to be finished in the six years suggested by the literary sources, the whole of this central block had to go up together. Simply co-ordinating the large numbers of builders working side by side must have been difficult. In his treatise on the building of the mythical city Sforzinda, the Renaissance architect Filarete recommended that masons were placed no closer than two arms lengths to stop fights – the builders at the baths could have worked more comfortably a little further apart than that.[42]

A few points might illustrate some of the other problems in working on a building project of this size. The first is access to the superstructure. The simple free-standing scaffold from which the builders in the tomb of Trebius Iustus work is impractical and potentially dangerous if extended vertically over 20 m or more. Instead more sophisticated pole scaffolding was used, tied to the wall with horizontal putlogs which have left sufficient of their tell-tale holes in the fabric for the pattern to be reconstructed (Fig. 6.9). Altogether some 100,000 poles were needed, just one of the many hidden materials which went into making the Baths of Caracalla.[43]

Also difficult are those aspects of construction where the physical limitations of the human frame make it impossible to divide construction tasks into individual action, the most important one for our arguments being the lifting of large weights. One example is the large formwork on which the great concrete vaults of the central main hall were laid, which can be reconstructed from later parallels such as the formwork used in the construction of the nave of the new St Peter's in Rome.[44] The other example is the columnar orders which formed such an essential decorative role in the finished building. Column shafts, capitals and architrave blocks are usually monolithic and even small ones are beyond the carrying or lifting capacity of a single man, requiring co-operative effort with crowbars and simple lifting devices. The great columns of the *frigidarium* in the baths, over 40 feet tall, weighed more in

Fig. 6.9: Rome: Baths of Caracalla, north facade of central block showing putlog holes for scaffolding (Photo: author).

the order of 100 tons; yet the limit of a five-man treadmill as shown on the relief from the tomb of the Haterii was 10 to 12 tons.[45]

The problems of moving objects of this size and weight in the days before steam, diesel or electricity are not to be treated lightly. When the last intact column from the Baths of Caracalla was removed in 1561 and sent as a gift by Pope Pius IV to Cosimo de Medici in Florence (where it stands to this day in the Piazza della Iustitia), it took three months to complete the journey; the Romans had used 250 columns for the central block of the Baths, all of which came from distant parts of the empire such as Greece, North Africa, Asia Minor and of course Egypt, the source of the largest monoliths.[46] The Vatican obelisk, weighing perhaps 500 tons, brought over from Egypt originally to adorn the circus of the emperor Caligula, took four months using 800 men and 120 horses to move a few hundred metres in the 16th century.[47] In Roman terms, simply using such giant monolithic columns was pushing technology to its limits and at the same time making a spectacle out of construction which carried an unmistakable message about the power of imperial Rome.

Altogether, excluding the elaborate decoration, the Baths of Caracalla required on average about 6,000 men working on site for 12 hours each day for 300 days over four years, with almost 10,000 at peak periods of construction.[48] The largest number – as many as half – were unskilled or partly skilled (builders' assistants and the like). The single largest group of workers were the skilled builders, as many as 4,600 of whom were needed at peak periods, when almost as many unskilled labourers were also employed. The project would also have given work to about 700 marble workers over four years, and a further 500 decorators in the final stages. But if we want to extend this picture, as we did for Ostia, from the single building to the totality of construction, we need to take into account other major imperial projects, such as the large baths at Albano, built of the same materials and by workmen trained in the same traditions as the Baths of Caracalla.[49] Obviously we do not have the same detailed record for Rome as we have for Ostia, but the presence of imperial brickstamps dating to the time of Caracalla in a number of poorly documented structures suggests that we would not be far wrong if we doubled the numbers employed on the Baths alone, so that in round numbers some 12,000 to 20,000 men might have been employed at Rome directly in construction – an order of magnitude greater than the workforce of 1,000 calculated for Ostia.

So how do these figures relate to the size of the association of builders with which we began – the 1,300 members of the *fabri tignarii* in Rome or the 350 in Ostia? If we consider just the actual builders and carpenters and their assistants, then each member of the guilds represents from three to no more than five or six workers, reinforcing the idea put forward at the beginning that these members are the heads of small building 'firms' similar to that represented on the painting from the tomb of Trebius Iustus. This is of course an average figure, and allowance must be made for both larger and smaller groups. It does, however, fit in very well with the picture of a building industry composed of many small units, each unit contracting alone, or with one or two others, for small scale projects like the building of an *insula*. The Insula of the Paintings at Ostia would have needed two or at the most three such groups if built in the time suggested.

Projects the size of the Baths of Caracalla, however, required more large-scale organization. Ancient historians have concentrated on the social and burial function of the *collegia*, tending to deny them any real role in the working lives of their members, but it is difficult to imagine a better ready-made if informal structure to encourage co-operation beyond the capabilities of any single member in this particular case. The *collegium* of the *fabri tignarii* at Rome is notable for its almost military organization, divided into 60 *decuriae*, each with its own officials which form the general administrative body under the control of six magistrates, the *magistri quinquennales*, each elected for a five-year term of office.[50] The original foundation of the *collegium* was thought to go back to Numa (Plutarch, *Numa* 17), and according to Asconius (*Corn.* p. 67) the *fabri* were one of the very few *collegia* not to be banned by the senate in the difficult circumstances of 64 BC, specifically because of their value to the state. At the time of Septimius Severus, the *collegium* was thought to exist for the benefit of public building works (*Digest* 50.6.6.5.12) and this was still true in 364 (*Codex Theodosianus* 12.1. l. 62). By the 3rd century, in exchange for certain immunities the poorer members at least owed days of labour to the state.

The evidence is, however, very tenuous and there is no information on how the system operated in detail. What is clear is that both at the level of public building requiring the co-operation of many builders and their teams and with private contracts involving only a few groups of builders, the existence of the *collegium* would have facilitated the gathering together of workers to fulfil a contract.[51] It would certainly have simplified the procuring of a large skilled workforce for one-off imperial projects, many of whom were already used to working together and thus presumably to a similar standard – one way at least of explaining the remarkable uniformity of building techniques in the city of Rome. The benefits of such an informal system would have been mutual – both to the emperor who wanted the building and to the members of the guild who wanted to participate in the no doubt lucrative state contracts. This makes the presence of an imperial contractor like the Tiberius Claudius Onesimus mentioned earlier as the chief magistrate of the guild perfectly understandable. The contractor Quintus Haterius Tychicus may also be important in this respect. If as Coarelli suggests he is the freedman of the consul of AD 53[52] then there is a clear role for the

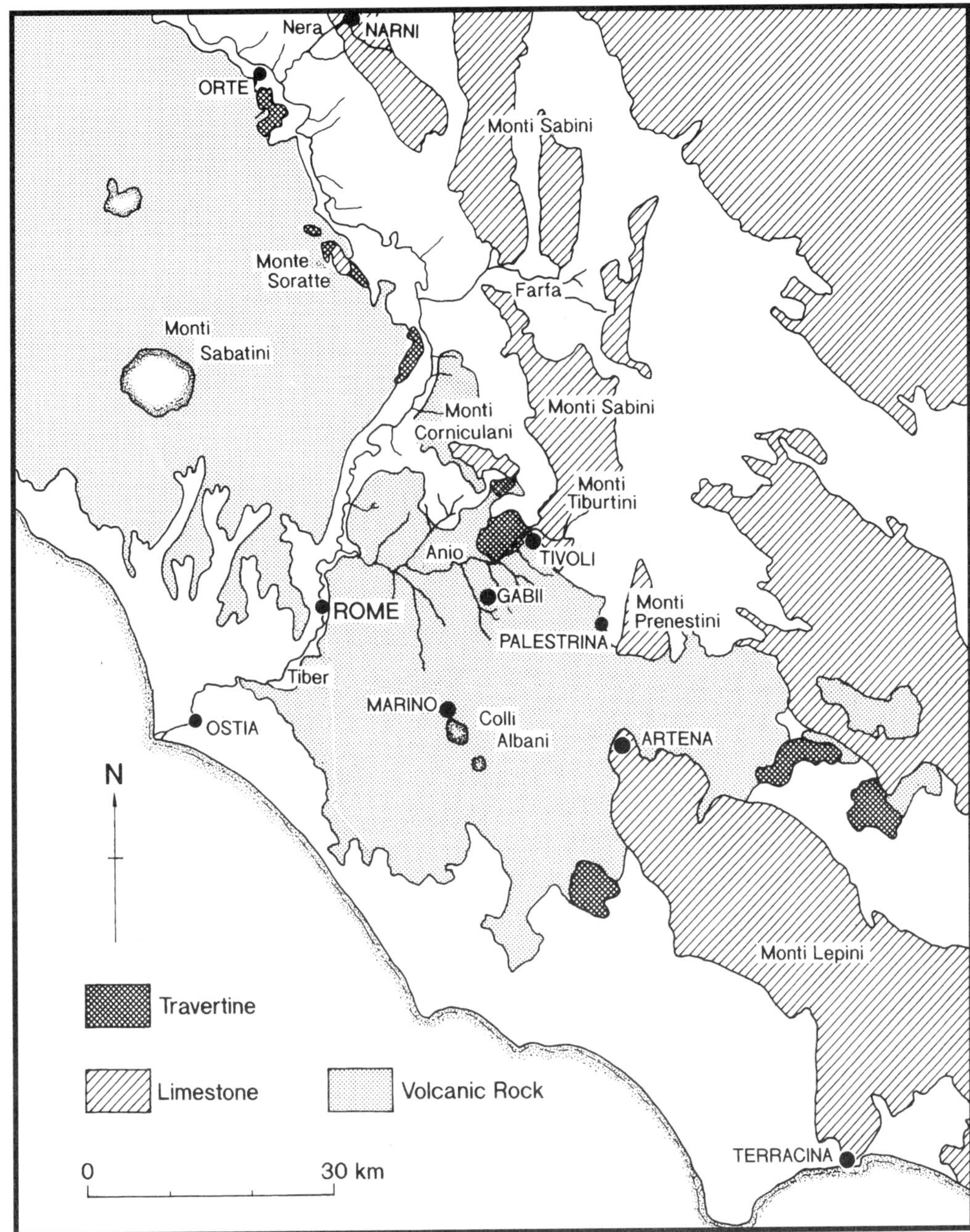

Fig. 6.10: Geological map of Rome and surrounding districts (Drawing: S. Allen).

otherwise absent elite in extending patronage to builders through the intermediary of contractors who were once their slaves.

The underlying role of the elite as facilitators in the building industry becomes even clearer if we now turn to look briefly at the production of building materials. Most of the basic building materials of Rome could be supplied reasonably locally (Fig. 6.10).[53] The

Fig. 6.11: Train of empty ox-carts returning to the selce *quarries on the Via Appia (Photo: G. Primoli, courtesy of the Fondazione Primoli).*

Latial and Sabatini volcanoes provided the various volcanic tuffs which formed the bulk of the cut stone construction of the Republic and the rubble for the concrete, as well as the all-important pozzolana which gave the mortar its great strength. The heavy basaltic lava used as rubble in large foundations (more familiar as paving for the great road system) and the aerated lava used for lightening vaults and domes were also products of the same volcanic systems, while sulphurous springs in the region of Tivoli deposited a porous limestone, the famous travertine. Brick was produced all along the Tiber valley especially north of Rome as far as Orte, while lime for the mortar was produced from the limestone of the Apennine chain, possibly north in the Sabina, east near Tivoli, or around Terracina where ready access to the sea made transport easier.[54]

The literary and epigraphic sources tell us little about the organization of the supply of these basic building materials, with the exception of what can be gleaned from the enigmatic texts of the brickstamps. Steinby's interpretation of these stamps as documentation of a legal contract between the landowner as owner of the raw materials and the brickmakers as producers working under contract does however give us a potential model for the other types of materials.[55] There is no reason why the quarrying of tufa or the production of lime could not have been contracted out in the same way as brick production, just as the contract system also operated at the level of construction, as we have seen. Our only ancient description of lime production is in Cato's treatise on agriculture (*On Agriculture* 38), emphasising the link between the production of building materials and agriculture. The density of villas of the imperial period in the areas notable as sources of building materials, such as Collatia near the Anio tufa quarries,[56] reminds us how important land ownership in Italy was for the senatorial order, and it is difficult to imagine them not being involved also in the exploitation of its resources. Varro is quite specific on this point (*On Farming* 1.2.22–3): while he excludes stone quarries and clay pits from agriculture proper, he adds "which is not to say that they are not to be worked on land where it is suitable and profitable". This involvement went to the highest levels of society including the emperor himself, who by the time of Caracalla had all the urban brickfields in his private possession.[57]

Given the quantities of materials required for construction, the exploitation was likely to have been highly profitable. The most straightforward illustration of this is the production of travertine. The great Italian archaeologist Rodolfo Lanciani studied the quarries as the modern exploitation of them was beginning in the late 19th century, and estimated that the Romans had quarried 5.5 million cubic metres over some four centuries;[58] one hundred thousand cubic metres of that were needed for the Colosseum alone.[59] We have no way of estimating how much tufa or pozzolana or brick or lime was needed altogether to build Rome, but the basic materials for the Baths of Caracalla required an additional workforce of roughly a thousand men for their production, including 200 brickmakers and about the same number of lime producers.

In addition, and in economic terms perhaps more importantly, all the building materials had to be transported to the city, and for that matter also within it. If all the travertine from the Tivoli quarries went by road to Rome – as has often been suggested – then a heavily laden cart would have left the quarry every few minutes of every day for 400 years, causing no doubt enormous traffic jams on the busy Via Tiburtina along which the elite travelled to their summer retreats. The more obvious solution was to go by water, as in fact happened in the Renaissance when the quarries further along the Anio were exploited for the building of St Peter's in Rome.[60] Still, there were no suitable waterways serving the southern tufa and basalt quarries, and nose to tail ox-carts were probably a common sight, as they were again when Rome was expanding rapidly after the Risorgimento to fill her role as capital of a united Italy (Fig. 6.11). If we include the carts needed within the city, moving materials which had come by water from the Tiber to the building site, as many as 2,500 to 3,500 ox-carts were needed on average to keep the builders of the Baths of Caracalla at work.[61] Builders' carts supplying public works were one of the very few categories of wheeled vehicles allowed in the city of Rome during daylight hours, and the references in Tibullus, Horace and Juvenal to the threats imposed by these carts suggest that they were a normal occurrence. Juvenal's account, as usual, is especially graphic:

> "…up comes a huge fir swaying on a wagon, and then another cart carrying a pine, towering on high and threatening the people. And if that axle with its load of Cararra marble breaks and dumps its load onto the crowd, what is left of their bodies?" (*Satires* 3.254–59)

All these animals (two to a cart, and more for large loads) had to be fed, watered, and stabled, and each cart needed its driver. The numbers involved make it unlikely that we are talking here just of ploughing oxen used on an *ad hoc* basis. Both animals and carts were relatively expensive items, as was their maintenance; according to the *Price Edict* of Diocletian, a single two-wheeled cart without its iron fittings (whatever that means) and a pair of oxen would cost the equivalent of the basic ration of corn for a man for nearly three years.[62] Once again we can suspect elite involvement.

Intensive building programmes can therefore, I believe, be seen to benefit the elite financially, and through their power to exercise patronage it also advantaged those of their freed slaves who had gone into the construction industry. But it also perhaps benefited the 'little' people, the ordinary free-born builder working with a couple of slaves and scraping a living as a jobbing builder, or the casual unskilled day labourer for whom large-scale building projects perhaps presented one of the few alternatives to work on the docks – a position recognisable to us from our own relatively recent past. It can be argued that here too a kind of mutual benefit society was operating between elites, and in particular the emperors and the people. The percentage of the population involved in the building industry was, on my very rough calculations, some 3–6% of the total population at both Rome and Ostia, perhaps 15%

of the adult males, similar to that in Renaissance Rome during the building of new St Peter's; this is historically large for pre-industrial societies. In absolute terms, if we include the producers of building materials around Rome and the transport drivers, at the time of Caracalla as many as 20,000 men may have been supported by the building industry at any one time, most of them presumably able-bodied; there is reason to think that the numbers may have been even higher in earlier periods, for example during periods of intensive building under Trajan.

The builders would therefore have normally formed the largest common interest group outside of the imperial household and the troops stationed in and around the city. The emperor and senate would have had good reason to fear concerted action on their part, although there is no record of any disturbance of this kind. The benefits accruing to the individual members of the builders' guild and their dependants through access to large public building contracts would have been more than enough to keep the ordinary builder sweet, adding a bonus to what must have been his normal income from small-scale private building projects; all of this would have had a 'knock-on' effect reaching also to the anonymous free urban poor employed on very large projects like the Baths of Caracalla on a daily basis, that part of the population for whom the daily wage for their labours might have made the difference between life and death.

The building and rebuilding of Rome, in terms of both great public monuments and the endless apartment blocks and warehouses, was a continuous process still showing signs of vitality into the 4th century; the great baths of Diocletian and of Constantine, and the major Constantinian churches, are evidence enough of this.[63] It is perhaps fitting that the latest epigraphic evidence we have for the *fabri tignarii* at Rome is a dedication to Lucius Aelius Helvius Dionysius, once commissioner for public works under Diocletian and Maximian and urban prefect in 301/2, for his many acts of patronage towards them.[64]

NOTES

1 *Lexicon* V, *s.v.* 'Subura', 379–85.

2 The standard basic accounts of Roman architecture in English are BROWN 1961; WARD-PERKINS 1981, 21–140, 415–39; MACDONALD 1982; SEAR 1982, 49–102, 134–84. For Roman construction, see BLAKE 1947 and 1959; LUGLI 1957; BLAKE and BISHOP 1973; GIULIANI 1990; ADAM 1994.

3 For an overview of the building industry at Rome which summarizes much of the previous literature, see ANDERSON 1997. Although LING 1985 is written in the context of Roman Britain, much of this very useful study relates to Italy, especially Rome and Pompeii.

4 See PEARSE 1975a, 100–20 and Appendix 1 for architects at Rome, and MACDONALD 1982, 122–37 for a discussion of the major practitioners in the imperial period, with further references. ANDERSON 1997, 15–67 collects the evidence for named architects.

5 STUART JONES 1912, 75, no. 6 and pl.15; *CIL* 6.10588 for the inscription.

6 For *redemptor* as the technical term for contractors in public works, see Festus p. 370M.

7 ANDERSON 1997, 68–94. The best preserved example of a public contract from the Republic is the *lex parieti faciundo Puteolana* (*CIL* 1.577 = *ILS* 5317 = *ILLRP* 518; WIEGAND 1894) which details the dimensions, materials, structure and decoration of a wall of a precinct near the Temple of Serapis in Puteoli. For a discussion of contracts under the empire, see BRUNT 1980, 84–8.

8 This is the obvious implication of *Digest* 50.8.11 and 50.10.2.1. This post seems, like the *curator aquarum*, to be more concerned with maintenance than with overseeing new building works (ROBINSON 1992, 54), with special officers or boards being established to take care of major new projects or rebuilding; for example, the equestrian officer appointed by Vespasian to see to the repair of the Capitoline Temple, damaged during the Civil War of AD 69 (Tacitus, *Histories* 4.53).

9 For these private contracts, see MARTIN 1989.

10 COARELLI 1979, 266–69. However appealing, the identification is not proved as the cognomen is missing from the funerary inscription (*CIL* 19148); *CIL* 6.607 supplies the *redemptor* Q. Haterius Tychicus. For another possible member of the same *familia* engaged in the building industry, see *CIL* 6.9408 (Quintus Haterius Evagogus). ANDERSON 1997, 103–12 provides a descriptive list of *redemptores* whose names are known.

11 *CIL* 6.9034, late 1st to early 2nd century AD.

12 For the *fabri tign(u)arii* of Rome and Ostia, see WALTZING 1896, II, 115–21; 1900, IV, 21–2; WILSON 1935, 52–65 (Ostia); MORE 1969 (with a summary in *Harvard Studies in Classical Philology,* Rome, 1971, 202–5); PEARSE 1975a, 123–35; ANDERSON 1997, 115–16 (Rome). The size of the *collegium* at Rome is deduced from *CIL* 6.1060 and 10300 which list the officers of *decuriae* 24–60, and 9405 which lists all 22 members of the tenth *decuria*; at Ostia, the minimum size is given by *CIL* 14.4569 which lists the 22 members of 16 *decuriae* (AD 198).

13 Evhodus – *CIL* 14.37; he was *magister quinquennalis* in 158–162. Tyrannus – *CIL* 14.370, *Notizie degli Scavi di antichità*, 1880, 474 (found reused in the theatre); he was *magister quinquennalis* in AD 163–176. Marcus Licinius Privatus, *magister quinquennalis* in AD 203–207, had a public statue set up to him by the members of the *collegium*, and was later given the *decurionatus ornamenta*, the nearest a freedman could come to being made a member of the town council; his son became both an *eques romanus* and a member of the Ostian *ordo*, as did his grandson (*CIL* 14.374).

14 *CIL* 6.6283–85 (*faber*); 6318 (*marmorarius*); 6321 (*mensor*); 6354 (a freedman *faber, structor, parietarius*); 6363–5 (*faber tignarius*). Uncertain is the *structor* of 6353 as this can also indicate a waiter or carver. *CIL* 6.6365a concerns Titus Statilius Tauri l. Antiochi, a *faber tignarius*, and either he or a namesake had his own separate burial plot near the Lateran from which came several boundary *cippi* (*CIL* 6.9412–15). Note that there is nothing to indicate that the three slave *fabri tignarii* were members of the guild. It may not be coincidence that the consul of 26 BC was also the builder of Rome's first permanent amphitheatre in the Campus Martius and *praefectus urbi* (urban prefect) in 16 BC.

15 Cat. fot. Parker n. 3304.

16 The builders possibly belonging to this family are: Titus Statilius Isochrysus, Titus Statilius Onesimus, and Titus Statilius Hieroni f., all in the tenth *decuria* of the *collegium* at the same time, presumably in the ?mid-1st century AD to judge by the number of Tiberii Iulii and Caii Iulii in the list (*CIL* 6.9405); and Titus Statilius L.l. Chrestus (PIETRANGELI 1939, 101–7), magistrate in the ninth *lustrum* which can be dated somewhere in the period AD 38–56 (see PEARSE 1975b, 116–23 for the problems with dating). Several slaves of a Titus Statilius Chrestus are commemorated in the Monumentum Statilii (*CIL* 6.6390, 6402, 6406), but there is no clear link to the *faber tignarius*.

17 See STUART JONES 1912, 76, no. 8. The sides of the tombstone are decorated with a Roman foot measure and other instruments; it dates to the ?3rd quarter 1st century AD, possibly from the Janiculum (*CIL* 6.1975 = 3233 = *ILS* 7737).

18 BRUNT 1980. For further discussion, see SKYDSGAARD 1983 and STEINBY 1983.

19 Literary references to architect's plans and models: Cicero, *Letters to Quintus* 2.2.1 and 2.5.4, *Letters to Atticus* 2.3.2 and 12.18.1; Plutarch, *Moralia* 498E.3, *Pompey* 42.4; Pliny, *Letters* 9.39.5–6; Aulus Gellius, *Attic Nights* 19.10.2–4.

20 See HASELBERGER 1997 for a detailed discussion. The plans are collected conveniently in VON HESBERG 1984, and the models in AZARA 1997. The function of the marble model of the inner shrine of Temple A at Nisa, which has been claimed to be an architect's model by WILL 1985, is not clear; it is hard to imagine the practicalities of working out design changes on marble.

21 CARETTONI 1960, 206–7, 221–31; RODRIGUEZ-ALMEIDA 1981.

22 See most recently ROCKWELL 1989 and HASELBERGER 1994, and note KALAYAN 1971 for material from Syria, and KRAUSE 1985 for the profile of an arch incised in the plaster covering a wall of *opus reticulatum*.

23 DELAINE 1997, 64–5; *Lexicon* V, *s.v.* 'Thermae Antoninianae', 42–8.

24 BURFORD 1969, 110–13.

25 This material is collected and discussed in MARTIN 1989, with a summary in ANDERSON 1997, 68–75.

26 MARTIN 1989, 90–101.

27 In *Digest* 19.2.60.4 the estimated overrun was 50% of the contract price; the builder had stopped work after spending the first half of the contract price, and the client took this as an opportunity of nullifying the agreement but without claiming the money already spent. With Cicero's brother Quintus, it was Nicephorus the contractor who withdrew when Quintus added work not covered by the contract price (Cicero, *Letters to Quintus* 3.2.5).

28 For apartment housing at Ostia, see PACKER 1971; MEIGGS 19732, 235–52; HERMANSEN 1982, 17–53; PAVOLINI 1986, 167–89.

29 Two years is the hypothetical time limit in *Digest* 45.1.124. For the Insula of Serapis, see BLOCH 1959, 231–34.

30 For the tomb and its paintings, see MARUCCHI 1911.

31 The main sources used here are SCAVIZZI 1983; PEGORETTI 1869; HURST 1865.

32 The following figures are based on DELAINE 1996, with more detailed justification for the assumptions used here. For a detailed description of the Insula of the Paintings and its building history, see DELAINE 1995a.

33 *CIL* 1^2. 590, 2.26–31.

34 THORNTON and THORNTON 1989 attempt to put some values on the size and cost of public building projects in Rome, but their attempt is flawed by being based on an arbitrary set of relative values of dubious validity.

35 For the Baths of Caracalla in general, see DELAINE 1997, especially chapter 1; *Lexicon* V, *s.v.* 'Thermae Antoninianae', 42–8.

36 The Baths of Trajan were dedicated in 109 (BARGAGLI and GROSSO 1997, 37, *s.v.* 109 AD), but are unlikely to have been begun before the fire of 104 which destroyed part of Nero's Golden House (Hieron. *Chron. a. Abr.* 2120); the dedicatory inscription for the Baths of Diocletian (*CIL* 6.1130 = 31242) can be dated between May 305 and July 306, and places the commencement of building after Maximian's return to Rome in late 298. See also *Lexicon* V, *s.v.* 'Thermae Traiani', 67–9; 'Thermae Diocletiani', 53–8.

37 Preliminary details are in PETRASSI 1985, and cf. LOMBARDI and CORAZZA 1995, 44–5.

38 DELAINE 1997, 175.

39 For the use of baskets on Trajan's Column, see LEPPER and FRERE 1988, pls.11–2, 15, 37, 42, and cf. the scene from the Tomb of Trebius Justus, Fig. 6.6. On the lack of wheelbarrows, see WHITE 1984, 127.

40 DELAINE 1997, 228.

41 DELAINE 1997, 127 and 176, tables 12 and 15.

42 SPENCER 1965, IV.23v.

43 DELAINE 1997, 145–49.

44 DELAINE 1997, 166–69. A list of the timbers required for the nave vault of St Peter's is given in SCAVIZZI 1983, 107–8.

45 COTTERELL and KAMINGA 1990, 41 give the power output per man on a treadmill as 70 Watt over a 12-hour day, based on 19th century records from Australia where treadmills were used in prisons. For the type of treadmill shown on the Haterii relief, this should give a rate of 26 tons/m/hour, assuming 100% efficiency. In reality, the pulleys alone lose 20%, and the total may only have been 50%. LANDELS 1978, 87–9 suggests a rate of 12 tons/m/hour, about half the maximum possible rate.

46 For a short general account of the imperial marble trade and the sources of stone with detailed bibliography, see DODGE 1991; see also FANT 1993 for some idea of the ideological importance attached to these stones. PEÑA 1989 discusses problems experienced in transporting large columns from the quarries in Egypt.

47 See DIBNER 1970 for this and other examples of moving large obelisks.

48 For the detailed figures, see DELAINE 1997, 175–94.

49 The details of these other Caracallan projects are given in DELAINE 1997, 198.

50 For a discussion of this material, see WALTZING 1896, II, 117–22, and cf. PEARSE 1975a, 68–71.

51 See LANCASTER 1998 for a recent attempt to identify different building teams in the Markets of Trajan.

52 COARELLI 1979, 266.

53 See DELAINE 1995b and bibliography for more details; the major source is VENTRIGLIA 1973. ANDERSON 1997, 127–65 gives a summary account.

54 For a general discussion of Roman lime production, see DIX 1982; see FONTANA 1995 for a possible commercial limekiln near Rome.

55 STEINBY 1993.

56 See QUILICI 1974, 73–7, Fig. 18, for the details of imperial Roman finds in the vicinity of the Anio tufa quarries.

57 For the organisation of the brick industry, see HELEN 1975; SETÄLÄ 1977; STEINBY 1978; 1982; 1983; 1993. ANDERSON 1997, 160–64 gives a brief summary.

58 LANCIANI 1897, 35–6.

59 *Lexicon* V, *s.v.* 'Via Tiburtina', 146–47; COZZO 1928, 212.

60 CASCIOLI 1923, 12.

61 BECCHETTI and PIETRANGELI 1982, 54, no. 48. BURFORD 1960 has long argued convincingly that the ox-cart was the normal means of heavy-duty transport in antiquity.

62 *Price Edict* 15.44 and 30.14.

63 *Lexicon* V, *s.v.* 'Thermae Diocletiani', 53–8; 'Thermae Constantinianae', 49–51.

64 *CIL* 6.1673: L . AELIO . HELVIO / DIONYSIO . C . V / IUDICI . SACRARUM . COG / NITIONUM . TOTIUS . ORIEN / PRAESIDI SYRIAE COELE / CORRECTORI . UTRIUSQ / ITALIAE . CURATORI AQ / ET MINICIAE . CURAT / ... / OPERUM PUBLICORUM / PONTIFI DEI SOL / ... / COLLEGIUM / FABRORUM . TIGNUAR / MULTIS IN SE PATRONCINIIS . CO
To L. Aelius Helvius Dionysius, judge in charge of hearing imperial appeals for all the east, governor of Syria Coele, governor of the two Italies, commissioner of the water board and of the corn supply, commissioner for public works, priest of the sun god. The *collegium* of the builders [set this up] for his many acts of patronage to it.

BIBLIOGRAPHY

ADAM, J.-P. 1994: *Roman Building. Materials and Techniques*, London, 1994.

ANDERSON, J.C. 1997: *Roman Architecture and Society*, Baltimore and London, 1997.

AZARA, P. 1997: *Las casas del alma – Maquetas arquitectónicas de la antigüedad (5500 AC/300 DC)*, Barcelona, 1997.

BARGAGLI, B. and GROSSO, C. 1997: *I Fasti Ostienses. Documento della storia di Ostia*, Itinerari Ostiensi VIII, Roma, 1997.

BECCHETTI, P. and PIETRANGELI, C. (ed.) 1982: *Tevere e Agro Romano dalle fotografie di Giuseppe Primoli*, Roma, 1982.

BLAKE, M.E. 1947: *Ancient Roman Construction in Italy from the Prehistoric Period to Augustus*, Washington, 1947.

BLAKE, M.E. 1959: *Roman Construction in Italy from Tiberius through the Flavians*, Washington, 1959.

BLAKE, M.E. and BISHOP, D.T. 1973: *Roman Construction in Italy from Nerva through the Antonines*, Philadelphia, 1973.

BLOCH, H. 1959: 'The Serapeum at Ostia and the brick-stamps of 123 AD', *AJA* 63, 1959, 225–40.

BROWN, F.E. 1961: *Roman Architecture*, New York, 1961.

BRUNT, P. 1980: 'Free labour and public works at Rome', *JRS* 70, 1980, 81–100.

BURFORD, A. 1960: 'Heavy transport in classical antiquity', *Economic History Review* 13, 1960, 1–18.

BURFORD, A. 1969: *The Greek Temple Builders at Epidauros,* Liverpool, 1969.

CARETTONI, G., COLINI, A. M., COZZA, L. and GATTI, G. (ed.) 1960: *La Pianta Marmorea di Roma Antica*, Roma, 1960.

CASCIOLI, G. 1923: *Bibliografia di Tivoli. Studi e Fonti per la Storia della Regione Tiburtina*, Tivoli, 1923.

COARELLI, F. 1979: 'La riscoperta del sepolcro degli Haterii: una base con dedica a Silvano', in *Studies in Classical Art and Archaeology: A Tribute to P. H. Von Blanckenhagen*, New York, 1979, 255–69.

COTTERELL, B. and KAMMINGA, J. 1990: *Mechanics of pre-industrial technology*, Cambridge, 1990.

COZZO, G. 1928: *Ingegneria romana*, Roma, 1928.

DELAINE, J. 1995a: 'The Insula of the Paintings at Ostia (I.iv.2–4). Paradigm for a city in flux', in T. Cornell and K. Lomas (ed.), *Urban Life in Roman Italy*, London, 1995, 79–106.

DELAINE, J. 1995b: 'The supply of building materials to the city of Rome. Some economic implications', in N. Christie (ed.), *Settlement and Economy in Italy 1500 BC to AD 1500. Papers of the Fifth Conference of Italian Archaeology*, Oxbow Monograph 41, Oxford, 1995, 555–62.

DELAINE, J. 1996: 'The Insula of the Paintings. A model for the economics of construction in Hadrianic Ostia', in A. Gallina Zevi and A. Claridge (ed.), *'Roman Ostia' Revisited. Archaeological and Historical Papers in Memory of Russell Meiggs*, London, 1996, 165–84.

DELAINE, J. 1997: *The Baths of Caracalla. A study in the design, construction and economics of large-scale building projects in imperial Rome*, JRA Supplementary Series 25, Portsmouth R. I., 1997.

DIBNER, B. 1970: *Moving the Obelisks*, Cambridge Mass., 1970.

DIX, B. 1982: 'The manufacture of lime and its uses in the western Roman provinces', *Oxford Journal of Archaeology* 1, 1982, 331–45.

DODGE, H. 1991: 'Ancient Marble Sudies: Recent Research', *JRA* 4, 1991, 28–50.

DUNCAN-JONES, R. 1982: *The Economy of the Roman Empire*, (ed. 2), Cambridge, 1982.

FANT, J. C. 1993: 'Ideology, gift, trade: a distribution model for the Roman imperial marbles', in W. V. Harris (ed.), *The Inscribed Economy. Production and distribution in the Roman empire in the light of instrumentum domesticum*, JRA Supplementary Series 6, Ann Arbor, 1993, 145–70.

FONTANA, S. 1995: 'Un impianto per la produzione della calce presso *Lucus Feroniae* (Roma)', in N. Christie (ed.), *Settlement and Economy in Italy 1500 BC to AD 1500. Papers of the Fifth Conference of Italian Archaeology*, Oxbow Monograph 41, Oxford, 1995, 563–70.

GIULIANI, C.F. 1990: *L'edilizia nell'antichità*, Studi Superiori NIS, Architettura 81, Roma, 1990.

GOLDTHWAITE, R.A. 1980: *The Building of Renaissance Florence*, Baltimore, 1980.

HASELBERGER, L. 1994: 'Ein Giebelriss der Vorhalle des Pantheon: die Werkrisse vor dem Augustmausoleum', *RM* 101, 1994, 279–308.

HASELBERGER, L. 1997: 'Architectural likenesses: models and plans of architecture in classical antiquity', *JRA* 10, 1997, 77–94.

HELEN, T. 1975: *The Organisation of Roman Brick Production in the First and Second Centuries AD: an Interpretation of Roman Brickstamps*, Helsinki, 1975.

HERMANSEN, G. 1982: *Ostia. Aspects of Roman City Life*, Edmonton, 1982.

HURST, J.T. 1865: *A Handbook of Formulae, Tables and Memoranda for Architectural Surveyors and others engaged in Building*, London, 1865.

JONES, A.H.M., MARTINDALE, J.R., and MORRIS, J. 1971: *The Prosopography of the Later Roman Empire Vol. 1 AD 260–395*, Cambridge 1971.

KALAYAN, H. 1971: 'Notes on assembly marks, drawings and models concerning the Roman period monuments in Lebanon', *Annales Archeologiques Arabes Syriennes* 21, 1971, 269–74.

KRAUSE, C. 1985: 'Das graffito in Terracina', in C. Krause (ed.), *La prospettiva pittorica*, Biblioteca Helvetica Romana 22, 1985, 131–33.

LANCASTER, L. 1998: 'Building Trajan's Markets', *AJA* 102, 1998, 283–308.

LANCIANI, R. 1897: *The Ruins and Excavations of Ancient Rome*, Boston and New York 1897.

LANDELS, J.G. 1978: *Engineering in the Ancient World*, Berkeley and Los Angeles, 1978.

LEPPER, F.A. and FRERE, S.S. 1988: *Trajan's Column*, Gloucester, 1988.

LING, R. 1985: 'The mechanics of the building trade', in F. Grew and B. Hobley (ed.), *Roman Urban Topography in Britain and the Western Provinces*, Council for British Archaeology Research Report 59, London, 1985, 14–26.

LOMBARDI, L. and CORAZZA, A. 1995: *Le terme di Caracalla*, Roma, 1995.

LUGLI, G. 1957: *La tecnica edilizia romana con particolare riguardo a Roma e Lazio*, Roma, 1957.

MACDONALD, W.L. 1982: *The Architecture of the Roman Empire I: an Introductory Study*, revised edition, New Haven, 1982.

MARUCCHI, O. 1911: 'L'ipogeo sepolcrale di Trebio Giusto', *Nuovo Bullettino di Archeologia Cristiana* 17, 1911, 209–35.

MARTIN, S.D. 1989: *The Roman Jurists and the Organization of Private Building in the Late Republic and Early Empire*, Collection Latomus 204, Bruxelles, 1989.

MEIGGS, R. 1973: *Roman Ostia*, (ed. 2), Oxford, 1973.

MORE, J.H. 1969: *The Fabrii Tignarii of Rome*, PhD thesis, Harvard, 1969.

PACKER, J.E. 1971: 'The Insulae of Imperial Ostia', *MAAR* 31, 1971.

PAVOLINI, C. 1986: *La vita quotidiana a Ostia*, Roma and Bari, 1986.

PEARSE, J.D.L. 1975a: *The Organisation of Roman Building during the Late Republic and Early Empire*, unpublished DPhil. thesis, Cambridge, 1975.

PEARSE, J. D.L. 1975b: 'A forgotten altar of the *collegium fabrum tignariorum* of Rome', *Epigraphica* 37, 1975, 100–23.

PEARSE, J.D.L. 1976–77: 'Three *alba* of the *collegium fabrum tignariorum* of Rome', *BollCom*, 1976–77, 163–76.

PEGORETTI, G. 1869: *Manuale pratico per l'estimazione dei lavori architettonici, stradale, idraulici, e di fortificazione, per uso degli ingegneri ed architetti*, (ed. 2, revised by A. Cantalupi), Milan, 1869.

PEÑA, J.T. 1989: '*P.Giss* 69: evidence for the supplying of stone transport operations in Roman Egypt and the production of 50 foot monolithic column shafts', *JRA* 2, 1989, 126–32.

PENSABENE, P. 1996: 'Committenza pubblica e committtenza privata a Ostia', in A. Gallina Zevi and A. Claridge (ed.), *'Roman Ostia' Revisited. Archaeological and Historical Papers in Memory of Russell Meiggs*, London, 1996, 185–222.

PETRASSI, L. 1985: 'Terme di Caracalla. Indagini geotecniche', *Lavori e Studi di Archeologia* 6.2, Roma, 1985, 601–4.

PIETRANGELI, C. 1939: 'Frammento dei Fasti del Collegio romano dei fabri tignarii', *BullCom* 67, 1939, 101–7.

QUILICI, L. 1974: *Forma Italia I.10. Collatia*, Roma, 1974.

ROBINSON, O. 1992: *Ancient Rome. City Planning and Administration*, London, 1992.

ROCKWELL, P. 1989: 'Carving instructions on the Temple of Vespasian', *RendPontAcc* 60, 1989, 53–70.

RODRIGUEZ-ALMEIDA, E. 1981: *Forma Urbis Marmorea: Aggiornamento generale*, Roma, 1981.

SCAVIZZI, C.P. 1983: *Edilizia nei secoli XVII e XVIII a Roma*, (*Quaderni* 6), Roma, 1983.

SEAR, F. 1982: *Roman Architecture*, London, 1982.

SETÄLÄ, P. 1977: *Private Domini in Roman Brickstamps of the Empire*, (*Acta Institutum Romanum Finlandiae* 9.2), Helsinki, 1977.

SKYDSGAARD, J.E. 1983: 'Public building and society', in K. de Fine Licht, *Città e Architettura nella Roma Imperiale*, Analecta Romana Instituti Danici Supplementi 10, 1983, 223–27.

SPENCER, J.R. 1965: *Filarete's Treatise on Architecture*, New Haven, 1965.

STEINBY, M. 1978: 'Ziegelstempel von Rom und Umgebung', *Reale Encyclopaedia*, Supplement 15, cols. 1489–1531.

STEINBY, M. 1982: 'I senatori e l'industria laterizia urbana', *Tituli 4: Epigrafia e Ordine Senatorio* 1, 1982, 227–37.

STEINBY, M. 1983: 'L'edilizia come industria pubblica e privata', in K. de Fine Licht, *Città e Architettura nella Roma Imperiale*, Analecta Romana Instituti Danici Supplementi 10, 1983, 219–21.

STEINBY, M. 1993: 'L'organizzazione produttiva dei laterizi: un modello interpretativo per l'*instrumentum* in genere?', in W. V. Harris (ed.), *The Inscribed Economy. Production and distribution in the Roman empire in the light of instrumentum domesticum*, JRA Supplementtary Series 6, Ann Arbor, 1993, 139–44.

STUART JONES, H. (ed.) 1912: *A Catalogue of the Ancient Sculptures preserved in the Municipal Collections of Rome. The Sculptures of the Museo Capitolino*, Oxford, 1912.

THORNTON, M.K. and J L. 1989: *Julio-Claudian Building Programs: a Quantitative Study in Political Management*, Wauconda Ill., 1989.

VENTRIGLIA, U. 1971: *La Geologia della città di Roma,* Roma, 1971.

VON HESBERG, H. 1984: 'Römische Grundrissplane auf Marmor', *Bauplanung und Bautheorie der Antike*, Diskussionen zur archäologischen Bauforschung 4, Berlin, 1984, 120–33.

WALTZING, J.-P. 1895–1900: *Etude Historique sur les Corporations Professionnelles chez les Romains*, 4 Vols., Louvain, 1895–1900.

WARD-PERKINS, J.B. 1981: *Roman Imperial Architecture*, Harmondsworth, 1981.

WIEGAND T. 1894: 'Die puteolanische Bauinschrift', *Jahrbüch für Klassische Philologie*, Suppl. 20, 1894, 660–778.

WILL, E. 1985: 'La maquette de l'adyton du Temple A de Nisa (Beqa)', in *Le dessin d'architecture dans les sociétés antiques. Actes du Colloque de Strasbourg, 26–28 janivier 1984*, Leiden, 1985, 277–81.

WILSON, F. 1935: 'Studies in the social and economic history of Ostia', *PBSR* 13, 1935, 41–68.

7. The Feeding of Imperial Rome: The Mechanics of the Food Supply System

David J. Mattingly and Gregory S. Aldrete

INTRODUCTION

One of the most impressive achievements of the Roman Empire was simply the fact that for over 400 years it managed to sustain and supply its capital city, which by the early 2nd century AD had an estimated population of around 1 million people.[1] This was a notable accomplishment in a largely unmechanized pre-industrial society where long-range transportation of goods was hazardous and costly.[2] The requirements of the city of Rome far outstripped the available local resources, however, and necessitated imports on an enormous scale. The most essential of these items was food; the threat of famine was never far away. But while the supply of grain, and the operation of the grain dole in particular, have received considerable attention, grain was only one of many foods and other commodities imported on a large scale.[3] From the reign of Augustus onward, Rome imported great quantities of marble and other decorative stones, which adorned its public buildings and the houses and villas of the rich.[4] Timber was another bulky item that was imported in vast amounts in all periods of Roman history for use in cooking, heating, construction, cremation and a variety of other purposes.[5]

While we shall focus primarily on food-related supply problems, it must be stressed that this was but one part of a larger logistical structure for the city. The minimalist nature of the central Roman administration has often been emphasized,[6] and some scholars have questioned whether the bureaucracy of Rome's supply system was ever very sophisticated. we shall argue to the contrary, that the sheer scale of the system, together with what we can infer about the complexity of its organization, strongly suggests that the state took an active role in encouraging and overseeing the supply of both foodstuffs and other materials to the city of Rome.

THE PROBLEM

By the end of the Republic, Rome's greatly increased population had far outstripped local resources and was ever more dependent on imported goods to sustain itself. The dietary needs of these *c.* 1 million people are normally assessed in terms of grain consumption, though modern estimates of this vary since it is impossible to be certain of the precise proportion of daily calorie intake fulfilled by cereals. The normal assumption is that cereals provided at least two thirds of calorie intake.[7] Figures have been advanced in recent years of between 200–270 kg of grain per person per year.[8] Other principal forms of nutrition included olives (and especially olive oil) and wine.[9] The advantage of all three of these crops was that their products were relatively easy to store, an important consideration in an age when methods of food preservation were fairly rudimentary. For this reason in particular, grains, oil and wine were the key components of the Roman diet, supplemented by other foods as and when in season or available on the open market. Meat was not a significant component of the everyday subsistence of the poorer sectors of society and, in a huge city such as Rome, the degree of reliance on the three staples (oil, wine and grains) was probably very high, especially during the winter months. The total annual requirement of these foodstuffs was thus colossal, in excess of 400,000 metric tons.[10] Even if the government had wished to avoid direct involvement in the mechanics of the food supply, the scale of the problem and the potential of food shortages to spark serious unrest impelled the state to play an increasingly active role in the logistical arrangements for feeding the city. The supply system that was developed is commonly referred to as the *annona*.[11]

A further problem related to the demography of the city was that the poor had limited means with which to buy food, particularly at the inflated prices that often operated in the capital.[12] There is a common misconception that the urban plebs led an entirely indolent existence, surviving on a diet of free shows and handouts of cash and grain. In reality, it is clear that work was a necessity for most people, though many jobs were seasonal in nature and continuous employment for unskilled workers was hard to come by.[13] The state, particularly from the time of Augustus onwards, was able to generate jobs in various sectors (notably the construction industry),[14] but there was also a necessity for more interventionist policies. In the late 2nd century BC, the Roman state adopted the principle of distributing some food free or at reduced prices to qualifying male citizens in times of shortage. Although not at first a commitment to regular distributions, the tendency over time was for the citizen plebs to expect increased state involvement in the food supply of the city. The precedent of distributing some free food was in a sense a point of no return for the Republican government. The state thus assumed not only the responsibility for ensuring that adequate food was on sale at reasonable prices in the markets, but also the collection, transport and distribution of a proportion of the total foodstuffs required.

Even meeting the minimum needs for these commodities imposed severe burdens on a pre-industrial state. Food shortage and famine were recurrent threats to an urban population as dependent on imports as that of ancient Rome. Incidents of food shortage frequently led to riots and other social disturbances. In the period from the end of the Second Punic War to the start of the Principate (201–31 BC) there are at least 37 attested incidents of food shortage in Rome.[15] The causes of these shortages were varied, including crop failure in the main producing areas, the effects of war (both external and civil), disruption of the shipping lanes by pirates, official negligence or corruption, and natural disasters such as fire or floods destroying supplies. A common response to the early signs of impending shortage was for merchants to hoard supplies causing food prices to soar.[16] Such shortages often resulted in serious social unrest and rioting, since basic foods quickly became unaffordable or unobtainable for the poorer people in society while large stocks were known to remain in the warehouses.

Food crises continued to afflict the city of Rome even after the creation of the Principate, with 10 incidents attested in the reign of Augustus alone and a total of 23 in the period down to Septimius Severus (31 BC–AD 193).[17] For much of Roman history, then, the availability of food and its cost on the market at Rome was a necessary preoccupation of both the populace at large and those responsible for maintaining public order. The Roman state, notoriously

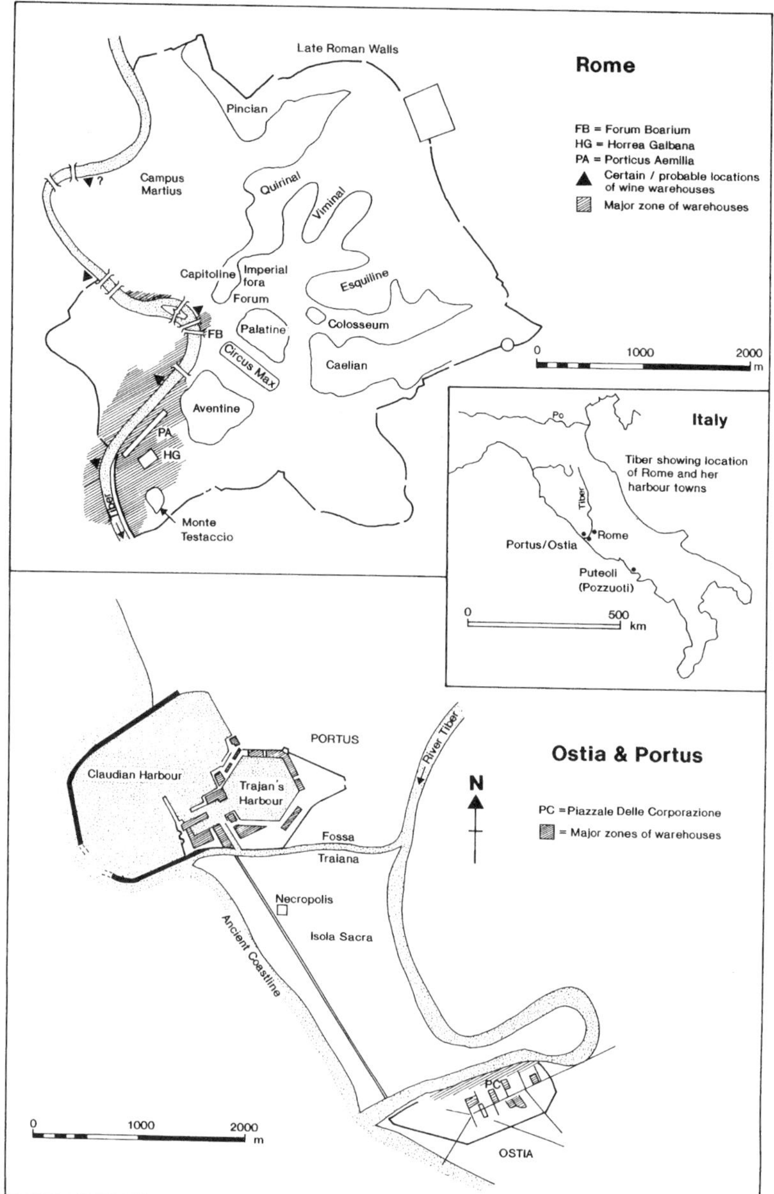

Fig. 7.1: Map of Rome and Ostia/Portus, indicating the commercial quarters.

non-interventionist and unbureaucratic in many areas of life, was forced to address the problems associated with feeding the city.

Overland transport of bulk foodstuffs was clearly expensive in antiquity and the major part of Rome's needs beyond what was supplied by her immediate hinterland came by water.[18] Rome was located about 15 miles (22 km) inland as the crow flies, on the left bank of the Tiber river. The river was navigable for ship and boats of shallow draft, though not for the larger sea-going ships. Unfortunately there was no good natural harbour at the mouth of the

Tiber, where the town of Ostia served as Rome's river port. In Republican times ships tied up at riverside wharfs or had their cargoes off-loaded onto lighters while riding at anchor offshore.[19] Some of the goods were temporarily stored at Ostia, others transported in the small river boats upstream to Rome. Only the smaller merchant ships could proceed directly up river to Rome without unloading in the hazardous and poorly sheltered conditions at Ostia. As a result of the inadequate facilities, crowded berths and dangerous conditions at Ostia, many of the largest ships had to dock some way from Rome at Puteoli on the Bay of Naples. From there, their cargoes had to be transhipped into smaller boats for onward transport to Rome. The absence of more substantial harbour installations close at hand thus further complicated the considerable problems involved in supplying the city (Fig. 7.1).[20]

The uncertainties of crop production, the perils of navigation, the organizational difficulties of co-ordinating the transport, storage and delivery of the huge quantities of foodstuffs imposed major constraints on the Roman state's response to the recurrent threat of shortage. These problems are neatly summed up by Tacitus: "Italy relies upon external resources and the life of the Roman people is tossed daily upon the uncertainties of sea and storm."[21]

THE SOLUTION

The Dole. The problem of the food supply for the city of Rome was closely related to the availability of the main staples. Through the acquisition and governance of empire, Rome was in an unrivalled position to regulate and direct trade in foodstuffs. Rome also received a considerable volume of surplus cereal production as tax or rent from the provinces, notably Egypt, Africa and Sicily.[22] Surplus production of other needed commodities expanded in the provinces; for example, Spain and Africa emerged as major exporters of olive oil under the Principate.[23]

The state never developed its own merchant fleet, relying instead on private shipping agencies to transport the goods to Rome.[24] It is clear, however, that a number of inducements were offered to encourage this trade: direct payments and subsidies, tax breaks and social distinctions (such as the grant of citizenship).[25] The stages by which these measures were introduced and the details of their application are not fully understood, but it is evident that in the late Republic and early Principate the state did adopt measures that amounted to the underwriting or subsidization of transport costs on a significant amount of goods being brought to Rome. Much 'trade' activity at the ports of Rome was thus founded on redistributive principles or could be described as 'tied' in nature. In this manner the state sought to guarantee that adequate supplies of a range of foodstuffs were available in the city.

The distribution of food (whether free or at a reduced price) is a separate but related issue. The first grain law in Rome was passed at the urging of Gaius Gracchus in 123 BC, and introduced the principle of monthly sales of grain at a reduced price.[26] The main threats to the grain supply in the 1st century BC came from the series of civil wars that led to the demise of the Republic and piracy, and at various points the Gracchan system of subsidized cereals fell into abeyance, only to be revived in modified form through popular pressure when conditions allowed.[27] It is important to stress that the initial schemes were all limited to 'adult' male citizens (with some citizen groups, such as freedmen, perhaps excluded) and provided grain at a reduced price, not free. A large percentage of the free poor, even if eligible, may not have been able to take full advantage of these schemes due to poverty.

A major change occurred in 58 BC with the passage of the grain law of Clodius.[28] This seems to have introduced a number of novel concepts: the free distribution of grain, the inclusion of freedmen of citizen status, the lowering of the minimum qualifying age to 10. All these measures greatly expanded the list of those eligible to this form of state assistance, while for the first time making the system more favourable for poorer citizens. The cost of such an expanded system was seen by many conservatives as exorbitant and the new measure met some determined opposition in the senate. By 46 BC there were 320,000 eligible for the individual allotment of 5 *modii* per month (an annual total of *c.* 400 kg per person – enough to keep two people at subsistence level). Consequently, Caesar reduced this number by half[29] and Augustus likewise seems to have limited his distributions to a male citizen pool that numbered *c.* 150,000–200,000, excluding some groups such as recently manumitted slaves from those eligible.[30] Although there were some additions and some growth in the size of this privileged group under the Principate, it probably never exceeded 250,000 again. To put it another way, only one quarter of the estimated populace of the city was eligible for free grain (though perhaps twice that number could be sustained on the grain distributed). At the beginning of the 3rd century AD, Septimius Severus added a ration of free olive oil to the grain dole, and later in the same century, Aurelian added pork and wine to the list of foods given to dole recipients.[31]

The needs of those ineligible for the grain dole, notably the non-citizen free poor, could not be ignored entirely by the state. As we shall see, the supply system that was developed to bring the dole grain to Rome had a wider remit. To an increasing extent, the state undertook to ensure that adequate supplies of a range of foods were available at reasonable prices in the markets of Rome. It is important not to focus on the detail of the dole to the exclusion of this significant additional role of the *annona* system.

Harbours and Warehouses. The unsatisfactory harbour arrangements for Rome continued until AD 42, when the pressing need for a good harbour at the mouth of the Tiber compelled the emperor Claudius to undertake the construction of an enormous artificial harbour. About 4 km north of Ostia, Claudius excavated out of the coastline a gigantic basin over 1,000 m wide. He also cut canals connecting the new harbour with the Tiber and had two moles built up to shelter the harbour from the sea.[32] Even in this new harbour, known as 'Portus', ships were still not immune from storms, since Tacitus records that 200 ships within the moles were sunk in a storm in AD 62 (*Annals* 15.18). Evidently, some part of the important Alexandrian grain fleets continued to unload at Puteoli.[33] The problem of storms was finally solved by Trajan, who excavated a hexagonal inner harbour basin 700 m in diameter, within which ships were evidently safe (Fig. 7.1).[34]

At Rome itself, both banks of the Tiber to the south of Tiber Island served as an extensive unloading zone for ships. Excavations have revealed quays of finely dressed stone along the riverbanks, with giant stone rings to which the ships tied up, as well as ramps to facilitate unloading. Such facilities were especially concentrated in the area to the south of the Aventine hill, known as the Emporium district (Fig. 7.2).[35]

Ostia, Portus, and Rome all contained numerous warehouses (*horrea*) and, indeed, the sophistication, number, and size of these storage structures are eloquent testimony to the scale and importance of Rome's imports.[36] Although there is some variation, the structure of most *horrea* was an open courtyard with small rooms opening onto it from four sides. Warehouses were frequently multi-storied structures, with the upper levels accessible by staircases and ramps. Some of the Roman warehouses were truly enormous structures. The *Horrea Galbana* contained 140 rooms on the ground floor alone, which covered *c.* 20,000 m^2.[37]

Fig. 7.2: General view of the wharves in the Emporium area (Photo: editors).

Fig. 7.4: Monte Testaccio: detail (Photo: editors).

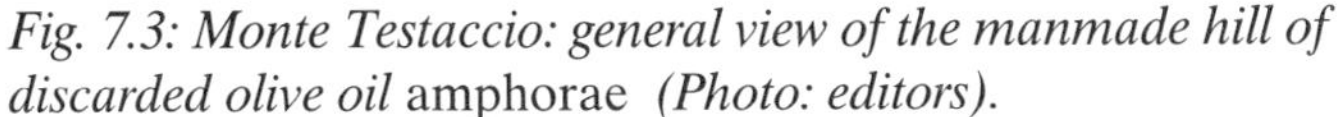

Fig. 7.3: Monte Testaccio: general view of the manmade hill of discarded olive oil amphorae *(Photo: editors).*

Fig. 7.5: Dressel 20 amphorae, *Tarragona, Spain (Photo: editors).*

These *horrea*, particularly those used to store grain, were constructed with considerable care. Since grain must be kept dry and free of vermin to prevent spoilage, many warehouses had raised floors which helped to keep the grain free of moisture and at an optimal temperature. In addition, warehouses were very solidly built, with thick walls (at least 60 cm, and frequently 1 m thick), and usually a space was left between adjoining warehouses as a deterrent to fire. Finally, in keeping with the value and importance of the items stored within them, the Roman *horrea* demonstrate a great concern with security. Within the structure, large square windows connected one room to another for ventilation, but the windows which pierced the outer walls were always placed high on the wall and were very narrow to prevent theft. There were also only the minimum number of exterior windows necessary for ventilation. The door frames of the *horrea* at Ostia preserve traces of elaborate systems of locks and bolts on both the doors to the individual rooms and on those to the warehouse complex as a whole. Also, probably for security purposes, entrances connecting the *horrea* to the outside were remarkably few, and these doors had locks which were fastened from both the outside and the inside. Often, there were only two or three external doors, even for very large complexes. In addition, the doorways themselves were quite narrow, often less than 1.5 m in width. As Rickman stresses, the narrow entrances and multiple levels of Roman warehouses demonstrate that goods were transported by manpower alone without the use of carts or draft animals.[38] Such a system would have required an enormous number of labourers employed solely as porters.

This scale of portage is particularly impressive when the mountain of ceramic 'empties' (Monte Testaccio) south of the Aventine is considered. This is 35m high and covers 20,000 square metres. It is made up entirely of broken olive-oil *amphorae* discarded over a comparatively short period (*c.* AD 140–250), and represents approximately 53 million vessels! (Figs. 7.3 & 7.4)[39] The latter are mainly 'Dressel Type 20' from southern Spain, which, because they are particularly thick-walled and durable, may be over-represented (Fig. 7.5).[40] Oil *amphorae* were usually discarded and broken up after the contents were decanted because their inner surface absorbed oil which went rancid. However, from the Hadrianic period onwards, one reuse of complete Dressel 20s was to lighten architectural vaulting, for example in the Circus of Maxentius (Fig. 7.6).[41]

Commercial Organization of the Supply System: The Guilds. The complexity of Rome's logistical system can be illustrated by tracing the path of commodities once the ships carrying them arrived at the mouth of the Tiber.[42] As Casson points out, when a ship arrived at the mouth of the harbour, "it had to present its ship's papers, be acknowledged by the harbourmaster, be assessed the appropriate port fees, and, most immediately, be assigned and conducted to a berth."[43] He suggests that the boat that met the incoming ship was also the one that would tow it to its assigned berth. Once the ship was tied up, the cargo had to be unloaded by gangs of men and then either trans-shipped to river barges for the journey to Rome, or transported to and stored in a warehouse. Eventually, the cargo was taken from the warehouse and loaded into specialized river boats, which were then towed up the Tiber to Rome; this stage could, and probably often did, take place a considerable time after the ship had first been unloaded. The journey-time was anything between 2 and 3 days, compared with half a day by road.[44] Once at Rome, the process of unloading and storing at warehouses had to be repeated. Finally, of course, the cargo was distributed to its actual place of consumption. At every stage of this process, there were officials and overseers monitoring the exchanges, comparing the commodity to official weights and measures, perhaps collecting taxes, and insuring that none of the cargo mysteriously disappeared. This process involved many thousands of people, including imperial officials, commercial associations, individual merchants, various guilds of boatmen, and a great many porters and dockworkers.

There appear to have been three main types of boats used in the harbours and on the Tiber: the *scaphae* and *lintres*, the *lenunculi*, and the *codicariae*. The *scaphae*, *lintres*, and *lenunculi* seem to have all been rowboats; *scaphae* and *lintres* simply designate any one of a variety of light rowboats used for a myriad of purposes around harbours, whereas the *lenunculi* were larger boats with multiple oarsmen.[45] There were five guilds of *lenuncularii* at Ostia.[46] The largest and most important of these was the *lenuncularii tabularii auxiliarii*. In AD 192, this guild had 258 members and listed Roman senators among its patrons.[47] The *lenuncularii tabularii auxiliarii* were probably the boats that met incoming merchant ships at the mouth of the harbour and towed them to their assigned berths.[48] A second guild was the *lenuncularii pleromarii auxiliarii*, which in AD 200 had only sixteen members.[49] Meiggs identifies these as the boats which lightened larger merchantmen at sea before entering the Tiber.[50] This was undoubtedly a much larger guild prior to the construction of Claudius' harbour. A third guild was the *lenuncularii traiectus Luculli*, who were ferrymen.[51] The function of the remaining two guilds of *lenuncularii* is uncertain, although there are three additional ferry services mentioned in inscriptions: the *traiectus marmorariorum*, the *traiectus togatensium*, and the *traiectus rusticelius*.[52]

The final important group of boats was the *naves codicariae*. These were the highly specialized vessels used to transport goods from Ostia and Portus up the Tiber to Rome, and which were towed upriver by teams of men or animals. The 22-mile trip (32 km) up the Tiber took up to three days, and the average size of these boats may have been about 70 tons.[53] *Codicariae* are easily identifiable in sculptural reliefs and mosaics by their lone, lowerable mast stepped extremely far forward, which was used for towing. Another distinctive feature of *codicariae* was a series of cleats on the mast, which enabled the crew to climb up it. These cleats were necessary since, because the mast could be lowered, the ship lacked standing rigging which was normally used for this purpose.[54] The guild of the *codicarii* lasted at least into the 4th century AD, indicating the vital role they played in supplying the city's food.[55] The *codicariae* were apparently hauled by manpower rather than by animals.[56] Martial alludes to the rhythmic chant of these boathaulers, known as *helciarii*, as they trudged along the towpaths by the Tiber (Martial 4.64). In addition to the Ostian *codicarii*, there was an entirely separate group of *codicarii* who transported goods between Rome and points further upriver.[57]

The size, variety, and specialization of the boats used at the harbours and on the Tiber were impressive. However, the boatmen made up only one group of guilds out of many. Their subdivisions and duties have been described at some length to serve as a representative example illustrating the complexity of the Ostian guilds involved in the transportation of goods to Rome. In the other guilds as well, a similar degree of specialization and complexity probably existed. There were many guilds associated with the construction and maintenance of ships. The *fabri navales*, the shipbuilders' guild, listed 320 ordinary members in the late 2nd century AD.[58] Other related guilds include the *stuppatores* (the caulkers), and the *restiones* (the ropemakers).[59] Not surprisingly, porters' guilds were particularly numerous; among these were the *saccarii* (the carriers of sacks of grain), the *phalangarii* (the carriers of *amphorae*), the *saburrarii* (who carried the sand used for ballast on and off the ships), and the *geruli* (the stevedores). Other important guilds connected to the harbour activity included the *mensores frumentarii* (who measured grain as it was unloaded from the ships and also when it was loaded onto the *codicariae*), the *horrearii* (the warehouse workers), the *custodiarii* (the warehouse guards), the *lignarii* (the timber dealers), the *collegium fabrum tignuariorum* (the general construction workers, whose guild listed 350 members in AD 198[60]), and finally, the *urinatores*, divers whose job was to recover goods that fell overboard while being unloaded.

These were some of the guilds associated with the actual physical handling of merchandise or with the construction of equipment and buildings around the docks. There were, of course, also guilds for the owners of the goods, most notably the grain, wine, and oil merchants. In Ostia, many of these guilds appear to have had offices located in the so-called Piazzale delle Corporazioni, a large rectangular colonnade with 61 small rooms opening off it.[61] In front of each room was a mosaic apparently illustrating or advertising the type of guild or the commercial services of the owner. Also many of these offices seem to have been occupied by merchants or shippers from various cities in Gaul and North Africa associated with the supply of commodities to Rome.[62] Grain merchants are heavily represented, but so are shippers in other goods including possibly exotic animals.[63]

Merchants and Shippers. The role and particularly the identity and status of the 'middlemen' who brought the grain and other foodstuffs to Rome are matters of debate. Further, the distinctions between ship owners, captains, and merchants are not always clear.[64] The state possessed a navy, but not a merchant marine. Therefore even state-owned grain from imperial estates intended for the dole had to be shipped by private merchants and shippers working under contract to the state. The very fact that there were enough shippers to keep Rome supplied with sufficient food indicates that there were profits to be made in shipping foodstuffs to Rome. The potential for making a considerable profit in overseas trade is attested in numerous literary sources.[65] One way to attempt to determine who these traders were is to consider who possessed the capital necessary to invest in such ventures.

Overseas trade entailed a substantial risk in terms of capital due to the expense of both cargo and ships.[66] However, the group that probably possessed the most wealth, the senatorial aristocracy, was at least technically forbidden from engaging in overseas trade by the *plebiscitum Claudianum* of 219–218 BC, which decreed that no senator or senator's son could own an ocean-going ship with a capacity of more than 300 *amphora*e, since trade was thought to be beneath the senators' dignity.[67] Perhaps a stronger impediment to senatorial involvement in trade, however, was the prevailing social ethos which considered trade a sordid occupation in which gentlemen should not participate. According to this ethos, the only proper source of wealth for aristocrats was land-ownership and agriculture. According to Cicero, "of all things from which one may acquire, none is better than agriculture, none more fruitful, none sweeter, none more fitting for a free man." (*De Officiis* 1.151). The most eloquent description of this attitude and the most forceful expression of its primacy is to be found in Finley's influential book, *The Ancient Economy*.[68] In his view, the possibility of loss of status effectively precluded direct senatorial involvement in trade for profit.

Most of the *negotiatores*, *mercatores*, and *navicularii* engaged in trade appear to be freedmen, foreigners and other low-status individuals.[69] One solution to the dilemma of funding is the suggestion that senators served as invisible partners in commerce, providing the financial backing for the freedmen and slaves whose names appear on inscriptions as merchants and shippers. Thus the freedmen and others acted as 'agents' for the senators.[70] While the solid evidence for such transactions is meagre, it certainly seems possible that silent partnerships between senators and their agents existed. It is unlikely, however, that the majority of merchants and shippers were simply agents for senators, if for no other reason than the scale of trade.[71] It seems entirely possible that many of these merchants and shippers were independent operators, as suggested by the numerous dedications and funerary monuments that they left.[72]

Although the state did not have a merchant marine service of its own, the emperors were clearly concerned with ensuring that there were adequate numbers of shippers bringing essential supplies to the city of Rome. Claudius passed legislation aimed at encouraging shippers to import grain to Rome. His legislation decreed that anyone who owned a ship with a capacity of at least 10,000 *modii* (about 70 tons) and who employed that ship in bringing grain to the city for at least six years would, if he were a Roman citizen, gain exemption from the *lex Papia Poppaea* which penalized the childless. If the owner were a woman, she would gain the privileges granted to mothers of four children. Non-citizens would be rewarded with Roman citizenship itself.[73] Similar incentives offering exemptions from various taxes and liturgies were added by Nero and by several 2nd century emperors.[74]

It has also been suggested that a considerable percentage of Rome's population was supported by an 'internal supply' operating outside of regular market mechanisms. This 'internal supply' consisted of the senatorial and equestrian upper classes acting out the aristocratic ethos of self-sufficiency by importing foodstuffs from their own estates for the consumption of themselves and their extended households, including such dependants as slaves and other retainers.[75] Again, while this mechanism may have accounted for some of the supply for the city, the size of the overall demand was much greater (for the scale of foodstuffs, see below). Additionally even if a sizeable percentage of Rome's supply were privately imported from the estates of the wealthy for consumption by their households, the foodstuffs still had to be transported to Rome by shippers, most of whom were probably private contractors.

One likely source of merchants and shippers is the local provincial elites around the empire, particularly those from important port cities in regions that exported goods to Rome. The wealthy *Augustales* found in coastal cities in Spain, Gaul, Italy, and Africa, whose benefactions adorned their local towns, may well have made their fortunes in overseas trade.[76] For these men the wealth gained in trade and then invested in land led to local magistracies, particularly for their sons, and sometimes ultimately to high status in Rome itself. The prosperity of gateway cities such as Lepcis Magna in Tripolitania, with their luxurious public buildings and private villas adorned with expensive marbles, indicates the wealth that could be gained by local elites controlling large-scale agricultural surpluses and engaging in maritime trade.[77] Therefore, while trade was viewed as an improper occupation for an aristocrat, wealthy men including senators were probably often at least indirectly involved in overseas trade, and such commerce offered an opportunity for others to join the ranks of the wealthy which could lead ultimately even to elite status itself.

The Administration of the Supply System. Another way of gauging the complexity and sophistication of Rome's food supply system is to attempt to determine the size and the degree of active involvement by the imperial administration.[78] In the Republic, there was a *quaestor Ostiensis* whose job was to oversee the transport and storage of grain at Ostia.[79] Around AD 7 or 8, Augustus first created the office of *praefectus annonae*, the official of equestrian status, primarily responsible for overseeing and ensuring an adequate grain supply.[80] It is interesting to note that the first *praefectus annonae*, C. Turranius Gracilius, held the post of prefect of Egypt immediately before being assigned the prefecture of the *annona*. On account of the importance of Egypt to the grain supply, his experience and connections in Egypt certainly made him a logical choice for the job of overseeing the food supply of Rome.[81] Various subordinate posts quickly multiplied. In the 1st century AD, the chief assistant to the *praefectus annonae* was termed an *adiutor*. By the end of the 2nd century, this official had become the *sub-praefectus annonae*, was directly appointed by the emperor, and received a salary of 100,000 sesterces.[82] From the time of Claudius, there were various special financial officers based at the main harbours, including the procurator of the port (*procurator portus*), and the procurator of the grain supply at Ostia (*procurator annonae Ostis*).[83] It is somewhat surprising that in addition to the numerous honorific inscriptions dedicated to the *procurator annonae Ostis* by the corn merchants,[84] there are many dedications from the *fabri tignuarii*, the construction workers' guild.[85] These honorific inscriptions certainly suggest that the official duties of these procurators extended beyond simply overseeing the grain *annona*. Beneath each procurator were a variety of lesser officials such as *cornicularii, dispensatores, beneficiarii,* and a whole range of *tabularii*, official measurers.[86] One of these *tabularii* of Ostia advanced through a series of financial posts, eventually rising to the procuratorship of Belgica.[87]

Many of these officials seem to have made careers specializing in supply posts. Sextus Julius Possessor was, at various points during his career, assistant to the prefect of the

Fig. 7.6: Re-used amphorae *(form Dressel 23, the successor to Dressel 20) in vaulting beneath the seating of the Circus Maxentius (Photo: editors).*

*Fig. 7.7: Ostia: large storage jars (*dolia*) for storage of olive oil or wine, set into the floor of a warehouse in* Reg. *I.iv.5. Such warehouses attest to the scale of oil and wine consumption in ancient Rome (Photo: editors).*

annona in charge of warehouses at Portus and Ostia (*adiutor praefecti annonae ad horrea Ostiensia et Portuensia*), procurator in charge of the banks of the river Baetis in southern Spain (*procurator ad ripam Baetis*), procurator of the *annona* at Ostia (*procurator Augusti ad annonam Ostis*), and *procurator ad Mercurium*, a district of Alexandria associated with grain storage.[88] Plainly, he fashioned an entire career in the administrative posts involved with the supply of the city. He began at Rome itself as an *adiutor* to the prefect of the *annona*. After this post he was dispatched to Spain. Baetica in southern Spain was one of the most important suppliers to Rome of several essential commodities, including olive oil, wine, and *garum*, a popular salty, fermented fish sauce. The river Baetis (modern Guadalquivir) was the main transport link between the agricultural heartlands of Baetica and the sea.[89] As procurator of the river banks, his primary duty would probably have been to facilitate the steady movement of these supplies, whose ultimate destination was Rome. His next post was back in Italy as a procurator at the port of Ostia. Finally, since the single most important part of Rome's supply system was probably the annual grain fleets from Alexandria in Egypt, it is no surprise to find that this specialist in the supply of Rome is next known to have been in charge of the Alexandrian grain warehouses. Although his career comprised a variety of posts both in Rome and in several provinces, Possessor clearly specialized throughout his life in the supply of food to the city of Rome.

There were probably many other imperial officials with specialized duties. One example of this is recorded on the tombstone of T. Flavius Stephanus who, between inscribed pictures of two camels and an elephant, is described as having been the *praepositus camelorum*.[90] Meiggs suggests that this was a post in charge of overseeing the supply of exotic animals to the city.[91] There was certainly an active trade in animals for beast hunts and arena displays, so that the existence of such a post is not surprising.[92] It does, however, indicate the extensive and active role of the state in supervising the supply of all commodities, no matter how unusual or specialized. The presence and involvement of such administrators was not limited to Ostia alone. There were officials in charge of the banks and river bed of the Tiber itself, the *curatores alvei Tiberis et riparum* and their *adiutors*.[93] They had a variety of duties, including the drawing of boundaries along the riverbank,[94] the monitoring of the *lenuncularii*,[95] and also probably overseeing the dredging of the river and tow-path maintenance. The *annona* officials had offices at both Ostia and Rome, and many of the other imperial officials undoubtedly did as well. The imperial organization formed a coherent unit encompassing Portus, Ostia, the Tiber, and Rome itself.

Dedications by construction workers to the *procurator annonae Ostis* suggest that the duties of officials connected with the *annona* extended far beyond simply overseeing the supply of grain for the dole. The construction and maintenance of port and warehouse facilities is but one such area of their work. The comprehensiveness of their duties is best illustrated by examining the interest shown by *annona* officials in ensuring and promoting the supply of olive oil to the city long before this commodity was first officially distributed by the state by order of Septimius Severus.[96] An inscription dating to the reign of Hadrian, three-quarters of a century before the olive oil dole was instituted, records an honorific dedication to the *praefectus annonae*, C. Junius Flavianus, by the grain and olive merchants of Africa, (*mercatores frumentarii et olearii Afrari*).[97] That the grain and olive merchants would set up a joint monument to the *praefectus annonae* indicates that these two groups had parallel relationships to the prefect.[98] It is easy to think of reasons why the grain merchants would be grateful to the *praefectus annonae,* but the fact that the olive merchants were similarly grateful strongly suggests that he also played an active role in the importation of olive oil, and that the olive merchants had frequent interactions with him even before olive oil became a part of the dole. This type of connection is made even more explicit by an honorific inscription to M. Petronius Honoratus, the prefect of the *annona* from AD 144–146/7, in which he is hailed as a patron (*patronus*) by the olive merchants from Baetica (*negotiatores olearii ex Baetica*).[99] He subsequently went on to become the prefect of Egypt, in which post the experience and connections he had developed as prefect of the *annona* were no doubt very useful.

Not only were *annona* officials interested in and involved with the oil supply, but there were also state officials specifically charged with guaranteeing an adequate supply of olive oil. During the reign of Antoninus Pius, one C. Pomponius Turpilianus is identified as the *procurator ad oleum in Galba Ostiae portus utriusque*.[100] His job was evidently to supervise the passage of oil through the enormous *Horrea Galbana*.[101] Because oil was constantly moving through these warehouses, and since ensuring a sufficient supply of oil was clearly a concern of the state, his appointment to this post represents not merely a short-term or exceptional case, but rather his job is probably a permanent position. Antoninus Pius once gave free distributions of grain, wine, and olive oil to the populace and no doubt such imperial distributions were greatly facilitated by the existence of imperial officials such as Turpilianus who were already deeply involved in the supply of these basic foodstuffs (SHA, *Antoninus Pius* 8.11).

Finally, there is even evidence that the state dispatched officials to the provinces to promote the export of olive oil in the period before it had become a part of the *annona*. An inscription from Hispalis dating to about AD 166 records that Sextus Julius Possessor was assistant to the prefect of the *annona*, Ulpius Saturninus, and that Possessor was in charge of counting and perhaps meeting quotas in Spanish and African oil, for overseeing its transportation, and for paying the shippers.[102] That a high official of the *annona*, an *adiutor praefecti annonae,* was sent on a mission to Spain and Africa to promote the supply of olive oil is a clear indication that the officials of the *annona* were intimately involved in ensuring an adequate supply of a range of foodstuffs to Rome – not just grain.[103] Additionally, it is important to note that this inscription contains an explicit reference to shippers being contracted and paid by the state to transport oil to Rome long before oil had become a part of *annona* distributions.[104]

SCALE

In addition to its complexity, a second significant aspect of the supply of Rome was its scale. Although attempts at quantifying ancient trade are highly dangerous and the results are often questionable, determining general orders of magnitude can be illuminating as long as one keeps in mind that these are only rough approximations. Undoubtedly, the three main foods imported to Rome were those staples of the Mediterranean diet, grain, olive oil, and wine.[105] In this section, we shall attempt to determine a rough order of magnitude for the scale of imports of these three essential items to the city of Rome, and then point out some of the implications which can be drawn from these calculations.

Assuming that the average inhabitant of Rome consumed 237 kg of wheat per year, multiplied by a million people (the estimated population of the city in the imperial period), yields 237,000 metric tons of wheat required for the city of Rome per year.[106] If this number is divided by the estimated average ship capacity of 250 tons, the wheat supply of Rome would necessitate a minimum of 948 shiploads of wheat each year.[107] The risk of a high rate of loss or spoilage at sea would have required the state to arrange for transport of substantially more than this minimum figure. The total number of ships carrying grain to Rome would have been higher still since large amounts of barley were also being imported, particularly for use as animal fodder.

For olive oil, we have used an average consumption rate of 20 litres per person per year.[108] As a figure for personal consumption, this could easily be a low estimate. In a study of modern Methana, average olive oil consumption was 50 kg per person per year.[109] In addition to its value as food, olive oil had many other significant functions in antiquity, such as its usage in medicine, for bathing, for lighting, and for perfumes. In Rome, with its gigantic imperial baths and its concentration of elite households, many thousands of litres would surely have been consumed for these purposes.[110] But the minimal figure of 20 litres per person per year multiplied by a million people yields 18,000 metric tons of oil (Fig. 7.7). To this must be added an additional 8,000 metric tons weight to account for the weight of the 285,714 *amphorae* in which the oil was transported,[111] for a total annual cargo of 26,000 tons. Divided by 250 tons per ship, this yields an absolute minimum of 104 shiploads of oil per year. Once again, the transport of larger quantities will have been necessary in order to guarantee this minimum level of provision.

For wine, we have somewhat arbitrarily chosen an average rate of consumption of 100 litres per person per year. While adult males probably drank more, this figure allows for children, women, and slaves, all of whom most likely consumed far less than adult males.[112] Again, multiplied by one million inhabitants, this results in 100,000,000 litres per year of wine or about 100,000 metric tons. Adding another 60,000 tons for the weight of the 4,000,000 *amphorae* results in a total weight of 160,000 metric tons per year.[113] Again, dividing by an average ship weight of 250 tons yields a total of 640 shiploads per year of wine.

Therefore, an absolute minimum figure for the number of shiploads necessary to carry a year's supply of wheat, oil, and wine for the city of Rome is 1,692. The prime sailing season, when most of Rome's imports arrived, probably lasted only a little over 100 days (April to September);[114] thus, during this period an average of *c.* 17 ships per day would have been arriving at Rome's ports.[115]

As a check on our computations, we calculated the calories provided by our hypothetical diet of grain, oil, and wine. Using the caloric values of 9,000 cal/kg of oil, 3,000 cal/kg of wheat, and 500 cal/kg of wine, resulted in a daily intake of 2,326 calories per person.[116] This figure is lower than those suggested by modern subsistence data: 3,822 cal/day for an extremely active male, 3,337 cal/day for a very active male, and 2,852 cal/day for a moderately active male.[117] However, once adjusted for the presence of other foods in the diet, such as fruits and vegetables, as well as for the lower requirements of women and children, our average caloric figure of 2,326 cal/day seems reasonable, or at least of the right order of magnitude for a minimum value.

Such quantification is also useful for attempting to estimate the scale of labour necessary in order to move all of these goods from the ships to Rome. Since this transportation involved numerous loadings and unloadings between the merchant vessels and the warehouses in Rome, *amphorae* and grain sacks were made to be about the maximum weight that an individual porter, or pair of porters, could carry. A year's supply of 20,000,000 litres of oil translates into about 285,714 *amphorae*, and 100,000,000 litres of wine would require 4,000,000 *amphorae*.[118] 237,000 tons of wheat equals 4,740,000 sacks.[119] Totalling the number of annual individual man-size loads of these commodities results in over 9,300,000 'porter-loads' per year.[120] Although the eventual transport of these commodities up the Tiber could be stretched out over the entire year, the ships had to be unloaded as soon as possible and the goods stored in a nearby warehouse. If the ships were unloaded in the 100-day peak sailing period, this process would necessitate 93,000 porter-loads per day. To push this calculation a bit further, if each trip by each porter took 15 minutes, and they worked nine hours a day with one hour off for lunch and other breaks, simply unloading the ships in the most basic way would have demanded a force of around 3,000 labourers.[121] This process of loading and unloading had to be repeated many times before the commodities eventually were distributed at Rome. While this type of calculation is extremely speculative, it does suggest the enormous amounts of labour demanded by the system.

The trip up the Tiber in the *codicariae* offers another opportunity for quantification. Assuming an average tonnage of 70 tons per boat,[122] 6,043 Tiber trips would be required to transport the 423,000 metric tons of grain, oil, and wine to Rome. At a minimum round trip time of one week, allowing time for loading and unloading, and assuming that this transport was spread out evenly over the entire year, a minimum of 116 *codicariae* would have been needed. Since the Tiber's ease of navigability varied throughout the course of the year, river transport was probably concentrated in the more favorable months. If the river shipping season were 10, 8, or 6 months long, the number of *codicariae* needed would have been 151, 189 or 252 respectively. How much of an underestimate these calculations might be is indicated by Tacitus' comment that in AD 62 a storm sank 200 vessels at Portus and a fire destroyed an additional 100 at Rome itself (*Annals* 15.18). All of the boats burnt at Rome were *codicariae*, but it seems likely that many of the ships sunk by the storm at Portus were other types of vessel. Yet, despite the loss of 300 boats, enough remained to ensure that there was no resultant food shortage.

All of these calculations are probably underestimates. As previously mentioned, we have not taken into account oil used for non-ingestive purposes, nor other grains such as barley. There was also certainly considerable spoilage and loss which occurred during shipping and at all stages of transport, necessitating arrangements for overprovision of these commodities above and beyond the minimum requirements. There were innumerable minor goods also passing through the system, ranging from exotic foods to manufactured goods and luxury wares. The daily requirements of the city were frequently augmented by lavish imperial handouts at public feasts or religious festivals. In 46 BC, in celebration of one of his triumphs, Julius Caesar is said to have given away 10 *modii* of grain (about 67 kg) and 10 Roman pounds of olive oil (about 3.3 kg) to every member of the Roman plebs then receiving the grain dole; at this time this may have numbered over 300,000 (Suetonius, *Julius Caesar* 38).[123] Only a few distributions of this scale would quickly boost the import calculations, and the emperors often gave such largesse.[124]

The confusion and bustle at Portus and Ostia would have been even more intense than we have described because the ships tended to arrive in multiples or even in great fleets rather than being spread evenly through the sailing season. If we accept that at the peak of the season, ships were arriving at Ostia and Portus far in excess of our notional average of 17 ships per day, then it follows that labour provision, storage capacity, and river haulage must have been organized on a far grander scale in order to cope with the volume of traffic. Seneca (*Letters* 77.1–3) offers an eyewitness account of such an occasion at Puteoli:

> "Unexpectedly, today, Alexandrian ships appeared within sight, those which are usually sent ahead and announce the arrival of a fleet behind them; they call them mail-boats, a welcome sight in Campania. A vast mob stood on the docks at Puteoli and spotted the Alexandrians from the configuration of their sails, despite the great mob of ships.....In the midst of this turmoil, as everyone rushed to the water's edge, I took great pleasure in my leisure."

This passage reveals a number of important points. First, the arrival of the grain ships was unexpected; this stresses the uncertain nature of ancient sailing. Second, the fleet sent messenger boats ahead, clearly in order to give the port time to prepare for its arrival (and perhaps time for people to gather from the countryside in expectation of employment unloading the ships). Finally, the passage suggests the excitement and importance of the arrival of the main supply fleets.

FOOD SUPPLY AND LABOUR PROVISION

As has been demonstrated above, the supply system would have demanded thousands of unskilled labourers in Ostia, Portus, and Rome, especially at the peak periods of activity during the summer. The sporadic nature of this demand required a large number of unemployed, or at least underemployed, people to be available whenever demand surged. The only group of potential labour that appears to meet these two requirements of size and constant availability was the urban plebs.[125] As Brunt has shown, the urban plebs cannot have subsisted solely on the grain dole. They would have both needed and wanted at least occasional employment as wage labourers.[126] While it would be theoretically possible for a segment of the urban populace to subsist on the grain dole, the urban plebs would have needed cash in order to pay for other basic essentials such as lodging and clothes. They would also certainly have wanted to earn money in order to supplement their free diet of bread and water with other foods such as wine, oil, fish, and the occasional vegetable or piece of meat.

The sheer number of workers required, together with the erratic nature of the demand, rules out the exclusive use of slave or criminal labour. Although some of the more permanent or skilled jobs were probably held by slaves, most of the labour cannot have been servile because the great seasonal fluctuations in labour would have left the slave owners with masses of idle or severely underemployed slaves to be fed, clothed, and housed during the periods of low labour demand. Therefore much of this labour must have been provided by the urban plebs themselves. That they also worked in addition to receiving the dole is supported by Suetonius (*Augustus* 40) who records that Augustus was concerned about the loss of work that occurred on the days when the plebs went to receive their ration. He attempted to alleviate this loss by distributing the grain three times a year rather than every month, but protests were so great that he abandoned the scheme. There may be another reference to this loss of work in a letter of Cicero to Atticus, in which Cicero complains that the builders working on his house have temporarily left in order to go collect their grain dole.[127] Clearly substantial numbers of the urban plebs found employment on public works as evidenced by Vespasian's famous rejection of a suggestion for a labour saving device to move columns by saying that he has an obligation to feed the plebs (Suetonius, *Vespasian* 18).[128]

In general the supply system of Rome must have provided employment for thousands both at Rome and all over the Mediterranean, particularly in the regions which were major exporters of foodstuffs such as southern Spain, North Africa, and Egypt. In each of these regions thousands of people were employed not only in the actual farming, but also in a variety of related occupations such as making *amphorae*, operating presses, transporting the agricultural products by land and river, overseeing production and transport, and shipping the goods to Rome.[129] Most of these people would have been aware that their livelihood was a result of the needs of the capital city, and of the special interest and involvement of the emperors and of the state in ensuring an adequate supply of food. This awareness and the resulting gratitude is exemplified by an incident in which Augustus, who had been a prominent figure in the institutionalization of Rome's supply system, was sailing in the gulf of Puteoli near the very end of his life. As his ship passed by a newly arrived Alexandrian ship, the crew of the Alexandrian ship, crowned with garlands and burning incense, hailed Augustus with lavish praise and good wishes, and declared that it was because of him that they lived, sailed the seas, enjoyed liberty, and made their fortunes (Suetonius, *Augustus* 98).

CONCLUSION

The size and complexity of both the guilds and the imperial bureaucracy concerned with the food supply of Rome, coupled with even minimalistic calculations of the scale of the goods that moved through this system, strongly suggest that the entire system was more complex and more deliberately organized than has often been admitted. The supply of the capital city was clearly an issue of concern to the emperors, who expended huge resources in order to insure that its inhabitants were fed.[130] The interest of the state was not limited to grain alone, and the duties of the *praefectus annonae* and his subordinates clearly extended to other foodstuffs. In addition, the variety of officials concerned with often rather specialized commodities, such as wild beasts, is another indication of both the size of the system and the involvement of the state. Another notable aspect of the imperial administration was the considerable professionalism achieved by some of its officials, particularly at middle and lower levels, who seem to have made entire careers specializing in the supply of the city. The contacts and informal networks with guilds and merchants that these officials built up in one post undoubtedly carried over from post to post, and played a role in the smooth operation of the system. Although much attention, both ancient and modern, has focused on food riots and shortages,[131] a far more significant point is how well the system worked. Despite the shortages, there were no real instances of widespread starvation for hundreds of years. Overall, the logistical institutions of Rome were remarkably successful in achieving the difficult feat of feeding a million people year after year in a pre-industrial society. The very success of the system and the enormous scale on which it operated imply a high degree of sophistication and organization. The size of this system demanded vast amounts of labour at all stages. Much of this labour was drawn from the freeborn population rather than from the slave sector, and this factor provides at least a partial counter to the popular image of a huge mass of idle urban plebs concerned only with 'bread and circuses.'[132] Many must have found at least occasional work in the organization which existed to provide subsidized or free handouts of food for them. Much of the information gathered in this paper is fairly well-known, but it is often presented separately; when put together, a coherent picture emerges of a system that was complex and sophisticated, and in which the state must have played an active role. The perception of the network which supplied commodities to Rome as a random or improvised patchwork is at odds with the realities of the organization and scale of the system itself.

ACKNOWLEDGEMENTS

This paper is a re-edited and revised version of the text given at the Oxford conference and subsequently published in 1999 (ALDRETE and MATTINGLY 1999). We are grateful to the University of Michigan Press for permission to adapt the paper for the present volume, and to the editors of this volume for their help in giving the text a fresh appearance. The editors would particularly like to acknowledge the great deal of work put into this paper by Emma Saunders to prepare it for publication.

NOTES

1 On the population of Rome in the early empire, see HOPKINS 1978, 96–8.

2 On the debate about transportation in the Roman world, and on the relative costs of water versus land transport, see note 18 below. On sea travel in general, see CASSON 1971 and ROUGE 1981. On speed of communication by water, see DUNCAN-JONES 1990, 7–29. On roads, see CHEVALLIER 1976.

3 On the grain supply in general, see RICKMAN 1980; GARNSEY 1983; 1988. On the administration of the grain dole, see D'ESCURAC 1976; CASSON 1980; SIRKS 1991. For the separate issue of military supply in the early empire, see REMESAL-RODRIGUEZ 1986. On grain as food, see FOXHALL and FORBES 1982. On wine and oil, see note 9 below. On fish products, see PONSICH 1988; CURTIS 1991; CORCORAN 1963.

4 See DODGE and WARD-PERKINS 1992; DODGE 1991; WARD-PERKINS 1971.

5 MEIGGS 1982.

6 For example, HOPKINS (1983a, 186) estimates that in the Roman Empire there was only one elite official for every 300,000 provincials. Nevertheless, when the lesser officials and servile civil servants are taken account of the bureaucracy appears less skeletal.

7 GARNSEY 1983, 118.

8 GARNSEY 1983, 118 (200 kg); FOXHALL and FORBES 1982, 69–72 (212–237 kg); PANELLA 1985, 180 (260 kg); RICKMAN 1980, 3–8 (270 kg).

9 On wine, see TCHERNIA 1986; ROSSITER 1981. On olive oil, see AMOURETTI 1986; MATTINGLY 1988a; 1988b; 1996; PEÑA 1998.

10 Our figures for order of magnitude (explained in more detail later in this chapter) are minimum estimates, based on bare subsistence needs. Changing the proportion of the main elements of the diet or substituting other commodities would not have a great affect on the overall tonnage of food required.

11 The term *annona* and the prefecture of the grain supply were introduced in the reign of Augustus, but the concept of grain distributions was already apparent in the 2nd century BC and it had become something of a permanent government concern by the time of Gaius Gracchus. For a discussion of this development, see ROBINSON 1994, 144–51; SIRKS 1991, 10–24.

12 For a discussion of the price of grain in Rome, see RICKMAN 1980, 143–55.

13 BRUNT 1980, 93–4.

14 See, for example, BRUNT 1980, 92, 96–8.

15 See GARNSEY 1988, 193–217 for incidents of food shortage or crisis in the years 189 (?), 182, 165, 142, 138, 129, 123 (?), 104, 100, 99, 91, 90, 89, 87, 86 (?), 82, 75, 74, 73, 67, 58, 57, 56, 54, 49, 48, 47, 46, 44, 43, 42, 41, 40, 39,

38, 37 and 36 BC. Since we lack detailed historical sources for much of this period, it is likely that we have considerably underestimated the scale of the problems. We should note that because the state did take measures to alleviate these crises, true famine was rare. On famine at Rome, see also VIRLOUVET 1985.

16 See, for example, GARNSEY 1988, 211. For the incidence of public disturbances in connection with the grain supply, see NIPPEL 1995, 49–50.

17 See GARNSEY 1988, 218–27 for crises under Augustus in the years 28 (?), 23, 22 and 18 BC and AD 5, 6, 7, 8 and 9; for crises under later emperors in AD 32, 41, 51, 62, 64, 69 and 70; and for undated incidents in the reigns of Domitian, Hadrian, Antoninus Pius and Marcus Aurelius in AD 161(?), 189, 193.

18 The classic calculation of costs by JONES (1964, 841–45) suggested that a wagonload of wheat would double in price after 300 miles of overland haulage charges. He also notes that the comparatively low sea freight made it "cheaper to ship grain from one end of the Mediterranean to the other than to cart it 75 miles overland". His figures were calculated in relation to cereals, however, and less bulky commodities would have been more competitive for overland transport. DUNCAN-JONES (1982, 366–69) has calculated relative cost ratios for sea:river:land transport as 1:4.9:34–42; that is, it was probably five times as costly to move goods by road as it was to shift them the same distance by inland waterway and 34–42 times more expensive than moving them by sea. Of course, the risk of loss was far higher with sea-borne traffic. See also GREENE 1986, 39–40; SPURR 1986, 144–46; HOPKINS 1983b.

19 Dionysius of Halicarnassus (3.44) and Strabo (231–2) both describe ships unloading offshore of Ostia while stressing the dangers of this procedure.

20 RICKMAN 1980, 18; MEIGGS 1973, 50–4; CASSON 1965.

21 Tacitus, *Annals* 3.54. The sentiment is repeated in *Annals* 12.43: "The life of the Roman people has been entrusted to ships and disasters."

22 GARNSEY 1983, 119–20. Warehouse facilities were located on both banks of the Tiber further upstream, e.g. the *Cellae Vinariae*, *CIL* 6.8826; *Lexicon* I, 259, Fig. 148; DUDLEY, Pl. 68.

23 MATTINGLY 1988a.

24 RICKMAN 1980, 17. On the general practice of the use of private contractors, see GARNSEY 1983, 121–26.

25 These inducements are discussed in more detail later in this chapter under 'Merchants and Shippers'.

26 See ROBINSON 1994, 151.

27 Grain laws were passed in the 90's BC (*Lex Octavia*), 73 BC (*Lex Terrentia Cassia*) and 62 BC (*Lex Porcia*). *The law of 62 either raised expenditure on grain distribution to 7.5 million denarii* or increased total outlay by this amount. In either case, it is evident that the state was by this date investing heavily. Perhaps as much as 50,000 tons of wheat could have been purchased outright for this sum. On the grain supply in the Republic, see also GARNSEY and RATHBONE 1985; GARSNEY 1986. On the threat to the grain supply posed by pirates, see RICKMAN 1980, 50–3.

28 RICKMAN 1980, 52–3.

29 Suetonius, *Julius Caesar* 41; Dio 43.21.4; RICKMAN 1980, 175–79.

30 Dio 55.10.1; RICKMAN 1980, 180–85.

31 SHA, *Septimius Severus* 18.3; SHA, *Aurelian* 35.2 and 48.1.

32 Suetonius, *Claudius* 20; Dio 60.11.1–5. The labour and expense required to build this harbour must have been vast. Claudius' other major project, the draining of the Fucine Lake, employed 30,000 men for 11 years (Suetonius, *Claudius* 20). MEIGGS (1973, 55) estimates that "the work involved in completing the Ostian harbour and its ancillary services was more extensive and more difficult."

33 Seneca, *Letters* 77.1–3. The excellent harbour and associated facilities at Puteoli ensured that this port continued to be used even after the construction of Rome's new harbours.

34 For a discussion of Trajan's harbour, see MEIGGS 1973, 162–71. For a full discussion of Ostia's role prior to Portus, see MEIGGS 1973, 16–54. MEIGGS (1973, 149–71) also has a useful description of the construction and lay-out of Portus.

35 For a discussion of Rome's port installations, see LYNGBY 1978; CASTAGNOLI 1980; LE GALL 1953, 194–204; RODRIGUEZ-ALMEIDA 1984, 23–106; *Lexicon* V, *s.v.* 'Tiberis', 69–73.

36 All information for this section on *horrea* is derived from RICKMAN 1971, particularly 1–15 and 76–86; see also RICKMAN 1980, 134–43; HERMANSEN 1982, 227–37.

37 RICKMAN 1971, 5, 97–104; *Lexicon* III, *s.v.* 'Horrea Galbana', 40–2.

38 RICKMAN 1971, 8, 79.

39 RODRIGUEZ-ALMEIDA 1980; 1984; CLARIDGE 1998, 367–68; *Lexicon* V, *s.v.* 'Testaceus Mons', 28–30. See also the smaller *amphora* hill of Monte Secco near Ponte Margherita (CLARIDGE 1998, 177).

40 PEACOCK and WILLIAMS 1986, 136–40. Some 10–15% of vessels are North African oil *amphorae*. See MATTINGLY 1988, 54–6 with supporting bibliography.

41 Known as *pignatte*, and seen also in the mausoleum at the Villa of the Gordians, and (eponymously) in the Tor Pignattura (Mausoleum of Helena): WARD-PERKINS 1981, 431; ADAM 1994, 183, Fig. 441.

42 Subsequently in this paper, we shall limit our discussion to the period after Portus superseded Puteoli, although Puteoli continued to be a port of importance and to serve as an auxiliary port for Rome for a long time. For the role of Puteoli as a harbour for Rome, see D'ARMS 1970, 73–165; 1981, 121–74; FREDERIKSEN 1984, 319–58.

43 CASSON 1965, 35.
44 CASSON 1965. The obvious advantage of river transport is that larger, and bulkier, cargoes could be transported with great ease.
45 MEIGGS 1973, 297.
46 *CIL* 14.352.
47 *CIL* 14.251; *CIL* 14.341.
48 CASSON 1965, 35.
49 *CIL* 14.252.
50 MEIGGS 1973, 298.
51 *CIL* 14.409.
52 *CIL* 14.425, 403; *CIL* 14, supp. 1, 4053–56.
53 RICKMAN 1980, 19.
54 CASSON (1965) discusses these and other characteristics of *codicariae* in greater detail as well as analyzing all the known iconographic representations of this specialized type of boat.
55 MEIGGS 1973, 293–94.
56 LE GALL 1953, 257.
57 This distinction is suggested by two inscriptions, one of which refers to *codicari naviculari infernates* (*CIL* 14.131) and the second of which specifies *codicari nav(iculari) infra pontem S(ublicium)* (*CIL* 14.185).
58 *CIL* 14.256.
59 *CIL* 14, supp. 1, 4549. For a complete listing of the many inscriptions mentioning these guilds as well as the epigraphic citations for those guilds referred to in the remainder of this paragraph, see FRANK 1940, 248–52; HERMANSEN 1982, 55–75. On Ostian guilds, see MEIGGS 1973, 311–36.
60 ANDERSON 1997, 116.
61 MEIGGS 1973, 282–89.
62 See, for example, *CIL* 14, supp. 1, 4549^{32} (Gaul); $4549^{10,12,17,18,34}$ (North Africa).
63 One mosaic from Sabratha depicts an elephant (*CIL* 14, supp. 1, 4549^{14}), and another from an unidentified city shows a boar, stag, and elephant (MEIGGS 1973, 289 and pl. 23b).
64 For a discussion of such distinctions and their complexity, see RICKMAN 1980, 124–27, 141–43. He also gives examples of men who combined categories such as Sextus Fadius Musa who was both a *navicularius* and a *negotiator* (*CIL* 12.4393; cf. RICKMAN 1980, 125). It is interesting to note that even the *codicarii* were sometimes also merchants; M. Caerellius Iazymis of Ostia identifies himself as a *codicarius* and a grain merchant: *codicarius item mercator frumentarius* (*CIL* 14.4234).
65 For example, Pliny the Elder (*Natural History* 2.118) comments that innumerable people were engaged in trade, hoping to make a profit. Juvenal (*Satires* 14.267–78) mocks those who, lured by dreams of enormous profits, sail the seas as merchants, and says that wherever hope for profit calls, fleets will follow. In a list of ways to gain wealth quickly, Seneca (*Letters* 119.5) puts overseas trade first. Petronius' vulgar freedman, Trimalchio, increased his inherited fortune by shipping wine to Rome (Petronius, *Satyricon* 76).
66 HOPKINS 1983b, 100–2. There were, however, several methods widely used by the Romans to reduce these financial risks. Often merchant ships were owned by a number of individuals who bought shares in the ship, thus spreading the potential losses among multiple investors (see, for example, Plutarch, *Cato the Elder* 21.6–7). Also, to reduce the loss incurred by any single shipwreck, a merchant could transport his goods in several ships rather than putting all of them into one vessel. One result of these strategies was that ships typically carried mixed cargoes consisting of a variety of different goods belonging to multiple owners. On mixed cargoes in general, see PARKER 1984; 1992. For a case study of a wrecked ship with an extremely varied cargo (Port Vendres II shipwreck off the south coast of France), see COLLS 1977. Sometimes a number of merchants would even pour their grain in common into a ship's hold (*Digest* 19.2.31). On maritime commerce in general, see CASSON 1971; SIRKS 1991.
67 Livy 21.63.3–7. Livy records that this measure met with considerable hostility from the senators, indicating that at least at this time, senators were involved in overseas trade. On this law, see D'ARMS 1981, 31–9; YAVETZ 1962. By the late Republic, although this law was still on the books, it seems to have lost its force, since Cicero (*Second Verrine* 5.45) refers to it as 'outdated and dead' (*Antiquae sunt istae leges et mortuae*).
68 FINLEY 1985; see particularly 35–62. Finley's analysis of Roman social attitudes is based on close reading of upper-class literary sources, especially Cicero.
69 See FINLEY 1985, 58–60.
70 On such senatorial agents, see D'ARMS 1981, 154–59; D'ESCURAC 1977, 339–55. For a sceptical view of the use of agents, see GARNSEY 1983, 129–30.
71 Although senators were concentrated at Rome, and while they certainly possessed a disproportionate amount of wealth, this class was numerically quite small. MACMULLEN (1974, 88) has estimated that only about 0.002% of the population of the Roman Empire was of senatorial rank. There were many equestrians, successful freedmen, and provincial aristocrats who amassed considerable fortunes, as attested by their

numerous, and often lavish, public dedications. See, for example, the lists compiled by DUNCAN-JONES 1982, 156–237 (Italian costs), 89–119 (African costs).

72 MEIGGS (1973, 275–98) cites many of these inscriptions from merchants found at Ostia. On merchants as independent operators, see also GARNSEY 1983, 121–30.

73 Suetonius, *Claudius* 18–9; Gaius, *Institutes* 1.32c; *Digest* 3.6 (Ulpian); GARNSEY 1983, 123–24.

74 Tacitus, *Annals* 13.51; *Digest* 50.5.3, 50.6.6.5–6 and 8–9. For a discussion of some of these exemptions, see GARNSEY 1983, 124–25; ROBINSON 1994, 149.

75 WHITTAKER 1985.

76 On such local elites who were clearly connected with overseas trade, and whose wealth led to local aristocratic status, see GARNSEY 1983, 124–26; D'ARMS 1981, especially 121–48, 175–81. For a detailed view of two such men, see TCHERNIA 1980. See also RODRIGUEZ-ALMEIDA 1980 (for a study of the *tituli picti* on *amphorae* from Monte Testaccio); 1984.

77 MATTINGLY 1988a; 1988c.

78 On all aspects of the imperial administration's role in the supply system of Rome, see D'ESCURAC 1976.

79 RICKMAN 1980, 47–8.

80 Dio 55.26.2–3 and 55.31.4. On the dating of the creation of the prefecture of the *annona*, see D'ESCURAC 1976, 29–32.

81 For the career of C. Turranius Gracilius, see D'ESCURAC 1976, 317–19.

82 RICKMAN 1980, 221.

83 On imperial procurators, see PFLAUM 1961 and supplement, 1982.

84 See, for example, *CIL* 14.154.

85 *CIL* 14.160. For further examples, see MEIGGS 1973, 300.

86 These include the offices of *tabularii, tabularii adiutor, tabularii portus,* and *tabularii Ostis ad annonem*. For a complete analysis of the imperial offices involved in the supply of the city, see particularly D'ESCURAC 1976, 89–152. For a more succinct description, see MEIGGS 1973, 298–310; RICKMAN 1980, 218–25.

87 *CIL* 6.8450, cited by MEIGGS 1973, 301.

88 *CIL* 2.1180; *PIR*[2] 1.480. See also PFLAUM 1982, 50–1, no. 185; RICKMAN 1980, 224.

89 The scale and complexity of the trade mechanisms at work on the river Baetis are suggested by epigraphic evidence indicating the existence of guilds of boatmen and of others involved with river transport similar to those that operated on the Tiber. The link between these guilds and the imperial administration is made explicit by dedications by the guilds to imperial officials involved with the *annona* and food supply (*CIL* 2.1168–69, 1180, 1183). On the importance of Baetica as an agricultural region in general, see BLASQUEZ-MARTINEZ and REMESAL RODRIGUEZ 1980; 1983. On the Tiber guilds, see LE GALL 1953, 216–83.

90 BLOCH 1953, 37.

91 MEIGGS 1973, 302.

92 The capture and difficult transport of exotic wild beasts for the games at Rome must have been a considerable industry in its own right. Numerous animals including elephants, tigers, lions, panthers, rhinos, hippopotami, crocodiles, giraffes, bears, and even ostriches were slaughtered in the arena, often in staggering numbers. Even the transport of a single elephant or hippo cannot have been an easy matter, and Augustus alone claimed that he gave 26 beast shows in which around 3,500 animals were killed (*Res Gestae* 22). Trajan is said to have given games which lasted 123 days and included the slaughter of 11,000 animals (Dio 68.15.1). On the subject of the capture and transport of wild beasts for the games in Rome, see most recently BERTRANDY 1987. An older work on the same topic is JENNISSSON 1937. The mosaics at a villa in Sicily dating from the early 4th century AD vividly depict the capture, caging, and shipping of wild beasts for the arena and provide useful iconographic information on these subjects; see CARANDINI 1982.

93 ROBINSON 1994, 85–94, 118.

94 BRAUND 1985, 810a and b.

95 *CIL* 14, supp. 1, 5320.

96 SHA, *Septimius Severus* 18.3. Aurelian subsequently added rations of pork and wine to the dole (SHA, *Aurelian* 35.2 and 48.1).

97 *CIL* 6.1620.

98 D'ESCURAC 1976, 189.

99 *CIL* 6.1625b.

100 *CIL* 14.20.

101 D'ESCURAC 1976, 191; RODRIGUEZ-ALMEIDA 1984, 53–65.

102 *Adiutor Ulpii Saturnini praefecti annonae ad oleum Afrum et Hispanum recensendum item solamina transferenda item vecturas navicularis exsolvenda* (*CIL* 2.1180).

103 RICKMAN (1980, 224) disagrees with this interpretation. He believes that Possessor never left Rome, but was simply in charge of keeping the accounts of Spanish and African oil that reached Rome. Rickman is unable,

however, to offer any support for his view, and it seems rather difficult to understand why the inscription honouring Possessor would be erected in Hispalis if he never left Rome. There is evidence that *annona* officials were indeed sent to the provinces from Rome; a 2nd-century inscription from Arles refers to a *procurator Augusti ad annonam provinciae Narbonensis et Liguriae* (*CIL* 12.672). The availability of surplus oil in Spain and Africa is attested by archaeological evidence for large-scale production; see MATTINGLY 1988a; 1988c.

104 On the developed system of shipping the oil for the *annona* from North Africa, see the important study by PEÑA 1998.

105 On the ancient diet, see above all FOXHALL and FORBES 1982. On grain, oil, and wine, see note 3 above. On Roman agriculture in general, see SPURR 1986; MORITZ 1958; WHITE 1970. Interesting comparative data is offered by several studies of modern diets in underdeveloped Mediterranean areas; see ALLBAUGH 1953; MACDONALD and RAPP 1972.

106 For grain consumption, we have used the average figure suggested by FOXHALL and FORBES 1982, 72. Other modern estimates range from 150,000 to 400,000 tons of grain consumed per year. For a summary of these alternative views, see GARNSEY 1983, 118–19.

107 The average size of Roman merchant ships is a matter of considerable debate. HOPKINS (1983b, 97–102) suggests an average cargo capacity of 250–400 tons. CASSON (1971, 170–73, 183–200) thinks that the majority of ships had a capacity of 100–150 tons. He believes, however, that some ships, in particular the largest of the grain freighters from Alexandria, could have had a capacity of over 1,000 tons. There is in fact no archaeological evidence for ships above about 650 tons capacity; the evidence for these very large grain ships comes from Lucian, *The Ship* 5 in which he describes the Isis, a ship which sought shelter in the harbour at Piraeus and whose size caused much amazement. In our calculations we have used a figure of 250 tons capacity, since although the average merchant ship was likely to have been much smaller, the largest ships were probably the very ones engaged in the transport of staples to the city of Rome, and therefore, those that we are concerned with in this study. It is worth noting that while larger capacity ships may have been most efficient, efficiency alone may not have been the most significant factor in determining ship size. A ship and its cargo were very valuable and therefore the larger the ship, the greater the financial risk. Due to the hazards of ancient maritime travel and the apparent frequency of shipwrecks, in many cases, modestly sized ships may have been preferable to larger ones (HOPKINS 1983b, 100–2).

108 AMOURETTI 1986, 177–96; MATTINGLY 1988b; 1996.

109 FOXHALL and FORBES 1982, 68.

110 One hint at the amount of oil used in baths and gymnasiums is that the gymnasium at Tauromenium from 195–167 BC consumed about 3,700 litres of oil each year (*IG* 14.422). In the 4th century AD, Rome contained over 800 baths of varying sizes. For baths in Rome, see YEGÜL 1992, 128–183; FAGAN 1999, particularly 69–74, 95–127, 193–97, 357–67; *Lexicon* V, 40–69 (*thermae*).

111 We have based these calculations on Dressel type 20 *amphorae* with an average capacity of 70 litres of olive oil and an empty weight of 28 kg. See PEACOCK and WILLIAMS 1986, table 1, 52; RODRIGUEZ-ALMEIDA 1984, 186–87.

112 FOXHALL and FORBES (1982, 68) note that in modern Methana, the adult males drank well over a litre per day of homemade wine.

113 Based on Dressel type 2–4 *amphorae* with an average volume of 25 litres and empty weight of 15 kg (PEACOCK and WILLIAMS 1986, table 1, 52).

114 RICKMAN 1980, 15, 128; CASSON 1994, 150.

115 Our calculations, although arrived at independently, tally very closely with similar calculations made by PANELLA (1985, 181), who estimated that eight ships per day would arrive carrying wine, one and a half with oil, and ten with grain, compared to our figures of six ships per day of wine, one of oil, and nine and a half of grain. In reality, many (perhaps most) ancient ships carried mixed cargoes, not a single commodity. One wrecked ship (Port Vendres II of the south coast of France), for example, was found to have been carrying a cargo of metal, pottery, oil, wine, and fish sauce (COLLS 1977).

116 The extremely high nutritional value of olive oil for a given unit of weight makes it one of the most efficiently packaged foods available to the Romans. This was certainly a significant factor in its ready marketability in long-distance trade.

117 FOXHALL and FORBES 1982, 48–9.

118 These numbers of *amphorae* are certainly not improbable. RODRIGUEZ-ALMEIDA (1984, 109–19) has estimated that Monte Testaccio contains the remains of over 50,000,000 olive oil *amphorae*. For a similar quantitative study of *amphorae* fragments from Ostia, see PANELLA 1983.

119 At 50 kg/sack after CASSON 1965, 32.

120 Since a Dressel 20 *amphora* loaded with olive oil would weigh about 91 kg, we have assumed that it would require two porters to transport each oil *amphora*. Examples in Roman art illustrate how two porters could transport a large *amphora* by passing a stick through one of its handles and then carrying it suspended between them on the stick. We have assumed that the 50 kg grain sacks and 40 kg loaded wine *amphorae* were carried by individual porters.

121 Fifteen minutes is perhaps an optimistic estimate for a single trip, which would have consisted of the porter picking up his burden of a sack or an *amphora*, checking it off with an official on the boat, carrying it down the narrow gangplank, bearing it to a nearby warehouse where he would again need to have it checked off and perhaps inspected by an official, depositing it in the warehouse, which often entailed bearing it up narrow ramps to upper levels, and finally returning to the ship for another load. He may well have had to wait in line at the many narrow passages involved in this route, such as the gangplank and the warehouse entrance, as well as at the official measuring and accounting posts. Naturally this procedure would be considerably complicated and lengthened if the warehouse were not immediately adjoining the dock.

122 RICKMAN 1980, 19.

123 Conversion from Roman measures is based on tables in FOXHALL and FORBES 1982, 43 and 86–9, table 3.

124 On imperial distributions, see BERCHEM 1939. Augustus, for example, twice gave grain distributions equivalent to a year's worth of the grain dole (23 BC and AD 6); see *Res Gestae* 15; Dio 55.26.1–3.

125 On the urban plebs in general during the early empire, see YAVETZ 1988; VEYNE 1990. On urban living conditions, see SCOBIE 1986 and Patterson in this volume.

126 BRUNT 1980. Although Brunt's article focuses on casual employment on imperial building projects, his arguments apply equally well to employment opportunities in the supply system of the city.

127 The meaning of this passage is uncertain; all the Latin says is that they went off '*ad frumentum*' (Cicero, *Letters to Atticus* 14.3 = SB 357). CASSON (1978, 47) suggests that the meaning could not be that they went off harvesting since the letter was written at least a month before harvesting could have begun. His interpretation is that they went to buy corn. This passage is admittedly ambiguous, but it may well refer to the same problem that concerned Augustus.

128 See BRUNT 1980 for a more detailed discussion of this passage.

129 For a good discussion of the varying groups associated with the African oil trade (oil weighers, warehousemen, shippers, overland hauliers, makers of amphorae and oil skins, etc), see PEÑA 1998, 193–217.

130 Even Tiberius, who of the Julio-Claudians was the least interested in the people of Rome and who spent the most time away from the city, is reputed to have called the supply of Rome a particular concern of the *princeps* (Tacitus, *Annals* 3.54). On Tiberius and Rome, see YAVETZ 1988, 103–13.

131 See, for example, NIPPEL 1995; GARNSEY 1988, 198–211; EVANS 1981.

132 Juvenal, *Satires* 10.81. This image has haunted the urban plebs from antiquity to the present. Typical of modern historians who accept this view is CARCOPINO (1941, 210) who states that, "In the city of Rome there were 150,000 complete idlers supported by the generosity of the public assistance." Both halves of this image are incorrect, since the plebs were neither unemployed, nor did they spend all their time at public amusements. In the early empire, a mere 3% of the total populace could have attended the theatres at the same time (if all the theatres were in use simultaneously), 5% could fit into the Colosseum (in which most of the seats were reserved for the upper classes, with room for only about 5,000 of the poor out of the Colosseum's total capacity of around 50,000), and although around 200,000 could be present at the Circus Maximus, there were only about 20 days per year on which races were held. However the plebs may have used their time, only a very small portion of it could have been spent at the games (BALSDON 1969).

BIBLIOGRAPHY

ADAM, J.P. 1994: *Roman Building Materials and Techniques*, London, 1994.

ALLBAUGH, L.G. 1953: *Crete: A Case Study of an Underdeveloped Area*, Princeton, 1953.

ALDRETE, G.S. and MATTINGLY, D.J. 1999: 'Feeding the City: the organization, operation and scale of the supply system for Rome', in D.S. Potter and D.J. Mattingly (ed.), *Life, Death and Entertainment in the Roman Empire*, Ann Arbor, 1999, 171–204.

AMOURETTI, M.-C. 1986: *Le Pain et l'Huile dans la Grèce Antique*, Paris, 1986.

ANDERSON, J.C. Jr. 1997: *Roman Architecture and Society,* Baltimore, 1997.

BALSDON, J.P.V.D. 1969: 'Panem et Circenses', in J. Bibauw, *Homages à Marcel Renard II*, Collection Latomus 102, Bruxelles, 1969, 57–60.

BERCHEM, D. van 1939: *Les Distributions de Blé et d'Argent à la Plèbe Romaine sous l'Empire*, Geneva, 1939.

BERTRANDY, F. 1987: 'Remarques sur le Commerce des Bêtes Sauvages entre l'Afrique du Nord et l'Italie', *MEFRA* 99, 1987, 211–41.

BLASQUEZ-MARTINEZ, J.M. and REMESAL-RODRIGUEZ, J. 1980: *Produccion y Comercio del Aceite en la Antigüedad* I, Madrid, 1980.

BLASQUEZ-MARTINEZ, J.M. and REMESAL-RODRIGUEZ, J. 1983: *Produccion y Comercio del Aceite en la Antigüedad* II, Madrid, 1983.

BLOCH, H. 1953: 'Ostia: Iscrizioni rinvenute tra il 1930 e il 1939', *Notizie degli Scavi di Antichita* 7, 1953, 239–306.

BRAUND, D.C. 1985: *Augustus to Nero: a source book on Roman history 31 BC–AD 68*, London, 1985.

BRUNT, P.A. 1980: 'Free Labour and Public Works at Rome', *JRS* 70, 1980, 81–100.

CARANDINI, A., RICCI, A. and DE VOS, M. 1982: *Filosofiana, la villa de Piazza Armerina, Imagine di un Aristocratico Romano al Tempo di Constantino*, Palermo, 1982.

CARCOPINO, J. 1941: *Daily Life in Ancient Rome*, (translated by E.O. Lorimer), London, 1941.

CASSON, L. 1965: 'Harbour and River Boats of Ancient Rome', *JRS* 55, 1965, 31–9.

CASSON, L. 1971: *Ships and Seamanship in the Ancient World*, Princeton, 1971.

CASSON, L. 1978: 'Unemployment, the Building Trade, and Suetonius *Vesp.* 18', *Bulletin of the American Society of Papyrologists* 15, 1978, 43–51.

CASSON, L. 1980: 'The Role of the State in Rome's Grain Trade', *MAAR* 36, 1980, 21–33.

CASTAGNOLI, F. 1980: 'Installazioni Portuali a Roma', *MAAR* 36, 1980, 35–42.

CHEVALLIER, V. 1976: *Roman Roads*, London, 1976.

CLARIDGE, A. 1998: *Rome: An Oxford Archaeological Guide*, Oxford, 1998.

COLLS, D. *et al.* 1977: 'L'Epave Port Vendres II', *Archaeonautica* 1, 1977.

CORCORAN, T.H. 1963: 'Roman Fish Sauces', *CJ* 58, 1963, 204–10.

CURTIS, R.I. 1991 'Salt Food Products around the Strait of Gibralter', *JRA* 4, 1991, 299–305.

D'ARMS, J. 1970: *Romans on the Bay of Naples*, Cambridge Mass., 1970.

D'ARMS, J. 1981: *Commerce and Social Standing in Ancient Rome,* Cambridge Mass., 1981.

D'ESCURAC, H.P. 1976: *La Préfecture de l'annone. Service administratif imperial d'Auguste à Constantin*, Paris, 1976.

D'ESCURAC, H.P. 1977: 'Aristocratie senatoriale et profits commerciaux', *Ktema* 2, 1977, 339–55.

DODGE, H. 1991: 'Ancient Marble Studies: Recent Research', *JRA* 4, 1991, 28–50.

DODGE, H. and WARD-PERKINS, B. (ed.) 1992: *Marble in Antiquity, Collected Papers and lectures of J.B. Ward-Perkins*, British School at Rome Archaeological Monograph No 6, London, 1992.

DUDLEY, D.R. 1967: *Urbs Roma*, Aberdeen, 1967.

DUNCAN-JONES, R. 1982: *The Economy of the Roman Empire: Quantitative Studies*, ed. 2, Cambridge, 1982.

DUNCAN-JONES, R. 1990: *Structure and Scale in the Roman Economy*, Cambridge, 1990.

EVANS, J.K. 1981: 'Wheat Production and its Social Consequences in the Roman World', *CQ* 31, 1981, 428–42.

FAGAN, G.G. 1999: *Bathing in Public in the Roman World*, Ann Arbor, 1999.

FINLEY, M. 1985: *The Ancient Economy*, revised ed., London, 1985.

FOXHALL, L. and FORBES, H.A. 1982: '*Sitometreia*: the Role of Grain as a Staple Food in Classical Antiquity', *Chiron* 12, 1982, 41–90.

FRANK, T. 1940: *An Economic Survey of Ancient Rome* V, Paterson NJ, 1940.

FREDERIKSEN, M. 1984: *Campania*, London, 1984.

GARNSEY, P. 1983: 'Grain for Rome', in P. Garnsey, K. Hopkins and C.R. Whittaker (ed.), *Trade in the Ancient Economy*, London, 1983, 118–30.

GARNSEY, P. 1988: *Famine and Food Supply in the Graeco-Roman World*, Cambridge, 1988.

GARNSEY, P. and RATHBONE, D. 1985: 'The Background to the Grain Law of Gaius Gracchus', *JRS* 75, 1985, 20–5.

GARNSEY, P., GALLANT, T. and RATHBONE, D. 1986: 'Thessaly and the Grain Supply of Rome During the Second Century BC', *JRS* 76, 1986, 30–44.

GREENE, K. 1986: *The Archaeology of the Roman Economy,* London, 1986.

HERMANSEN, G. 1982: *Ostia: Aspects of Roman City Life*, Edmonton, 1982.

HOPKINS, K. 1978: *Conquerors and Slaves*, Cambridge, 1978.

HOPKINS, K. 1983a: *Death and Renewal*, Cambridge, 1983.

HOPKINS, K. 1983b: 'Models, Ships, and Staples', in P. Garnsey, K. Hopkins and C.R. Whittaker (ed.), *Trade in the Ancient Economy*, London, 1983, 84–109.

JENNISSON, G. 1937: *Animals for Show and Pleasure in Ancient Rome*, Manchester, 1937.

JONES, A.H.M. 1964: *The Later Roman Empire,* Oxford, 1964.

LE GALL, J. 1953: *Le Tibre: Fleuve de Rome dans l'Antiquité*, Paris, 1953.

LYNGBY, H., POLIA, M. and SARTORIO, G.P. 1978: 'Richerche sulla porta flumentana', *Opuscula Romana* 8, 1978, 33–52.

MACDONALD, W.A. and RAPP, G.R. (ed.) 1972: *The Minnesota Messenia Expedition*, Minneapolis, 1972.

MACMULLEN, R. 1974: *Roman Social Relations, 50 BC–AD 284*, New Haven, 1974.

MATTINGLY, D.J. 1988a: 'Oil for Export? A Comparison of Libyan, Spanish, and Tunisian Olive Oil Production in the Roman Empire', *JRA* 1, 1988, 33–56.

MATTINGLY, D.J. 1988b: 'Olea Mediterranea?', *JRA* 1, 1988, 153–61.

MATTINGLY, D.J. 1988c: 'The Olive Boom. Oil Surpluses, Wealth, and Power in Roman Tripolitania', *Libyan Studies* 19, 21–41.

MATTINGLY, D.J. 1996: 'First Fruit? The Olive in the Roman World', in G. Shipley and J. Salmon (ed.), *Human Landscape in the Ancient World*, London, 1996, 213–53.

MEIGGS, R. 1973: *Roman Ostia*, Oxford, 1973.

MEIGGS, R. 1982: *Trees and Timber in the Ancient Mediterranean World*, Oxford, 1982.

MORITZ, L. 1958: *Grain Mills and Flour in Classical Antiquity*, Oxford, 1958.

NIPPEL, W. 1995: *Public Order in Ancient Rome*, Cambridge, 1995.

PANELLA, C. 1983: 'I contenitori oleari presentati ad Ostia in età antonina: Analisi tipologica, epigraphica, quantitativa', in BLASQUEZ-MARTINEZ and REMESAL RODRIGUEZ 1983, 225–61.

PANELLA, C. 1985: 'I commerci di Roma e di Ostia in età Imperiale (Secoli I–III): Le derrate alimentari', in R. Bussi and V. Vandelli, *Misurare la Terra: centuriazione e coloni nel mondo romano: città, agricoltura, commercio: materiali da Roma e dal suburbio*, Modena, 1985, 180–88.

PARKER, A.J. 1984: 'Shipwrecks and Ancient Trade in the Mediterranean', *Archaeological Review from Cambridge* 3.2, 1984, 99–113.

PARKER, A.J. 1992: *Ancient Shipwrecks of the Mediterranean and Roman Provinces. BAR International Series* 580, Oxford, 1992.

PEACOCK, D.P.S. and WILLIAMS, D.F. 1986: *Amphorae and the Roman Economy*, London, 1986.

PEÑA, J.T. 1998: 'The mobilization of state olive oil in Roman Africa: the evidence of late 4th century ostraca from Carthage', in J.T. Peña, J.J. Rossiter, A.I. Wilson and C.M. Wells, *Carthage Papers. The early colony's economy, water supply, a public bath and the mobilization of state olive oil*, JRA Supplementary Series 28, Portsmouth RI, 1998, 116–238.

PFLAUM, H.-G. 1961: *Les carrières procuratoriennes equestres sous le haut-empire romain*, Paris, 1961.

PFLAUM, H.-G. 1982: *Les carrières procuratoriennes equestres sous le haut-empire romain, Supplément*, Paris, 1982.

PONSICH, M. 1988: *Aceite de Oliva y Salazones de Pescado. Factores Geo-Economicos de Betica y Tingitania,* Madrid, 1988.

REMESAL-RODRIGUEZ, J. 1986: *La annona militaris y la exportacion de aceite Betico a Germania*, Madrid, 1986.

RICKMAN, G. 1971: *Roman Granaries and Store Buildings*, Cambridge, 1971.

RICKMAN, G. 1980: *The Corn Supply of Ancient Rome*, Oxford, 1980.

ROBINSON, O.F. 1994: *Ancient Rome: City Planning and Administration*, London, 1994.

RODRIGUEZ-ALMEIDA, E. 1980: 'El Monte Testaccio, Hoy: Nuevos Testimonios Epigraphicos', in BLASQUEZ-MARTINEZ and REMESAL-RODRIGUEZ 1980, 57–103.

RODRIGUEZ-ALMEIDA, E. 1984: *Il Monte Testaccio: ambiente, storia, materiali*, Roma, 1984.

ROSSITER, J. 1981: 'Wine and Oil Processing at Roman Farms in Italy', *Phoenix 35*, 1981, 345–61.

ROUGÉ, J. 1981: *Ships and Fleets of the Ancient Mediterranean*, Middletown Conn., 1981.

SCOBIE, A. 1986: 'Slums, Sanitation, and Mortality in the Roman World', *Klio* 68, 1986, 399–433.

SIRKS, A.J.B. 1991: *Food for Rome. The legal structure of the transportation and processing of supplies for Rome and Constantinople,* Amsterdam, 1991.

SPURR, M.S. 1986: *Arable Cultivation in Roman Italy*, London, 1986.

TCHERNIA, A. 1980: 'D. Caecilius Hospitalis et M. Iulius Hermesianus', in BLASQUEZ MARTINEZ 1980, 155–61.

TCHERNIA, A. 1986: *Le Vin de l'Italie Romaine*, Roma, 1986.

VEYNE, P. 1990: *Bread and Circuses: Historical Sociology and Political Pluralism*, (translated by B. Pearce), London, 1990.

VIRLOUVET, C. 1985: *Famines et Emeutes à Rome des Origines de la Republique à la Mort de Neron*, Roma, 1985.

WARD-PERKINS, J.B. 1971: 'Quarrying in Antiquity: Technology, Tradition, and Social Change', *Proceedings of the British Academy* 57, 1971, 3–24.

WARD-PERKINS, J.B. 1981: *Roman Imperial Architecture*, Harmondsworth, 1981.

WHITTAKER, C.R. 1985: 'Trade and the Aristocracy in the Roman Empire', *Opus* 4, 1985, 49–75.

WHITE, K.D. 1970: *Roman Farming*, London, 1970.

YAVETZ, Z. 1962: 'The Policy of C. Flaminius and the Plebiscitum Claudianum', *Athenaeum* 40, 1962, 325–44.

YAVETZ, Z. 1988: *Plebs and Princeps*, ed. 2, Oxford, 1988.

YEGÜL, F. 1992: *Baths and Bathing in the Roman World*, Cambridge Mass., 1992.

8. 'Greater than the Pyramids': the Water Supply of Ancient Rome

Hazel Dodge

Since antiquity the water supply of ancient Rome has attracted much admiration and amazement. Dionysius of Halicarnassus, writing in the 1st century BC, said "In my opinion indeed, the three most significant works of Rome, in which the greatness of her empire is best seen, are the aqueducts, the paved roads, and the construction of sewers" (3.67.5; in particular, he is referring to the Cloaca Maxima at this point). The Roman geographer Strabo wrote that "Romans had the best foresight in those matters which the Greeks made but little account of, such as the construction of roads and aqueducts, and of sewers that wash away the filth of the city to the Tiber" (5.3.8). He goes on to say that "water is brought into the city through aqueducts in such quantities that veritable rivers flow through the city and the sewers". Perhaps the best-known acclamation of the aqueducts of Rome was made by Frontinus: "With such an array of indispensable structures carrying so many waters, compare, if you will, the Pyramids or the useless, though famous, works of the Greeks!" (*On Aqueducts* 16). Rome's greatness was being measured by these vast examples of hydraulic expertise which have left their not insignificant mark on the Roman countryside even today. Obviously at its most basic level water is a necessity of life, but as the city of Rome, and other cities in the Empire, grew, water became essential not only as a means to stay alive but also as an important cultural symbol. The construction of aqueducts and fountains were a matter of civic pride, often being provided by both the authorities and private individuals.[1]

Our main, and indeed only specific source on Roman water supply is Sextus Julius Frontinus who was appointed *curator aquarum* (Water Commissioner) at Rome by Nerva. Vitruvius also discussed aspects of Roman hydraulic technology, but the passages are not always very clear nor are they specific to Rome (*On Architecture* 8). Frontinus was a distinguished military commander who had been governor of Britain from AD 74–77 (or 78), and had been given the post of proconsul of Asia by Domitian in 85/86, but had no experience in hydraulic engineering. He was appointed *curator aquarum* in AD 97. The importance of this post was immense. Obviously it bestowed a good deal of prestige on the holder, but more importantly upon this office depended the health and sanitation of the city (see below). Frontinus' published work *De aquis urbis Romae* (*On the Aqueducts of Rome*, henceforth *On Aqueducts*) was the result of his tenure of the post. He had already written works dealing with military matters and land surveying, the latter perhaps being one of a number of reasons for his appointment.[2] He was faced with a highly technical field that any engineer would have told him needed a lifetime to master. Frontinus makes clear his own view of his published work; it was intended as a personal handbook and one which would hopefully be of use to his successors (*On* Aqueducts 2.3).[3] As well as descriptions of the individual aqueduct lines, their sources, delivery points and capacity he gives invaluable information on the uses and misuses of water in the city; it is clear that he felt these to be important issues to address. However, a major drawback is that because the work concentrates on the city of Rome it is not a source applicable to the rest of the empire. Nor is it a good source for some of the standard features of Roman aqueducts elsewhere.[4] He gives little space to the day-to-day maintenance of the aqueducts and does not discuss at all the construction of aqueducts and the accompanying work of surveyors. But then that was not his purpose. He was put in office to overhaul a system which had been badly affected by corruption and neglect; in that respect he has left us with a great legacy. His work survives in a corrupt text which provides conflicting figures on the amount of water entering Rome and the distribution of the individual lines; but despite these problems, Frontinus remains a formidable source which must form the basis of any study of Rome's water supply.[5]

In more recent times our knowledge of the Roman aqueduct system owes much to the work of Esther van Deman, published as *The Building of the Roman Aqueducts* in 1934, and the companion work by Thomas Ashby, *The Aqueducts of Ancient Rome*, published posthumously in 1935. Since their work was carried out, Rome has changed dramatically and the monuments have suffered accordingly, but Ashby's work in particular still remains the standard work nearly 70 years after its original publication.[6] Work continues to be carried out on the structures themselves, but now scholars are beginning to ask different questions of the material. Why were aqueducts introduced into the city in the first place? Where did they deliver their water and how? What different needs did they meet and how did these change over time? The answers give a broader context for the structures, an insight into the advantages of a piped water supply for the general population, and a greater understanding of urbanization in the Roman world. In this chapter a range of concerns will be explored. Firstly, the technology, distribution and circumstances of the construction of the aqueducts which supplied Rome; secondly, the administration of this water supply and the application of Frontinus in modern studies; and thirdly, the broader significance of the ancient water supply to Rome in more modern times.

THE OFFICE OF *CURATOR AQUARUM*

The functioning of the aqueducts and the provision of a water supply was as important a factor in the city's government and the well-being of the population as 'bread and circuses'. The office of *curator aquarum*, to which Frontinus was appointed, was established under Augustus, with a remit to maintain the water supply of Rome and a body of imperial slaves to carry out the necessary tasks.[7] In the Republic the provision of aqueducts and the maintenance of Rome's water supply was one of the duties of the censors; the Aqua Appia in 312 BC and the Aqua Tepula in 125 BC were both the work of the censors.[8] The Aqua Anio Novus (272 BC) was supplied by the *duumviri aquae perducendae* (Livy 9.29; Frontinus, *On Aqueducts* 5–8). For the Aqua Marcia (144 BC) a praetor was put in charge commissioned by the senate and the project was financed by a specific grant from the Senate.[9] The Aqua Appia was probably financed by tribute and the Tepula probably from general revenue. Thus although maintaining an adequate water supply to the city was one of the censors' duties, the details of funding could vary. Further, the censors were only in office for 18 months every five years, so many of the day-to-day matters (for example the right to take water) were dealt with by the aediles.[10] The maintenance work was contracted out and it was the responsibility of the censors and aediles to ensure the work was carried out properly (Frontinus, *On Aqueducts* 96).[11]

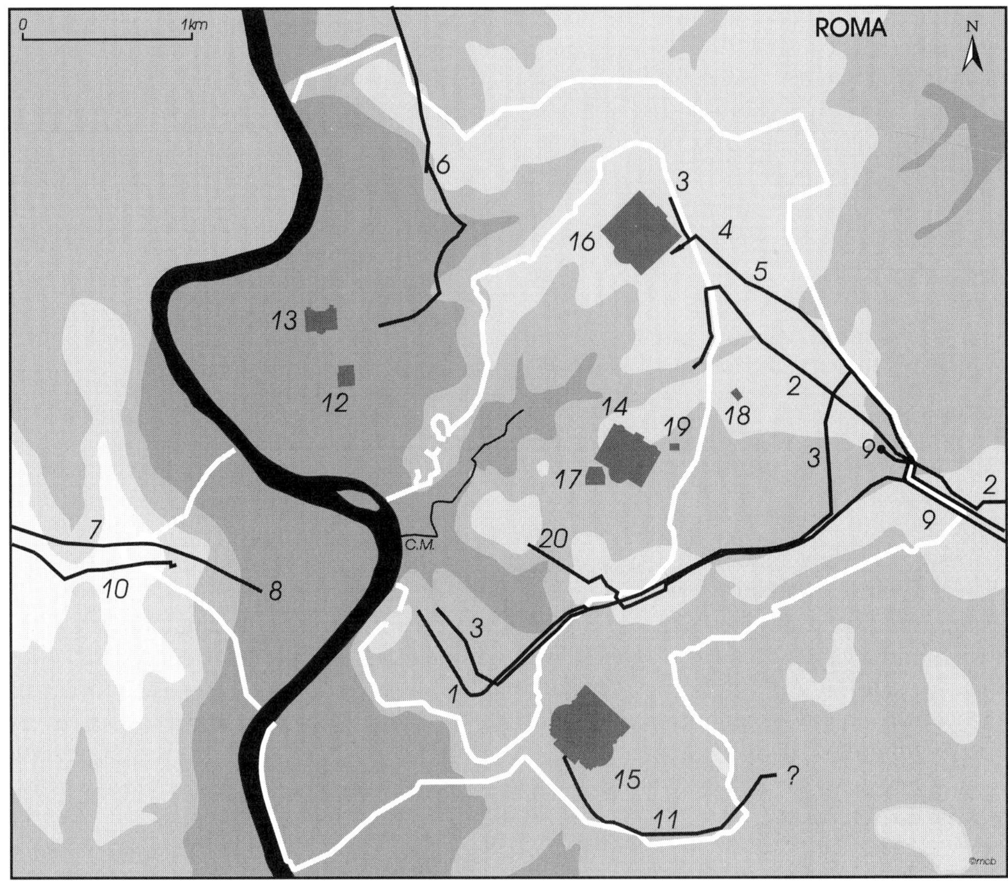

Fig. 8.1: Map of aqueducts. 1 Aqua Appia, 2 Aqua Anio Vetus, 3 Aqua Marcia, 4 Aqua Tepula, 5 Aqua Iulia, 6 Aqua Virgo, 7 Aqua Alsietina, 8 Naumachia Augusti, 9 Aqua Claudia & Anio Novus, 10 Aqua Traiana, 11 Aqua Antoniniana, 12 Stagnum and Baths of Agrippa, 13 Baths of Nero and Severus Alexander, 14 Baths of Trajan, 15 Baths of Caracalla, 16 Baths of Diocletian, 17 Baths of Titus, 18 Nymphaeum 'Trofei di Mario', 19 Sette sale, 20 Arcus Caelimontani. C.M. Cloaca Maxima.

In 33 BC as aedile Agrippa had not only built the Aqua Iulia but also repaired the existing aqueducts and maintained them with his own gang of slaves (240 men strong); these he bequeathed to Augustus who made them public property.[12] From these Augustus established the *cura aquarum*. This was a commission of three men of senatorial rank with a president, and it was provided with a staff which included architects and surveyors, clerks and the public slaves.[13] Under Claudius the post of *procurator aquarum* came into existence (Frontinus, *On Aqueducts* 105) which had executive control of the water supply and was concerned with it permanently; the *curatores* were often serving as part of their senatorial careers and all but one in the 1st century AD was of consular rank when he took up office. The post of *procurator* was held by imperial freedmen until the time of Trajan when the first equestrian *procurator* is encountered.[14] At first the appointment of *curator* was for life, an unusual phenomenon in Roman administration; it may be that the post was more honorary in nature, at least at this time. From the time of Nero, the *curator aquarum* was in office for an average of two years. For a large part of the 2nd century AD no *curatores aquarum* are known to us, but under Septimius Severus and Caracalla a new title is recorded, *curator aquarum et Minuciae*.[15]

It has been suggested that in the later 2nd century AD the headquarters for the *statio aquarum* was fixed at the Porticus Minucia, sharing its location with the *statio annonae*, and from the 4th century epigraphic evidence suggests it was at the Lacus Iuternae in the Forum Romanum.[16]

Being in charge of the water commission involved tasks in three main areas. The *curator aquarum*'s primary concern was to guarantee the water supply to the city and therefore he commanded a workforce of 700 slaves. He had control over private water lines and acted as judge in cases concerning aqueducts and water supply (Frontinus, *On Aqueducts* 17, 103, 104, 105, 109, 129). One of Frontinus' main concerns was to cut down on fraud.[17]

IN THE BEGINNING

Frontinus begins the main part of his treatise with the words: "For 441 years after the city was founded, the Romans were content with water supplies drawn from wells, springs or the river Tiber" (*On Aqueducts* 4.1). The site of Rome was well-provided with springs and streams, for example the Lacus Iuternae and the Lacus Curtius in the Forum Romanum. Springs, water deities and nymphs were closely linked with the foundation and growth of the city.[18] Such water sources retained their importance even after the construction of the aqueducts, and the well-watered site of the city was still discussed in glowing terms in the 1st century BC by Cicero (*On the Republic* II.3.5;5.10;6.1) amongst others.[19] The Tiber is not a particularly attractive prospect as a water source, but it was a logical one for early Rome. However, its waters also provided the easiest method of refuse disposal, either directly or indirectly via the sewers. This might involve anything from human waste to the odd dead body or two,[20] and it was a fact of which the inhabitants of Rome were reminded every time the river flooded. The Tiber was both threat and benefit to the citizens of Rome. It was a major transport route, particularly for the food brought not only from other parts of Italy but also from elsewhere in the Mediterranean and on which, by the imperial period, the city had become so heavily dependent. The regular flooding of the river was a constant threat to this food supply. There are constant references in Livy, Tacitus and Dio to flooding; in 193 BC the lower part of the city was flooded causing a number of buildings to collapse (Livy 35.9.2). The following year two bridges were washed away by the swollen river (Livy 35.21.5). In 23 BC the Pons Sublicius was destroyed for the second time in 40 years and for three days the city was navigable more easily by boat than by foot (Dio 53.33).[21]

The causes of such devastating inundations were partly natural and partly man-made. The Tiber, relatively fast-flowing in antiquity, rises in the Apennines and the water travels fast across a relatively wide flood plain before it reaches the rather narrower gorge formed by the hills at Rome coming close to the river banks. The site of Rome, of course, was originally very marshy and the valleys were only made habitable after a massive drainage and landfill scheme in the later 7th century.[22] Added to this was the rubbish which accumulated on the banks of the rivers, particularly in the port areas, and which restricted flow. Julius Caesar planned to alter the channel of the river in order, so Cicero claims, to double the size of the Campus Martius;[23] what effect this would have had is anyone's guess. Augustus dredged and cleared the river bed early on in his reign to facilitate flow and make the river less likely to flood (Suetonius, *Augustus* 30.1), but the floods continued.[24] We have very little evidence of who was responsible during the Republic for the care of the river and river banks, and although the importance of the river could not be overstated it may have been on a relatively *ad hoc* basis. In the early 1st century AD the *cura riparum et alvei Tiberis*, the commission for the Tiber, was created, comprising originally five senators who were charged with the supervision of the river and its banks.[25] However, from the time of Vespasian the commission appears to have been in the hands of one man of consular rank, and it continued its work into the 4th century when it became part of and answerable to the Urban Praefecture.[26] Under Trajan the care of sewers (*cura cloacarum urbis*) was made over to the *curator riparum et alvei Tiberis*, clearly demonstrating the authorities' awareness of the importance of co-ordinating these two closely connected concerns.[27]

The areas which suffered most in these floods were the low-lying areas such as the Campus Martius and the Emporium area, the latter of great importance for Rome's food supply. Even the heart of the city, the Forum Romanum, however, could also be affected; in AD 217 people in the Forum were swept away by the force of the waters (Dio 79.25). Hadrian raised the ground level of the northern Campus Martius, effectively creating a raised bank which would presumably have acted as a flood barrier.[28] The floods continued and it was not until the late 19th century and the canalisation of the river channel that such regular and devastating floods ceased.[29]

THE AQUEDUCTS

Long and impressive arcaded structures marching across the countryside in order to supply water to a city are often thought of as a characteristic of Roman urban design, though it would be true to say that not all Roman towns had an aqueduct.[30] It would also be true to say that not all aqueducts were high-level prominent structures; earlier Greek parallels for Roman aqueducts bringing water from outside were nearly all underground pipelines.[31] This is not because the Greeks lacked the technology; the Hellenistic aqueducts of Pergamum are clear witness to the fact that the Greek engineers were both familiar with, and skilled in, hydraulic technology.[32] It was more to do with the unstable and insecure times at which such pipelines were built. Aqueducts were vulnerable to enemy attack and very visible arcades could easily be destroyed or the water poisoned; hence such eye-catching arcades, so symbolic of Rome throughout the Empire, were projects of peace-time. The danger was shown very clearly during the 537 siege of Rome when the besieging Goths not only cut the aqueduct water supply to the city but also very nearly managed to enter the city along the channel of the Aqua Virgo (Procopius, *Gothic War* 1.1913, 18; 2.9.1–11). It has been commented on how early the Romans felt confident enough to build supply lines bringing water into the city of Rome.[33] These aqueducts became a necessity in order to supply baths, fountains, pools and basins which became so characteristic of the city and a symbol of its wealth. This is well illustrated by a passage relating to Agrippa's activities in 33 BC from Pliny the Elder (*Natural History* 121). In addition to renovating existing aqueducts and building the Aqua Iulia, he built 500 ornamental fountains, 300 of which were decorated with marble and bronze statues, as well as 700 basins and pools for public use. Such an abundance of water was impossible without a constant running water supply. By the early 3rd century AD Rome had 11 major aqueducts supplying her with water (Figs 8.1 and 8.2), nine of these are mentioned and described by Frontinus. In the Regionary

Name	Date	Length (m)	Source	Altitude of Source (m)	Level on entry into Rome	Average slope (m per km)	Length on arches (km)	Distribution within city
Appia	312 BC	16444.60	springs	30	20	0.6	0.1	II, VIII, IX, XI, XII, XIII, XIV
Anio Vetus	272–269 BC	63704.50	R Anio	280	48	3.6	–	I, III, IV, V, VI, VII, VIII, IX, XII, XIV
Marcia	144–140 BC	91424.10	springs	318	58.63	2.7	10	I, III, IV, V, VI, VII, VIII, IX, X, XIV
Tepula	125 BC	17745.40	springs	151	60.63	5.0	9	IV, V, VI, VII
Iulia	33 BC	22853.60	springs	350	63.73	12.4	10	II, III, V, VI, VIII, X, XII
Virgo	19 BC	20696.60	springs	24	20	0.2	1.2	VII, IX, XIV
Alsietina	2 BC	32847.80	Lake Alsietinus	209	71	6.0	0.5	XIV
Claudia	AD 38–52	68750.50	springs	320	67.40	3.8	14	ALL
Anio Novus	AD 38–52	86964.00	R Anio	400	70.40	3.8	11	ALL
Traiana	AD109	57700.00	springs	300	71.16	3.8	–	ALL
Alexandrina	AD 226	22,000.00	springs	65	43	1.0	2.4	IX

Fig. 8.2: Rome's aqueducts: statistics and features.

Catalogues of the early 4th century, 19 aqueducts are listed feeding 1352 public fountains, 15 *nymphaea*, 11 imperial *thermae*, 856 public baths and 254 reservoirs.[34]

Aqua Appia. By the latter part of the 4th century BC Rome's wells and springs were no longer sufficient providers of water, or perhaps of good drinking water; Rome's population was on the increase and it was felt necessary to supplement supply with water brought in from outside the city. The first of Rome's aqueducts, the Aqua Appia, was built in 312 BC by the censor Appius Claudius Caecus.[35] This aqueduct, fed by springs near Albano to the south, was technologically very simple. It ran underground for 11,190 paces (16.5 km), entering the city in the area of the Spes Vetus near the Porta Maggiore and is reported to have been carried on arcades for a distance of 60 paces (100 m) of its course within the city. It terminated at the place called the Salinae near the Porta Trigemina in the southern Forum Boarium (Frontinus, *On Aqueducts* 5–6). There is some disagreement among scholars over the exact course taken within the city, though most agree that the arcade (the term used by Frontinus is '*substructio*') was located in the valley between the Caelian and the Aventine very close to the Porta Capena.[36] There is no evidence for an elaborate terminus, but it was at a height of only 15m above sea level, meaning that its original distribution would have been much restricted. It probably supplied the Forum Boarium itself, the foot of the north-western part of the Aventine as well as the Campus Martius. These areas were developing fast at this time and presumably made worthwhile the extraordinary measures by Appius Claudius to bring water in from a source only 10 to 15 m higher than the delivery point (Fig. 8.2).[37] We know that a century later there were high rise residential blocks in the Forum Boarium area (Livy 24.47.15) and this seems to have been the main target area.

By Frontinus' day the Appia had been repaired three times: in 144 BC by Q Marcius Rex, 33 BC by Agrippa and 11–4 BC by Augustus. It supplied seven of the fourteen Augustan regions,[38] made possible by a number of secondary lines, including a conduit which was carried over the Pons Aemilia to Transtiberim.[39] One of the most important of these secondary lines was a branch added by Augustus to augment the supply of the original water line (Frontinus, *On Aqueducts* 5.7). This was known as the Appia Augusta and had a separate source, but it is doubtful that it had a separate line into the city.

Over the next 400 years the amount of water brought to Rome was to increase by a factor of 15. It has been demonstrated that the construction of new aqueducts in the last 250 years BC can be tied in to periods of population growth in the city; such periods are prefaced by major episodes of military campaigning and a lull in building in the city.[40] However, although the suggested sequence of war, population growth, aqueduct (and other) building activity does fit the general scheme, the sequence of war, which brings in booty (i.e. finance), leading to building activity which leads to population growth, equally fits the evidence (and is certainly the case with the Aqua Anio Vetus). From the time of Agrippa and Augustus, the emphasis was on providing a better and more abundant supply of water with a wider distribution, but the construction of a large imperial bath building became a prime factor.[41]

Aqua Anio Vetus. The construction of Rome's second aqueduct was an altogether more ambitious enterprise. This was the Anio Vetus, built in 272 BC by the censors M'. Curius Dentatus and L. Papirius Carbo, and funded with the spoils taken from Pyrrhus.[42] As its name implies the intake for the aqueduct was from the Aniene River (the ancient Anio) above Tivoli. Like the Appia most of the channel ran underground, but it was almost 4 times the latter's length with a meandering course to maintain a steady gradient; by Frontinus' time it was 64 km long, but it had been shortened by the addition of bridges and arcades (Fig. 8.2).[43] According to Frontinus (*On Aqueducts* 21.3), it came into the city underground at the Spes Vetus and distributed its water just inside the Servian Wall at the Porta Esquilina. Remains of a *castellum* as well as traces of the *specus* (channel) were found in the 1970s which seem to corroborate Frontinus' account.[44] Its original distribution is rather more difficult to ascertain, though as its delivery point was fairly low (48 m above sea level) it was probably restricted to those areas easily within reach by gravity flow of the Porta Esquilina. However, it gives good evidence for the expansion of the city and this time towards the higher ground to the east.[45] Its distribution by the end of the 1st century AD had been much extended, presumably through the addition of later branch lines, and it supplied water to 10 regions.[46] Despite this broad distribution, the quality of its water was rather poor; river water anyway could be heavily laden with sediment and the Aniene was particularly muddy after storms. From the late 1st century AD at least its supply was as far as possible restricted to the irrigation of gardens and "the meaner services of the city".[47]

Aqua Marcia. The first half of the 2nd century BC was a busy time overseas for Rome, culminating in the sack and destruction of Corinth and Carthage in 146 BC. Now Rome was not just mistress of the Mediterranean; as capital her population had been growing since the Second Punic War and with the successes over Carthage and Macedonia it swelled rapidly.

Building was also on the increase and there is literary evidence that a new aqueduct had been planned in 179 BC by the censors for that year;[48] the project was blocked when Licinius Crassus refused a right of way across his land. Livy mentions the planned construction of arches, a significant feature on two counts, given that Rome's first two aqueducts were underground lines, at least outside the city. Firstly this implies the introduction of a relatively high line, representing a much more ambitious project. Secondly, it was also a physical display of Rome's new-found status and accompanying confidence after the Second Punic War. In 144 BC work finally started on the construction of a new aqueduct by the praetor Q. Marcius Rex, thus named the Aqua Marcia.[49] It was the first of Rome's high-level aqueducts and an astonishing engineering achievement which cost more than 180,000,000 sesterces (a figure which Platner and Ashby in 1929 reckoned to be in the region of $1,800,000); most scholars agree that the enterprise was most probably funded by booty from Corinth and Carthage.[50] The aqueduct, renowned for the clarity and quality of its water,[51] was fed by springs high up in the Aniene valley and its channel was 61710½ paces (91 km) long (Frontinus, *On Aqueducts* 7.6), making it the longest of all Rome's aqueducts (Fig. 8.2). The ancient installations at the source of the Marcia were destroyed when the modern line of the Acqua Marcia Pia was constructed in the 1870s, but some of the ancient remains were documented by Lanciani and Ashby.[52] Initially the route of the Marcia followed more or less that of the Anio Vetus. Near Romavecchia, the channel emerged from underground to be carried on arcades the remaining *c.* 10 km into the city (Fig. 8.3).[53] The most impressive trace of the Aqua Marcia, which very well demonstrates the constant repair, renovation and maintenance required by these supply lines, is the Ponte Lupo.[54] This carried the channel (*specus*) across the Valle dei Morti south-east of Tivoli. This is a massive structure 110–115 m long, with a maximum height of over 29 m. Van Deman neatly summarised the nature of this construction: "This colossal structure, an epitome in stone and concrete of the history of Roman construction for almost nine centuries, is composed of two lofty arches of early cut stone over the stream with heavy abutments of Augustan concrete on both banks, enclosed but a few years later in walls of concrete of the same general type which in their turn were reinforced by massive walls at least three times in as many centuries, with extensive later repairs".[55] Essentially the remodelling of the bridge reflects the major repair programmes of Agrippa and Augustus. The bridge was originally built of tufa blocks quarried from the banks of the valley; the two tall central arches are constructed of the original neatly squared blocks. A century later Agrippa replaced much of the original bridge using concrete for the first time in an aqueduct arcade.[56] However, only a few years later this structure required shoring up and Augustus increased the thickness. Much of this was similarly replaced by Titus in concrete faced with *opus reticulatum*, and more buttressing was added by Hadrian. In AD 212 a massive retaining wall, 8–15 m thick, was constructed under Caracalla. At the end of the 3rd century another such wall was built on the opposite side, 6 m thick and built up to the height of the channel. It was probably designed as a counter-weight to Caracalla's wall.[57] Another bridge, also built as part of the original line in 144 BC and similarly renovated and encased by later repairs, can be seen at Ponte S. Piero which carried the Marcia across the Valle della Mola.[58]

At Romavecchia, where the Marcia emerged from underground, stretches of the arcade can still be seen with the channels of the later Aqua Tepula and Aqua Iulia above, and the 1585 channel of the still functioning Acqua Felice which runs on the north side (Fig. 8.3).[59] The Marcia came into Rome at the Spes Vetus (Fig. 8.4) and it terminated at the highest point on the Viminal Hill within the Servian Wall near the Porta Viminalis (near the later Baths of Diocletian), though the exact location is unknown.[60] A branch, the Rivus

Fig. 8.3: The channel and arcade of the Aqua Marcia at Romavecchia. The channel of the Aqua Tepula partially survives on top (Photo: author).

Herculaneus, left the main line near the Porta Tiburtina and crossed the Caelian to the Aventine.[61] In the early 3rd century Caracalla brought a branch from the Marcia, the Aqua Antoniniana, to supply his baths, and the Baths of Diocletian may also have been supplied from its terminal reservoir by a channel. A large reservoir, 91m by 16 m, known as the Botte di Termini and destroyed in 1876, was built by Diocletian as part of the construction programme.[62]

The Marcia served the northern parts of Rome especially the Quirinal and Viminal (Frontinus, *On Aqueducts* 19.3–5); visible and in place until 1992 near Termini was a small circular distribution point built of tufa and travertine. The exact function of this is unknown though it did have two lead pipes issuing from the north sides.[63] Perhaps most importantly, waters from the Marcia reached the Capitoline Hill, probably by siphon.[64] By Frontinus' time the Marcia had a very wide distribution and supplied the Palatine, the first of Rome's aqueducts to do so; the higher delivery point of the supply probably made this possible, using a siphon. The Aqua Marcia greatly improved the supply to the city centre and southern Campus Martius.[65]

With the building of the next two aqueducts we can see a development of the arcade system which is without parallel elsewhere in the Roman world. As the needs of the city increased, these extra requirements were met by tapping new springs. Additional supplies were not fed into the existing system, but completely new channels were constructed. In their upper courses aqueducts followed the hillsides, but once they emerged out onto the Roman Campagna they required expensive masonry arcades. To reduce materials, effort and cost a new channel was simply carried on top of an existing one, piggy-back fashion. In Agrippa's rebuilding work in 33 BC the Marcia acquired the Tepula and the Iulia to form a triple-decker, though the Tepula may have used the arcades of the Marcia from the beginning (see below).

Aqua Tepula. The Aqua Tepula is the most problematic of all the republican aqueducts. It was constructed in 125 BC but because it was radically altered by Agrippa, most of the information given by Frontinus refers to its 1st century AD state; equally there is very little archaeological evidence for its original form.[66] In addition the original purpose of the aqueduct is difficult to ascertain. Its construction only 20 years or so after that of the Marcia must indicate a fairly

Fig. 8.4: A pier of the Aqua Marcia preserved in the later Aurelianic Wall. The smaller channels of the Tepula and Iulia are visible above the stone channel of the Marcia (Photo: author).

rapid growth in the city's population, as well as the fact that it also apparently supplied the Capitoline, probably to supplement the rather limited supply of the Marcia.[67]

The springs that fed the Tepula were located on the northern slopes of the Alban Hills at the foot of Monte Cimino;[68] the water was warm (60°F) giving the aqueduct its name. As a result the water was probably not suitable for drinking and the aqueduct may well have been introduced originally for industrial uses to free up the Marcia for drinking. Given that the Tepula supplied the Capitoline, it would have had to have come into the city at a high level. It has been suggested, therefore, that in order to cut down on the expense of building more arcades (which had been built for the Marcia only 20 years before), the arcades of the Aqua Marcia were used even at this early stage; Agrippa's rebuilding work, however, makes it very difficult to elucidate the exact situation.[69]

Aqua Iulia. The Aqua Tepula was completely reworked in 33 BC when Agrippa was aedile in conjunction with his construction of the Aqua Iulia (Frontinus, *On Aqueducts* 9). The 1st century BC had been riven with political strife and civil war and by the 30s BC Rome's water system was in desperate need of attention. Agrippa repaired the Appia, Anio Vetus and Marcia whose channels were in a very bad state (Frontinus, *On Aqueducts* 9.3). It was also at this time that he laid the foundations of the administrative system for Rome's water supply, *the cura aquarum* which was established in 11 BC (see above).[70]

The source of the Aqua Iulia was a set of abundant springs near modern Grottaferrata and Agrippa added the waters of the Tepula, the combined waters running for 6 km to a settling tank near Capanelle.[71] From here the two lines were separated and carried into Rome on the arcade of the Marcia. Both these additional channels were much narrower than the original cut-stone channel of the Marcia. Further, they were not placed centrally over the bottom channel. One side wall was directly above the side wall of the Marcia below, while the other rested upon the Marcia's cover slabs. When the Marcia was built it had not been anticipated that it would have to bear such extra weight and these slabs often cracked. The Tepula's channel had to be narrower because the aqueduct had a smaller discharge, but the height had to be the same to permit access for maintenance. If it had been as wide as the Marcia, with the smaller volume of water, the flow would have been reduced and the risk of silting up of the channel increased.[72]

The Iulia was the third highest of all the lines (Frontinus, *On Aqueducts* 18.4) and had a capacity almost double that of the Tepula. Its terminus was near that of the Marcia near the

Porta Viminalis[73] and it had a wide distribution via a number of secondary *intra urbem* branches by the time of Frontinus (*On Aqueducts* 83.2) (Figs 8.2 and 8.5). The Iulia was very important in Agrippa's general reworking of Rome's water supply and it made a significant contribution to the total volume of water coming into Rome at the time. The Iulia supplied a large proportion of its waters to public areas, in contrast to the Tepula the water of which was destined more for private users. Certainly by mixing the waters of the two lines, Agrippa much improved the earlier aqueduct, increasing its capacity and lowering the temperature of the water. Further, the Iulia had a specific function, that of supplying water for the Augustan building programme.[74]

Aqua Virgo. In 19 BC Agrippa added the Aqua Virgo to Rome's water system, the purpose and distribution of which was quite different from the Tepula and Iulia (Frontinus, *On Aqueducts* 10; Dio 54.117).[75] This aqueduct is noteworthy on a number of counts; it is the only ancient aqueduct which has continuously functioned since antiquity; it was the only one to enter Rome from the north; and it was the first aqueduct line to be built to supply a specific complex of buildings in a specific area (the Baths of Agrippa, the Stagnum and the Euripus on the Campus Martius).[76] Further, apart from the Alsietina and the Appia, this was also one of the lowest aqueducts in terms of elevation (20 m above sea level) (Frontinus, *On Aqueducts* 18) (Fig. 8.2). For an aqueduct to be most effective and reach most of any city it needed to enter the city at or close to the highest point, a reality of which Frontinus was certainly aware (*On Aqueducts* 18). However, the purpose of this line, to supply a very low-lying area, negated this need to some extent.[77] Pliny the Elder particularly comments on the special suitability of its water for the purposes of bathing in comparison to the Marcia which was ideal for drinking water (*Natural History* 31.42). The springs which supplied the Virgo were 10.5 km from Rome. According to Frontinus (*On Aqueducts* 10) the aqueduct received its name as a result of a young girl showing Agrippa's engineers the hidden source which supplied good quality, clear, cool water in abundance. Pliny the Elder (*Natural History* 31.42) gives another explanation: "The springs are close to the stream of Hercules, but because the waters of the Virgo run away from this, it was so named". The water channel was underground for most of its course until it emerged in the area of the modern Piazza di Spagna. The channel was then carried on a low arcade to the area of the Saepta Iulia whence the water was distributed.[78] The complex supplied by the aqueduct was large indeed. The Stagnum, essentially an artificial lake, was extensive enough for boating; swimming is only mentioned by the sources in connection with the Euripus.[79]

The distribution of water from the Virgo complemented that of the Aqua Iulia, supplying water to three regions.[80] It was clearly planned to meet the specific requirements of districts only marginally supplied by earlier aqueducts, as well as to supply Agrippa's new set of buildings (Fig. 8.5). At this time the Campus Martius was undergoing major monumentalization and until this time had been badly served by Rome's water supply lines.[81] The Transtiberim was supplied by a branch of the Virgo carried across the Pons Agrippae, and it has been suggested that this was the reason for the bridge's construction.[82] By Frontinus' time the Transtiberim region was supplied by the Appia, the Anio Vetus and the Marcia, the pipes being carried across the Tiber on bridges.[83] However, the distribution from the Virgo via the Pons Agrippae started further upstream and therefore could have had a much wider delivery into the northern region of Transtiberim.[84]

Aqueduct	Castella	Delivery extra urbem		Total delivery intra urbem	nomine Caesaris intra urbem	privati intra urbem	usibus publicis intra urbem	opera publica (Total 95)	lacus (Total 591)
		Caes. nom.	priv.						
Appia	20	5		699	151	194	354	123 (14)	226 (92)
Anio Vetus	35	169	404	1508.5	64.5	490	552	196 (19)	218 (94)
Marcia	51	261.5		1472	116	543	491	61 (15)	113 (256)
Tepula	14	58	56	331	34	237	50	7 (3)	32 (13)
Iulia	17	85	121	597	18	196	383	181 (11?)	65 (28)
Virgo	18	200		2304	509	338	1457	1380 (16)	51 (25)
Alsietina		254	138						
Claudia & Anio Novus	92	728	439	3498	816	1567	1115	374 (18)	585 (226)

Fig. 8.5: Capacities and distribution of Rome's aqueducts according to Frontinus.

Aqua Alsietina. Agrippa's provision and repair of the Tepula, Iulia and Virgo reflect supplies for particular needs, although they also provided water more generally. The last Augustan aqueduct was the most specialised of all. This was the Aqua Alsietina, built by Augustus to supply his *naumachia* on the west bank of the Tiber, the only aqueduct to deliver water to a point outside the city limits.[85] The source for this aqueduct was the Lacus Alsietinus, the modern Lago Martignano to the north of Rome. Most of the 33 km course was underground and it came into the urban area near the later Porta Aurelia, after which it was carried on an arcade before again going underground to Trastevere.[86] The aqueduct arrived at the city at a high elevation (71 m above sea level) and as such would have had a wide distribution throughout the Transtiberim region.[87] The *naumachia* was at a much lower level (*c*. 16 m above sea level), and in order to achieve this much lower elevation over such a short distance, the water was probably used to irrigate gardens on the hillslopes; it has also been suggested that it was used to power mills on the slopes of the Janiculum (see below).[88]

The *naumachia* basin itself was inaugurated with a magnificent show of naval warfare in 2 BC in connection with the dedication of the Temple of Mars Ultor. It was located in the area bounded by S. Cosimato, S. Francesco a Ripa and the Janiculum 1800 Roman feet by 1200 Roman feet.[89] The water of the Alsietina was considered unwholesome in the extreme and Frontinus (*On Aqueducts* 11.2) says it was not used for public needs but was fit only for industrial uses and for watering gardens. However, although the population of Transtiberim was usually by this time supplied by water from the Marcia and the Virgo which was piped across from the east bank, when these were cut during bridge maintenance, the people had no choice but to use the Alsietina's doubtful supplies.[90] Frontinus in fact gives very little detail of the Alsietina.[91] It is true to say that the line would have declined in importance after the introduction of the Aqua Traiana in the early 2nd century AD, possibly even going out of use. Philip the Arab is recorded as having constructed a *naumachia* in the Transtiberim region to celebrate the millennium of Rome in AD 247, but it could easily have been supplied by the Aqua Traiana – if this notice has any truth at all.[92]

Aqua Claudia and Aqua Anio Novus. In the early 1st century AD water was becoming increasingly important for display and decorative purposes, so much so that within 50 years Agrippa's aqueducts were no longer sufficient. In AD 38 Caligula started the construction of probably the two greatest aqueducts in terms of volume of water carried into Rome – the Aqua Claudia and the Aqua Anio Novus.[93] The project was completed by Claudius in 52; in Frontinus' description the two lines are seen as a single project although they have very different sources.[94] The Claudia was fed by springs in the Aniene valley further upstream from those serving the Marcia and considered in quality second only to the Marcia.[95] It also emerged from underground at Capanelle to cross the Campagna near Romavecchia on a lofty arcade for a distance of 10 km to the city (Fig. 8.6).[96] At Spes Vetus it was carried across the Via Labicana and Via Praenestina on the Claudian monumental arch now known as the Porta Maggiore (Fig. 8.7).[97] The Anio Novus, as the Anio Vetus before it, was fed by the Aniene river itself and was initially troubled by the infiltration of mud despite special settling tanks at the point of intake (Frontinus, *On Aqueducts* 15.1–2; 90; 93.4). The intake was remodelled by Trajan to deal with the sediment problem and indeed the quality was improved immeasurably. The source was moved upstream to one of the lakes formed when Nero had dammed the Aniene for a pleasure lake at his villa at Subiaco.[98] Near Capanelle the channel passed through a settling tank (see below) and for the approach to Rome across the Campagna was carried piggy-back by that of the Claudia;[99] the consequences of carrying two channels on one arcade not designed for the purpose can be clearly seen. The arcade and *specus* of the Claudia were constructed of neatly cut blocks of *peperino* tufa; the channel of the Anio Novus was of concrete, clearly indicating that this arrangement had not been part of the original plan.[100] The tendency was for the arches to settle or even crack from the extra weight causing leaks in the conduits above. Various later repairs and reinforcements were designed to correct the problem. Under Hadrian bracing arches were built between the piers, and support was inserted where necessary in the form of arches of brick as a liner to the stone arcades. This was not wholly successful because the liner often settled more than the arch it was supposed to support, leaving gaps between the two. [101]

The Aqua Claudia and Aqua Anio Novus were, with the Aqua Traiana, the highest of Rome's aqueducts in terms of urban elevation, and their waters were mixed within the city before distribution, much to the disapproval of Frontinus (*On Aqueducts* 72.6; 91.1–4; see below) (Fig. 8.2). The terminal *castellum* was located near the 'Temple of Minerva Medica' and was recorded in a famous engraving of Piranesi; it was unfortunately destroyed in a fire in 1880 (Fig. 8.8).[102] Despite some of its waters being mixed with the Anio Novus, a branch left the Claudia before this occurred and the water from this supply line was distributed under the name of Claudia. This is the Arcus Caelimontani. This branch diverted from the main conduit just south of the Porta Maggiore. It maintained a high elevation for 2 km across the ridge of the Caelian to terminate behind the platform of the Temple of the Deified Claudius at the area known as 'Aqueductium' on the *Forma Urbis* (Fig 8.9). Nero was responsible for this line, hence Frontinus referring to it as Arcus Neroniani (Fig 8.10). The purpose of this line is one which has been questioned in recent times.[103] Most scholars have assumed that Nero built the branch line to supply his Domus Aurea and its extensive water systems, in particular the lake in the valley of the Colosseum and the *nymphaeum* on the north-west slopes of the Caelian (actually the unfinished Temple of the Deified Claudius). After Nero's death and the dismantling of much of these systems, the line continued to be useful, delivering good quality water to the centre of the city. However, the lake could have been just as easily formed by damming the stream which flows between the Caelian and the Esquiline

Fig. 8.6: The arcade of the Aqua Claudia at Romavecchia. The partially preserved channel of the Anio Novus runs above that of the Claudia (Photo: author).

(whose presence is still in evidence in the lowest levels beneath S Clemente nearby); an aqueduct could have topped it up but it was not absolutely necessary.[104] Indeed, given that Roman aqueducts could not be turned off,[105] if this branch line supplied the lake as well there must have been various and substantial installations to allow the water to drain away without causing flooding. The aqueduct might therefore have been constructed as part of the general welfare programme instituted by Nero after the Great Fire in 64.[106] It is interesting to note that nowhere does Frontinus say that Nero built this branch to supply the Domus Aurea. However, clearly its high elevation meant it could supply good quality water to a wide area, and it perhaps replaced in some areas the water supplied by the Marcia which could then be delivered more selectively.[107] Under Domitian this branch was extended to the Palatine; much of that standing today is a Severan rebuild.[108] Certainly the combined Claudia and Anio Novus supplied all regions of Rome and had a considerable capacity (Frontinus, *On Aqueducts* 20.5; 76.3) (Figs 8.2 and 8.5). From the Caelian, the Aventine and Transtiberim region could be easily supplied and it is significant that no new water supply-line was felt necessary for 60 years.[109]

Aqua Traiana. The Aqua Traiana, the last of the great aqueducts to supply the city, was constructed in AD 109.[110] Built after the time that Frontinus was writing, we know very little about it, a fact which underscores the value of the water commissioner's writings. The Aqua Traiana brought high quality water from springs above the Lacus Sabatinus (Lake Bracchiano) to the north of Rome. The channel has been traced at various locations along its course to the Janiculum, including its association with mills which were reported by Lanciani in 1886 and which are depicted on the *Forma Urbis*.[111] A large *castellum* or receiving tank was found on the Via Aurelia just inside the city wall.[112] With its point of entry high above the Transtiberim region, the water of the Aqua Traiana vastly improved the lot of the inhabitants of the west bank who had increased considerably in numbers during the 1st century AD. Particularly if supplies from across the river were cut, this may have been its primary purpose (Fig. 8.2).[113] However, its elevation meant that it could deliver water to all 14 regions (as the Claudia and Anio Novus) , and for the first time water was piped to the east bank from the west.[114] The Aqua Traiana also supplied water to the new Baths of Trajan on the Esquiline Hill, although the details of how this was achieved are lacking. What is clear is that it was not the main supplier. The Sette Sale, the huge cistern to the north-east of the baths and built

Fig. 8.8: Piranesi's engraving of the reservoir (castellum) *of the Aqua Claudia and Aqua Anio Novus (destroyed in 1880).*

Fig. 8.7: The Claudian Porta Maggiore which carried the channels of the Aqua Claudia and Aqua Anio Novus across the Via Praenestina and the Via Labicana (Photo: author).

contemporaneously with them, was not supplied by the Aqua Traiana, but by one of the aqueducts entering the city at Spes Vetus, possibly the Aqua Claudia (see below).[115]

Aqua Alexandrina. The Aqua Traiana was the last of the great aqueduct lines of imperial Rome. One further aqueduct was built, the Aqua Alexandrina, constructed by Severus Alexander in the early 3rd century.[116] Most scholars assume, on the basis of the *Historia Augusta*, that it was brought in specifically to supply his rebuilding of the Baths of Nero in the Campus Martius, but there are several problems with this assumption. The passage in the SHA (*Severus Alexander* 25) mentions the construction of the aqueduct in the same sentence but does not specifically state that it was built to supply the refurbished baths; many modern commentators seem to ignore the fact that the earlier Baths of Nero had to have been supplied with water. This, coupled with a major lack of knowledge of the course of the Aqua Alexandrina within the city, makes the situation far less certain than is often made out.[117] The source of the Alexandrina was at springs in a marshy area south of the 14th milestone of the Via Praenestina; in certain locations it was carried on arcades with the most impressive surviving section at Viale Palmiro in Centocelle.[118] It entered the city at ground level in the vicinity of Spes Vetus, but little is known of its course after that; a structure close to the Saepta has been identified as the terminal *castellum*.[119] In 1585–7 the waters of the Alexandrina were regathered by Sixtus V as the Acqua Felice (see below).

Fig. 8.9: The area to the south-east of the temple of Claudius depicted on the FUR and labelled 'Aqueductum' (Photo: author).

QUALITY, TANKS AND MAINTENANCE

Frontinus goes into some detail in *On Aqueducts* about the quality of the water provided by these supply lines and the problems involved in keeping supplies uncontaminated. The Marcia was universally lauded as the best; it was clear, cool and pure.[120] Indeed, Nero outraged public opinion by bathing in the springs which supplied the aqueduct (Tacitus, *Annals* 14.22). The Alsietina, on the other hand, was universally despised.[121] There were therefore good reasons for keeping the channels separate. However, there were provisions along a number of the aqueduct lines for the diversion of water from one channel to another to facilitate maintenance and to reduce flow.[122] The level of the water in the channels varied with rainfall and since the sources were in a variety of areas, the rate of flow was complicated by both seasonal and regional peaks. This variation has also been noted in the study of the aqueducts supplying Lyon.[123] Whilst diversion made practical sense in theory, it was not always intelligently carried out; good water could be wasted or contaminated by bad. Frontinus (*On Aqueducts* 67, 90–2) says that the Anio Vetus which ran at a lower level than the others kept its pollution to itself, though by the end of the 1st century AD it did draw some of its water from the Marcia. Not so the Anio Novus. Being the highest of all the aqueducts and also very abundant, it was used to make up any shortage in the others.[124] Frontinus laments the fact that the waters of the Claudia, which were also plentiful, were mixed with those of the Anio Novus when the two channels entered the city.[125] With obvious anger he says "even the Marcia, so charming in its brilliancy and coldness, is found serving baths, fullers, and even purposes too vile to mention" (Frontinus, *On Aqueducts* 91).

This switching of water from one channel to another was facilitated by the channels being placed one on top of the other. The problem was that the better quality water ran in the bottom channel – the Marcia and the Claudia; any maintenance work required in the upper channels would almost certainly mean diversion of the inferior water into the far better quality supply. This can also happen in more complicated arrangements. At Grotto Sconce there is a settling tank on the Anio Novus.[126] Two channels run out from it, one carrying the Anio Novus, the second running out to supply the Claudia and the Marcia via cross-link channels. These last

Fig. 8.10: Piranesi's engraving of the Arcus Neroniani or Arcus Caelimontani which carried a branch of the Claudia onto the Caelian.

two aqueducts ran at a lower level – and both carried water of much higher quality. The Anio Novus was notoriously sandy and the reservoir would have served as a settling tank to rid it of as much of the impurities as possible before being mixed with the purer waters of the Claudia and Marcia. At S. Cosimato, the channel of the Claudia crossed over that of the Marcia; a vertical shaft, 1.2 by 1.08 metres, at the crossing point allowed water, controlled by a sluice-gate, from the Claudia to drop through the floor into the Marcia.[127]

Such settling tanks along the route of an aqueduct were important so that the water could arrive in the city rid of the worst of its impurities, though not all aqueducts may have had them.[128] The importance of these settling tanks can probably be best demonstrated by the example on the course of the Anio Novus discovered in 1884 at the Villa Bertone, Capanelle.[129] The tank comprised two chambers, 6 by 6.70 m and 12 by 6.70 m and both were completely full of small, completely round, pea-sized pebbles. These seem to have travelled from Subiaco in the Sabine Hills, a distance of some 70 km, along the bed of the Anio Novus. What is amazing here is that not only were the tanks full when discovered but the Villa Bertone itself seems to have been built on an artificial platform made up of the debris from numerous cleaning operations of the settling tank. With the material surrounding the tank, which also included sand, the owner of the villa was able to plaster six or seven buildings on his farm, without appearing to diminish the deposit, and to gravel about a kilometre of avenues.[130] In fact one of the improvements under Trajan was to realign the intake for this aqueduct so that water was taken from the middle of three large dammed pleasure lakes created by Nero which could thereafter act as giant settling tanks.[131] This great mass of sand and pebbles at the Villa Bertone merely represents the final residue that still managed to escape this screening process. A major, and never-ending, task for the maintenance teams was not only the removal of this kind of debris, but also of lime incrustation (*sinter*) from the inside of the conduit; a build-up of lime could severely restrict the flow of water.[132]

GRADIENT AND SPEED OF FLOW

Nine of Rome's eleven major aqueducts drew their water from sources in the Sabine Hills and their course then followed the valley of the Aniene to Tivoli; the water ran in large, covered conduits, either rock-cut or closed by slabs. All were gravity-flow aqueducts and the speed of flow was determined by the gradient of the channel which must not be too shallow or too great (the water might 'burst its banks' or lie still and become stagnant).[133] At Tivoli the aqueducts were confronted by an escarpment which abruptly dropped 180 m; the river itself negotiates this in the celebrated Tivoli cascade. The aqueducts avoid this by swinging to the south-west and maintaining the same gradient, taking a route which slopes down the face of the escarpment.[134] For Vitruvius (*On Architecture* 8.6.1) the minimum slope was ½ foot per 100 feet or 5 m per km (0.5%); for Pliny (*Natural History* 31.57) it is ¼ inch per 100 feet or 20 cm per km (0.02%). Archaeological evidence suggests that Pliny's figure is more accurate, though it is rather shallow. For the principal aqueducts of Rome, an average gradient of 3m per km (0.3%) is common (Fig. 8.2). The difference in slope along an aqueduct line is mainly the result of topographical factors but the quality of the water (for example if it is laden with silt) could also be a consideration.[135] On the Anio Novus gradients varied quite considerably (the highest estimated velocity was 4.08 m per second and in some tunnels the gradients were very steep indeed).[136] Hodge suggests that the usual speed of water in a channel was about 1–1.5 m per second (average speed 3.5–5.5 km per hour),[137] which means that it might take up to 24 hours for water to travel from source to city in the longest aqueducts (obviously this would be considerably less for shorter lines).

DISTRIBUTION *INTRA* AND *EXTRA URBEM* (FIG. 8.5)

According to Frontinus (*On Aqueducts* 78–86) just over a quarter of water delivered by Rome's aqueducts never reached Rome, but was drawn off outside the city (*extra urbem*); this was a considerable amount considering that Frontinus probably reckoned the area up to the 7th milestone as *intra urbem*.[138] Private consumers who owned estates along an aqueduct could arrange to draw off water at certain times; payment for water rights helped pay for maintenance costs.[139] Land irrigated unlawfully, that is by drawing water off illegally, was a problem mentioned by Frontinus and one which continued into late antiquity.[140] There are a number of instances of private lines taken off main aqueducts. An imperial example is provided by the Commodan period (180–192) branch off the Aqua Claudia which supplied the earlier Villa of the Quintilii on the Via Appia.[141] Private examples include the estate of Manlius Vopiscus at Tivoli which was supplied with water by a branch off the Aqua Marcia, and the mid-2nd century AD large villa of Sette Bassi at Casale Romavecchia which was served by a branch from the Anio Novus.[142] The Hadrianic villa at La Vignacce was very close to the line of the Marcia from which water was taken into a very large cistern, so designed that water could only be drawn off if the *specus* of the Marcia was running at two-thirds full.[143] In his discussion of the Aqua Iulia (*On Aqueducts* 9) Frontinus mentions the Aqua Crabra, a small aqueduct which supplied all the villas in the area of Tusculum. Apparently the supply for this aqueduct had received the attentions of some of the watermen who had used it for illegal distributions. Frontinus put a stop to the practice and restored the supply to the area of Tusculum. The Anio Vetus supplied through a branch *in Tiburtium usum* (for the use of Tibur (Tivoli), and presumably the surrounding district); the poorer quality water from the Anio Vetus was recommended only to be used for irrigating gardens. The Alsietina was employed almost exclusively for irrigation outside Rome.[144]

Most of Rome's aqueducts entered the city from the east; only the Alsietina and the Traiana came in on the west bank. The Transtiberim region was well-served with springs and until the late Republic this was sufficient for its small population. However, in the imperial period the population of Regio XIV greatly increased, necessitating other measures.[145] Six pipelines are known to have been taken across the Tiber, five of which can be deduced from Frontinus; the earliest are the Appia, Anio Vetus and Marcia (Frontinus, *On Aqueducts* 79.2; 80.2; 81.2).[146] The Aqua Virgo was taken across by Agrippa; the Aqua Claudia was extended by Nero (Frontinus *On Aqueducts* 20). After Frontinus' time the Aqua Traiana was taken across in the other direction and supplied the Baths of Trajan.[147] One of the most complex aspects of Roman water supply was how water was distributed within towns, a feature further complicated by how little it has been studied.[148] Another problem is the almost complete lack of survival *in situ* of the lead pipes used to convey the water. Closed pipe-lines were not the only way of conveying water within the city; free-flow channels were also used, for example the Arcus Neroniani of the Claudia/Anio Novus and the Rivus Herculaneus of the Aqua Marcia.[149]

FRONTINUS' FIGURES AND THE CAPACITY OF ROME'S WATER SUPPLY (Figs 8.5 and 8.11)

Reference has already been made to Frontinus' figures for the volume of water delivered by each of the aqueducts, but the problem is that scholars cannot agree on how much water this actually constituted.[150] "Students of Frontinus correct him at their own peril"[151] is advice which is not always followed. Frontinus' description of measurement and capacity uses three basic concepts: *modus* (quantity), *conceptio* (supply available), *erogatio* (amount delivered); he gives his figures in the form of *quinariae*. According to Frontinus (*On Aqueducts* 24–30) there were two main methods of measuring the size of a water-pipe which were relevant to Rome. The first, possibly introduced by Agrippa and certainly mentioned by Vitruvius (*On Architecture* 8.6.4), was based on the width of the sheet of lead from which the pipe was made. The *quinaria* was the smallest lead pipe in use; its name derives from the fact that the lead sheet from which it was made was 5 *digiti* in width (a *digitus* is approximately 1.85 cm); the diameter of the pipe was 2.3125 cm.[152] The second method, apparently in use since Augustus (Frontinus, *On Aqueducts* 99), still used the *quinaria* as the basic unit, indicating a diameter of 5 *quadrantes*. The method was only used for pipes with a diameter up to 20 *quadrantes*; after this the pipe was named according to the area of the pipe measured in *digiti*. The *quinaria* is therefore used as the basic unit of measurement and reflects the diameter of the pipe; it does not reflect the volume or time, but merely a cross-section.[153] This is really at the heart of the problem. How can a simple pipe and its linear diameter dimension be used to measure volume of water? Frontinus is using the *quinaria* pipe as a measurement of volume, that is the amount of water passing through pipe under a fixed given head. On the factor of rate of flow, Frontinus has not been sympathetically treated by modern commentators; one goes so far to say that the Romans must have been aware of something so obvious, and Frontinus got it wrong because he was a civil servant and not an engineer.[154] The Romans could, and did, measure volume (for example of wine and olive oil); they could also measure time. But it was the two together, velocity, for which there was no convenient method, although the concept and effect were known.[155] Further, the rate of flow in an aqueduct is influenced by a number of factors, for example the local conditions of the channel itself, and by the situation both upstream and downstream of it. One could therefore have varying depths of water flowing in a channel along its course, as well as varying rates of flow, as has been well demonstrated in recent studies.[156] As a result of this, we now face a situation where we have widely differing estimates of how much water the Roman aqueducts carried – from

322,000 m^3 per day to 1,010,000 m^3 per day.[157] These modern estimates are based on the *capacity* of the aqueducts estimated from Frontinus' measurements taken at source (given here in Fig. 8.11 with a sample of modern estimates; Grimal's figures include modern estimates for the Traiana and Alexandrina). Any estimates on a *per capita* basis are based on these figures of capacity and rarely on the actual amount delivered. Frontinus' figures for the actual amount of water delivered by each aqueduct, and therefore available for use by Rome's population, are set out in Fig. 8.5; these rarely figure in modern calculation of Rome's water supply.[158] Further, modern estimates do not take into account that the amount of water available to the upper classes, who could afford their own private connection and private bath suites, was many times greater than the amount reaching (and being used by) the ordinary person who had to rely on the nearest fountain. Blackman's very meticulous set of figures suggests that we should be looking at the lower end of these estimates, but the margin of error is still too great for these figures to have any real meaning.[159] One particular problem with Frontinus' figures (*On Aqueducts* 2, 4–5, 80–81, 90–2, 101–2, 125, 135) is that they reflect the situation in his own time rather than the original capacities of the aqueducts; repairs would presumably have improved their capacity and efficiency. A further problem is that his figures are sometimes misquoted, adjusted or rounded up by modern scholars. The aqueducts of his day had a capacity of 24,413 *quinariae*; he gives the figure of 14,018 *quinariae* for the amount delivered (Frontinus, *On Aqueducts* 87.3; 64.4). These two figures are most often used for modern calculations, overlooking the fact that the amount delivered includes 4063 *quinariae* drawn off *outside* the city.[160] Moreover, Frontinus wrongly assumed that the quantity of water in open-flow channels could be reckoned in the same way as for closed pipes in an urban distribution system.[161] The lack of any exact figure (and lack of consistency in expression of that figure) for the water delivery to the city of Rome therefore makes it difficult to try to calculate how much water was available on a *per capita* basis (added to which estimates of the population of Rome also vary widely!)[162] Given the above discussion, one has to ask whether *any* of these calculations has any value. However, Frontinus' figures do afford an extremely valuable body of evidence for where, when and why water was needed, and the relative quantities delivered to different consumers.

Part of Frontinus' duties as curator of Rome's aqueducts was to correct any discrepancies in the records as well as address the problem of abuse of the system by both private individuals and the employees of the water office. He refers on a number of occasions to where the imperial records do not tally with his own measurements (*On Aqueducts* 64–76). And he lays the blame fairly and squarely on the "dishonesty of the water men, whom we have detected diverting water from the public conduits for private use" and also "a large number of landed proprietors, past whose fields the aqueducts run, who tap the conduits; whence it comes that the public water-courses are actually brought to a standstill by private citizens, just to water their gardens".

That is not to say that it was not possible to legally tap into the system outside the city. Frontinus states that of the total delivery of 14,018 *quinariae* of Rome's aqueducts, only 9,955 were divided *intra urbem* (71%).[163] Of the 4063 *quinariae* delivered outside Rome just under half (1718 *quinariae* or 42.3%) was subject to the disposition of the Emperor, the rest went to private individuals (2345 *quinariae*) (Fig. 8.5).[164] One final point to bear in mind is that Rome had a high water table and never had to entirely depend on aqueducts for its water. There is now little way of knowing how significant a role wells and cisterns might have played in the lives of the city's population.

CASTELLA

However much water actually came into Rome, a settling tank was normally positioned at the end of an aqueduct's run when it entered the city, although in some cities elsewhere in the Roman world aqueducts delivered water into very large cisterns.[165] This slowed the flow sufficiently to allow any material carried in suspension to drift to the bottom. The water was then piped off to different parts of the city. Arrangements within the structure varied although a common principle was to have at least two chambers. Pliny the Elder (*Natural History* 36.173) recommends two chambers for a *castellum divisiorum*, but in the terminal *castellum* for the Aqua Virgo, recorded in the 17th century at the foot of the Pincian, the water circulated through 4 chambers in turn, allowing impurities to settle by gravity.[166] The water flowed into one of the upper chambers but had to pass through the two lower chambers before leaving via a channel in the second upper chamber, having deposited debris and impurities in the lower chambers; one of these lower chambers had an opening low on one side running directly into the sewers. With chambers arranged on different levels the water would become less and less contaminated; certainly the Virgo ranked after the Marcia and Claudia for purity (Pliny, *Natural History* 31.42). Presumably grills or some such mechanism could have been fitted; there is no evidence on any of the Rome aqueducts, where of course the volume of water to be treated is enormous, that the water was filtered in some way. The water was then carried to secondary *castella* sometimes on arcades, sometimes underground.[167]

The various terminal *castella* were obviously in different locations but all were fairly high to facilitate distribution within the city. For example, the Claudia and Anio Novus discharged into a *castellum* near the Minerva Medica, which is recorded in an engraving of Piranesi. It was destroyed in 1880, but it was an imposing structure 21.5 by 14.2 m and consisting of 5 rectangular cisterns with semi-circular niches on the façade (fig. 8.8).[168] From here the waters were distributed through a shared network of secondary *castella* from which pipes supplied individual customers (Fig. 8.5).

Rome in the time of Frontinus had 247 *castella*, with the Claudia and Anio Novus combined waters supplying 92, the Marcia 51 and the Anio Vetus 35 (Fig. 8.5).[169] Vitruvius' prescription for a *castellum* requires three chambers, all supplied by an aqueduct and so arranged that when the two outer chambers overflow, the water goes into the middle one (Vitruvius, *On Architecture* 8.1–2). From the middle one, pipes go off to serve the public fountains; the other two serve the baths and private homes. The priorities are clearly established. But what is clear from Vitruvius' account is that it does not recognise the priority of public fountains usually inferred by modern commentators in that his design makes no effort to ensure that they are served first; in time of dearth all three go short. If we look at the *castellum* at Pompeii we here see in plan the three divisions as outlined by Vitruvius, but the difference from his prescription is that the three outlets are at different heights with the lowest supplying the public fountains and therefore the last to dry up. For Rome we know very little about this side of the water supply despite having Frontinus' account. He does talk of fountains with two water jets, each supplied by a different aqueduct so that if one was out of commission the provision of water was not interrupted, so there were contingency plans. The pipelines from the *castellum* might be lead or terracotta pipes; the *castellum* marks the end of the open channel and the beginning of the low pressure pipe system of urban distribution [170]

Name	Total capacity at intake (*quinariae*)	m³ (Grimal)	m³ (Forbes)	m³ (Aicher)
Appia	1825	73000	75737	75000
Anio Vetus	4398	175920	182517	180000
Marcia	4690	187600	194365	190000
Tepula	445	17800		17800
Iulia	1206	48240	50043	48000
Virgo	2504	100160	103916	100000
Alsietina	392	15680	16228	16000
Claudia	4607	184280	191190	185000
Anio Novus	4738	189520	196627	190000
Traiana		113920		
Alexandrina		21160		
Total	24805	1127220	1010623	1001800

Fig. 8.11: Comparative figures of aqueduct capacities.

CONSUMERS, PIPES AND FOUNTAINS

Frontinus specified three clearly separate groups of water consumers within the city.[171] The first, which included selected public baths, was accorded special privileges by the emperor (*c.* 17% of the water). The second group consisted of public users such as military and official establishments, theatres, fountains and baths (*c.* 44%). The third was private users, houses and industries (*c.* 38%).[172] Basic fountains would have been near enough on every street corner and are marked as circles on the *Forma Urbis Romae*; but decorative fountains were not introduced into Rome until the 1st century BC.[173] Frontinus (*On Aqueducts* 78.3) lists a total of 591 open water basins (*lacus*) within the city. We know of one from an inscription, the *fons cuniculi*; presumably the wall from which the feed pipe emerged was carved with the figure of a rabbit. Similar types of fountain head can still be seen at Pompeii. A number of other fountains are listed in the Regionary Catalogues, but of a total of 1212 (or 1352) fountains known to have existed in ancient Rome, only a few can be identified now.[174] One which is known and excavated is the Lacus Servilius in the Forum Romanum which was fed by the Aqua Marcia and drained into the Cloaca Maxima. The Lacus Iuternae was also situated in the Forum and was fed by springs.[175] Ovid (*Fasti* 1.708) clearly indicated the position of the fountain but it was not known until 1900 with Boni's excavations of the Forum Romanum.[176] One exceptional fountain, perhaps more properly called a *nymphaeum*, still stands in what is now the Piazza Vittorio Emanuele. This is a brick-faced concrete structure, popularly known as the Sedia del Diavolo or Trofei di Mario, which has been dated to the 3rd century AD (Fig. 8.12). Traditionally described as the terminus of the Aqua Iulia, this is now very much in doubt.[177] This comprised a number of chambers on several levels; the upper storey consists of a large apsidal niche flanked by open arches. Below this water poured from niches into a broad channel and from there it flowed to the lower storey, largely taken up by a large basin. Five main outlets are still visible – one on the 2nd storey, three in the first and one on each side. This building is an excellent illustration of the importance of large water-providing installations with a combined display function. The parallels are numerous around the Mediterranean and indeed this may be the only surviving example in Rome of a type of fountain called '*munera*' by Frontinus (*On Aqueducts* 79–86).[178] Such terminal display fountains have traditionally been provided since the post-Roman period for each aqueduct serving as a public memorial to the whole hydraulic achievement of the aqueduct; but as an ancient Roman practice this may not have been usual.[179] Probably the most famous large fountain in Rome was the Meta Sudans, destroyed in 1936 (Fig. 8.13). This stood south-west of the Colosseum and in its final form was built in the Flavian period. It consisted of an elongated cone with bowed sides, 7 m in diameter at the base and possibly three times as high. The original basin was over 13m in diameter and was surrounded by an open drain that caught the overflow. The aqueduct which supplied it is unknown.[180]

Given all the problems in calculating how much water was coming into Rome, is it possible to work out in very rough terms how much water was available to each person? From figures given by Frontinus (*On Aqueducts* 78.3), there were 591 *lacus* served by the aqueducts in his day. Estimates vary from 67 litres per person per day to over 1,000 litres per person per day.[181] But what does this mean? Do the figures only reflect domestic use? What about industrial use and the baths? How certain can we be of the discharge from each *lacus*? Comparisons with modern consumption, although they are dramatic, have limited value. All that seems clear is that, drawing the analogy of Pompeii, anywhere in the city a consumer would not find himself far away from a public fountain.[182]

According to Frontinus, water was conveyed to private customers' houses, usually from a secondary *castellum*, or sometimes from a conduit, by means of a *calix*.[183] Private consumers paid a tax or subscription to draw water from the public supply line. The *calix* was a bronze nozzle or tube at least 12 digits (21.6 cm) long and of standardized size which was fitted onto the lead pipe (Frontinus, *On Aqueducts* 36, 105, 112, 113, 129).[184] It was mounted into the side of the *castellum* or conduit and governed the amount of water the user could receive. The *calix* was effectively a water meter, and through it the customer would receive water day and night. The *calices* came in regular sizes to match the different gauges of pipe in use, and since they controlled the distribution and consumption of the water, it is not surprising that Frontinus spends about a third of his *On Aqueducts* (39 chapters out of 130) setting out the niceties of this arrangement.[185] In theory the *calix* was stamped with its nominal size, and a pipe connected to it was repeatedly marked for the first 50 feet of its length to certify that it too was the correct size.[186]

In practice, however, the opportunities for cheating and abusing the system were boundless; if Frontinus is anything to go by the Rome City Waterworks staff were expert in all of them! The *calix* might carry the wrong stamp, or not be stamped at all, or it might be of a larger size than that authorised if the gang carrying out the work had been well-bribed.[187] As a result, says Frontinus, "We have found irrigated fields, shops, garrets even, and last of all brothels fitted up with fixtures through which a constant supply of flowing water might be assured" (*On Aqueducts* 76).

Within the city, water was conveyed by both lead pipes and free-flow channels both above and below ground; a good above-ground example is the Arcus Neroniani (see above). There is a major problem in that evidence for these major free-flow channels survives in a patchy manner. Lead was the usual material, at least in Rome, for water pipes.[188] This has raised a number of interesting questions amongst modern scholars concerning the risk of lead poisoning with the assertion that this may have contributed to the decline of the Roman aristocracy.[189] Certainly Vitruvius (*On Architecture* 8.6.11) was aware of the poisonous nature of lead and it is perhaps surprising therefore that lead was used for piping. Lead is a plentiful by-product in the refinement of silver and the ancient world was not short of the material;

utilising it to make water pipes was a logical and practical solution to this glut.[190] But the water, of course, was flowing through and was not stationary within the pipe line. Therefore the amount of time it is actually in contact with the lead is minimal. Further, many pipes, including aqueduct channels themselves, in hard water areas develop a coating of lime scale. This insulating effect of the deposit inside lead pipes is well-known to modern water engineers.[191] Rome's aqueducts are notorious for heavy lime incrustation, and it did not escape the notice of Frontinus either.[192] It is only if water was left standing in a lead or lead-lined basin that there might be a problem – and only if this was to be drunk. The Roman aqueduct system was designed on the principle of continuous flow and off-take with no peak or slack hours. Thus, lead-poisoning is not really an issue in this situation.[193]

AQUEDUCTS AND BATHS

By the imperial period the largest single users of water within the city were the baths, and according to Frontinus (*On Aqueducts* 94, 107, 108) supplying water to them was of major concern for the aqueduct administration. Bathing for the Romans was in the full sense of the word, an institution, going far beyond considerations of hygiene.[194] Public baths became popular in Rome in the 3rd and 2nd centuries BC; Frontinus (*On Aqueducts* 65–68) says that water consumption had doubled by the later 2nd century, presumably partly for this reason. An aqueduct was not essential for the functioning of smaller bath buildings but for the larger baths and the *thermae* in Rome it was critical; the final abandonment and disuse of the *thermae* and many smaller baths of Rome only came in 537 when the aqueducts were cut by the Goths (Procopius, *Gothic War* 5.19.13).[195] In the Republic all water entering the city in aqueducts was designated for specific public uses (Frontinus, *On Aqueducts*, 94); baths are not individually mentioned but lumped in with fullers' shops as consumers which were granted the use of run-off water from public troughs, although not without having to pay. This seems to indicate that at this time the baths were private enterprises as opposed to public services; indeed there is no evidence for the authorities in the Republic providing public baths for the city.[196] By the 4th century AD there were 11 *thermae* and 856 *balnea*, according the the Regionary Catalogues.[197]

The great volume of water used in a Roman bath did not only serve strictly bathing needs, but also fed large and small fountains; Seneca (*Letters* 86.7) describes the fashionable baths of his day and comments on the amount of water flowing from fountains.[198] Frontinus does not mention baths explicitly in his discussion of consumers; under 'public use' he includes public basins (*lacus*), camps (*castra*) and ornamental fountains (*munera*), but there is no mention of baths (*On Aqueducts* 79–86). A big unknown is whether privately owned public access baths would come under 'public use' or 'private citizens'.[199] The water was brought to the baths either by a main line from the *castellum* or by a branch of an aqueduct. A major reservoir was necessary for the collection and distribution of the water to various parts of the building. The Aqua Virgo was the first of Rome's aqueducts to be built specifically to supply a bath building, the Baths of Agrippa, which, until they were bequeathed to the Roman people on Agrippa's death in 12 BC, were privately owned and funded. The Virgo also supplied the Stagnum Agrippae and the Euripus Canal, which with the Baths were set within sumptuous gardens on the Campus Martius.[200] The Aqua Virgo may also have supplied the Baths of Nero built in 62, also on the Campus Martius.[201]

The Baths of Trajan on the Oppian Hill were dedicated in 109; they were supplied mainly from the reservoir known as the Sette Sale, fed by one of the aqueducts coming into Rome at

Fig. 8.12: The nymphaeum *known as La Sedia del Diavolo or Trofei di Mario (early 3rd century AD) in Piazza Vittorio Emanuele (Photo: author).*

Spes Vetus, perhaps the Claudia/Anio Novus. The Traiana did supply water to the baths themselves, although not to the Sette Sale.[202] The Sette Sale was contemporary with the baths and comprised nine interconnecting chambers with overall dimensions of nearly 30 m by 40 m; the vaulted chambers are 8m high, and the capacity is approximately 15,000 m^3. Predictably one of the most impressive of these reservoirs is that serving the Baths of Caracalla, fed by the Aqua Antoniniana.[203] The reservoir is situated on the west side of the outer terrace. It was double-storeyed and had 18 chambers with an estimated capacity of 30–40,000 m^3, roughly 30 times the quantity required to fill the great *natatio*.[204] The Aqua Marcia also served the great reservoir of the Baths of Diocletian on the Quirinal via another branch; this was later known as the *Botte di Termini* and was demolished in 1876 during the construction of the railway station. It was a trapezoidal structure, measuring approximately 16 by 91 m, situated just outside the south-east side of the baths precinct. [205]

AQUEDUCTS AND MILLS

Feeding the population of Rome was a constant battle against shortages and famine (see Mattingly and Aldrete in this volume), the accompanying problems becoming more acute as the empire started to disintegrate. A large mill complex on the slopes of the Janiculum operated from the later 3rd to the 5th century AD; excavation in the 1990s has clarified the form and chronology of these structures. The complex can be dated on pottery finds to some time after the early 3rd century AD and was powered by water from the Aqua Traiana (the channel of the aqueduct actually flows through the building), not the Alsietina as has sometimes been thought. The mills went out of use sometime in the late 4th/early 5th century, but were back in action in the 7th, 8th and 9th centuries (see below). [206]A small water-mill was located in a subterranean room of the Baths of Caracalla, powered by outflow water from the baths, though the exact chronology is unclear.[207] After the mills could no longer be used because the aqueducts had been cut, Belisarius came up with an ingenious solution to the provision of much needed grain

Fig. 8.13: View from the Colosseum of the foundations of the Meta Sudans, the large and elaborate fountain built by Domitian and destroyed in 1936 (Photo: author).

for the beleaguered city. He built floating mills on the Tiber itself at the Pons Aurelius with the mill mechanisms attached to a line of boats across the river (Procopius, *Gothic War* 5.19–27). The Goths tried to destroy them by throwing debris into the river further upstream. Belisarius acted swiftly and suspended a chain across the river on which the debris caught and was then brought safely to the river bank. All mills ceased to function in the middle of the 6th century. Pope Honorius I in the 7th century repaired the Aqua Traiana in conjunction with the construction of a mill outside the walls at S. Pancrazio, and smaller mills were built across the slopes of the Janiculum.[208] Floating mills were installed on the Tiber for the second time from the 10th century and there were still such structures in the 19th century.[209]

DIRTY WATERS

There is very little literary evidence on the form and administration of sewers and latrines (*foricae* or *latrinae*) in the Roman world; Vitruvius is noticeably, but discreetly, silent. The practice of incorporating latrines into bath structures, apart from the obvious advantages to the bathers, had very practical technical advantages of sharing drainage facilities and using discharge water for flushing.[210] However, latrines in baths would not have been sufficient and there were certainly other public latrines around the city.[211] In the Regionary Catalogues 144 public latrines are recorded in the city,[212] though only a few are known from archaeological evidence. One of Hadrianic date can still be seen above shops in the Forum Iulium and another is situated in the Largo Argentina/Portico of Pompey area (Fig. 8.14). A presumably public latrine was discovered in 1963 in the Via Garibaldi in Trastevere. Its painted decoration (giving a date of the 2nd to 3rd century AD) and black and white mosaic floors were very rich, giving an air of opulence which was presumably not always the case in such structures.[213] The value of the figure in the Regionary Catalogues is severely limited by a number of factors. Firstly, the seating capacity is not known for each facility, nor is it certain what proportion of the population used public latrines. It is usually assumed that many private dwellings in Rome, particularly the high rise dwellings, did not have latrines; they were not furnished with a running water supply, which, though not absolutely necessary to flush a

Fig. 8.14: Latrine in the south-east corner of the Portico of Pompey, now visible in the north-west corner of the Largo di Torre Argentina excavations (Photo: author).

Fig. 8.15: The Cloaca Maxima emptying into the Tiber (Photo: author)

latrine, was obviously a distinct advantage.[214] However, given that we have so little evidence surviving it seems rather inadvisable to make any definitive statements on this subject.[215]

In the modern world there is an obvious connection between latrines and sewers; in the Roman world other arrangements are also found. The law codes distinguish between public sewers maintained by the state, and private sewers the upkeep of which was the responsibility of individual property owners. The latter had the right to connect a private to a public sewer without having to receive permission from the authorities.[216] On the other hand, there was no *legal* obligation for a home-owner to connect his dwelling to a public street sewer, and archaeological evidence from Rome, Ostia and Pompeii indicates that very few dwellings were directly connected to street drains. Latrines feeding into internal cesspits seem to have been more normally in use. At Pompeii the combination of kitchen and latrine has been noted with some alarm about health risks, but there is the practical advantage that cooks could conveniently dispose of kitchen waste.[217]

The expense of installing drains would seem at first sight to have been well worth the consequent improvement in hygiene within a property, but why was this not more commonly done? There are probably several explanations. For one, Roman drains lacked traps to prevent gases such as hydrogen sulphide and methane escaping from the sewers and thereby causing not only an odour nuisance but also the danger of explosions – a consequence known from Victorian toilets in London![218] The ideal was that Roman *cloacae* were self-cleansing but it is clear that some had to be cleaned manually (*Digest* 43.23.2). There were two other potentially disagreeable consequences of being connected to the main drain system. In Rome, in low-lying areas, sewers could back up when the level of the Tiber rose (and this could be quite a considerable rise). Thus sewage and waste water which normally fed into the Tiber would be forced back up the network and into any houses connected to it. Vermin and other animals could enter a house via these connections – a spectacular and fanciful case being one referred to by Aelian (*HA* 13.6) whereby a rather enterprising octopus swam up a house drain each night from the sea to eat pickled fish stored in the house of an Iberian merchant!

However, there was one factor which may have outweighed all others: human waste was a valuable commodity as a fertilizer.[219] The contents of a domestic cesspit could therefore be sold on. Having your latrine connected to the public sewers could mean that you were literally throwing money down the drain.

The Romans have frequently been charged with wasting a large amount of the water which they brought into the city. This accusation stems from the fact that in principle in the Roman aqueduct system the water could not be turned off, as we can in modern water supply networks, it could only be diverted.[220] As we have seen, water *could* be stored in cisterns, but the major problem for modern scholars is that the water ran day and night, particularly from the fountains, even though demand must have been drastically reduced during the hours of darkness. Arguably, the Romans considered constant water flow as a particular sign of richness and a high standard of living.[221] The fact that Frontinus makes no reference to taps and similar devices should not be taken as supporting evidence; archaeology has brought to light a range of such devices – though they should be thought of as more like stopcocks than as the taps we might have in the bathroom or kitchen. These allowed for the *diversion* of water to either a place of storage or to where it *was* needed.[222]

Indeed Frontinus clearly states "There must necessarily be some overflow from the reservoirs, this being proper not only for the health of our city, but also for use in the flushing of the sewers" (*On Aqueducts* 111). If the literary sources are to be believed, even allowing for gross exaggeration, it is very clear that such an overflow was vital not only to the cleansing of the drains but also of the streets themselves. Juvenal (*Satires* 3.296–305) outlines the way in which a man dices with death as he walks along a street, especially at night: "It is a long way up to the roof tops, and a falling tile can brain you – not to mention all those cracked or leaky pots that people toss out of windows. So hope and make your miserable prayer, that the women are content to empty out their basin" (that is not drop the pot as well). This is the 'gardez l'eau' practice of the Roman world.[223] If you did not have a cesspit in which to rid yourself of waste, the street was the next best place.

Thus overflow from the fountains would flush such detritus down into the drains. The most famous Roman drain is the Cloaca Maxima, the original construction of which is attributed to Tarquinius Priscus.[224] This was an open ditch to help drain the marshy land particularly in the Forum Romanum area and the Subura, debouching into the Tiber near the Pons Aemilius/Ponte Rotto (Juvenal *Satires* 5.104–6; Fig. 8.15). Although it was meant to carry off surplus water it was inevitable from its early days that it also carried sewage. In the later Republic the Cloaca Maxima was enclosed in a subterranean channel which is still in use today. As the crow flies the distance between start and outflow is over 900 m, but its course meanders as a result of it being artificially diverted where buildings made this necessary. Thus its actual length is approximately 1600 m. Its size is noteworthy; in places it is 4.2m high and 3.2m wide, and Roman writers agree that it was large enough for a wagon load of hay to pass through. Agrippa is reported to have sailed in a boat through the underground world of Rome's drainage system on a tour of inspection.[225]

THE AQUEDUCTS AND WATER SUPPLY AFTER ANTIQUITY

Rome's aqueducts continued to function into the 6th century AD when Vigitis is recorded to have cut them and Belisarius to have deliberately blocked them to prevent their use as a means of infiltrating the city.[226] Many claim that after these events Rome lacked the resources, and perhaps the demand, to maintain an artificial water supply, but there is both archaeological and documentary evidence for the subsequent repair of at least some of the aqueduct lines, as well as of the Tiber

Fig. 8.16: La Fontana di Trevi, completed in 1762 and supplied by the Acqua Vergine which reuses the Roman Aqua Virgo (Photo: author).

embankments.[227] Belisarius may have restored them after the siege, although the main evidence is in the form of surviving masonry which is notoriously difficult to date accurately.[228] Within 60 years of the Gothic siege the aqueducts were running again, according to a letter of Gregory the Great dated 602 (*Letters* 12.6), but who and what they supplied seems to have changed. There is no evidence for the great public baths having continued in use after this time; the chief consumers in the early Middle Ages were the city's mills and the church (baptisteries and baths for the clergy and the poor). For drinking water the city relied on wells.[229] By the late 8th century the papacy had taken charge of the city's aqueducts, though the church had carried out earlier repairs on several branch lines.[230] Property documents from as late as the 11th century mention functioning aqueducts both inside and outside the city, but such references slowly disappear after the 12th century.[231] Rome's population became concentrated in the low-lying bend of the Tiber, an area which came to be known as the *abitato* and the river itself increased in importance.[232] The supply of domestic water played a very minor role in papal aqueduct repairs. Those aqueducts which were repaired did not for the most part reach this densely populated area; Trastevere was supplied by the Aqua Traiana but all sources point to the prime importance of the mills and the S. Pietro in Vaticano complex . Wells were the most likely replacement for domestic water supply. Although there does not seem to be evidence of Christian patronage of aqueducts to supply ordinary drinking water, there is clear evidence of such patronage of wells.[233] Christian hydraulic patronage in the form of the provision of fountains in church atria was of importance at this time; clearly this was for washing hands. The Pine Cone fountain, set up in the 5th century in the middle of the atrium of S. Pietro, survived until the demolition of the Constantinian church; the pine cone sculpture is now the centrepiece of the Cortile della Pigne in the Vatican. It was almost certainly supplied by the Aqua Traiana and the fountain functioned into the early Middle Ages, making it, it has been suggested, the only public fountain to do so in western Christendom.[234] Pope Symmachus (498–514) set up a public lavatory in St Peter's Square which was possibly flushed by water from the fountain (*Liber Pontificalis* 1.262).

The papal Lateran palace enjoyed an elaborate water supply for its bath-house. It is first mentioned in 667 in the *Liber Pontificalis* (1.343) when Constans II is recorded to have bathed there. It was supplied by the Aqua Claudia which was repaired under Hadrian I (772–95; *Liber Pontificalis* 1.502–3). Leo III added a porphyry fountain in one of the palace dining rooms (795–816; *Liber Pontificalis* 2.11). Sumptuous rebuilding took place under

Gregory IV (827–44) when the bath house was described as being much in need of repair (*Liber Pontificalis* 2.81).[235]

The mills on the Janiculum are first recorded in an inscription, probably of 5th century date, and vividly described by Procopius in the 6th century:

> "... across the Tiber there is a great hill where, for a long time, all the mills of the city have been built, as a great deal of water is brought by an aqueduct to the crest of the hill and rushes down the slope with great force" (Procopius, *Gothic War* 1.19.8).

They continued to function intermittently, fed by the Aqua Traiana, and there were a number of papal repairs: under Honorius I (625–38), Hadrian I and Gregory IV.[236] The papal interest in these mills was understandable; they were vital for the provision of the city's bread. The last mention of the Aqua Traiana is under Nicholas I (827–44) when repairs were carried out; it presumably fell out of use soon after this along with most of the other aqueducts.[237] It is not referred to again until the later 15th century when it was first repaired by Innocent VIII (1484–96) and then by Paul V in 1611. It still supplies the fountains in Trastevere and the Vatican as the Acqua Paola with a great and imposing terminal fountain, a *mostra*, the Fontana Paola.[238]

Major repair work was carried out on the Aqua Virgo into the 14th century, but by as early as the 8th century much of the arcades had fallen, so that a relatively short stretch was left running as far as modern Piazza di Trevi. A modest fountain was established at the foot of the Quirinal Hill and by the 10th century a small suburb had developed around it complete with several churches serving a neighbourhood of one-storeyed dwellings with gardens; Rome was changing and the Aqua Virgo gave way to the Acqua Vergine (Fig. 8.16).[239] It is not until Sixtus V (1585–90) that new aqueducts were constructed, the first being the Acqua Felice, regathering the springs of the Aqua Alexandrina, with an imposing *mostra,* the Fountain of Moses. Predictably, these post classical *mostre* were much influenced by the great Trofei di Mario *castellum*.[240]

The supply of water to ancient Rome was not something planned as an overall scheme but grew and developed with the city and as the population's needs and demands changed. The fact that three of the eleven great aqueducts of the ancient city in effect (with major modifications) still function today (Aqua Virgo as the Acqua Vergine Antica, the Aqua Alexandrina as the Acqua Felice, and the Aqua Traiana as the Acqua Paola) is testament to the skill and planning of the ancient hydraulic engineers. As Pliny the Elder (*Natural History* 36.123) declared:

> " But if anyone will note the abundance of water skilfully brought into the city, for public uses, for baths, for public basins, for houses, runnels, suburban gardens and villas; if he will note the high aqueducts required for maintaining the proper elevation; the mountains which had to be pierced; the levelled valleys; he will admit that there has never been anything more marvellous in the whole world".

ACKNOWLEDGEMENTS

The research for this paper has been carried out over a number of years. I am grateful to Amanda Claridge, Peter Connolly, Jon Coulston, and Andrew Wilson who have played a part in the formation of my thoughts on watery subjects over the years. Travel and Research Grants were generously awarded by the Craven and Meyerstein Funds of the University of Oxford, the British Academy and the British School at Rome. Jon Coulston and Christopher

Smith read and commented on a draft of the chapter and rescued me from many errors and illogical arguments; any that remain and the opinions expressed are mine alone.

NOTES

1 A practice taken on with zealous vigour in the provinces and especially in Asia Minor; a particularly telling example is the aqueduct at Ephseus built between AD 4 and 14 and supervised with a colleague by Sextilius Pollio, who paid for the very visible part of the aqueduct where the channel was carried across the main road from Ephesus to Magnesia and the Maeander further south (*IGR* 4.242). For other examples in Asia Minor see COULTON 1987, 81. For *nymphaea* in Greece: WALKER 1987. See PURCELL 1996 for a general discussion of the management of water by the Romans as a symbol of power.

2 BRUUN 1991, 10–19; HODGE 1992, 16–7; RODGERS 1996, 395–8. For a discussion of Vitruvius and aqueducts: HODGE 1992, 13–16; LEWIS 1999.

3 ASHBY 1935, 26–7; BRUUN 1991, 11–13; LLOYD 1979, 408. HODGE 1992, 17, feels that it was clearly intended to demonstrate that he really had mastered the intricate technicalities of Rome's water supply. For a full discussion of the aims and purpose of Frontinus' *On Aqueducts*, see GRIMAL 1961, xv–xvi, who sees it clearly as a piece of political writing despite its format as a technical treatise.

4 For example the siphon, HODGE 1982: LEWIS 1999, 162–67 for Vitruvius and the siphon.

5 See REYNOLDS 1986, 166–70, for the manuscript tradition. LANCIANI 1881, a magisterial commentary of Frontinus, is still important; the subject of Roman water supply generally has been recently well-served by (amongst others) BRUUN 1991; HODGE 1992; EVANS 1994; AICHER 1995, all usefully discussed with supporting bibliography by WILSON 1996.

6 DEMAN 1934; ASHBY 1935. This was published in Italian 10 years ago (ASHBY 1991). AICHER 1995, essentially a guide to the remains at the end of the 20th century, provides a very valuable companion to Ashby.

7 Frontinus, *On Aqueducts* 1; BRUUN 1991; RODGERS 1996, 398–400.

8 CORNELL 1995, 373–377 and 385. Livy (39.44) records that Cato in 184 BC, when he was censor, repaired channels and reservoirs.

9 Q. Marcius Rex, responsible for the Marcia, was the only urban praetor recorded as the builder of an aqueduct. Further, the Marcia is the only Republican water supply line built following a *senatus consultum*. For the tradition that this line goes back to Ancus Marcius, Pliny, *Natural History* 31.41.

10 ROBINSON 1992, 96.

11 For the problems which had to be dealt with as a result of this system, see the activities of Marcus Caelius Rufus (Cicero, *Ad familiares* 8.6.4; Frontinus, *On Aqueducts* 76).

12 Frontinus, *On Aqueducts* 98–99; BRUUN 1991, 148–52; 190–94.

13 There were apparently two gangs of slaves – about 240 state-owned slaves descended from those bequeathed by Agrippa and another of about 460 created by Claudius which remained imperial property (Frontinus, *On Aqueducts* 116). BRUUN 1991, 190–99.

14 BRUUN 1987; ROBINSON 1992, 100–101. Under Claudius there were three *curatores aquarum* in office (*CIL* 6.1248). See BRUUN 1991, 150, 174–89, 207–9 and 218–20 for *procuratores*. For the title *curator aquarum et Minuciae*: *CIL* 5.7783.

15 Frontinus (*On Aqueducts* 102) lists the *curatores aquarum* from the 1st century AD, making 17 in all including Frontinus himself. There were long periods of time when the office does not appear to have been filled: BRUUN 1991, 179; RODGERS 1996, 398–9.

16 ROBINSON 1992, 101; *Lexicon* IV, *s.v.* 'Statio Aquarum', 346–49. For the location at the Porticus Minucia *CIL* 5.7783; 6.1532;14.3902; for location in the Forum Romanum *ILS* 8943, 9050. BRUUN 1989; 1991, 195–6 doubts the existence of any special headquarters for the water administration and suggests that we should think about it in a more abstract and general sense. The term is not used by Frontinus, but it is attested epigraphically: *CIL* 6.8489, 36781; 14.7338.

17 Frontinus, *On Aqueducts* 69, 72, 75–77 on fraud and abuse. On private and public users see Frontinus, *On Aqueducts* 79–86. For a general discussion see BRUUN 1991, 183–87; ROBINSON 1992, 99–10.

18 Frontinus, *On Aqueducts* 4. *Lexicon* I, *s.v.* 'Lacus Iuternae', 168–70; *s.v.* 'Lacus Curtius', 166–7.

19 RAMAGE 1983, 62–4; WENTWORTH RINNE 1996, 145–6; PURCELL 1996.

20 Cicero (*For Sestius* 77) gives a lurid picture of urban violence in 57 BC; the Tiber was filled with bodies and the sewers stuffed with more. See also Tacitus, *Annals* 6.19 in AD 33 after Sejanus' downfall.

21 RAMAGE 1983, 72–4. Other instances: 13 BC (Dio 54.25), when Balbus was unable to enter his theatre except by boat; AD 5 (Dio 55.22), when a bridge (unspecified) was destroyed and the city was navigable for seven days; AD 12 (Dio 56.27), when the Circus was flooded and the Ludi Martiales had to be held in the Forum Augustum.

For a list of the floods known from antiquity see LE GALL 1953, 29–30. For the Tiber generally, see LE GALL 1953; D'ONOFRIO 1970.

22 AMMERMAN 1990; HOLLOWAY 1994, 86–7; SMITH 1996, 101–2. This drainage was partially achieved through the construction of the Cloaca Maxima.

23 Cicero, *Letters to Atticus* 13.33a; FAVRO 1996, 73–5; the plain of the Campus Martius, despite the flooding problems, was the obvious place and direction for expansion.

24 Dio 55.22; 56.27.4. For the *cura riparum* and Augustan activity *CIL* 6.31541;31542. *CIL* 14.85 records Claudius building canals in AD 46 in conjunction with the construction of the harbour at Portus, stating hopefully that they would "free the city from floods".

25 Tacitus, *Annals* 1.76 and 79, and Dio 57.14.7–8 both credit Tiberius for its creation. ROBINSON 1992, 86–88. *CIL* 1.766a; *CIL* 6.31451.1 – censors and consuls delimiting banks.

26 The post was held by Pliny the Younger before his departure for Bithynia *ILS* 2927. For the 4th century, see *Notitia Dignitatum, Occ.* IV.6.

27 ROBINSON 1992, 88.

28 BOATWRIGHT 1987, 40–42.

29 D'ONOFRIO 1970.

30 For example there is no evidence for aqueducts at Ampurias, Tiddis or London (HODGE 1992, 61) where wells, cisterns and springs were the main sources of water.

31 CROUCH 1993.

32 The bibliography on the Pergamum aqueduct is quite extensive and conveniently collected together in HODGE 1992, 368.

33 COULTON 1987, 73. However, the early lines may not have been that much of a risk. By the end of the 4th century BC the Latins had been pacified and there was limited external threat to Roman territory. Added to which most of the length of these early lines was underground.

34 NORDH 1949, 100.15–101.10 (11 *thermae*); 101.11–102.11 (19 aqueducts); 104.11 (15 *nymphaea*); 105.6 (856 *balneae*); 105.7 (1352 *lacus*); 105.9 (254 *pistrina*). These are the figures listed in the concluding section, but the individual figures given by region produce the following, slightly different, figures: 942 public baths (*balneae*), 1204 public fountains, 257 reservoirs; the figures for *nymphaea* and *thermae* are the same. See also Zachariah of Mitylene, *The Syriac Chronicle* 10.16. The situation is further complicated by the indiscriminate, combined use by modern scholars of Frontinus' figures (which are similarly flawed) and those from the later sources.

35 For the urban population of Rome in the Republic see BRUNT 1971, 376–388. Aqua Appia: Frontinus, *On Aqueducts* 5, 22 & 65; *Lexicon* I, *s.v.* 'Aqua Appia', 61–2; DEMAN 1934, 23–28, 368, 365; ASHBY 1935, 49–54; RICHARDSON 1992, 15–16; MUCCI 1986a; EVANS 1991, 22–25; 1994, 65–74; AICHER 1995, 34–5.

36 PARKER (1876, 8–9, Pl. XVIII) claimed to have seen this structure and recorded it in 1867. See also LANCIANI 1881, 249–50; DEMAN 1934, 26–27; ASHBY 1935, 52–53; PACE 1983, 120.

37 This reflects a drop over the entire course of not more than 0.5–0.6% – the absolute minimum prescribed by Vitruvius (*On Architecture* 8.6.1). See HODGE 1992, 178–184 for a discussion of aqueduct gradients. It is interesting to note that Appius Claudius also interfered with cult activity in the Forum Boarium by transforming the Ara Maxima from a private concern into a publicly administered cult (Livy 9.29.9–11; COARELLI 1988, 80–2; CORNELL 1995, 385).

38 144 BC: Frontinus, *On Aqueducts* 7.3. Agrippa: Frontinus, *On Aqueducts* 9.9; Pliny, *Natural History* 36.121. Augustus: Frontinus, *On Aqueducts* 5.6–8; *Res Gestae* 20.2; *CIL* 6.1244. Regions supplied (Frontinus, *On Aqueducts* 79.2): Caelius (II), Forum Romanum (VIII), Circus Flaminius (IX), Circus Maximus (XI), Piscina Publica (XII), Aventinus (XIII), Transtiberim (XIV).

39 EVANS 1982, 409; 1991, 24–5; 1994, 107. TAYLOR 1995, 78–9, however, disagrees pointing out that this would be overloading this one bridge; there were other bridges which could have been used.

40 HODGE 1992, 274.

41 For example the Aqua Virgo and the Baths of Agrippa on the Campus Martius. The large imperial *thermae*, requiring constantly running water, were huge consumers of water.

42 Frontinus, *On Aqueducts* 6.2; *Lexicon* I, *s.v.*. 'Anio Vetus', 44–45; ASHBY 1935, 54–87; RICHARDSON 1992, 11; EVANS 1994, 75–82; AICHER 1995, 35–36. The work was unfinished at the end of the censors' term of office; the two men were elected *duumviri aquae ducendae* two years later to finish the project.

43 For the course see RONCAIOLI LAMBERTI 1986. For the improvements and additions ASHBY 1935, 54–87. For new *cippi* marking the course see MARI 1991. BLACKMAN 1979 estimates the length at 81 km, but has a discussion of the various lengths arrived at by different scholars.

44 SANTA MARIA SCRINARI 1979, 61–2; AICHER 1995, 36.

45 EVANS 1994, 77. See also BRUNT 1971, 384 for a reflection of the city's population growth in the increased water supply.

46 Distribution (Frontinus, *On Aqueducts* 80.2): Porta Capena (I), Isis and Serapis (III), Templum Pacis (IV), Esquiliae (V), Alta Semita (VI), Via Lata (VII), Forum Romanum (VIII), Circus Flaminius (IX), Piscina Publica

(XII) and the Transtiberim (XIV). For the aqueduct crossing to the Transtiberim region and a discussion of which bridge was used: TAYLOR 1995. Frontinus (*On Aqueducts* 21) mentions a branch called the Octavianus, which from its name probably dates from the Agrippan or Augustan overhaul of the system; its purpose seems to have been to serve the growing residential area outside the Servian Wall to the south-east (EVANS 1994, 78–9).

47 Frontinus, *On Aqueducts* 92. Unlike the later Anio Novus, the Anio Vetus was never given a major overhaul to address this problem. For repairs on the Anio Vetus: 144 BC: Frontinus, *On Aqueducts*, 7; Pliny, *Natural History* 36.121. Agrippa: Frontinus, *On Aqueducts* 9; Dio 49.43.

48 Livy 40.51.7. Population increase: BRUNT 1971; NOY 2000. For increases in building activity see COARELLI 1977.

49 Aqua Marcia: Frontinus, *On Aqueducts* 7; Pliny, *Natural History* 36.121; Martial 6.42.18; *Lexicon* I, *s.v.*. 'Aqua Marcia', 67–69; ASHBY 1935, 88–159; MORGAN 1978; RICHARDSON 1992, 17–18; EVANS 1994, 83–93; AICHER 1995, 36–7; VOLPE 1996. MORGAN 1978, 25–6 points out that the circumstances surrounding the actual construction of this aqueduct line are unclear, partly as a result of problems with Frontinus' text.

50 Frontinus, *On Aqueducts* 7.4; PLATNER and ASHBY 1929, 24–7. FRANK 1933, 226–7 estimates the cost at $9 million. FORBES 1964, 180, gives the figure of £3.5 million. See also BLACKMAN 1979; ROBINSON 1980, 49.

51 Pliny, *Natural History* 31.41; Propertius 3.2.14; Vitruvius, *On Architecture* 8.31. Nero swam in the source, much to people's disgust (Tacitus, *Annals* 14.22).

52 ASHBY 1935, 95–8 and references.

53 Frontinus, *On Aqueducts* 7.8 says that 7,463 paces (10 km) were carried on arcades. For *cippi* along the course of the Marcia see MARI 1991.

54 ASHBY 1935, 117–21; AICHER 1995, 116–122.

55 DEMAN 1934, 95.

56 AICHER 1995, 118.

57 AICHER 1995, 121–2.

58 AICHER 1995, 126–28. These various repairs to the Marcia were recorded at the Porta Tiburtina (*CIL* 6.1244 (Augustus 4 BC))and on *cippi* (*CIL* 6.1250, 1251 and 31750c; 1246 (Titus AD 79); 1245 (Caracalla AD 212)).

59 AICHER 1995, 99–101.

60 EVANS 1994, 85. Frontinus refers to the immediate area of the Porta Maggiore as *ad Spem Veterem* because of its proximity to an old temple of Hope (for example *On Aqueducts* 5, 19, 20).

61 See EVANS 1994, 87–9 for the problems relating to this branch; AICHER 1995, 37.

62 *Lexicon* I, 68; ASHBY 1935, 151. It was almost certainly the Marcia-Tepula-Iulia line which supplied the later Castra Praetoria. For the Aqua Antoniniana: *CIL* 6.29843; AICHER 1995, 74–5. This branch was brought from the Marcia near the 3rd milestone on the Via Latina and crossed the Via Appia on the Arch of Drusus (*Lexicon* I, *s.v.* 'Arcus Drusi (Via Appia)', 93; AICHER 1995, 75–6).

63 For the course of the Aqua Marcia within the city DEMAN 1934, 116–22; ASHBY 1935, 146–49; CATTALINI 1986a, 49–50; EVANS 1994, 85; VOLPE 1996, 64–81.

64 Nothing remains of this branch which probably delivered a very small supply: EVANS 1994, 86. MORGAN 1978 48–51 discusses opposition at the time to the provision of water to the Capitoline. On the course of this section of the Marcia between the Quirinal and the Capitoline see TORTORICI 1993. For the use of siphons in Roman aqueducts see HODGE 1982. More properly this is the inverted siphon which made it possible to supply water to locations at a higher level than the supply-line itself.

65 Siphon: BRUUN 1991, 134. For the Marcia being carried across the river on bridges: TAYLOR 1995, 78–82.

66 Frontinus, *On Aqueducts* 8; 67–9; *Lexicon* I, *s.v.*. 'Aqua Tepula', 70; ASHBY 1935, 160–1; RICHARDSON 1992, 18; EVANS 1982, 403–406; CATTALINI 1986c; EVANS 1994, 95–98; AICHER 1995, 38.

67 Frontinus, *On Aqueducts* 8; EVANS 1982, 404. Competition in building between Roman elite families may also have played a part, rather than this aqueduct actually being required (*pers.comm.* Christopher Smith).

68 CATTALINI 1986c, 60. Frontinus (*On Aqueducts* 68) says that the water came from rivulets (*venae*) from these springs.

69 EVANS 1994, 95–8; cf AICHER 1995, 38; 92–5 (Romavecchia). For the course of the Marcia-Tepula-Iulia see ASHBY 1935, 128–58; EVANS 1982, 404.

70 *Cura Aquarum*: Frontinus, *On Aqueducts* 99.1–5; SHIPLEY 1933, 24–26; BRUUN 1991, 148–49. For a discussion of Agrippa's work in general, SHIPLEY 1933; LLOYD 1979; EVANS 1982.

71 *Lexicon* I, *s.v.* 'Aqua Iulia', 66–67; EVANS 1982, 406–408; RICHARDSON 1982, 17. For the course of the Iulia see ASHBY 1935, 128–58 (Marcia-Tepula-Iulia),161–66; CATTALINI 1986d; EVANS 1994, 99–103; AICHER 1995, 38–9, 92–5. For *cippi* dating to Augustus: *CIL* 6.31563a, b, c.

72 ASHBY 1935, 130–2; HODGE 1992, 168–70.

73 ASHBY 1935, 149–50; EVANS 1994, 100.

74 For the general distribution of the Iulia see ASHBY 1935, 149–58; EVANS 1994, 102–103. Although there is no direct physical evidence, the building complexes almost certainly supplied were the Forum of Caesar, the

Forum of Augustus and the Augustan buildings in the Forum Romanum. Presumably these supply lines would also have been useful during the construction of these areas.

75 *Lexicon* I, *s.v.* 'Aqua Virgo', 72–3; ASHBY 1935, 167–83; LLOYD 1979; EVANS 1982, 408–409; RICHARDSON 1992, 19; QUILICI 1986; EVANS 1994, 105–109; AICHER 1995, 39–41. Pliny, *Natural History* 36.121 erroneously gives the date as 33 BC.

76 In Frontinus' day this was the third largest of the aqueducts (*On Aqueducts* 83). Feeder channels along the course of the aqueduct might help to explain why it could still deliver water in the Middle Ages (AICHER 1995, 40; COATES-STEPHENS 1998). For the papal and modern reworkings of the Aqua Virgo see TOLOMEO 1986; CAMBEDDI 1986; PINTO 1986. For the Agrippan building programme: SHIPLEY 1933; EVANS 1982, 409–411.

77 For the height of entry into a city see HODGE 1992, 104. The fact that the Virgo also delivered a substantial amount *extra urbem* (to suburban areas) may have had some influence (QUILICI 1986, 65–6).

78 LLOYD 1979, 193–5; AICHER 1995, 40. The aqueduct was carried across the Via Lata on the Arch of Claudius (*Lexicon* I, *s.v.*. 'Arcus Claudii', 85–6) which commemorated Claudius' 'conquest' of Britain: *CIL* 6.920, 31203.

79 The Stagnum may have been fed by run-off water from the baths (LLOYD 1979, 195). Tacitus, *Annals* 15.37 describes an extravagent and notorious banquet held at the Stagnum during Nero's reign. For swimming in the Euripus: Ovid, *Tristia* 3.12.22; Martial, *Epigrams* 11.47.5–6. Seneca in his youth would start the year off with a plunge in its cold waters (*Letters* 83.5)!

80 Frontinus, *On Aqueducts* 84.2: Via Lata (VII), Circus Flaminius (IX) and Transtiberim (XIV).

81 The Appia, Anio Vetus and Marcia did partially serve these areas but in a limited way (Frontinus, *On Aqueducts* 79–81; EVANS 1994, 106–7).

82 SHIPLEY 1933, 66–68; COARELLI 1977, 842–43; LLOYD 1979, 195–201; EVANS 1994, 107.

83 EVANS 1982, 409; 1991, 24; 1994, 71, 77 identifies the Pons Aemilia as the one bridge used. However, TAYLOR 1995 disagrees feeling that this is overload and that other bridges were available.

84 LLOYD 1979, 201; BRUUN 1991, 117 and n.5; TAYLOR 1995, 82–90.

85 The Alsietina is sometimes also called the Aqua Augusta. Frontinus, *On Architecture* 11.1; Res *Gestae* 23.1; *Lexicon* I, *s.v.* 'Aqua Alsietina', 61; RICHARDSON 1992, 15; LIBERATI SILVERIO 1986, 72–73; EVANS 1994, 111–113; AICHER 1995, 41; TAYLOR 1997. For the Aqua Alsietina and the *naumachia* of Augustus see TAYLOR 1997.

86 AICHER 1995, 41; TAYLOR 1997, 482–3, for a section of tunnel uncovered near S. Cosimato in Trastevere.

87 EVANS 1994, 112. LANCIANI 1897, 58; AICHER 1995, 165 give the elevation as 16.60 m and 17 m respectively, the level of the *naumachia* and final destination of the supply line.

88 EVANS 1994, 112. It also probably supplied a fish hatchery discovered near the modern Stazione di Trastevere (DEMAN 1934, 184–5; LIBERATI SILVERIO 1986, 75), though the Aqua Traiana may have provided its water (ASHBY 1935, 307).

89 *Lexicon* III, *s.v.* 'Naumachia Augusti', 337–8; RICARDSON 1992, 265; TAYLOR 1997; COLEMAN 1993, 50–55. According to Dio (62.20; 66.25) the *stagnum* was used by both Nero and Titus; see Coleman in this volume.

90 For discussions of which bridges were used see EVANS 1982; 1991;1994; and for a more correct assessment of the archaeological evidence, see TAYLOR 1995. The construction of the Aqua Claudia and Aqua Anio Novus and the Aqua Traiana served to redress this situation.

91 TAYLOR 1997, 468–73.

92 *Lexicon* III, *s.v.* 'Naumachiae Philipporum', 338; QUILICI 1989, 79; Aurelius Victor, *Caes.* 28; LIBERATI SILVERIO 1986, 73. For the course and distribution of the Alsietina: TAYLOR 1997, 483–4.

93 *Lexicon* I, *s.v.* 'Aqua Claudia', 63–5; *s.v.* 'Anio Novus', 42–4; RICHARDSON 1982, 11, 16; EVANS 1994, 115–128; AICHER 1995, 42–44. BRUNT 1971, 385 points out that the construction of these two aqueducts need not indicate an increase in population; Claudius was substantially raising standards.

94 Frontinus, *On Aqueducts* 13.1–2; BLACKMAN 1978.

95 Frontinus, *On Aqueducts* 13.4. Even in the 3rd century the high quality of the water of the Aqua Claudia was well-known; the emperor Severus Alexander would drink a pint of cold Aqua Claudia before taking food (SHA, *Severus Alexander* 30.44).

96 ASHBY 1935, 224–6; AICHER 1995, 42, 97–98.

97 *CIL* 6. 1256 records the construction and completion of both the Claudia and the Aqua Anio Novus.

98 SMITH 1970; AICHER 1995, 162–164. For the source of both the Anio Vetus and the Anio Novus see RONCOAIOLI LAMBERTI 1987.

99 DEMAN 1934, 237–50; ASHBY 1935, 224–42; MUCCI 1986b, 84–86; AICHER 1995, 97–8.

100 Frontinus, *On Aqueducts* 124 draws attention to the problems of maintenance and repair that this situation called for.

101 The buttressing to the piers are original to the structure. *CIL* 6.1257 and 1258 on the Porta Maggiore record repairs to the Claudia under Vespasian and Titus, which they claim was due to the inadequate functioning of the Claudia. No mention is made of the Anio Novus which would also have been affected by this work and EVANS

(1994, 116–117) suggests that these inscriptions reflect Flavian propaganda and perhaps minor repairs and work to the line. See also VODRET 1987.

102 ASHBY 1935, 243–44 ; MUCCI 1986b. The mixing of water carried by different supply lines of course had already occurred with Agrippa's combining of the waters of the Tepula and the Iulia.

103 Frontinus, *On Aqueducts* 20.3–4; *Lexicon* I, *s.v.* 'Aqueductium', 73–4; EVANS 1983; 1994, 118. For the course of this branch: DEMAN 1934, 266–70; ASHBY 1935, 244–49; MUCCI 1986c, 95–99. For the Aqueductium on the *Forma Urbis*: CARETTONI 1960, 63, pl. 16. Remains of the terminal *castellum* are still visible in the garden of the Passionist Fathers. For discussion of the purpose of this line: EVANS 1983; 1994, 119; ELSNER 1994.

104 PLATNER and ASHBY 1929, 361; EVANS 1983, 395–7; RICHARDSON 1992, 268.

105 HODGE 1992, 3. Roman aqueducts worked on the principle of constant supply and off-take 24 hours a day; they could not be turned off in the way we today can turn water on and off in our homes. The water could only be diverted to another location or destination.

106 ELSNER 1994. EVANS 1994, 120 suggests that this branch was part of the original Claudian plan and that Nero was upgrading and improving an already existing system; Frontinus, *On Aqueducts* 76.5–7 says that *castella* were adopted for the Arcus Caelimontani which had supplied water from the Marcia and Iulia to the Caelian and the Aventine.

107 EVANS 1994, 120. For Nero's concern to provide adequate water supplies for public needs, see Tacitus, *Annals* 15.43. The silence in the sources in this regard is even more striking, given that abuse of natural resources for private gain was a fairly strong and standard charge against Nero.

108 *CIL* 6.1259 (AD 201).

109 For a discussion on the supply across the river, see TAYLOR 1995, 91.

110 *Lexicon* I, *s.v.* 'Aqua Traiana', 70–2; CIL 6.1260; ASHBY 1935, 299–307; RICHARDSON 1992, 18–19; VIRGILI 1986, 118–9; EVANS 1991, 25–6; 1994, 129–33; AICHER 1995, 44, 76–9.

111 On the mills: LANCIANI 1893–1901, 127; WIKANDER 1979, 13–36; *Lexicon* V, *s.v.* 'Molinae', 277. These apparently produced much of Rome's flour in late antiquity and the early medieval period (see below).

112 EVANS 1994, 130 and n. 8; *Lexicon* I, *s.v.* 'Aqua Traiana', 71. TAYLOR 1995, 97, 102 thinks that although this might have been the terminus of the aqueduct and therefore the main distribution tank, after some of the water had been distributed to Transtiberim, the bulk of the water was taken to the east bank; the construction of the baths alone, however, did not justify the large amount of water taken across to the east bank.

113 The supply of the Naumachia Traiani is often cited as the main reason for the construction of the Aqua Traiana (TAYLOR 1995, n. 73; *Lexicon* III, *s.v.* 'Naumachia Traiani', 338–9).

114 BRUUN 1991, 135, states there is no trace of an arcaded river crossing. However, TAYLOR 1995, 98 suggests that the crossing was via a specially constructed aqueduct bridge just downstream from the Aventine. LANCIANI 1893–1901, Pl. 34, shows ancient piers in the river which Taylor suggests are the remains of a hitherto unidentified aqueduct bridge for the Aqua Traiana. If this is so, it is the only example of an exclusive aqueduct bridge in the city.

115 Epigraphic evidence (BLOCH 1944; EVANS 1994, 131) confirms the connection between the Aqua Traiana and the Baths of Trajan. For a recent detailed discussion of the river crossing and supply to the baths see TAYLOR 1995, 91–102. See also CONNOLLY and DODGE 1998, 240–1. For the Sette Sale: FINE LICHT 1990.

116 ASHBY 1935, 308–15; CARUSO 1986, 308–15; CARUSO and GIUSBERTI 1993; EVANS 1994, 132–3; AICHER 1995, 45, 74–5; *Lexicon* I, *s.v.* 'Aqua Alexandrina', 60–61; *Lexicon* V, *s.v.* 'Thermae Neronianae/Alexandrinae', 60.

117 According to COATES-STEPHENS 1998, 176 n.29 the Baths of Nero were supplied by the Aqua Virgo; FAGAN 1999, 73 says the complex was supplied by the Claudia/Anio Novus.

118 AICHER 1995, 104–112.

119 *Lexicon* V, *s.v.* 'Thermae Neronianae/Alexandrinae', 60. COATES-STEPHENS 1998, 176–77 suggests that the Alexandrina and the Antoniniana were in fact the same aqueduct, referred to in later sources as the Aqua Iovia.

120 Frontinus, *On Aqueducts* 7; Pliny, *Natural History* 31.41; Propertius 3.2.14; Tibullus 3.6.58; Vitruvius, *On Architecture* 8.3.1; Plutarch, *Coriolanus* 1.

121 Frontinus, *On Aqueducts* 11.1; EVANS 1994, 112–13.

122 For flow, velocity and gradient in general HODGE 1992, 215–45.

123 HODGE 1992, 169, 226–7; BLACKMAN 1979, 55–7.

124 BLACKMAN 1979, 55.

125 EVANS 1994, 117.

126 ASHBY 1935, 278; HODGE 1992, 120–1; AICHER 1995, 136–39; EVANS 1994, 117.

127 ASHBY 1935, 101–2; HODGE 1992, 120–1.

128 HODGE 1992, 274. The Appia, Virgo and Alsietina had no settling tanks and the water arrived unfiltered; Frontinus (*On Aqueducts* 1,11 and 22) did not consider the Alsietina worth cleaning up.

129 ASHBY 1935, 226; HODGE 1992, 124–5.

130 ASHBY 1935, 226–7.

131 SMITH 1970; AICHER 1995, 43. SMITH 1991, 124 claims it was the biggest of all Roman dams; it was overcome by floods in 1305.

132 This work was further complicated by the need to divert the flow of water to allow access into the channel (LEVEAU 1991, 152–3). See ASHBY 1935, 272 and Plate XIX for major lime incrustation of the channel of the Anio Novus.

133 For a discussion of gradient and velocity see BLACKMAN 1979; SMITH 1991, 120–23; HODGE 1992, 216–221. For a discussion of Vitruvius and aqueduct gradients see LEWIS 1999, 152–56. It was important for aqueduct channels to be covered to prevent evaporation, debris from falling in and blocking the channel or fouling the water, and the growth of algae as a result of the effect of sunlight on the water.

134 HODGE 1992, 218.

135 FRENCH 1985, 285; an average velocity of 2–3 ft per second (0.61–0.91 m per second) is enough to prevent sedimentation when there is a low silt load.

136 ASHBY 1935, 271, 287.

137 HODGE 1992, 94, 220–1. Average speeds in modern aqueducts are not normally above 1.2–1.3 m per second.

138 Frontinus, *On Aqueducts* 19; BRUUN 1991, 116–8, 148; for deliveries *extra urbem* generally: WILSON 1999.

139 Frontinus, *On Aqueducts* 18; 9.5; *CIL* 6.1261, 31566; 14.3676. For the use of aqueduct water for irrigation, see HORDEN and PURCELL 2000, 247–9.

140 Frontinus, *On Aqueducts* 97; WIKANDER 1991, 144–5. This was a problem even in the Republic; Plutarch, *Cato* 19 says that the censor in 184 BC cut off the pipes which were being used by private individuals to rob the aqueducts of water for their own houses and gardens. This might have caused a diminished flow in the Appia and Anio Vetus, necessitating the planning of a new line and the eventual construction of the Aqua Marcia (MORGAN 1978, 28–9).

141 WILSON 1999, 316–7. Villa of the Quintilii: ASHBY 1935, 223–4; AICHER 1995, 103–4.

142 Manlius Vopiscus: Statius, *Silvae* 1.3.66–7; this included a siphon beneath the river Anio itself (HODGE 1982, 157). Sette Bassi: ASHBY 1935, 228 (who dates it to the late 3rd or early 4th century AD); AICHER 1995, 103.

143 ASHBY 1935, 133–4; SARTORIO 1986; AICHER 1995, 93–5; WILSON 1999, 316. See also THOMAS and WILSON 1994.

144 Frontinus, *On Aqueducts* 11; 92; EVANS 1993; TAYLOR 1997, 488–92.

145 For population in this region HERMANSEN 1978, 160–2.

146 TAYLOR 1995 for aqueduct river crossings, which as he points out, is a much neglected area of the subject. EVANS 1982, 409, thinks that these 3 lines were all initially carried on the Pons Aemilius, but TAYLOR 1995, 78 points out that the evidence in Frontinus makes this unlikely; neither the Anio Vetus nor the Marcia supplied Regio XI, an the eastern end of the Pons Aemilius (*On Aqueducts* 80.2; 81.2).

147 BLOCH 1944; EVANS 1994, 131.

148 HODGE 1992, 275–303. The subject is always going to be hindered as much as helped by the survival of Frontinus. See also HODGE 1996.

149 BRUUN 1991, 118–25.

150 FORBES 1964; BLACKMAN 1978; 1979; HODGE 1984; 1992, 298–300; RODGERS 1986; BRUUN 1991, 51–55. Added to which, as FAGAN 1999, 71 has pointed out, some scholars (eg YEGÜL 1992, 393–4) give more credence to modern interpretations of Frontinus' figures as opposed to Frontinus' original figures. See SMITH 1991, 120–1; BRUUN 1991; 1997, 126–30; EVANS 1994, 140–44 for a much more measured discussion of this subject.

151 TAYLOR 1997, 468.

152 BRUUN 1991, 51–5; HODGE 1992, 296–7 (on pipes in general 308–15); LANDELS 1978, 42–57.

153 We, of course, tend to think in terms of quantity = units per period of time. A standard of 0.48 l/sec (based on a minimum head of 12 cm) is now more or less universally accepted by scholars as a minimum value for the *quinaria* (DIFENIZIO 1916). As RODGERS 1986, 355, points out, we have no *evidence* for any standard except for capacity; we, therefore, are basing much of these calculations on ignorance. See generally on this subject RODGERS 1986, 353–4; SMITH 1991, 120–1; HODGE 1992, 299. BRUUN 1991 has an Appendix aptly titled 'The impossibility of reaching the exact value for the Roman *quinaria* measurement'.

154 HODGE 1984, 205–6. See TAYLOR 1997, 468–71 for a more recent, and very useful, discussion.

155 HODGE 1984; RODGERS 1986, 354.

156 BLACKMAN 1978, 71.

157 GRIMAL 1961: 1,127,220 m^3 per day; PACE 1983: 1,010,000 m^3 per day; GARBRECHT 1982, 33: 525,000–635,000 m^3 per day; BLACKMAN 1978: 560,000–620,000 m^3 per day for the four largest aqueducts (Anio Vetus, Marcia, Claudia, Anio Novus); it does not help the situation that these estimates are often difficult to compare as they are expressed in different ways (SCOBIE 1986, 423; HODGE 1989, 130; BRUUN 1991, 98–104; 1997, 137–41). FAGAN 1999, 74, following FORBES 1964, 174, gives the following water consumption figures for 1936 – Rome 150 gallons per head per day; London 35.5 gallons per head per day; Munich 55 gallons; New York 120 gallons, and compares this with an estimated 198 gallons per head per day for Rome in 50 BC. On the other hand YEGÜL 1992, 393 says that the 9 aqueducts of Frontinus supplied nearly 1 million m^3, an estimated 300 gallons per person per day. BRUUN 1991, 103–4 suggests the figure of 67 litres per person per

day, much lower than other estimates, for example ADAM 1994, 268: 1,100 litres per person/day. Whilst such figures help to gain an appreciation of the overall scale, they can only be guesstimates.

158 The approach used by EVANS 1994, expressing Frontinus' figures as percentages, seems to be a far more valuable, accurate and honest use of the water commissioner's data.

159 BLACKMAN 1978. See HODGE 1992, 304–7 for Pompeii. SMITH 1991, 120–2 provides a very pragmatic approach.

160 RODGERS 1996. The 10,000 *quinariae* discrepancy between the amount which could be supplied and the amount actually delivered is explained by Frontinus as being the result of fraud (*On Aqueducts* 74.2). HERSCHEL 1913, 203, points out that Frontinus' data is at times too general and vague to give us a clear idea of how he reconciled these different figures.

161 RODGERS 1986, 360.

162 A further example is given by HODGE 1989, 130, who provides a set of calculations the results of which suggest that 1st century AD Rome's water supply was twice that of New York in 1986. This completely ignores the fact that water use has changed and in modern New York is completely different. On population estimates for Rome, see most recently Noy 2000, 15–22. See FAGAN 1999, 71 for a very sensible discussion of this whole problem.

163 Frontinus, *On Aqueducts* 78.3, though as EVANS 1994, 139 points out, when the individual deliveries in 79–86 are added up a higher figure, 10,409½, is achieved.

164 EVANS 1994, 140.

165 Cisterns: HODGE 1992, 58–60, 79, 89 (274–294 for urban distribution).

166 This structure is probably Hadrianic (DEMAN 1935, 173) and was certainly added after Frontinus who says that the Virgo had no settling tanks along its course (*On Aqueducts* 1.11. See ASHBY 1935, 174; ADAM 1994, 571; AICHER 1995, Fig. 6).

167 This whole process would be somewhat negated when two supply lines of differing qualities are mixed before they came into the city. Filtering: the water could flow across a bed of sand or pass through some porous cleansing agent. There is evidence for this process surviving from Ampurias in Spain and Cirta (Constantine) in Algeria; in the latter case a filter, constructed on sandbags, was fitted across the aqueduct channel (BERTHIER 1955–56; see also HODGE 1992, 275–6). For secondary *castella*, see HODGE 1992, 280.

168 ASHBY 1935, 242: AICHER 1995, 55. The *castellum* of the Marcia was on top of the Porta Capena (ASHBY 1935, 155). Juvenal, *Satires* 3.11 refers to the Porta Capua as 'dripping' (*madida*), reflecting one of the constant problems of maintenance.

169 Frontinus, *On Aqueducts*, 79–86; EVANS 1994, 139–41.

170 HODGE 1994, 282–91.

171 Frontinus, *On Aqueducts* 78.3; EVANS 1994, 139–144. For a full study of the stamps on pipes (*fistulae*) and their importance in our understanding of Rome's urban water supply, see BRUUN 1991.

172 BRUUN 1991, 58; 101–4; YEGÜL 1992, 393–4; EVANS 1994, 140. FORBES 1964, 173, followed by HODGE 1992, 257–8; it should be noted that aqueduct water was put to a wide variety of uses in the city rather than being restricted to bathing or drinking.

173 HODGE 1994, 304–307; *Lexicon* II, *s.v.* 'Fons', 255; EVANS 1991, 25.

174 NORDH 1949, 104.11 (15 *nymphaea*); 105.7 (1352 *lacus*). The discrepancy in the figures is a problem with the Catalogues themselves.

175 *Lexicon* II, *s.v.* 'Fons', 255–61; III, *s.v.* 'Lacus Servilius', 172–3; 'Lacus Iuternae', 168–70; RICHARDSON 1992, 162–3. Pompeii is very much the model which modern scholars follow. See also MORTON 1966, 46–52.

176 NASH 1961–2 vol. 2, 18–20. The direct connection with a sewer increased the potential for contamination.

177 *Lexicon* IV, *s.v.* 'nymphaeum Alexandri', 351–3; RICHARDSON 1992, 270–1. The topography and general urban layout was much changed in the 18th century, presenting major problems of interpretation. TEDESCHI GRISANTI 1986a, 126 has excluded the Iulia from supplying this structure on the grounds that the channel is at a lower level than that actually supplying the *nymphaeum*. It was more likely supplied by the Claudia and Anio Novus. See also CATTALINI and TEDESCHI GRISANTI 1986; TEDESCHI GRISANTI 1987; AICHER 1993, 348–350; EVANS 1994, 127, 407.

178 AICHER 1993, 350–1. It is from this monument that Pope Sixtus V in 1590 removed the marble trophies which are now set on the balustrade of the Piazza del Campodoglio, hence its medieval name 'Trofei di Mario'; see TEDESCHI GRISANTI 1977; 1986a; AICHER 1995, 60–1.

179 TEDESCHI GRISANTI 1986b; AICHER 1993.

180 *Lexicon* III, *s.v.*. 'Meta Sudans', 247–9. Water was brought probably from the Esquiline in concrete-built channels, rather than lead pipes. For the results of recent excavations: PANELLA 1990; 1996. For a possible connection with the Domus Aurea: LEONE 1985. Gladiators are said to have been in the habit of drinking there after a fight in the Colosseum.

181 SCOBIE 1986, 423; HODGE 1989, 130.

182 HODGE 1992, 304–7, Fig. 213.

183 HERSCHEL 1913, 203–11; FORBES 1964, 170–3; BRUUN 1991, 41–44; HODGE 1992, 294–300. See TAYLOR 1997, 484–6 for a discussion of legal rights and aqueducts.

184 No bronze pieces have been found which correspond to the details given by Frontinus either in Rome or Ostia, and there are a number of places where no *calices* were used at all (BRUUN 1991, 41–44).

185 For different pipe sizes: Frontinus, *On Aqueducts* 39–45; LANDELS 1978, 42–44. GRIMAL 1961 lists some of the commonest *calix* sizes as listed by Frontinus with modern measurements. See also LANDELS 1978, 53–57.

186 BRUUN 1991, 41–44. Frontinus (*On Aqueducts* 113) admits that *calices* were not always applied. The archaeological evidence is difficult and contradictory. BRUUN 1991, 44 suggests that Frontinus' account of the *calix* is prescriptive not descriptive.

187 LANDELS 1978, 52. See Frontinus *On Aqueducts*, 112–115 on cheating; 105 on legal provisions for stamping *calices* and lead pipes connected to them.

188 LANDELS 1978, 42–5; BRUUN 1991 124–127; 304–309 (manufacture of Roman lead water pipes); HODGE 1992, 307–17.

189 HODGE 1981; BRUUN 1991, 127–30. If the daily intake of lead exceeds 0.6 mg, the body becomes saturated and can no longer eliminate the excess which gradually accumulates, poisoning the system.

190 Vitruvius, and other ancient writers, are in fact more concerned with the poisonous nature of white lead (*cerussa*): HODGE 1981, 486. See COULTON 1987, 76–80 for a discussion of why lead is not used everywhere in the empire for piping.

191 HODGE 1981, 488. Lead is soluble in water but if the water has been flowing over sedimentary rocks, as is the case with Roman period water supply lines, the calcium carbonate makes it less likely for the lead to dissolve.

192 ASHBY 1935, 271–2 and Pl. XIX; HODGE 1992, 72; 227–32.

193 HODGE 1981, 489–91 points out that this does not mean that the Romans were necessarily free from lead poisoning. NEEDLEMAN 1985 provides an exhaustive discussion on Roman infertility and concludes that it was caused by gonorrhea. There still remains the possibility, however, that this is just another literary *topos*.

194 For baths and bathing generally see YEGÜL 1992; NIELSEN 1993; FAGAN 1999, 85–103 on baths and the Romans' perception of their medical value; 107–117 on the construction of the imperial baths; 357–67 for non-imperial baths in Rome; DELAINE 1999.

195 The Stabian Baths at Pompeii illustrate how a bath building can be well supplied with water from cisterns and wells and how the supply system can change and adapt. When the aqueduct was built under Augustus a specific channel carried water from the *castellum aquae* to the baths: ESCHEBACH 1979; NIELSEN 1993, 23.

196 See BRUUN 1991, 72–6 for *fistula* evidence; FAGAN 1999, 105–6 and Appendix 2 for evidence for non-imperial baths in Rome in the imperial period. This was partly due to senatorial conservatism; cf the ban in the late Republic on the construction of permanent theatres which were seen by ancient commentators as incitements to indolence and dissent (Tacitus, *Annals* 14.20, FRÉZOULS 1983).

197 NORDH 1949, 100.15–101.10, 105.6; the *thermae* listed are Traianae, Titianae, Commodianae, Antoninianae, Syranae, Decianae, Agrippianae, Alexandrinae, Diocletianae, Constantinianae and Severianae . For ownership of public baths: BRUUN 1991; 1999; YEGÜL 1991, 43–46. For the imperial *thermae* in Rome, see YEGÜL 1991, 128–83. For the new excavations on the Baths of Titus, see CARUSO and CECCHERELLI 1987–88.

198 YEGÜL 1992, 395. See PURCELL 1996 for discussion of water as a symbol of wealth and luxury. MANDERSCHEID 1988 and 1991 explores within the context of the Baths of Caracalla the theme of abundant water display and is firm in the belief that at least the imperial *thermae* in Rome were supplied with fresh running water, making it unnecessary to change the water in the plunge pools on a daily basis.

199 FAGAN 1999, 72; BRUUN 1991, 73.

200 *Lexicon* V, *s.v.* 'Thermae Agrippae', 40–42; SHIPLEY 1933 says that 19,000 m^3 of water per day was delivered to the baths – over one third of the total flow of the Virgo.

201 *Lexicon* V, *s.v.* 'Thermae Neronianae/Alexandrinae', 60–62. There is some dispute about the supply of water to this complex under Nero and under Severus Alexander who restored the baths (SHA, *Severus Alexander* 24.5). Traditionally, the Aqua Alexandrina is described as the main supply line for the later rebuilding but there are major problems with this assumption (see above Aqua Alexandrina). FAGAN 1999, 73 suggests that the Baths of Nero were supplied by the Claudia and Anio Novus.

202 *Lexicon* V, *s.v.* 'Thermae Traiani', 67–9; ANDERSON 1985; CONNOLLY and DODGE 1998, 238–47. For the Sette Sale: FINE LICHT 1990. For epigraphic evidence for the connections between the aqueduct and the baths: BLOCH 1944; EVANS 1994, 131. Exactly how the baths were fed by the Traiana is unknown, though see recent work by TAYLOR 1995, 95–102, who suggests the line after crossing the river was taken around the southern slopes of the Aventine and through the valley between the Palatine and the Caelian. He also notes (99 and n. 83) that a number of baths, significant enough to be mentioned in the Regionary Catalogues, were built along this route, particularly in the area of the Aventine soon after the completion of the aqueduct; clearly this region benefited much from the large capacity and wide distribution of the Aqua Traiana.

203 *Lexicon* I, *s.v.* 'Aqua Marcia', 67–9; V, *s.v.* 'Thermae Antoninianae', 42–8; ASHBY 1935, 158; CONFORTO and IACOPI 1987; MANDERSCHEID 1988; 1991; GARBRECHT and MANDERSCHEID 1992; 1995; DELAINE 1997, 16–17 and bibliography.

204 YEGÜL 1992, 394. GARBRECHT and MANDERSCHEID 1992 give an estimated capacity of 11,500m^3, whilst *Lexicon* I, 68 gives 8 million litres, yet another indication of how scholars complicate the issue by using different methods to describe volume and quantity.

205 ASHBY 1935, 151; *Lexicon* V, *s.v.* 'Thermae Diocletiani', 53–8. For the reservoir see AURIGEMMA 1974, 3–10.

206 For a discussion of the Alsietina and the mills see WIKANDER 1979; BELL 1994, 73–89. For the new work being carried out by Andrew Wilson, and the new interpretations of the evidence: *Lexicon* V, *s.v.* 'Molinae', 277. For the mills in the early medieval period: WARD-PERKINS 1984, 143.

207 WIKANDER 1979, 28–9.

208 WIKANDER 1979, 34–5; *Lexicon* V, *s.v.* 'Molinae', 277. WARD-PERKINS 1984, 143–4, who also believes that the Traiana would never have been maintained purely to power the mills; the fact that water from the Traiana also supplied St Peter's was the all-important factor.

209 KRAUTHEIMER 1980, 241 and fig. 190. The mills were concentrated by the Tiber Island where the current is at its fastest.

210 SCOBIE 1986, 407–18, 427–30; HODGE 1992, 270–2; FAGAN 1999, 77–78.

211 SCOBIE 1986, 413 estimates 40–50,000 kg of human waste, produced by a population of about 1 million, would have gone into the Tiber per day through the Cloaca Maxima by the imperial period.

212 NORDH 1949, 105.11.

213 SCOBIE 1986, 413; ROBINSON 1992, 119–22. Forum Iulium: BLAKE 1973 18–19. Largo Argentina/Portico of Pompey BLAKE 1947, 135–6; for a reconstruction see CONNOLLY and DODGE 1998, 133. For the Via Garibaldi latrine: CHINI 1993; PORTELLA 2000, 258–61. The Domus Transitoria had a very large latrine, apparently able to accommodate 60 occupants at any one time and thought to have been for palace servants; it is now located benath the *triclinium* and peristyle of the Domus Flavia (NASH 1961–2, 375).

214 Obviously people did not run out in the middle of the night if they got caught short! Some *insulae* at Ostia had communal ground floor latrines, although PACKER 1971 frustratingly gives few details.

215 116 latrines or *necessariae* were incorporated into the Aurelianic Wall at the level of the rampart (when the wall was heightened in the 4th century), a position suggesting that they were for the wall garrison. There was no provision to remove the waste from where it fell at the base of the wall, making these areas particularly unpleasant! Only one of these latrines survives today, to the east of the Porta Salaria: RICHMOND 1930, 84–6; NASH 1961–2 vol 2, 288.

216 *Digest* 43.23 *de cloacis* 1.2–3; ROBINSON 1992, 118. On the *cloacae* of Rome generally see MOCCHEGIANI CARPANO 1984.

217 SCOBIE 1986, 409–11; JANSEN 1991, 155–8: nearly every house or apartment at Herculaneum and many at Pompeii, including those above ground floor, has a latrine. Very few at Pompeii were flushed by running water but fed into a cesspit. Similar arrangements for latrines with cesspits were also found at Cosa (BROWN 1980, 42).

218 SCOBIE 1986, 412 and accompanying bibliography.

219 ROBINSON 1992, 122–24. Columella 1.6.24; 11.3.12; Varro, *On Farming* 1.13.4. GOWERS 1995, 27 says there were few latrines and few cesspits, thereby falling into the trap of argument from the non-survival of evidence; ROBINSON 1992, 120 for wagons taking out the night soil. For the mechanics of this in a modern setting (in 19th century Hamburg), see EVANS 1990, 129–31, particularly on how horrible the situation could be with the contents of chamber-pots, as well as the pots themselves, in the street.

220 Frontinus, *On Aqueducts* 104; HODGE 1992, 3.

221 HODGE 1992, 1, 5, 32.

222 HODGE 1981, 489–91; 1992, 322–6. Roman taps can range from stopcocks to discharge taps. A number of Roman taps have been discovered, but they mainly fall into the stopcock category.

223 Although *Digest* 43.10.1 prohibits the throwing of excrement, corpses and animal skins onto the streets, clearly it did happen.

224 Overflow: Frontinus, *On* Aqueducts 111; ASHBY 1935, 46. BAUER 1989; *Lexicon* I, ' Cloaca Maxima', 288–290; Strabo 5.8; Pliny, *Natural History* 36.108. Pliny (*Natural History* 36.24) ascribes its construction to Tarquinius Priscus, whilst Livy (1.38.6 and 1.56.2) credits Tarquinius Superbus. For a fanciful discussion of the symbolism of the Cloaca in literature, see GOWERS 1995.

225 Pliny, *Natural History* 36.104–108; Dio 49.31. Cassiodorus (*Variae* 3.30.1–2) was still singing the praises of Rome's sewers in the 6th century (see Christie in this volume).

226 Procopius, *Gothic* Wars 5.19.1, 18; Lexicon V, *s.v.* 'Molinae', 277; COATES-STEPHENS 1998.

227 See generally WARD-PERKINS 1984, 250–55; COATES-STEPHENS 1998. The reason for this apparent lack is that the evidence just has not been looked for until recently (WARD-PERKINS 1984, 153). For a particularly grim picture at the time of Gregory the Great see LLEWELLYN 1971, 97.

228 DEMAN 1934, 20, 330, 334; ASHBY 1935, 99, 240, 310. WARD-PERKINS 1984, 130, is highly sceptical.

229 The cutting of the aqueducts by Vitigis was mainly felt by the Romans in the closing of the baths (Procopius, *Gothic War* 1.20.5). It is clear from *Liber Pontificalis* 1.291 that wells and springs provided sufficient drinking water. On the baths: KRAUTHEIMER 1980, 111; WARD-PERKINS 1984, 135–49 (eg baths attached to churches built

by Pope Symmachus at S. Paolo fuori le muri, S. Michele and S. Pancrazio); COATES-STEPHENS 1998, 171–6. For wells, see HUBERT 1990, 78–9.

230 *Liber Pontificalis* 62.5, 91.2; AICHER 1995, 28–9. The aqueducts were often referred to as *formae* in the medieval period. Pope Honorius I built a mill on the Janiculum supplied by the Traiana and Gregory II restored the water supply to the baths at S. Lorenzo fuori le muri, originally built by Pope Hilarus (461–8) (WARD-PERKINS 1984, 137). In the 770s Pope Hadrian I repaired the Claudia, the Virgo, the Traiana and the 'Iovia' (*Liber Pontificalis* 97.59, 61–2, 65). The Claudia had a wide distribution supplying private water mills, houses at the Porta Maggiore, on the Esquiline and along the course of the Arcus Neroniani towards the Palatine (WARD-PERKINS 1984, 254–5; COATES-STEPHENS 1998, 173–4). The 'Iovia' is a name which first appears in 7th century sources and is generally believed to correspond to the Antoniniana, the branch of the Marcia built by Caracalla to supply his baths. COATES-STEPENS 1998, 174–6 suggests that the Aqua Iovia might in fact refer to the Aqua Alexandrina and that this and the Antoniniana are in fact the same line; he also claims that it is wrong to think that the Alexandrina was built to supply the refurbished baths of Nero by Alexander Severus. WARD-PERKINS 1984, 255, argues that the medieval name Iovia refers to the whole of the Marcia, possibly acquiring it after radical repairs under Diocletian (see RICHARDSON 1992, 18).

231 HUBERT 1990, 76–8; COATES-STEPHENS 1998, 172–3.

232 KRAUTHEIMER 1980, *passim,* but especially 271–288. Rome was exceptional at this time in the abandonment of the hills for settlement on low-lying ground, presumably because of the security offered by the Aurelianic walls. As WARD-PERKINS 1984, 125 points out, the drainage of the land was a much more important factor, a function superbly carried out by the Cloaca Maxima.

233 WARD-PERKINS 1984, 144–5.

234 KRAUTHEIMER 1980, 251–2; WARD-PERKINS 1984, 141–3. See also MORTON 1966, 202–205 (for the Pine Cone fountain); 202–216 (for St Peter's and fountains generally).

235 KRAUTHEIMER 1980, 251–2; AICHER 1995, 29. It was the Neronian branch of the Claudia which supplied the palace, hence its mediavel name, the 'Forma Lateranensis'.

236 5th century inscription: *CIL* 6.1711. RICHARDSON 1982, 258–9; WARD-PERKINS 1984 143–44. They were also referred to in the 8th century *Einsiedeln Itinerary*.

237 WARD-PERKINS 1984, 253.

238 LANCIANI 1881, 166–8; MORTON 1966 164–201.

239 PINTO 1986, 21–27 and *passim*; LANCIANI 1880, 128–30; MORTON 1966, 73–116.

240 MORTON 1966, 117–63.

BIBLIOGRAPHY

ADAM J.-P. 1994: *Roman Building. Materials and Techniques*, London, 1994.

AICHER, P.J. 1993: 'Terminal Display Fountains (*Mostre*) and the Aqueducts of Ancient Rome', *Phoenix* 47.4, 1993, 339–352.

AICHER, P.J. 1995: *Guide to the Aqueducts of Ancient Rome*, Wauconda Illinois, 1995.

AMMERMAN, A.J. 1990: 'On the origins of the Forum Romanum', *AJA* 94, 1990, 627–45.

ANDERSON, J.C. 1985: 'The date of the *Thermae Traianae* and the Topography of the *Oppius Mons*', *AJA* 89, 1985, 499–509.

ASHBY, T. 1935: *The Aqueducts of Rome*, London, 1935.

ASHBY, T. 1991: *Gli acquedotti dell'antica Roma*, Roma, 1991.

ASTIN, A.E. 1961: 'Water to the Capitol: a Note on Frontinus *De Aquis* 1,7,5', *Latomus* 20, 1961, 541–548.

AURIGEMMA, S. 1974: *Le Terme di Diocleziano e il Museo Nazionale Romano*, Roma, 1974.

BAUER, H. 1989: 'Die Cloaca Maxima in Rom', *Mitteilungen des Leichtweiss-Institutes für Wasserbau der Technischen Universität Braunschweig* 103, 1989, 45–67.

BELL, M. 1994: 'An Imperial Flour Mill on the Janiculum', in *Le ravitaillement en blé de Rome et des centres urbains des débuts de la République jusqu'au Haut Empire*, Roma, 1994, 73–89.

BERTHIER, A. 1955–56: 'Note sur un filtre romain découvert à Constantine', *Recueil des notices et mémoires de la Société Archéologique de Constantine* 69, 1955–56, 175–8.

BLACKMAN, D.R. 1978: 'The volume of water delivered by the four great aqueducts of Rome', *PBSR* 46, 1978, 52–72.

BLACKMAN, D.R. 1979: 'The length of the four great aqueducts of Rome', *PBSR* 47, 1979, 12–18.

BLAKE, M.E. 1947: *Ancient Roman Construction in Italy from the Prehistoric Period to Augustus*, Washington, 1947.

BLAKE, M.E. 1973: *Roman Construction in Italy from Nerva through the Antonines*, Philadelphia, 1973.

BLOCH, H. 1944: 'Aqua Traiana', *AJA* 48, 1944, 337–41.

BOATWRIGHT, M.T. 1987: *Hadrian and the City of Rome*, Princeton, 1987.
BROWN, F.E. 1980: *Cosa. The Making of a Roman Town*, Ann Arbor, 1980.
BRUNT, P. 1971: *Italian Manpower 225 B.C.–A.D. 14*, Oxford, 1971.
BRUUN, C. 1987: 'Water for the Castra Praetoria', *Arctos* 21, 1987, 7–18.
BRUUN, C. 1989: 'Statio aquarum', in E. Steinby (ed.), *Lacus Iuternae* I, Roma, 1989, 127–47.
BRUUN, C. 1991: *The Water Supply of Ancient Rome*, Helsinki, 1991.
BRUUN, C. 1997: 'Acquedotti e Condizioni Sociali di Roma Imperiale: Immagini e Realtà', *La Rome Impériale. Démographie et Logistique*, Collection de L'École Française de Rome 230, Roma, 1997, 121–155.
BRUUN, C. 1999: 'Ownership of Baths in Rome: the evidence from lead-pipe installations', in DELAINE and JOHNSTON, 1999, 75–85.
CAMBEDDI, A.1986: 'L'Acquedotto Vergine (sec. XVIII–XX)' , in PISANO SARTORIO and LIBERATI SILVERIO 1986, 208–13.
CARDELLI ALLOISI, L. 1986: 'La Mostra dell'Acqua Vergine (fontana di Trevi)', in PISANO SARTORIO and LIBERATI SILVERIO 1986, 235–40.
CARETTONI, G., COLINI, A.M., COZZA, L. and GATTI, G. 1960: *La pianta marmorea di Roma antica (Forma Urbis Romae)*, 2 vols, Roma, 1960.
CARUSO, G. 1986: 'Aqua Alexandriana', in PISANO SARTORIO and LIBERATI SILVERIO 1986, 120–23.
CARUSO, G. and CECCHERELLI, A. 1987–88: 'Terme di Tito', *BullCom* 92, 1987–88, 317–23.
CARUSO, G. and GIUSBERTI, P. 1993: 'Acquedotto Alessandrino. Restauro del tratto tra via del Fossa di Centocelle e Via dei Pioppi', *BullCom* 95.2, 1993, 116–121.
CATTALINI, D. 1986a: 'Aqua Marcia', in PISANO SARTORIO and LIBERATI SILVERIO 1986, 42–52.
CATTALINI, D. 1986b: 'Aqua Antoniniana', in PISANO SARTORIO and LIBERATI SILVERIO 1986, 57–59.
CATTALINI, D. 1986c: 'Aqua Tepula', in PISANO SARTORIO and LIBERATI SILVERIO 1986, 42–52.
CATTALINI, D. 1986d: 'Aqua Julia', in PISANO SARTORIO and LIBERATI SILVERIO 1986, 62–54.
CATTALINI, D. and TEDESCHI GRISANTI, G. 1986: 'Trofei di Mario', *BullCom* 91, 1986, 343–49.
CHINI, P. 1993: 'Latrina romana in Via Garibaldi', *BullCom* 95.2, 1993, 211–15.
COARELLI, F. 1977: 'Il Campo Marzio occidentale. Storie e topografie', *MEFRA* 89.2, 1977, 807–46.
COARELLI, F. 1988: *Il Foro Boario: dalle origini alla fine della Repubblica*, Roma, 1988.
COATES-STEVENS, R. 1998: 'The Walls and Aqueducts of Rome in the Early Middle Ages, A.D. 500–1000', *JRS* 88, 1998, 166–178.
COLEMAN, K. M. 1993: 'Launching into History: Aquatic Displays in the early Empire', *JRS* 83, 1993, 48–74.
CONFORTO M.L. AND IACOPI, I. 1987: 'Terme di Caracalla: studi e proposte per il controllo idrico', in PISANO SARTORIO and LIBERATI SILVERIO 1987, 198–98.
CONNOLLY, P. AND DODGE, H. 1998: *The Ancient City*, Oxford, 1998.
CORNELL, T.J. 1995: *The Beginnings of Rome: Italy and Rome from the Bronze Age to the Punic Wars (c 1000–264 BC)*, London, 1995.
COULTON, J.J. 1987: 'Roman Aqueducts in Asia Minor', in S. Macready and F.H. Thompson (ed.), *Roman Architecture in the Greek World*, London, 1987, 72–84.
CROUCH, D. 1993: *Water Management in Ancient Greek Cities*, Oxford, 1993.
DELAINE, J. 1997: *The Baths of Caracalla*, JRA Supplementary Series 25, Portsmouth RI, 1997.
DELAINE, J. 1999: 'Bathing and Society', in DELAINE and JOHNSTON 1999, 7–16.
DELAINE, J. and JOHNSTON, D.E. (ed.) 1999: *Roman Baths and Bathing, 1, Bathing and Society*, JRA Supplementary Series 37, Portsmouth RI, 1999.
DEMAN, E.B. van 1934: *The Building of the Roman Aqueducts*, Washington, 1934.
DIFENIZIO , C. 1916: 'Sulla portata degli acqudotti romani e determinazione della *quinaria*', *Giornale del Genio Civile* 14, 1916, 226–331.
D'ONOFRIO, C. 1970: *Il Tevere e Roma*, Roma, 1970.
ELSNER, J. 1994: 'Constructing decadence; the representation of Nero as imperial builder', in J. Elsner and J. Masters (ed.), *Reflections of Nero: culture, history, & representation*, London, 1994, 112–27.
ESCHEBACH, H. 1979: *Stabianer Thermen in Pompeji*, Berlin, 1979.
EVANS, H.B. 1982: 'Agrippa's Water Plan', *AJA* 86, 1982, 401–411.
EVANS, H.B. 1983: 'Nero's *Arcus Caelimontani*', *AJA* 87, 1983, 392–399.
EVANS, H.B. 1991: 'Water distribution in ancient Rome: *Quorsum et Cui Bono*?' in HODGE 1991, 21–7.
EVANS, H.B. 1993: '*In Tiburtium usum*: special arrangements in the Roman water system (Frontinus, *Aq*.6.5)', *AJA* 97, 1993, 447–55.
EVANS, H.B. 1994: *Water distribution in ancient Rome. The evidence of Frontinus*, Ann Arbor, 1994.

EVANS, R.J. 1990: *Death in Hamburg*, London, 1990.
FAGAN, G.G. 1999: *Bathing in Public in the Roman World*, Ann Arbor, 1999.
FAVRO, D. 1996: *The Urban Image of Augustus*, Cambridge, 1996.
FINE LICHT, K. de 1990: *Untersuchungen an den Traiansthermen zu Rom II. Sette Sale*, Analecti Romani Danici Supplement 19, Roma, 1990.
FORBES, R.J. 1964: *Studies in Ancient Technology*, Leiden, 1964.
FRANK, T. (ed.) 1933: *Economic Survey of Ancient Rome* I, Baltimore, 1933.
FRENCH. H. 1985: *Open Channel Hydraulics*, New York, 1985.
FRÉZOULS, E. 1983: 'La construction du *theatrum lapideum* et son contexte politique', in *Théâtre et spectacles dans l'antiquité. Actes du Colloque de Strasbourg 5–7 novembre 1981*, Leiden, 1983, 193–214.
GARBRECHT, G. 1982: 'Wasserversorgungstechnik in römischer zeit', in *Wasserversorgung im antiken Rom*, München, 1982, 9–43.
GARBRECHT, G. and MANDERSCHEID, H. 1992: '*Etiam fonte novo Antoniniano*. L'acquedotto Antoniniano alle Terme di Caracalla', *Archeologia Classica* 44, 1992, 193–234.
GARBRECHT, G. and MANDERSCHEID, H. 1995: 'Die Wasserversorgung der Caracallathermen durch die Aqua Antoniniana', *Antike Welt* 26, 1995, 195–202.
GOWERS, E. 1995: 'The anatomy of Rome from Capitol to Cloaca', *JRS* 85, 1995, 23–32.
GRIMAL, P. 1961: *Frontin, les aqueducs de la ville de Rom*, ed 2, Paris, 1961.
HERMANSEN, G. 1978: 'The population of imperial Rome: the regionaries', *Historia* 27, 1978, 129–68.
HERSCHEL, C. 1913: *The Two Books on the Water Supply of Sextus Julius Frontinus*, ed. 2, London, 1913.
HODGE, A.T. 1981: 'Vitruvius, lead pipes and lead poisoning', *AJA* 85, 1981, 486–91.
HODGE, A.T. 1982: 'Siphons in Roman aqueducts', *PBSR* 51, 1983, 174–221.
HODGE, A.T. 1984: 'How did Frontinus measure the quinaria?' *AJA* 88, 1984, 205–16.
HODGE, A.T. 1989: 'Aqueducts', in I. M. Barton (ed.), *Roman Public Buildings*, Exeter, 1989, 127–49.
HODGE, A.T. (ed.) 1991: *Future Currents in Aqueduct Studies*, Leeds, 1991.
HODGE, A.T. 1992: *Roman Aqueducts and Water Supply*, London, 1992.
HODGE A.T. 1996: 'In Vitruviam Pompeianum: urban water distribution reappraised', *AJA* 100, 1996, 261–276.
HOLLOWAY, R.R. 1994: *Early Rome and Latium*, London, 1994.
HORDEN P. and PURCELL, N. 2000: *The Corrupting Sea*, Oxford, 2000.
HUBERT, E. 1990: *Éspace urbain et habitat à Rome du Xe siècle à la fin du XIIIe siècle*, Roma, 1990.
JANSEN, G.C.M. 1991: 'Water systems and sanitation in the houses of Herculaneum', *Mededelingen van het Nederlands Institut te Rome* 50, 1991, 145–166.
KRAUTHEIMER, R. 1980: *Rome: Profile of a City, 312–1308*, Princeton, 1980.
LANCIANI, R. 1881: *I commentarii di Frontino intorno le acque e gli acquedotti*, Roma, 1881.
LANCIANI, R. 1893–1901: *Forma Urbis Romae*, Milano, 1893–1901.
LANCIANI, R. 1897: *The Ruins and Excavations of Ancient Rome*, London, 1897.
LANDELS, J. 1978: *Engineering in the Ancient World*, Berkeley, 1978.
LE GALL, J. 1953: *Le Tibre, fleuve de Rome dans l'antiquité*, Paris, 1953.
LEONE, E 1985: 'Domus Aurea e Meta Sudans', *Roma. Archeologia nel Centro, I: L'Area Archeologia Centrale*, Roma, 1985, 13–19.
LEVEAU, P. 1991: 'Research on Roman Aqueducts in the past ten years', in HODGE 1991, 149–62.
LEWIS, M. 1999: 'Vitruvius and Greek Aqueducts', *PBSR* 67, 1999, 145–72.
LIBERATI SILVERIO, A. 1986: 'Aqua Alsietina', in PISANO SARTORIO and LIBERATI SILVERIO 1986, 72–79.
LLEWELLYN, P. 1971: *Rome in the Dark Ages*, Oxford, 1971.
LLOYD, R.B. 1979: 'The *Aqua Virgo* and *Pons Agrippae*', *AJA* 83, 1979, 193–204.
MANDERSCHEID, H. 1988: '*Quantum aquarum per gradus cum fragore labentium*. Überlegungen zu Wasserversogung und Wassernutzung der Caracallathermen', *Archäologisches Korrespondenzblatt* 13.3, 1988, 291–99.
MANDERSCHEID, H. 1991: 'La gestione idrica delle terme di Caracalla: alcuni osservazioni', in *Les Thermes Romains*, Collection de l'École française de Rome 142, Roma, 1991, 49–60.
MARI, Z. 1991: 'Nuovi *cippi* degli acquedotti Aniensi', *PBSR* 59, 1991, 151–75.
MOCCHEGIANI CARPANO, C. 1984: 'Le cloache dell'antica Roma', in *Roma Sotterranea,* Roma, 1984, 164–78.
MORGAN, M.G. 1978: 'The Introduction of the Aqua Marcia into Rome, 144–140 B.C.', *Philologus* 122, 1978, 25–58.
MORTON, H.V. 1966: *The Waters of Rome*, London, 1966.
MUCCI, A. 1986a: 'Aqua Appia', in PISANO SARTORIO and LIBERATI SILVERIO 1986, 30–2.
MUCCI, A. 1986b: 'Aqua Claudia', in PISANO SARTORIO and LIBERATI SILVERIO 1986, 80–88.

MUCCI, A. 1986c: 'Arcus Caelimontani Aquae Claudiae', in PISANO SARTORIO and LIBERATI SILVERIO 1986, 95–99.

MUCCI, A. 1986d: 'Anio Novus', in PISANO SARTORIO and LIBERATI SILVERIO 1986, 100–106.

NASH, E. 1961–62: *Pictorial Dictionary of Ancient Rome*, I–II, London, 1961–62.

NEEDLEMAN, L. and D. 1985: 'Lead Poisoning and the decline of the Roman aristocracy', *Classical Review* 29, 1985, 63–94.

NIELSEN, I. 1993: *Thermae et Balnea: the architecture and cultural history of Roman public baths*, Aarhus, 1990.

NORDH, A. 1949: *Libellis de regionibus urbis Romae*, Lund, 1949.

NOY, D. 2000: *Foreigners at Rome*, London, 2000.

PACE, P. 1983: *Gli aquedotti di Roma e il "De Aquaeductu" di Frontin*, Rome, 1983.

PACKER, J. 1971: *The Insulae of Imperial Ostia*, MAAR 31, Roma, 1971.

PANELLA, C. 1990: 'La Valle del Colosseo nell'antichità', *Bollettino di Archeologia*, 1990, 34–88.

PANELLA, C. 1996: *Meta Sudans I. Un'area sacra in Palatio e le valle del Colosseo primo e dopo Nerone*, Roma, 1996.

PARKER, J.H. 1876: *The Aqueducts of Ancient Rome*, Rome, 1876.

PINTO, J.A. 1986: *The Trevi Fountain*, New Haven, 1986.

PISANO SARTORIO, G. and LIBERATI SILVERIO, A. (ed.) 1986: *Il trionfo dell'acqua: Acque e acquedotti a Roma, IV sec. a.C.–XX sec.*, Roma, 1986.

PISANO SARTORIO, G. and LIBERATI SILVERIO, A. (ed.) 1987: *Il trionfo dell'acqua. Gli antichi acquedotti di Roma: problemi di conoscenza, conservazione e tutela,* Roma, 1987.

PLATNER, S.B. and ASHBY, T. 1929: *A Topographical Dictionary of Ancient Rome*, Oxford, 1929.

PORTELLA, I. della 2000: *Subterranean Rome*, Roma, 2000.

PURCELL, N. 1996: 'Rome and the management of water: environment, culture and power', in G. Shipley and J. Salmon (ed.), *Human Landscapes in Classical Antiquity. Environment and Culture*, London, 1996, 180–212.

QUILICI, L. 1968: 'Sull'acquedotto Vergine dal monte Pincio alle sorgente', *Studi Topografica romana*, Roma, 1968, 125–60.

QUILICI, L. 1986: 'Aqua Virgo', in PISANO SARTORIO and LIBERATI SILVERIO 1986, 65–70.

QUILICI, L. 1989: 'Gli acquedotti di Roma', *Archeo: attualità del passato* 53, 1989, 51–97.

RAMAGE, E. S. 1983: 'Urban problems in Ancient Rome', in M. Marchese (ed.), *Aspects of Greco-Roman Urbanism: essays on the Classical City*, BAR International Series 188, Oxford, 1983, 61–92.

REYNOLDS, L.J. 1986: *Texts and Transmission: a survey of the Latin Classics*, Oxford, 1986.

RICHARDSON, L. 1992: *A New Topographical Dictionary of Ancient Rome*, Baltimore, 1992.

RICHMOND, I. 1930: *The City Wall of Imperial Rome*, Oxford, 1930.

ROBINSON, O. 1980: 'The Water Supply of Ancient Rome', *Studia et Documenta Historiae et Iuris* 46, 1980, 44–86.

ROBINSON, O. 1992: *Ancient Rome: City Planning and Administration*, London, 1992.

RODGERS, R.H. 1986: 'Copia Aquarum: Frontinus' Measurements and the Perspective of Capacity', *TAPA* 116, 1986, 353–360.

RODGERS, R.H. 1996: 'Sidestepping the long shadow of Frontinus', *JRA* 9, 1996, 395–408.

RONCAIOLI LAMBERTI, C. 1986: 'L'Aqua Anio Vetus', in PISANO SARTORIO and LIBERATI SILVERIO 1986, 33–40.

RONCAIOLI LAMBERTI, C. 1987: 'Osservazioni e proposte sul sito dell'incile dell'Anio Vetus e sul ramo di derivazione dell'Anio Novus', in PISANO SARTORIO and LIBERATI SILVERIO 1987, 83–92.

SANTA MARIA SCRINARI, V. 1979: 'Brevi note sugli scavi sotto la chiesa di S. Vito', *AL* 2, 1979, 61–2.

SARTORIO, G. 1986: 'Punto di derivazione dell'acqua Marcia alla cisterna della c.d. villa delle Vignacce sulla via Latina: strada di manutenzione e cippo terminale delle acque Marcia, Tepula e Iulia', in PISANO SARTORIO and LIBERATI SILVERIO 1986, 55–6.

SCOBIE, A. 1986: 'Slums, Sanitation, and Mortality in the Roman World', *Klio* 68, 1986, 399–433.

SHIPLEY, F.W. 1933: *Agrippa's Building Activities in Rome*, St Louis, 1933.

SMITH, C.J. 1996: *Early Rome and Latium: Economy and Society c. 1000 to 500 BC*, Oxford, 1996.

SMITH N.A.F. 1970: 'The Roman Dams of Subiaco', *Technology and Culture* 11, 1970, 56–68.

SMITH, N.A.F. 1991: 'Problems of Design and Analysis', in HODGE 1991, 113–28.

STAMBAUGH, J.E. 1988: *The Ancient Roman City*, Baltimore, 1988.

TAYLOR, R. 1995: '*A citeriore ripa aquae*: Aqueduct River Crossings in the Ancient City of Rome', *PBSR* 63, 1995, 75–103.

TAYLOR, R. 1997: 'Torrent or Trickle? The Aqua Alsietina, the Naumachia Augusti, and the Transtiberim', *AJA* 101, 1997, 465–492.

TEDESCHI GRISANTI, G. 1977: *I 'trofei di Mario': il ninfeo dell'Acqua Giulia sull'Esquilino*, Roma, 1977.

TEDESCHI GRISANTI, G. 1986a: 'Le mostre degli antichi acquedotti: I 'Trofei de Mario'', in PISANO SARTORIO and LIBERATI SILVERIO 1986, 126–35.
TEDESCHI GRISANTI, G. 1986b: 'I terminali degli acquedotti', in PISANO SARTORIO and LIBERATI SILVERIO 1986, 151–55.
TEDESCHI GRISANTI, G. 1987: 'Primo contributo ad una livellazione urbana sistematica degli antichi acquedotti dei Roma', in PISANO SARTORIO and LIBERATI SILVERIO 1987, 59–69.
THOMAS, R. and WILSON, A. 1994: 'Water supply for Roman farms in Latium and South Etruria', *PBSR* 62, 1994, 139–96.
TOLOMEO, M.G. 1986: 'L'Acquedotto Vergine (sec. XVI–XVII)', in PISANO SARTORIO and LIBERATI SILVERIO 1986, 205–8.
TORTORICI, E. 1993: 'La "Terrazza domizianea", *l'aqua Marcia* ed il taglio della sella tra Campidoglio e Quirinale', *BullComm* 95.2, 1993, 7–24.
VIRGILI, P. 1986: 'Aqua Traiana', in PISANO SARTORIO and LIBERATI SILVERIO 1986, 113–119.
VODRET, A. 1987: 'L'acquedotto Claudio. Dal degrado al cantiere di restuaro', in PISANO SARTORIO and LIBERATI SILVERIO 1987, 199–210.
VOLPE, R. 1996: *Aqua Marcia. Lo scavo di un tratto urbano*, Firenze, 1996.
WALKER, S. 1987: 'Roman Nymphaea in Greece', in S. Macready and F.H. Thompson (ed.), *Roman Architecture in the Greek World*, London, 1987, 60–71.
WARD-PERKINS, B. 1984: *From Classical Antiquity to the Middle Ages*, Oxford, 1984.
WENTWORTH RINNE, K. 1996: 'Aquae Urbis Romae: an historical overview of water in the public life of Rome', in N. De Haan and G.C.M. Jansen (ed.), *Cura Aquarum in Campania*, Roma, 1996, 145–51.
WIKANDER, Ö. 1979: 'Water-Mills in ancient Rome', *Opuscula Romana* 12, 1979, 13–36.
WIKANDER, Ö. 1991: 'Water mills and aqueducts', in HODGE 1991, 141–148.
WILSON, A.W. 1999: 'Deliveries *extra urbem*: aqueducts and the countryside', *JRA* 12, 1999, 314–331.
WILSON, R.J.A. 1996: '*Tot aquarum tam multis necessaris molibus* .... Recent Studies on Roman aqueducts and water supply', *JRA* 9, 1996, 5–29.
YEGÜL, F. 1992: *Baths and Bathing in Classical Antiquity*, Cambridge Mass., 1992.

9. Entertaining Rome

Kathleen Coleman

INTRODUCTION

The street-entertainers of Antiquity have left behind few traces, save passing references in literature and occasional iconographic depictions.[1] Their spectators were few enough in number to cluster around the performer on street-corners or in the courtyard of a tavern. Bear-baiters, street-musicians, jugglers, conjurors – they must all have passed through the city of Rome as they pursued their itinerant occupation along the great arterial routes and side-roads linking the towns and villages of Italy. But the forms of entertainment that have left their mark upon the fabric of Rome in brick and stone served a religious or political function that required the witness of massed spectators: circus-games that originated to celebrate Rome's first victory over the Latins; theatrical performances to appease the gods who were deemed responsible for a plague; gladiatorial combat at the funeral of a prominent senator; and, by the end of the Republic, the whole complex tapestry of *ludi publici* (games put on for the people by the city magistrates), woven from strands of public policy and religious observance.[2]

The evolution of custom-built structures to accommodate spectators was a gradual process that reflected the ambitions of wealthy and powerful benefactors, of whom the Roman emperor is the supreme example.[3] The principal building-types and venues associated with public entertainment came into use at distinct stages during the evolution of the city of Rome. Many of them were concentrated in the Campus Martius, which was not yet built over by the end of the Republic and was therefore available to accommodate large public buildings, including structures for mass entertainment (Fig. 9.1). The discussion below reflects the order in which the different types of entertainment-building evolved in the city of Rome. It offers a brief introduction to all the known examples of each type, set within the context of the performances that took place in them.

CIRCUS

Circus Maximus. Two areas designated by the term *circus* are associated with the earliest recorded *ludi*: the Circus Maximus and the Circus Flaminius. They seem, however, to have been quite different in both appearance and function. The Circus Maximus[4] is associated with the legendary 'rape of the Sabine women', carried out on the occasion of games staged by Romulus with the intention of furthering the Roman race (Livy 1.9). Its more 'historical' association with the Ludi Romani may date from the Etruscan domination of Rome under the dynasty of the Tarquins (Livy 1.35.8–9). The location of the Circus Maximus, in the valley between the Palatine and the Aventine, was the site of cults to deities in whose honour the earliest races were presumably staged, chief amongst them Murcia, Consus, and Sol (the

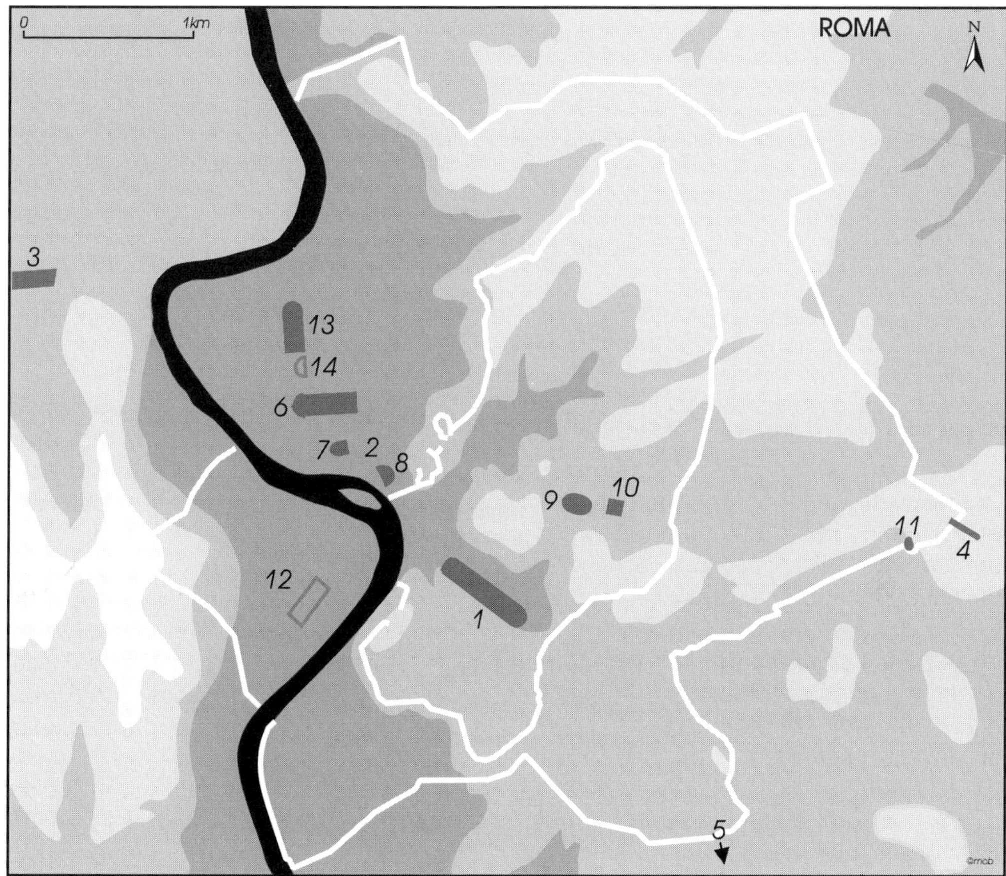

Fig. 9.1: Map showing distribution of spectacle-buildings in Rome. 1 Circus Maximus, 2 Circus Flaminius, 3 Circus Gai et Neronia, 4 Circus Varianus, 5 Circus of Maxentius, 6 Theatrum Pompeii, 7 Theatrum Balbi, 8 Theatrum Marcelli, 9 Amphitheatrum Flavium, 10 Ludus Magnus, 11 Ludus Gallicus, 12 Ludus Dacicus/Ludus Matutinus, 13 Amphitheatrum Castrense, 14 Naumachia Augusti, 15 Stadium Domitiani, 16 Odeum Domitiani

Sun). Their identification with the site persisted throughout Antiquity. What were perhaps at first merely altars to Murcia and Consus became shrines, and a temple to the Sun (and the Moon) was also built into the fabric of the monumental circus.[5]

The route of the races was determined by the elongated shape of the valley; originally the spectators must have been accommodated on the neighbouring slopes or on portable wooden stands. In the latter half of the 4th century BC the first set of starting-gates (*carceres*) was installed, probably made of wood (Varro, *On the Latin language* 5.153; Livy 8.20.2). The first embellishment to be attributed to a named individual was the arch (*fornix*) installed together with gilded statues by L. Stertinius in 196 BC out of *manubiae* won in Hispania Ulterior (Livy 33.27.3–5). Such a public benefaction was an appropriate use of that share of the booty that was entrusted to the general on behalf of the Roman people;[6] and the erection of an arch in a building of this type is an early example of a trend manifest in all entertainment buildings, whereby particular notice accrues to a benefactor by virtue of the

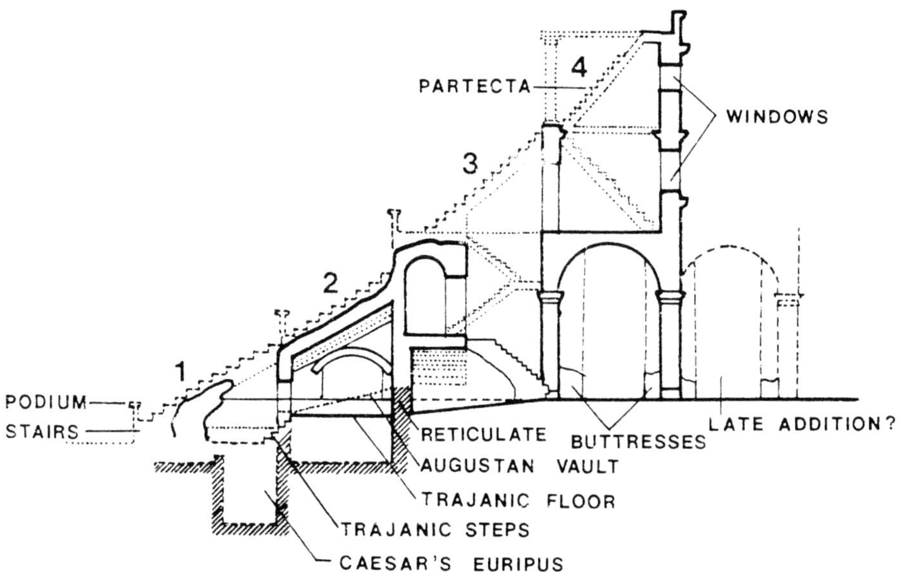

Fig. 9.2: Cross-section of the seating at the south-east end of the Circus Maximus showing the major datable components (reproduced from Humphrey 1986, Fig. 45, by kind permission of the author).

prominent display of his generosity before a stationary (and hence 'captive') audience (see Cornell in this volume).

The first substantial structural developments were effected by Julius Caesar. He constructed the first tier of stone seating, and in front of it he dug a channel (*euripus*) ten feet wide around the perimeter of the track (Fig. 9.2) to protect the spectators from wild beasts to be displayed in *venationes* (Dionysius of Halicarnassus 3.68.1–4; Pliny, *Natural History* 8.21, 36.102; Suetonius, *Julius Caesar* 39.2). The eggs (*ova*) for counting the laps had already been established by the 2nd century, since in 174 BC the censors restored them (Livy 41.27.6); but it was Augustus' general, Agrippa, who gave monumental form to the central platform running down the centre of the track and introduced the other characteristic set of lap-markers, which were shaped like dolphins (Dio 49.43.2). Also in Augustus' reign the *pulvinar* was given monumental form. Originally this was a raised platform for displaying images of the gods and cult objects. Augustus built it into the seating in the form of a small shrine, and watched the races from there. In practical terms it offered a good vantage point, since it was located opposite the finishing-line, which was two-thirds of the way down the track; and in ideological terms the traditional association of the *pulvinar* with the images of the gods implicitly presented Augustus as a focus for public veneration.[7]

Successive emperors added their own embellishments, testifying to the symbolism attaching to this building as one of the most ancient amenities in the city. In trying to identify the most beautiful building in the world, the Elder Pliny explicitly leaves out of consideration the Circus Maximus (*Natural History* 36.102); hence, by implication, he judges it to surpass his three top candidates: the Basilica Aemilia, the Forum of Augustus, and the Templum Pacis built by Vespasian. The Circus that Pliny so admired must have looked, in part, very smart and clean, since under Nero it had been substantially altered, and then it had almost

Fig. 9.3: Sestertius of Trajan commemorating his renovation of the Circus Maximus (reproduced by courtesy of the Trustees of the British Museum).

immediately undergone extensive repairs after the 'Great Fire' of AD 64, which started in shops adjacent to the Circus on the side facing the Mons Caelius (Tacitus, *Annals* 15.38). Nero's alterations prior to the fire attest the Roman sensitivity to hierarchy in seating-arrangements, especially evident in the seating in the theatre (see below). He had removed Caesar's *euripus* so as to install permanent seating for the *equites* at the front of the viewing-area (Pliny, *Natural History* 8.21; Tacitus, *Annals* 15.32.1). Since the *euripus* had been designed to prevent beasts from escaping into the audience, its removal must have necessitated alternative security-arrangements, perhaps on an *ad hoc* basis.

Although the depredations of the Great Fire had been made good by AD 68 (Suetonius, *Nero* 25.2; Dio 62.20.4, 21.1), the Circus Maximus was still presumably constructed largely of wood, since it burnt down again under Domitian. The repairs and improvements that were effected by Trajan (AD 98–117) elicited a rhetorical flourish from the Younger Pliny, who complimented the emperor on installing seating that was "no less noteworthy than the spectacles to be seen from there".[8] Trajan did not rely on the hazards of literary transmission to give him credit for these improvements; he issued a *sestertius* (Fig. 9.3) that bears a precious image of what the Circus looked like in AD 103. It depicts a three-storey structure with arcading on the ground floor and engaged pilasters on the floors above; we shall return to this image below. By now, if not earlier, the Circus comprised a structure approximately 600 m long and 180 m wide.[9] In the 4th-century Regionary Catalogues it is estimated to contain 385,000 and 485,000 *loca* respectively. The formula for calculating these figures is not clear, but modern estimates reckon a capacity of approximately 150,000 spectators.[10] Sadly, throughout Antiquity it continued to be subjected to fire and intermittent structural failure, culminating in a disaster under Diocletian in which the wall of the uppermost tier of seating (*partecta*) collapsed and 13,000 victims are said to have perished.[11]

The function of the circus as a race-track dictated a division lengthwise down the middle of the arena, around which the chariots performed seven laps to complete a race. The resulting barrier that could be erected to connect the turning-posts (*metae*) at either end was therefore visible to the entire body of spectators, and its axis readily accommodated the display of items with a practical or symbolic function (such as the lap-markers mentioned above).[12] By the 1st century AD a permanent barrier was installed along this axis, and at some point between the reign of Nero and that of Septimius Severus it was equipped with a series of basins (*euripi*) that became its distinguishing characteristic, so that *euripus* ('channel') probably developed as the correct term for what is nowadays, by a common misnomer, usually termed *spina*

Fig. 9.4: Augustus' obelisk in the Piazza del Popolo (Photo: editors).

('backbone').[13] The dominating feature that came to be associated with circus architecture from Augustus onwards was the obelisk. Following a serious fire in 31 BC (Dio 50.10.3), his renovations included the installation of an obelisk of Rameses II on the barrier.[14] This obelisk had been transported from Heliopolis, the centre of the Egyptian cult of the Sun, and was hence an appropriate monument for display in a Roman building associated with solar cult, the site of chariot-races in honour of the divine charioteer who runs his eternal course across the heavens. When the obelisk was moved to Piazza del Popolo in 1587 (Fig. 9.4), Augustus' dedicatory inscription on two faces of the base was preserved (*CIL* 6.701–2); it records both his piety in dedicating it to the Sun "as a gift" (*Soli donum dedit*) and his political and military achievement in bringing Egypt "back into the power of the people" (*Aegypto in potestatem / populi Romani redacta*).

The suitability of the Circus Maximus for a major ideological statement is conveyed by the triumphal arch that was erected by the senate and people of Rome at the eastern (curved) end in AD 81 in honour of the emperor Titus. It bore an inscription commemorating the sack of Jerusalem in AD 70. Though no longer extant, this inscription is known from a copy made by a traveller in the 9th century (*CIL* 6.944 = *ILS* 264).[15] It reaches a forceful climax:

> quod praeceptis patri[is?] consiliisq(ue) et auspiciis gentem / Iudaeorum domuit et urbem Hierosolymam omnibus ante / se ducibus regibus gentibus aut frustra petitam aut / omnino intemptatam delevit.

> because in accordance with his father's[16] precepts, planning and auspices he tamed the nation of the Jews, and the city of Jerusalem – which all generals, kings, and nations before him had either assaulted in vain or avoided altogether – he utterly destroyed.

The periodic structure and rhetorical power of this climactic sentence are a forceful and insistent expression of the Flavians' claim to be the heirs and custodians of Rome's traditional imperialist ideology; the complementary theme of the accompanying triumphal frieze is attested by a surviving fragment, excavated in 1934, representing the helmeted head of a Roman soldier bearing the symbol of the *legio XII Fulminata* commanded by Titus in the Jewish War (Josephus, *Jewish War* 5.16).[17] But the arch may have gained another point for Flavian propaganda by scoring one off Nero, if it was on the site of an earlier arch that Nero's supporters had demolished so that he could effect a triumphant progress into the circus after he had won 1,808 *coronae* on the games-circuit in Greece (Suetonius, *Nero* 25; Dio 63.20).[18] In other respects too (e.g. by constructing the Colosseum on the site of the Stagnum attached to the Domus Aurea: see below) the Flavians showed themselves concerned to make good what they interpreted as depredations wreaked by Nero.[19]

It is now time to return to the coin minted by Trajan after he had enlarged the seating (Fig. 9.3). It is not only facilities for accommodating the spectators that are commemorated in this coin. The Circus is depicted from the north; the viewpoint is that of the emperor himself on the Palatine. At the curved end (left) is the Arch of Titus, at the other end are the two towers flanking the *carceres* and crowned with *quadrigae*, just like triumphal arches. Augustus' obelisk is prominent in the middle of the track, and in the background is the Temple of the Sun. The features that the die-engraver wished to emphasize are of course magnified; if the image were to scale, no detail would be easily visible. Hence what appears to be a faithful rendering lays stress upon three crucial aspects: the Circus was an imperial benefaction, its monuments honoured the emperors, and its games were a ritual of divine cult.[20]

Spectacles in the Circus. All these propagandistic aspects of the Circus Maximus are an index of the popularity of the races that were put on there, since it was the presence of thousands of spectators that made the Circus a suitable venue for advertising the strength of the empire and the achievements of its rulers, from the erection of obelisks miraculously transported from Augustus' new province of Egypt to Titus' arch proclaiming the destruction of Jerusalem. The origins of chariot-racing at Rome are obscure.[21] By the middle of the 4th century BC a pattern of self-financed individual entrants was replaced by a form of centralized organization, whereby the state began to pay breeders to supply horses; this may be when the four colours of the circus 'factions' were introduced, stables identified respectively as red, white, green, and blue. The new form of organization meant that by the end of the Republic the spectators had three possible goals for their allegiance – faction, charioteer, team of horses – and the greatest glory accrued to the organizers and sponsors.[22] Under the empire prizes increased, perhaps financed in part by a fee paid by breeders to the state for the right to enter horses. In the 2nd century AD the charioteer C. Appuleius Diocles, from Lusitania (modern Portugal), "the champion of all charioteers" (*omnium agitatorum eminentissimus*), earned over 35,000,000 HS in a career spanning 24 years, in which he entered 4,257 races and won 1,462 times.[23] Charioteers were largely exempt from the legal disabilities that applied to other categories of public performer (see under 'Theatrical performances' and 'Amphitheatre displays' below); this may be partly because of the ancient tradition attaching to

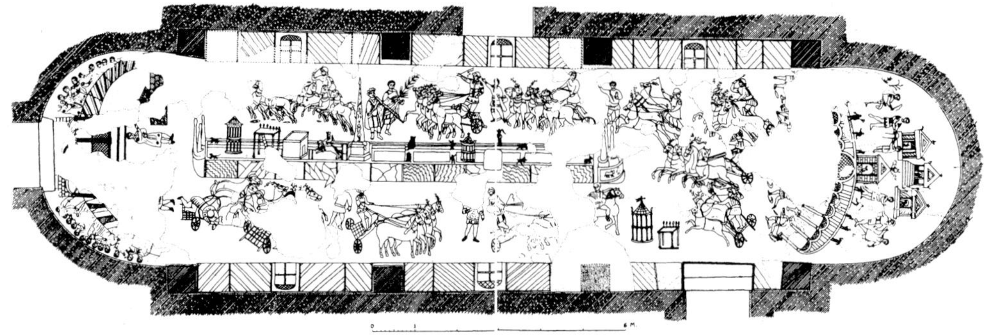

Fig. 9.5: Mosaic of the Circus Maximus from Piazza Armerina, Sicily, showing the monuments on the central barrier and an accident at the turning-posts (Fototeca Unione, neg. 14409).

chariot-racing at Rome, and partly – perhaps – because charioteers were not exhibiting their bodies in the same way as actors and gladiators.[24]

The atmosphere of the Circus Maximus was always busy; it was a focal point even when no races were scheduled, since on these days it was thronged by stall-holders, fortune-tellers, buskers, and hawkers.[25] The races themselves provoked fanatical interest: the chariots, light and unstable because they were designed for speed, were especially prone to accidents at the hazardous turn at either end of the track; graphic depictions in mosaic of a jumble of wheels, legs, and tangled reins suggests that the circus catered to the same morbid fascination with risk and violence that drew spectators to the more notorious displays of the amphitheatre (Fig. 9.5).[26] The disparaging tone of the Younger Pliny's remarks about the vacuity of the common man who pins his hopes on the colours of a faction (*Letters* 9.6.2) is somewhat belied by his pride in recounting an anecdote told to him by Tacitus: a stranger with whom Tacitus fell into conversation at the Circus guessed that he must be either Tacitus or Pliny (*Letters* 9.23.2–3); clearly Pliny was shocked neither by Tacitus' presence at the Circus nor by the expectation that he might be there himself.[27]

Not that chariot-racing was all that there was to see at the Circus. Even after amphitheatres had become the regular venue for certain types of beast-display, the massed hunts that had been staged in the Circus Maximus under the Republic still continued to be held there on special occasions. In a glamorous spectacle lasting seven days that was probably part of the Ludi Saeculares in AD 204, Septimius Severus constructed a massive ship in the Circus that was designed to fall apart, releasing a total of 700 animals belonging to seven different species. This piece of stage-craft is vivid testimony to the Romans' taste for creating a plausible context for their spectacles. Exotic beasts were delivered to Rome by sea, so that a 'shipwreck' in the middle of the circus would be a wittily appropriate means for releasing a large number of animals simultaneously, as well as a theatrical *tour de force* in its own right.[28] And if *naufragium* ('shipwreck') was a colloquial expression for a chariot-accident, the Severan display was also a pun on the nature of the spectacles associated with the Circus. To commemorate this event a special series of *aurei* and *denarii* was minted. On the reverse were depicted chariot-races, the ship, and the ensuing *venatio*; the legend around the rim, *laetitia temporum* ("What happy times!") epitomizes the central role that spectacle played in the lives of the entire citizen body. An emperor who provided spectacles on a lavish scale was the guarantor of what would now be called the 'feel-good factor'. Significantly, that sensation is associated today with material comfort. But to an audience for whom material comfort was largely unattainable, the games provided a different category of satisfaction; and the spectators' sense of psychological fulfilment was no doubt enhanced by surroundings that were exponentially more magnificent than the humble contexts in which they lived their daily lives.[29]

Circus Flaminius. If the Circus Maximus was dedicated to racing and comparable spectacles, and steadily acquired the canonical shape and installations that became standard in circus buildings across the empire, very different, apparently, was Rome's other Republican 'circus', the Circus Flaminius.[30] Labelled 'Cir(cus) Flami(nius)' on a fragment of the Marble Plan (*FUR* 30 = 31 ii), it gave its name to the ninth of the *regiones* into which Augustus divided the city. The Circus comprised an open space on the site of the *prata Flaminia*, perhaps originally roughly circular,[31] that was used for a variety of functions: performing banking transactions (*CIL* 6.9713); delivering funeral speeches (Dio 55.2.2); conducting *contiones*, i.e. public meetings;[32] distributing decorations and donatives to military troops (Livy 39.5.17); displaying captured booty (Plutarch, *Lucullus* 37.2); and even accommodating soldiers (Seneca, *On Benefits* 5.16.5). While the major *ludi circenses* were associated exclusively with the Circus Maximus, Varro identifies the Circus Flaminius as the site of the quinquennial Ludi Taurii (*On the Latin Language* 5.154), horse-races in honour of the *di inferi* (gods of the underworld); the chthonic connection meant that they could not be held within the walls of Rome. Varro implies that these were the only *ludi* that were regularly associated with the Circus Flaminius. A claim by Valerius Maximus (1.7.4) that the Ludi Plebeii were held there matches the plebeian associations of this site; the games may have started as horse-races rather than chariot-races, and could therefore have been held in the Circus Flaminius until they developed a more sophisticated format requiring the facilities of the Circus Maximus.[33]

In 2 BC Augustus 'flooded' the Circus Flaminius for the display and subsequent slaughter of 36 crocodiles (Dio 55.10.8). Whether or not it had been reduced from its original size by encroaching buildings,[34] he may simply have had a basin dug in the middle rather than flooding the entire area; there must have been room left for bleachers to accommodate spectators, since it can hardly have been expected that they would all watch from neighbouring buildings. Hence it is not necessarily correct to infer from the crocodile-display that by this stage the Circus must have had a retaining wall, though some sort of permanent structure seems required to justify Varro's allusion to a process of construction (*aedificatus est*).[35] Indeed, the way Augustus' contemporary Livy refers to it suggests that the name 'Circus Flaminius' does not imply any monumental structure (3.54.15): *ea omnia in pratis Flaminiis concilio plebis acta, quem nunc Circum Flaminium appellant* ("All this business was transacted at a meeting of the plebs in the Flaminian fields, which people nowadays call the Circus Flaminius"). Nor are there any traces, either literary or archaeological, of any central feature like the barrier down the middle of the Circus Maximus and the monuments upon it. The *metae* (turning-posts) mentioned by Varro in connection with the Ludi Taurii can plausibly be assumed to have been set up for the occasion and dismantled immediately afterwards. The only recorded installation is a type of sundial (*plinthium sive lacunar*: Vitruvius, *On Architecture* 9.8.1), an amenity better suited to the business transactions of a market than to chariot-racing.[36] Hence with respect to the circuses at Rome a cardinal distinction has to be observed: the location that became dedicated to the mounting of chariot-races and installations for spectators was the Circus Maximus; the open area known as the Circus Flaminius, on the other hand, accommodated chariot-races but much else besides, and was therefore never hemmed in by the restrictive provision of seating.

Circus Vaticanus and Circus Varianus. Two other circuses from the city of Rome are of the monumental type exemplified by the Circus Maximus. The Circus Gai et Neronis was a race-track created by Caligula on the right bank of the Tiber in the Horti Agrippinae and adapted by Nero, who may have converted it from a private to a public space (Pliny, *Natural History* 16.201, 36.74; Suetonius, *Claudius* 21.2).[37] It lay on part of the site occupied by the Vatican today, hence its alternative name of Circus Vaticanus. It was long believed to be an open recreational space rather than a monumental circus, though it was clearly associated with conventional circus decoration: the obelisk that now stands in the middle of Piazza S. Pietro was brought from Egypt[38] by Caligula to decorate it, in clear imitation of Augustus' obelisk in the Circus Maximus. The obelisk may have preserved the identity of the site, which became known as *Gaianum* in the Middle Ages and is presumably the place called Γαιανόν where Caligula is said to have practised driving chariots (Dio 59.14.6). Walls near St. Peter's Square have now been identified with the *carceres*, and a monumental design seems certain.

Remnants of another circus building survive south of Porta Maggiore near the church of S. Croce in Gerusalemme abutting the Aurelian Wall and the palatial villa complex known as the Sessorium (discussed further under 'Amphitheatrum Castrense' below). The dimensions of the circus (565 × 125 m) are nearly as large as those of the Circus Maximus (600 × 150 m).[39] This structure, which was perhaps started by Caracalla, has been identified as the circus in which Elagabalus used to race *in hortis Spei Veteris* under his family name of Varius (SHA, *Elagabalus* 14.5), hence the designation of the site as 'Circus Varianus'. Recorded among its ruins in the 16th century was an obelisk 9.25 m high that had originally been located at the tomb of Hadrian's favourite, Antinous, and was moved to the Horti by Elagabalus; in 1632 it was removed to the Palazzo Barberini, from there to the Vatican in 1769, and finally to its current location in the park of Monte Pincio in 1822.[40]

Circus of Maxentius. A third structure that is modelled upon the Circus Maximus is mentioned only once in documentary sources (by the Chronographer of AD 354),[41] but its archaeological remains have been excavated more fully than any other circus from the environs of Rome. It lies outside the ancient confines of the city along the Via Appia. It is part of the complex constructed by Constantine's rival Maxentius during his reign as princeps, AD 306–312, comprising a villa, a circus, and a mausoleum for his son Romulus. Hence the association of palace and circus which developed for the Circus Maximus is replicated by both Elagabalus and Maxentius. In the case of Maxentius' circus, the elevated pulvinar projecting from the adjacent palace is supported on walls that are pierced at ground-level by doorways, thereby accommodating access around the entire perimeter of the circus instead of creating a barrier at the point of contact between circus and palace.

The maximum external dimensions of Maxentius' circus are 520 × 92 m; the maximum dimensions of the arena are 503 × 79 m. Since the rows of seats are comparatively low and narrow (37–40.5 cm high and 30 cm deep), each alternate row may have been intended exclusively as a footrest for the spectators seated on the row above, which would allow a maximum capacity of 10,000 spectators, significantly smaller than most monumental circuses in the Roman world. Nevertheless, it was clearly intended for more than 'private' displays for the exclusive entertainment of the emperor and his court, and while the Circus Maximus remained the obvious venue for regular racing, events associated with the imperial house could have been staged here for an audience comprising the *crème* of contemporary society. In conjunction with the adjacent mausoleum to Maxentius' son, the complex would have made a powerful dynastic statement in the politically unstable and volatile climate of the early 4th century.[42]

Arval Circus. The distinction that we draw between 'public' and 'private' sits uneasily with another circus that was physically located outside the city-precinct but was intimately connected with one influential sector of Rome's ruling class. This is the race-track located in the grove of the Fratres Arvales (Arval Brethren) sacred to Dea Dia *c*. 7.5 km out of Rome along the Via Campana, at what is now La Magliana in the suburbs of the modern city. The circus lay to the west of the main sanctuary. The remaining traces have been dated to the reign of Tiberius or Claudius, though it is likely that the circus was included in the major renovations and extensions to the sanctuary under Caracalla and Severus Alexander.[43] But although little survives *in situ*, some of the features of the circus are attested in inscriptions, including the starting-gates.[44] It is uncertain whether it was equipped with monumental seating. The earliest inscription to mention circus-races there dates from the reign of Claudius (AD 38).[45] Possibly these races were part of the old Republican practices associated with the Arval ritual that Augustus had revived when he effectively re-invented it as an instrument of the imperial cult, thereby giving this section of the aristocracy a mechanism for demonstrating their loyalty towards the Julio-Claudian dynasty.[46]

THEATRE

Temporary theatres. In a pre- or semi-literate society theatrical spectacles are a crucial context for the formation and transmission of cultural memory. Theatrical performances are attested at Rome from at least the 3rd century BC, their audiences marked by an inclusiveness that contrasts with the narrow exclusivity of contemporary literate circles; while the concept of a 'reading public' is an anachronism in Republican Rome, that of a 'theatrical public' is not.[47] If the theatre was a vehicle for moulding the Romans' view of themselves as a nation, it also bred a politicized atmosphere in which audience response could invest the spoken word with highly-charged political and ideological overtones. To estimate the political mood of the people Cicero watched their behaviour at theatrical performances and gladiatorial shows, and witnessed their enthusiastic reception of a single line with a devastating double-entendre that undermined Pompey's reputation.[48] Audiences swift to put a contemporary spin on the script invited an equally rapid response from their political leaders: when an audience applauded a line acclaiming a "just and good master",[49] the emperor Augustus immediately gestured to them to stop, and the next day issued an edict forbidding anyone to refer to him by a term with these connotations of despotism. In moral terms the intelligentsia might deride the theatre as an incubus of enervating pleasure and lascivious indecency,[50] but from its roots in Atellane farce and imported Greek models to the imperial craze for dance and comedy-sketches the theatre was a constant element in the cultural formation and self-expression of the Roman people.

The Republic was on the brink of extinction when the first permanent theatre was eventually constructed in the city, by Pompey in 55 BC. A theatre *tout court* is a luxury, occupying urban space and yet fully functional only sporadically throughout the year (which is no doubt why Pompey integrated his theatre in a complex that fulfilled many functions simultaneously: see under 'Theatre of Pompey' below). Yet the reasons why the Romans relied upon *ad hoc* arrangements for so long have as much to do with religion and politics as with pragmatism. The original context of *ludi scaenici* at Rome was either a festival in honour of a deity or some other ceremony in the religious calendar, or else the funeral of a prominent citizen. The earliest recorded Latin play was almost certainly composed by L. Livius Andronicus, a Greek from Tarentum, for performance at the Ludi Romani in 240 BC (Cicero, *Brutus* 72; Aulus Gellius, *Attic Nights* 17.21.42).[51] *Ludi* at a festival were performed at the site associated with that festival (usually at the temple of the relevant deity), and funerary *ludi* were usually performed in one of the *fora* (to be discussed below in conjunction with the evolution of the amphitheatre). If the space in front of a temple were adequate for the staging of a drama, spectators could be accommodated on the steps leading up to the *podium* (the platform supporting the superstructure); if not, temporary facilities might be erected in the vicinity upon the occasion of the festival. Such appears to have been the case with the Ludi Megalenses, which were celebrated simultaneously in two venues by the end of the Republic: in the narrow space in front of the Temple of the Great Mother on the Palatine at the edge of the cliff above the Lupercal, which was presumably their original venue, and immediately beneath at the bottom of the cliff in a temporary structure erected for the purpose.[52] The exclusive association between a festival and its *ludi* would be a strong factor militating against the construction of a permanent theatre in the city: the theatrical performance had to be located in the god's vicinity, and the short duration of each festival could be argued to render a custom-built structure superfluous.

Attempts to construct a permanent theatre in Rome in the 2nd century BC suggest that the link between site and spectacle was weakening, at least for some people. But the fact that such attempts were thwarted indicates the strength of conservative opinion. In 174 BC the censors contracted for a *scaena* to be used by the aediles and praetor, i.e. the authorities in charge of the Ludi Romani, Plebeii, Megalenses and Apollinares (Livy 41.27.6). In 154 BC the censors, M. Valerius Messalla and C. Cassius Longinus, began a permanent theatre near the Palatine which the senate ordered to be aborted at the behest of P. Cornelius Scipio Nasica Corculum (Livy, *Periochae* 48; Valerius Maximus 2.4.2). There is an apparent doublet of this story at Appian, *Civil Wars* 1.28, with some significant deviations: the initiative to build a permanent theatre was taken by a Cassius with a different *praenomen* (Lucius), the name of his opponent was probably not Scipio but Caepio,[53] and opposition to the project was based on fear of class-conflict and suspicion regarding decadent Greek influences. If this is in fact a separate incident dating from the last decade of the century (108–106 BC), it matches the prevailing atmosphere of class-conflict that was the legacy of the Gracchi.[54] Meanwhile, in 154 BC an apparently regressive step was taken in forbidding spectators to sit down at *ludi scaenici* (Valerius Maximus 2.4.2; Orosius 4.21.4). Tacitus says it was feared that seating encouraged the people to spend all day lolling in idleness, although eventually the economic advantages of installing permanent seating prevailed over the waste of money involved in repeated installation and removal of temporary stands (Tacitus, *Annals* 14.20–21).

There were other reasons too for retaining the custom of erecting *ad hoc* structures and demolishing them afterwards. Conspicuous consumption was flaunted by these temporary theatres, which became increasingly elaborate in the course of the 1st century BC. The acme was reached with the theatre erected by the flamboyant entrepreneur M. Aemilius Scaurus in 58 BC: this marvel boasted a *scaenae frons* three storeys high embellished with marble on the lowest storey, mosaics in the middle, and gilded wood on top, and no fewer than 360 columns, with 3,000 bronze statues in the spaces between them (Pliny, *Natural History* 36.114–15).[55] The tribune Curio, on the other hand, erected a structure remarkable not for its decoration but for its technical wizardry: on the occasion of his father's funeral in 52 BC he built two theatres back to back that could revolve on pivots to re-form in a shape approximating to that of an amphitheatre (Pliny, *Natural History* 36.117).[56] And even though Rome possessed three permanent theatres by 13 BC (those of Pompey, Balbus, and Marcellus: see below), temporary structures continued to be built in the city well into the empire,[57] perhaps for events tied to specific locations on a very occasional basis, such as the Ludi Palatini (Josephus, *Jewish Antiquities* 19.90). Practical considerations also determined the choice of venue, as in the case of the Diribitorium. This was a roofed building at the south end of the Saepta, more than 120 m long and 33 m wide on the inside, that was begun by Agrippa and completed by Augustus in 7 BC.[58] It was designed for counting the votes cast in the Saepta, but in times of excessive heat Caligula moved theatrical performances into its shaded interior, which had been furnished with benches for this purpose (Dio 59.7.8).

Theatre of Pompey. The stone theatres built at Rome contributed a markedly hellenistic atmosphere to the topography of the city,[59] though contemporaries may have been reminded in the first instance of the stone theatres closer to home in Campania and Sicily. It is also likely that the dazzling ostentation of some of the temporary theatres in the city (see above) may have made these stone structures seem slightly less astounding than one might otherwise expect. But certainly the ostentation evident in the temporary structures of the late Republic, and the concomitant glory accruing to their sponsors, must have been a powerful stimulus to Pompey in erecting Rome's first permanent theatre,[60] whether or not he conceived it as an amenity with particular appeal for the *plebs*.[61] Since the most common designation by which it was known to contemporary and succeeding generations was 'Pompey's theatre',[62] this raises the question of ownership, which is in turn connected with the type of building that it was conceived to be. Pompey is said to have justified the auditorium as a grand approach to the Temple of Venus Victrix at the top, though the nomenclature shows that it was recognized for what it was: a theatre. The combination of temple and stepped approach is paralleled in some of the great sanctuaries of the 2nd and 1st centuries BC like that of Juno at Gabii, 15 km from Rome.[63] The artificiality of Pompey's ruse, however, is reflected in the chronology: the theatre, dedicated in 55 BC (Cicero, *Letters to Friends* 7.1.3), pre-dated the 'temple' by three years (Aulus Gellius, *Attic Nights* 10.1.6–7). Even though he is likely to have begun planning it immediately after he returned to Rome to celebrate his triumph over Mithradates in 62 BC, there is no evidence that it was conceived as a manubial temple.[64] There is therefore little doubt that Pompey financed the project out of his own personal fortune, though we may still ask who owned the land on which it stood, and whether Pompey rented it or purchased it. Presumably he owned the entire property. The intention, to draw attention to Pompey's 'greatness' (his *cognomen* was 'Magnus'), is reflected in the colossal dimensions of the building. The capacity is estimated by the Regionary Catalogues at 17,500 *loca*, which is calculated to have accommodated 11,000 people. The diameter of the *cavea* (auditorium) is estimated at 150–160 m, with a space 95 m wide for the *scaenae frons* (stage building).

The theatre has not been excavated, though some of the modern buildings in the area are built into the radiating concrete vaults and walls that supported the seating, and in their basements there is still some fine facing in *opus reticulatum* to be seen.[65] At ground level the position of the theatre can be traced in the contours of the streets and buildings between Piazza Campo dei Fiori and Via Grottapinta.[66] Both the internal and the external curve of the *cavea* are visible, and the bulge at the west end of the block bounded on the north by Piazza dei Biscione and on the south by Via dei Giubbonari corresponds to the apse of the temple of Venus Victrix.[67] It is calculated that the roof of this temple must have towered 45 m above the Campus Martius, equivalent to the height of the Capitol. The grandiloquence of Pompey's project is attested also by the dimensions of the stage, which must have covered the equivalent of nearly half the arena in the Colosseum (see below). Perhaps Pompey's theatre was indeed designed to accommodate gladiatorial displays; Caesar's assassins assembled gladiators here on the day of his murder, though their intention is disputed. It has been suggested that nothing beyond the initial parade of gladiators was to be held in the theatre. Alternatively, we know that at Pompeii the portico attached to the theatre was converted into a *ludus* for gladiators, and so in 44 BC perhaps gladiators were being temporarily billetted in the adjacent *porticus*.[68]

The magnificence and singularity of the theatre depended for its full impact upon its position within the entire complex that Pompey erected in the south-east sector of the Campus Martius. Behind the *cavea* Pompey built himself a magnificent residence that must have been located at a little distance from the theatre, since Plutarch compares it to a tender towed behind a great ship (*Pompey* 40.5).[69] Behind the space for the *scaenae frons* stretched Pompey's portico, traceable still in the layout of the modern streets between Campo dei Fiori and Largo Argentina.[70] The eastern end of the *porticus* opened onto the complex of Republican temples in Largo Argentina, which were intimately associated with the triumphal route and the achievements of past generations,[71] an association that Pompey clearly wished to exploit. The *porticus* comprised a 'double grove' (*nemus duplex*, Martial 2.14.10), planted with plane trees and shrubs, and decorated with statuary and fountains. It was flanked by colonnades where works of art were put on display (Pliny, *Natural History* 35.59, 114, 126, 132), perhaps a combination of war booty and commissioned pieces. The art-work was carefully chosen to construct a thematic 'programme': the sculptures emphasized the cult of Venus, and the world of poetry and the theatre; beyond that, Pompey's *imitatio* of Pergamene art in his *porticus* contributed to his self-image as the successor of the hellenistic kings; and the ensemble that the sculptures formed with the plantings has recently been shown to celebrate his achievements in Roman Asia, and to place his unmistakeable imprint on the landscape of the Campus Martius.[72]

The *scaenae frons* on the Marble Plan is probably the replacement for one that burnt down in AD 64 (Dio 66.24).[73] It is not known whether the *scaenae frons* of the original theatre was conceived as a permanent fixture of stone or a temporary wooden installation, though the scale and magnificence of the building might seem to have required a permanent *scaenae frons*. If, however, it had originally been a temporary installation to be erected on an *ad hoc* basis, visitors approaching the theatre through the *porticus* would have seen a vista dominated by the temple to Venus Victrix.[74] It is crucial to see the complex as an integrated whole: the combination of portico, temple, and auditorium was more akin to a Roman forum than to the modern concept of an entertainment building.[75] On a basic level the relationship of theatre and portico corresponds to Vitruvius' recommendation that in the construction of a theatre a *porticus* should be extended behind the *scaenae frons* to afford the audience shelter in wet weather (Vitruvius, *On Architecture* 5.8). More than that, Pompey's *porticus* was intended to provide a pleasant amenity for theatre-goers and, generally, for the population at large strolling in the Campus Martius.[76] But the entire complex was also a carefully orchestrated advertisement of Pompey's influence and prestige; not only stage-productions but even their architectural setting could convey a political message. The whole complex was ostensibly conceived to honour Venus; but even though she was the goddess of love, Pompey might have been disappointed that his *porticus* would be known to posterity as promising territory for meeting members of the opposite sex.[77]

Theatre of Balbus. The concept of a 'recreation-complex' is repeated in the smallest of the three stone theatres constructed in the Campus Martius. This is the combined theatre and *cryptoporticus* completed in 13 BC by L. Cornelius Balbus, who had celebrated a triumph for his campaign against the Garamantes in Africa in 19 BC.[78] The Theatre of Marcellus was probably also dedicated in 13 BC; for the significance of the date, see under 'Theatre of Marcellus' below. Balbus' theatre-complex comprised the last of the great projects funded by *manubiae* awarded to Octavian's generals after the civil wars.[79] For Tacitus, it was evidence that individual gestures of civic munificence (*publica munificentia*) could still occur after the collapse of the Republic, despite a decline in the wealth of the old Republican families and Augustus' tendency to limit such displays by anyone other than himself (*Annals* 3.72.1). The theatre used to be identified with a building visible in Via di S. Maria dei Calderari, until surviving fragments of the Marble Plan (*FUR* 39a–b) yielded a new location for it underneath the Palazzi Mattei, Caetani, and Paganica, and for the *crypta* underneath the church of S. Caterina dei Funari.[80] The Regionary Catalogues state the capacity of the theatre as 11,510 *loca*, which is calculated to accommodate about 7,700 spectators.

The sole surviving mention of the *cryptoporticus* occurs in the entry 'Crypta Balbi' in the Regionary Catalogues for Regio IX, and so it is not certain what its original name was. Balbus' *cryptoporticus* extended behind the *scaenae frons* (located at the east end of the theatre). It comprised an *ambulatio tecta* (covered walk) 10.65 m wide that ran all the way round, except on the side abutting upon the theatre. At the eastern end of the east-west axis there was an *exedra* that was later converted into a public latrine.[81] It has been suggested that the name of Via delle Botteghe Oscure may preserve an ancient memory of shops in the arcades of the *cryptoporticus* on the side facing the street. The *cryptoporticus* was virtually square, 93.6 m long on its north-south axis, and the effect must have been quite different from that in the *porticus* behind Pompey's theatre, which was rectangular, with a much longer east-west axis. The *porticus* behind Balbus' theatre would have created an impression of intimacy in contrast to the imposing vistas afforded by Pompey's *porticus*.

Theatre of Marcellus. The third element in the geographical and chronological cluster comprising Rome's three stone theatres was the Theatre of Marcellus.[82] It was originally conceived by Julius Caesar, who demolished temples in the south-east corner of the Campus Martius to make space for a theatre adjacent to the Temple of Apollo (Dio 43.49.3). This project was finally realized by Augustus, while Caesar's other theatrical ambition, clearly intended to outdo Pompey's theatre, was never fulfilled at all: a theatre on the Capitol overlooking the Forum (Suetonius, *Julius Caesar* 44.1). By 17 BC construction was sufficiently advanced for the theatre to host some of the events at the Ludi Saeculares, though it was not formally inaugurated until several years later (see below). It is likely that the impetus for its construction was connected with the Lex Julia Theatralis of *c*. 20 BC; if the theatre was designed to conform to the provisions of that law (see below, on the Colosseum), it must have been the first theatre at Rome to reflect Augustus' strict hierarchy in its seating.[83]

What survives of the Theatre of Marcellus constitutes one of the most striking remnants of the ancient city. It has been continuously inhabited ever since it was adapted to dwelling-space at some point in its post-antique phase, so that the arcades of the lowest storey, buried to a depth of 4 m before excavation in the late nineteen-twenties,[84] very clearly support converted apartments and households on the upper floors (Fig. 9.6). Externally the building provides something of a template for the Colosseum, since the theatre's three storeys exhibit features that are expanded into four storeys in the amphitheatre. The Tuscan capitals of the arcading on

Fig. 9.6: Theatre of Marcellus after excavation (Fototeca Unione, neg. 541).

Fig. 9.7: Model of the Theatre of Marcellus, Museo della Civiltà Romana (Deutsches Archäologisches Institut, neg. 73.998).

the lowest storey of the theatre give way to Ionic on the storey above, and on the top storey engaged pilasters with Corinthian capitals embrace panels alternating between a blank façade and one pierced by a square window (Fig. 9.7). In the Colosseum the first two storeys correspond to those of the theatre; the third comprises arcading with Corinthian capitals; and the fourth storey incorporates engaged pilasters on a blank façade, demarcating panels that are pierced by windows placed alternately in the centre or at the bottom of each panel. The absence of arcading on the top storey of both buildings provides mounting-space for the corbels supporting the masts from which the cables for the roof-awnings were slung. Inside the theatre, the stone seating (partially surviving in the private apartments of Palazzo Savelli-Orsini) originally comprised three main zones. Around the *orchestra* at the bottom were extra rows of broader steps for distinguished patrons. At the top, under a roofed balcony, wooden seats were erected for the humblest spectators, a feature that was again to be replicated in the Colosseum. The Regionary Catalogues give the capacity of the theatre as 20,500 *loca*; modern estimates allow 13,000–14,000 spectators. The stage-building has not been excavated, so the only evidence for it comes from the Marble Plan, which shows a rather cramped *porticus* behind it on the river-front.[85]

As was fitting for a theatre, both the arcaded storeys of the Theatre of Marcellus were originally decorated with masks, those of the second storey having survived into the Renaissance to be recorded in the engravings of Du Pérac;[86] traces of the fixtures still survive on some of the keystones. Displayed at a height of 7 m above ground-level on the lowest storey and 16.5 m on the middle floor, the masks were fashioned with exaggerated features and angled at a downward tilt so as to be recognizable from below. The range of types represented by the surviving fragments corresponds to an exclusively classical repertoire: of the twenty masks that have survived in substantial fragments, ten represent characters from comedy, five from tragedy, and five from satyr plays. But this is an example of the stylized repertoire of theatrical elements in artistic decoration, and should not be taken to indicate the type of drama that was performed in this theatre; indeed, the genre that captivated the audience at the inauguration was the innovative pantomime spectacle.[87]

Exactly when the theatre was inaugurated is an important question: 13 BC (Dio 54.26.1) or 11 BC (Pliny, *Natural History* 8.65)? Either date would imply a delay, since it was already in use in 17 BC (see above). The inauguration of the Theatre of Balbus, which is securely dated to 13 BC (Suetonius, *Augustus* 29.5; Dio 54.25.2), may also imply a delay, since the *manubiae* out of which it was funded had been won six years previously. 13 BC has been shown to be a significant choice, coinciding with a series of anniversaries important to Augustus' regime:[88] his fiftieth birthday; the tenth anniversary of his assumption of tribunician power and the fifth anniversary of Agrippa's; and the seventh birthday of Augustus' grandson Gaius, now halfway to manhood at fourteen. Furthermore, Augustus was returning to Rome after a three-year absence in the western provinces, and the consuls for the year had been carefully chosen: one of them was Augustus' stepson Tiberius, the other was P. Quinctilius Varus, and both were married to daughters of Agrippa. If the inauguration of Balbus' theatre was timed to coincide with a year that was significant to the Augustan regime, it seems even more likely that the Theatre of Marcellus was inaugurated in the same year. It was dedicated to the memory of Augustus' nephew M. Claudius Marcellus, who had died in 23 BC, and so it could just as easily have been dedicated to his memory before it was put into use for the Ludi Saeculares of 17 BC. But it looks as though Augustus did not wish such an august celebration in the Roman calendar to eclipse a dedicatory ceremony that could, by careful timing, be connected with the key figures in Rome's new dynasty.

The sources may seem to imply that an implausibly wide range of spectacles was performed in this theatre. Apart from events staged during the Ludi Saeculares, the Ludi Romani are recorded as having been performed there too (Dio 53.30.6); but this must mean just the *ludi scaenici* on the programme, since the *ludi circenses* were presumably held in the Circus Maximus. The inaugural spectacles included two that must have been performed at a more spacious venue: the equestrian event known as the Lusus Troiae,[89] and a *venatio* (beast-hunt) involving 600 African animals (Dio 53.30.6, 54.26.1). The Lusus Troiae may have been held in what remained of the open space of the adjacent Circus Flaminius, though the Circus Maximus, being the regular location for *ludi circenses*, seems more likely.[90] The *venatio* must have been put on in the Circus Maximus, where protection for the spectators could easily be erected and *venationes* are frequently attested.[91] Splitting a set of games among multiple venues was a regular occurrence with *ludi sollemnes* by this date; an analogy for an inaugural celebration is furnished about a century later by the Colosseum, when events were staged in the Stagnum Augusti as well as in the amphitheatre itself (see below).

Theatrical performances. The increasing scope for dramatic productions in the 3rd century BC had led to the founding of a guild for authors and actors (*collegium scribarum histrionumque*).[92] In 207 BC it was given a public meeting-place in the Temple of Minerva on the Aventine (Festus 446L); of course Minerva was a deity suitably associated with crafts and intellectual processes, but perhaps this gesture of respect also disguised the senate's intention of monitoring any potentially subversive freedom of speech among the members of the *collegium*.[93] In the early 2nd century at the time of Plautus and Terence, who wrote plays in Latin adapted from the scripts of Greek New Comedy, dramatic performances had mainly taken place on occasions associated with religious ceremonial: the regular *ludi scaenici*, *instaurationes* of the Ludi Romani and the Ludi Plebeii, votive games in honour of Jupiter Optimus Maximus, and the dedication of a temple.[94] In addition, drama was among the spectacles that could be staged at aristocratic funerals as a means to eulogize the family: the prologue to the *Hecyra* of Terence records that its second production (staged, presumably in the Forum, on the occasion of the funeral of L. Aemilius Paullus in 160 BC) had to compete with mime-artistes, gladiators, acrobats, and like attractions.[95] Rome's permanent theatres are also a measure of the increasing importance of theatrical entertainment by the late 1st century BC.[96] The 11 days that were the official minimum devoted every year to 'scenic

Fig. 9.8: Terracotta statuette depicting a troupe of actors (reproduced by courtesy of the Arthur M. Sackler Museum, Harvard University Art Museums, gift of Dr. Harris Kennedy, Class of 1894. © President and Fellows of Harvard College, Harvard University).

entertainment' in Plautus' youth had grown to 55 by the time Julius Caesar was assassinated, and would increase to 101 by the mid-4th century AD.[97]

The presiding magistrate paid for the performance, assisted by a contribution from the state treasury; or, in the case of a funeral, the honorand's heirs sponsored the production. Playwrights were paid for their scripts, and actor-managers for the production. By the early empire, however, the earning-capacity of actors became limited by praetorian edict. Individual actors might enjoy the patronage of leading *nobiles*, and receive *beneficia* (perks and advantages) as tokens of friendship (*amicitia*), but it was strictly understood that it was degrading for a Roman citizen to be seen to receive payment for his services, because this was tantamount to servitude. Actors were deemed *infamis*, legally disgraceful ('without reputation'), if they received monetary reward in public for appearing on the stage; rewards in kind were respectable, cash payments were not.[98] No legal disability attached to well-born Romans who acted and danced at private or semi-private occasions; nor to noble amateurs who appeared on the public stage, as Nero did, without receiving a fee.

As the Republic gave way to the empire, the nature of dramatic performances changed. Mime and pantomime developed alongside the traditional forms of tragedy and comedy until gradually they came to dominate the Roman stage.[99] Mime (*μῖμος*, 'imitator') was the name for both the genre and for the type of entertainer who performed it, likewise pantomime (*παντόμιμος*, 'imitator of all things'). Mimes dealt largely with themes from everyday life, and were something akin to modern soap-operas. A team of actors either spoke or sang, with or (usually) without a choral accompaniment (Fig. 9.8). Pantomimes generally drew their themes from mythology, and the actor mimed and danced his solo role to the accompaniment of music played on a variety of instruments. The epic poet Statius wrote at least one pantomime libretto, on the theme of Agave, who killed her own son in a Dionysiac frenzy; it starred the renowned pantomime artiste of Domitianic Rome, Paris.[100] The satirist Juvenal implies that although readings from Statius' epic, the *Thebaid*, provoked a reaction akin to sexual excitement among their audience, to earn hard cash he had to stoop to composing the *Agave* (Juvenal, *Satires* 7.82–7):

"When Statius has made the city happy by fixing a date, there is a rush to hear his charming voice reciting his beloved *Thebaid*. Everyone is captivated and transfixed by the sweetness of his verse, and the audience listening to him is overwhelmed by pleasure. But although the reaction to his recital has caused the seating to collapse, he is going to starve unless he sells Paris the rights to his *Agave*".[101]

This testifies not only to the popularity of pantomime but also to a contemporary craze for staging advertised readings from contemporary works of literature. Later the Christian fathers would rail against the theatre as immoral pagan entertainment, though it was not until the 6th century that cultural attitudes and economic factors caused theatrical productions to cease.[102]

AMPHITHEATRE

The Forum as an arena. From at least the 2nd century BC the popularity of drama was challenged by the attractions of gladiatorial combat. Where the Romans first encountered it is a matter of scholarly debate;[103] but Roman sources are unanimous in tracing its first appearance at Rome to funerary displays in honour of a deceased aristocrat, specifically M. Iunius Brutus Pera, whose sons (Livy, *Periochae* 16; Valerius Maximus 2.4.7) or grandson (Servius, *Commentary on the Aeneid* 3.67) staged gladiatorial combat in the Forum Boarium at Rome to mark his death in 264 BC. The Forum Romanum became the regular venue at Rome for *ludi funebres* – and hence for gladiatorial combat[104] – in the late Republic, and it continued to be used for this purpose even after Rome's first permanent amphitheatre was constructed early in the reign of Augustus in 29 BC. The amphitheatre as an architectural form, however, is attested at least forty years earlier in Campania, at Pompeii, where Sulla had established a military colony (*CIL* 10.852 = *ILS* 5627). It is now recognized that the other known sites of monumental amphitheatres built during the Republic were also Roman colonies or *municipia*,[105] which argues strongly for the theory that the colonists conceived of the amphitheatre as a symbol of Roman identity that helped to establish their cultural claims to their new territory.

In support of this theory it has also been suggested that the elliptical shape of the arena is to be explained by the temporary seating erected within the trapezoidal space flanked by the Basilica Aemilia and the Basilica Sempronia in the Forum Romanum at Rome, which would have accommodated a structure that was essentially oval.[106] The upper storeys of the basilicas themselves provided some of the viewing-space, the term *maenianum* for a horizontal band of seating in the arena apparently deriving from the name of the enterprising Maenius who was the first person to erect an upstairs balcony as a vantage-point for watching the games in the Forum (pseudo-Asconius, *On the Speech of Cicero Against Q. Caecilius* 16–50; Festus 134b.22 M).[107] Under the Forum are galleries consisting of a central corridor with four lateral arms bisecting it at regular distances 15 m apart. The alignment of the central corridor parallel to the Basilica Iulia, which was inaugurated in 46 BC, suggests that the galleries may have been installed at about the same time.[108] They give access into the Forum through twelve openings. Traces of installations in these galleries are reminiscent of the system of cages and pulleys that would be installed beneath some amphitheatres in the imperial period for winching animals into the arena.[109] At least one spectacle in the Forum involved beasts, the execution of the Sicilian bandit Selurus, 'son of Etna', that was witnessed by Strabo under the Second Triumvirate or soon afterwards (Strabo 6.273); in a spectacle that mocked Selurus' reputation he was displayed on a collapsible contraption that 'erupted' to deposit him into cages of animals.[110]

Amphitheatre of Statilius Taurus. It is noteworthy that at Rome the amphitheatre, like the theatre, was for a long time an exclusively temporary construction.[111] Actors and gladiators were both classified as *infamis*, though the penalties they suffered under the law were not identical;[112] the same inhibitions that kept a permanent theatre at bay may also have hindered the introduction of a stone amphitheatre. The wooden 'hunting theatre' (*θέατρον κυνηγετικόν*) that Julius Caesar erected for the spectacles associated with his quadruple triumph in 46 BC (Dio 43.22.3) was presumably a temporary structure in the Forum.[113] The first stone amphitheatre in Rome was built in the Campus Martius in 29 BC by one of Octavian's generals, Statilius Taurus, out of *manubiae* awarded to him upon the triumph he celebrated in 34 BC for securing the province of Africa for Octavian (Dio 51.23.1). Since it burned down completely in Nero's fire of AD 64 (Dio 62.18.2), the seating may have been wooden and only the outer shell built of stone.[114] Because it was a manubial project, it may have belonged nominally to the Roman people. But it remained under the management of its founder's heirs, since slaves belonging to the Statilii are commemorated in the family *columbarium* in various capacities associated with the amphitheatre (*CIL* 6.6226–8, 6258).

Statilius' amphitheatre, however, did not become the exclusive venue for gladiatorial displays, which continued to be held in the Forum. For example, Tiberius held two funerary spectacles, one in the Forum in honour of his father Tiberius Claudius Nero, who died between 34 and 32 BC, and the other in Statilius' amphitheatre in honour of his maternal grandfather Drusus, who had died in 42 BC (Suetonius, *Tiberius* 7.1); both occasions should probably be dated early in the reign of Augustus, i.e. soon after 27 BC.[115] It is not clear what determined the choice of venue; Suetonius implies that both occasions, and some *ludi* that Tiberius held *in absentia*, were all equally magnificent, so there can have been no sense that Statilius' amphitheatre was in any way inadequate. After the date in Augustus' reign when the Forum was paved over, however, it would no longer have been possible to hold spectacles there that required access from underground, though gladiatorial spectacles could presumably have continued to be staged at this venue.[116] When the buildings in the vicinity of the Forum were damaged by fire in 7 BC, Augustus used the Saepta Iulia on the Campus Martius for his funerary games in honour of Agrippa (Dio 55.8.5); this was a building with a suitably prestigious public character.[117] Augustus is said also to have planned a major amphitheatre for the centre of Rome (Suetonius, *Vespasian* 9.1). Such a project seems a plausible item on his agenda for transforming the city into an elegant and sophisticated metropolis; his failure to realize it is one of the enigmas of his reign.[118]

Amphitheatres of Caligula and Nero. Caligula used Statilius' amphitheatre (Suetonius, *Caligula* 18.1), though on at least one occasion in AD 38 he is said to have disdained it and used the Saepta instead, which he excavated and filled with water in order to display a single ship (Dio 59.10.5); Claudius seems regularly to have used the Saepta (Suetonius, *Claudius* 21.4). Perhaps because he had sequestered the Saepta for an aquatic display, Caligula also demolished a number of buildings elsewhere in order to erect a temporary structure of wooden stands (Dio 59.10.5). This may be different from the amphitheatre that he is said to have begun 'next door to the Saepta' (*iuxta Saepta*: Suetonius, *Caligula* 21), i.e. in the Campus

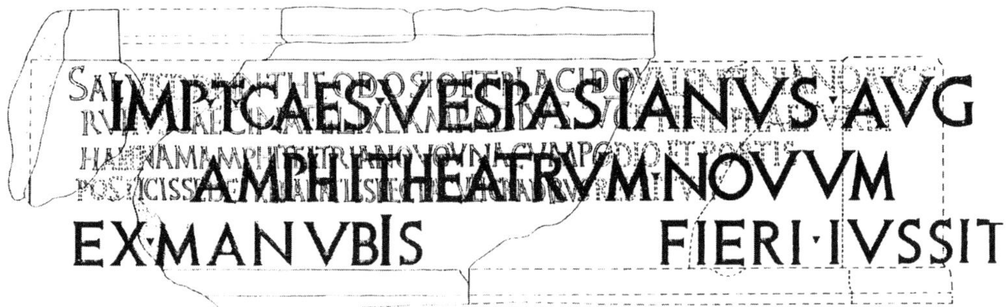

*Fig. 9.9: Reconstructed dedication superimposed over 5th-century inscription from the Colosseum (*CIL *6.32089: reproduced from* ZPE *109, 1995, 213, Fig. 6, by courtesy of Dr. Rudolf Habelt GmbH, Bonn).*

Martius; this project was abandoned by Claudius after Caligula's death.[119] Perhaps Nero used Caligula's site for his wooden amphitheatre on the Campus Martius, a building of considerable sophistication in which he is even said to have staged aquatic displays (Dio 61.9.5). It was built of wood, which probably accounts for the speed with which it was completed within a single year in AD 57 (Tacitus, *Annals* 13.31.1, Suetonius, *Nero* 12.1). It was a showpiece, boasting timbers from the largest tree ever exhibited at Rome and slung with star-spangled awnings, blue like the sky (Pliny, *Natural History* 16.200, 19.24). It must have been a casualty of the great fire in AD 64.[120]

Colosseum. After the fire of AD 64 had destroyed both Statilius Taurus' amphitheatre and Nero's, a major permanent arena in Rome became an urgent requirement. The ornamental lake in the grounds of Nero's Domus Aurea furnished Vespasian with a site for the building and an occasion for propaganda. A recent attempt to restore the original dedicatory inscription from the peg-holes surviving beneath a 5th-century re-dedication in the Colosseum postulates evidence that the new amphitheatre was – astonishingly and anachronistically – conceived as a manubial construction. The reconstruction reads: *I[mp(erator)] T(itus) Caes(ar) Vespasi[anus Aug(ustus)] / amphitheatru[m novum (?)] / [ex] manubi(i)s* (vac.) *[fieri iussit (?)]* ("The emperor Titus Caesar Vespasian Augustus ordered the new amphitheatre to be constructed out of the spoils of war", Fig. 9.9). The phrase *ex manubiis*, redolent of Republican practice, would have to refer to the booty captured in the campaign waged by Vespasian and Titus in Judaea in AD 70;[121] prisoners of war brought to Rome may be conjectured to have provided manpower.

Nero the showman had had a popular following; the Flavians had to counter nostalgia for his reign with due attention to mass entertainment. They took the opportunity to package this necessity as a democratic impulse to contrast with what they characterized as Nero's autocratic self-interest (Martial, *Book of Spectacles* 2).[122] The ground on which the new amphitheatre stood was already imperial property, since it had belonged to Nero. But if Vespasian conceived it as a manubial project, the building may have formally belonged to the Roman people. Certainly that is the general impression that Martial, avoiding technicalities, wished to give (*Book of Spectacles* 2.11–12): *reddita Roma sibi est et sunt te praeside, Caesar, / deliciae populi, quae fuerant domini* ("Rome has been restored to herself, and under your guidance, Caesar, what used to be the master's fun is now the people's"). So powerful a symbol of imperial generosity was the amphitheatre, that Titus tried to claim it as his own benefaction; on the

Fig. 9.10: Coin of Gordian III showing the Colosseum, with the colossal statue of the Sun to the left (Deutsches Archäologisches Institut, neg. 10736F).

Fig. 9.11: Exterior of the Colosseum in its present state (Deutsches Archäologisches Institut, neg. 79.2682).

Fig. 9.12: Sestertius commemorating the dedication of the Colosseum by Titus in AD 80 (Fototeca Unione, neg. 4267F).

restored dedication it is apparent that the first line of the inscription was re-configured to accommodate the 'T' that distinguishes his nomenclature from that of his father.[123]

The amphitheatre that Vespasian built is usually designated by modern scholars as 'Amphitheatrum Flavium' or 'Flavian Amphitheatre'. If the restored dedication is correct, the designation *amphitheatru[m novum]* may stress the originality of the design as well as the initiative of the Flavians in replacing the razed amphitheatres of Julio-Claudian Rome with a brand new one.[124] But contemporaries may simply have called it *amphitheatrum*, since there was none other surviving in Rome when it was constructed.[125] 13 fragments of the Marble Plan have been pieced together to show this building and its label, *[AMPHITHE]ATRVM*.[126] By the early Middle Ages it acquired the nickname 'Colosseum', first attested in an 8th century epigram in Bede's *Collectanea* (Migne 94.543): *quandiu stat Colisaeus, stat et Roma; / quando cadet Colisaeus, cadet et Roma; / quando cadet Roma, cadet et mundus*.[127] One explanation is that it acquired this name from the colossal statue beside it, originally a representation of Nero that stood in the *vestibulum* of his Golden House (Domus Aurea). This statue was later moved to its new position adjacent to the Colosseum, and modified to represent the Sun (Fig. 9.10).[128] But an alternative explanation posits a direct connection between the size of the building, truly 'colossal', and its nickname:[129] the main axes of the entire structure measured 188 × 156 m, and the arena (86 × 54 m) occupied an area of 3,357 m^2. It was the tallest building in the city, rising four storeys to a height of 52 m (Fig. 9.11). Its impact on the physical landscape of the ancient city, and on the mental landscape of its inhabitants, is still perceptible in the towering hulk of the modern ruin.[130]

A 4th-century source, the Chronographer of AD 354, preserves a jumbled summary in faulty Latin that appears to ascribe the fourth storey to Domitian. Probably, however, there is no need to suppose that he modified the design that he inherited from his father and brother (except, possibly, for the basement: see below).[131] The exterior of the amphitheatre is built of travertine, the interior of brick and concrete, with marble seating. The whole structure rests on a travertine podium of two steps surrounded by a travertine pavement 17.5 m wide. The arcades of the second and third storeys were occupied by statues, evidently of gods and heroes, that are clearly visible on contemporary representations (Figs. 9.12 and 9.13).[132] Mythologizing decor, in keeping with the religious rituals that underpinned Roman spectacle, is also characteristic of the *scaenae frons* in the theatre, and perhaps even of the building housing the *carceres* in the circus; the mosaic from Piazza Armerina shows statues of gods and athletes on the roof, and classicizing herms between the boxes themselves (Fig. 9.5).[133] A different atmosphere is conveyed by the blank façade of the fourth and tallest storey. Pierced by windows (described in connection with the Theatre of Marcellus above), it created an impression of weight and solidity on top of the three arcades beneath. At the top the shields decorating every alternate bay must have flashed impressively as they caught the sun. The monumental entrance supporting a *quadriga* features prominently on the relief sculpture on the Tomb of the Haterii (Fig. 9.13), even though the amphitheatre depicted here has been shorn of one storey, perhaps so as to fit the space available on the stone.[134]

Under legislation promulgated by Augustus (Suetonius, *Augustus* 44), seating in the theatre and the amphitheatre at Rome was strictly allocated, though it is not clear whether the distinctions were as rigid in the amphitheatre as they were in the theatre, where seats were demarcated according to status (slave or free, civilian or soldier, layman or priest), rank (*plebs*, *eques*, or senator), age (adult or child), marital circumstances, and gender; further sub-divisions might pertain within each discrete category.[135] Comparative evidence from elsewhere in Italy suggests that individual guilds and fraternities (*collegia*) may have had

Fig. 9.13: Haterii Monument: detail of amphitheatre (Deutsches Archäologisches Institut, neg. 39.566).

Fig. 9.14: Model of Colosseum, with cut-away section showing access routes beneath the cavea, *Museo della Civiltà Romana (Deutsches Archäologisches Institut, neg. 73.1002).*

their own seats too. These distinctions notwithstanding, permanent exceptions might be made, as with the Vestal Virgins, whose priestly status took precedence over their gender. Whether or not this reflection of an ideally ordered society was subsequently modified by changes in the rules, there is abundant evidence that reserved seating in the Colosseum continued to be a tenaciously guarded privilege: some of the seats still have the names of individual senators from the late empire carved on them, and there is a 'block booking' reserved for spectators from Gades (modern Cadiz).[136] The most advantageous position, on the short axis, was occupied by the imperial box, gorgeously decorated with coloured marble and occupied by the supreme patron whose munificence guaranteed the populace the spectacles in the arena. The stratification of the amphitheatre, between *cavea* and arena, and

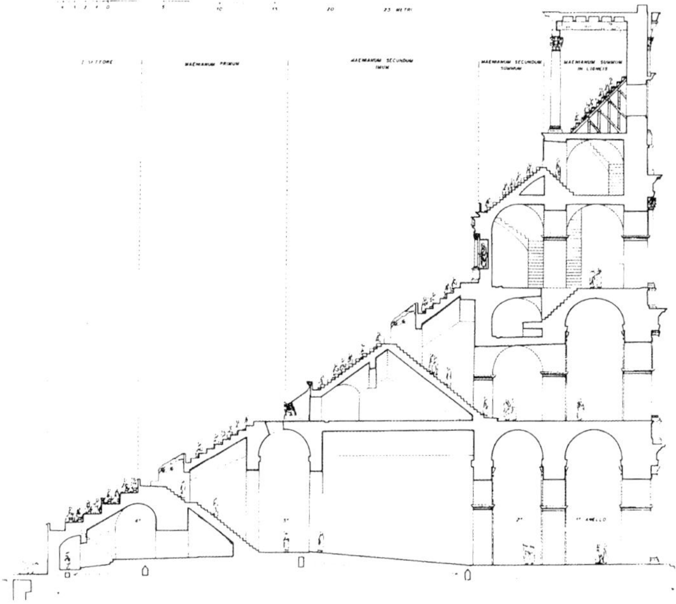

Fig. 9.15: Diagram of cross-section of the interior of the Colosseum (reproduced from Rea 1988, 32–3, by courtesy of Edizioni Quasar).

Fig. 9.16: View of the Ludus Magnus (Photo: editors).

within the *cavea* itself, reflected Roman society, properly ordered; and the spectacles themselves reinforced Roman cultural values (see below).[137]

A system of stream-lined access to individual seating-areas, frequently extolled by scholars for its efficiency, also served to protect social distinctions (Fig. 9.14). Five stone posts survive of the row that originally encircled the amphitheatre on the outer edge of its surrounding pavement; similar posts are attested outside the Italian amphitheatres at Puteoli (modern Pozzuoli) and Capua (S. Maria Capua Vetere).[138] On top of each post is a hole in which a ring is believed to have been inserted; it is more likely that a chain for crowd-control would have been looped between these rings than that they would have been strong enough to anchor the cables for the awning over the *cavea* (see below). Four pairs of holes visible in each post on the side facing the amphitheatre also seem to have facilitated crowd-control by providing moorings for a wooden barrier.[139] Numerals above each arch of the lowest arcade indicated which entrance a spectator should use in order to gain immediate access to the row in which he was seated, an expedient that was essential for the efficient management of an audience numbering up to 50,000.[140] Inside, a complicated series of vaulted sub-structures beneath the *cavea* created staircases leading to a series of openings (*vomitoria*) that gave access to four tiers of seats, the two uppermost being more steeply raked than the lower tiers. At the top was a balcony that provided standing-room beneath a wooden roof (see Fig. 9.15).

The spectators on the terracing sat beyond the overhang of the roof, and so to protect them from sun and rain there was provision for an awning (*velum*) like those installed in Roman theatres and at other amphitheatres too. A fresco from Pompeii in the Museo Nazionale at Naples illustrating the riot in the amphitheatre at Pompeii in AD 59 (Tacitus, *Annals* 14.17) furnishes a multiple perspective that accommodates a view of the exterior, the interior, and the *velum* all at once.[141] In the Colosseum masts mounted on corbels set into the blank façade of the fourth storey projected above the roof-line to support a web of cables connected to a pulley-system for rigging and lowering the *velum*.[142] This embellishment is clearly visible among the details proudly rendered on a *sestertius* issued by the senate to commemorate the dedication of the amphitheatre in AD 80 (Fig. 9.12) and on the coin minted by Gordian III advertising his *munificentia* (Fig. 9.10), and the same mast-supports are visible in other amphitheatres, such as those at Nîmes (ancient Nemausus) in the south of France and at Pula (Pola) in Croatia.[143] At the Colosseum the *velum* was operated by a detachment of marines from the fleet at Misenum (SHA, *Commodus* 15.6), who were barracked in the vicinity, probably on the slopes of the Oppian Hill between the Baths of Trajan and the ancient street running beneath the modern Via Labicana (Coulston in this volume). A fragment of the Marble Plan (*FUR* 6a) attests two contiguous structures that must have belonged to the accretion of support-buildings in the vicinity of the Colosseum: the barracks for the marines (Castra Misenatium)[144] and the gladiatorial armoury (Armamentaria: see below). The marines' expertise in rigging the sails on ships would clearly be a valuable asset in their role in the amphitheatre, though that is unlikely to have been the sole reason for their presence in Rome; as a unit of the military they were available also for police-duty in an emergency.[145]

Underneath the arena there was a *hypogeum* (basement) 6 m deep, the shell partly of *opus quadratum*, the rest brick. It was laid out in a series of elliptical corridors that would have housed a system of lifts and cages for hoisting apparatus and animals into the arena through trapdoors in the arena floor.[146] It seems likely, however, that the *hypogeum* in its present form was a later addition, perhaps dating to the reign of Domitian (AD 81–96). His predecessor Titus (AD 79–81) staged a miniature naval battle in the arena (the clash between Corinth and Corcyra at the beginning of the Peloponnesian War: Dio 66.25.3, cf. Martial, *Book of Spectacles* 27). He also put on an aquatic pantomime featuring Nereids who described various conformations in the water; the venue for this was probably also the Colosseum, since the patterns would have created a striking spectacle when viewed from high up in the *cavea* (Martial, *Book of Spectacles* 30). He is even reported to have staged a type of aquatic dressage performed by terrestrial animals (Dio 66.25.2).[147] Unless, however, we are to imagine that Titus water-proofed the arena-floor, it is clear that the *hypogeum* was too deep, and the installations in it too precious, for it to have been flooded for an aquatic display.

Surviving evidence for aquatic installations comes from the amphitheatres at Verona (Italy) and Mérida (ancient Augusta Emerita, in Spain). Each is equipped with a shallow basin in the middle of the arena that does not resemble the underground storage areas and facilities associated with a regular *hypogeum*. The shallow depth of these basins (approximately 1.25 m), and the presence of a water-supply, suggests that they may have been used for aquatic displays.[148] The floorboards could presumably have been removed for an aquatic event and put back again for the rest of the programme, though they must have rested on supports that have disappeared, and it is hard to imagine that such supports would not have got in the way during an aquatic performance. At all events, any aquatic display performed in such a basin would have been a very modest affair; full-scale re-enactments of naval battles were staged on custom-built lakes (see under *Naumachia* below). Domitian constructed his own *stagnum* for aquatic displays in the area of the Vatican (Suetonius, *Domitian* 4.1–2), which lends credence to the theory that he was responsible for the conversion of the Colosseum into the structure with a *hypogeum* that we know today. If by then Augustus' *naumachia* in Trastevere was falling into disrepair, it was imperative for Domitian to construct his own aquatic venue.

But even if there is no sign that the Colosseum in its final form was equipped to host aquatic displays, there is detailed evidence of a hydraulic system to supply water for drinking-fountains (and perhaps latrines) and to drain rain-water from the building.[149] Nero had built an extension from the Aqua Claudia to convey water into a reservoir on the Caelian Hill in order to supply the Temple of Claudius, the Palatine, and Nero's own lake in the grounds of the Domus Aurea (see Dodge in this volume). The system of siphons that the Flavian engineers used to convey water from the reservoir to the Colosseum was probably the same system that had been designed to feed Nero's lake. Pipes supplied water for fountains at regular distances throughout the first two storeys of the amphitheatre. The gallery between the second and third storeys, easily accessible from the *summa cavea* and the balcony in the attic, may have accommodated a latrine. In such a large building with no permanent roof the evacuation of rain-water was critical. In the Colosseum rain-water that collected in the arena or the *hypogeum* was led through a system of drains and tanks into a large channel about 10 m beneath the paving outside the building, from where it ultimately flowed into the Tiber. Even if this meant that the Colosseum was occasionally inundated by flood-waters from the river, under normal circumstances it remained well drained and serviceable throughout the year.

Support-buildings. Adjacent to the Colosseum on its east side, and connected to the *hypogeum* by a tunnel, was the Ludus Magnus, one of four gladiatorial training-schools and barracks founded by Domitian to service the Colosseum;[150] we have already noted that Domitian may have been responsible for the *hypogeum* of the Colosseum as we know it. The Ludus Magnus was completed by Trajan, altered by Hadrian, and repaired by Caracalla. It was first uncovered in 1937, but more than half still remains to be excavated (Fig. 9.16). It was a three-storey building similar to the premises of the *Vigiles* (fire-fighters) in Ostia, with a portico opening inwards on the two lower storeys and possibly an open gallery on the top storey. Opening onto the portico on the two lower storeys were cells and other facilities for the gladiators. The longer sides (north and south) probably comprised 14 cells on each storey; on the west side there were probably 10. These cells measure more than twice the size of the cells in the gladiatorial barracks at Pompeii, which may have housed one or two gladiators each; so in the Ludus Magnus there may have been three or four gladiators to a cell. Hence the building may have accommodated several hundred gladiators. The east side was occupied by larger facilities, including a shrine for the imperial cult. On the north and south sides behind the cells there was a row of shops opening on to the street. In the middle of the quadrangle formed by the porticoes there was a training-arena measuring 62.15 × 41.45 m, i.e. with a surface area of approximately 2,000 m^2 (a ratio of 1:2.5 in comparison with the

Colosseum).[151] Its *cavea* consisted of nine rows of seats accessible via four external staircases. On the short axis there was seating for VIPs. In all, the *cavea* could have held approximately 3,000 spectators. Its existence demonstrates that the gladiators were given the opportunity to practise in front of an audience; and the spectators were afforded a preview of the protagonists whom they were later to see in combat in the Colosseum.[152]

To the south, aligned along the Vicus Capitis Africae very close to the Templum Divi Claudii, lay a smaller barracks-building, now no longer visible, which was almost certainly the Ludus Matutinus, located in Regio II or III by the Regionary Catalogues.[153] Its name suggests that it was intended for the training and housing of the *bestiarii* who performed against beasts in the morning shows. Maybe it was built on the site of the *ludus bestiarius* mentioned by Seneca (*On Benefits* 70.20). The Ludus Gallicus, listed by the *Notitia* in Regio II, is assumed to have stood nearby.[154] More secure is the identification of the Ludus Dacicus: by combining two fragments of the Marble Plan it has been ascertained that it was located in Regio III between the Ludus Magnus and what was to be the site of the Thermae Traiani.[155] The names of these last two *ludi* suggest that they were probably intended respectively for gladiators from Gaul and for prisoners captured during Domitian's Dacian campaigns.[156] Without knowing the dimensions of all the *ludi* it is impossible to calculate how many gladiators were barracked in the vicinity of the Colosseum, but a figure of a thousand for all four *ludi* is probably conservative. Clearly the presence of these men in the city-centre was a risk, to which the inward-facing design of the *ludi* was perhaps in part a response. It is also noteworthy that their weapons were stored away from their barracks: the fragment of the Marble Plan that attests the Armamentaria ('weapons-stores') together with the Castra Misenatium (see above) is believed to fit to the north-east of the Ludus Magnus.[157] The plural designation *armamentaria* suggests that this was a central depot for storing collections of weapons belonging to the individual gladiatorial schools; an inscription records a *libertus Augusti* who was *praepositus armamentario Ludi Magni* (*CIL* 6.10164 = *ILS* 5153), so the Ludus Magnus at least – if not each of the other *ludi* too – apparently had its own *armamentarium*.[158]

The site of three other support-buildings associated with the Colosseum is not known precisely, though they are to be located in the general area of the *ludi* and the Armamentaria. The Regionary Catalogues assign to Regio II the Spoliarium and Saniarium (or Samiarium). The Spoliarium (from Latin *spoliare*, "to strip") was where the corpses of gladiators who had been killed in the arena were stripped of their armour (SHA, *Commodus* 18.3–5; 19.1, 3), and where defeated gladiators who had not been spared were taken to have their throats slit (Seneca, *Letters* 93.12).[159] It was supervised by a *curator spoliarii* (*CIL* 6.10171). The Saniarium, if the reading preserved in the *Curiosum* is correct, would be the place where wounded gladiators who had either won or been spared were taken for treatment. The alternative reading *samiarium*, preserved in the *Notitia*, would designate a workshop where the weapons were sharpened and polished (cf. *samiare*, "to buff up"), though the Armamentaria would seem the appropriate place for this.[160] A little more certainty attaches to the last of the support-buildings, the Summum Choragium, for which epigraphic evidence survives as well as an entry in both Regionary Catalogues, under Regio III. On the basis of the findspots of the inscriptions that mention it, the Summum Choragium is to be located east of the Castra Misenatium and west of the Ludus Magnus. It was the depot where scenery and equipment for the Colosseum was assembled and stored. The name is a Greek loanword, *χορήγιον* (originally the place where the chorus was trained, later the word for a stage-building in a theatre). The Summum Choragium was administered by imperial slaves and freedmen in various capacities, of which the most revealing is the position occupied by the *medicus rationis Summi*

Fig. 9.17: Campana plaque depicting bestiarii *fighting lions and a bear, with a spectator-building in the background (reproduced by courtesy of Teatro La Scala, Milan).*

Choragii (*CIL* 6.10085 = *ILS* 1770); if the office for stage properties had its own doctor, that is because the stage-hands in charge of special effects (not to mention the performers) were at considerable risk from machinery that malfunctioned.[161] The epithet *summum* in the name of this building used to be thought to distinguish it from the other *choragia* in Rome, which would have been under the control of the senate instead of the emperor. Recently, however, it has been suggested that *summum* indicates that this *choragium* was bigger than those attaching to the individual theatres in the city.[162]

Amphitheatre displays. The complex infrastructure that supported the spectacles of the arena has left a rich, if fragmentary, epigraphic record of some of the sponsors, support-staff and combatants who contributed to the spectacles mounted in the Colosseum, and in the Julio-Claudian amphitheatres that were its forerunners in Rome.[163] Even a few graffiti and their accompanying cartoons survive, scratched onto what were once the marble facings of the Colosseum; they offer informal testimony to the popular interest in following individual gladiators' fortunes, from acclamation of a victorious *retiarius* down to the morbid *theta nigrum* ('black theta') that tersely symbolized death in the arena.[164] A highly specialized system of fighting styles, requiring distinctive weaponry and armour, inspired fierce partisanship among gladiators' fans across the empire, from the scribblers who totted up gladiators' tallies on the walls of Pompeii[165] to a figure as august as the emperor Titus, who made no secret of his favour towards gladiators fighting in the Thracian style (Suetonius, *Titus* 8.2). And the gladiators themselves, living, training, and fighting together in their *ludi*, formed close-knit fraternities. Such a bond is eloquently attested in funerary monuments such as that for Macedo, a Thracian gladiator who died in his first fight (presumably in the Colosseum) aged twenty years, eight months, and twelve days, and was commemorated by the entire company of Thracians.[166]

Ambiguity pervades the notion of a gladiator: he was admired for his physical courage (*virtus*), but despised for his incapacity to aspire to civic status; he was trained for mortal combat, but he was too precious to be summarily despatched; he was a social outcast, and yet equestrians and senators had to be legally prevented from participating in gladiatorial combat for monetary gain.[167] Fine distinctions governed grades into which gladiators were classified; matches were closely controlled by a referee (*summa rudis*).[168] Gladiators are to be distinguished from *bestiarii*, who were engaged in beast-fighting (Fig. 9.17).[169] A further category comprised the condemned criminals or prisoners of war who were executed in the arena by one of the aggravated death-penalties: crucifixion, *crematio* or *vivicomburium* (burning alive), and *damnatio ad bestias* (condemnation to the beasts).[170]

It is impossible now to re-capture the sensation of attending a spectacle in the Colosseum, even though we may understand that gladiatorial combat provided a spectacle of bravery and skill, beast-displays an image of nature pitted against Man and ultimately controlled by him, and criminal punishment an endorsement of the power of the state and the rule of law.[171] If whores plied their trade in the arcades on the ground floor, that is because their discreet shelter was traditionally associated with prostitution (fornication 'under the arches', *fornices*).[172] The assumption that they would have been there, catering to a heightened sexual drive experienced by spectators after the thrill of the show, must remain purely conjectural. But certainly the spectators felt an irrational excitement: St. Augustine's friend Alypius became 'drunk on blood-stained pleasure' (*cruenta voluptate inebriebatur*) after attending a spectacle at Rome, surely in the Colosseum (Augustine, *Confessions* 6.8). The 'philosopher-emperor' Marcus Aurelius, on the other hand, simply found gladiatorial displays boring;[173] but at the same time he recognized their fundamental importance as an economic force and a social institution. Since the reign of Augustus, the provision of spectacles in the capital had been carefully controlled by the emperor or his agent (Dio 54.2.3–4, 17.4), though technically it was the senate that controlled the number of gladiators in a *munus*. But it was Marcus Aurelius in AD 177 or 178 who introduced legislation across the empire to keep expenditure on spectacles within practical limits, in order to encourage candidates for those municipal magistracies that required the incumbent to provide public spectacles out of his own resources.[174] Throughout the empire, displays of two or three pairs of gladiators or a handful of wild beasts reflected – however modestly – the magnificence of the displays of the Colosseum at the heart of the Roman world.[175]

Most of the literary references to arena spectacles are purely incidental, and it is very difficult to get a sense of a dawn-to-dusk programme. But, fortunately, the magnificent displays staged by Titus at the inauguration of the Colosseum in AD 80 were commemorated by Martial in a series of epigrams that survive (partially, at least) in the collection known as the *Liber spectaculorum* or *Liber de spectaculis* (*Book of Spectacles*).[176] The staples of the programme were gladiatorial combat, animal displays,[177] and public executions staged as mythological enactments[178] (chiefly enacting a sentence of *damnatio ad bestias*), accompanied by the traditional distribution of largesse (*missilia*) among the spectators.[179] But there were novel additions: a grand political gesture in the form of public humiliation of the dreaded *delatores* who were widely regarded as the emperor's secret agents (Martial, *Book of Spectacles* 4–5);[180] female beast-fighters (*Book of Spectacles* 8); a water-ballet (mentioned above) that featured a troupe of Nereids; an enactment of Leander's intrepid swim to Hero, with an uncanonical outcome (*Book of Spectacles* 28–9); naval battles, both in the amphitheatre (see above) and at the artificial lake dug by Augustus beside the Tiber in Trastevere (see under '*Naumachia*' below). Titus' inaugural displays lasted 100 days, a series characterized by unprecedented extravagance to match the splendours of the Flavian benefaction that was being celebrated. With epigrammatic hyperbole Martial declares that the new amphitheatre eclipses all seven wonders of the world rolled into one (*Book of Spectacles* 1.7–8), and each successive spectacle he presents as a miracle of the emperor's devising. Titus' extravaganza was to be eclipsed in the next generation by the spectacles celebrating Trajan's Dacian victory in AD 107, which lasted 123 days, involved 10,000 gladiators, and despatched 11,000 beasts (Dio 68.15.1). And in between, during the reign of Domitian, the Colosseum was the venue for at least one banquet, at which all the social orders enjoyed the emperor's hospitality, feasting and watching a cabaret featuring mock blood-sports, musicians, dancing-girls, and other theatrical entertainments (Statius, *Silvae* 1.6).[181]

The Christian fathers complained vociferously of the idolatrous nature of Roman spectacles and of their brutalizing effects on the spectators, though they paid scant attention to the participants. As one of the categories of miscreant punished sporadically in the arena, not to mention their professed belief in the brotherhood of Man, the Christians might have been expected to close the amphitheatres after the Christianization of the empire under Constantine (AD 312). But Christian authors voice what are essentially the same objections as pagan detractors, with the added complaint that the arena is a pagan institution, and the gradual decline of gladiatorial combat may have been influenced by political and economic factors (e.g. the need for a continuing supply of criminals to work the mines). But although gladiatorial combat disappeared from the eastern empire by the middle of the 4th century, it continued into the 5th century in the west, fuelled in part – perhaps – by the reluctance of the élite to give up their gladiatorial bodyguards (Christie in this volume).[182] The resulting vacuum was soon filled: *venationes* continued into the Byzantine empire, and chariot-racing reached unprecedented levels of popularity. The hagiographic tradition of the 6th and 7th centuries recounts a series of martyrdoms that are purported to have taken place in the Colosseum during the Christian persecutions of the 3rd century. The veracity of these accounts is highly dubious, but they do illustrate Christian attitudes towards the Colosseum in the post-antique phase. For the 6th century hagiographers the Colosseum was a symbol of pagan cruelty and bigotry. The contempt in which the Christians held this towering monument is vividly conveyed by the reactions attributed to Abdon and Sennen, two Persian Christians who were allegedly martyred under Decius. When they were brought to the foot of the colossal statue of the Sun outside the amphitheatre and ordered to perform a sacrifice, they are said to have spat at the statue and chosen to face two lions and four bears in the arena instead; their courage was apparently vindicated when the animals came roaring and growling to their protection.[183]

Amphitheatrum Castrense. Like the Circus Varianus (see above), an amphitheatre also survives in the vicinity of the church of S. Croce in Gerusalemme. It was later incorporated into the Aurelian Wall, whereupon it presumably ceased to host spectacles and assumed the function of a fortification. It was smaller than the Colosseum (88 × 75.8 m), only three storeys high, and constructed of brick-faced concrete.[184] Excavations in the 18th century revealed a *hypogeum* beneath the arena filled with the bones of large animals, which suggests that the spectacles staged here included *venationes*. The Regionary Catalogues ascribe to Regio V an "Amphitheatrum Castrense", which may mean "amphitheatre attached to the imperial residence". Both the amphitheatre and the so-called Circus Varianus (see above) were part of the palatial villa known as Sessorium.[185] From a water-pipe stamped with the consular date corresponding to AD 202 (*CIL* 15.7364), it appears that construction of this complex began under Septimius Severus. Work continued under Caracalla and Elagabalus. The amphitheatre and the circus were connected by a long corridor, until the whole complex was bifurcated by the Aurelian Wall. There are precedents for constructing spectacle-buildings for the private (or semi-private) use of wealthy and influential groups or individuals, such as the racetrack in the precinct of the Fratres Arvales or Caligula's Vatican circus (see above). The construction of such a building, to be used for its original purpose, should be distinguished from the taste for incorporating private versions of spectacle buildings into the emperor's residence as purely decorative spaces. This trend goes back at least to Domitian, whose palace on the Palatine

Fig. 9.18: Model of Stadium of Domitian, Museo della Civiltà Romana (Photo: Deutsches Archäologisches Institut, neg. 73.994).

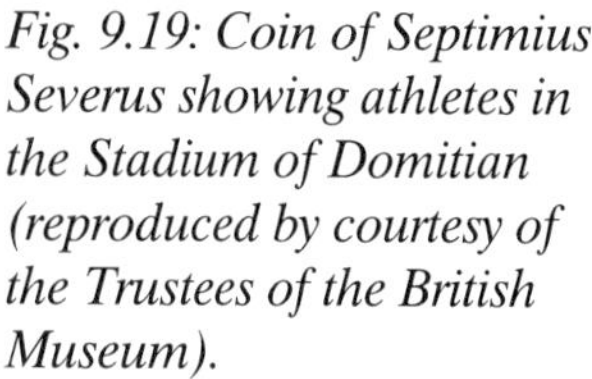

Fig. 9.19: Coin of Septimius Severus showing athletes in the Stadium of Domitian (reproduced by courtesy of the Trustees of the British Museum).

incorporated a so-called 'hippodromos'.[186] Hadrian's magnificent villa at Tibur (Tivoli) incorporates a similar structure, known as the 'stadium garden'. These were probably no more than ornamental spaces for walking and conversation amid sumptuous garden statuary and elegant plantings, but they evoked an atmosphere of Greek competitive spectacle consonant with the preferences of avowedly hellenophile emperors.[187]

NAUMACHIA

Naumachiae of Caesar and Augustus. The dominant characteristic of public entertainment at Rome under the empire is the striving after novelty and extravagance, and one structure above all others captures its essence: the *naumachia* or *stagnum*, an artificial basin constructed for large-scale aquatic displays.[188] Here again Julius Caesar led the way for his heir: he had a basin excavated in the Campus Martius[189] in order to stage a naval battle between 'Tyrian' and 'Egyptian' fleets as part of the celebrations following his quadruple triumph in 46 BC (Suetonius, *Julius Caesar* 39.4); the context for this engagement, albeit fictitious rather than historical,[190] is characteristic of the Roman preference for the realistic over the symbolic (i.e. rather an historicizing context than 'reds' vs. 'greens', or 'spots' vs. 'stripes'). Caesar's basin was filled in after his death, but in 2 BC Augustus had one excavated in Trastevere[191] of enormous dimensions (536 x 357 m, as large as a modern city-block) in order to re-enact the battle of Salamis with 3,000 marines (not counting oarsmen) as part of the inaugural celebrations for the Temple of Mars Ultor (*Res Gestae* 23; Dio 55.10.7). This basin continued in use at least down to the reign of Titus, since some of the aquatic spectacles for the inauguration of the Colosseum were held there (Martial, *Book of Spectacles* 34). These included a re-enactment of the attack by Athens on Syracuse in the Peloponnesian War in which the 'Athenians' took advantage of an island in the middle of the basin (which had presumably originally represented Salamis) in order to effect a landing and a terrestrial engagement as well as the canonical naval battle (Dio 66.25.4). In the 3rd century traces of this basin were still visible (Dio 55.10.7).

Naumachiae of Domitian and Trajan. Domitian's *naumachia* (mentioned in the section 'Amphitheatre' above) was an excavated basin with a retaining wall, perhaps stepped to accommodate spectators.[192] Already by Suetonius' day it had been demolished and the stone used to repair fire-damage to the Circus Maximus.[193] Without being able to assess the comparative amenities of this *naumachia* and Augustus', it is impossible to be certain why the older basin was retained at the expense of the newer. It is, however, tempting to suppose that Augustus' reputation preserved his *naumachia*, whereas the basin constructed by Domitian was doomed by the *damnatio memoriae* that he suffered. If its demolition was total, then Trajan cannot have appropriated it.[194] In that case the *naumachia Traiani* that was dedicated in AD 109[195] must be yet another building, probably to be identified with the remnants of a spectacle-building that have been discovered NW of Castel Sant'Angelo in the vicinity of the 8th-century church S. Pellegrino in Naumachia. Waterproof facing in *opus signinum* in a corridor below the performance-area, and facilities for drainage, have led to this identification.[196] If it is correct, this indicates the extent to which individual emperors wished to be associated with the glamour of aquatic displays (however infrequently performed), and with the construction of a building for staging them.

STADIUM

Stadia in Italy. If the amphitheatre was a Roman architectural type seldom attested in the Greek East, the same – in reverse – is true of the stadium: this Greek structure appears only rarely in the West.[197] In Italy stadia were built in Magna Graecia at Puteoli and at Naples, the latter the site of the Sebasta, Greek games founded by Augustus in AD 2.[198] For occasional athletic displays at Rome a permanent venue was not necessary: a temporary stadium on the Campus Martius served for Julius Caesar's three days of athletic contests during the celebration of his quadruple triumph in 46 BC (Suetonius, *Julius Caesar* 39.3); his heir Augustus made similar provision (Dio 53.1.5). Rome eventually acquired the character of a πόλις ἑλληνίς ('Greek city') when Nero brought it onto the Greek games circuit by establishing the short-lived Neroneia, a gymnastic, equestrian, and musical competition in his own honour (Suetonius, *Nero* 12.3). It seems likely that Nero built a stadium to accommodate the athletic aspects of this event, but in default of any traces it is assumed to have occupied the site where a stadium was later constructed by Domitian. Together with his *odeum*, Domitian's stadium provided the facilities for his Agon Capitolinus (see below, under '*Odeum*'), which was perpetuated for three centuries as the city's oldest permanent Greek competition (Suetonius, *Domitian* 4.3).[199] The long duration of this institution, and the founding of three more Greek-style competitions in the 3rd century, demonstrate that Domitian's hellenophile tastes found a response at Rome.[200]

Stadium of Domitian. The modern Piazza Navona preserves the outline of Domitian's stadium beneath it.[201] In 1936 the demolition of houses at the curved end revealed that Domitian's structure was the first stadium to be raised on vaults instead of being banked in earth, a sophisticated development to match the theatres and amphitheatre of contemporary Rome (Fig. 9.18). From its dimensions (external: 275 × 228 m; internal: 106 × 53 m; height: 18.5 m)

Domitian's stadium is estimated to have been among the largest stadia known from Antiquity, with a capacity of approximately 30,000 spectators. When the Colosseum was damaged by fire under Macrinus in AD 217, the stadium temporarily and exceptionally hosted gladiatorial spectacles (Dio 79.25.2–3), but its canonical function was to stage the athletics associated with Greek contests. The musical events that were part of this programme required a more compact and acoustically sensitive venue (see under 'Odeum' below).

A rare coin testifies to the appearance and function of this building. An image on a coin of Septimius Severus dating from AD 202–210[202] has been identified as an aerial view of the stadium from the East (Fig. 9.19). It shows a two-storey arcaded building in the shape of an elongated 'U'. Four monumental entrances are depicted, one at the end of either arm of the *cavea*, one midway down the length of the near side, and one along the curve. Statues are depicted in the arches of the upper storey, and masts project above to support the awning. Inside the performance space nine figures, symmetrically arranged, are engaged simultaneously in various activities characteristic of a stadium: there is a solo figure at each end (to the left a runner, to the right the seated figure of the emperor); on the inner side of each of these figures there is a pair of contestants (to the left boxers, to the right wrestlers); in the centre is a trio of figures performing a ceremony to award the victorious athlete his crown (to the left a musician, in the middle the winner, and to the right the presiding official performing the coronation). The depiction of these athletes, together with the absence of a central barrier, confirms the identification as Domitian's stadium.[203]

Greek athletics. Roman attitudes towards the contests associated with the Greek gymnasium are complicated.[204] Boxing and wrestling had long been admired at Rome, and were known from Etruscan, Latin, and Campanian culture.[205] A boxing-match (*athletarum certamen*) had been put on at Rome as early as 186 BC, by M. Fulvius Nobilior (Livy 39.22.1–2). Increasing contact between the great generals of the late Republic and the Greek East encouraged the Romans to associate the Greek athletic repertoire with true 'Greekness', so that Augustus established athletic events in his Actian games at Nicopolis on the Adriatic coast of Greece, and in his Sebasta, the games that he founded in the Greek city of Naples. Yet in AD 60 when Nero introduced athletic contests at Rome in the context of a true *certamen Graecum* ('Greek competition', including musical and equestrian events), he met some fierce resistance (Tacitus, *Annals* 14.20). It was not Greek gymnastic contests *per se* but certain aspects of their performance that aroused Roman contempt, most obviously their association with nudity, and a perception that some categories, such as throwing the discus, had no practical application.[206]

Yet, of the five categories in Domitian's Agon Capitolinus that did not survive beyond the age of Hadrian, only one was athletic: the girls' footrace (Suetonius, *Domitian* 4.4).[207] It evidently foundered upon a moral objection; the girls of course ran naked. At least one prominent senator, however, would have liked to abolish the Agon Capitolinus altogether (Iunius Mauricus, quoted at Pliny, *Letters* 4.22.3). And the increasing popularity of Greek athletic contests in the western provinces was stamped out in at least one centre, at Vienne, at the behest of a local magistrate, Trebonius Rufinus, whose action was referred all the way to Rome, where it was subsequently endorsed by Trajan's circle of advisers.[208] Yet the survival of the Agon Capitolinus itself (assisted, no doubt, by the absence of Domitian's nomenclature from their title) shows that Roman society could accept athletics in the context of Greek games at Rome,[209] and further *agones* that were established in the city from the Severan age onwards (n. 200 above) were also doubtless intended to be performed in the venues that Domitian had donated to the city.[210]

ODEUM

Odeum of Domitian. The function of a concert-hall for the '*eisteddfod*' aspect of Domitian's Greek games (recitations and recitals) required a venue with exquisite acoustics. This demand was fulfilled by another Greek structure that was adopted and refined by the Romans, the roofed theatre known as an ᾠδεῖον ('odeion').[211] Such may have been the *theatrum peculiare* that Nero built for his private use in the Vatican valley (Pliny, *Natural History* 37.19); but Domitian's *odeum* in the Campus Martius was the first such public amenity in Rome (Suetonius, *Domitian* 5; *Chron. min.* 146 Mommsen; Hieron. *Chron. a. Abr.* 2105). The claim that it was built by Apollodorus of Damascus, the architect closely associated with Trajan (Dio 69.4.1), has led some scholars to suppose that Apollodorus was responsible for renovating it,[212] or that he built another theatre altogether.[213] Perhaps Trajan's Forum provides an analogy, since Domitian reputedly started it (Aurelius Victor, *On the Caesars* 13.5) and Apollodorus is attested as having worked on it too (Dio 69.4.1).

The old identification of the *odeum* with the artificial mound known as 'Monte Giordano'[214] has seemed rather far from the stadium which it was presumably intended to complement, hence the alternative suggestion of the curved façade of the Palazzo Massimo alle Colonne on the Corso Vittorio Emanuele.[215] Two late Roman sources regard the *odeum* as one of the architectural marvels of Rome (Ammianus Marcellinus 16.10.14; Polemius Silvius 545). Its capacity in late Antiquity is estimated by the *Curiosum* at 10,600 *loca*, i.e. accommodation for approximately 7,000 spectators, whereas the capacity of the largest surviving *odeum*, that of Herodes Atticus at Athens, is estimated at 5,000.[216] Yet the estimate of the *Curiosum* is probably correct: the diameter of the *cavea* in Domitian's *odeum* is estimated at 100 m, which is at least 30% wider than that of the *odeum* of Herodes Atticus, and since the top rows of the *cavea* would have held more spectators than the lower rows, an increase of 2,000 spectators is sustained by the dimensions.[217] It seems technically impossible, however, for such a large structure to have been roofed over in its entirety. The roof of the *odeum* of Herodes Atticus probably covered no more than the upper tiers of seating and the stage, leaving a semi-circular *oculus* (opening, lit. 'eye') over the rest of the structure; hence the *odeum* of Domitian must also have been no more than partially roofed.

Agon Capitolinus. Despite the *damnatio memoriae* that he suffered, Domitian's legacy of the Capitoline contest[218] survived down to the 4th century, except for the girls' footrace (mentioned above), competitions in Greek and Latin oratory, recitals on the *cithara*, and solo and choral singing to *cithara* accompaniment, all of which had been discontinued by Suetonius' day, i.e. in the time of Hadrian (Suetonius, *Domitian* 4.4). A rich record (mainly epigraphic) attests 65 known competitors over a period of 300 years, and another 10 possible participants.[219] Nobody of senatorial or equestrian rank is known to have competed in the category for Latin poets, perhaps because of the disgrace that traditionally attached to appearance on the stage, though many may in any case have been put off by the narrow parameters of the prescription – an extempore poem in praise of Jupiter.[220]

But talents were attracted from a different quarter: the ambitions that the poetic categories nurtured are perhaps best captured on the tombstone of Q. Sulpicius Maximus (apparently the child of freedman parents), which records the 43 hexameters that he delivered extempore in the Greek poetry section in AD 94 at the age of eleven.[221] The title of his entry was 'The words Zeus would use in censuring the Sun for giving the chariot to Phaethon'. His solemn person, clutching an open papyrus roll in his left hand, gazes out from

Fig. 9.20 Tomb of Q. Sulpicius Maximus, aged eleven, inscribed with his entry for the Agon Capitolinus (reproduced by courtesy of the Musei Capitolini).

the central niche, surrounded by the lines of his poem that his grieving parents had inscribed to immortalize his precocious effort (Fig. 9.20). The poignancy of this advertisement becomes more acute in the context of another inscription, put up nearly sixty years later to commemorate L. Valerius Pudens, who had risen to be *curator rei publicae Aeserninorum* under Antoninus Pius; the achievements of his illustrious career are headed by his victory in the Latin poetry section of the Agon Captolinus in AD 106, when he was thirteen years old.[222] Like Q. Sulpicius Maximus, this child should be envisaged performing before an audience of 7,000 in one of the architectural marvels of Rome.

Recitations. Domitian's hellenophile construction, custom-built to accommodate his Greek *agon*, draws attention to the fact that until then Rome had had no building dedicated to the nearest Roman equivalent, the *recitatio*. It seems likely that recitations often took place before an invited audience in a private house. On a grand scale the facilities might approximate those of the so-called 'Auditorium' in the Horti Maecenatis; the design, which is typical of the *triclinia* (dining-rooms) of the grand houses of the late Republic and early empire, includes at one end an apse comprising seven steps in concentric semi-circles, and at the other a transept suitable for dramatic performances and declamations.[223] A public facility where poetic recitals and declamations are believed to have been delivered is the Augustan complex dedicated to Palatine Apollo, either in the temple itself or in one of the libraries attached to it.[224] Nor should we overlook Caligula's opportunistic use of the Diribitorium as a theatrical space (see above, under 'Temporary theatres'); and the basilicas of Rome, centres for administrative business and for commercial transactions, could also perhaps have served a similar *ad hoc* purpose. Even the brand-new cultural foundation of a hellenophile emperor was not inaugurated in a building of its own: when Hadrian established his school of Greek grammar and rhetoric at Rome he apparently located it in the Atrium Minervae, adjoining the Curia; only in the 4th century, after

Diocletian rebuilt the Curia, was the Athenaeum re-housed in a building that may have incorporated an *odeum* for epideictic oratory in Greek and Latin.[225] And, finally, in considering public entertainment at Rome and its architectural context we would under-estimate the pervasive nature of spectacle and the spectacular element in public life if we were to disregard rhetorical performances at *contiones*, on the *rostra*, and in the law-courts.[226]

CONCLUSION

Entertainment was monumentalized at Rome by the last generation of the Republic and its survivors: Pompey built Rome's first permanent theatre and Julius Caesar transformed the Circus Maximus from a grassy depression into a solid formal structure; of Octavian's generals, Statilius Taurus built Rome's first stone amphitheatre and Balbus a theatrical complex, while Augustus himself sponsored the Theatre of Marcellus and endowed Rome with a custom-built lake for aquatic spectacles that was still a landmark more than two centuries later. This monumentalization – coinciding with the transition from Republic to Empire, from oligarchy to autocracy – marks a shift in the attitudes of the ruling class towards the provision of public entertainment: spectacles, and their venues became a status-marker for the benefactor and a regular expectation of the beneficiaries. Within the first post-Republican generation the role of supreme benefactor in the city of Rome became the prerogative of the emperor, so that his predilections shaped both the nature of entertainment and the physical fabric that evolved to accommodate its development. Hence Domitian, the last representative of Rome's second dynasty, not only introduced to the city Greek-style competitions in music and athletics but also left a monumental legacy in the form of Rome's first (and probably only) stadium and *odeum*. It is a significant paradox that, in catering for the ephemeral pleasures of the volatile urban population, the most ambitious figures of late Republican Rome, and the emperors who succeeded them, created some of the greatest surviving landmarks of the ancient city.

ACKNOWLEDGEMENTS

I am very grateful to the editors and Katherine Welch, who were a great help answering queries and supplying bibliography, and most especially to William Slater, who read a draft of the entire article, and made numerous important comments and suggestions with unstinting patience and generosity.

NOTES

1 BLÜMNER 1918.
2 The development of these festivals is complex and obscure, but by the mid-1st century BC some clarity emerges. There were by then seven of them, each celebrated with *ludi scaenici* (dramatic performances) followed by *ludi circenses* (chariot-races and beast-hunts): the Ludi Megalenses, for the Magna Mater ('Great Mother'), 4–9 April; the Ludi Cereales, for Ceres, 12–18 April; the Ludi Florales, for Flora (28 April – 2 May); the Ludi Apollinares, for Apollo (6–12 July); the Ludi Romani, for Jupiter (4–12 September); the Ludi Victoriae, for Victory (26–31 October); and the Ludi Plebeii, also for Jupiter (4–12 November). Overview: *RE* Suppl. 5.608–30 *s.v.* 'Ludi publici' (Habel).
3 KLOFT 1970.
4 The monumental study by HUMPHREY 1986 is supplemented by CIANCIO ROSSETTO 1987. Overview: RICHARDSON 1992, 84–7; *Lexicon* I, *s.v.* 'Circus Maximus', 272–77. Further bibliography at *Lexicon* V, *s.v.* 'Circus Maximus', 236–37.

5 HUMPHREY 1986, 60–4 (the early valley and its deities); 91–5 (temple of the Sun); 95–7 (shrine of Murcia); 258–59 (shrine of Consus). A recent study has explored the relationship between the topography of the valley and some of the performances enacted there (the Consualia, a ritual celebrating Consus as the deity of the storehouse; the Floralia in honour of Flora, whose temple was located at the west end of the valley; and the Lusus Troiae, exploiting the connections of the site with Rome's foundation myth): FAVRO 1999.

6 On *manubiae*: SHATZMAN 1972 and 1975. For the important distinction that *manubiae*, and what they were spent on, did not become the property of the general: CHURCHILL 1999.

7 HUMPHREY 1986, 78–83; DAREGGI 1991.

8 Pliny, *Panegyric of Trajan* 51.3: *sedes nec minus ipsa visenda quam quae ex illa spectabuntur.*

9 Reconstructions and cross-section: CONNOLLY and DODGE 1998, 176, 178, 181.

10 Conflicting figures in the ancient sources: HUMPHREY 1986, 126.

11 Recorded by the Chronographer of AD 354 (*Chronica Minora* ed. Mommsen, p. 148). For the identification of the *partecta*, see HUMPHREY 1986, 115.

12 An entire chapter is devoted to the barrier at HUMPHREY 1986, 175–294 (summarized at 292–94).

13 HUMPHREY 1986, 175. The only instance of *spina* to designate the barrier in the circus is post-antique (Cassiodorus, *Selected Letters* 3.51).

14 IVERSEN 1968, 65–75; RICHARDSON 1992, 273; *Lexicon* III, *s.v.* 'Obeliscus Augusti', 355–56.

15 Re-published with bibliography and masterly discussion at *CIL* 6 Pt. 8 Fasc. 2, under the same number (944).

16 The translation imposes a limitation not present in the Latin, since the supplement *patriis* simultaneously conveys both a strictly Flavian reference ('his father's', i.e. Vespasian's) and a more universal sense ('ancestral').

17 LA ROCCA 1974.

18 CIANCIO ROSSETTO 1987, 44. She goes on to argue that coins depicting this arch with a single *fornix* are a symbolic design, and that the surviving remnants bear out the triple *fornix* represented on the Marble Plan, *Forma Urbis Romae* (*FUR*).

19 Flavian partisanship may have played a considerable role in constructing the predominantly negative view of Nero in the surviving tradition. For a balanced account of the merits and defects of his reign, see GRIFFIN 1984. For a collaborative attempt to reconstruct a positive view, see ELSNER and MASTERS 1994.

20 ZANKER 1997, 27.

21 RAWSON 1981, 15–16 = 1991, 406–7 (Etruscan origins); POTTER 1999, 288 (indigenous developments).

22 Disputed origins of the colours of the factions: HUMPHREY 1986, 137; POTTER 1999, 292. Spectator allegiance: CAMERON 1976.

23 *CIL* 6.10048 = *ILS* 5287; FRIEDLÄNDER 1913, 154–64; POTTER 1999, 296–300. For a translation of the first part of the inscription, see LEWIS and REINHOLD 1966, 230–32.

24 EDWARDS 1997, 75.

25 For a vivid tapestry woven from the ancient sources, see WISEMAN 1980, 12. The equally vivid account of circus spectacles by FRIEDLÄNDER 1908, 19–40, ends with a striking description of the desolate remains of the Circus Maximus in his day.

26 Other mosaics depicting crashed chariots: Lyons (HUMPHREY 1986, Fig. 36) and Gerona (WEEBER 199, Fig. 98).

27 For the view in the ancient literary sources that chariot-racing was an essentially trivial preoccupation of the common man, see WISTRAND 1992, 41–7.

28 The rigging of a 'shipwreck' is most famously attested by Nero's attempt to drown his mother in the Bay of Naples (Tacitus, *Annals* 14.5). The shipwreck is a popular literary and dramatic theme whose presence here blends mime with *venatio*. For dramatic elements fused with the spectacles of the arena see under 'Amphitheatre displays' below.

29 Dio 76.1.4–5, dating the event to the tenth anniversary of Septimius' accession (AD 202). But the same spectacle is reported in the *acta* of the Ludi Saeculares: *L'Année Épigraphique* 1932, 70 = SABBATINI TUMOLESI 1988b, no. 43, with pl. XIII.1. The ship was presumably constructed around the central barrier, which must have remained *in situ*. The seven species comprised lion, lionesses (counted as a separate species), leopards, bears, bison, wild asses, and ostriches. Coin: KÜTHMANN and OVERBECK 1973, no. 71. Fragmentary terracotta mould commemorating the same event: HUMPHREY 1986, 249–50. Discussion and interpretation: HUMPHREY 1986, 115–16; ZANKER 1997, 40–1.

30 HUMPHREY 1986, 540–45; RICHARDSON 1992, 83; *Lexicon* I, *s.v.* 'Circus Flaminius', 269–72. Further bibliography at *Lexicon* V, *s.v.* 'Circus Flaminius', 236.

31 If the designation *Circus* (= 'circle') alludes in this case to its shape, as implied by Varro, *On the Latin Language* 5.154: see WISEMAN 1974a, 3. The western edge of the Circus, presumably limited at first by the *amnis Petronia* (WISEMAN 1974a, 8), may have been extended once the watercourse was diverted into a culvert. The Circus apparently reached as far as S. Salvatore in Campo, if this was the site of the Temple of Neptune that is described *in circo Flaminio* (Pliny, *Natural History* 36.26; *CIL* 6.8423; Livy 28.11.4): see WISEMAN 1976, 45–7.

32 Livy 27.21.1; Cicero, *Letters to Atticus* 1.14.1; *Speech for Sestius* 33; *Speech before the Senate on his return from exile* 13, 17. Cicero says that Pompey addressed a crowd that had gathered on a market-day, from which WISEMAN (1974a, 4) infers that the Circus Flaminius was used for holding a market.

33 The genesis of the *Ludi Plebeii* before the outbreak of the Second Punic War in 218 BC seems to coincide with the construction undertaken in the Circus Flaminius by the distinguished plebeian C. Flaminius in 220 BC: see QUINN-SCHOFIELD 1967; BERNSTEIN 1998, 158–63.

34 Deduced by WISEMAN 1974a, 5 from the designation *in circo Flaminio* to describe buildings erected in this area.

35 Cf. the construction (of a perimeter wall?) attributed to the censor C. Flaminius (Livy, *Periochae* 20: *exstruxit*).

36 WISEMAN 1974a, 4.

37 MAGI 1972/73; HUMPHREY 1986, 545–52; RICHARDSON 1992, 83–4.

38 Presumably from Alexandria, since an earlier inscription underneath the later duplex inscription in honour of the deified Augustus and Tiberius celebrates the construction of a Forum Iulium by Cornelius Gallus, probably to be identified with what became the Forum Augusti at Alexandria: see FRASER 1972, II.96–7 (= I.30 n. 218); GORDON 1983, no. 35; RICHARDSON 1992, 275–76 ('Obeliscus Vaticanus').

39 HUMPHREY 1986, 552–57; RICHARDSON 1992, 87 and Fig. 78; *Lexicon* III, *s.v.* 'Horti Spei Veteris', 85, with Fig. 54 (map of the Horti); *Lexicon* V, *s.v.* 'Circus Varianus', 237–38.

40 RICHARDSON 1992, 272; *Lexicon* III, *s.v.* 'Obeliscus Antinoi', 355.

41 *Chronica Minora* ed. Mommsen, p. 148: *fecit et circum in catecumbas* (locating the Circus opposite the catacombs of S. Sebastiano).

42 IOPPOLO 1980; HUMPHREY 1986, 582–602. This circus also had an obelisk positioned on its *euripus*, not in this case a pharaonic one brought direct from Egypt, but one appropriated from the Iseum Campensis in Rome. The obelisk was Domitianic and fell and broke into pieces after the 4th century. In 1650 it was repaired and re-erected on Bernini's Fontana dei Quattro Fiume in a commensurate position in the Piazza Navona (*Lexicon* III, *s.v.* 'Obeliscus Domitiani', 357–58).

43 BROISE and SCHEID 1993, 147–48, with Fig. 2 (schematic plan of the complex in the Severan period).

44 In the extant *acta* the word *carcer* is attested 22 times in the formula *supra carceres escendit/ascendit* or *e carceribus ... misit*, e.g. *CIL* 6.2065 col. 2 lines 15–40 (at line 36) = *ILS* 5037 = SCHEID 1998, no. 55 = BEARD 1998, 87–8 (AD 87): *sup[r]a carcares escidit (viz. escendit)*.

45 *CIL* 6.2028d.8–10 = SCHEID 1998, no. 12c lines 50–1.

46 HUMPHREY 1986, 567.

47 On the importance of the *ludi scaenici* in forming and preserving Roman identity, see WISEMAN 1995, 129–41. For the role of the theatre in forming an intellectual consciousness among sub-élite groups at Rome, see HORSFALL 1996.

48 Cicero, *Letters to Atticus* 2.19.3: *populi sensus maxime theatro et spectaculis perspectus est ... ludis Apollinaribus Diphilus tragoedus in nostrum Pompeium petulanter invectus est: 'nostra miseria tu es magnus' miliens coactus est dicere* ("Popular sentiment has been most apparent at the theatre and the shows ... At the Games of Apollo the actor Diphilus attacked our friend Pompey quite frankly: "By our misfortune art thou Great" – there were a dozen *encores*").

49 Suetonius, *Augustus* 53.1: *o dominum aequum et bonum!* ("Oh what a fair and excellent master!").

50 WISTRAND 1992, 30–40.

51 Cicero rejects Accius' date of 198 BC for Livius' play and claims to have seen documentary evidence assigning it to 240 BC. The first year of peace after the First Punic War coheres with the tendency for innovations in *ludi publici* to be stimulated by public policy. For a clear exposition of the chronological difficulty see BEARE 1940.

52 The implications of the double venue were first explored by HANSON 1959, 14 and developed by WISEMAN 1974b, 168, interpreting Cicero, *Speech concerning the response of the augurs* 25–6 (the celebration of the *Ludi Megalenses* by P. Clodius as curule aedile in 56 BC). The dramaturgical significance of performing plays in the limited space of a temple precinct is explored by GOLDBERG 1998.

53 The better manuscripts (BV) prefer *και πίων* over *σκιπίων* (C); the less frequently attested 'Caepio' would probably be more easily corrected to 'Scipio' than the other way round.

54 NORTH 1992. If there were two incidents rather than one, the anomalies in the report by Velleius Paterculus 1.15.3 become explicable as a conflation of the two.

55 On the temporary theatres erected 100–50 BC, see Pliny, *Natural History* 34.36; 35.23; 36.5, 50, 114–15, 189; Valerius Maximus 2.4.6. On Scaurus' theatre see RICHARDSON 1992, 385; *Lexicon* V *s.v.* 'Theatrum Scauri', 38–9. On his resourcefulness in acquiring exotica abroad to display on his return to Rome, see COLEMAN 1996, 61–2.

56 GOLVIN 1988, 30–2 and pl. 4.

57 RAWSON 1985, 100, n. 18 = 1991, 472, n. 18.

58 RICHARDSON 1992, 109–10; *Lexicon* II, *s.v.* 'Diribitorium', 17–18. Further bibliography at *Lexicon* V, *s.v.* 'Diribitorium', 242.

59 GROS 1987.

60 Principal literary and epigraphic sources (translated): DUDLEY 1967, 181–84. Overview: RICHARDSON 1992, 383–85; *Lexicon* V, *s.v.* 'Theatrum Pompei', 35–8.

61 Pompey is said to have been inspired by the theatre at Mytilene (Plutarch, *Pompey* 42.4). It has been suggested that he conceived the project upon his return from the East in 62 BC as a venue guaranteeing freedom of expression to the *plebs*, in compensation for the political muzzle applied by the *senatus consultum* banning the *collegia* and *ludi compitalicii* in 64 BC (subsequently restored in 58 BC, three years before Pompey's theatre was dedicated): see FRÉZOULS 1983, 204–7.

62 *Pompeium theatrum*: Augustus, *Res Gestae* 20.1. *Theatrum Pompeianum*: Pliny, *Natural History* 34.40, 36.115; Martial 6.9.1, 10.51.11, 14.29.1, 14.166.1; Suetonius, *Tiberius* 47.1. Other epithets: *Lexicon* V, *s.v.* 'Theatrum Pompei', 35.

63 Pompey's theatre as an approach to the temple: Suetonius, *Claudius* 21.1; Aulus Gellius, *Attic Nights* 10.1.7 (quoting loosely from a letter by Tiro in which the theatre is referred to as *aedes Victoriae*); Tertullian, *On the Spectacles* 10. Sanctuary at Gabii: COARELLI 1987, 11–21, Fig. 3 (reconstructed plan), Fig. 4 (reconstructed view).

64 On *manubiae* see n. 6.

65 CLARIDGE 1998, 214. Exploration of the entire complex involving extensive site survey and selected 'key-hole' excavations at targeted locations has been initiated by Theatron Ltd., based in Coventry, UK; the results are to be continuously updated on the project's website (http://www.theatron.co.uk/romeperm.htm).

66 NASH 1968, II.424, Fig. 1217.

67 CENCETTI 1979, Fig. 19 (outline of the theatre superimposed on the modern street plan), Fig. 25 (photograph of the building corresponding to the apse of the temple); GOLDBERG 1998, 12, n. 35. There may have been more than one shrine in Pompey's theatre: cf. *Inscr. Ital.* xiii 2.493–94 = *Fasti Allifani* for 12 August (sacrifices appointed at five temples *in theatro*), Suetonius, *Claudius* 21.1 (Claudius worshipped in shrines at the top of the auditorium, *apud superiores aedes*), RICHARDSON 1987, 123.

68 Dio 44.16.2; Appian, *Civil War* 2.17.118. Parade of gladiators: VILLE 1981, 72. Porticus as a temporary barracks: *Lexicon* IV, *s.v.* 'Porticus Pompei', 149–50.

69 A tree-lined avenue linking Pompey's theatre and house has been proposed for the parallel lines projecting from the *cavea* on the Marble Plan: RICHARDSON 1987, 126.

70 RICHARDSON 1992, 318–19; *Lexicon* IV, *s.v.* 'Porticus Pompei', 148–49.

71 FAVRO 1994, 157 and n. 22–3.

72 COARELLI 1971/72; FUCHS 1982; KUTTNER 1999.

73 SEAR 1993.

74 GLEASON 1994, 21.

75 PURCELL 1993, 125–26.

76 GLEASON 1990; 1994. For a restored plan of the whole complex, based on the Marble Plan and superimposed upon a modern map, see GLEASON 1994, 16, Fig. 3.

77 Martial 11.47.3–4 (of a sexual deviant called Lattara): *cur nec Pompeia lentus spatiatur in umbra? ... ne futuat* ("Why doesn't he stroll slowly along in Pompey's shade? ... So that he needn't make love"). This association was already current in Pompey's lifetime (Catullus 55.6–7) and was frequently made in the Augustan period (Propertius, *Elegies* 4.8.75; Ovid, *The Art of Love* 1.67–68, 3.387–88).

78 Overview: RICHARDSON 1992, 381–82; *Lexicon* I, *s.v.* 'Crypta Balbi', 326–29; *Lexicon* V, *s.v.* 'Theatrum Balbi', 30–1.

79 ECK 1984.

80 GATTI 1960.

81 RICHARDSON 1992, Fig. 80 (outline of theatre, *cryptoporticus*, *exedra*, and surroundings superimposed on the modern street-plan); *Lexicon* I, Fig. 193 (axonometric drawing of the *exedra* and latrine). On the relationship between the theatre and the Crypta Balbi, see GATTI 1979.

82 Principal literary and epigraphic sources (translated): DUDLEY 1967, 178–80. Overview: SEAR 1989, 53 and Fig. 25; RICHARDSON 1992, 382–83; *Lexicon* V, *s.v.* 'Theatrum Marcelli', 31–5. Plan, cross-section, and external elevation: CLARIDGE 1998, 244, Fig. 113. Reconstruction and cut-away: CONNOLLY and DODGE 1998, 186–87.

83 For the tensions inherent in this imposed order, especially among the fourteen rows reserved for the *equites*, some of whose number had deliberately incurred legal disability so as to perform on the stage, see SLATER 1994, 129–32.

84 For an account of the phases of the excavation, see CALZO BINI 1953; his appendix comprises a valuable digest of the ancient literary sources for this building.

85 *Lexicon* II, Fig. 126a (= *FUR* frg. 31, superimposed on modern street-plan).

86 CIANCIO ROSSETTO 1984.

87 JORY 1996, 6.

88 PURCELL 1999, 185–86.

89 Manoeuvres performed down to the end of the Julio-Claudian period at triumphs, dedicatory ceremonies, funerals, and circus games by the sons of senators and equestrians up to the age of seventeen: FORTUIN 1996, 161–75.

90 A display of the Lusus Troiae in the reign of Claudius is explicitly located in the Circus Maximus (Suetonius, *Claudius* 21.3). The fit between the Lusus Troiae and the cultural overtones of this site is argued by FAVRO 1999, 213.

91 A total of 600 animals would suggest that the majority were hunted in a mass spectacle, so that the suggestion (by RICHARDSON 1992, 383) that this event was staged in the theatre for maximum visibility seems unlikely.

92 Meeting-place of the *collegium scribarum histrionumque*: JORY 1970, 226–27. Summary of the evolution of associations of athletes and stage-performers in the Roman world: POTTER 1999, 265–83.

93 PANSIERI 1997, 752–53.

94 TAYLOR 1937, 285–300.

95 Funerals might seem to be the obvious occasion for *fabulae praetextae*, panegyric pieces glorifying the role in history of the chief protagonist: ZEHNACKER 1983, 47. Recently, however, it has been argued persuasively that they would have derived greater impact from a context such as votive games (performances in fulfilment of a vow), in which the role of the honorand was played alongside a conventional cast of gods and heroes, and before an audience that probably included the honorand himself: FLOWER 1995; PURCELL 1999, 184.

96 Translated sources for the staging of ancient dramatic productions (emphasis on Greek; coverage also of Roman): CSAPO and SLATER 1995. General account of theatrical life at Rome: FRIEDLÄNDER 1908, 90–117.

97 TAYLOR 1937, 301; JORY 1986a, 144. It is impossible to calculate actual totals, which would have to include various types of *munera*, *instaurationes*, and private games of which we have only the most partial evidence.

98 LEBEK 1996, with much interesting detail on the social distinction between writing for the stage, which was respectable, and acting, which was not. For speculation on the social risks of exhibiting one's body for the pleasure of others see EDWARDS 1997, 78–81, 83–5. For a succinct account of the early history of Roman drama, see CONTE 1994, 29–38.

99 JORY 1986a, 147–49.

100 For the mute solo dancer, see JORY 1996 (with the modification that evidence such as Statius' *Agave* demonstrates that there must have been some accompanying *libretto*, perhaps sung by a chorus or delivered by a narrator).

101 *curritur ad vocem iucundam et carmen amicae / Thebaidos, laetam cum fecit Statius urbem / promisitque diem: tanta dulcedine captos / adficit ille animos tantaque libidine volgi / auditur. sed cum fregit subsellia versu, / esurit intactam Paridi nisi vendit Agaven*.

102 BARNES 1996.

103 For a good summary of the controversy between proponents of Samnite and Etruscan origins, see WELCH 1994, 59, n. 3; for extended discussion, see VILLE 1981, 1–51. For a suggested link with Greek culture, see MOURATIDIS 1996.

104 JORY 1986b.

105 See the table at WELCH 1994, 66–7.

106 GOLVIN postulates an irregular shape determined by the different alignment of the two basilicas (1988, 59; WELCH 1994, Fig. 5b); WELCH proposes an oval shape that would be 'proportionally more harmonious ... better suited to the performance requirements of single combat' (1994, 76 and Figs. 6–9).

107 On *maeniana*, see COARELLI 1985, 143–45. For the distinction between these balconies and the Columna Maenia, with which they are often conflated, see *Lexicon* I, *s.v.* 'Columna Maenia', 301–2. On the forum as a setting for formal spectacle see *Lexicon* II, *s.v.* 'Forum Romanum (the Republican period)', 331–32.

108 COARELLI 1985, 222–25.

109 CARETTONI 1959.

110 COLEMAN 1990, 53.

111 For Curio's hybrid 'amphitheatre' concocted from two revolving theatres, see n. 56.

112 EDWARDS 1993, 123–25.

113 VILLE 1981, 70; GOLVIN 1988, 48–9.

114 GOLVIN 1988, 52; RICHARDSON 1992, 11; *Lexicon* I, *s.v.* 'Amphitheatrum Statilii Tauri', 36–7.

115 Suetonius says that the expense was borne by Tiberius' mother and step-father, which suggests that the father whom he was honouring was his natural father, not Augustus: VILLE 1981, 100–1.

116 For the inscription on the paving recording its completion by L. Naevius Surdinus during his praetorship (12 BC?), see NASH 1968, I.397, Fig. 485 (= *CIL* 6.1468, 31662); VERDUCHI 1987, 93–4, Figs. 119 (photograph) and 120 (reconstruction); *Lexicon* II, Fig.169.

117 VILLE 1981, 103; GOLVIN 1988, 58–9.

118 Lack of funds may perhaps be adduced.

119 VILLE 1981, 131–34; GOLVIN 1988, 54; RICHARDSON 1992, 6–7; *Lexicon* I, *s.v.* 'Amphitheatrum Caligulae', 35.

120 GOLVIN 1988, 55–6; RICHARDSON 1992, 10–11; *Lexicon* I, *s.v.* 'Amphitheatrum Neronis', 36. The gorgeously-decorated amphitheatre described by Calpurnius Siculus, apparently a wooden structure (*Eclogue*

7.23–24), has traditionally been identified as Nero's amphitheatre: see TOWNEND 1980, 169–73. For a rival identification as the Colosseum, see CHAMPLIN 1978, 107; BALDWIN 1995, 160–62.

121 ALFÖLDY 1995, 217–22.

122 Despite Flavian propaganda, under Nero there was apparently public access to the grounds of the Domus Aurea, if not to all the buildings: see GRIFFIN 1984, 139–41.

123 ALFÖLDY 1995, 208–10, 212–13. The regular spacing of the first two items in Vespasian's nomenclature (Abb. 3 and 5) is compressed to accommodate Titus' initial (Abb. 4, and Fig. 9 above).

124 ALFÖLDY 1995, 215–16.

125 Evidence for the contemporary designation *amphit(h)eatrum*: *Lexicon* I, *s.v.* 'Amphitheatrum', 30.

126 *FUR* frgs. 13a–o = *Lexicon* I, Fig. 13.

127 Famously quoted by Byron, with cynical comment (*Childe Harold*, 4.145): ""While stands the Coliseum, Rome shall stand; / When falls the Coliseum, Rome shall fall; /And when Rome falls – the World." From our own land / Thus spake the pilgrims o'er this mighty wall / In Saxon times, which we are wont to call /Ancient; and these three mortal things are still / On their foundations, and unalter'd all; / Rome and her Ruin past Redemption's skill, / The World, the same wide den – of thieves, or what ye will."

128 For the theory that the verses quoted by Bede refer not to the building but to the statue (reading *Colossus* instead of *Colisaeus*), see RICHARDSON 1992, 94, *s.v.* 'Colossus Solis (Neronis)'; *Lexicon* I, *s.v.* 'Colossus: Nero', 295–98.

129 CANTER 1930.

130 Principal literary and epigraphic sources (translated): DUDLEY 1967, 142–45. Overview: GOLVIN 1988, 173–80 and pls. 36–7; SEAR 1989, 135–44; RICHARDSON 1992, 7–10; *Lexicon* I, *s.v.* 'Amphitheatrum', 30–5; *Lexicon* V, *s.v.* 'Amphitheatrum', 223; DARWALL-SMITH 1996, 76–90, 215–16; FUTRELL 1997, 152–61; CONNOLLY and DODGE 1998, 190–217, illustrated with detailed photographs and drawings (especially 200–1: reconstructed cut-away section). The monumental impact of the building, even in its ruined state, and the brutality and magnificence of the spectacles that were performed in it, have made the Colosseum into a symbol *par excellence* for the power and futility of human endeavour, variously adapted from different ideological standpoints. For a brief history of its fortunes since Antiquity see FRIEDLÄNDER 1908, 85–90. The first systematic archaeological investigations, and the intrigues that accompanied them, are treated by RIDLEY 1992, 217–37. For the treatment of the Colosseum since the 17th century in literature, painting and (now) photography on both sides of the Atlantic, see VANCE 1989, 43–67; SZEGEDY-MASZAK 1992; LIVERSIDGE and EDWARDS 1996.

131 *Chronica Minora* ed. Mommsen, p. 146: *Divus Vespasianus ... tribus gradibus amphitheatrum dedicavit ... Divus Titus ... amphitheatrum a tribus gradibus patris sui duos adiecit ... Domitianus ... amphitheatrum usque ad clipea (fabricavit)* ("The divine Vespasian ... dedicated the amphitheatre with three levels ... The divine Titus ... added to the amphitheatre two levels starting from his father's three ... Domitian built the amphitheatre up to the shields"). For the theory that the fourth storey was added by Domitian to an original design of three storeys, see GERKAN 1925.

132 Numismatic evidence for sculpture displayed in architectural settings is surveyed by VERMEULE 1977, 103–8.

133 ZANKER 1997, 31–2.

134 SINN and FREYBERGER 1996, No. 8. For a discussion of contemporary representations of the Colosseum, see REA 1988.

135 The most detailed study of the evidence for the city of Rome is by RAWSON 1987.

136 CHASTAGNOL 1966. The corpus of seating-inscriptions from the Colosseum still awaits comprehensive publication and analysis.

137 EDMONDSON 1996.

138 GOLVIN 1988, 182 (Puteoli), 204 (Capua).

139 Clearly described by REA 1996, 137; both purposes (awnings and crowd-control) are adduced by GOLVIN 1988, 179.

140 Detailed discussion of amenities for the spectators: SCOBIE 1988.

141 Frequently illustrated, e.g. HÖNLE and HENZE 1981, 135, Fig. 115; WEEBER 1994, 4, Fig. 3; CONNOLLY and DODGE 1998, 199 (detail).

142 GRAEFE 1979; GOLDMAN 1982; SEAR 1989, 143–44 and Fig. 83.

143 GOLVIN 1988, 172 (Pula), 186 (Nîmes).

144 RICHARDSON 1992, 77–8; *Lexicon* I, *s.v.* 'Castra Misenatium', 248–49, with Fig. 69; *Lexicon* III, Fig. 133.

145 REDDÉ 1986, 451–53. Regular responsibility for maintaining order at public spectacles in the early empire probably devolved upon the Praetorian Guard: BINGHAM 1999. See Coulston in this volume.

146 Reconstructions: SEAR 1989, Fig. 82; CONNOLLY and DODGE 1998, 205–7; BESTE 1999, Fig. 23–4, 26–31.

147 On the aquatic displays in the Colosseum at its inauguration see COLEMAN 1993, 60–2, 63–5. 'Water-ballet' is probably a more accurate designation for the Nereids' pantomime than 'synchronized swimming' (both terms at COLEMAN 1993, 64).

148 GOLVIN 1988, 109–10 and pl. 30 (Mérida: 50 x 7.1 m), 169–71 and pl. 33 (Verona: 36.13 x 8.77 m), 334–36.

149 LOMBARDI 1999, with colour-coded diagrams illustrating the system of water-distribution and drainage.

150 Chronographer of AD 354 = *Chronica Minora* ed. Mommsen, p. 146; *FUR* frgs. 6b–f; COLINI and COZZA 1962 (with an appendix of literary sources and inscriptions); VILLE 1981, 282; GOLVIN 1988, 149–50; RICHARDSON 1992, 236–38; *Lexicon* III, *s.v.* 'Ludus Magnus', 196–97, with Figs. 131–33.

151 Diagram showing the comparative sizes of the two arenas: COLINI and COZZA 1962, Fig. 134. Model of the Ludus Magnus in the Museo della Civiltà Romana, showing the arena and the surrounding porticoes: REA 1996, Fig. 96.

152 Reconstruction and cut-away section: CONNOLLY and DODGE 1998, 209.

153 VILLE 1981, 282–83; GOLVIN 1988, 150–51; RICHARDSON 1992, 238; *Lexicon* III, *s.v.* 'Ludus Matutinus', 197–98. For the location of all four *ludi* relative to one another and to the Colosseum, see RODRÍGUEZ ALMEIDA 1977, 237–42 and Fig. 8 (= *Lexicon* III, Fig. 131); he points out (242) that the name of the Ludus Magnus implies that the others were smaller.

154 RICHARDSON 1992, 236; *Lexicon* III, *s.v.* 'Ludus Gallicus', 196.

155 *FUR* frgs. 142 and 161; RICHARDSON 1992, 236; *Lexicon* III *s.v.* 'Ludus Dacicus', 195–96.

156 VILLE 1981, 283.

157 *FUR* frg. 6a; RICHARDSON 1992, 39; *Lexicon* I, *s.v.* 'Armamentaria', 126, with Fig. 69; *Lexicon* III: Fig. 133.

158 The same concept of a central storage-depot for gladiatorial weapons, albeit probably not in the same location, may go back to the late Republic, if Cicero's reference to *armamentaria publica* during the consulship of Marius in 101 BC refers to gladiatorial equipment (*On behalf of Rabirius, accused of treason* 20): *Lexicon* V, *s.v.* 'Armamentaria publica', 229.

159 RICHARDSON 1992, 366 (whose conjecture that the Spoliarium also functioned as the gladiators' dressing-room is based on a false inference from the meaning of *spoliare*); *Lexicon* IV, *s.v.* 'Spoliarium', 338–39; VILLE 1981, 299–300, n. 172.

160 RICHARDSON 1992, 342 (favouring Samiarium); *Lexicon* IV, *s.v.* 'Saniarium', 233.

161 Malfunctioning equipment (and the added hazard of the emperor's wrath): Suetonius, *Claudius* 34.2: *praeterque destinatos etiam leui subitaque de causa quosdam committeret, de fabrorum quoque ac ministrorum atque id genus numero, si automatum uel pegma uel quid tale aliud parum cessisset* ("apart from those who were meant to be there he also consigned [to the arena], for a trivial reason and on the spur of the moment, people from among the staff of artisans and attendants and people like that, if a machine or a piece of scenery or some such thing did not work properly").

162 RICHARDSON 1992, 374; *Lexicon* IV, *s.v.* 'Summum Choragium', 386–87 (postulating the theory that 'Summum' refers to the size of the establishment).

163 SABBATINI TUMOLESI 1988b (catalogue with tabulated analyses, commentary, and comprehensive indices).

164 Victorious *retiarius* (gladiator armed with a net and trident): *CIL* 6.32261; *theta nigrum*: *CIL* 6.32260a. On the graffiti: SABBATINI TUMOLESI 1988a. On the probable origin of the *theta nigrum* as a barred O representing a Latin abbreviation (*o[biit]*, 'he died', or *[o]bitus*, 'dead') that was later mistakenly interpreted as a Greek *theta* (*θ[ανών]*, 'dead', or *θ[άνατος]*, 'death'), see WATSON 1952.

165 Summary of the arms and equipment of 17 different types of gladiator: FRIEDLÄNDER 1913, 171–80 (= App. XXIX). Gladiatorial graffiti from Pompeii: MAU 1890; COLEMAN 1999a.

166 *CIL* 6.10197 = *ILS* 5089 = Sabbatini Tumolesi 1988b, no. 97: *D(is) M(anibus) / Macedoni thr(aeci) / tiro(ni) Alexandrin(o) / ben(e) mer(enti) fec(it) / armatura thraecum /universa. vix(it) ann(is) XX / men(sibus) VIII dieb(us) XII* ("To the shades of the dead. To well-deserving Macedo, Thracian gladiator, novice, from Alexandria, the whole company of Thracian gladiators erected this monument. He lived 20 years, 8 months, 12 days").

167 Admiration for bravery exhibited in the arena: WISTRAND 1992, 15–29. Legal disability (*infamia*) attaching to stage-performers and gladiators: HORSMANN 1994; EDWARDS 1997, 77–8. Gladiators as a financial investment for their trainers (*lanistae*): POTTER 1999, 311–12. *Tabula* from Larinum (AD 19) banning élite participation in the theatre and the arena: LEVICK 1982; LEBEK 1990 and 1991.

168 For the acquisition of gladiators, their training, and their professional role, see VILLE 1981, 227–334; WIEDEMANN 1992, 102–27; POTTER 1999, 311–23 (summary).

169 *Bestiarius* is the regular term in classical Latin for someone who fights beasts in the arena, as opposed to *venator*, someone who hunts animals in the wild. *Venator* starts to be transferred to the context of spectacle in the 2nd century: the use at Juvenal, *Satires* 4.101 may be intended to draw attention to the disjunction between the man's high status and his participation in the arena; but at Apuleius, *Metamorphoses* 4.13 *venatores* seems unmarked alongside *gladiatores* and *noxii*, comprising the three categories of participant in the arena. Thereafter this usage becomes common, and is reflected in epigraphy: cf. *CIL* 12.1590 *coll(egium) venator(um) ... qui ministerio arenario fungunt*. *Bestiarius* is occasionally applied also to someone who had been condemned to the beasts (VILLE 1981, 465). Seneca uses the terms *ludus bestiariorum* and *ludus bestiarius* (*Letters* 70.20, 22), whereas by the time of Ulpian the penalty *damnatio ad ludum venatorium* is attested (*Digest* 48.19.8.11–2), The distinctions that are proposed between *venator* and *bestiarius* by FRIEDLÄNDER (1913,180) and JENNISON (1937, 194) seem to be based on an unsupported assumption that *venator* is attested of a beast-fighter in the arena throughout the classical period. On animal displays see

JENNISON 1937; BROWN 1992; WIEDEMANN 1992, 55–67; COLEMAN 1996. On the types of animals displayed in the arena: FRIEDLÄNDER 1913, 181–89 (= App. XXX).

170 Execution of criminals: COLEMAN 1990; VISMARA 1990; WIEDEMANN 1992.

171 COLEMAN 1997. The punitive aspect is emphasized by KYLE 1998. For the theory that the spectacles of the arena introduced danger into the middle of the city in order to control it, see PLASS 1995. For a blend of lower-class leisure with aristocratic ideals of military training and the pursuit of hunting, see TONER 1995, 34–52. Links between gladiatorial and military cultures are discussed by COULSTON forthcoming.

172 WALLACE-HADRILL 1990, 145.

173 *Meditations* 6.46: "The shows in the amphitheatre and similar places grate upon you as an everlasting impression of the same sight, and the constant repetition makes the spectacle uninteresting".

174 Funding under the Julio-Claudian emperors: CAVALLARO 1984. Legislation of Marcus Aurelius: OLIVER and PALMER 1955; POTTER 1999, 318–19.

175 On the spread of amphitheatre displays in Italy and the provinces see FRIEDLÄNDER 1908, 82–5.

176 References to the *Liber spectaculorum* follow the numeration in the Teubner edition by D. R. Shackleton Bailey (1990), which is replicated in his edition with facing translation in the Loeb Classical Library (1993). For the literary and historical context, see COLEMAN 1998.

177 All gladiatorial displays (*munera*) and staged hunts (*venationes*) at Rome down to AD 96 are fully documented and discussed by VILLE 1981.

178 COLEMAN 1990.

179 For the manner of distributing gifts or tokens by means of cloth receptacles strung on cables over the spectators' heads, see KILLEEN 1959.

180 COLEMAN 1999b.

181 JONES 1991, 194.

182 Christian attitudes: MACMULLEN 1986, 330–33; CHADWICK 1992. Decline of gladiatorial combat: VILLE 1960; WIEDEMANN 1992, 128–64, and 1995 (canvassing the questionable theory that the Christians saw the arena as a rival means of offering salvation from death). Aristocrats recruiting bodyguards from gladiatorial schools: *Theodosian Code* 15.12.3 (law of AD 399): *si quos e gladiatorio ludo ad servitia senatoria transisse constabit, eos in extremas solitudines amandari decernimus* ("If any persons are proved to have passed from a gladiatorial school into private service with a senator, we decree that they are to be subjected to the most stringent terms of exile"); VILLE 1960: 322–25.

183 DELEHAYE 1933; *Lexicon* I, *s.v.* 'Amphitheatrum', 35.

184 RICHARDSON 1992, 7 and Fig. 78; *Lexicon* I, *s.v.* 'Amphitheatrum Castrense', 35–6; *Lexicon* IV, Fig. 158.

185 RICHARDSON 1992, 361–62; *Lexicon* IV, *s.v.* 'Sessorium', 304–8.

186 For an alternative interpretation, that Domitian wanted to mirror the relationship between his "would-be holy palace (*sacrum palatium*)" and the "quasi-sacred place where Romulus and Remus raced (the Circus Maximus)", see MACDONALD 1982, 68, n. 70.

187 Domitian's *'hippodromos'*: DARWALL-SMITH 1996, 199–201 and Fig. 91; VERMEULE 1977, 51–3 (statuary). Hadrian's 'stadium garden': MACDONALD and PINTO 1995, 767, Figs. 87 (plan), 88 (photograph looking north-east). On the development of this design-feature, see GIERÉ 1986.

188 Overview: FRIEDLÄNDER 1908, 74–6. Detailed discussion: COLEMAN 1993.

189 RICHARDSON 1992, 265; *Lexicon* III, *s.v.* 'Naumachia Caesaris', 338. Further bibliography at *Lexicon* V, *s.v.* 'Naumachia Caesaris', 278.

190 There is no historical record of a naval engagement between Tyre and Egypt. For a discussion of the 'historicizing' atmosphere of naval spectacles at Rome, see COLEMAN 1993, 69–71.

191 In what was to become the Nemus Caesarum after the death of Augustus' grandsons Gaius and Lucius (*Res Gestae* 23). See RICHARDSON 1992, 265; *Lexicon* III, *s.v.* 'Naumachia Augusti', 337. Further bibliography at *Lexicon* V, *s.v.* 'Naumachia Augusti', 278. The site (in Regio XIV) was identified by Lanciani in the area of level ground at the foot of the Janiculum between the churches of S. Cosimato and S. Francesco a Ripa. A rival identification further west near the Porta Portuensis, on what is a blank space on frg. 28 of the Marble Plan (COARELLI 1992, 47), is disqualified on the basis that the space between Via Portuensis and the slope of the Janiculum is too narrow for such a large structure (TAYLOR 1997, 475). Lanciani's conjecture has now been refined to locate the Naumachia more precisely in relation to four ecclesiastical landmarks in modern Trastevere: S. Francesco at the SE corner, S. Crisogono at the NE corner, S. Cosimato along the western edge, and Piazza S. Maria in Trastevere at the NW corner. For a map combining the modern street-plan with the relevant fragments of the Marble Plan see TAYLOR 1997, 478, Fig. 4.

192 Suetonius, *Domitian* 4.2: *effosso et circumstructo iuxta Tiberim lacu* ("a lake was excavated and built up next to the Tiber"). See RICHARDSON 1992, 265–66; *Lexicon* III, *s.v.* 'Naumachia Domitiani', 338. Further bibliography at *Lexicon* V, *s.v.* 'Naumachia Domitiani', 278.

193 Suetonius, *Domitian* 5: *excitavit ... naumachiam, e cuius postea lapide maximus circus deustis utrimque lateribus extructus est* ("He constructed an artificial lake, and afterwards its stone was used to build up the Circus Maximus, which had been burnt down along both sides").

194 As supposed by BUZZETTI 1968, 109.

195 *Notizie degli Scavi*, 1932, 194–96 = *Fasti Ostienses*, fragment recording the period AD 108–113, lines 9–10: *III id. Nov. / [im]p. Traianus naumachiam suam dedicavit*; *Lexicon* III, *s.v.* 'Naumachia Traiani', 338.

196 RICHARDSON 1992, 266; TAYLOR 1997, 480–81.

197 Summary of the evolution of the stadium from its Greek origins to the form attested at Rome: AUPERT 1994.

198 FREDERIKSEN 1984, 353 (Puteoli), map 5 (Naples).

199 For the name of Domitian's contest Latin sources either borrow a Greek term (*Capitolia*/*Καπιτώλεια* or *agon Capitolinus*), or else they use the Latin translation *certamen Capitolinum*: CALDELLI 1993, 1–2.

200 Antoninia Pythia, founded by Elagabalus *c.* AD 119/120: ROBERT 1970, 18–27; CALDELLI 1993, 45–7. Agon Minervae (= agon Athenas Promachou), founded by Gordian III upon his departure for the Persian expedition in AD 242: CALDELLI 1993, 48–50. Agon Solis, founded by Aurelian, AD 274: CALDELLI 1993, 50–2. It is not known whether the agon Herculeus, founded by Alexander Severus at an unknown date in his reign (AD 222–235), was held only once or became a periodic event in the calendar: CALDELLI 1993, 47–8.

201 Literary sources (translated): DUDLEY 1967, 184–85. Detailed study: BOSTICCO 1978. Overview: RICHARDSON 1992, 366–67; *Lexicon* IV, *s.v.* 'Stadium Domitiani', 341–43.

202 KÜTHMANN-OVERBECK 1973, 70–1, no. 135.

203 The specificity of the contests depicted suggests that the coin celebrates a particular occasion. A date of AD 206, suggested by an obverse die link, would coincide with the thirty-first occasion of the Agon Capitolinus, i.e. the one hundred and twentieth anniversary of its foundation, although this does not seem to be an anniversary of sufficient significance to justify such an unusual coin-issue. Alternative anniversaries that the coin may have been commemorating are suggested by DAMSKY 1990, 85–9.

204 Fundamental discussion at FRIEDLÄNDER 1908, 122–30.

205 Some confusion is caused by the ambiguity of the Greek loan-word *athleta* in Latin, which can designate an athlete in general or a boxer (or wrestler) in particular.

206 WISTRAND 1992, 48–54.

207 Categories at the Agon Capitolinus: FRIEDLÄNDER 1913, 264–67 (= App. XLII); CALDELLI 1993, 68–78 (*agon musicus*), 78–82 (*agon equestris*), 83–9 (*agon gymnicus*).

208 Gymnastic contests in the western provinces: FRIEDLÄNDER 1913, 268–70 (= App. XLIV). At Vienne: Pliny, *Letters* 4.22.1–3, 7. South of the gymnasium at Vienne traces of a stadium (as yet unpublished) demonstrate that the contests abolished by Trebonius Rufinus had been a serious undertaking, the legacy of the Greek influence in Gallia Narbonensis. A mosaic and a Severan wall-painting with athletic themes illustrate that the taste for athletics at Vienne survived despite the Domitianic ban (LANDES 1994b, 13, and 306–7, no. 109); but they do not prove that contests were still held there after that.

209 Continuation of the Agon Capitolinus: FRIEDLÄNDER 1913, 267–68 (= App. XLIII).

210 On the introduction of Greek athletic guilds at Rome, and their role in the Agon Capitolinus, see FORBES 1955; PLEKET 1973; POTTER 1999, 276–83 (summary).

211 The Roman *theatrum tectum* or *odeum* is described as "structurally, architecturally, visually and acoustically ... the most versatile and sophisticated, as well as the most successful of the theaters of all kinds, both outdoor and roofed, that have come down to us from classical antiquity": IZENOUR 1992, 169.

212 MEINEL 1980, 299.

213 TAMM-FAHLSTRÖM 1959, 68.

214 PLATNER and ASHBY 1929, 371.

215 RICHARDSON 1992, 276; *Lexicon* III, *s.v.* 'Odeum, Odium', 359–60. Not having been excavated, Domitian's *odeum* is not treated in the most recent study of *odea*, except to be included under 'Partial Listing of Known Roofed Auditorium Sites of Classical Antiquity': IZENOUR 1992, 220–22 (= Appendix H).

216 TRAVLOS 1971, *s.v.* 'Odeion of Herodes Atticus', 378–86; IZENOUR 1992, 136.

217 If the estimate of 100 m for the diameter of the *cavea* of Domitian's *odeum* (*Lexicon* III, *s.v.* 'Odeum, Odium', 360) is restricted to the seating, the corresponding dimension in the *odeum* of Herodes Atticus is 60 m; if it includes the supporting wall at the back, the corresponding dimension is 75 m (both figures calculated from the cross-section at IZENOUR 1992, 138, Fig. 2.13f).

218 This competition is distinct from the Ludi Capitolini, which were games celebrated annually on the Ides of October in the precinct in front of the Temple of Jupiter Feretrius on the Capitoline: *RE* Suppl. V, *s.v.* 'Ludi Capitolini', 607–8.

219 See the catalogue at CALDELLI 1993, 123–61, with the *addendum* at WHITE 1998, 84, n. 1 (= *Epigraphica Anatolica* 17, 1991, 144–49, an inscription honouring the *xystarch* T. Aelius Aurelius Maron, whose achievements on the games circuits of the later 2nd century included two victories at the Agon Capitolinus).

220 WHITE 1998.

221 *IG* 14.2012 = KAIBEL 1878, 250–53, no. 618; cf. *CIL* 6.33976 = *ILS* 5177 = GORDON 1983, 130–31, no. 52 (Latin epitaph only) = CALDELLI 1993, 126, no. 7 (catalogue entry without text).

222 *CIL* 9.2860 = *ILS* 5178 = CALDELLI 1993, 131, no. 17 (catalogue entry without text), pl. 7.

223 *Lexicon* III, *s.v.* 'Horti Maecenatis. "Auditorium"', 74–5, with Fig. 44.

224 Scholiast to Horace, *Satires* 1.10.38: *in aede Musarum ubi poetae carmina sua recitabant* ("in the temple of the Muses where poets used to recite their poetry"); Calpurnius Siculus, *Eclogue* 4.157–59; *Lexicon* I, *s.v.* 'Apollo Palatinus', 54–7. Alternatively, however, it was first suggested by Bentley that the scholiast is referring to the *aedes Herculis Musarum*, where the enclosed courtyard might have been a suitable venue for meetings of the *collegium poetarum* and perhaps also for recitations: TAMM 1961; HORSFALL 1976, 86; *Lexicon* III, *s.v.* 'Hercules Musarum, aedes', 17–19. For the use of the Bibliotheca Ulpia for public recitations in the 7th century see *Lexicon* II, 349.

225 *Lexicon* I, *s.v.* 'Atrium Minervae', 135–36; BOATWRIGHT 1987, 207.

226 BELL 1997.

BIBLIOGRAPHY

ALFÖLDY, G. 1995: 'Eine Bauinschrift aus dem Colosseum', *ZPE* 109, 1995, 195–226.

AUPERT, P. 1994: 'Évolution et avatars d'une forme architecturale', in LANDES 1994a, 95–105.

BALDWIN, B. 1995: 'Better late than early: reflections on the date of Calpurnius Siculus', *Illinois Classical Studies* 20, 1995, 157–67.

BARNES, T.D. 1996: 'Christians and the theater', in SLATER 1996, 161–80.

BEARD, M., NORTH, J. and PRICE, S R.F. 1998: *Religions of Rome. Volume 2: A Sourcebook*, Cambridge, 1998.

BEARE, W. 1940: 'When did Livius Andronicus come to Rome?', *CQ* 34, 1940, 11–19.

BELL, A.J.E. 1997: 'Cicero and the spectacle of power', *JRS* 87, 1997, 1–22.

BERGMANN, B. and KONDOLEON, C. (ed.) 1999: *The Art of Ancient Spectacle*, Washington, 1999.

BERNSTEIN, F. 1998: *Ludi publici. Untersuchungen zur Entstehung und Entwicklung der öffentlichen Spiele im republikanischen Rom*, Stuttgart, 1998.

BESTE, H.J. 1999: 'Neue Forschungsergebnisse zu einen Aufzugssystem im Untergeschoss des Kolosseums', *RM* 106, 1999, 249–76.

BINGHAM, S. 1999: 'Security at the games in the early imperial period', *Échos du Monde Classique* n.s. 18, 1999, 369–79.

BLÜMNER, H. 1918: 'Fahrendes Volk im Altertum', *Sitzungsberichte der Bayerischen Akademie der Wissenschaften* 6, 1918, 3–53.

BOATWRIGHT, M.T. 1987: *Hadrian and the City of Rome*, Princeton, 1987.

BOSTICCO, S., COLINI, A.M. *et al.* 1978: *Piazza Navona, Isola dei Pamphilj*, Roma, 1970.

BROISE, H. and SCHEID, J. 1993: 'Étude d'un cas: le *lucus deae Diae* à Rome', in O. de Cazanove and J. Scheid (ed.), *Les Bois sacrés*, Napoli, 1993, 145–57.

BROTHERS, A.J. 1989: 'Buildings for entertainment', in I.M. Barton (ed.), *Roman Public Buildings*, Exeter, 1989, 97–126.

BROWN, S. 1992: 'Death as decoration: scenes from the arena on Roman domestic mosaics', in A. Richlin (ed.), *Pornography and Representation in Greece and Rome*, New York, 1992, 180–211.

BUZZETTI, C. 1968: 'Nota sulla topografia dell'ager Vaticanus', *Quaderni dell'Istituto di Topografia Antica della Università di Roma* 5, 1968, 105–11.

CALDELLI, M.L. 1993: *L'Agon Capitolinus. Storia e protagonisti dall'istituzione domizianea al IV secolo*, Roma, 1993.

CALZO BINI, A. 1953: 'Il teatro di Marcello. Forma e strutture', *Bollettino del Centro di Studi per la Storia dell'Architettura* 7, 1953, 3–46.

CAMERON, A. 1976: *Circus Factions: Blues and Greens at Rome and Byzantium*, Oxford, 1976.

CANTER, H.V. 1930: 'The Venerable Bede and the Colosseum', *TAPA* 61, 1930, 150–64.

CARETTONI, G.F. 1959: 'Le gallerie ipogee del Foro Romano e i ludi gladiatori forensi', *BullCom* 76, 1959, 23–44.

CAVALLARO, M.A. 1984: *Spese e spettacoli. Aspetti economici-strutturali degli spettacoli nella Roma guilio-claudia*, Bonn, 1984.

CENCETTI, A.M.C. 1979: 'Variazioni nel tempo dell'identità funzionale di un monumento: il teatro di Pompeio', *Rivista di Archeologia* 3, 1979, 72–85.

CHADWICK, H. 1992: 'Augustine and Almachius', in *De Tertullien aux Mozarabes: mélanges offerts à Jacques Fontaine*, Paris, 299–303.

CHAMPLIN, E. 1978: 'The life and times of Calpurnius Siculus', *JRS* 68, 1978, 95–110.

CHASTAGNOL, A. 1966: *Le Sénat Romain sous le règne d'Odoacre: Recherches sur l'Épigraphie du Colisée au Ve Siècle*, Bonn, 1966.

CHURCHILL, J.B. 1999: '*Ex qua quod vellent facerent*: Roman magistrates' authority over *praeda* and *manubiae*', *TAPA* 129, 1999, 85–116.

CIANCIO ROSSETTO, P. 1984: 'Les masques du Théâtre de Marcellus', *Histoire et archéologie. Les dossiers*, 82, April 1984, 94–7.

CIANCIO ROSSETTO, P. 1987: 'Circo Massimo. Il circo Cesariano e l'Arco di Tito', *AL* 8, 1987, 39–46.

CLARIDGE, A. 1998: *Rome. An Oxford Archaeological Guide*, Oxford, 1998.

CLAVEL-LÉVÈQUE, M. 1984: *L'Empire en jeux. Espace symbolique et sociale dans le monde romain*, Paris, 1984.

COARELLI, F. 1971/72: 'Il complesso pompeiano del Campo Marzio e la sua decorazione scultorea', *RendPontAcc* 45, 1971/72, 99–122.

COARELLI, F. 1985: *Il foro romano II: periodo repubblicano e augusteo*, Roma, 1985.

COARELLI, F. 1987: *I santuari del Lazio in età repubblicana*, Roma, 1987.

COARELLI, F. 1992: 'Aedes Fortis Fortunae, Naumachia Augusti, Castra Ravennatium. La via Campana Portuensis e alcuni edifici adiacenti nella pianta marmorea Severiana', *Ostraka* 1, 1992, 39–54.

COLEMAN, K.M. 1990: 'Fatal charades: Roman executions staged as mythological enactments', *JRS* 80, 1990, 44–73.

COLEMAN, K.M. 1993: 'Launching into history: aquatic displays in the early Empire', *JRS* 83, 1993, 48–74.

COLEMAN, K.M. 1996: 'Ptolemy Philadelphus and the Roman amphitheater', in SLATER 1996, 49–68.

COLEMAN, K.M. 1997: '"The contagion of the throng": absorbing violence in the Roman world', *European Review* 5, 1997, 401–17 = *Hermathena* 164, 1998, 65–88.

COLEMAN, K.M. 1998: 'The *liber spectaculorum*: perpetuating the ephemeral', in F. Grewing (ed.), *Toto Notus in Orbe. Perspektiven der Martial-Interpretation*, Stuttgart, 1998, 15–36.

COLEMAN, K.M. 1999a: 'Graffiti for beginners', *Classical Outlook* 46, 1999, 41–7.

COLEMAN, K.M. 1999b: '"Informers" on parade', in BERGMANN and KONDOLEON 1999, 230–45.

COLINI, A.M. and L. COZZA 1962: *Ludus Magnus*, Roma, 1962.

CONNOLLY, P. and DODGE, H. 1998: *The Ancient City. Life in Classical Athens and Rome*, Oxford, 1998.

CONTE, G.B. 1994: *Latin Literature. A History*, Baltimore, 1994.

COULSTON, J.N.C. forthcoming: 'Gladiators and soldiers: personnel and equipment in *ludus* and *castra*', *Journal of Roman Military Equipment Studies*, forthcoming.

CSAPO, E. and W.J. SLATER 1995: *The Context of Ancient Drama*, Ann Arbor, 1995.

DAMSKY, B.L. 1990: 'The stadium aureus of Septimius Severus', *American Journal of Numismatics* ser.2, 2, 1990, 77–105.

DAREGGI, G. 1991: 'Genesi e sviluppo della tipologia del loggiato imperiale nelle raffigurazioni degli edifici circensi', *MEFRA* 103, 1991, 71–89.

DARWALL-SMITH, R.H. 1996: *Emperors and Architecture: a Study of Flavian Rome*, Bruxelles, 1996.

DELEHAYE, H. 1933: 'Recherches sur le légendier Romain. La Passion de S. Polychronius', *Analecta Bollandia* 51, 1933, 34–98.

DODGE, H. 1999: 'Amusing the masses: buildings for entertainment and leisure in the Roman world', in POTTER and MATTINGLY 1999, 205–55.

DUDLEY, D.R. 1967: *Urbs Roma. A source book of classical texts on the city & its monuments selected & translated with a commentary*, Oxford, 1967.

ECK, W. 1984: 'Senatorial self-representation: developments in the Augustan period', in F. Millar and E. Segal (ed.), *Caesar Augustus. Seven Aspects*, Oxford, 1984.

EDMONDSON, J.C. 1996: 'Dynamic arenas: gladiatorial presentations in the city of Rome and the construction of Roman society during the early Empire', in W.J. Slater (ed.), *Roman Theater and Society*, Ann Arbor, 1996, 69–112.

EDWARDS, C. 1993: *The Politics of Immorality in Ancient Rome*, Cambridge, 1993.

EDWARDS, C. 1997: 'Unspeakable professions: public performance and prostitution in ancient Rome', in J.P. Hallett and M.B. Skinner (ed.), *Roman Sexualities*, Princeton, 1997, 66–95.

ELSNER, J. and MASTERS, J. 1994: *Reflections of Nero: culture, history, and representation*, London, 1994.

ÉTIENNE, R. 1965: 'La naissance de l'amphithéâtre: le mot et la chose', *Revue des Études Latines* 43, 1965, 213–20.

FAVRO, D. 1994: 'The street triumphant. The urban impact of Roman triumphal parades', in Z. Çelik, D. Favro, and R. Ingersoll (ed.), *Streets of the World. Critical Perspectives on Public Space*, Berkeley-Los Angeles-London, 1994, 151–64.

FAVRO, D. 1999: 'The city is a living thing: the performative role of an urban site in Ancient Rome, the Vallis Murcia', in BERGMANN and KONDOLEON 1999, 205–19.
FLOWER, H. 1995: '*Fabulae praetextae* in context: when were plays on contemporary subjects performed in republican Rome?', *CQ* n.s. 45, 1995, 170–90.
FORBES, C.A. 1955: 'Ancient athletic guilds', *CP* 50, 1955, 238–52.
FORTUIN, R.W. 1996: *Der Sport im augusteischen Rom: philologische und sporthistorische Untersuchungen (mit einer Sammlung, Übersetzung und Kommentierung der antiken Zeugnisse zum Sport in Rom)*, Stuttgart, 1996.
FRASER, P.M. 1972: *Ptolemaic Alexandria*, I–III, Oxford, 1972.
FREDERIKSEN, M. 1984: *Campania*, Roma, 1984.
FRÉZOULS, E. 1983: 'La construction du *theatrum lapideum* et son contexte politique', in *Théâtre et spectacles dans l'antiquité. Actes du Colloque de Strasbourg 5–7 novembre 1981*, Leiden, 1983, 193–214.
FRIEDLÄNDER, L. 1908: *Roman Life and Manners*, II, translated by J.H.Freese and L.A. Magnus, London, 1908.
FRIEDLÄNDER, L. 1913: *Roman Life and Manners*, IV, translated by A.B. Gough, London, 1913.
FUCHS, M. 1982: 'Eine Musengruppe aus dem Pompeius-Theater', *RM* 89, 1982, 69–80.
FUTRELL, A. 1997: *Blood in the Arena. The Spectacle of Roman Power*, Austin, 1997.
GATTI, G. 1960: 'Dove erano situati il Teatro di Balbo e il Circo Flaminio?', *Capitolium* 35.7, 1960, 3–12.
GATTI, G. 1979: 'Il teatro e la crypta di Balbo in Roma', *MEFRA* 91, 1979, 237–313.
GERKAN, A. 1925: 'Das Obergeschoss des flavischen Amphitheaters', *RM* 40, 1925, 11–50 = Boehringer, E. (ed.), *Von antiker Architektur und Topographie. Gesammelte Aufsätze von Arnim von Gerkan*, Stuttgart, 1959, 29–43.
GIERÉ, A. 1986: *Hippodromos und Xystus*, Zurich, 1986.
GLEASON, K. 1990: 'The garden portico of Pompey the Great. An ancient public park preserved in the layers of Rome', *Expedition* 32.2, 1990, 4–13.
GLEASON, K. 1994: 'Porticus Pompeiana: a new perspective on the first public park of Ancient Rome', *Journal of Garden History* 14, 1994, 13–27.
GOLDBERG, S.M. 1998: 'Plautus on the Palatine', *JRS* 88, 1998, 1–20.
GOLDMAN, N. 1982: 'Reconstructing the Roman Colosseum awning', *Archaeology* 35.2, 1982, 57–65.
GOLVIN, J.-C. 1988: *L'Amphithéâtre romain*, I–II, Paris, 1988.
GORDON, A.E. 1983: *Illustrated Introduction to Latin Epigraphy*, Berkeley, 1983.
GRAEFE, R. 1979: *Vela erunt. Die Zeltdächer der römischen Theater und ähnlicher Anlagen*, I–II, Mainz, 1979.
GRIFFIN, M. 1984: *Nero. The End of a Dynasty*, London, 1984.
GROS, P. 1987: 'La fonction symbolique des édifices théâtraux dans le paysage urbain de la Rome augustéenne', in *L'Urbs. Espace urbain et histoire (Ier siècle av. J.-C. – IIIe siècle ap. J.-C.). Actes du colloque international organisé par le centre national de la recherche scientifique et l'École française de Rome (Rome, 8–12 mai 1985)*, Roma, 1987, 319–43.
HANSON, P.A. 1959: *Roman Theater-Temples*, Princeton, 1959.
HÖNLE, A. and HENZE, A. 1981: *Römische Amphitheater und Stadien. Gladiatorenkämpfe und Circusspiele*, Feldmeilen, 1981.
HORSFALL, N. 1976: 'The collegium poetarum', *BICS* 23, 1976, 79–95.
HORSFALL, N. 1996: *La cultura della* plebs *romana*, Barcelona, 1996.
HORSMANN, G. 1994: 'Die Bescholtenheit der Berufssportler im römischen Recht. Zur Bedeutung von 'artem ludicram facere' und 'in scaenam prodire' in den juristischen Quellen', *Nikephoros* 7, 1994, 207–27.
HUMPHREY, J.H. 1986: *Roman Circuses: Arenas for Chariot Racing*, London, 1986.
IOPPOLO, G. 1980: 'Il circo', in *La Residenza imperiale di Massenzio. Villa, Circo e Mausoleo*, Roma, 1980, 133–38.
IVERSEN, E. 1968: *Obelisks in Exile, I: The Obelisks of Rome*, Copenhagen, 1968.
IZENOUR, G.C. 1992: *Roofed Theaters of Classical Antiquity*, New Haven-London, 1992.
JENNISON, G. 1937: *Animals for Show and Pleasure in Ancient Rome*, Manchester, 1937.
JONES, C.P. 1991: 'Dinner theater', in W.J. Slater (ed.), *Dining in a Classical Context*, Ann Arbor, 1991, 185–98.
JORY, E.J. 1970: 'Associations of actors in Rome', *Hermes* 98, 1970, 224–53.
JORY, E.J. 1986a: 'Continuity and change in the Roman theatre', in J.H. Betts, J.T. Hooker and J.R. Green (ed.), *Studies in Honour of T.B.L. Webster* I, Bristol, 1986, 143–52.
JORY, E.J. 1986b: 'Gladiators in the theatre', *CQ* n.s. 36, 1986, 537–39.
JORY, E.J. 1996: 'The drama of the dance: prolegomena to an iconography of imperial pantomime', in SLATER 1996, 1–27.
KAIBEL, G. 1878: *Epigrammata Graeca ex lapidibus conlecta*, Berlin, 1878, (reprint, Hildesheim, 1965).
KILLEEN, J.F. 1959: 'What was the *linea dives* (Martial, 8.78.7)?', *AJP* 80, 1959, 185–88.
KLOFT, H. 1970: *Liberalitas Principis: Herkunft und Bedeutung. Studien zur Prinzipatsideologie*, Köln, 1970.
KÜTHMANN, H. and OVERBECK, B. 1973: *Bauten Roms auf Münzen und Medaillen: Antike*, München, 1973.

KUTTNER, A.L. 1999: 'Culture and history at Pompey's museum', *TAPA* 129, 1999, 343–73.
KYLE, D.G. 1998: *Spectacles of Death in Ancient Rome*, London, 1998.
LA ROCCA, E. 1974: 'Un frammento dell'Arco di Tito al Circo Massimo', *Bollettino dei Musei Comunali di Roma* 21, 1974, 1–5.
LANDES, C. 1994a: *Le stade romain et ses spectacles*, Lattes, 1994.
LANDES, C. 1994b: 'Les spectacles dans le monde romain, IV: le Stade romain et ses spectacles', in LANDES 1994a, 11–14.
LEBEK, W.D. 1990: 'Standeswürde und Berufsverbot unter Tiberius: Das SC der Tabula Larinas', *ZPE* 81, 1990, 37–96.
LEBEK, W.D. 1991: 'Das SC der Tabula Larinas: Rittermusterung und andere Probleme', *ZPE* 85, 1991, 41–70.
LEBEK, W.D. 1996: 'Money-making on the Roman stage', in SLATER 1996, 29–48.
LEVICK, B. 1983: 'The *senatus consultum* from Larinum', *JRS* 73, 1983, 97–115.
LEWIS, N. and REINHOLD, M. 1966: *Roman Civilization. Sourceboook II: The Empire*, New York, 1966.
LIVERSIDGE, M. and EDWARDS, C. (ed.) 1996: *Imagining Rome: British Artists and Rome in the Nineteenth Century*, London, 1996.
LOMBARDI, L. 1999: 'L'impianto idraulico del Colosseo', in A. Gabucci (ed.), *Il Colosseo*, Milano, 1999, 234–40.
MACDONALD, W.L. 1982: *The Architecture of the Roman Empire*, revised ed., I–II, New Haven, 1982.
MACDONALD, W.L. and PINTO, J.A. 1995: *Hadrian's Villa and its Legacy*, New Haven, 1995.
MACMULLEN, R. 1986: 'What difference did Christianity make?', *Historia* 35, 1986, 322–43.
MAGI, F. 1972/73: 'Il circo Vaticano in base alle più recenti scoperte, il suo obelsico e i suio "carceres"', *RendPontAcc* 45, 1972/73, 37–73.
MAU, A. 1890: 'Iscrizioni gladiatorie di Pompei', *RM* 5, 1890, 25–39.
MEINEL, R. 1980: *Das Odeion. Untersuchungen an überdachten antiken Theatergebäuden*, Frankfurt-Bern-Cirencester, 1980.
MOURATIDIS, J. 1996: 'On the origin of the gladiatorial games', *Nikephoros* 9, 1996, 111–34.
NASH, E. 1968: *Pictorial Dictionary of Ancient Rome*, I–II, London, 1968.
NORTH, J.A. 1992: 'Deconstructing stone theatres', in *Apodosis: Essays presented to Dr. W.W. Cruickshank*, London, 1992, 75–83.
OLIVER, J.H. and PALMER, R.E.A. 1955: 'Minutes of an act of the Roman senate', *Hesperia* 24, 1955, 320–49.
PANSIERI, C. 1997: *Plaute et Rome, ou, Les ambiguités d'un marginal*, Bruxelles, 1997.
PLASS, P. 1995: *The Game of Death in Ancient Rome. Arena Sport and Political Suicide*, Madison, 1995.
PLATNER, S.B. and ASHBY, T. 1929: *A Topographical Dictionary of Ancient Rome*, London, 1929.
PLEKET, H.W. 1973: 'Some aspects of the history of the athletic guilds', *ZPE* 10, 1973, 197–227.
PONTRANDOLFO, A. and ROUVERET, A. 1992: *Le Tombe dipinte di Paestum*, Modena, 1992.
POTTER, D.S. 1999: 'Entertainers in the Roman Empire', in POTTER and MATTINGLY 1999, 256–325.
POTTER, D.S. and MATTINGLY, D.J. (ed.) 1999: *Life, Death and Entertainment in the Roman Empire*, Ann Arbor, 1999.
PURCELL, N. 1993: '*Atrium Libertatis*', *PBSR* 61, 1993, 125–55.
PURCELL, N. 1999: 'Does Caesar mime?', in BERGMANN and KONDOLEON 1999, 181–93.
QUINN-SCHOFIELD, W.K. 1967: 'Observations upon the Ludi Plebeii', *Latomus* 26, 1967, 677–85.
RAWSON, E. 1981: 'Chariot-racing in the Roman Republic', *PBSR* 49, 1981, 1–16 = RAWSON 1991, 389–407.
RAWSON, E. 1985: 'Theatrical life in Republican Rome and Italy', *PBSR* 53, 1985, 97–113 = RAWSON 1991, 468–87.
RAWSON, E. 1987: '*Discrimina ordinum*: the *Lex Julia theatralis*', *PBSR* 55, 1987, 83–114 = RAWSON 1991, 508–45.
RAWSON, E. 1991: *Roman Culture and Society*, Oxford, 1991.
RAWSON, E. 1993: 'The vulgarity of the Roman mime', in H.D. Jocelyn (ed.), *Tria Lustra*, Liverpool, 1993, 255–60.
REA, R. 1988: 'Le antichi raffigurazioni dell'Anfiteatro', in REGGIANI 1988, 23–46.
REA, R. 1996: *Anfiteatro Flavio*, Roma, 1996.
REDDÉ, M. 1986: *Mare Nostrum. Les infrastructures, le dispositif et l'histoire de la marine militaire sous l'Empire romain*, Roma, 1986.
REGGIANI, A.M. (ed.) 1988: *Anfiteatro Flavio. Immagine Testimonianze Spettacoli*, Roma, 1988.
RICHARDSON, L. 1987: 'A note on the architecture of the Theatrum Pompei in Rome', *AJA* 91, 1987, 123–26.
RICHARDSON, L. 1992: *A New Topographical Dictionary of Ancient Rome*, London-Baltimore, 1992.
RIDLEY, R.T. 1992: *The Eagle and the Spade: archaeology in Rome during the Napoleonic era*, Cambridge-New York, 1992.

ROBERT, L. 1970: 'Deux concours grecs à Rome', *CRAI, 1970, 6–27* = *Opera Minora Selecta* V, Amsterdam, 1989, 647–68.

RODRÌGUEZ ALMEIDA, E. 1977: '*Forma Vrbis Marmorea*: nuovi elementi di analisi e nuove ipotesi di lavoro', *MEFRA* 89, 1977, 219–56.

SABBATINI TUMOLESI, P. 1988a: 'Gli spettacoli anfiteatrali alla luce di alcune testimonianze epigrafiche', in REGGIANI 1988, 91–9.

SABBATINI TUMOLESI, P. 1988b: *Epigrafia anfiteatrale dell'occidente romano I. Roma*, Roma, 1988.

SCHEID, J. 1998: *Recherches archéologiques à la Magliana: Commentarii Fratrum Arvalium qui supersunt*, Roma, 1998.

SCOBIE, A. 1988: 'Spectator security and comfort at gladiatorial games', *Nikephoros* 1, 1988, 191–243.

SEAR, F. 1989: *Roman Architecture*, revised ed., London, 1989.

SEAR, F.B. 1993: 'The *scaenae frons* of the theater of Pompey', *AJA* 97, 1993, 687–701.

SHATZMAN, I. 1972: 'The Roman general's authority over booty', *Historia* 21, 1972, 177–205.

SHATZMAN, I. 1975: *Senatorial Wealth and Roman Politics*, Bruxelles, 1975.

SINN, F. and FREYBERGER, K.S. 1996: *Vatikanische Museen. Museo Gregoriano Profano ex Lateranense. Katalog der Skulpturen I.2, Die Grabdenkmäler 2, Die Ausstattung des Hateriergrabes*, Mainz, 1996.

SLATER, W.J. 1994: 'Pantomime riots', *Classical Antiquity* 13, 1994, 120–44.

SLATER, W.J. (ed.) 1996: *Roman Theater and Society*, Ann Arbor, 1996.

SZEGEDY-MASZAK, A. 1992: 'A perfect ruin: nineteenth-century views of the Colosseum', *Arion* ser.3, 2, 1992, 115–42.

TAMM, B. 1961: 'Le temple des Muses à Rome', *Opuscula Romana* 3, 1961, 157–67.

TAMM-FAHLSTRÖM, B. 1959: 'Remarques sur les odéons de Rome', *Eranos* 58, 1959, 67–71.

TAYLOR, L.R. 1937: 'The opportunities for dramatic performances in the time of Plautus and Terence', *TAPA* 68, 1937, 284–304.

TAYLOR, R. 1997: 'Torrent or trickle? The Aqua Alsietina, the Naumachia Augusti, and the Transtiberim', *AJA* 101, 1997, 465–92.

TONER, J.P. 1995: *Leisure and Ancient Rome*, Cambridge, 1995.

TOWNEND, G.B. 1980: 'Calpurnius Siculus and the *munus Neronis*', *JRS* 70, 1980, 166–74.

TRAVLOS, J. 1971: *Pictorial Dictionary of Ancient Athens*, London, 1971.

VANCE, W.L. 1989: *America's Rome*, New Haven, 1989.

VERDUCHI, P. 1987: *L'area centrale del Foro Romano*, Firenze, 1987.

VERMEULE, C.C. 1977: *Greek Sculpture and Roman Taste. The Purpose and Setting of Graeco-Roman Art in Italy and the Greek Imperial East*, Ann Arbor, 1977.

VILLE, G. 1960: 'Les jeux de gladiateurs dans l'empire chrétien', *MEFRA* 72, 1960, 273–335.

VILLE, G. 1981: *La Gladiature en Occident des origines à la mort de Domitien*, Roma, 1981.

VISMARA, C. 1990: *Il supplizio come spettacolo*, Roma, 1990.

WALLACE-HADRILL, A. 1990: 'Roman arches and Greek honours: the language of power at Rome', *Proceedings of the Cambridge Philological Society*, 216 = n.s. 36, 1990, 143–81.

WATSON, G.R. 1952: 'Theta nigrum', *JRS* 42, 1952, 56–62.

WEEBER, K.-W. 1994: *Panem et circenses. Massenunterhaltung als Politik im antiken Rom*, Mainz, 1994.

WELCH, K. 1994: 'The Roman arena in late-Republican Italy: a new interpretation', *JRA* 7, 1994, 59–80.

WHITE, P. 1998: 'Latin poets and the *Certamen Capitolinum*', in P. Knox and C. Foss (ed.), *Style and Tradition. Studies in Honor of Wendell Clausen*, Stuttgart-Leipzig, 1998, 84–95.

WIEDEMANN, T. 1992: *Emperors and Gladiators*, London-New York, 1992.

WIEDEMANN, T. 1995: 'Das Ende der römischen Gladiatorenspiele', *Nikephoros* 8, 1995, 145–59.

WISEMAN, T.P. 1974a: 'The Circus Flaminius', *PBSR* 42, 1974, 3–26.

WISEMAN, T.P. 1974b: 'Clodius at the theatre', in *Cinna the Poet and other Roman Essays*, Leicester, 1974, 159–69.

WISEMAN, T.P. 1976: 'Two questions on the Circus Flaminius', *PBSR* 44, 1976, 44–7.

WISEMAN, T.P. 1980: 'Looking for Camerius: the topography of Catullus 55', *PBSR* 48, 1980, 6–16.

WISEMAN, T.P. 1995: *Remus. A Roman Myth*, Cambridge, 1995.

WISTRAND, M. 1992: *Entertainment and Violence in Ancient Rome. The attitudes of Roman writers of the first century AD*, Göteborg, 1992.

ZANKER, P. 1997: *Der Kaiser baut fürs Volk*, Opladen, 1997.

ZEHNACKER, H. 1983: 'Tragédie prétexte et spectacle romain', in *Théâtre et spectacles dans l'antiquité. Actes du Colloque de Strasbourg 5–7 novembre 1981*, Leiden, 1983, 31–48.

10. Living and Dying in the City of Rome: houses and tombs

John R. Patterson

The population of the city of Rome was vast – perhaps a million inhabitants in the early imperial period[1] – and this meant that housing the living and disposing of the deceased residents of such a metropolis presented significant problems. Concentrating primarily on the last two centuries of the Republic and the first two centuries of the Empire, this chapter examines the ways in which Rome's inhabitants, rich and poor, were provided with the basics of human existence – somewhere to live and a suitable last resting place. In the first half, I will be examining how the housing and burial arrangements of the Romans related to their political and social identity within the city, and how this was affected by the change from a Republican system of government to the principate. In the second, the focus will be on the ways in which family ties, patronage, and membership of *collegia* (professional, religious and social organizations) all contributed in different ways to making both life – and death – more bearable for the inhabitants of the city below the political elite.

The study of the Roman political elite, in terms of the relationships of its members both with each other and with the emperor, has always been a major concern of ancient historians, and the study of the structures of Roman society in a broader sense has in recent years become another focus of particular attention. Significant work has been done on the organization of family life[2] and the role of patronage;[3] while the role of the *collegia* in public and private life, a topic for many years unjustly neglected, is now being re-examined.[4] The study of housing and its social implications at Pompeii has provided illustrations of and models for the understanding of housing arrangements at Rome;[5] at the same time, the upsurge in archaeological activity in Rome during the 1980s, whilst primarily concerned with the public buildings of the city, has also contributed to an improved understanding of the residential areas as well – in so far as the two can meaningfully be distinguished.[6] Several major recent publications have been devoted to the grave-monuments of Rome,[7] and the problems involved in the interpretation of the data provided by tombstones.[8] A study of the links between housing, burial and social structure thus provides an opportunity to examine recent trends in both the historical topography of the city of Rome and the historiography of Roman society. It further allows an insight into the circumstances of the vast majority of the people of Rome, whose lives were individually below the concern of literary authors.

ARISTOCRATIC HOUSES

Aristocratic houses both reflected and contributed to the distinction of their occupant – both in terms of their design and their location.[9] They were typically organized around a central *atrium* where the Roman politician could meet clients and hold informal political meetings. Vitruvius, writing in the Augustan period, comments:

> "for distinguished men who are obliged to fulfil their duty to their fellow citizens by holding public offices and magistracies, we must build lofty vestibules in regal style, and spacious *atria* and peristyles ... also libraries and basilicas comparable with the magnificence of public buildings, because very often public meetings and private trials and judgements take place within their houses" (*On Architecture* 6.5.2).[10]

Pliny the Elder describes how under the Republic the *atrium* was traditionally decorated with reminders of the distinguished past of the family which occupied the house: family trees, wax masks of ancestors, portraits and archive rooms with records of magistrates' achievements.[11] The façade might be decorated with spoils taken from the enemy in battle by earlier occupants of the house, which even a new owner of the property was forbidden to remove (*Natural History* 35.6–7);[12] after Pompey's death, his house in the Carinae district of Rome, which had been decorated with the prows of the pirate ships he had captured in 67 BC, was occupied by M. Antonius, and Cicero drew attention to the discrepancy between the heroic deeds of its former owner and Antonius' debauched lifestyle (*Philippics* 2.68–9).[13] Suetonius tells us that some of the houses destroyed in the great fire of AD 64 still had ancient spoils attached to them (Suetonius, *Nero* 38). In the same way, tradition had it that those aiming at tyranny at Rome were not only punished as individuals; their houses too were destroyed, as a way of blotting out the offender from the collective memory of the community.[14] When Cicero was exiled from Rome in 58 BC for having had the Catilinarian conspirators executed without a formal trial in 63 BC, his house was demolished, and a shrine of Liberty established on the site.[15]

Under the Republic, the homes of wealthy citizens involved in public life tended to be situated near to the centre of political activity in the Forum Romanum. Pompey had a house on the Carinae, Julius Caesar lived in the Subura before becoming Pontifex Maximus (Suetonius, *Julius Caesar* 46.1), and other well-known individuals owned houses on the slopes of the Capitol, including T. Annius Milo (*For Milo* 64), or in the immediate vicinity of the Forum itself. P. Cornelius Scipio Africanus lived in a house on the south side of the Forum, which in 169 BC was demolished to make way for the Basilica Sempronia (Livy 44.16.10).[16] Gaius Gracchus was said to have moved to the Forum area because it was 'more democratic' (Plutarch, *C. Gracchus* 5); and the house of Octavian (before he moved to a house on top of the Palatine hill which had formerly belonged to the celebrated orator Q. Hortensius Hortalus), was also located by the Forum above the *scalae Anulariae* (Suetonius, *Augustus* 72).[17] However, it was the Palatine which, in the last century of the Republic, was the pre-eminent location for aristocratic residence. The topography of the summit of the hill in republican times is difficult to reconstruct because of the impact of the later imperial palaces on the site, but the remains of several republican houses, for example the 2nd century 'House of the Griffins', and the 1st century 'Aula Isiaca', have been discovered underneath the Flavian Palace.[18]

Excavations conducted by Carandini on the slopes of the Palatine during the 1980s (down the hill from where the later Arch of Titus stands) have revealed the remains of an impressive house, which has convincingly been identified with that of M. Aemilius Scaurus (aedile in 58 BC).[19] We know from Asconius' commentary on Cicero's speech *For Scaurus* that Scaurus' house, famous in antiquity for its lavish scale and decoration, was to be found "on that part of the Palatine which is located when you come down the Via Sacra and take the first turning on the left side" (Asconius 27C), and the house excavated does indeed stand at the junction of the Via Sacra and the road leading up to the summit of the Palatine hill.[20] In 53 BC, the house was purchased by Scaurus' next-door neighbour P. Clodius Pulcher (tribune in 58 BC) for the enormous sum of 14,800,000 *sestertii* (Pliny, *Natural History* 36.103).[21] On the other side of Clodius' house was the property which had once belonged to M. Livius Drusus (tribune in 91 BC) and had been acquired in 62 BC by Cicero, who had moved here from the Carinae;[22] and Cicero was followed in his move to the Palatine by his brother Quintus, who had by 59 BC acquired the property next door to Cicero's (Cicero, *Letters to Atticus* 2.4.7).[23] Clodius' house had evidently been in the family for generations, so he was able to sneer at Cicero for having bought a house, as opposed to having inherited it (Cicero, *Letters to Atticus* 1.16.10); and excavations do indeed suggest that houses may have existed on the site since the 6th century BC.[24] It was apparently not uncommon for such fierce political rivals to live close to each other: Pliny the Elder records a dispute between the censors of 92 BC, Cn. Domitius Ahenobarbus (who was notorious for his bad temper) and L. Licinius Crassus, whom Domitius accused of having too lavish a house (*Natural History* 17.1–4). The house in question seems to have been part of the property on the slopes of the Palatine subsequently owned by Scaurus, while the remains of a Republican house found beneath the Hadrianic Temple of Venus and Rome have now been identified with that of Ahenobarbus,[25] so it seems that the two censors owned properties on opposite sides of the Via Sacra. Neighbours might not always be enemies; Cicero paints a pathetic picture of the dying Q. Caecilius Metellus Celer beating on the party wall connecting his house with that of his late neighbour, Q. Lutatius Catulus, and calling his name (Cicero, *For Caelius* 59) – but competition between Roman aristocrats was probably exacerbated and certainly more overt because they tended to live close to one another. Indeed, the increasingly bitter political rivalry of the 1st century BC was reflected in the building of more and more lavish houses, often formed by acquiring neighbours' dwellings and combining them:[26] Pliny notes that the home of M. Aemilius Lepidus, the finest in Rome in 78 BC, was only thirty-five years later not even in the first hundred (*Natural History* 36.110).

The advent of the principate brought about significant changes in patterns of aristocratic housing, but this was a gradual process. Augustus' residence took in a number of houses on the Palatine in addition to that of Hortensius (Velleius Paterculus 2.81.3), and eventually the imperial palace, extended by successive emperors, came to occupy the whole of the hill.[27] Some areas around the Forum continued to be occupied by aristocratic housing in the Julio-Claudian period, such as the site overlooking the Forum adjacent to the Porta Fontinalis where Cn. Piso was living in AD 20 (Tacitus, *Annals* 3.9.3),[28] and we hear that Salvidienus Orfitus (consul in AD 51) was put to death for letting out *tabernae* near his house by the Forum to foreign states (Suetonius, *Nero* 37). Likewise senators continued to occupy in significant numbers the slopes which led up to the Palatine from the Forum – the area in which the houses of Scaurus, Clodius, Cicero and others were to be found under the Republic.[29] For example, we know that Cicero's house came into the possession of L. Marcius Censorinus; by AD 30 it was owned by Sisenna Statilius Taurus (Velleius Paterculus 2.14.3).[30] Similarly, the house of Aemilius Scaurus was eventually acquired by C. Caecina Largus, consul in AD 43 (Asconius 27C; Pliny, *Natural History* 17.5).[31] The great fire in AD 64, however, destroyed many of the buildings around the Palatine (Tacitus, *Annals* 15.41), and Nero's subsequent construction of the Domus Aurea, which extended the imperial residence from the Palatine to the Oppian hill, had the effect of largely removing the housing of individual senators from these areas. Even when parts of the Domus Aurea were destroyed by Nero's successors, the land it occupied was given over to public monuments rather than to private housing. Carandini's excavations show that between AD 70 and AD 90 the house of Scaurus was replaced with a *horreum* (storage-building), perhaps to be connected to the construction of the nearby Colosseum.[32]

Under the High Empire aristocratic houses were, it appears, increasingly located on hills which lay further away from the political centre of the city: senatorial properties are known to have been located on the Lateran (which itself took its name from the estates of the Plautii Laterani), the Caelian (including that of L. Marius Maximus Perpetuus Aurelianus) and the Aventine (which in the Republic was principally thought of as an area of plebeian housing, but now included the houses of the 2nd century consuls L. Licinius Sura and L. Fabius Cilo; the latter residence became at a later period the church of S. Balbina).[33] The Quirinal too appears to have been particularly densely populated with the houses of the wealthy, including T. Pomponius Bassus and T. Avidius Quietus.[34] Pliny the Younger lived in a property on the Esquiline near the Porticus Liviae, which has now been identified on a fragment of the Marble Plan of Rome; nearby lived L. Arruntius Stella and the Neratii, an influential consular family from Saepinum in Samnium.[35] Those wealthy individuals who chose not to live on the Palatine had always been dispersed across the city, surrounded by the houses and workshops of their clients and freedmen in the pattern familiar from Pompeii, and this continued to be true into the imperial period.[36] This greater geographical spread can be seen not only as a consequence of the encroachment of the imperial palace on traditional areas of aristocratic housing, but perhaps also the declining need for senators to be involved in day-to-day political activity in and around the Forum, which under the Republic had been a major element in their day's programme. There were still regular meetings of the senate in the Curia, but now elections were conducted in the senate, so it was necessary to canvass fellow senators discreetly, rather than to seek the support of members of popular assemblies publicly on the streets of Rome. In the early imperial period, the requirements of a wealthy man's house were much as they had been under the Republic. Patronage over ordinary voters was no longer of any great political importance (if it ever had been);[37] now the patronage which counted was that which emanated from the imperial palace.[38] Nevertheless the reception of clients by patrons was still an essential element in day-to-day social relations, and houses had to be spacious and impressive enough to cope with influxes of visitors, grand and humble. As Tacitus put it: "the more impressive a man's wealth, house and apparel, the more his name and *clientela* became more eminent" (*Annals* 3.55). Even in the Severan period, unaltered *atrium*-type houses are still visible on the Marble Plan (Fig. 10.1);[39] the house on the Cispian which has produced celebrated frescoes depicting scenes from the Odyssey seems not to have been significantly altered between the 1st century BC and the 3rd century AD, and it may well have continued to belong to the Papirii, a distinguished and ancient noble family.[40] Statues and inscriptions were under the empire increasingly erected in the honorand's house, rather than in a public space: a statue was set up to L. Cornelius Pusio, consul in the early 70s AD, in his house on the Quirinal by a centurion of the Sixteenth Legion who had served under his command in Germany.[41] There are, however, some indications even in the 1st century AD of a trend towards a decreasing emphasis on the *atrium* in domestic design, and greater emphasis placed on peristyles and rooms for entertainment;[42] by the 4th century, the chief room in a wealthy house – such as that of Junius Bassus on the Esquiline, or the late antique *domus* under S. Pietro in Vincoli – tended to be a massive audience room, often apsidal in design, which reflects the greater formalization of patronage rituals in late antiquity.[43]

Fig. 10.1: Residential area on the Viminal depicted on the Forma Urbis. *Three houses with atrium and peristyle indicated (Modified from Rodriguez-Almeida 1981).*

Wealthy men who had retired from politics for ideological or practical reasons in the latter years of the Republic – such as Lucullus or Sallust – sometimes took up residence in *horti*.[44] These were luxurious residences set in gardens which lay in the *suburbium* of Rome, beyond the Servian wall and the *pomerium*, which allowed them both to live in grand style in a marginally more discreet way than was possible in an urban *domus*, and symbolically to distance themselves from the sordid competitiveness of political life.[45] Lucullus, who had acquired enormous wealth during his campaigns in the East (and also owned substantial properties on the Bay of Naples and at Tusculum), led the way in this respect, with his creation of the Horti Lucullani on the Pincio (Plutarch, *Lucullus* 39), and others followed, like Sallust's Horti Sallustiani to the north of the Quirinal.[46] Under Augustus and his successors, *horti* became an increasingly popular form of residence for affluent (and influential) members of the senatorial elite such as Statilius Taurus, L. Aelius Lamia, and others close to the imperial family like Maecenas, whose gardens on the Esquiline were built over the city wall and an old cemetery for the poor (Horace, *Satires* 1.8.14–6).[47] Many of the *horti*, however, soon came under the control of the emperors themselves, whether by gift, legacy or confiscation. In AD 38, we hear of Caligula receiving a Jewish embassy from Alexandria in the Horti Lamiani on the Esquiline (Philo, *Embassy to Gaius* 351–52); the Horti Sallustiani were (according to Dio's portrayal) Vespasian's favoured residence in the city (Dio 65.10.3).[48] In the 2nd century, some of the wealthiest senators, who had often originated from outside Italy, preferred to live in suburban properties even more distant from the centre of the city, such as the Villa of the Quintilii on the Via Appia (Fig. 10.2) and the Sette Bassi and Santo Stefano villas off the Via Latina.[49] In an era characterized by potentially jealous and unpredictable emperors, there were obvious attractions in maintaining a comparatively low profile in the city; but many of these villas, like the *horti* before them, had fallen into imperial hands by the end of the 2nd century AD.

Fig. 10.2: General view of the Villa of the Quintilii on the Via Appia (Photo: editors).

Fig. 10.3: Relief from Amiternum depicting the funerary procession of a member of the elite (Museo Archeologico di L'Aquila: I.N. 30.516).

ARISTOCRATIC FUNERALS AND TOMB-MONUMENTS

In many significant ways, the treatment of the Roman dead seems to have reflected their roles and activities when alive.[50] These links between burial and social status can be seen most clearly in the case of Roman senators. Like their housing arrangements, the funerary rituals of Roman aristocrats reflected their role as public figures with an identity primarily defined by their political role.[51] Polybius, a Greek historian living at Rome in the mid-2nd century BC, gives a fascinating description of the funeral of a Roman aristocrat (6.53–4), while the depiction of a funeral procession on a relief from the central Italian town of Amiternum, probably of late republican date, seems to have been influenced by Roman elite practice, and provides a graphic illustration (Fig. 10.3).[52] The deceased would be laid out in the *atrium* of his house (where he had received his clients when alive) and then a procession of relatives and friends would set out for the Forum, accompanied by musicians and actors wearing masks representing eminent members of his family, with insignia and ceremonial dress appropriate to the offices they had held when alive. There, the procession would stop at the *rostra*, where the deceased would be propped up, and a funeral oration would be delivered to the crowd (and the images of his ancestors, now sitting on ivory chairs) by his son or other close male relative. Afterwards, the cortège would continue to the family tomb, where the cremation or burial would take place.[53]

The earliest cemeteries at Rome had been located on the fringes of the scattered communities which they served. When these disparate settlements coalesced to form the city that was Rome, the cemeteries were abandoned (the so-called Sepulcretum on the edge of the Forum for example, located in front of the Temple of Antoninus and Faustina) in favour of other *necropoleis*, notably beyond the walls on the Esquiline hill. Burial within the *pomerium*, the sacred boundary of the city, was only permitted in highly exceptional circumstances (Cicero, *On the Laws* 2.58). We know of only a handful of families who had been granted this privilege by special dispensation during the Republic, notably those of Valerius Publicola (one of the first consuls of the Republic) and C. Fabricius Luscinus (noted for his victories in southern Italy in the 3rd century BC, and for his celebrated austerity)[54], but it appears that (by the imperial period at least) the honour was purely a ceremonial one and the physical burial or cremation took place elsewhere (Plutarch, *Publicola* 23; *Roman Questions* 79). The right to be buried within the *pomerium* was granted to Julius Caesar by the senate (Dio 44.7.1), but in the event he was to be buried in the tomb of his daughter Julia on the Campus Martius. The Column of Trajan, where that emperor's ashes were deposited, was however within the *pomerium* (Eutropius, *Breviarium* 8.5),[55] and it seems that Domitian too was secretly buried in the Temple of the Gens Flavia, again within the city (Suetonius, *Domitian* 1.17).[56]

Individuals of particular distinction might, by decree of the senate, be granted a place of burial or an honorary monument on the Campus Martius.[57] Those so honoured included the Scipio brothers, killed in Spain in 211 BC (Silius 13.658–60), Sulla (Plutarch, *Sulla* 38; Appian, *Civil War* 1.106), Julia, Caesar's daughter and Pompey's wife (who was buried there without proper approval: Dio 39.64), and Aulus Hirtius and C. Vibius Pansa, consuls of 43 BC, who both met their deaths at the battle of Mutina.[58] Another favoured location for burial of this kind was the Campus Esquilinus, just outside the Porta Esquilina (Cicero, *Philippics* 9.17), and it may be that the 3rd century BC Esquiline tomb of the Fabii or Fannii, decorated with military scenes, was an example of such an honorific burial.[59]

Aristocratic families often had their own traditional burial places; the Tomb of the Claudii, for example, was located below the Capitol near the Campus Martius (Suetonius, *Tiberius* 1).[60] Some of these tombs seem to have been set up in locations where the deceased's family had property; the Tomb of Ser. Sulpicius Galba (the consul of 144 BC or 108 BC) was close to the family's warehouses, the *Horrea Galbana* below the Aventine.[61] Aristocratic tombs were very often located along the main roads leading out of the city: the family monuments of the Claudii Marcelli, the Servilii, the Metelli (Fig. 10.4), of Atilius Calatinus (victor in the First Punic War) and, most notably, the Scipios (Fig. 10.5), were located in a small area close to and between the Via Appia and the Via Latina outside the Porta Capena (Cicero, *Tusculan Disputations* 1.7.13).[62] Not far away, but away from the Via Appia, was the Tomb of P. Cornelius Scapula (consul in 328 BC), suggesting that the Cornelii may have had estates here even before the construction of the road in 312 BC.[63] Like their houses on the Palatine, the tombs of the aristocracy on the Via Appia were clustered together, expressing their rivalry in death as well as in life. The Tomb of the Scipios, excavated in the 18th century and still visible beside the Via Appia, revealed a series of sarcophagi of members of the family from Cn. Cornelius Scipio Barbatus (cos. 298 BC) onwards, with inscribed texts recording their victories and other achievements (Fig. 10.6). Tombs of the mid-Republic seem normally to have been modest in external appearance; the sarcophagi would have been visible only to those entering the monument, it seems. However, the exterior was often embellished later as political competition became stronger and styles of ornamentation derived from the hellenistic world were increasingly employed.[64] The exterior of the Tomb of the Scipios appears to have been remodelled in this way in the mid-2nd century BC, presumably in the context of the political rivalries of that time.[65]

Like their houses, then, the tombs of Roman aristocrats can be seen to reflect the competitive ethos of the republican senate in the commemoration of the achievements of individuals within the context of the family.[66]

Similarly, the advent of the principate led to some subtle changes in the form of funerary commemoration adopted by members of the Roman elite. Ancestor masks continued to be

Fig. 10.4: Mausoleum of Caecilia Metella on the Via Appia (Photo: editors).

Fig. 10.5: Fresco depicting military figures (shown waist-downwards) on the façade of the Tomb of the Scipios, scale 30 cm (Photo: editors).

displayed at funerals into the imperial period: the masks of twenty distinguished families were carried at the funeral of Junia Tertia in AD 22 (Tacitus, *Annals* 3.76), and there are indications that the practice continued into the 2nd century AD.[67] However, the impressive *tumuli* which were frequently constructed by wealthy Romans in the third quarter of the 1st century BC (the best-known example is the Tomb of Caecilia Metella on the Appian Way; Fig. 10.4) were little used in and around Rome after the construction of Augustus' massive Mausoleum on the Campus Martius, though they continued to be found in Italian cities into the 1st century AD.[68] Presumably competition by senators over the scale of tombs was no longer feasible (or advisable) in the capital, though there are a few exceptional examples of tombs in the old ostentatious style dating from the Augustan period, notably the pyramid-shaped monument of C. Cestius, built between 18 and 12 BC on the Via Ostiensis (Fig. 10.7).[69] Instead, the senatorial tombs of the early empire often tend to be smaller in scale (for example the Tomb of Minicius Fundanus on Monte Mario, and that of the Calpurnii on the Via Salaria[70]), while another tendency which prevailed from the Augustan period onwards was for tombs to become more inclusive, providing spaces for the burial of members of the extended family of slaves and freedmen as well as the members of the nuclear family for whom the late-republican *tumulus*-style tomb was normally reserved. In general, tombs of the empire tended to be more

Fig. 10.6: Sarcophagus of L. Cornelius Scipio Barbatus, Rome (after Nash 1968. By permission of Ernst Wasmuth GMbH).

Fig. 10.7: Pyramid of Cestius, built c. 18–12 BC (Photo: editors).

restrained in their exterior appearance and more lavishly decorated inside than their late republican predecessors; and often they were located away from major roads, suggesting that visibility was less of a priority than in former times.[71] This may reflect not only the changed political circumstances of the early empire, but also a cyclical pattern of funerary commemoration in which the senators began to prefer a rather more understated form of monument, and left the more ostentatious type of monument to the upwardly mobile.[72] Several major tombs of the Augustan era (e.g. those of the Statilii Tauri or of Maecenas) were located close to the *horti* in which the deceased lived when alive.[73]

THE POOR AND THE NOT-SO-POOR

At the other end of the social scale, the squalid conditions endured by the very poorest in Rome were likewise reflected both in housing provision and death-ritual.[74] The destitute seem to have 'lived rough'; late imperial evidence suggests that they lived either in shacks around the city, under the awnings of the theatre, or in tombs (Ammianus Marcellinus 14.6.25; *Digest* 47.12.3.11), and we must imagine that the same may have been true under the Republic too. The poorest citizens – those without the means to afford an individual burial, or those without ties of family or friendship which would allow the organization of funeral arrangements – might be buried in mass graves such as those on the Esquiline, especially when epidemic or other disaster struck the densely packed urban population or at times of high seasonal mortality.[75] Those slightly more fortunate seem to have been buried in graves marked by tiles or *amphorae* such as those found in the cemetery of Portus at Isola Sacra near Ostia (Fig. 10.8);[76] but the anonymity and horror of a pauper's burial persisted into the empire: Martial paints a grim picture of a party of *vespillones* (corpse-bearers) carrying a body "like a thousand that the pauper's pyre receives" (Martial, *Epigrams* 8.75). The body of the assassinated emperor Domitian was similarly carried away on a simple stretcher by the *vespillones* (Suetonius, *Domitian* 17). How the bodies of the indigent were disposed of under the Empire is still somewhat mysterious; the most likely possibility is that the mass graves which characterized the Esquiline under the Republic (in an area which had largely been taken over by *horti* by Augustus' time) were replaced by public crematoria.[77]

The vast majority of the population must of course have occupied a position somewhere between the wealthy political class on the one hand and the destitute on the other. Tacitus, in an analysis of reactions in the city of Rome to the death of Nero, drew a distinction between what he described as the *pars populi integra* (the "respectable element of the population") which he represents as pleased at the demise of the emperor, and the *plebs sordida* ("the filthy plebs") which was "gloomy and eager for rumours" (*Histories* 1.4). Pliny, likewise, in a discussion of the spread of a disease known as *mentagra*, observes that the nobles were primarily affected rather than the slaves or *plebes humilis aut media* "the lower or middling classes of the urban population" (*Natural History* 26.3). Both writers were of course analyzing the *plebs* from an aristocratic perspective,[78] but there were clearly vast differences in wealth and social location between the different elements in the *populus Romanus*, and it is the upper element within this middle group about which we tend to know most, in particular from the archaeology of tombs and from epigraphy. Here too there are close links between burial practice and social identity.

Many tombs from Rome either record the deceased's profession in an inscription, and/or depict it in sculptural form.[79] Perhaps the best known of these (and certainly one of the most ostentatious) is the Tomb of M. Vergilius Eurysaces (30–20 BC) located between the Via Praenestina and Via Labicana next to the Porta Maggiore, in the form of a granary (Fig. 10.9). It was decorated with a frieze showing scenes in a bakery, and statues of Eurysaces and his wife Antistia (*CIL* 1^2.1203–5 = *ILS* 7460a–c = *ILLRP* 805).[80] Similarly, the tomb of the celebrated 2nd century AD charioteer P. Aelius Gutta Calpurnianus (*CIL* 6.10047 = *ILS* 5288), which stood on the Via Flaminia, depicted a *quadriga* (four-horse chariot) and horses.[81] On a less lavish scale, several tombs from Isola Sacra depict scenes of trade or manufacture.[82] The Tomb of Verria Zosime and Verrius Euhelpistus (no. 29) shows scenes of tool-making in a blacksmith's forge (Fig. 10.10),[83] while no. 78, the Tomb of Ti. Claudius Eutychus and Claudia Memnon, depicts a boat and grain mill; presumably Claudius Eutychus was involved in the import and milling of grain (Figs. 10.11 & 10.12).[84] Similarly, the monument of Naevoleia Tyche and C. Munatius Faustus in the cemetery outside the Herculaneum gate at Pompeii[85] depicts both a ship and the *bisellium* (an honorific chair) with which Munatius Faustus was honoured by the *decuriones* of the city. Perhaps the most striking example of the 'autobiographical' tomb, however, comes from literature. Petronius' *Satyricon* provides us with a fictional (and satirical) account of the tomb of a wealthy freedman – Trimalchio. In the latter stages of a lavish banquet held at Trimalchio's house, known as the *Cena Trimalchionis,* the host tells his guests about the tomb he has designed for himself. It will depict Trimalchio's pet dog, famous gladiatorial fights, ships in sail (trade was the source of Trimalchio's wealth), and Trimalchio himself wearing the *toga praetexta* and five gold rings distributing money to the people; there will be a dining room with couches, with the people enjoying a meal, "and let there be a sundial in the middle, so that anyone who looks at the time will read my name whether he likes it or not" (*Satyricon* 71). The whole tomb thus reflects Trimalchio's career as shipowner, Augustalis, and benefactor (as well as his vanity and tasteless ostentation).[86] The large and impressive tomb found near Chieti of C. Lusius Storax, a *sevir* of the mid-1st century AD, decorated with a bust of the deceased and a depiction of Storax presiding at a gladiatorial show with the magistrates and councillors of his city,[87] shows that commemoration of the type favoured by Trimalchio was not solely a figment of Petronius' imagination. Nevertheless the scale and ostentation of the individuals mentioned here should not be seen as typical of freedmen as a whole. Freedmen were keen to be commemorated on stone and with a permanent tomb-monument, probably to draw attention to their newly

Fig. 10.8: Isola Sacra cemetery, Portus: tile and amphora *graves (Photo: editors).*

Fig. 10.9: Tomb of Eurysaces, Rome, built c. *30 BC (Photo: author).*

Fig. 10.10: Isola Sacra cemetery, Portus: tomb no. 29 (Photo: author).

acquired citizen status, and indeed a disproportionate number of funerary inscriptions at Rome are erected by or for ex-slaves; but most of their monuments were comparatively restrained. The early 1st century BC tombs on the Via Caelimontana found in the grounds of the Villa Wolkonsky at Rome aimed at similarity instead of idiosyncrasy.[88]

These examples illustrate the close links which can be identified between social identity and funerary practice even below the political elite, the identity of whose members was perceived as primarily political. For ex-slaves, by contrast, their sense of identity was more likely to be linked with their profession, as they were unable to engage in formal political activity or take on public office (and even involvement in the imperial

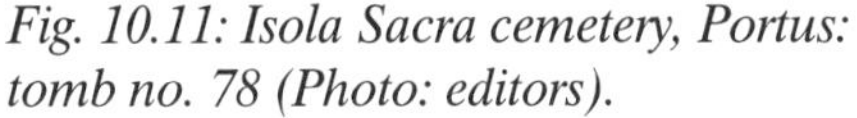

Fig. 10.11: Isola Sacra cemetery, Portus: tomb no. 78 (Photo: editors).

Fig. 10.12: Isola Sacra cemetery, Portus: façade of tomb no. 78. Detail of plaque depicting a grain mill (Photo: author).

cult was excluded in the capital, by contrast with the towns of Italy where they could serve as *seviri*).[89] But as well as illuminating the social identity of individual citizens, the pattern of commemoration also illustrates the importance of three institutions which were of major importance in the social integration of the *plebs* in the city of Rome: the family, patronage and the *collegia*. The remainder of this chapter examines their role in the provision of housing and burial for the urban populace.

HOUSING, BURIAL AND THE FAMILY

At Rome, as in pre-industrial societies generally, the family was central to the life of the individual and the community, and this seems to have been particularly true in respect both of housing and burial. Even the terminology used in Latin implies the close association of the concepts of 'family' and 'home' for the Romans; as Saller demonstrates, the word *domus* can mean not only 'the physical house' but also 'the household', 'the kinship group' and the 'patrimony'.[90] Many Roman families must have been of the nuclear type (i.e. husband, wife and children), largely because the effects of high mortality rates and consequent low level of life expectancy at Rome would have meant that few families would have had more than two generations living at the same time,[91] though other forms of 'extended' family must have existed too. Some families composed of brothers living together are attested in literature – for example, the case of the young M. Licinius Crassus who lived with his parents and his married brothers (Plutarch, *Crassus* 1) – but these seem to be mentioned because they were exceptional, at least among the upper classes.[92] However, it is possible that such arrangements might have been more widespread on small family-run rural estates, or in urban workshops. Similarly, divorce, death and remarriage might have led to a situation in which (for example) children of a single father by two successive wives might live under the same roof, and nurses and others loosely attached to the nuclear family might also live in the household.[93] Besides, for the Romans, the *familia* included slaves and ex-slaves as well as direct relations of the *paterfamilias*. Their

Fig. 10.13: Isola Sacra cemetery, Portus: general view of the tombs (Photo: editors).

inclusion would in practice have meant that many Roman houses contained 'multi-conjugal' households, albeit of differing statuses.[94] Aristocratic houses were designed to make provision for large slave households; Tacitus reports that Pedanius Secundus, urban prefect in AD 61, had 400 slaves apparently living under the same roof (he was murdered by one of them: *Annals* 14.42–3). The House of Aemilius Scaurus on the Palatine had about 50 rooms for slaves in the basement,[95] while a complex of rooms found close to the Temple of Antoninus and Faustina also seems to represent the slave quarters of a *domus*.[96]

Just as the family was basic to the provision of housing at Rome, so it was considered to have the major responsibility with regard to the burial and commemoration of the dead.[97] The vast majority of those who died at Rome and whose names were recorded on a funerary inscription were commemorated by members of their family. Saller and Shaw estimate that 72–8 % of non-elite epitaphs in Rome were erected by members of the immediate family of the deceased.[98] Husbands and wives commemorated each other, as did parents and children. Nuclear families are often depicted on the tombstones of freedmen in the Late Republic and Early Empire, again emphasizing the importance of the ideology of the family in the commemoration of the dead, and perhaps underlining the fact that they – unlike slaves – had a family.[99] In addition to the burial rites themselves, members of the family were also expected to carry out the annual ceremonies in memory of the dead, which included the *Parentalia* (in February), the *Lemuria* (in May) and other observances of the anniversary of the deceased's birth or death;[100] a funerary garden might be laid out in the vicinity of the tomb for the celebration of these rituals.[101] Concern was evidently felt where an estate passed to an heir who was not biologically related, lest the rites be neglected or the tomb misused; often tomb-inscriptions included the formula *hoc monumentum heredem non sequitur* ("this monument does not descend to the heir"), abbreviated *h.m.h.n.s.*. Alternatively, family tombs could be expressly designated for the future use not only of the immediate family of the deceased, but also the broader household of their freedmen, freedwomen and *their* descendants, in the hope that the freedmen's families, bearing the same name as the original master, would be able to maintain the rites.[102] In particular, under the early empire, *columbaria* ('dove-cote tombs') were often built to hold the ash-urns of the extended *familia* of slaves and freedmen. The most spectacular examples are the tombs of the Roman aristocracy. For example, the Tomb of the Statilii Tauri on the Via Praenestina contained the remains of hundreds of freedmen and slaves of the household of Statilius Taurus, consul in 37 and in 26 BC; located nearby was the similarly extensive Tomb of the Arruntii, built by the consul of AD 6.[103] Likewise, the Vigna Codini *columbarium* located near the Tomb of the Scipios between the Via Appia and Via Latina contained the ashes of numerous slaves and freedmen of the imperial house.[104] This may have reflected a genuine concern for members of the wider *familia*; but equally, just as it was prestigious for an aristocrat to have a substantial house with a grand *atrium*, and a grand household of slaves and other dependants, so the scale of one's establishment could be displayed in a tomb for members of the household.[105] The same pattern can be found on a smaller scale at Isola Sacra, the cemetery of the port of Ostia (Fig. 10.13): the tombs of Verrius Euhelpistus and Claudius Eutychus are also reserved for their freedmen, freedwomen and *their* descendants in turn. Examination of the Isola Sacra tombs suggests that while in many cases the epigraphic text on the facade referred only to a husband, wife or child, the monument often contained large numbers of burial spaces, many more than would be needed to accommodate all those mentioned on the inscription. Ideological considerations evidently led to the privileging of the nuclear family in epigraphic commemoration, while in practice many outside the nuclear family were accommodated within the tomb.[106]

In the perilous conditions of life at Rome, however, not everyone was able to rely on the support and resources of their families, whether nuclear or extended, naturally or legally defined, to provide housing or burial. Many inhabitants of the city must have been migrants from Italy or overseas, potential victims of the diseases endemic in the city, and left their families behind; premature death, sudden poverty, and other disasters must have befallen individual families.[107] Other strategies for the provision of housing and burial were often needed.

HOUSING, BURIAL AND PATRONAGE

In recent years, much effort has been devoted to understanding the role of patronage in Roman society. The existence of patronage relationships was believed by the Romans themselves to go back to the time of Romulus,[108] and it has conventionally been thought that patronage was of central importance in the political struggles of the Late Republic. The increased emphasis in recent scholarship on the role of popular participation in Roman politics has led to a playing-down of the specifically political importance of the patronage of the poor by the rich,[109] but it is clear that it continued to be of major social significance into the imperial period.[110]

The importance of patronage in defining the organization of the aristocratic house – allowing the reception of large numbers of clients – has already been stressed. Cicero speaks of "the home of an eminent man in which many guests must be entertained and a multitude of every sort of people received" (*De Officiis* 1.139). The continuing importance of public spaces such as peristyles, dining rooms and reception rooms in houses of imperial date shows the continuing importance of the relationships between patrons and clients in aristocratic life under the empire and into late antiquity.[111] But patronage might also potentially have been of major importance in the provision of housing for the poor at Rome. Wallace-Hadrill has argued that the key function of patronage is "the manipulation of scarce resources".[112] Access to housing at Rome might plausibly be thought of as falling into this category, since it was both scarce (given the vast population of the city and its limited area) and expensive

Fig. 10.14: Clivus Scauri: embedded insula-*block below the later SS. Giovanni e Paolo (Photo: editors).*

(judging by parallels in other pre-industrial cities). Juvenal comments that "you can buy an excellent house at Sora or Fabrateria or Frusino for what you now pay to rent a dark garret for a year" (*Satires* 3.223–25). Similarly, providing for the dead with more than a summary burial was a costly business, in which we might expect the assistance of a patron to have been welcome. The cost of land around the city for a tomb was substantial, and in the period under examination, the predominant rite for the disposal of the dead was cremation, so wood and perfumes would have had to be acquired for the pyre; and an inscription and permanent monument would have added to the cost significantly.[113]

However, two types of patronage relationship need to be distinguished, even in very schematic terms; and a variety of arrangements for the provision of housing and burial evidently existed within (and beyond) the scope of patronage. Some relationships were long-term in nature, for example those between a freedman and his former master, as they were still tied by some legally defined obligations and responsibilities. Indeed in many ways, as we have seen, the relationship could be better characterized as one of family ties than one of patronage. Similarly close were those between members of the elite and their immediate social inferiors – the *pars populi integra* "the respectable element in the population" in Tacitus' formulation, which he describes as being "attached to the great houses". These clients were, under the Republic, best placed to provide political backing for the patron, and must have formed the most distinguished element at his social functions, though they themselves might well have referred to their relationship with the patron in terms of *amicitia* 'friendship' rather than clientship.[114]

Other patronage relationships might well be less firm and long-lasting. Clients of lower status, without the moral and legal ties established by the bond of ex-slave and master, would be less closely tied to a particular patron. They had less to give a patron, perhaps attending at the *salutatio*[115] or escorting him through the city, and received less in return, perhaps a place at an occasional meal or a share in a distribution of food or money. As a result, it would be in their interests to seek support from as many potential patrons as possible.

Two main types of popular housing can be identified from the literary and archaeological record: accommodation attached to the aristocratic *domus*, and the purpose-built *insulae* (apartment blocks)[116] which came to be particularly characteristic of Rome and Ostia (though there were also other possibilities, including the *domus* which had been converted

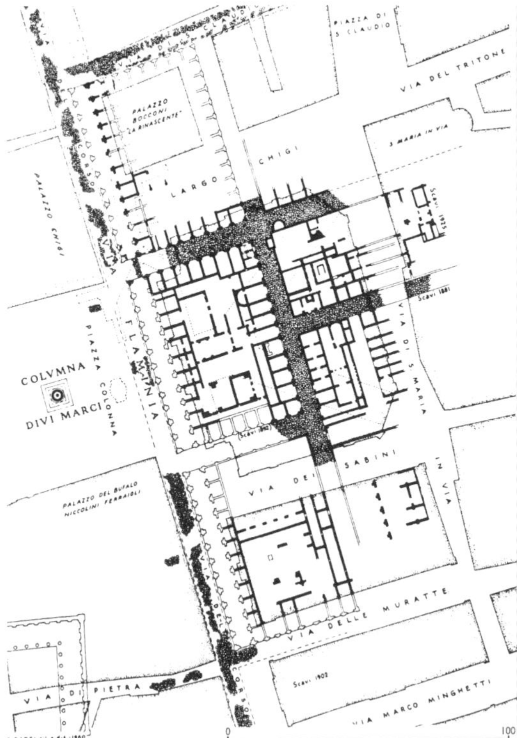

Fig. 10.15: Plan of the insulae *on the east side of the Via Lata, Galleria Colonna site (after Nash 1961–62).*

Fig. 10.16: Insula*-block on the Via Giulio Romano, early 2nd century AD (Photo: editors).*

for multiple occupation known from the Severan Marble Plan).[117] Unfortunately, few examples have been archaeologically well preserved at Rome itself.[118]

For the first type, we have to rely primarily on the evidence from Pompeii and Herculaneum, where poorer households in the form of *cenacula* ('upstairs apartments') and *tabernae* ('shops or workshops') have been identified adjacent to wealthy residences. Some were reached through these houses themselves, others seem to have been separate entities, identified as such on the basis of their independent entrance stairs, hearths and their own shrines to the divinities of the

Fig. 10.17: Shops fronting onto Salita del Grillo behind the Markets of Trajan. The shop in the foreground has two ovens and was probably a bakery (Photo: editors).

household, the Lares. Here we may imagine that patronage relationships played a major role in housing provision, given the proximity of the landlord's property.[119]

By contrast, the scope for the operation of patronage in connection with residence in *insulae* is less immediately apparent, although it is likely that many of them were owned by wealthy individuals, who were well placed to dispense patronage. The capital investment and the risks involved in the ownership of urban rental property were substantial; *insulae* were purpose-built structures, and the ever-present hazards of fire and collapse made total loss a real possibility, especially since it was common practice to build the upper floors in wood or wattle-work because of the weakness of the main walls (Vitruvius, *On Architecture* 2.8.17–20). Aulus Gellius describes a scene of an *insula* ablaze on the Cispian hill, and has an onlooker observe that "the returns from city property are great, but the hazards are far greater" (*Attic Nights* 15.1). Nevertheless, the attractions of urban property ownership were evidently enough to outweigh these risks; they provided a substantial – and instant – regular income in cash to complement the longer-term returns from rural properties (Cicero obtained an income of 80,000 *sestertii* annually from his *insulae* in the Argiletum (near the Forum) and on the Aventine (Cicero, *Letters to Atticus* 12.32.2, 16.1.5). If *insulae* were sufficiently widely distributed in the city (as Cicero's evidently were), rather than being concentrated in one area, the overall level of risk involved for the proprietor was significantly reduced.[120] Several *insulae* are known to have belonged to high status Romans under the Empire, for example those of the Volusii and of M. Vettius Bolanus, consul in AD 66.[121]

Some foundations of *insula*-blocks have recently been identified at Rome, for example on the Quirinal and Caelian hills, and adjacent to the Via Flaminia (Fig. 10.15);[122] remains of others have been discovered built into later structures such as the churches of SS. Giovanni e Paolo (on the ancient Clivus Scauri, Fig. 10.14)[123] and S. Anastasia, in the Velabrum area below the Palatine.[124] One example, however, located at the foot of the Capitol (known as the Via Giulio Romano house) is comparatively well preserved and has been studied in detail;[125] and there are also many good examples from Ostia.[126] Juvenal gives a graphic account of the squalor and danger of life in a jerry-built attic with the ever-present risk of fire and collapse (Juvenal, *Satires* 3.190–211), but it would be a mistake to identify the *insulae* as being characteristically the homes of the poor (Fig. 10.15). At the Via Giulio Romano *insula*, four floors survive. The ground floor was occupied by shops with residential mezzanines above, the first floor by two apartments, and the second and third floors by smaller rooms (Fig.

10.16). In general, *insula* blocks at Roma and Ostia seem to have been vertically zoned: the higher up the building one went, the cheaper and more squalid the property; water-supply was only likely to be available on the ground floor.[127] Both the comparatively well-off, and the comparatively poor, might well therefore have occupied rented apartments in the same *insula*. Though the relationship with the proprietor was less overt than where a *cenaculum* was attached to an aristocratic *domus*, the *insulae* nevertheless neatly reflected the hierarchical nature of Roman society below the elite.[128]

The apparently parallel prevalence of renting properties among both the rich and the less rich is however deceptive. Researches into the legal sources for property rental have revealed that two distinct systems operated. Some tenants (the wealthier, we may imagine) paid a single annual payment to their landlord, in arrears; the lease might be for a year or several years. We might think of the case of M. Caelius Rufus, who in the 50s BC rented a property from P. Clodius, which was perhaps attached to Clodius' own *domus* on the Palatine at a rent of 30,000 *sestertii* (inflated, according to Cicero, *For Caelius* 17–8).[129] The less wealthy, on the other hand, rented rooms in lodging houses, on short term leases; there was no security of tenure and rent was collected every few days.[130]

This distinction – between 'long-term' tenants of high prestige and poorer and less prestigious occupants – seems in some ways to reflect the two types of patronage relationship outlined earlier. Clients of higher status were established in properties on a long-term basis, paying rent at the end of the year as a marker of their reliability; lower status clients were less close to their patron, had a more fluid relationship with him, and their potential unreliability was reflected in regular payment of small amounts of rent, presumably in case they absconded. Indeed, for this group, the borderline between a very loose variety of 'patronage' and what we might term a 'market economy' must have been quite indistinct.[131] We must imagine the existence of a spectrum of possible relationships, from owner-occupier to short-term casual tenant. A high-status client or *amicus* might occupy the most prestigious quarters in an *insula*; likewise a favoured freedman or client might perhaps live within, or in a property adjoining, his master's house free of charge. The latter situation, where a property is 'let out gratis to their own or their wife's freedmen or clients' is envisaged by Ulpian in a discussion of the problem of identifying liability where injury was caused by objects or liquids being thrown or poured from a building in multiple occupation (*Digest* 9.3.5.1).[132] At the other end of the spectrum, a poor client's relationship with a landlord might amount purely to paying the rent (or *not* paying the rent) on a regular basis (Fig. 10.17).

These schematic distinctions may well be reflected in the situation at Pompeii, too. Analysis of patterns of housing there suggests that adjacent workshops and smaller properties were let out by the owners of the larger houses, but that distinctions can potentially be identified between categories of tenants. Those who were most closely tied to the family of the *domus* might be imagined living in properties with direct access to the *atrium*, but the Pompeiian evidence also suggests the existence of what might be termed a housing market.[133] Some dwellings were openly advertised on street corners, for example in the Insula Arriana Polliana where *tabernae cum pergulis suis et cenacula equestria et domus* ('workshop/shop units with mezzanine floors, equestrian-style upstairs apartments, and houses') were advertised (VI, 6, 1: *CIL* 4.138), and in the Praedia of Julia Felix, where *tabernae*, *pergulae* and *cenacula* were available to rent (II, 4: *CIL* 4.1136).

In the same way, we might expect arrangements for burial for those below the elite to reflect the distinction between close, long-term patronage relationships and the more tenuous links of more casual relationships.[134] This indeed seems to have been the case.

Fig. 10.18: Isola Sacra cemetery, Portus: tomb 15. Dining couches for funerary banquets (Photo: editors).

Although most of those buried in the Tomb of the Statilii Tauri were members of that extended family, some of those interred in the monument have (so far as we can tell from their names) no clear relation (either as freedmen or relatives) with the Statilii; some of the niches may have been sold off at a later date,[135] or improperly occupied by interlopers, but it is also quite possible that some of these are particularly well-deserving clients. Similarly, in the tombs studied at Isola Sacra, Hope identified burials of individuals who (to judge by their names) were not obviously part of the family who set up the tomb: "Friends and outsiders came to occupy the tomb just as the house might be subdivided and let out to lodgers or tenants".[136] It is difficult to be sure, though, since clients would have been unlikely to have drawn attention to their subservient status on their tombstone; as Cicero observed, "those who consider themselves wealthy... think it is as bad as death to make use of a patron or be called clients" (*De Officiis* 2.69). Other possibilities existed for the successful client beyond burial in the master's tomb. The better off the freedmen or clients, the more we would expect them to be able to finance their own funerary monuments (perhaps in part due to the patron's generosity); while the poorer client would rarely have shown the commitment to an individual patron which might have justified a permanent commemoration of the relationship. In general, then, the importance of patronage in enabling burial to take place seems to have been limited, except where very close links existed between the patron and the deceased, and in particular in the quasi-familial relationship between the patron and the ex-slave, or where there was a close individual relationship, perhaps best defined in terms of *amicitia* (friendship). The case of the poet Horace, who was buried close to the Tomb of Maecenas on the Esquiline, might be one such example (Suetonius, *Life of Horace*).[137]

THE ROLE OF THE *COLLEGIA*

Collegia were popular associations which derived their identity from association with a particular shrine or form of religious observance, residence in a particular area of the city, or membership of a particular profession.[138] Ancient tradition ascribed their creation to Numa, the second king of Rome, as an initiative to integrate the Roman and the Sabine elements in the city's population (Plutarch, *Numa* 17), and similar organizations can be identified in Italian towns such as Praeneste, at least as early as the 2nd century BC (*ILLRP* 103–7).[139] They seem to have become increasingly important in Rome during the 1st century BC, as the population of the city grew, but they were regarded with grave suspicion by the authorities, no doubt because of their role as associations of the *plebs*, their position outside the formal political structures of the Roman state, and as a result their potential for subverting the established order. This concern is particularly apparent in the years leading up to and following Catiline's conspiracy in 63 BC, when the associations and their members were often mobilized for political or violent ends: most *collegia* were banned by order of the senate, probably in 64 BC (Asconius 7C),[140] revived in 58 BC by P. Clodius Pulcher, but then prohibited again under Julius Caesar and (with some exceptions) by Augustus (Suetonius, *Julius Caesar* 42; *Augustus* 32). Even in the imperial period, *collegia* continued to be regarded with suspicion, and were blamed, for example, for the riot in the amphitheatre at Pompeii in AD 59 (Tacitus, *Annals* 14.17); in the time of Trajan, we find the emperor refusing to authorize the setting up of a fire-brigade in Bithynia in case it became a *collegium* and caused disruption (Pliny, *Letters* 10.33–4).

Since *collegia* were operating on the borders of the law in this way, certainly under the late Republic and to a lesser extent under the Empire, it is difficult to build up an very clear picture of exactly what their functions and activities were, though it is clear that they played an increasingly significant role in civic life, illustrated most graphically by the multiplicity of associations attested at Ostia in the High Empire.[141] Their names, recorded in inscriptions, give us some clues. Some were named after specific trades, like the *fabri* (builders) or *centonarii* (rag-makers); others after religious observances, like the *dendrophoroi* (literally 'tree-bearers'), who derived their name from the cult of Cybele. *Commorientes* ('fellows in death') and *convictores* ('fellow diners') suggest funerary and festive concerns respectively (Fig. 10.18).[142] However, such an analysis would seem to be too simplistic: *collegia* named after specific professions or dedicated to deities often seem to have provided festive banquets for their members when living and burial after their death, just as much as their counterparts whose names suggested specifically funerary or festive concerns.[143] In fact it is these aspects of *collegia* activities which are best attested in the epigraphic sources. For example, a document from Lanuvium, just south of Rome, preserves the rules of the *collegium* of Diana and Antinous, from AD 136. Members have to pay an entry fee of 100 *sestertii* and an *amphora* of wine,[144] followed by a monthly contribution of 5 *asses*. On the death of a paid-up member, the society would organize his funeral at a cost of 250 *sestertii,* and provide 50 *sestertii* to be distributed to the mourners. Regular banquets took place for the members of the association, on six fixed dates during the year. Fines were laid down to punish disorderly conduct on these occasions: 4 *sestertii* for moving one's place at dinner, 12 *sestertii* for abusing other members, and 20 *sestertii* for abusing the club presidents (*CIL* 14.2112 = *ILS* 7212).[145] Thus club members could enjoy the conviviality of the meetings in the knowledge that that the club would pay for their funeral and burial, often in a designated burial ground or *columbarium*.

The members of the *collegia* seem to have been of varying statuses and might include free men, ex-slaves and indeed those who were still slaves (slave members who were granted their freedom were required to donate an *amphora* of good wine to the association, presumably so they could collectively celebrate his good fortune). The requirement to pay joining fees and regular subscriptions implies that the membership came from a stratum above the very poorest in society, although the provision of the sum of 250 HS to members of the club at Lanuvium, equivalent to the very cheapest funerals attested by inscriptions elsewhere in Italy, and the burial grant introduced by the emperor Nerva,[146] perhaps suggests that the members were of comparatively low social status; some *collegia*, especially those within the city of Rome, would have had much more affluent members.

Like the support of the family and that of the patron, membership of a *collegium* allowed some of those below the elite, but above the poverty line, to be commemorated after their death – and also to enjoy the sociable benefits of membership when they were alive. We should however be cautious about seeing the *collegium* as primarily an *alternative* to the family or the patron as a source of burial provision; rather, all three seem to have operated together. In some cases it seems that wives and children of club members were themselves buried in a club's monument.[147] According to the rules of the Lanuvium *collegium*, if a member died without leaving a family, the club would make arrangements for his burial. If, however, the deceased had a surviving heir, the latter could celebrate the funeral and claim the burial fee payable on the death of a club member. The *collegium* acted as a back-up for the family, not as a replacement for it: one role of the club was to provide an institution which (it was hoped) could be relied upon to provide a cash sum to pay for the funeral without (much) danger of misappropriation or loss. In the insecure conditions of imperial Rome, this was a considerable benefit; othcrwise, those below the elite must have found it extremely difficult to keep safe a sum of money sufficient to pay for their funeral. In many cases, however, those buried by their *collegia* must have been sufficiently affluent to have had a choice whether to organize their funeral in this way or to opt for entirely private burial arrangements.[148] Membership of the *collegium* must therefore have had its own attractions, which might include the provision of a more impressive (and better attended) funeral than might otherwise be feasible, the opportunity to socialize and to enhance their social identity with fellow workers in the same trade or profession, and – especially attractive to the recently freed, we might imagine – to participate in an organization which mimicked the structures of civic politics from which they were excluded.

Just as the family and the *collegia* together combined in the provision of burial, so the *collegia* themselves were closely involved in ties of patronage and in particular relied on patrons to maintain their financial well-being.[149] For example, the rules of the *collegium* of Diana and Antinous were published in response to a benefaction of L. Caesennius Rufus, patron of the city of Lanuvium, who donated to the club the annual interest on a lump sum of 15,000 *sestertii*. Helping a collective group might potentially have had greater – or at least different – attractions for a benefactor than helping poor individuals: a *collegium* could reciprocate in a more visible way, perhaps by holding an annual dinner on the donor's birthday or by decking his tomb with flowers. Near the monumental Tomb of Lusius Storax at Chieti was an enclosure containing the (evidently less grand) tombs of the *soci monimenti* (the 'Fellows of the Tomb-Monument'), and it may be that in life Storax had a close association with this group, perhaps as its patron.[150] Sometimes the distinction between patron, benefactor and *paterfamilias* was blurred still further: the households of some wealthy individuals were organized on the model of *collegia*. In the imperial palace itself the different grades of staff had their own organizations, a *collegium* of cooks for example (*CIL* 6.7458 = *ILS* 1798; *CIL* 6.8570);[151] and several inscriptions record the *collegium quod est in domo Sergiae Paullinae* 'the *collegium* in the house of Sergia Paullina' probably the sister or daughter of L. Sergius Paullus, consul for the second time in AD 168 (*CIL* 6.9148 = *ILS* 7333; 6.9149; 6.10260–62; 6.10263 = *ILS* 7334). In the Tomb of the Statilii Tauri, the *collegium commorientium* ('fellows in death') seems to have been involved in the organization of burial arrangements (*CIL* 6.6215–16 = *ILS* 7360–60a).

Collegia should therefore be seen as only one element in a complex nexus of relationships which involved family and patronage, as well as the popular associations in the provision of burial for those below the elite at Rome. They did, however, have a significant impact on the urban landscape, as *scholae* ('clubhouses') were set up all over the city.[152] Many of those known from epigraphy and excavation in the city were substantial buildings, often in affluent areas of the city – such as the Quirinal or the Caelian, where the 'Basilica Hilariana', clubhouse of the *dendrophoroi*, stood in the mid-2nd century AD.[153] These must have belonged to associations with substantial resources of their own and/or wealthy patrons. There are, however, indications that even smaller clubs had their own clubhouses, although these were often modest affairs close to the burial places of their members. The *schola* of the Sodales Serrenses, a small chamber five metres square with an altar at the centre, which might have held some 40 people, was discovered by the Via Nomentana, for example; the burial ground of the association may have been located nearby. The clubhouse seems to have belonged to an association of people who had emigrated to the city from the Vicus Serrensis in Africa, demonstrating how in some circumstances the *collegia* could act as a support network for those far away from their families.[154] Similarly an inscription of AD 153 which records a gift by Salvia Marcellina in memory of her late husband M. Ulpius Capito and his superior Flavius Apollonius, procurator of the imperial picture-galleries, provides an idea of the facilities acquired by the Collegium of Asclepius and Hygia, and reminds us how much the *collegia* themselves relied on benefactors. Salvia Marcellina presented a shrine with a pergola, a statue of Asclepius, and a roofed terrace nearby where the members of the association could dine, and donated the sum of 50,000 *sestertii* for distributions of cash, bread and wine to the members of the club. The site was located "between the first and second milestones of the Via Appia, near the Temple of Mars, on the left hand side for those leaving the city" (*CIL* 6.10234 = *ILS* 7213).[155]

Although the *collegia* could own property in addition to their own *scholae*, and periodically gifts and legacies of both urban and rural properties were made to the associations, it is interesting that despite their concern for the provision of burial for their members, the *collegia* seem (so far as we can detect) not to have been interested in providing housing for them, though there is an intriguing reference in a 4th century AD inscription to the *Insulae Coriariorum* ('apartment blocks of the leather-workers', *CIL* 6.1682 = *ILS* 1220). The properties acquired by the clubs seem to have been regarded as a source of income rather than a privilege for members. When a benefactor donated *tabernae cum cenaculis* ('workshops with upstairs apartments') in the Vicus Herculius at Brixia, which produced an annual income of 200 *denarii* to the *centonarii* of that city, he stipulated that 100 *denarii* be spent on distributions of wine, and 100 *denarii* on the upkeep of the properties (*CIL* 5.4488). The major capital investment involved in building or acquiring an *insula* or other multi-tenanted property, and then the recurrent expenditure involved in maintaining it, must have discouraged the *collegia* from involvement in the provision of housing for their members, but additionally such a project might not commend itself to a patron as much as the festive or commemorative aspects of an association's activities.

CONCLUSION

The house and the tomb were very closely related in Roman thought. At the beginning of the first millennium, urns in the form of huts were used for the deposition of cremated remains;[156] funerary monuments built in the style of houses are found in imperial period cemeteries on the Vatican at Rome and at Isola Sacra.[157] Some funerary portraits of the Late Republic appear to show the deceased looking out of the window of the house/tomb;[158] the image of a half-open door is a common motif on ash-urns and sarcophagi of the 1st and 2nd centuries AD.[159] Similarly, the equation of house and tomb was a common motif on Roman epitaphs.[160] Petronius' Trimalchio, making plans for this tomb, observed: "it is quite wrong for a man to decorate his house when he is alive, and not to be concerned about that house where he must stay for longer" (*Satyricon* 71). At a lower social level, we find an echo of the same idea, even more graphically expressed, in the epitaph of Ancarenus Nothus, buried in a *columbarium* on the Via Latina: "My body knows no longer hunger or gout; now it is no longer a deposit on the rent, but enjoys for free an eternal lodging" (*CIL* 6.7193a).[161]

Three institutions combined to assist the Roman *plebs* in their aspirations towards adequate housing and commemoration after their death – the family, patronage and the *collegia*. It is clear, however, that these did not operate independently of one another, but instead formed a complex series of inter-relationships. Patrons provided housing for their freedmen and clients, who might also be buried within the family tomb; patrons supported *collegia* with funds which would allow them to provide burial for their members; *collegia* assisted families in providing burial for their relatives. In particular, the relationship between patron and freedmen might combine the form of the *collegium* and characteristics of the family with the structures of patronage. In the insecure, chaotic, insanitary and dangerous conditions of ancient Rome, those below the elite needed all the support they could find firstly to obtain a place to live and then to secure decent burial, and they made the most of every possibility.

ACKNOWLEDGEMENTS

I am very grateful to Peter Garnsey, Keith Hopkins, Felix Pirson, and the Editors for their comments on successive drafts of this chapter; to Scott Perry, Onno van Nijf, and Andrew Wallace-Hadrill, for letting me see work in advance of publication; and to Angela Heap for improving the final text. None of these is responsible for any errors which remain.

NOTES

1 HOPKINS 1978, 96–8; STAMBAUGH 1988, 89–90; MORLEY 1996, 33–9.
2 See, for example, the books reviewed in PARKIN 1994; also RAWSON and WEAVER 1997.
3 For example SALLER 1982; BRUNT 1988, 382–442; WALLACE-HADRILL 1989.
4 The fundamental study is WALTZING 1895–1900; more recently, see AUSBÜTTEL 1982; ROYDEN 1988; KLOPPENBORG and WILSON 1996; NIJF 1997; PERRY 1999.
5 WALLACE-HADRILL 1994; LAURENCE and WALLACE-HADRILL 1997.
6 Recent work is reviewed by PATTERSON 1992a, especially 200–4.
7 HESBERG and ZANKER 1987; HESBERG 1992; 1994; KOCKEL 1993.
8 SALLER and SHAW 1984; HOPKINS 1987; MEYER 1990; PARKIN 1992, 5–19; MORRIS 1992, 156–73; SCHEIDEL 1994; 1996; SHAW 1996.
9 WISEMAN 1987; STAMBAUGH 1988, 157–82; CLARKE 1991, 2–11; EDWARDS 1993, 150–57; WALLACE-HADRILL 1994, 4–7; *Lexicon* II, 22–217; PATTERSON 2000, 38–43; GUILHEMBET forthcoming; WALLACE-HADRILL forthcoming.
10 COARELLI 1989; ZACCARIA RUGGIU 1995, 370–77.
11 FLOWER 1996, 185–222.
12 RAWSON 1990.
13 On the location of Pompey's house and the prows of the pirate ships, see GUILHEMBET 1992; *Lexicon* II, *s.v.* 'Domus Pompeiorum', 159–60; for the archaeology of this region of the city in general, see PALOMBI 1997.
14 EDWARDS 1993, 155–57; SALLER 1994, 93; MUSTAKALLIO 1994, 78; BODEL 1997, 7–11.
15 *Lexicon* II, *s.v.* 'Domus: M. Tullius Cicero", 202–4; *Lexicon* III, *s.v.* 'Libertas', 96–7.

16 For the House of Pompey, see note 13; *Lexicon* II, *s.v.* 'Domus: Caesar', 73–4; 'Domus: T. Annius Milo', 32; 'Domus: P. Cornelius Scipio Africanus', 88.

17 CORBIER 1992; *Lexicon* II, *s.v.* 'Domus: C. Sempronius Gracchus', 176; 'Domus: Q. Hortensius', 116–17; 'Domus: C. Licinius Macer Calvus', 129.

18 COARELLI 1995, 169–70; IACOPI 1997; CLARIDGE 1998, 135; ROYO 1999, 9–117; *Lexicon* IV, *s.v.* 'Palatium (età repubblicana – 64 d.C)', 22–8.

19 CARANDINI 1988, 359–87; see CARANDINI and TERRENATO 1994 for a brief account of the work in English; also CLARIDGE 1998, 111–12; *Lexicon* II, *s.v.* 'Domus: M. Aemilius Scaurus', 26.

20 CARANDINI 1988, 368–69; *Lexicon* IV, *s.v.* 'Via Sacra', 223–28; see PATTERSON 1992a, 200–3 for a discussion.

21 *Lexicon* II, *s.v.* 'Domus: P. Clodius Pulcher', 85–6.

22 *Lexicon* II, *s.v.* 'Domus: M. Tullius Cicero', 202–4.

23 *Lexicon* II, *s.v.* 'Domus: Q. Tullius Cicero', 204.

24 CARANDINI 1990.

25 CARANDINI 1988, 370–71.

26 PAPI 1998, 46.

27 CLARIDGE 1998, 128–30; ROYO 1999; *Lexicon* II, *s.v.* 'Domus: Augustus (Palatium)', 46–8.

28 *Lexicon* II, *s.v.* 'Domus: Cn. Calpurnius Piso', 96–7; *Senatus consultum de Cn. Pisone* 106–7 in ECK 1996; FLOWER 1998, 169–70; BODEL 1999, 58–60.

29 WISEMAN 1987, 406–7; ECK 1997b, 180.

30 *Lexicon* II, *s.v.* 'Domus: Sisenna Statilius Taurus', 182.

31 CARANDINI 1988, 369.

32 CARANDINI 1988, 371–81.

33 Lateran: LIVERANI 1988; *Lexicon* II, *s.v.* 'Domus: Laterani', 127. Caelian: *Lexicon* II, *s.v.* 'Domus: L. Marius Maximus Perpetuus Aurelianus', 137–38. Aventine: *Lexicon* II, *s.v.* 'Domus: L. Licinius Sura', 129–30; 'Domus: L. Fabius Cilo', 95–6; see also ECK 1997a, 77.

34 ECK 1997b, 181; *Lexicon* II, *s.v.* 'Domus: T. Pomponius Atticus', 161–62; 'Domus: T. Avidius Quietus', 67.

35 RODRIGUEZ ALMEIDA 1987, 421–23; *Lexicon* II, *s.v.* 'Domus: C. Plinius Caecilius Secundus', 158–59; 'Domus: L. Arruntius Stella', 37–8; 'Domus: Neratii', 144.

36 WALLACE-HADRILL 1994, 118–42; see WALLACE-HADRILL forthcoming.

37 WALLACE-HADRILL 1989; BRUNT 1988.

38 WALLACE-HADRILL forthcoming.

39 STAMBAUGH 1988, 168; CARETTONI 1960, No. 543 = RODRIGUEZ-ALMEIDA 1981, No. 11e–f.

40 COARELLI 1998.

41 *Lexicon* II, *s.v.* 'Domus: L. Cornelius Pusio', 88; ECK 1997b, 185.

42 WALLACE-HADRILL 1994, 51–7.

43 GUIDOBALDI 1986, 171–75, 184–86, 206–7; *Lexicon* II, *s.v.* 'Domus: Iunius Bassus', 69; ELLIS 1988; GUIDOBALDI 1993.

44 On *horti*, see especially GRIMAL 1984; CIMA and LA ROCCA 1986; 1998; *Lexicon* III, 51–88; ROYO 1999, 195–207, Fig. 36.

45 WALLACE-HADRILL 1998. On the *suburbium*, see CHAMPLIN 1982; PURCELL 1987; CARANDINI 1988, 339–57.

46 BROISE and JOLIVET 1998; *Lexicon* III, *s.v.* 'Horti Lucullani', 67–70; 'Horti Sallustiani', 79–81; TALAMO 1998.

47 HÄUBER 1990; *Lexicon* III, *s.v.* 'Horti Tauriani', 85; 'Horti Lamiani', 61–4; 'Horti Maecenatis', 70–4.

48 BEARD 1998, 30.

49 COARELLI 1986, 45–55; *Lexicon* V, *s.v.* 'Via Appia', 130–33; 'Via Latina', 141.

50 TOYNBEE 1971; DAVIES 1977; MORRIS 1992, 1–30.

51 FRIEDLAENDER 1908–28, II, 210–18; TOYNBEE 1971, 46–8; SCULLARD 1981, 218–21; NICOLET 1980, 352–56; HOPKINS 1983, 201–2; PATTERSON 2000, 43–8.

52 BIANCHI BANDINELLI 1963–64, 23–32.

53 *Lexicon* IV, *s.v.* 'Rostra (età repubblicana)', 212–14; 'Rostra Augusti', 214–17.

54 *Lexicon* IV, *s.v.* 'Sepulcrum: Valerii', 301; 'Sepulcrum: Fabricii', 288–89; VERZÁR-BASS 1998, 404–5.

55 LABROUSSE 1937, 191–92.

56 *Lexicon* IV, *s.v.* 'Pomerium', 96–105, particularly 100.

57 COARELLI 1997, 591–602; FRISCHER 1982–83; EISNER 1986.

58 *Lexicon* IV, *s.v.* 'Sepulcrum: L. Cornelius Sulla', 286; 'Sepulcrum: Iulia (Tumulus)', 291; 'Sepulcrum: A. Hirtius', 290; 'Sepulcrum: C. Vibius Pansa', 302.

59 *Lexicon* I, *s.v.* 'Campus Esquilinus', 218–19; COARELLI 1973; LA ROCCA 1984; COARELLI 1990, 171–77.
60 *Lexicon* IV, *s.v.* 'Sepulcrum: Claudii', 279.
61 VERZÁR-BASS 1998, 409–10; *Lexicon* IV, *s.v.* 'Sepulcrum: Ser. Sulpicius Galba', 299.
62 *Lexicon* IV, *s.v.* 'Sepulcrum: M. Claudius Marcellus', 279–80; 'Sepulcrum: A. Atilius Calatinus', 276; 'Sepulcrum: (Corneliorum) Scipionum', 281–85; PURCELL 1987, 27–8.
63 PISANI SARTORIO and QUILICI GIGLI 1987–88.
64 HESBERG 1994, 32–4.
65 COARELLI 1972; FLOWER 1996, 160–66; CLARIDGE 1998, 328–32; *Lexicon* IV, *s.v.* 'Sepulcrum: (Corneliorum) Scipionum', 281–85.
66 WISEMAN 1985, 3–19; PATTERSON 2000.
67 FLOWER 1996, 263–64.
68 HESBERG 1994, 124–25; HESBERG and PANCIERA 1994; *Lexicon* III, *s.v.* 'Mausoleum Augusti: das Monument', 234–37; 'Mausoleum Augusti: le sepolture', 237–39; *Lexicon* V, 275–76; CLARIDGE 1998, 181–84, 341–42.
69 ZANKER 1988, 291–92; RIDLEY 1992; CLARIDGE 1998, 364–66; *Lexicon* IV, *s.v.* 'Sepulcrum: C. Cestius', 278–79; *Lexicon* V, *s.v.* 'Via Ostiensis', 143; cf. *Lexicon* III, *s.v.* 'Meta Romuli', 278 and references. For the so-called 'Meta Romuli', another perhaps even larger pyramidal mausoleum, see PLATNER and ASHBY 1929, 340; NASH 1968, II, 59–60.
70 ECK 1997a, 86; RICHARDSON 1992, 353; *Lexicon* V, *s.v.* 'Via Salaria', 144–45.
71 HESBERG 1994, 57–8.
72 RAWSON 1997, 210–11.
73 *Lexicon* IV, *s.v.* 'Sepulcrum: Maecenas (Tumulus)', 292; 'Sepulcrum: Statilii', 299; see also VERZÁR-BASS 1998, 415–16.
74 YAVETZ 1958; SCOBIE 1986; WHITTAKER 1993; PURCELL 1994.
75 LE GALL 1980–81; ALBERTONI 1983; BODEL 1994, 38–54; SCHEIDEL 1994; SHAW 1996.
76 CALZA 1940, 44.
77 BODEL 1994, 114, n. 194.
78 PURCELL 1994, 657.
79 JOSHEL 1992, 78–85.
80 CIANCIO ROSSETTO 1973; ZANKER 1988, 15; RICHARDSON 1992, 355; BRANDT 1993; CLARIDGE 1998, 359–61; *Lexicon* IV, *s.v.* 'Sepulcrum: M. Vergilius Eurysaces', 301–2; *Lexicon* V, *s.v.* 'Via Praenestina', 144; 'Via Labicana', 138–39.
81 NASH 1968, II, 308; *Lexicon* IV, *s.v.* 'Sepulcrum: P. Aelius Gutta Calpurnianus', 272–73; *Lexicon* V, *s.v.* 'Via Flaminia', 135–37.
82 CALZA 1940; PAVOLINI 1983, 260–70; BALDASSARE 1987; D'AMBRA 1988; HOPE 1997, 73–82.
83 D'AMBRA 1988, 87–97; HOPE 1997, 75.
84 D'AMBRA 1988, 97–9.
85 KOCKEL 1983, 100–9.
86 BIANCHI BANDINELLI 1963–64, 16, 19; D'ARMS 1981, 108–16; CHAMPLIN 1991, 171–75; HOPE 1997, 70–1.
87 GHISLANZONI 1908; BIANCHI BANDINELLI 1963–64, 72–84.
88 ZANKER 1988, 15; *Lexicon* V. *s.v.* 'Via Caelemontana', 135.
89 GARNSEY 1970, 243, 262; BRADLEY 1994, 154–65.
90 SALLER 1994, 80–8.
91 TREGGIARI 1991, 410; HOPKINS 1983, 100–1, 146–49.
92 RAWSON 1986, 14; BRADLEY 1991a, 163; BANNON 1997, 49–51.
93 RAWSON 1986; BRADLEY 1991a, 76–102, 125–76; 1991b.
94 WALLACE-HADRILL 1994, 113.
95 CARANDINI 1988, 363–64; *Lexicon* II, *s.v.* 'Domus: M. Aemilius Scaurus', 26.
96 GEORGE 1997, 17.
97 SALLER 1994, 95–101.
98 SALLER and SHAW 1984, 134; though note the critique of the methodology employed made by MARTIN 1996.
99 SHAW 1991, following ZANKER 1975 and KLEINER 1977; KOCKEL 1993, 3–4.
100 HARMON 1978, 1600–1603; SCULLARD 1981, 74–6, 118–19.
101 TOYNBEE 1971, 94–100, especially 98–9 for depictions of funerary gardens.
102 CROOK 1967, 136; CHAMPLIN 1991, 176–77; DIXON 1992, 114.
103 NASH 1968, II, 359–69; RICHARDSON 1992, 360; *Lexicon* IV, *s.v.* 'Sepulcrum: Statilii', 299; 'Sepulcrum: Arruntii', 275.
104 NASH 1968, II, 333–39; RICHARDSON 1992, 356.

105 PURCELL 1987.
106 HOPE 1997, 77–8.
107 SCOBIE 1986; PURCELL 1994, 650, 655–56; SCHEIDEL 1994, 166.
108 DRUMMOND 1989.
109 For example in MILLAR 1984; 1998; see also NORTH 1990.
110 SALLER 1982, 1–6; BRUNT 1988, 382–442; WALLACE-HADRILL 1989, 63–88.
111 For this subject generally see SLATER 1991.
112 WALLACE-HADRILL 1989, 73.
113 MORRIS 1992, 31–69; MEIGGS 1982, 237; DUNCAN-JONES 1982, 127–31 discusses the cost of tombs and funerals.
114 SALLER 1989, 57.
115 SALLER 1982, 128–29; LAURENCE 1994, 125.
116 HERMANSEN 1978, 129–31.
117 Fragment 543 of the Marble Plan: see RODRIGUEZ ALMEIDA 1981, 89.
118 STAMBAUGH 1988, 174–78.
119 WALLACE-HADRILL 1994, 103–10; PIRSON 1997; PARKINS 1997, 102–7.
120 GARNSEY 1976; FRIER 1980, 23–4; PARKINS 1997, 92–7.
121 *Lexicon* III, *s.v.* 'Insula Volusiana', 102–3; 'Insula Bolani', 96–7.
122 PATTERSON 1992a, 204; WALLACE-HADRILL forthcoming.
123 *Lexicon* II, *s.v.* 'Domus SS. Iohannis et Pauli', 117–18; CLARIDGE 1998, 313–17.
124 CLARIDGE 1998, 261–62; *Lexicon* I, *s.v.* 'S. Anastasia: titulus', 37–8.
125 PACKER 1968–69; see also the reconstruction in CONNOLLY and DODGE 1998, 141–43; CLARIDGE 1998, 232–34.
126 PACKER 1967, 80; FRIER 1980, 3–20; DELAINE 1995; 1996.
127 PACKER 1971; HERMANSEN 1981, 17–53; CLARKE 1991, 26–9.
128 WALLACE-HADRILL 1994, 117.
129 AUSTIN 1960, 66–7.
130 FRIER 1977; 1980.
131 PURCELL 1994, 667–69.
132 WHITTAKER 1993, 291–92.
133 PIRSON 1997.
134 PATTERSON 1992b, 17–19.
135 *Lexicon* IV, *s.v.* 'Sepulcrum: Statilii', 299.
136 HOPE 1997, 86–7.
137 *Lexicon* IV, *s.v.* 'Sepulcrum: Maecenas (Tumulus)', 292.
138 LINTOTT 1999, 77–83; PATTERSON 1992b, 19–22; NIJF 1997; see Delaine in this volume for *collegia* in the building industry.
139 WALTZING 1895–1900, I, 85–9.
140 WALTZING 1895–1900, I, 90–113; FLAMBARD 1977; VANDERBROECK 1987; FRASCHETTI 1990, 216–17.
141 MEIGGS 1973, 311–36; for the *collegia* in the towns of Italy more generally, see PATTERSON 1994.
142 WALTZING 1895–1900, I, 323.
143 FLAMBARD 1987, 210.
144 The amount of wine contained by an *amphora* might be estimated to be between 15 and 30 litres, depending on the type of *amphora*. The Dressel 2–4 type common in Italy in the 1st century contained on average 28–30 litres; the 'Spello' *amphorae* produced in the Tiber valley, and characteristic of the 2nd century, were smaller, containing some 15 litres. See PANELLA 1989, 144.
145 FLAMBARD 1987, 225–34; see LEWIS and REINHOLD 1955, II, 273–75 for a translation of the text. See also HOPKINS 1983, 211–17.
146 DUNCAN-JONES 1982, 127–31.
147 WALTZING 1895–1900, I, 277.
148 NIJF 1997, 33.
149 CLEMENTE 1972.
150 BIANCHI BANDINELLI 1963–64, 61–71.
151 *Lexicon* IV, *s.v.* 'Schola: collegium cocorum', 246.
152 BOLLMANN 1997; 1998; *Lexicon* IV, 243–61 (*scholae*).
153 *Lexicon* I, *s.v.* 'Basilica Hilariana', 175–76.

154 FLAMBARD 1987, 216–17; *Lexicon* IV, *s.v.* 'Schola: Sodales Serrenses', 258; *Lexicon* V, *s.v.* 'Via Nomentana', 142.
155 FLAMBARD 1987, 234–39.
156 BARTOLONI 1987; SMITH 1996, 35–6.
157 TOYNBEE and WARD-PERKINS 1956, 24–62; HOPE 1997, 69–70.
158 ZANKER 1988, 15; KOCKEL 1993, 7, 11.
159 HAARLØV 1977.
160 LATTIMORE 1962, 165–67.
161 FRIER 1980, 45.

BIBLIOGRAPHY

ALBERTONI, M. 1983: 'La necropoli esquilina arcaica e repubblicana', in *Roma Capitale 1870–1911: l'archeologia in Roma tra sterro e scavo*, Roma, 1983, 140–55.

AUSBÜTTEL, F. 1982: *Untersuchungen zu den Vereinen im Westen des römischen Reiches*, Frankfurt, 1982.

AUSTIN, R.G. 1960: *M. Tulli Ciceronis Pro Caelio Oratio*, ed. 3, Oxford, 1960.

BALDASSARE, I. 1987: 'La necropoli dell'Isola Sacra (Porto)', in HESBERG and ZANKER 1987, 125–38.

BANNON, C. 1997: *The brothers of Romulus: fraternal pietas in Roman law, literature and society*, Princeton, 1997.

BARTOLONI, G. *et al.* 1987: *Le urne a capanna rinvenute in Italia*, Roma, 1987.

BEARD, M. 1998: 'Imaginary horti: or up the garden path', in CIMA and LA ROCCA 1998, 23–32.

BIANCHI BANDINELLI, R., COARELLI, F., FRANCHI, L., GIULIANO, A., REGINA, A. la and TORELLI, M. 1963–64: *Sculture municipali dell'area sabellica tra l'età di Cesare e quella di Nerone,* Studi Miscellanei 10, 1963–64.

BODEL, J. 1994: *Graveyards and groves: a study of the Lex Lucerina*, Cambridge, Mass., 1994, = AJAH 11, 1986 [1994].

BODEL, J. 1997: 'Monumental villas and villa monuments', *JRA* 10, 1997, 5–35.

BODEL, J. 1999: 'Punishing Piso', *AJP* 120, 1999, 43–63.

BOLLMANN, B. 1997: 'La distribuzione delle *scholae* delle corporazioni a Roma', in C. Virlouvet (ed.), *La Rome impériale: démographie et logistique*, Collection de l'École Française de Rome 230, Roma, 209–25.

BOLLMANN, B. 1998: *Römische Vereinshäuser: Untersuchungen zu den Scholae der römischen Berufs-, Kult- und Augustalen-Kollegien in Italien*, Mainz, 1998.

BRADLEY, K.R. 1991a: *Discovering the Roman family: studies in Roman social history*, Oxford, 1991.

BRADLEY, K.R. 1991b: 'Remarriage and the structure of the upper-class Roman family', in RAWSON 1991, 79–98.

BRADLEY, K.R. 1994: *Slavery and Society at Rome*, Cambridge, 1994.

BRANDT, O. 1993: 'Recent research on the tomb of Eurysaces', *Opuscula Romana* 19, 1993, 13–7.

BROISE, H. and JOLIVET, V. 1998: 'Il giardino e l'acqua: l'esempio degli horti Lucullani', in CIMA and LA ROCCA 1998, 189–202.

BRUNT, P.A. 1988: *The Fall of the Roman Republic*, Oxford, 1988.

CALZA, G. 1940: *La necropoli del porto di Roma nell' Isola Sacra*, Roma, 1940.

CARANDINI, A. 1988: *Schiavi in Italia*, Roma, 1988.

CARANDINI, A. 1990: 'Domus aristocratiche sopra le mura e il pomerio del Palatino', in M. Cristofani (ed.), *La grande Roma dei Tarquini: Palazzo delle esposizioni, Roma 12 giugno – 30 settembre 1990*, Catalogo della mostra, Roma, 1990.

CARANDINI, A. and TERRENATO, N. 1994: 'The Forum of Rome', *Current Archaeology* 139, June/August 1994, 261–65.

CARETTONI, G., COLINI, A.M., COZZA, L. and GATTI, G. 1960: *La pianta marmorea di Roma antica. Forma Urbis Romae*, Roma, 1960

CHAMPLIN, E. 1982: 'The *suburbium* of Rome', *AJAH* 7, 1982, 97–117.

CHAMPLIN, E. 1991: *Final judgements: duty and emotion in Roman wills, 200 BC – AD 250*, Berkeley, 1991.

CIANCIO ROSSETTO, P. 1973: *La tomba del fornaio Marco Virgilio Eurisace a Porta Maggiore*, Roma, 1973.

CIMA, M. and LA ROCCA, E. 1986: *Le tranquille dimore degli dei*, Roma, 1986.

CIMA, M. and LA ROCCA, E. (ed.) 1998: *Horti Romani: atti del convegno internazionale, Roma, 4–6 maggio 1995*, Roma, 1998.

CLARIDGE, A. 1998: *Rome. An Oxford Archaeological Guide*, Oxford, 1998.

CLARKE, J.R. 1991: *The Houses of Roman Italy 100 BC – AD 250*, Berkeley, 1991.

CLEMENTE, G. 1972: 'Il patronato nei *collegia* dell'impero romano', *Studi Classici e Orientali* 21, 1972, 142–229.
COARELLI, F. 1972: 'Il sepolcro degli Scipioni', *DialArch* 6, 1972, 36–106 = COARELLI 1996, 179–238.
COARELLI, F. 1973: 'Frammento di affresco dall'Esquilino con scena storica', in *Roma medio-repubblicana: aspetti culturali di Roma e del Lazio nei secoli IV e III a.C*, Catalogo della mostra, Roma, 1973, 200–8.
COARELLI, F. 1986: 'L'urbs e il suburbio', in A. Giardina (ed.), *Società romana e produzione schiavistica* II, Roma/ Bari, 1986, 1–58.
COARELLI, F. 1989: 'La casa dell'aristocrazia romana secondo Vitruvio', in H. Geertman and J.J. De Jong, *Munus non ingratum: proceedings of the international symposium on Vitruvius' De Architectura and the Hellenistic and Republican architecture*, Leiden, 1989 = COARELLI 1996, 344–59.
COARELLI, F. 1990: 'Cultura artistica e società', in G. Clemente, F. Coarelli and E. Gabba (ed.), *Storia di Roma 2.1: L'impero mediterraneo. La repubblica imperiale*, Torino, 1990, 159–85.
COARELLI, F. 1995: *Roma*,Guide archeologiche Laterza, ed. 2, Roma/Bari, 1995.
COARELLI, F. 1996: *Revixit ars: arte e ideologia a Roma. Dai modelli ellenistici alla tradizione repubblicana*, Roma, 1996.
COARELLI, F. 1997: *Il Campo Marzio dalle origini alla fine delle repubblica*, Roma, 1997.
COARELLI, F. 1998: 'The Odyssey frescoes of the Via Graziosa: a proposed context', *PBSR* 66, 1998, 21–37.
CONNOLLY, P. and DODGE, H. 1998: *The Ancient City: life in classical Athens and Rome*, Oxford, 1998.
CORBIER, M. 1992: 'De la maison d'Hortensius à la *curia* sur le Palatin', *MEFRA* 104, 1992, 871–916.
CROOK, J. 1967: *Law and life of Rome*, London, 1967.
D'AMBRA, E. 1988: 'A myth for a smith; a Meleager sarcophagus from a tomb in Ostia', *AJA* 92, 1988, 85–100.
D'ARMS, J.H. 1981: *Commerce and social standing in ancient Rome*, Cambridge Mass., 1981.
DAVIES, G. 1977: 'Burial in Italy up to Augustus', in R. Reece (ed.), *Burial in the Roman World*, Council for British Archaeology Research Reports 22, London, 1977.
DELAINE, J. 1995: 'The Insula of the Paintings at Ostia I.4.2–4: paradigm for a city in flux', in T.J. Cornell and K. Lomas (ed.), *Urban society in Roman Italy*, London, 1995, 79–106.
DELAINE, J. 1996: 'The Insula of the Paintings. A model for the economics of construction in Hadrianic Ostia', in A. Gallina Zevi and A. Claridge (ed.), *'Roman Ostia' Revisited: Archaeological and Historical Papers in memory of Russell Meiggs*, London, 1996, 165–84.
DIXON, S. 1992: *The Roman Family*, Baltimore, 1992.
DRUMMOND, A. 1989: 'Early Roman clientes', in WALLACE-HADRILL 1989, 89–116.
DUNCAN-JONES, R. 1982: *The Economy of the Roman Empire*, ed. 2, Cambridge, 1982.
ECK, W. 1984: 'Senatorial self-representation: developments in the Augustan period', in F. Millar and E. Segal (ed.), *Caesar Augustus: seven aspects*, Oxford, 1984.
ECK, W., CABALLOS, A. and FERNANDEZ, F. 1996: *Das Senatus Consultum de Cn. Pisone patre, Vestigia* 48, München, 1996.
ECK, W. 1997a: 'Rome and the outside world: senatorial families and the world they lived in', in RAWSON and WEAVER 1997, 71–99.
ECK, W. 1997b: '*Cum dignitate otium*: senatorial *domus* in imperial Rome', *Scripta Classica Israelitica* 19, 1997, 162–90.
EDWARDS, C. 1993: *The politics of immorality in ancient Rome*, Cambridge, 1993.
EISNER, M. 1986: *Zur Typologie der Grabbauten im Suburbium Roms*, RM Supplement 26, Mainz, 1986.
ELLIS, S.P. 1988: 'The end of the Roman house', *AJA* 92, 1988, 565–76.
FLAMBARD, J.M. 1977: 'Clodius, les collèges, la plèbe et les esclaves. Recherches sur la politique populaire au milieu du 1er siècle', *MEFRA* 89, 1977, 115–56.
FLAMBARD, J.M. 1987: 'Élements pour une approche financière de la mort dans les classes populaires du Haut-Empire: analyse du budget de quelques collèges funéraires de Rome et d'Italie', in HINARD 1987, 209–44.
FLOWER, H.I. 1996: *Ancestor masks and aristocratic power in Roman culture*, Oxford, 1996.
FLOWER, H.I. 1998: 'Rethinking '*damnatio memoriae*': the case of Cn. Calpurnius Piso pater in AD 20', *Classical Antiquity* 17, 1998, 155–87.
FRASCHETTI, A. 1990: *Roma e il principe*, Roma/Bari, 1990.
FRIEDLAENDER, L. 1908–28: *Roman Life and Manners under the Early Empire*, ed. 2, London, 1908–28.
FRIER, B. 1977: 'The rental market in early Rome', *JRS* 67, 1977, 27–37.
FRIER, B. 1980: *Landlords and tenants in imperial Rome*, Princeton, 1980.
FRISCHER, B. 1982–83: '*Monumenta et arae honoris virtutisque causa*: evidence of memorials for Roman civic heroes', *BullCom* 88, 1982–83, 51–86.
GARNSEY, P. 1970: *Social Status and Legal Privilege in the Roman Empire*, Oxford, 1970.

GARNSEY, P. 1976: 'Urban property investment', in M.I. Finley (ed.), *Studies in Roman Property*, Cambridge, 1976, 123–36.

GEORGE, M. 1997: '*Servus* and *domus*: the slave in the Roman house', in LAURENCE and WALLACE-HADRILL 1997, 15–24.

GHISLANZONI, E. 1908: 'Il rilievo gladiatorio di Chieti', *MonAnt* 19, 1908, 542–614.

GIARDINA, A. 1993: *The Romans*, Chicago, 1993.

GRIMAL, P. 1984: *Les jardins romains*, ed. 3, Paris, 1984.

GUIDOBALDI, F. 1986: 'L'edilizia abitativa unifamiliare nella Roma tardoantica', in A. Giardina (ed.), *Società romana e impero tardoantico* II, Roma/Bari, 1986, 165–237.

GUIDOBALDI, F. 1993: 'Roma: il tessuto abitativo, le *domus* e i *tituli*', in A. Carandini, L. Cracco Ruggini, and A. Giardina (ed.), *Storia di Roma 3.2: L'età tardoantica. I luoghi e le culture*, Torino, 1993, 69–83.

GUILHEMBET, J.-P. 1992: 'Sur un jeu de mots de Sextus Pompée: *domus* et propagande politique lors d'un épisode des guerres civiles', *MEFRA* 104, 1992, 787–816.

GUILHEMBET, J.-P. forthcoming: *Habitavi in oculis: recherches sur la résidence urbaine des classes dirigeantes romains des Grécques à Auguste*, Rome, forthcoming.

HAARLØV, B. 1977: *The half-open door. A common symbolic motif within Roman sepulchral sculpture*, Odense, 1977.

HARMON, D.P. 1978: 'The family festivals of Rome', *ANRW* 16.2, Berlin, 1978, 1592–1603.

HÄUBER, C. 1990: 'Zur Topographie der Horti Maecenatis und der Horti Lamiani auf dem Esquilin in Rom', *Kölner Jahrbuch* 23, 1990, 11–107.

HERMANSEN, G. 1978: 'The population of imperial Rome: the regionaries', *Historia* 27, 1978, 129–68.

HERMANSEN, G. 1981: *Ostia: aspects of Roman city life*, Edmonton, 1981.

HESBERG, H. von 1992: *Römische Grabbauten*, Darmstadt, 1992.

HESBERG, H. von 1994: *Monumenta: i sepolcri romani e la loro architettura*, Milano, 1994 (Italian translation of HESBERG 1992).

HESBERG, H. von and PANCIERA, S. 1994: *Das Mausoleum des Augustus: der Bau und seine Inschriften*, München, 1994.

HESBERG, H. von and ZANKER, P. (ed.) 1987: *Römische Gräberstrasse*, München, 1987.

HINARD, F. (ed.) 1987: *La mort, les morts et l'au-delà dans le monde romaine*, Caen, 1987.

HOPE, V. 1997: 'A roof over the dead: communal tombs and family structure', in LAURENCE and WALLACE-HADRILL 1997, 69–88.

HOPKINS, K. 1978: *Conquerors and Slaves*, Cambridge, 1978.

HOPKINS, K. 1983: *Death and Renewal*, Cambridge, 1983.

HOPKINS, K. 1987: 'Graveyards for historians', in HINARD 1987, 113–26.

IACOPI, I. 1997: *La decorazione pittorica dell'Aula Isiaca*, Milano, 1997.

JOSHEL, S.R. 1992: *Work, identity and legal status at Rome: a study of the occupational inscriptions*, Norman Oklahoma, 1992.

KERTZER, D. and SALLER, R.P. (ed.) 1991: *The family in Italy from antiquity to the present*, New Haven, 1991.

KLEINER, D.E.E. 1977: *Roman group portraiture: the funerary reliefs of the late Republic and early Empire*, New York, 1977.

KLOPPENBORG, J.S. and WILSON S.G. 1996: *Voluntary associations in the Greco-Roman world*, London, 1996.

KOCKEL, V. 1983: *Die Grabbauten vor dem Herkulaner Tor in Pompeji*, Mainz am Rhein, 1983.

KOCKEL, V. 1993: *Porträtreliefs stadtrömischer Grabbauten*, Mainz am Rhein, 1993.

LABROUSSE, M. 1937: 'Le pomerium de la Rome impériale: notes de topographie romaine', *MEFRA* 54, 1937, 165–99.

LA ROCCA, E. 1984: 'Fabio o Fannio. L'affresco medio-repubblicano dell' Esquilino come riflesso dell'arte rappresentativa e come espressione di mobilità sociale', *DialArch* series 3.1, 1984, 31–53.

LATTIMORE, R. 1962: *Themes in Greek and Latin epitaphs*, Urbana, 1962.

LAURENCE, R. 1994: *Roman Pompeii: space and society*, London, 1994.

LAURENCE, R. and WALLACE-HADRILL, A. (ed.) 1997: *Domestic space in the Roman world: Pompeii and beyond*, JRA Supplementary Series 22, Providence RI, 1997.

LE GALL, J. 1980–81: 'Sépulture des pauvres à Rome', *Bulletin de la société nationale des antiquaires de France*, 1980–81, 148–52.

LEWIS, N. and REINHOLD, M. 1955: *Roman civilization* I–II, New York, 1955.

LINTOTT, A.W. 1999: *Violence in Republican Rome*, ed.2, Oxford, 1999.

LIVERANI, P. 1988: 'Le proprietà private nell'area Lateranense fino all'età di Costantino', *MEFRA* 100, 1988, 891–915.

MARTIN, D.B. 1996: 'The construction of the ancient family: methodological considerations', *JRS* 86, 1996, 40–60.
MEIGGS, R. 1973: *Roman Ostia*, ed. 2, Oxford, 1973.
MEIGGS, R. 1982: *Trees and timber in the ancient Mediterranean world*, Oxford, 1982.
MEYER, E.A. 1990: 'Explaining the epigraphic habit in the Roman empire: the evidence of epitaphs', *JRS* 80, 1990, 74–96.
MILLAR, F. 1984: 'The political character of the classical Roman Republic', *JRS* 74, 1984, 1–19.
MILLAR, F. 1998: *The crowd in Rome in the late Republic*, Ann Arbor, 1998.
MORLEY, N. 1996: *Metropolis and Hinterland: the City of Rome and the Italian Economy 200 BC – AD 200*, Cambridge, 1996.
MORRIS, I. 1992: *Death-ritual and social structure in Classical antiquity*, Cambridge, 1992.
MUSTAKALLIO, K. 1994: *Death and disgrace: capital punishment with post mortem sanctions in early Roman historiography*, Helsinki, 1994.
NASH, E. 1968: *Pictorial Dictionary of Ancient Rome* I–II, ed. 2, London, 1968.
NICOLET, C. 1980: *The world of the citizen in Republican Rome*, London, 1980.
NIJF, O.M. van 1997: *The civic world of professional associations in the Roman East*, Amsterdam, 1997.
NORTH, J. 1990: 'Democratic politics in Republican Rome', *P&P* 126, 1990, 3–21.
PACKER, J. 1967: 'Housing and population in imperial Ostia and Rome', *JRS* 57, 1967, 80–95.
PACKER, J. 1968–69: 'La casa di via Giulio Romano', *BullCom* 81, 1968–69, 127–48.
PACKER, J. 1971: *The insulae of Imperial Ostia,* MAAR 31, 1971.
PALOMBI, D. 1997: *Tra Palatino ed Esquilino: Velia Carinae Fagutal*, Roma, 1997.
PANELLA, C. 1989: 'Le anfore italiche del II secolo d.C.', in M. Lenoir, D. Manacorda and C. Panella (ed.), *Amphores romaines et histoire économique*, Roma, 1989, 139–78.
PAPI, E. 1998: '" Domus est quae nulli villarum mearum cedat" (Cic. *Fam*. 6.18.5). Osservazioni sulle residenze del Palatino alla metà del 1. secolo a.C.', in CIMA and LA ROCCA 1998, 45–70.
PARKIN, T.G. 1992: *Demography and Roman Society*, Baltimore, 1992.
PARKIN, T.G. 1994: Review of books on the Roman family, *JRS* 84, 1994, 178–85.
PARKINS, H.M. 1997: 'The 'consumer city' domesticated? The Roman city in élite economic strategies', in H. M. Parkins (ed.), *Roman urbanism: beyond the consumer city*, London, 1997, 83–111.
PATTERSON, J.R. 1992a: 'The City of Rome: from Republic to Empire', *JRS* 82, 1992, 186–215.
PATTERSON, J.R. 1992b: 'Patronage, collegia and burial in Imperial Rome', in S. Bassett (ed.), *Death in Towns: urban responses to the dying and the dead, 100–1600*, Leicester, 1992, 15–27.
PATTERSON, J.R. 1994: 'The *collegia* and the transformation of the towns of Italy in the second century AD', in *L'Italie d'Auguste a Dioclétien*, Collection de l'École Française de Rome 198, Roma, 1994, 227–38.
PATTERSON, J.R. 2000: *Political life in the City of Rome*, Bristol, 2000.
PAVOLINI, C. 1983: *Ostia*, Guide archeologiche Laterza, Roma/Bari, 1983.
PERRY, J.S. 1999: *A death in the familia: the funerary colleges of the Roman Empire*, unpublished Ph.D. thesis, University of North Carolina at Chapel Hill, 1999.
PIRSON, F. 1997: 'Rented accommodation at Pompeii: the evidence of the *Insula Arriana Polliana* VI 6', in LAURENCE and WALLACE-HADRILL 1997, 165–81.
PISANI SARTORIO, G. and QUILICI GIGLI, S. 1987–88: 'A proposito della Tomba dei Cornelii', *BullCom* 1987–88, 247–64.
PLATNER, S.B. and ASHBY, T. 1929: *A Topographical Dictionary of Rome*, Oxford, 1929.
PURCELL, N. 1987: 'Tomb and suburb', in HESBERG and ZANKER 1987, 25–41.
PURCELL, N. 1994: 'The city of Rome and the *plebs urbana* in the late Republic', *CAH*² 9, 1994, 644–88.
RAWSON, B. 1986: *The family in ancient Rome: new perspectives*, London, 1986.
RAWSON, B. 1991: *Marriage, divorce and children in ancient Rome*, Oxford, 1991.
RAWSON, B. 1997: 'The iconography of Roman childhood', in RAWSON and WEAVER 1997, 205–38.
RAWSON, B. and WEAVER, P. (ed.) 1997: *The Roman Family in Italy: status, sentiment, space*, Oxford, 1997.
RAWSON, E. 1990: 'The antiquarian tradition: spoils and representations of foreign armour', in W. Eder (ed.), *Staat und Staatlichkeit in der frühen römischen Republik*, Stuttgart, 1990, 157–73 = *Roman Culture and Society: Collected Papers*, Oxford, 1991, 582–98.
RICHARDSON, L. 1992: *A new topographical dictionary of ancient Rome*, Baltimore, 1992.
RIDLEY, R.T. 1992: 'The praetor and the pyramid. The tomb of Gaius Cestius in history, archaeology and literature', *BA* 13–5, 1992, 1–29.
RODRIGUEZ ALMEIDA E. 1981: *Forma Urbis Marmorea: aggiornamento generale 1980*, Roma, 1981.

RODRIGUEZ ALMEIDA, E. 1987: 'Qualche osservazione sulle Esquiliae patrizie e il Lacus Orphei', in C. Pietri (ed.), *L'Urbs: espace urbain et histoire*, Collection de l'École Française de Rome 98, Roma, 1987, 415–28.

ROYDEN, H.L. 1988: *The magistrates of the Roman professional collegia in Italy from the first to the third century AD*, Pisa, 1988.

ROYO, M. 1999: *Domus Imperatoriae. Topographie, formation et imaginaire des palais impériaux du Palatin*, Roma, 1999.

SALLER, R.P. 1982: *Personal patronage under the Roman Empire*, Cambridge, 1982.

SALLER, R.P. 1989: 'Patronage and friendship in early imperial Rome: drawing the distinction', in WALLACE-HADRILL 1989, 49–62.

SALLER, R.P. and SHAW, B.D. 1984: 'Tombstones and Roman family relations in the principate: civilians, soldiers and slaves', *JRS* 74, 1984, 124–56.

SALLER, R.P. 1994: *Patriarchy, property and death in the Roman family*, Cambridge, 1994.

SCHEIDEL, W. 1994: 'Libitina's bitter gains: seasonal mortality and endemic disease in the ancient city of Rome', *Ancient Society* 25, 1994, 151–75.

SCHEIDEL, W. 1996: *Measuring sex, age and death in the Roman Empire*, JRA Supplementary Series 21, Ann Arbor, 1996.

SCOBIE, A. 1986: 'Slums, sanitation, and mortality in the Roman world', *Klio* 68, 1986, 399–433.

SCULLARD, H.H. 1981: *Festivals and ceremonies of the Roman Republic*, London, 1981.

SHAW, B.D. 1991: 'The cultural meaning of death: age and gender in the Roman family', in KERTZER and SALLER 1991, 66–90.

SHAW, B.D. 1996: 'Seasons of death: aspects of mortality in imperial Rome', *JRS* 86, 1996, 100–38.

SLATER, W.J. (ed.) 1991: *Dining in a Classical Context*, Ann Arbor, 1991.

SMITH, C. 1996: *Early Rome and Latium: economy and society c. 1000–500 BC*, Oxford, 1996.

STAMBAUGH, J.E. 1988: *The Ancient Roman City*, Baltimore, 1988.

TALAMO, E. 1998: 'Gli orti di Sallustio a Porta Collina', in CIMA and LA ROCCA 1998, 113–69.

TOYNBEE, J.M.C. and WARD-PERKINS, J.B. 1956: *The Shrine of St Peter and the Vatican excavations*, London, 1956.

TOYNBEE, J.M.C. 1971: *Death and burial in the Roman world*, London, 1971.

TREGGIARI, S. 1991: *Roman marriage: iusti coniuges from the time of Cicero to the time of Ulpian*, Oxford, 1991.

VANDERBROECK, P.J.J. 1987: *Popular leadership and collective behaviour in the late Roman republic,* Amsterdam, 1987.

VERZÁR-BASS, M. 1998: 'A proposito dei mausolei negli *horti* e nelle *villae*', in CIMA and LA ROCCA 1998, 401–24.

WALLACE-HADRILL, A. (ed.) 1989: *Patronage in Ancient Society*, London, 1989.

WALLACE-HADRILL, A. 1994: *Houses and Society in Pompeii and Herculaneum*, Princeton, 1994.

WALLACE-HADRILL, A. 1998: 'Horti and hellenization', in CIMA and LA ROCCA 1998, 1–12.

WALLACE-HADRILL, A. forthcoming: 'Case e abitanti a Roma', in E. Lo Cascio (ed.), *Roma: metropoli preindustriale*, Roma, forthcoming.

WALTZING J.-P. 1895–1900: *Étude historique sur les corporations professionelles chez les romains*, I–IV, Bruxelles/ Louvain, 1895–1900.

WHITTAKER, C.R. 1993: 'The poor', in GIARDINA 1993, 272–99.

WISEMAN, T.P. 1985: *Roman political life 90 BC – AD 69*, Exeter, 1985.

WISEMAN, T.P. 1987: '*Conspicui postes tectaque digna deo*: the public image of aristocratic and imperial houses in the late Republic and early Empire', in C. Pietri (ed.), *L'Urbs: espace urbain et histoire*, Collection de l'École française de Rome 98, Roma, 1987, 393–413 = *Historiography and imagination: eight essays on Roman culture*, Exeter, 1994, 98–115.

YAVETZ, Z. 1958: 'The living conditions of the urban plebs in Republican Rome', *Latomus* 17, 1958, 500–17 = R. Seager (ed.), *The crisis of the Roman republic: studies in political and social history*, Cambridge, 1969, 162–79.

ZACCARIA RUGGIU, A. 1995: *Spazio privato e spazio pubblico nella città romana*, Collection de l'École Française de Rome 210, Roma, 1995.

ZANKER, P. 1975: 'Grabreliefs römischer Freigelassener', *Jahrbuch des Deutschen Archaeologischen Instituts* 90, 1975, 267–315.

ZANKER, P. 1988: *The power of images in the age of Augustus*, Ann Arbor, 1988.

11. Religions of Rome

Simon Price

The city of Rome used to be a great black hole in our understanding of Roman imperial history: we knew more about the periphery than the centre. Fortunately, over the past few years this gap has begun to be filled (and is further filled, we hope, by this volume). One aspect of our ignorance concerned the religious life of Rome during the principate (the period with which this chapter is concerned). Histories of Roman religion have traditionally petered out with the reign of Augustus, and attention has shifted to 'Oriental cults', and to Judaism and Christianity. The challenge facing us now is both to argue for the importance of official cults of Rome under the empire, and also to integrate into a general picture material (of very different types) on the various cults of Rome. But before such integration is possible it is necessary to establish a clear model of those cults. Though it is conventional to talk of them as homogeneous and exclusive entities, this chapter argues that such an assumption is very misleading and that they were neither homogeneous nor exclusive.[1] This chapter is structured round three questions: (1) is it right to think of religious groups at Rome as homogeneous? (2) were they exclusive at the theological level? (3) were individual allegiances to these groups exclusive?

Religion was important in the ancient world to everyone's sense of identity, whether one thinks of classical Athenians, Jews or republican Romans. Religion was an element of a more general identity: 'Athenian', 'Greek', 'Jewish', or 'Roman', which is characteristic of a situation in which religion was embedded in other, social and political, institutions. This role for religion remained important throughout antiquity. Immigrants from Palmyra in Syria established a sanctuary to a number of Palmyrene gods at Rome in Trastevere, on the west bank of the Tiber; there they made dedications to 'their ancestral deities' in a combination of languages, Latin, Greek and Aramaic (the common language of the near east).[2] At the highest level, the state cults of imperial Rome should not be seen as a formality of interest at most to emperors and senators; in fact they and the official religious festivals were deeply entwined into the rhythms of urban life. Processions in honour of the gods of Rome (e.g. Jupiter, Mater Magna or deified emperors) wound their way through the streets of Rome to the circus, where the associated games were watched by tens or hundreds of thousands of spectators.[3]

In addition to the official cults, there developed in both Greece and Rome other religious choices, outside the framework of civic cults, which offered possibilities for new religious identities. In Rome such choices existed from at least the early 2nd century BC onwards, and were well established by the imperial period. Cults allegedly originating in Egypt, Syria and Asia Minor were located across the city (Fig 11.1); there is also evidence for some twenty-five Mithraic sanctuaries in Rome (Fig. 11.2).[4] A good example of this type of private religious meeting place is probably the so-called Underground Basilica at Porta Maggiore (Fig. 11.1, no. 31 & Fig. 11.3). This miraculously preserved building, of early 1st-century AD date, might be the meeting place of a religious association, which shared arcane, perhaps Pythagorean, beliefs.[5] The state cults and these religious groups coexisted, but the new groups were also novel: with their demands of personal commitment, they offered a new sort of identity.

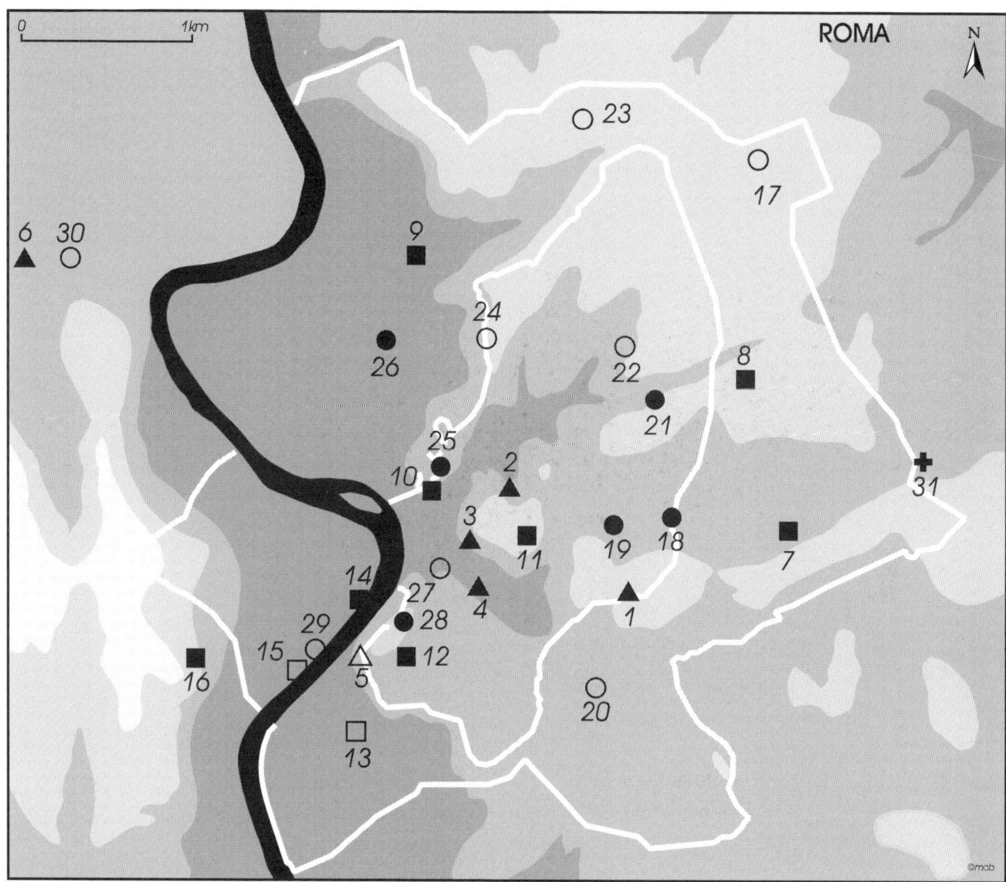

Fig. 11.1: Map showing the distribution of oriental cults at Rome (after Coarelli 1982 and Beard, North and Price 1998). A symbol in outline indicates uncertain location. ● Egyptian cults, ■ Syrian-Phoenician cults, ▲ Magna Mater, ✚ Underground basilica. 1. 'Basilica' Hilariana; 2. Shrine of Magna Mater in Via Sacra; 3. Temple of Magna Mater on Palatine; 4. Image of Magna Mater in Circus Maximus; 5. Cult of Magna Mater and Navisalvia ('Ship Saver'); 6. Phrygianum in Vatican; 7. Jupiter Dolichenus in Castra Priora Equitum Singularium; 8. Jupiter Dolichenus on Esquiline; 9. Temple of Sol built by Aurelian; 10. Cult of Caelestis and Jupiter Africanus on Capitoline; 11.Temple of Elagabalus; 12. Jupiter Dolichenus on Aventine; 13. Syrian cults near Horrea Galbana; 14. Palmyrene sanctuary in Trastevere; 15. Syrian cults of Trastevere; 16. Syrian sanctuary on Janiculum; 17. Isis in Castra Praetoria; 18. Isis and Serapis; 19. Isium Metellinum; 20. Isis Athenodoria; 21. Shrine near S. Martino ai Monti; 22. Isis Patricia; 23. Sanctuary in Gardens of Sallust; 24. Serapis on the Quirinal; 25. Isis on Capitolium; 26. Isis and Serapis in Campus Martius; 27.Isis in Circus Maximus; 28. Isis below S. Sabina; 29. Isis in Trastevere; 30. Isis in Vatican; 31. Underground Basilica.

Religion was not just one of a bundle of characteristics defining ethnic or civic identity, it was *the* defining characteristic. The cults offered, in short, *religious* identity to their members.

The interesting issue is to see how these identities relate to one another, and to ethnic or civic identities. Here it is crucial to be as comprehensive as possible. We shall never make

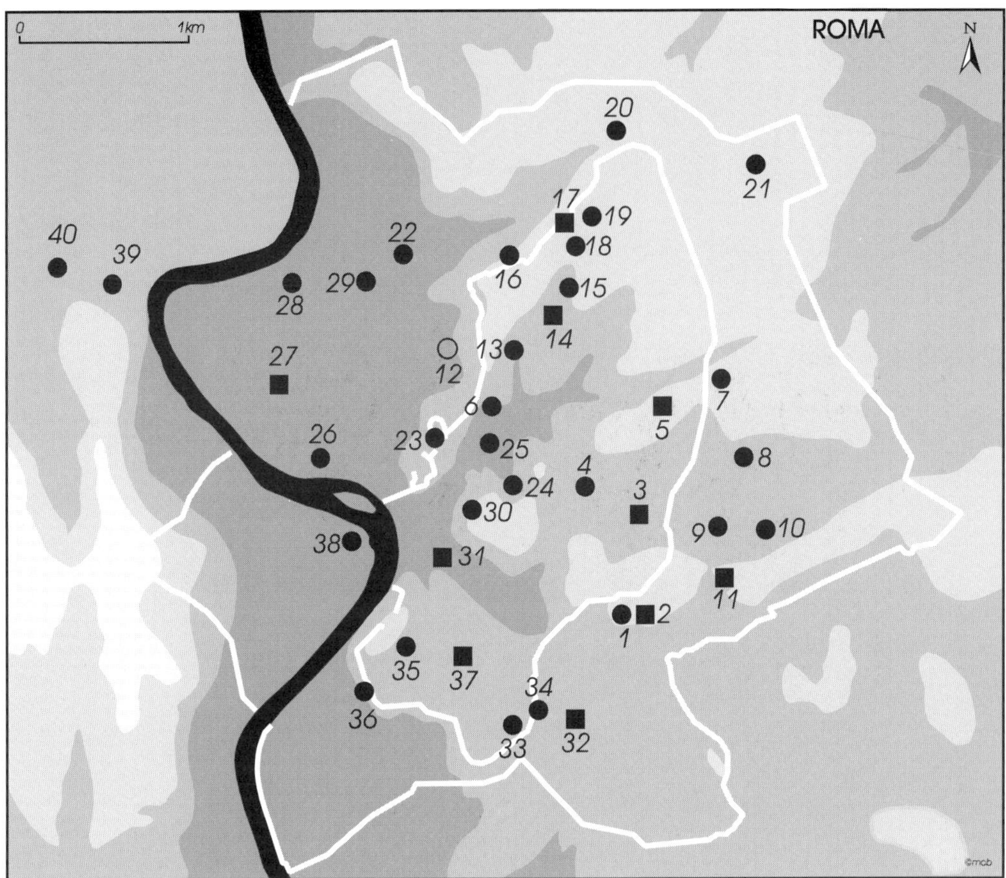

Fig. 11.2: Map showing the distribution of Mithraic sanctuaries and monuments in Rome (after Coarelli 1979 and Beard, North and Price 1998). A symbol in outline indicates uncertain location. ■ *Mithraic sanctuaries,* ● *Other Mithraic monuments. 1. Piazza della Navicella, in Castra cohors V vigilum; 2. S. Stefano Rotondo in Castra Peregrinorum; 3. S. Clemente; 4. Baths of Titus; 5. Private house near S. Martino ai Monti; 6. Palazzo del Grillo; 7. Between S. Eusebio and S. Vito; 8. Piazza Dante, on imperial property; 9. SS. Pietro and Marcellino; 10. Scala Santa in Castra Priora Equitum Singularium; 11. Hospital of S. Giovanni; 12. Temple of Serapis; 13. Via Mazzarino, in or near the Baths of Constantine; 14. S. Vitale; 15. Via Nazionale; 16. Via Rasella; 17. Palazzo Barberini, in public building?; 18. Private house in Via XX Septembre; 19. S. Susanna, perhaps connected with Baths of Diocletian; 20. Via Sicilia, on imperial property; 21. Castra Praetoria; 22. Piazza S. Silvestro, probably inside Temple of Sol; 23. Arx Captitolina; 24. Via Sacra, an inscription probably not in situ; 25. 4th century shrine in Forum of Nerva; 26. S. Maria in Monticelli; 27. S. Lorenzo in Damaso; 28. Palazzo Primoli (uncertain); 29. Palazzo Montecitorio; 30. Palatine, north-west slopes; 31. Circus Maximus; 32. Baths of Caracalla; 33. S. Saba, Castra cohors IV vigilum; 34. S. Balbina, in a private house; 35. Jupiter Dolichenus on Aventine; 36. Arch of S.Lazarro; 37. S. Prisca, in private house; 38. Ponte Emilio; 39. Via della Conciliazione; 40. S. Pietro, related to Phrygianum.*

progress if we remain locked into particular specialisms: historians of Isis, of Mithras, of Judaism, of Christianity. To exclude any of these at the outset is to prejudge the issues: in particular, it is important to have Judaism and Christianity in the picture, otherwise one is liable to uphold *a priori* a dichotomy between 'paganism' and 'Christianity' which is deeply unhelpful. In examining such connections we need to avoid the conventional category 'Oriental religions'. In the hands of the brilliant Franz Cumont, the category seemed to be the key to understanding the religious history of the period.[6] But in fact the category conflates things that need to be kept separate and is founded on arbitrary premises. Even though several of the cults proclaimed an eastern 'origin' for their wisdom, the 'origins' were quite different (Egypt, Syria, Persia) and do not constitute a homogeneous 'Orient'. Some of the cults (Mater Magna, Isis) began as public cults and only later acquired private mysteries, which were quite distinct. These mysteries, even if they claimed an eastern origin, are in fact descended from earlier Greek initiation cults. Nor can one assume a common preoccupation with 'salvation', which made the 'Oriental cults' precursors of and rivals to Christianity. For there is no real body of evidence to show this, and the assumption is illicitly Christianizing.

HOMOGENEITY

In the past scholars have assumed that ancient religious groups, especially Judaism and Christianity, were homogeneous and exclusive entities. That is, their theological and practical positions each had a normative core, consistent across place and time; round that were a number of awkward heretical or deviant groups which could be treated as simply marginal. They were exclusive of each other and of other religious groups of the time. The current trend in the study of Judaism and Christianity is firmly against the normative assumptions of the old picture. Many scholars would now wish to talk not of core and periphery, but of clusters of ideas and people for each cult.[7] This trend means that it is right to rethink the old model for understanding other cults of the period. For reasons of space, this chapter will be concerned mainly with Mater Magna, Jupiter Dolichenus, Isis and Mithras, as well as Jews and Christians.

The background to the issue of homogeneity is the wide geographical spread of these cults, though the precise distribution pattern varies widely from cult to cult.[8] The cult of Isis is found in the hellenistic period in Greece, but its expansion under the empire was largely western, in Italy, Africa, Spain, Gaul and Britain. Jupiter Dolichenus proclaimed its origin at Doliche in North Syria, and some 17 sanctuaries of the cult have been found, ranging from Dura Europus on the Euphrates to Germany. There were three sanctuaries in Rome: on the Aventine, the Caelian and the Esquiline, of which that on the Aventine is the best known (Fig. 11.1, no. 12; see below).[9] Mithras was common in Italy (especially Rome and Ostia) and along the Rhine-Danube and British frontier zones, but appears hardly at all in Greece, Asia Minor, Syria, Egypt, North Africa or Spain.

The relative uniformity of these cults is easily established. Dedications to Jupiter Dolichenus from various parts of the empire employ a very similar iconography.[10] Or the inscribed hymns to Isis from the Greek world, which range in date from the 2nd century BC to the 2nd or 3rd centuries AD, are similar both to each other and to the version in Apuleius' *Metamorphoses* (11.25).[11] And when, in that novel, Lucius went from Corinth to Rome, at the instruction of Isis, the cult at Rome into which he was initiated was clearly related to that at Corinth (11.26–30). The cults of Mithras also display a striking degree of uniformity. Shrines excavated in Britain or Germany are much the same as those in Rome or even at Dura

Fig. 11.3: Underground Basilica (Basilica Sotteranea) outside Porta Maggiore (Photo: editors).

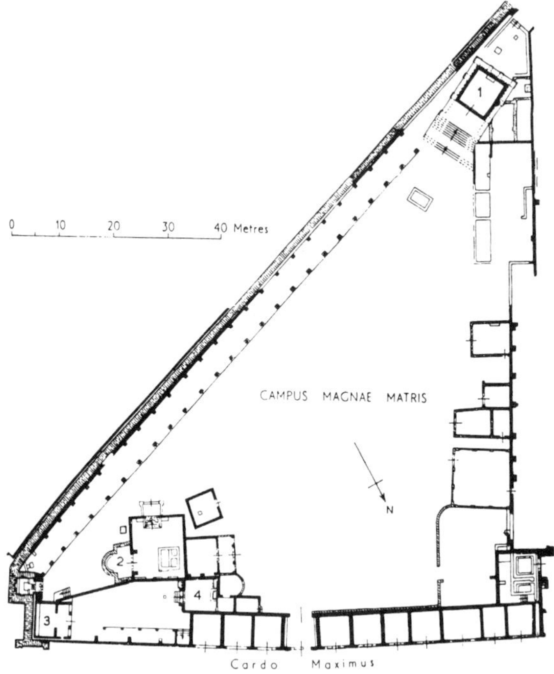

Fig. 11.4: Ostia IV.i.1: Sanctuary of the Magna Mater (after Meiggs 1973; Vermaseren 1977–89).

Europus: a long cave-like building with benches along the side and a relief or painting at the far end of Mithras slaying the bull. This is true even of the sanctuary at Dura Europus, once seen as a meeting place for putative 'eastern' and 'western' traditions. In the second phase of the shrine, when it was patronized by soldiers, the iconography, if not the idiom, of the frescoes follows a standard pattern found in the west.[12]

All that is obvious enough, but how far did such homogeneity go? How indeed are we to assess degrees of homogeneity? The fragmentary and disparate nature of our evidence makes it almost inevitable that those seeking to interpret the cults should set up clear and unitary models within which the individual items of evidence can fit. The assumption of homogeneity is almost a necessary heuristic device. But for how long should one maintain it?

The best example for exploring the issue of homogeneity is the cult of Mithras, one of the most complex, and most complexly documented, cults of the Roman empire.[13] This cult, allegedly originating in Persia in the remote past, in fact developed in the Latin west in the 2nd century AD. Though the bull-slaying scene was an easily recognizable icon wherever the cult existed, the extent of iconographical uniformity should not be exaggerated. The side scenes round the representation of Mithras and the bull do not appear in a fixed sequence; there seem to be two major groupings, found primarily in the Rhine and in the Danube areas, but Italy was different and even within the two areas there was much diversity.[14] Such diversity might be taken as regional variations, drawing on a common repertoire of images, but more worrying for 'unitarians' are the sequences of planetary gods, which are placed centre stage by Beck 1988. He bravely attempts to make the maximum degree of order, but the evidence just does not fit together as neatly as he hoped. In fact there are different sequences in different contexts which it is not possible to reduce to a central normative core with peripheral elaborations.[15]

If one does not start from the assumption that there is a core of 'real' Mithraic doctrines and a penumbra of divergences or misunderstandings, a possible solution would be to say that the mysteries of Mithras consist of a cluster of overlapping readings, offering different (and sometimes incompatible) systems. If that is the correct interpretation of some rather thorny aspects of Mithraism, it suggests that one should return to the so-called 'Mithras liturgy', preserved as part of a long sequence of magical texts.[16] This is an amazing text which gives instructions about the gaining of divine revelation from a number of gods including Mithras. Early in the 20th century it was argued that it was an actual text of the Mithraic mysteries (hence its common name, the 'Mithras liturgy'). This idea was so roundly criticized that the text practically dropped out of discussions of Mithraism. In fact one should not try to decide if it was 'really' Mithraic (as was originally argued), but look at the way that it employs Mithraic themes. At a different level there is the issue of the role of women in the cult. They were not initiated into the cult, and indeed Porphyry says that they were classified as noxious hyenas.[17] However, the place of women is more complex than the image of the hyena might suggest. In the excavations of the S. Prisca Mithraic sanctuary in Rome (Fig. 11.2, no. 37), the sculpture included the portrait bust of an old lady.[18] She was not necessarily initiated, but hardly a hyena. Perhaps she was the mistress of the house in which the sanctuary was located. Another find from a different Mithraic sanctuary in Rome is the inscribed version of a prayer to Mithras by a woman, one Cascellia Elegans. "Not really Mithraic", some experts claim, but there is nothing in it that is impossible in a Mithraic context.[19] The ideology of the cult was perhaps not as homogeneous as modern theory would like, and there are indeed cases where women make dedications to Mithras.[20]

Space prevents analysis here of the other cults in terms of a non-unitary model, though the various hymns to Isis mentioned above do in fact all differ. Though the one from Kyme claims to be a copy of an archetype at Memphis in Egypt, the others do not and are not the same as it.[21] A cluster model does look rather helpful here too, and is in general a better initial assumption.

THEOLOGICAL EXCLUSIVITY

It is easy to assume that the peculiarities of each cult left no place for the ordinary Graeco-Roman pantheon, and that if any ordinary gods do appear in the cult they have to have peculiar interpretations placed on them. In fact, this assumption needs to be rejected. Consider, for example, the Sanctuary of Mater Magna at Ostia (Fig. 11.4). Within it there were not only temples of Mater Magna and of Attis, but also of Bellona, all of Antonine date.[22] What is Bellona doing here? Scholars sometimes say that she is here seen as an aspect of Mater Magna, but is this a necessary assumption? Then there are statues of other gods dedicated in the sanctuary: Pan (twice), Dionysus, Venus (five times) and perhaps Ceres. They certainly do not play a fixed part in the cult of Mater Magna, and there is surely no reason to deny that these gods carry with them all or most of the evocations they have in other contemporary contexts. But, one might argue, Mater Magna was an institutionalized if marginal cult, whose official acceptance at Rome makes it unsurprising to find other gods in her sanctuary.

What about Jupiter Dolichenus, whose cult was not institutionalized? The sanctuary on the Aventine in Rome (frequented by civilians) is perhaps the best known of his sanctuaries in the empire.[23] The adherents formed a tightly knit group, with a complex hierarchy: a 'father of candidates', priests, and 'patrons' presided over a series of candidates. Jupiter Dolichenus was there described as 'protector of the whole world', and is often called Optimus Maximus and his female partner Juno Regina, the technical names for the first two members of the Capitoline triad. So the cult borrowed (both in Rome and elsewhere in the empire) elements of the Capitoline triad, but to assert the overarching position of *this* deity. In addition, all sorts of other gods were also represented in this sanctuary. First, the ordinary Graeco-Roman gods: Heracles Victor, Artemis with Iphigeneia, Athena, Venus, Dionysus, Silvanus and Apollo; it is striking that the statue of Apollo was put up 'on the order of Jupiter Optimus Maximus Dolichenus'. Secondly, there were Egyptianizing statuettes, *uraei* of Isis, and Isis and Serapis themselves on a relief whose main figures are Jupiter Dolichenus and his female partner. Thirdly, there were four Mithraic reliefs.[24] Presumably the implication of these dedications is that Jupiter Optimus Maximus Dolichenus was simply the new head of the old pantheon, superior both to the gods like Artemis or Apollo, and to the Egyptian and Persian gods. This sort of cosmology would have no need to be exclusivist: indeed incorporation would reinforce its strength.

Mithras is more of a problem. Mithraic cosmology was radically novel and allowed no place for the ordinary gods of the pantheon. What mattered was the ascent of the initiate through the seven grades (Raven, Male Bride, Soldier, Lion, Persian, Sun-runner, Father); as each grade was correlated with a different planet (e.g. Lion with Jupiter, Father with Saturn), the soul of the initiate was probably conceived to rise during his lifetime further and further away from the earth, finally achieving *apogenesis*, or birth away from the material world.[25] Does that mean that for the Mithraic initiate (at least in certain contexts) the traditional Graeco-Roman gods had no role? Scholars sometimes, if only by their silence on this matter, give the impression that this is the case, but again the finds from the S. Prisca sanctuary show that the matter is more complex than theory would suggest. The excavations revealed, along with all the Mithraic material: stucco heads of Serapis, Venus and perhaps Mars; representations of Hecate, Fortuna, Dionysus, Asclepius, a statuette of Serapis, plus Serapis and Magna Mater on two lamps.[26] The text of the final report mentions only the three stucco heads, the rest are buried in the catalogue of finds and the problems they raise for the issue of Mithraic exclusivity has been little discussed.

There are however parallels for this range of dedications from other Mithraic sanctuaries. The Walbrook sanctuary in London contained, in addition to Mithraic images, images of Minerva, Serapis, Mercury, a Water-god, a Genius, and a Dioscorus.[27] Reliefs from Gaul and Germany sometimes feature an assembly of gods: for example, the great relief from Osterburken has Jupiter, Apollo, Mars, Heracles, Juno, Minerva, Venus and so on.[28] Mithraic sanctuaries were, at least from time to time, quite hospitable of other gods.

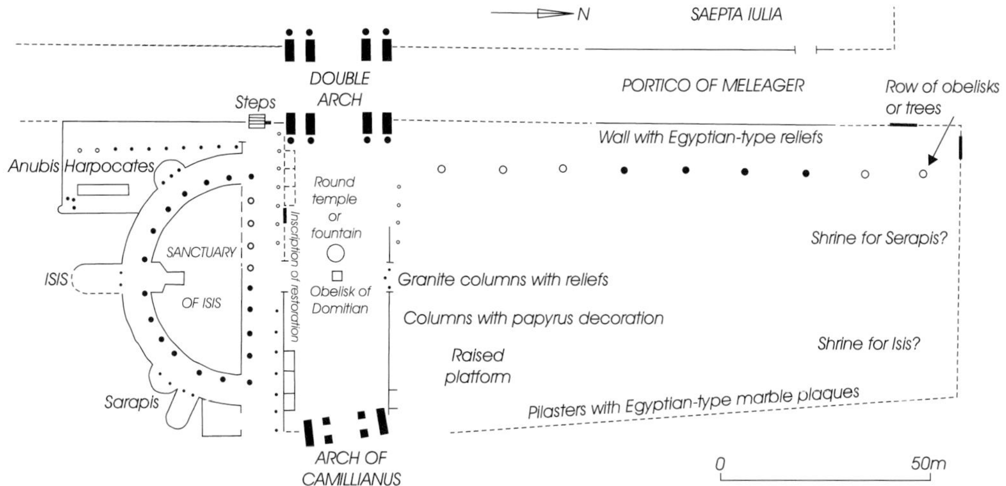

Fig. 11.5: Plan of the sanctuary of Isis and Serapis on the Campus Martius (after Beard, North and Price 1998).

Fig. 11.6: Marble elephant by Bernini (1667) in Piazza Minerva supporting a small 6th century BC Aswan red granite obelisk (H. 5.47 m) from the nearby Sanctuary of Isis and Serapis (Photo: editors).

Fig. 11.7: Domitianic Aswan red granite obelisk (H. 16.54 m) on Bernini's Fontana dei Quattro Fiumi (1651) in Piazza Navona. Probably first erected in the Campus Martius Temple of Isis and Serapis (Photo: editors).

Toynbee argued that the gods represented in the Walbrook sanctuary cohered with the basic ideology of the cult, in that all were concerned with salvation. That is a possible interpretation, though one has to press Minerva rather hard to make her fit, and it does not seem to account for the range of deities found either at S. Prisca or represented at Osterburken. Instead one might suggest that the current interpretations of the cult, which privilege the arcane and astronomical aspects of the cult, have to be seen as coexisting, rather messily no

Fig. 11.8: Bull (just over half life-size) from the Sanctuary of Isis at Benevento (Photo: editors).

doubt, with all sorts of gods familiar to the initiates from the rest of their lives. Presumably they were not structured, as in the cult of Jupiter Dolichenus, into a new pantheon (that was hardly possible with the overall Persian ideology of the cult), but individuals did think from time to time that particular Graeco-Roman gods had their place in a Mithraic sanctuary. There are in fact sporadic instances of images of local deities being dedicated in Mithraic sanctuaries: for example, a Mother Goddess at Carrawburgh on Hadrian's Wall or a Mercury at Stockstadt in Germany.[29] Thus the cult of Mithras, which is often implied to be exclusive, in fact turns out not to be so.

Isis is also surprising, but perhaps for exactly the opposite reasons. According to the ideology of the cult, Isis was all-encompassing. In the hymn from Kyme, Isis is made to say, "I taught humans to honour images of the gods, I founded sanctuaries of the gods", and in Apuleius' novel she says,

> "My unparalleled divine power is worshipped by the whole world in varied forms, with different rites and multifarious names. The first-born Phrygians call me Mother of the Gods at Pessinus; the indigenous Athenians, Minerva, daughter of Cecrops, ... and the Ethiopians, Arians and Egyptians, steeped in their ancient learning, worship me with their own rites and call me by my real name, queen Isis."[30]

So Isis, though of firmly Egyptian origin, was responsible for the apparatus of the ordinary Graeco-Roman pantheon, and indeed was worshipped under various names throughout the world. This cosmology is very inclusive, but we need to see what the actual sanctuaries of Isis were like.[31] At first sight those in Italy seem resolutely Egyptian in tone. The great Sanctuary of Isis and Serapis on the Campus Martius in Rome had a large obelisk, a Serapeum modelled on that at Alexandria and a sanctuary of Isis with a processional route lined with small obelisks and Egyptian statues (Figs. 11.5–11.7).[32] The Sanctuary of Isis at Beneventum had an obelisk, images of Isis, Apis bulls, lions, sphinxes, statues of priests or worshippers, and even images of Domitian as Pharaoh (Fig. 11.8).[33] The iconography could hardly be more resolutely Egyptian than that. The problem is evidential. No sanctuary of Isis in Italy has been properly excavated and published (those just mentioned in Rome and Beneventum have necessarily been reconstructed on the basis of chance finds), which means that we cannot know if there were also statues of non-Egyptian gods in those sanctuaries. The Iseum at Pompeii, which was excavated in the 18th century, is a little better known: it did include statuettes of Dionysus and Venus, perhaps because of the claim that Isis was worshipped under different names throughout the world.[34]

Where does this brief account of Mater Magna, Jupiter Dolichenus, Mithras and Isis leave us? The cosmologies of all four are quite different, three inclusivist, and one (Mithras) exclusivist. And yet at the level of sanctuary dedications, Mater Magna, Jupiter Dolichenus and even Mithras accommodated the ordinary Graeco-Roman gods; only Isis may have excluded them, perhaps to maintain the Egyptian allure of her sanctuaries, but perhaps also because (as we shall see) the level of allegiance to her was very high.

EXCLUSIVITY OF ALLEGIANCE

That brings us on to the third main question: how far did these cults claim exclusivity of allegiance? If one was initiated into one cult, did that preclude membership of others? Or did they serve different functions for the same people at different times? The second alternative is certainly what one would expect in the ordinary Graeco-Roman pantheon. The various gods of the Roman calendar had particular functions to serve; individuals, families and other groups would turn to one or another deity depending on the circumstances. On the other hand, exclusivity of allegiance is what one would expect to follow from the profound differences between the cosmologies of the different cults. Whereas the gods of the Roman calendar were perceived as belonging together in one pantheon, Isis and Mithras proclaimed that they were responsible for different and incompatible cosmologies. It is hard to imagine reconciling the two, but could individuals live with such inconsistencies?

There is some evidence that this was indeed possible. A fine Mithraic relief from Nersae in central Italy has an inscription on the bottom: "Apronianus the civic treasurer made it at his own expense". It so happens that we have another inscription from the same town in which Apronianus the civic treasurer proclaims that he paid for he erection of statues of Serapis and Isis.[35] This suggestion of multiple allegiances is reinforced by the terminology of the cults themselves. It seems that the initiates of most of the cults did not generally use any particular term of self-description, to define them as potentially exclusive adherents of the cult concerned. Modern scholars may talk of 'Mithraists', but there is no corresponding term in the ancient sources; while the grades of initiation were precisely that – not terms regularly used outside a specifically cultic context. The most we can detect are some much vaguer terms of self-description (*syndexios* – 'he who has performed the ritual handshake', or *sacratus* – 'devotee').[36]

In some cults there is a difference between those whose religious, and maybe social, identity had come to depend on the worship of their particular deity (and who were rarely involved in more than one of the new cults) and those nearer the margins (who were much less likely to be so exclusive). In the cult of Mater Magna, for example, we can detect a difference between the *dendrophori*, 'tree-bearers' (who formed a sub-group within the cult with particular ritual duties) and the castrated cult servants, the *galli*: the *dendrophori* are found playing other roles; not so the *galli*. This exclusivity is predictable, insofar as their castration marked them out in perpetuity as belonging to this one deity; for the *galli*, that is, this religious role was their principal role, their claim to status and self-definition – as is suggested by the fact that some chose to have themselves represented on their tombstones in the costume of, and with the symbols of, their religious office.[37]

With the cult of Isis too there were some overachievers whose physical appearance was crucial. Those who had shaved their heads as priests of Isis also sought to display to the world that they belonged to Isis. And Lucius in Apuleius' novel is presented as having no time for any deity other than Isis. Lucius says to Isis before leaving her sanctuary in Corinth,

> "I shall make sure I do all the things a religious but poor person can: I shall for ever guard your sacred appearance and most holy divine power in the depth of my heart and gaze upon it".

When he went from Corinth to Rome, on the instruction of Isis, he was again initiated into her mysteries there.[38] The story presupposes and evokes the idea that some people were exclusively attached to the cult of Isis. Funerary inscriptions again help to confirm this impression. There are a significant number of funerary inscriptions that are Isiac in language or decoration: some 25 from Rome and 15 from the rest of Italy. Some begin with the traditional formula *Dis Manibus* ('To the Spirits of the Dead') and continue with references to attachment to Isis. But what is particularly striking about the texts is the range of positions that was commemorated on the tombstones. Unlike Magna Mater, where only the *galli* commemorate themselves, all sorts of Isiac offices are mentioned. In Rome there was a *fanaticus* of Isis and Serapis; an *aedituus* of Isis Pelagia, who had held office for 10 years; women described as Bubastiaca or Memfiana; a *pastophorus*; a man who as *nauarcus* had paid for the major procession of Isis, the *navigium*; and a wife commemorated in a long verse epigram as a "chaste and attentive worshipper of the Pharian goddess [i.e. Isis], with whom I spent thirty years of happiness".[39]

No other cult, it seems, generated such an extensive public display in funerary monuments. One might say that this is because of the connection between Isis and the after-life. There certainly was such a link. Isis promised Lucius that he would be subject to her for the rest of his life, which she would prolong beyond what the fates had appointed, and after death he would find her shining in the darkness of the underworld. His subsequent initiation took him down to the entrance of the underworld and back to life again.[40] So too in the funerary inscriptions from Rome there are a few which hope that Osiris will grant the deceased refreshment in the afterlife.[41]

So tombstones were at least an appropriate context in which to commemorate Isiac attachments, but they do not read like a form of Pascal's wager, to maximize the chances of the deceased. Rather, they pick out Isiac attachments as crucial attributes of the *living*. And the cult offered an extremely wide range of positions in which people could feel proud. Unlike the cult of Mater Magna, there were many ways in the cult of Isis of marking one's primary if not exclusive allegiance to the cult.

The argument as presented so far has implications for our understanding of Jews and Christians in this period. There are certainly monuments peculiar to each of the groups: for example, catacombs containing images of the Jewish *menorah*;[42] the memorial to Peter below S. Pietro; or the Memorial of Peter and Paul on the Appian Way, of 3rd century date, whose rear wall has contemporary graffiti such as "Peter and Paul pray for Victor".[43] But if one accepts the suggestion about the relative *lack* of homogeneity and exclusivity among at least some of the traditional cults, it perhaps becomes easier to understand the behaviour of some Jewish and Christian groups. That is, the 'cluster' or 'polythetic' approach to the two religions, which formed our starting point and which is normally applied *within* the context of Judaism and Christianity, can be extended to the relations between Jews and Christians and between them both and traditional cults.

If the experience of the cults of, for example, Jupiter Dolichenus or Mithras, let alone of the ordinary civic cults, was of a kind of inclusivity, it is perhaps easier to see how some individuals could be led to at least the fringes of Judaism or Christianity. 'Godfearers' or their

Christian equivalents might expect not to have to reject all their own religious heritage, however much hard-liners might denounce the whole apparatus of 'paganism'. Certainly if one looks forward to the 4th and 5th centuries, the picture is surely of at times some sort of attempted reconciliation of the two. After all, the *Codex Calendar of 354*, dedicated to a Christian, includes both the calendar of the traditional cults of Rome and a Christian calendar, and towards the end of the 5th century a bishop of Rome felt it necessary to pronounce that only pagans and not Christians could take part in the Lupercalia.[44]

In the 2nd and 3rd centuries there were debates about how much traditional thought should be taken over by Christians. Followers of the Christian Theodotus in Rome in the early 3rd century apparently diligently studied Euclid's geometry, admired Aristotle and Theophrastus, and revered Galen for his logic. Their stance was controversial, and we know of them only because Eusebius preserves a pamphlet attacking them.[45] So too some Christians felt that they could participate in traditional cults. Some (like the Valentinians) were said to eat sacrificial meat and gather at pagan festivals, imagining that they were beyond pollution.[46] Others held that traditional cults preserved part of the truth. The Naassenes were said to hold that performances of the mysteries of Attis were under the guidance of providence. Without themselves being castrated, they would attend the mysteries of Mater Magna "considering that they can actually observe their own mystery in those rites". Hippolytus, who reports their actions, is horrified, and most church historians have not really escaped from his perspective, but the attitude of the Naassenes should perhaps be seen as predictable, and perhaps even normal, in the religious life of the Roman empire.[47]

In conclusion three remarks. One, inconclusively, about change. It is very hard to see what things were like before the 2nd and 3rd centuries AD, on which this chapter has focused. We are well informed about this period because of the growth of the epigraphic and iconographic habits, but we are correspondingly poorly informed about the situation in earlier centuries. On the other hand, the situation was obviously different by the 4th century: some Roman senators had by then become very inclusivist, attempting to incorporate all sorts of 'traditional' cults, including Isis and Mithras, in the face of Christianity.[48] The tendency to bracket together all the non Judaeo-Christian cults was established by the mid-3rd century with Decius' promulgation of a universal sacrifice test, and was growing before then.[49] There was also a move on the Jewish and Christian sides towards greater homogeneity at this period.[50]

Second, gender. Did women and men have different religious identities at this period?[51] In terms of ethnic and civic identities the picture remained much as it had been in the classical period. The religious systems of Rome and of individual cities in the empire drew on women so far as was necessary for cults of a peculiarly 'female' nature, and permitted their attendance at public ceremonials.[52] Were women short-changed, and ready for new roles? Upper class men feared any activity by women outside these closely defined roles, and operated with a stereotype of extensive female participation in some elective cults.[53] But the extent of female participation was in fact not as great as in the stereotype. Though women, as we have seen, did take part in the cult of Isis, they did not predominate numerically and the principal offices were held by men.[54] Lower class women generally could not join the occupational or burial associations formed by slaves, ex-slaves and free poor; only in the purely domestic associations of the great households were women normally members.[55] It was the *mixed* membership of *some* of the cults (Isis, Judaism, Christianity) that differentiated them from the traditional cults of Greece and Rome, where the norm was segregated participation.

Third, homogeneity and the Roman empire. The evidence on the ground shows that the cults which are often seen as both homogeneous and exclusive are neither. The hypothetical creator of a cult like Mithraism may have expected both homogeneity and exclusivity for his new vision of the world (though this is pure guesswork), but the worshippers had quite different expectations, derived from ordinary polytheism. The worshippers treated the cults in part as neither homogeneous (the cults of any given Graeco-Roman god were not homogeneous) nor exclusive (any more than the traditional cults were exclusive). But even if this argument seems plausible, the cults do have a recognizable degree of cluster or polythetic cohesion. And, with the exceptions of Judaism, Christianity and Manichaeism, they are found only within the bounds of the Roman empire. Their adherents desired cults that were not limited to one town, but transcended particular places or regions. These cults offered new religious identities within the framework of the Roman empire. As was said in the cult of Mithras, "Hail to the Fathers from East to West".[56]

NOTES

1 The substance of this chapter, first written in 1993, has been incorporated in BEARD, NORTH and PRICE 1998, I, 245–312. Vol. II, a sourcebook, includes many of the sources, both textual and material, referred to here.

2 *IGUR* 117–25; SCHNEIDER 1987; CHAUSSON 1995, 661–718; *Lexicon* IV, *s.v.* 'Sol Malachbelus/Malakbel', 334–35.

3 BALSDON 1969, 244–339; BEARD, NORTH and PRICE 1998, I, 262–63; BERNSTEIN 1998. Cf. BEARD, NORTH and PRICE 1998, II, no. 5.7.

4 *Lexicon* III, 257–70 catalogues the evidence. Two good examples are the sanctuaries below S. Prisca (VERMASEREN and ESSEN 1965; *Lexicon* III, *s.v.* 'Mithra (S. Prisca; Reg. XIII)', 268–69) and that below S. Stefano Rotondo (LISSI CARONNA 1986; *Lexicon* I, *s.v.* 'Castra Peregrina: Mithraeum', 251; *Lexicon* V, *s.v.* 'S. Stephanus in Monte Celio', 373–77), the former in a private (senatorial?) house and the latter in the Castra Peregrina.

5 CARCOPINO 1926; BEARD, NORTH and PRICE 1998, I, 273–74. Alternatively, it has been argued that the building had a primarily funerary purpose.

6 CUMONT 1911. BURKERT 1987 also rejects the category 'Oriental cults'.

7 On classification in terms of family or sporadic resemblances, 'polythetic classification', see NEEDHAM 1975. For varieties of Judaisms, see NEUSNER 1987; LIEU 1992; GOODMAN forthcoming. For varieties of Christianity see BAUER 1971. For further information see SCHÜRER 1973–87 and FREND 1984.

8 Isis: MALAISE 1984. Jupiter Dolichenus: HÖRIG and SCHWERTHEIM 1987; BELLELLI 1997. Mithras: CLAUSS 1990, 31–7, with map at 34.

9 *Lexicon* III, 107–16; *Lexicon* IV, 302–3 (Serapis).

10 HÖRIG and SCHWERTHEIM 1987, nos. 5 (Doliche, Syria), 103 (Jasen, Moesia Superior), 201 (Lussonium, Pannonia Inferior), 371 (Aventine, Rome), 512 (Heddernheim, Germania Superior). Cf. DE BELLIS 1997.

11 LECLANT 1984; FOWDEN 1986, 45–52.

12 CUMONT 1975; BECK 1984, 2013–17.

13 For introductions, see VERMASEREN 1963; BECK 1984; HINNELLS 1985; TURCAN 1993.

14 GORDON 1980.

15 BECK 1988; PRICE 1990. See now GORDON 1994.

16 DIETERICH 1923; translated in BETZ 1992, 48–54, extracts trans. in BEARD, NORTH and PRICE 1998, II, no. 11.6.

17 TOYNBEE 1955–56; GORDON 1980, 42–3, 57–64. Porphyry, *On Abstinence from Animal Food* 4.16, trans. BEARD, NORTH and PRICE 1998, II, no. 12.5d.

18 VERMASEREN and ESSEN 1965, 454 no. 11.

19 MUSSIES 1982. The inscription comes from the S. Stefano Rotondo sanctuary (LISSI CARONNA 1986).

20 *CIMRM* I.284, 705, 1463.

21 Above, n. 11. *Inschriften von Kyme* 41, trans. BEARD, NORTH and PRICE 1998, II, no. 12.4a.

22 G. CALZA 1943; R. CALZA 1943; VERMASEREN 1977–89, III, 107–14. Mary Beard kindly drew my attention to this sanctuary.

23 HÖRIG and SCHWERTHEIM 1987, 221–63; *Lexicon* III, *s.v.* 'Iuppiter Dolichenus, Templum', 133–34; *Lexicon* V, 270; CHINI 1997; SANZI 1997.
24 For another Mithraic relief in a sanctuary of Jupiter Dolichenus, see HÖRIG and SCHWERTHEIM 1987, no. 97 (Egeta, Moesia Superior); cf. no. 431 (Rome).
25 VERMASEREN 1963, 138–53; TURCAN 1982.
26 VERMASEREN and ESSEN 1965, 134–37, 342 no. 20 (Hecate), 342 no. 21 (Fortuna), 343 no. 24 (Venus), 383 no. 966 (Dionysus), 435 no. 11 (Serapis), 447 no. 81 (Serapis, on lamp), 447 no. 82 (Asclepius), 447 no. 84 (Medusa), 476 no. 236 (Magna Mater, on lamp); *Opus* 4 (1985) for lamps; VERMASEREN 1977–89, III, no. 220 Attis walled in by AD 97.
27 See TOYNBEE 1986, who characteristically did discuss the issue of exclusivity; SHEPHERD 1998, 165–83, 228.
28 *CIMRM* 1292.
29 Carrawburgh: RICHMOND and GILLAM 1951, 30 (with further references); COULSTON and PHILLIPS 1988, No. 164; Stockstadt: SCHWERTHEIM 1974, 147 no. 117a.
30 *Inschriften von Kyme* 41, lines 25–6 (trans. BEARD, NORTH and PRICE 1998, II, no. 12.4a); Apuleius, *Metamorphoses* 11.5 (trans. BEARD, NORTH and PRICE 1998, II, no. 12.4b).
31 WILD 1984.
32 MALAISE 1972, 187–214; ENSOLI VITTOZZI 1990; LEMBKE 1994; *Lexicon* III, *s.v.* 'Iseum ct Serapeum in Campo Martio; Isis Campensis', 107–9, Fig. 69. For other sanctuaries of Isis in Rome, see *Lexicon* III, 110–16; *Lexicon* V, 269; BEARD, NORTH and PRICE 1998, I, 266.
33 MÜLLER 1969.
34 *Alla ricerca di Iside* 1992, 70. In the western empire only the sanctuary at Sabratha has been dealt with fully; that may have had a statue of Heracles: PESCE 1953; WILD 1984, 1817–18. The Temple of Isis at Dion (Macedonia) was flanked by one to Aphrodite Hypolympidia and one probably to Eros: PANDERMALIS 1982; WILD 1984, 1841–42.
35 *CIMRM* 650; *ILS* 4381 = VIDMAN 1969, no. 477.
36 GORDON 1994, 109–10. 'Isiacs' does have an equivalent ancient word, but it is only very rarely attested.
37 VERMASEREN 1977–89, III, nos. 422, 433, 446, 447 (Ostia).
38 Apuleius, *Metamorphoses* 11.25, 26–30.
39 VIDMAN 1969, nos. 373, 396, 422–24, 428, 433, 451 (trans. in BEARD, NORTH and PRICE 1998, II, no. 9.6b).
40 Apuleius, *Metamorphoses* 11.6, 23 (trans. BEARD, NORTH and PRICE 1998, II, no. 12.4b).
41 VIDMAN 1969, nos. 459–63.
42 GOODENOUGH 1953–68, II, 3–50 (e.g. Via Appia Antica). Cf. RAJAK 1994; RUTGERS 1995, 50–99, who argue that the Jewish catacombs were not exclusive.
43 TOYNBEE and WARD-PERKINS 1956, 127–82 (picture in BEARD, NORTH and PRICE 1998, II, no. 12.7f(iv)).
44 SALZMAN 1990; Gelasius, *Letter against the Lupercalia* (ed. Pomares, Paris, 1959, trans. BEARD, NORTH and PRICE 1998, II, no. 5.2e).
45 *Ecclesiastical History* 5.28.13–4 (trans. BEARD, NORTH and PRICE 1998, II, no. 12.7e(v)).
46 Irenaeus, *Against Heresies* 1.6.2–4 (trans. BEARD, NORTH and PRICE 1998, II, no. 12.7e(iii)).
47 *Refutation of All Heresies* 5.9.7–11 (trans. BEARD, NORTH and PRICE 1998, II, no. 12.7e(iv)).
48 BEARD, NORTH and PRICE 1998, I, 364–88.
49 RIVES 1999. For one document see BEARD, NORTH and PRICE 1998, II, no. 6.8c.
50 BEARD, NORTH and PRICE 1998, I, 304–6.
51 SAWYER 1996 discusses the relation between religion and gender.
52 SCHEID 1992.
53 EDWARDS 1993, 63–97; HENDERSON 1989.
54 MORA 1990, II, 1–29.
55 WALTZING 1895–1900, I, 348–49, IV, 254–57; AUSBÜTTEL 1982, 42.
56 VERMASEREN and ESSEN 1965, 155, 179–84.

BIBLIOGRAPHY

Alla ricerca di Iside 1992: *Alla ricerca di Iside: analisi, studi e restauri dell'Iseo pompeiano nel Museo di Napoli*, Roma, 1992.

AUSBÜTTEL, F.M. 1982: *Untersuchungen zu den Vereinen im Westen des römischen Reiches,* Frankfurter althistorischer Studien 11, Kallmünz, 1982.

BALSDON, J.P.V.D. 1969: *Life and Leisure in Ancient Rome*, London, 1969.

BAUER, W. 1971: *Orthodoxy and Heresy in Earliest Christianity*, Philadelphia, 1971 (London, 1972; German original 1934).

BECK, R. 1984: 'Mithraism since Franz Cumont', *ANRW* II.17.4, 1984, 2002–115.

BECK, R. 1988: *Planetary Gods and Planetary Orders in the Mysteries of Mithras*, Études preliminaires aux religions orientales dans l'Empire romain 109, Leiden, 1988.

BEARD, M., NORTH, J. and PRICE, S.R.F. 1998: *Religions of Rome* I–II, Cambridge, 1998.

BELLELLI, G.M. 1997: 'Les sanctuaires de Iuppiter Dolichenus à Rome', in BELLELLI and BIANCHI 1997, 305–28.

BELLELLI, G.M. and BIANCHI, U. (ed.) 1997: *Orientalia Sacra Urbis Romae: Dolichena et Heliopolitana. Recueil d'études archéologiques et hisorico-religieuses sur les cultes cosmopolites d'origine commagénienne et syrienne*, Roma, 1997.

BERNSTEIN, F. 1998: Ludi publici: *Untersuchungen zur Entstehung und Entwicklung der öffentlichen Spiele im republikanische Rom*, Historia Einzelschrift 119, Stuttgart, 1998.

BETZ, H.D. (ed.) 1992: *The Greek Magical Papyri in Translation*, ed. 2, Chicago and London, 1992.

BIANCHI, U. and VERMASEREN, J.R. (ed.) 1982: *La soteriologia dei culti orientali nell'impero romano*, Études preliminaires aux religions orientales dans l'Empire romain 92, Leiden, 1982.

BURKERT, W. 1987: *Ancient Mystery Cults,* Cambridge Mass., and London, 1987.

CALZA, G. 1943: 'Il santuario della Magna Mater a Ostia', *MemPontAcc* 6, 1943, 183–205.

CALZA, R. 1943: 'Sculture rinvenute nel santuario', *MemPontAcc* 6, 1943, 207–27.

CARCOPINO, J. 1926: *La basilique pythagoricienne de la Porte Majeure,* Paris, 1926.

CHAUSSON, F. 1995: '*Vel Iovi vel Soli* : Quatre études autour de la Vigna Barberini (191–354)', *MEFRA* 107, 1995, 661–765.

CHINI, P. 1997: 'Le Dolocenum de l'Aventin: interprétation des structures', in BELLELLI and BIANCHI 1997, 329–47.

CLAUSS, M. 1990: *Mithras, Kult und Mysterien,* München, 1990.

COARELLI, F. 1979: 'Topografia mitraica di Roma (con una carta)', in U. Bianchi (ed.), *Mysteria Mithrae. Atti del seminario internazionale sulla specificata storico-religiosa dei Misteri di Mithra, con particolare riferimento alle fonti documentarie di Roma e Ostia, Roma e Ostia 28–31 marzo 1978*, Études preliminaires aux religions orientales dans l'Empire romain 80, Leiden, 1979, 69–79.

COARELLI, F. 1982: 'I monumenti dei culti orientali in Roma. Questioni topografiche e cronologiche', in BIANCHI and VERMASEREN 1982, 33–67.

COULSTON, J.C.N. and PHILLIPS, E.J. 1988: *Corpus Signorum Imperii Romani, Great Britain I.6, Hadrian's Wall West of the River North Tyne and Carlisle*, Oxford, 1988.

CUMONT, F. 1911: *The Oriental Religions in Roman Paganism,* Chicago, 1911.

CUMONT, F. 1975: 'The Dura mithraeum' (ed. and trans. E. D. Francis), in J.R. Hinnells (ed.), *Mithraic Studies: Proceedings of the First International Congress of Mithraic Studies* I–II, Manchester, 1975, 151–214.

DE BELLIS, S. 1997: 'Sur la typologie des triangles votifs du culte de Jupiter Dolichénien', in BELLELLI and BIANCHI 1997, 455–68.

DIETERICH, A. 1923: *Eine Mithrasliturgie*, ed. 3, Leipzig and Berlin, 1923.

EDWARDS, C. 1993: *The Politics of Immorality in Ancient Rome*, Cambridge, 1993.

ENSOLI VITTOZZI, S. 1990: *Musei Capitolini: La collezione Egizia*, Roma, 1990.

FOWDEN, G. 1986: *The Egyptian Hermes*, Cambridge, 1986.

FREND, W.H.C. 1984: *The Rise of Christianity*, London, 1984.

GOODENOUGH, E.R. 1953–68: *Jewish Symbols in the Graeco-Roman Period* I–XIII, New York, 1953–68.

GOODMAN, M.D. forthcoming: *Varieties of Judaism*, Oxford, forthcoming.

GORDON, R.L. 1972: 'Mithraism and Roman society', *Religion* 2, 1972, 92–121, repr. in GORDON 1996.

GORDON, R.L. 1980: 'Panelled complications', *Journal of Mithraic Studies* 3, 1980, 200–27, repr. in GORDON 1996.

GORDON, R.L. 1989: 'Authority, salvation and mystery in the mysteries of Mithras', in J. Huskinson, P. Zanker and R. Gordon (ed.), *Image and Mystery in the Roman World,* Gloucester, 1989, 45–80, repr. in GORDON 1996.

GORDON, R.L. 1994: 'Mystery, metaphor and doctrine in the mysteries of Mithras', in J.R. Hinnells (ed.), *Studies in Mithraism,* Roma, 1994, 103–24.

GORDON, R. L. 1996: *Image and Value in the Graeco-Roman World: Studies in Mithraism and Religious Art*, Aldershot/Brookfield Vermont, 1996.

HENDERSON, J. 1989: 'Satire writes "woman": *Gendersong*', *Proceedings of the Cambridge Philological Society* n.s. 35, 1989, 50–80.

HINNELLS, J. R. 1985: *Persian Mythology*, ed. 2, London, 1985.

HÖRIG, M. and SCHWERTHEIM, E. 1987: *Corpus cultus Iovis Dolicheni*, Études preliminaires aux religions orientales dans l'Empire romain 106, Leiden, 1987.

LECLANT, J. 1984: 'Aegyptiaca et mileiux isiaques. Recherches sur la diffusion du matériel et des idées égyptiennes', *ANRW* 2.17.3, 1984, 1692–709.

LEMBKE, K. 1994: *Das Iseum Campense in Rom*, Archäologie und Geschichte 3, Heidelberg, 1994.

LIEU, J., NORTH, J. and RAJEK, T. (ed.) 1992: *The Jews among Pagans and Christians*, London and New York, 1992.

LISSI CARONNA, E. 1986: *Il mitreo dei* Castra Peregrinorum *(S. Stefano Rotondo)*, Études preliminaires aux religions orientales dans l'Empire romain 104, Leiden, 1986.

MALAISE, M. 1972: *Inventaire préliminaire des documents égyptiens découverts en Italie*, Études preliminaires aux religions orientales dans l'Empire romain 21, Leiden, 1972.

MALAISE, M. 1984: 'La diffusion des cultes égyptiens dans les provinces européennes de l'Empire romain', *ANRW* II.17.3, 1984, 1615–91.

MEIGGS, R. 1973: *Roman Ostia*, ed. 2, Oxford 1973.

MORA, F. 1990: *Prosopographia Isiaca* I–II, Études preliminaires aux religions orientales dans l'Empire romain 113, Leiden, 1990.

MÜLLER, H.W. 1969: *Der Isiskult im antike Benevent,* Münchner ögyptologische Studien 16, Berlin, 1969.

MUSSIES, G. 1982: 'Cascelia's prayer', in BIANCHI and VERMASEREN 1982, 156–67.

NEEDHAM, R. 1975: 'Polythetic classification: convergence and consequences', *Man* n.s. 10, 1975, 349–69.

NEUSNER, J., GREEN, W.S. and FRERICHS, E.S. (ed.) 1987: *Judaisms and their Messiahs at the Turn of the Christian Era*, Cambridge, 1987.

PANDERMALIS, D. 1982: 'Ein neues Heiligtum in Dion', *AA*, 1982, 727–35.

PESCE, G. 1953: *Il tempio d'Iside in Sabratha*, Roma, 1953.

PRICE, S.R.F. 1990: [Review of BECK 1988], *Phoenix* 44, 1990, 194–96.

RAJAK, T. 1994: 'Inscription and context: reading the Jewish catacombs of Rome', in J.W. van Henten and P.W. van der Horst (ed.), *Studies in Early Jewish Epigraphy,* Leiden, 1994, 226–41.

RICHMOND, I.A. and GILLAM, J.P. 1951: *The Temple of Mithras at Carrawburgh,* Newcastle upon Tyne, 1951.

RIVES, J.B. 1999: 'The decree of Decius and the religion of empire', *JRS* 89, 1999, 135–54.

RUTGERS, L.V. 1995: *The Jews in Late Antique Rome*, Leiden, 1995.

SALZMAN, M.R. 1990: *On Roman Time. The Codex-Calendar of 354 and the Rhythms of Urban Life in Late Antiquity*, Berkeley, 1990.

SANZI, E. 1997: 'Dimension sociale et organisation du culte Dolichénien', in BETELLI and BIANCHI 1997, 475–513.

SAWYER, D.F. 1996: *Women and Religion in the First Christian Centuries,* London and New York, 1996.

SCHEID, J. 1992: 'The religious roles of Roman women', in P. Schmitt Pantel (ed.), *A History of Women: from Ancient Goddesses to Christian Saints,* Cambridge Mass., 1992, 377–408.

SCHNEIDER, E.E. 1987: 'Il santuario di Bel e delle divinità di Palmira. Comunità e tradizioni religiose dei Palmireni a Roma', *DialArch* 3.5, 1987, 69–85.

SCHÜRER, E. 1973–87: *The History of the Jewish People in the Age of Jesus Christ* I–III, (revised ed. by G. Vermes, F. Millar and M. Goodman), Edinburgh, 1973–87.

SCHWERTHEIM, E. 1974: *Die Denkmäler orientalischer Gottheiten im römischen Deutschland*, Études preliminaires aux religions orientales dans l'Empire romain 40, Leiden, 1974.

SHEPHERD, J.D. 1998: *The Temple of Mithras, London*, English Heritage Archaeology Report 12, London, 1998.

TOYNBEE, J.M.C. 1955–56: 'Still more about Mithras', *Hibbert Journal* 54, 1955–56, 107–14.

TOYNBEE, J.M.C. 1986: *The Roman Art Treasures from the Temple of Mithras [London]*, London, 1986.

TOYNBEE, J. and WARD-PERKINS, J. 1956: *The Shrine of St. Peter and the Vatican Excavations*, London, 1956.

TURCAN, R. 1982: 'Salut mithriaque et sotériologie néoplatonicienne', in BIANCHI and VERMASEREN 1982, 173–91.

TURCAN, R. 1993: *Mithra et le mithriacisme,* ed. 2, Paris, 1993.

VERMASEREN, M.J. 1963: *Mithras, the Secret God,* London, 1963.

VERMASEREN, M.J. 1977–89: *Corpus cultus Cybelae Attidisque*, Études preliminaires aux religions orientales dans l'Empire romain 50, I–VII, Leiden, 1977–89.

VERMASEREN, M.J. and ESSEN, C.C. van 1965: *The Excavations in the Mithraeum of the Church of Santa Prisca in Rome*, Leiden, 1965.

VIDMAN, L. 1969: *Sylloge inscriptionum religionis Isiacae et Sarapiacae,* Religionsgeschichtliche Versuche und Vorarbeiten 28, Berlin, 1969.

WALTZING, J.-P. 1895–1900: *Etude historique sur les corporations professionnelles chez les romains* I–IV, Louvain, 1895–1900.

WILD, R.A. 1984: 'The known Isis-Sarapis sanctuaries of the Roman period', *ANRW* II.17.4, 1984, 1739–51.

12. Lost Glories? Rome at the End of Empire

Neil Christie

"After I had spent some time admiring this stunningly picturesque sight, I thanked God, mighty throughout the entire world, who had here rendered the works of man wondrously and indescribably beautiful. For although all of Rome lies in ruins, nothing intact can be compared to this."[1]

INTRODUCTION

All too frequent is the image of an unchanging imperial Rome, strewn with an astonishing array of monuments, amenities, services, bureaucracy and traders, enduring beyond the Roman heyday before being swept aside by uncouth barbarian soldiery in the 5th century. The transition from Roman to German is still perceived as a brutal rupture, with civilization and culture tumbling into the bleakness of the Dark Ages. The architectural grandeur is viewed as surviving more through its bulk and solidity than through any non-Roman input and churches alone are seen as beacons of residual Roman influence. The writings of Edward Gibbon speak gloomily of this transition, although they also show that he clearly understood that the decay had long before begun to make its mark on the social, military and monumental fabric of the Roman state. But how many of Rome's past glories were still evident at the end of the 5th century? How far was the monumentality of Augustan Rome maintained until the arrival of the Visigothic and Ostrogothic armies? To what degree did the incoming Germans disrupt and destroy the ancient Rome? How eternal was the Eternal City? By the late 5th century Rome was certainly old – nearly twelve hundred years old – but was she past her sell-by date? As will be shown, these questions are not always easy to answer: our evidence is at times fragmentary and at best suggestive, though these data do combine to offer a reasonably coherent guide to the format of late imperial Rome.

It is, firstly, important to note that in the final centuries of Roman rule, Rome herself was no longer even capital of Italy, let alone capital of the empire – in the late 3rd century Milan had usurped Rome's role of capital as the emperors turned to face the northern frontiers; in the early 5th century as the barbarians were beginning their sightseeing tours of the old Roman heartland, the emperor shifted from Milan to the marshes of Ravenna. Rome thus had long ago virtually been relegated to an out-of-the-way Museum city, still cram-packed with monuments, but with many of these fine public buildings in serious need of attention. Despite the emperors' good intentions to revamp Rome as an early Heritage Centre, the Eternal City lacked the money and the civil authorities to be rekindled. Indeed, few emperors (Honorius briefly, plus a few usurpers) even paid Rome the honour of a visit in the 5th century, undoubtedly thereby restricting the effectiveness of legislation regarding the preservation of the old monuments. Politically and economically Rome had been marginalized. Hence the glorious mosaics of 5th- and 6th-century Ravenna are not readily matched in old imperial Rome.

This is perhaps rather overstating the case, since Rome continued as the symbolic heart of the beleaguered empire, and, with the person of the Bishop of Rome or Pope, she claimed religious supremacy too. But the transfer of the imperial court to Milan in the late 3rd century, followed in the early 4th century by the foundation of Constantinople as capital of the Eastern Roman empire (and with this the creation of an eastern archepiscopal rival), combined to denude the old capital of enormous imperial income and favour. Revenue from Church lands and from pilgrim traffic clearly helped in the upkeep of the many early Christian churches but little may have been left for maintaining the mass of other, more ancient structures littered across the huge urban expanse.

The key question to be asked here, therefore, is whether the removal of immediate imperial patronage had a major impact on the city's monumentality. Was 5th-century Rome really so far removed from the glory days of Augustus? In what ways had the city changed and why? And can we see here already the emergence of the medieval *disabitato*[2] and the city 'of ruins' described by Magister Gregorius in the 13th century?

Problematic is the fact that the picture that can be drawn from historical and archaeological sources is not always clear enough to provide answers to these questions. There are relatively few good documentary sources to guide us neatly through into the 5th century: vital for the late empire are the laws of the *Codex Theodosianus* which tell us how the emperor viewed things and what problems the state sought to counter; but, in contrast, there are few nice straightforward 'no frills' histories to reveal everyday situations. Authors like Zosimus, Augustine and Ausonius offer us potted histories, clerical debate and sluggish poetry, but lack the depth and authority of earlier sources such as Livy, Pliny, or Juvenal. Ammianus Marcellinus alone offers a coherent guide to the politico-military and social upheavals of the 4th-century empire. For the Church the *Liber Pontificalis* charts us through the contributions of the early bishops, whilst Eusebius provides suitably sweeping praise for Constantine's early works. Inscriptions continue to be carved, although even this epigraphic habit is reduced from the later 3rd century and increasingly we hear only from state officials and, in particular, governors; early Christian epitaphs, meanwhile, offer rarely more than minimal information.[3] Thus relatively few sources adequately allow for an understanding of basic changes in everyday Roman culture. Nonetheless, some sources are at least available and so we are not forced to rely purely on archaeology to provide both bones and flesh to the image of late Rome.

This literary fall-back is in fact important, given that archaeology itself is only slowly contributing to the picture of the last centuries of imperial Rome. The main reason for this archaeological tardiness is the woeful neglect by 19th- and early 20th-century archaeologists of the poorer, less substantial layers of the period of *c.* AD 350 onwards. For example, in much of the Roman Forum early investigations had the primary aim of clearing down to the solid, unmissable and materially rich Roman imperial layers dating to the first centuries AD, with the result that few elements in the Forum apart from a number of later churches can be set to the period after AD 300.[4] Pockets of undisturbed and potentially fruitful stratigraphy survive away from the monumental heart of the city,[5] but there seems far too little to enable us easily to draw up a coherent archaeological image of the use of the Palatine and Forum areas in Late Antiquity and beyond.[6] Instead we rely heavily on stray finds, incomplete old excavation records and later references which offer hints only of the major changes occurring. Indeed, it is only in very recent years that proper academic interest has turned to examine the phases of decline, aided by the increase in systematic urban excavations which seek to record all periods of past activity.[7] Understandably things have been slow: unlike in England, where British archaeologists have long been keen to hunt out traces of

Anglo-Saxon ancestors, in Italy the emphasis has always been on the Roman prime – simply because there is just so much of it still extant. But questions of survival and continuity beyond the Roman fall now stimulate vital research into ceramics in particular, since pottery provides one of the most common and more tangible archaeological guides for human activity. A detailed understanding of the ceramics allows for discussion on the levels of trade activity, of local production and consumption, and thereby provides scope for understanding more of the character and needs of the population of Rome in the late empire.[8]

Pottery studies are essential because elsewhere we begin to lose sight of the urban and rural populations, due mainly to an evident material decline, manifested most strongly in the decline in stone building and a reversion to timber construction, primarily in the domestic context. At the same time, however, the loss of civic pride and a loss in patronage witnessed a significant decline in public building programmes, with individuals tending to keep their money to themselves.[9] In effect, the architectural splendour of the early empire falls away. Nonetheless there is one major source of data for the late empire which we can fortunately draw upon, namely the Church and Christianity. A large number of early Christian basilicas survive in one form or another in Rome – nearly intact as in the case of Sant'Agnese on the Via Nomentana or swamped out by later rebuilding, as with San Pietro in Vaticano – and present ample scope for studying the changing urban landscape of the Eternal City.[10] But even here there are problems in study, since churches have often been looked at purely from an architectural or an historical context and rarely have they been tied into the broader social context – it is too easy to be carried along by the descriptions of glorious new fittings, donations, etc. endowed to churches by each pope.[11] Churches can be a veritable mine of information architecturally, artistically and archaeologically: so many Roman basilica churches offer instant amalgams of Baroque, Renaissance, Romanesque, Carolingian, Byzantine and Early Christian features, either visible, stored up, part-shrouded or simply waiting to be found. In addition, church size, siting and building materials – including the use of *spolia*, material drawn from demolished buildings[12] – each provide essential clues regarding population and wider changes in the urban fabric.

These are some of the main sources at hand for analysing late imperial Rome. Next some of the key events which wrought drastic changes on the old capital in the last centuries of Roman rule can be summarized.

THE LATE ROMAN CONTEXT

The problems can in fact be traced back to the end of the 2nd century AD – the period at which Edward Gibbon properly commenced his monumental work *The Decline and Fall of the Roman Empire.* After a century and a half of peace and prosperity within the empire and stability along the distant Rhine and Danube river frontiers, Germanic tribes suddenly broke through at various points. In the case of one group, made up of Marcomanni and Quadi, these intruders made it down as far as Aquileia and Oderzo in north-east Italy. The shock-waves must have been tremendous – the very heartland of the empire had been penetrated by an enemy. Yet this was a mere taster of later events, with the turbulent 3rd century marking not just an escalation of these external threats from the wilds of northern, central and eastern Europe, but simultaneously an eruption of internal strife, of civil wars, usurpations, plague, and rocketing inflation, all resulting in a desperate succession of soldier-emperors, would-be emperors and puppets.[13] Few of these men made it to Rome;

Fig. 12.1: Basilica Nova, on the Via Sacra. Built by Maxentius and remodelled by Constantine I (Photo: editors).

Fig. 12.2: The late Roman defences of Rome, erected under Aurelian in the 270s and modified and heightened under Honorius in 402-404. View towards the Porta Appia (Photo: author).

many died on the frontiers or in battles against fellow Romans; only one or two of these fleeting emperors managed to die a natural death.[14] Military prowess against the enemy and dominance over one's own soldiery became prerequisites of imperial rule, but even these abilities could be curtailed in the bloodiness of war.

That the empire managed to survive these 3rd-century traumas was miraculous – but it did so at a price. So much now was geared to maintaining the military, feeding frontier troops and mobile armies behind, creating and reinforcing frontier fortifications, all to stall the barbarian onslaughts. This could not of course easily counter the internal disunion, which was in fact aggravated by the decision to split the empire into East and West and to create junior emperors – power made even brother emperors bitter rivals. Another result of these changes was the shift of the imperial capitals to face the delicate frontier zones. Suddenly then, from 284, Rome lost her all powerful status as Milan was selected as the new Western imperial seat – Rome was still the seat of the old Senate, but this wielded little authority anyway by the 4th century and power politics were played out elsewhere.[15]

This is not to say that Rome lost out immediately: in terms of building works Diocletian's Baths and the Basilica Nova of Maxentius attest that she continued as an imperial architectural showpiece, at least for a while (Fig. 12.1).[16] In addition, Rome had come to be endowed with a massive circuit of defensive walls – a quite remarkable engineering feat, accomplished within a decade in the course of the 270s under the initiative of the emperor Aurelian. These walls covered, and indeed still largely extend for, a length of not less than 18 km, were (in their final form) 15 m high, multi-turreted and pierced by various gates (Fig. 12.2).[17] Yet despite the powerful resources that these defences reflect, they also denote something more rudimentary, namely the drastic changes wrought upon the empire by the military upheavals of the 3rd century. In effect Rome's walls are a blatant statement of panic and of mistrust in the ability of the legions and gods to protect both the city and the empire.

There were in fact a few northern centres like Verona, close to the Alpine passes, which had seen defences installed slightly earlier to try and counter the enemy threat, but these had obviously failed to instill any substantial confidence to the elite population of Rome. It cannot be doubted, however, that Rome's show of distress must have been matched elsewhere in terms of new or revamped defensive walls. Here indeed is a first major contrast with the Roman glory days, when expansion of territory and culture was marked by the foundation of colonies – neat planned expressions of power and authority, defined indeed by walls, but walls which acted more as a symbol of Roman strength than as an inward-looking image of insecurity such as emerges in the late empire.[18]

FROM PAGAN STRONGHOLD TO CHRISTIAN CITADEL

As civil and military disorders spread it is perhaps not surprising to find that people turned again to religion. Against an array of mystical deities and oriental cults such as Mithras hoarded by the elite and by the army, we can observe the progressive growth and expansion of Christianity, already well enough established in the time of Trajan in the East, and making inroads into the larger urban nuclei of the West. This religion appealed more to the grass roots of society, given how it offered more hope in the next world than was present in this one and gave people more of a voice and a greater sense of community and belonging. Its rise in the early centuries AD despite periodic persecutions was remarkable, and one estimate suggests that a third of the empire was Christian before its official adoption as the state religion in the early 4th century.[19] It was also a fresh religion: in some ways the old Gods had become stale and many of the temples were suffering from neglect, with the basic problem of a lack of private patronage. Thus when Constantine declared himself in support of Christianity in AD 312 after the battle of the Milvian Bridge, he immediately secured for himself mass popular support, if only from the lower and middle echelons of society.[20] He nonetheless still had a fair struggle within the city, for Rome remained very much a pagan stronghold, headed by the old aristocratic clans and the Senate. What is clear in fact is that Constantine shied away from enforcing change and an all-new Christian image on Rome – he either respected the old order too much or feared their loyalty. Hence he was careful in his imperial manoeuvres, building churches outside the walls of Rome over the Christian cemeteries and holding back from intruding too far into the old urban fabric. The Lateran alone (with S. Croce in an imperial residence) represents an intramural Christian foothold of substance, although here it is notable that the Lateran's construction can also be regarded as a structural assertion of new order power in that its site selection meant the demolition of the barracks of the cavalry guard who had resisted Constantine's entry to Rome; the zone otherwise was relatively open ground, on state land, and this will have added to the visual impact of the new religion's official Rome headquarters.[21] Nonetheless, Constantine was duly honoured in 315 by the Rome Senate in the creation of the triumphal arch, suitably dominant between Colosseum and Forum on the triumphal route.[22] Constantine did meanwhile undertake new works (baths) and complete/modify some of Maxentius', most notably the Basilica Nova (Fig. 12.1).[23]

The pagan elite bided their time in Rome, at one moment fearing persecution from devout Christian emperors, at other times rejoicing in sympathy with a fully pagan ruler like Julian the Apostate in the 360s. Yet deprived of official imperial sanction and financial backing, paganism duly lost ground and prestige and the elite slowly peeled away to comply with the state's directives. Indeed, it is noticeable that it took until the mid-5th century before a full round of intramural church building (see below) began to make a monumental mark within the city walls.[24] (Figs. 12.3 and 12.4). This is not to claim that the elite were all pagans. There are many recorded instances of rich aristocrats seeking God and donating their properties to the Church rather than hoarding their wealth or investing it in plush villas; many 'pagan' senators had Christian leanings and likewise many Christian elite still maintained the 'traditional secular' ceremonies of ancient Rome.[25]

Constantine's building efforts and those of various bishops of Rome nonetheless had some early impact on pagan Rome, encircling it with an array of churches, catacombs and hallowed tombs: a somewhat less fearful foe than the barbarians or usurpers of the 3rd century, but one that exerted powerful pressure even so. Quite rapidly new prestige was gained through the exultation of the bones of the martyrs, with St. Peter's the obvious focus;[26] and there are signs of an early start to pilgrim traffic – a traffic which, in the course of the 8th and 9th centuries, perhaps formed a substantial precursor to modern tourism levels (see below).

Yet even in the context of the new Christian religion Rome did not exclusively hold centre stage. In the East empire, Constantine's foundation of Constantinople soon diverted much of the glory away: although an ancient seat with pagan elements, far greater scope existed here for the new Church to display itself within a capital's townscape. Similarly in the West there were Milan, Trier and Sirmium – all new imperial seats which swallowed up Rome's old revenues and offered scope firstly for major imperial palaces and, in time, Christian building programmes.[27] Constantine himself spent little time in Rome, the longest stay being in 312–13, and then briefly in 315 and 326.

LATE ROMAN ROME: IMAGES OF DECAY

It is rather difficult, in the absence of adequate documentary sources, to gauge exactly how contemporaries viewed or fully recognized this gradual decline of status and authority. Life still continued of course and so long as food still arrived in the city people cannot have been too aware of what appear – at least to us – as major changes. Nonetheless, in order to understand better these changes it is important first to try to understand something about the human content of Rome.

Had population levels changed much over time? Is the figure of one million souls for Augustan Rome valid still for Constantinian Rome? It seems more than plausible to maintain this estimate into the 3rd century, given the generally high level of peace and economic security throughout the Roman empire, as clearly reflected in ever continuous building activity throughout the 1st and 2nd centuries AD. However, in the course of the turbulent 3rd century the onset of civil wars, barbarian raids, economic crises and more importantly, the shift in the imperial court to Milan, must all have had some impact on

Fig. 12.3: The church of S. Sabina on the Aventine Hill (Photo: editors).

numbers – though potentially insecurity could also have seen people empty the countryside in favour of the towns. To a degree the few available figures for the 4th century seem to support this idea, suggesting an urban populus still somewhere between three-quarters of a million and a full million.[28] But overall this seems an indication more of relative stability within Rome, with little major disruption caused by the transfer of state rule to both north and east. These calculations can all be disputed in one way or another of course, and these are generous estimates; but nonetheless, even if one errs on the side of caution, it seems clear that Rome still remained the biggest city in the West, and was rivalled only by Constantinople in the East. In effect Rome still had to cope with the enormous logistical problems of looking after her huge population even in the absence of a resident emperor.

For the 5th century, the imperial lawcodes provide various figures, but of most value here are those laws decreeing the level of entitlements to free pork. Noticeably, calculations based on the documented figures point to a sharp fall in the population, at best half a million in the mid-5th century.[29] This somewhat diminished figure neatly ties in with reports in the laws of a depopulated or at least untended countryside, most notably across regions of southern Italy and even in once prosperous Campania.[30] The emperors are shown as being forced to remit taxes in a largely vain attempt to encourage farmers back onto the land – to get them to supply more food for Rome and for the army; desertion of the land also meant a reduction in potential recruits for the ever more essential armies. But by this date the empire was crumbling: Gaul was part-colonized by Franks, Visigoths were installed in Spain and, more seriously for Rome herself, North Africa (west of Libya) was now a Vandal kingdom. Vandal raids wore down Roman Sicily and virtually emptied the western coasts of the Italian peninsula.[31] Piracy was again rife on the seas, and the indications are that the big grain fleets of former times were gone – though Sicily rapidly became the new granary of Rome. Food shortages, already documented as a constant problem in the 4th century and bringing with them riots and looting, were exacerbated in the 5th century: the Visigothic assaults on Rome in 410 prompted cases of death by famine and even of cannibalism; the Vandal raids of the 440s and 450s forced people to sell off young relatives as slaves for money to pay the inflated prices for food; while droughts and bad harvests in Italy saw further denuding of the countryside.[32] Whilst this catalogue of disasters might be hard to visualize, a valid comparison – if of much shorter duration – might be

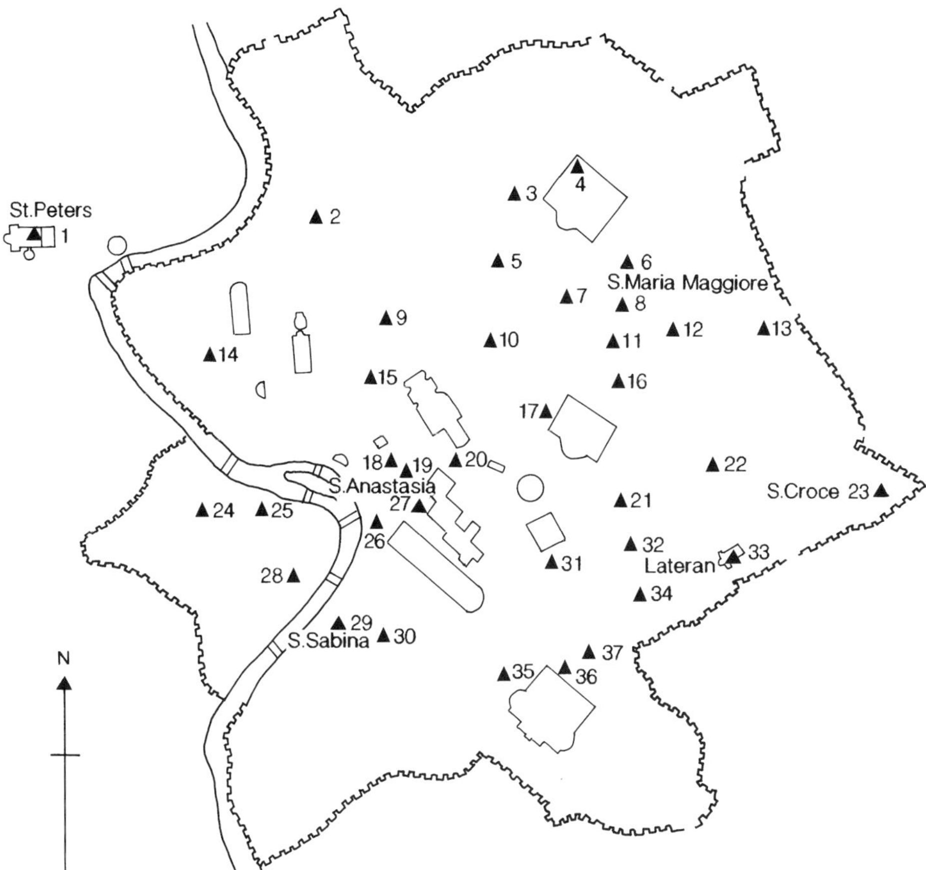

Fig. 12.4: The intramural churches of Rome and rebuilt secular/pagan buildings c. A.D. 500 (after Krautheimer 1980). KEY: 1. St Peter's (S. Pietro in Vaticano); 2. S. Lorenzo in Lucina; 3. S. Susanna; 4. S. Ciriaci; 5. S. Vitale; 6. S. Maria Maggiore; 7. S. Pudenziana; 8. S. Prassede; 9. S. Marcello; 10. S. Agata dei Goti; 11. S, Vito in Macello; 12. S. Eusebio; 13. S. Bibiana; 14. S. Lorenzo in Damaso; 15. S. Marco; 16. S. Martino ai Monti; 17. S. Pietro in Vincoli; 18. Porticus Deorum Consentium; 19. Temple of Saturn; 20. Praefectus Urbis (SS. Cosma e Damiano); 21. S. Clemente; 22. SS. Marcellino e Pietro; 23. S. Croce in Gerusalemme; 24. S. Maria in Trastevere; 25. S. Crisogono; 26. Statio Annonae; 27. S. Anastasia; 28. S. Cecilia; 29. S. Sabina; 30. S. Prisca; 31. SS. Giovanni e Paolo; 32. SS. Quattro Coronati; 33. Lateran (S. Giovanni in Laterano); 34. S. Stefano Rotondo; 35. S. Balbina; 36. SS. Nereo e Achileo; 37. S. Sisto Vecchio. Principal Roman secular monuments (e.g. Circus Maximus, Baths of Caracalla) are shown in outline.

found with the recent conflicts in former Yugoslavia which made plain the telling effects of warfare on settlements, their populations, and the land.

Striking is the fact that despite the failure of the grain fleets in the 4th and 5th centuries Rome failed to encourage increased crop and food production in her own hinterland; the results of archaeological field surveys in the area of South Etruria north of Rome instead show that the number of farms in this fertile region had in fact diminished from the 3rd century onwards and had all but dwindled away by the later 5th century.[33] Quite conceivably this matches a decline in activity within the city. Rome had for too long been a huge consumer city: unlike most other towns in the empire which utilized local agricultural resources to a high degree, Rome's population was totally urban – there was no longer (if there really ever had been) a healthy blend of townies and urban-based farmers. In this regard Rome contrasts with Milan, whose rise to imperial capital status in AD 284 prompted a major upsurge in rural activity in its territory.[34] Thus Rome continued to rely heavily on imported foodstuffs.[35]

In the case of Rome, however, it is very hard to imagine a drastic population decline from the 4th century. Some aristocrats certainly headed east, others perhaps moved to the provinces, but the poorer classes who made up the vast bulk of the urban population could afford to do neither and must have stayed put (again one need only view the resilience of townspeople in war-torn Bosnia to understand this). Perhaps the food shortages and plagues did have a devastating effect; perhaps people did head out to make a life in the countryside (though the archaeology sees no trace of them there); or perhaps the birthrate had dropped alarmingly from that of previous centuries. A detailed study of the bones of the late Roman population could give some interesting clues in this regard, but studies of this sort are still awaited.

Yet decline there undoubtedly was. Hence, Cassiodorus Senator, writing at the start of the 6th century under Ostrogothic rule, wonders at the disappearance of so many people over time, informing us that:

> "The great size of the population of the city of Rome in former times is clear from the fact that it required the provision of foodstuffs from different regions to supply its needs... The great extent of the walls, the seating capacity of the places of entertainment, the remarkable size of the public baths and the number of mills, bear witness to the hordes of citizens." (*Selected Letters* 2.39)

This letter and others indicate that quite clearly here was a rather altered urban landscape – not deserted, but clearly lacking the heaving hordes of the early and middle empire. At the same time, Cassiodorus also reveals that early 6th-century Rome was crowded with aged monuments, part decayed through neglect, part-cannibalized for other uses and part-demolished and quarried for building materials to be used in private houses elsewhere – quite possibly the Forum was almost then already in its current state of confused ruins.

This state of affairs was not a sudden event, however: 4th- and 5th-century laws in the *Codex Theodosianus* issued in Rome, Milan, Ravenna and Constantinople refer to decayed public edifices and dangerous ruins and legislate against robbing of materials from these, and against the building of private houses alongside or inside them and even pulling them down. "They are part of our heritage" the laws proclaim – but the fact that the laws are constantly re-issued emperor after emperor is a clear enough sign that heritage meant little to most people and that ruination or at least decay continued fairly unabated.[36] The laws certainly reflect an ideological desire to maintain the past – or at least those upstanding and thus workable remnants of this past: incorporation, maintenance or, where demolition had to occur, reuse were the means of preserving this past.[37] Despite this, illegal demolition and 'natural' decay no doubt continued apace, reflective of the wider economic and demographic downturn.

There is only a limited amount of archaeological evidence which we can draw upon to highlight this decay. Notable, however, are the enormously fruitful excavations undertaken in the Crypta Balbi, named after the theatre of Cornelius Balbus constructed at the end of the 1st century BC close to temples of Largo Argentina in the Campo Marzio.[38] From the 1st century AD the theatre adjoined the Porticus Minucia *frumentaria*, used in the distribution of the corn dole; this was still the case in the 230s although an inscription indicates that much repair-work had to be done on the (already) decaying buildings.[39] The role of *frumentaria* was given up around AD 300 and the structures were instead given over to storage and/or private workshops, resulting in a deteriorating structural condition and eventually leading in the early 5th century to the virtual abandonment of the zone. In the late 5th or early 6th century, however, there was some renewed activity in the form of a roadway running over the paving of the Porticus, with lime workshops adjoining.[40] As Manacorda points out, this industrial activity extended into the Early Middle Ages, and gave its name to the quarter, 'Calcarario'. Thus, here, right in the centre of Rome, workshops in and around the ruins of Roman period monuments were burning down travertine and marble drawn from other defunct monuments.[41]

Elsewhere, in the Forum area itself, the space behind the Curia or Senate House (from the 620s transformed into the church of S. Adriano: Fig. 12.5) was likewise being used in the 8th to 10th century as a storage dump for marble to be burnt down for lime; the lime kilns clearly overlay a level of abandonment covering the Forum in this zone.[42] Meanwhile, on the northern slopes of the Palatine signs of decay are also fairly evident in the absence of occupational debris between the 5th and 12th centuries; in addition there were identified a series of 12th-century robber trenches cut by workmen in search of travertine blocks, either for direct reuse as building materials or for burning down for lime. The fact that these trenches had to be cut down is a clear indication that the bulk of the buildings concerned had already been pillaged for their materials.[43]

Often it is possible to identify through the increasingly fleeting documentary references a general structural survival of the old Roman public edifices, and a degree of civil or public activity around them. In the case of the Forum of Trajan, despite pilfering under Constantine for architectural pieces for his arch, a continuing 'official' role can be perceived in 5th century inscriptions and statuary being erected as well as laws being promulgated here, while in the late 6th century Venantius Fortunatus talks of classical poetry recitals being on offer (Fig. 12.6).[44] After this we lose track of the complex until the 9th and 10th centuries when, although the column of Trajan and the Forum itself are evident, any political function is long past and the zone begins to be colonized by small churches, housing and gardens.[45]

Nonetheless, many ancient buildings did survive – and of course still survive – through their bulk and structural resilience, albeit modified,[46] but once their primary function had been lost it was often only a matter of time before they became cannibalized or colonized by the Church or by private dwellings. For 5th-century Rome, however, we presently have only a patchy image of this sequence of urban metamorphosis.

Similarly, only now is archaeology properly beginning to search for and recognize traces of 'late antique' or 'dark age' domestic structures in Rome.[47] To a degree church excavations are a guide, since various early churches overlie what had been in the 4th and 5th centuries fairly opulent *domus* complexes – these perhaps denote a progressive Christianisation of the city elite and the transferral of property to the Church; in a few cases, potentially, we may observe churches emerging over the seats of the earliest *domus ecclesiae* of the first three centuries AD. The principal pattern of evolution, however, is the recolonization of internal space – partitioning up old houses or public monuments, such as *horrea* and even porticoes; such actions imply an active population, fitting into or creating space within a decayed townscape. Rome, as elsewhere, had seen elites shift primary interests to the countryside in the mid-4th to early 5th century, with villas often far exceeding town houses in artistic display;[48] however, the various military threats of the 5th century must have instigated a return to the towns, still not fully recognized archaeologically.

Fig. 12.5: *The Senate House in its early medieval and pre-modern role as the church of S. Adriano (after Lanciani 1897). Medieval and post-medieval accretions have been removed to 'revive' its antiquity.*

Fig. 12.6: *Honorius Pedestal: inscription honouring the Emperor Honorus, Forum of Trajan. Inscriptions of the House of Theodosius are perhaps over represented because they formed the last major wave of public dedications (Photo: editors).*

The Rome data are better understood through comparison with key excavations in the northern towns of Milan, Verona and Brescia, where the sequence of 'scaling-down' of large *domus* residences has been examined, reflected in the blocking of doors and even porticoes and the creation of dividing walls; often this is at the expense of elegant floor mosaics which are unceremoniously rooted up or simply covered by dirt flooring.[49] Modest private housing seems also to have begun to cannibalize old and redundant public edifices such as theatres and amphitheatres, as evident at sites across Italy, such as Ventimiglia, Lucca, Spoleto and Sepino. The laws noted above show this process underway in the capitals during the 4th century; such transformation could have occurred earlier in lesser centres.[50]

Archaeology can, meanwhile, provide good evidence regarding the changing economy and material culture of Rome and Italy in the 5th century AD. Excavations on both urban and rural sites readily testify to a progressive economic decline in the late empire, running hand in hand with the gradual break-up and regionalization of the old empire. Although imports still reached Rome from all parts of her world, notably from North Africa, Syria, Palestine and Asia Minor, the level of such international trade (in olive oil, wine, ceramics and grain) began falling away in the 5th century, and yet continued to function adequately into the 7th. This can be matched by an apparent decline in the use of, or rather minting of, coins, with 3rd- and 4th-century copper and bronze issues continuing to circulate into the 5th century and probably beyond.[51] In all aspects there is a narrowing of interests, with each part of the empire becoming increasingly self-sufficient. Rome to some degree may be exceptional in that she had for so

Fig. 12.7: Schola Praeconum (Photo: editors).

long been a consumer rather than producer, reliant on imports for food in particular, and accordingly traders continued to look to Rome for a ready market – the state and Church after all still had the burden of Rome's poor to consider. Nonetheless, the severe reduction in scale must have had repercussions regarding the population levels within the walls.[52] Rome was thus forced to exploit more local resources to supplement the declining imports, and indeed there are numerous references to huge numbers of swine being bred in southern Italy and marketed in Rome to assist in the food dole.[53]

Good archaeological support for this image of gradual change comes from the excavations of the so-called Schola Praeconum at the foot of the Palatine hill near the church of Sant'Anastasia (Fig. 12.7).[54] This structure was used as a dump for building materials and domestic refuse on two occasions, the first in *c.* 430–440, and a second either soon after AD 500, or perhaps as late as *c.* 600. The origins of the refuse are unclear, but presumably relate to a relatively well-endowed town house nearby (the 475 kg of marble veneer from the first dump recommends a wealthy source). The animal bones from the earlier dump reflect the documented prominence of pig products in the Roman diet in the 5th century (although pork had long been an important element of the Roman diet) and interestingly showed that the household in question had not been limited to the choice cuts.[55] The comparison between the ceramic finds from the two rubbish deposits highlights a decline in the level of imports reaching Rome, particularly in terms of fine North African table-wares which lose out to local imitations; nonetheless oil and wine are still in demand, as reflected in *amphorae* from North Africa, Asia Minor and Syria.[56] For each dump, these data are useful in showing how, despite the contemporary political and military upheavals in the Mediterranean world (namely the break-up of the western provinces, the loss of Africa to the Vandals after *c.* 430 and the rise in piracy), long-distance trade did continue. Indeed, in other contexts, the Ostrogothic period reveals a particularly healthy exchange between Italy and Vandal Africa. Enterprise in a relatively free market allowed for this persistence.[57] Even with the onset of Arab expansion from the 640s the movement of oil, wine, *amphorae*, lamps, etc. continues, with signs from the Crypta Balbi in Rome that this trade endured to the very late 7th century.[58]

THE 5TH-CENTURY DISASTERS: VISIGOTHS AND VANDALS

> "I do not belong to the school which condemns the barbaric hosts, and holds them responsible for the material destruction of Rome and its immediate surroundings. The barbarians took gold, silver, bronze, jewellery, whatever could be easily moved and carried away; they may have set fire to a few monuments in the excitement of battle, or out of spite; in their ignorance and in their hatred of the Latin name, they may have knocked down from their pedestals statues of emperors and gods; but it would be folly to throw upon them the blame and the shame of the destruction of substantial marble, stone and brick buildings. They did not have time to indulge in that sort of sport; they did not possess the proper tools to accomplish such Titanic deeds; they did not care to commit acts of vandalism from which they could reap no benefit. Rome has been destroyed by its own inhabitants..." [59]

Two key episodes broke the back of 5th-century Rome: first the Visigothic capture of the city in AD 410, and second, the Vandal occupation of 455. Whilst it was bad enough to witness tramping Roman and barbarian armies within the peninsula, it was total disaster to see those armies within the ancient heart of the empire. Both events sent shock-waves around the decaying Roman world – though those shock-waves were perhaps not as intense as they would have been if Rome had still held real power. In both instances in fact Rome was let off fairly lightly: both episodes were short-lived, long enough for plunder but with no apparent attempt at permanent possession – either as a sign of respect for old age, or of a fear to intrude (if not to violate), or maybe a sign that Rome was no longer so important even in the barbarians' eyes. The western emperor held back from interfering, sitting tight behind the marshes of Ravenna, spending money on new churches to adorn the new capital, but scared of stepping into the outside world – a task instead left to his military officers, many of these now of barbarian or, more accurately, Romano-German stock, and most of whom were more intent on chasing power than on chasing the enemy.[60]

In the late 4th and early 5th centuries northern Italy was a veritable battleground between Romans and Visigoths – a situation which forced the weak-willed emperor Honorius to take refuge at Ravenna, away from an exposed Milan. The failure to defeat conclusively the Visigothic king Alaric over nearly a decade of campaigning eventually led Honorius to murder his Vandal general Stilicho, but in so doing he opened the floodgates, depriving Italy and Rome of her leading soldier. In 408 Alaric marched straight on Rome, capturing Ostia and starting a blockade of Rome – primarily Alaric was after booty and tribute, a nice major official appointment from the emperor and land for his people. Not too much to ask for perhaps, but too much for Honorius who preferred scheming over plans in the security of Ravenna. Rome was under virtual siege for three years on and off but in that time seems to have lacked any military support at all from Ravenna. Although Rome was well-enough defended by its walls (which had in fact just been substantially raised and reinforced in 402),[61] it lacked a large garrison and adequate food stores. The Visigoths probably also suffered from food shortages but at least had the Ostian grain depots to fall back on. In 409 Rome, in desperation, renounced Honorius' rule and chose an alternative emperor, Attalus, to treat with Alaric who was duly elevated by Attalus to the position of supreme military general in the West and endowed with suitable funds. The appointment was somewhat hollow, since Attalus' own empire covered only the confines of Rome's walls. Unsurprisingly, in 410 Attalus was deposed by Alaric and the siege and starvation of Rome resumed. Finally, someone opened the gates to the Visigoths and the Germans ploughed in, looting and murdering for three days, but bypassing the refuge centres of S. Paolo and S. Pietro, before withdrawing from a foodless and probably plague-ridden city for the more fertile lands of south Italy. Pagans blamed Christians, Christians blamed pagans, and Honorius still stayed away.[62]

How extensive the destruction was is not altogether clear. Parts of the Forum such as the Basilica Aemilia and the Senate House were damaged by fire – the basilica very neatly contained coins of this date in a destruction level – and other districts of Rome including the Aventine and Caelian hills suffered burning too (with houses at the former and the Castra Peregrina at the latter); but most of the destruction came in the removal of mobile wealth.[63]

Alaric died shortly afterwards and his successor Ataulf chose to take the Visigoths back northwards, this time into Gaul, where, astonishingly, Honorius accepted him as ally and general of Rome – the barbarians may have been tearing the empire apart and violating Rome, but the empire needed the barbarians as defenders. The final century of Roman rule in the West is indeed a frighteningly confused image of Romans and Germans as allies and enemies at each other's throats.

Nature also seems to have conspired against Rome: the sack of 410 is sandwiched between destructive floods by the Tiber river and also earthquakes.[64] Whilst we should not assume that this suggests the onset of a deteriorating climate, it does perhaps indicate that Rome now lacked the engineering skills which had in earlier centuries prevented frequent flooding of the city centre.

Rome and Italy staggered on still after 410. The senatorial poet, Rutilius Namatianus, writing in 417 as he journeyed home from a devastated Italy to a war-torn Gaul, puts on a very brave face when talking of old Rome, saying:

> "May misfortune be forgotten; may your wounds close and heal because you have ignored the pain. Surrounded by failure, hope for prosperity; may you be enriched by all your losses" (*De Reditu Suo* 1.119–22)

He further tries to cover up the cracks in the imperial edifice by claiming that

> "Even today Rome mingles victory with mercy; her enemies become her allies... Rome had wisdom and judgement. War and peace alike were prudently used to enhance a position that never weakened. Rome deserved to prevail but that she has prevailed to this extent is a mark of her strength, rather than a mark of her destiny" (*De Reditu Suo* 1.69, 88–94)

Yet at the same time Namatianus admits that the "land has become wild again", with brigands and Goths infesting the countryside, roads flooded or littered with land-slides and bridges collapsed (*De Reditu Suo* 1.35–40).

Although the military action had largely shifted westwards after the Visigoths, there was in fact little hope for revival, for new enemies took their place. In the 440s and 450s the Huns flooded across eastern and central Europe and their overlord Attila briefly invaded Italy and threatened Rome. Across the Mediterranean, once the Vandals had established themselves in North Africa, raids were sent out against Sicily, southern and western Italy and went largely unchecked. Rome inevitably fell again to a foreign army in 455, suffering 14 days of systematic looting with all manner of treasures (metals and princesses) being shipped back to Vandal Carthage.[65] In each of these cases – the Vandal looting and the Hunnic threat – there was little or no concerted military opposition forthcoming. But for each event notable were the actions of Pope Leo I. In 452 Leo is traditionally said to have persuaded Attila to withdraw from a bloodied Italy; in 455 he met the Vandal invaders at the gates of Rome, and although he could not stop the plunder, he did at least receive a promise of no bloodshed and no burning. Both episodes are perhaps half or full legend but nonetheless comprise a sign of the growing or subsequent prominence of the bishop of Rome at the head of the urban flock.

5TH-CENTURY ROME: IMAGES OF ACTIVITY

The pope had fast become both spiritual and practical guardian to Rome. Little surprise then that the Church of Rome displayed its prominence in architecture and art, maintaining an image of vitality within the city. As well as Church/state funded buildings, we also see an array of elite conversions and donations, whether money, land or buildings.[66] The new churches, among them Santa Sabina (Fig. 12.3) with its stunning early 5th-century carved wooden doors, were variously adorned with marble and mosaics and with architectural elements generally drawn from demolished temples or other public buildings.[67] Some material perhaps had already been stockpiled, others could have been accessed following the destructions of 410. It appears, however, that recovery after 410 and 455 was slow: for example, only under Celestine I (422–432) were suitable treasures restored to St. Paul's and St. Peter's, and only under Hilarus (461–468) were Vandal thefts fully replaced (though in 456 Leo did swiftly set about replacing lost consecrated vessels at the various *tituli* by melting down the huge water jars from the major basilicas).[68] Yet in between times, expansion of activity and revival is well attested, principally under pope Sistus III (432–440), whose monumental Santa Maria Maggiore preserves much of its original interior form, including its fine mosaic panels.[69]

Whilst veneration of the martyrs and the endowment of the extramural churches continued, we can recognize by the time of Sistus that the Church's intramural colonization of Rome was well advanced. This colonization was in part due to the official end of paganism in 395 and thus the removal of competition, but also, as noted, due to the granting of properties by elites within the walls. The array of shrines, catacombs, churches and monasteries combines to document a populous city – boosted by numerous visitors.[70] The distribution of intramural seats is of interest, however, in implying that some portions of the city were perhaps less active than others – notably the northern and southern districts – with most foundations set in a broad central band, in relatively close proximity to the old monumental foci (Fig. 12.4).

Donations – and occupations by enemies – meanwhile denote the persistence of wealth and a numerous elite within the city confines. Indeed, if we care to believe the words of Olympiodorus of Thebes in *c.* 420, Rome remained resplendent with elite *domus*, claiming that these contain all the elements to make a town, namely circus, forum, temple, fountain, baths, and thus Rome contains a thousand such towns.[71] This claim, however, has more validity for the 4th than the 5th century, when a progressive deterioration or at least a 'running-down' can be claimed for a variety of the elite *domus*.[72] Nonetheless, there was certainly enough to protect and even if Honorius failed to protect Rome with weapons and armies, he did at least ensure its walls were substantially raised, and these continued to serve Rome well beyond her 'fall'.[73] Likewise the Urban Prefect continued to undertake acts of public maintenance, ensuring that much of the old centre remained orderly and a suitable setting for the seat of the ancient Senate: hence in the years following the Visigothic seizure of Rome the Senate House was duly restored, its *secretarium* repaired, as well as the buildings of the Prefecture itself.[74]

Fig. 12.8: Church of SS. Cosma e Damiano (Photo: editors).

AFTER ROMAN ROME

The 5th-century image could, therefore, be considered somewhat bleak: malnourished Christians, a diminished elite, decayed pagan and public architecture, and a basic lack of prosperity. It could be argued that Rome was almost too vast to revive in the 5th century: a huge garrison would have been needed to man the circuit wall; provisioning this force and the mass of would-be urban poor far outstretched the resources then available; and mere maintenance of the architectural heritage would have strained the coffers still further – as is clear even in modern Rome. In any case, Rome was now poorly sited to cope with altered politico-military needs: seaborne communications were vital in this era and close surveillance of the northern passes imperative. Ravenna met these requirements far better than Rome. She was more defensively sited, with a more compact circuit wall, but possessed good water communications within the Adriatic and beyond. Endowed with new buildings to cater for the imperial court and the Church, she lacked the decayed array of pagan structures or redundant secular edifices of Rome. It was for these same reasons that Rome's Germanic successors towards the end of the 5th century, and likewise the Byzantine governors from the mid-6th century, persisted with Ravenna as the residential capital.[75]

Nonetheless, the transition to Germanic rule in fact benefited the old city of Rome: Theoderic (489/493–526) imposed stability once more within and beyond Italy through a strong and long rule, through careful diplomacy and through a good strategic scattering of his sisters and daughter in marriage alliances with western neighbours.[76] All this helped revive the Italian economy – even if not back to the bounteous levels of the mid-empire, trade overall seems to have flourished once more within the Mediterranean basin. In Italy this is reflected in renewed building activity within towns, particularly in the north, where Theoderic keenly demonstrated royal patronage and prompted private input once more – as is nowhere more obvious than at Ravenna, whose glorious church mosaics testify to high artistic survival.[77] Rome, meanwhile, in Theoderic's eyes, retained its old imperial charm and he treated it with all due respect, admiring its architectural treasures, whilst seeking to repair, restore and augment.[78] For him, buildings were "the delights of our power, the decorous face

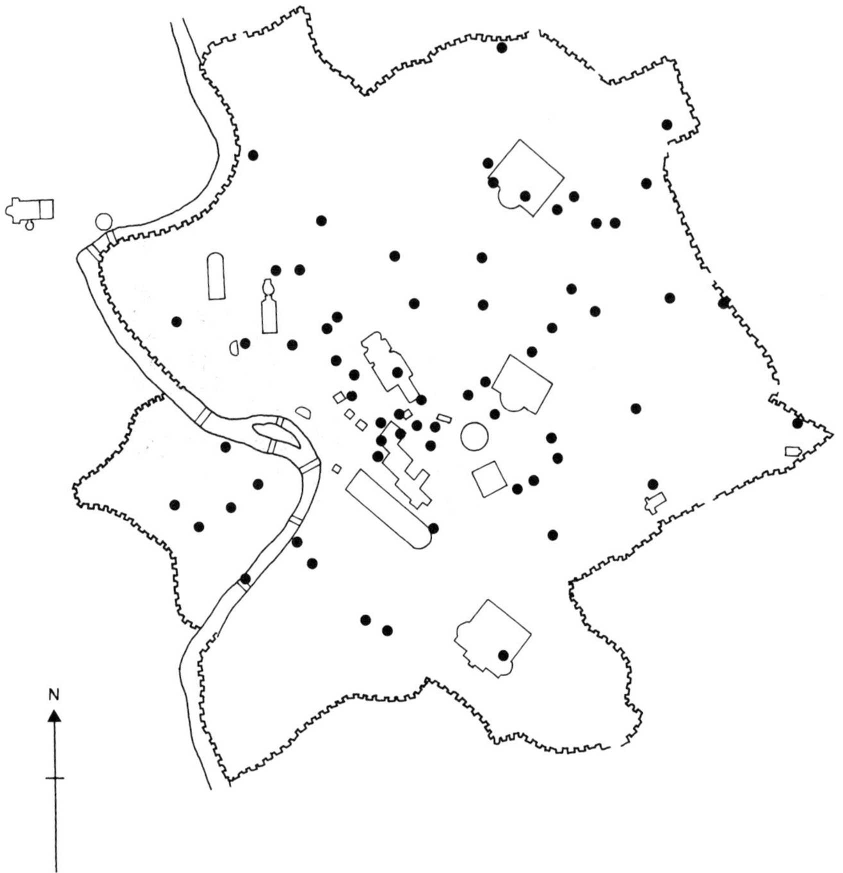

Fig. 12.9: Distribution of isolated tombs and burial plots of 5th to 7th century AD date within the walls of Rome. Principal Roman secular monuments and churches are shown in outline (after Meneghini and Santangeli Valenzani 1993).

of our realm, the prestigious testimonial of kingdoms".[79] In these actions Theoderic was showing himself to be a worthy successor to the emperors of old – indeed, he clearly considered the holding of circus and gladiatorial games a prerequisite of '*romanitas*'.

Despite this new input, Rome remained primarily a pilgrimage centre rather than a genuine source of authority. Its old institutions persisted largely as relics of the past, although all the time the Pope was slowly gathering up the reins of residual secular power, to emerge as a powerful figure in the following centuries, bolstered by the growing income from the Church. With the late 6th century Rome was once more established as an urban force.[80]

Although outside the scope of this contribution, the 6th century should not be overlooked, since this marks the period of more dramatic change in the urban landscape of Rome. For example, one corner of the Forum Pacis was converted into the earliest church located in the centre, SS. Cosma e Damiano (AD 526–530) (Fig. 12.8).[81] The long and bloody war (AD 535–554) between Ostrogoths and Byzantines, followed from 568 by the invasion and expansion of the Longobards, resulted in a disastrous economic instability within Italy which is reflected archaeologically in a near invisibility of urban life anywhere in Italy between *c.*

550 and 700. Rome was besieged many times, in particular during the early years of the Gothic War, and at one point the historian Procopius claims that Rome's population, decimated by war, starvation and bubonic plague, was reduced to a mere 500 persons.[82] It can never have sunk that low in reality, but a virtual desertion of the once heaving throughfares can easily be envisaged. The war also prompted the first organized appearance of burials within the walls, with the extramural catacombs and above-ground cemeteries no longer deemed secure.[83] Some earlier burial activity can nonetheless be attested, scattered in and around former – and even active – monumental zones such as the Colosseum. Here in fact 5th- and 6th-century graves were excavated in the 19th century, with the earlier tombs thought to relate to the first decade of the 5th century and marking an enforced act of intramural burial prompted by the blockades of the Visigoths.[84] Subsequent reuse of the zone for a more regulated cemetery is claimed to relate to the period of the Gothic Wars onwards, although three of the excavated graves did use tiles featuring stamps of king Theoderic, raising the possibility of an earlier resumption of burials. Nonetheless, the Flavian Amphitheatre was still being used as late as AD 523 and was indeed commemorated as having been restored after earthquake damage at the end of the 5th century;[85] it would seem strange therefore to have burials and games taking place in the same area contemporaneously and the strongest likelihood is that the disuse of the Colosseum from the 530s gave full scope for an alternative activity in the valle del Colosseo.[86] Other former monumental zones seem likewise to have been given over as burial plots for the locals from the first half of the 6th century – further signs of the developing *disabitato* and of the emergence of smaller settlement and burial foci within the vast walled area (Fig. 12.9).[87]

THE ROMAN PHOENIX

A useful conclusion to this paper is offered by the description given by the writings of Cassiodorus, Theoderic's minister in Rome. Cassiodorus was one of the last of the senatorial aristocracy and was clearly a proud citizen of Rome.[88] He is therefore suitably over-the-top in extolling the wondrous good old days without ever admitting to the decay of his own time. Cassiodorus here writes about the marvels of Rome's drains:

> "Care for the city of Rome keeps perpetual watch over my mind. For, of the proper subjects for my thought, what is worthier than to maintain the repairs of that place which clearly preserves the glory of my state? Hence, illustrious Prefect, you must know that I have despatched the distinguished John, for the sake of the glorious sewers of the city of Rome, which cause such amazement to beholders that they surpass the wonders of other cities. There you may see rivers enclosed, so to speak, in hollow hills, and flowing through huge plastered tunnels; you may even see men sailing the swift waters in boats... Hence, Rome, we may grasp your outstanding greatness. For what city can dare to rival your towers, when even your foundations have no parallel?" (*Selected Letters* 3.30 of AD 510)

Rome's star may have fallen but her greatness still shone through even in the bleakness of the last century of the old Roman empire. Even with the traumas of the Gothic and Longobard wars to follow in the 6th and 7th centuries it would only be a fairly short time before papal power put Rome once more back into merited prominence. Ruins may have abounded – and continued to abound even into the Middle Ages – within the vast expanse of Rome's walls, but these continued to attest the monumentality and power of Rome's imperial 'glory days'.

ACKNOWLEDGEMENTS

This paper in part draws on research carried out aeons ago at the University of Newcastle Upon Tyne during my tenureship of a Sir James Knott Research Fellowship (1987–89) and from research since periodically achieved at the British School at Rome as elsewhere. I would like to thank in particular Andrea Augenti for discussions on the fate of the Palatine and Rome in general and for his generosity in letting me read his manuscript on the medieval Palatine in advance of publication, plus various subsequent papers. Thanks also to those people who offered useful feedback on my paper at the conference in Oxford, plus of course the editors of this volume for their pointers for improving the text. Finally, it should be noted that the above chapter has not been able to incorporate materials published in the excellent volume edited by HARRIS 1999, which appeared well after the submission date of my text. However, I have incorporated references to the main papers in my footnotes. I hope that my chapter will thus serve as a useful introduction to the more detailed papers presented in that volume.

NOTES

1 Magister Gregorius, *Marvels* ch.1 – *c*. AD 1230.

2 KRAUTHEIMER 1980, 68–9, 237–59.

3 WARD-PERKINS 1984, 3–37. Cf. discussion on the reliability of rebuilding and restoration inscriptions – a form relatively prevalent in the late empire and viewed, by some scholars, as reflective of exaggerated pronouncements of interventions on behalf of the state, claiming rebuilding instead of mere repairs (as attested by archaeology): FAGAN 1996.

4 *Lexicon* II, *s.v.* 'Forum Romanum (età tarda)', 342–43; 'Forum Romanum (Lastricati)', 343–45. See also BAUER 1999.

5 MANACORDA 1990; 1993 on Crypta Balbi – discussed below.

6 AUGENTI 1992; AUGENTI 1994; 1996a. Nonetheless, the recent (unpublished as yet) clearances across the Forum of Nerva have yielded the extremely valuable evidence of two Carolingian (9th century) stone houses, of modest, not opulent form (see CRYPTA BALBI 2000, 89–90) – and in the meanwhile work has begun on unearthing what remains beside the Via dei Fori Imperiali of the Imperial Fora.

7 On the enormous rise of interest in the question of town survival/decay in the light of increased levels of urban archaeology, see for example, CHRISTIE and LOSEBY 1996; for Italy in WARD-PERKINS 1997; plus volumes in the ESF *Transformation of the Roman World* series, particularly BROGIOLO and WARD-PERKINS 1999.

8 For example, papers in GIARDINA 1986; LUSUARDI SIENA 1994; BROGIOLO and GELICHI 1996; and recently SAGUÌ 1998. The Crypta Balbi project, plus renewed research in both Portus and Ostia, have transformed our understanding of commerce to and industry in late antique and early medieval Rome: see CRYPTA BALBI 2000; PAVOLINI 1996; COCCIA 1996. On a much wider setting see the oft-cited HODGES and WHITEHOUSE 1983, particularly 1–53.

9 Cf. WARD-PERKINS 1984, 12–34.

10 WARD-PERKINS 1984, 51–84; KRAUTHEIMER 1937–77; 1983; *Lexicon* I, *s.v.* 'S. Agnes', 27–8. The Chrstianization of towns and town spaces is currently receiving much attention: see GAUTHIER 1999, and for Italy specifically CANTINO WATAGHIN 1996.

11 See introduction in DAVIS 1989 to his translation of the early entries of the *Liber Pontificalis*.

12 On *spolia* see the excellent survey by ALCHERMES 1994; discussed also by WARD-PERKINS 1984; 1999, and fully for Rome by PENSABENE and PANELLA 1993–94. There is the added advantage that architectural *spolia* were taken under cover early, and therefore their sculptural detail is very crisply preserved, e.g. in S. Giorgio in Velabro, S. Clemente and S. Lorenzo fuori le mura (KRAUTHEIMER 1980, Fig. 68; CLARIDGE 1983, n. 9).

13 COLLINS 1991, 1–15; CAMERON 1993, 12–32.

14 CICATRIX and ROWSON 1995 gives a suitably over-the-top illustrated guide to the varied fates of the emperors.

15 MILANO 1990, 17–23.

16 Summarized in COARELLI 1999 and FROVA 1990, noting Maxentius' substantial building programme – including his opulent villa complex on the Via Appia, notably set outside the new city walls – comprising residence and reception suites, baths, circus and mausoleum; *Lexicon* I, *s.v.* 'Basilica Constantini, B. Nova', 170–73; *Lexicon* V, *s.v.* 'Thermae Diocletiani', 53–8.

17 RICHMOND 1930; TODD 1983; COZZA 1987; *Lexicon* III, *s.v.* 'Muri Aureliani', 290–314; *Lexicon* V, 277.

18 CHRISTIE 1992; JOHNSON 1983, 9–54.

19 FREND 1984, 400–1, 413–14, noting for Rome the firm existence of parishes by the 260s, the opening of new catacombs around Rome, and with roughly forty churches within the city by the start of the 4th century. Frend overall offers a clear summary of the rise of the religion and the politics of adoption and conflict. For the 4th century see also papers in BONAMENTE and NESTORI 1988.

20 FREND 1984, 473–517 on Constantine's pro-Christian policies. The devout historian Eusebius of course paints the emperor as a fully-fledged Christian: *Ecclesiastical History* 10.8.

21 KRAUTHEIMER 1980, 18–31. The other sizeable intramural church, Santa Croce in Gerusalemme, was established over the Sessorian villa/palace – owned by Constantine, and again just inside the town defences: see VARAGNOLI 1995, 12–8; *Lexicon* IV, *s.v.* 'Sessorium', 304–8.

22 Much debate has centred recently on the Arch of Constantine, often seen in its reuse of older Trajanic and Hadrianic sculpture, stone and marble as a reflection of the start of late Roman artistic decline, with a lack of quality masons and artists to produce suitable new works; however, recent reappraisals prefer to see a substantial ideological statement being offered, a conscious combination of old and new, merging old powers with new, and in particular displaying a link with Trajan, viewed as one of the greatest emperors – hence the reworked busts of the emperor (of a high quality): PENSABENE and PANELLA 1993–94; WARD-PERKINS 1999, 227–33; *Lexicon* I, *s.v.* 'Arcus Constantini', 86–91.

23 FROVA 1990, 195; *Lexicon* I, *s.v.* 'Basilica Constantiniana, B. Nova', 17–73; *Lexicon* V, *s.v.* 'Thermae Constantinianae', 49–51. Repairs were also made to the circus.

24 KRAUTHEIMER 1980, 33–58; WARD-PERKINS 1984, 236–41; MILBURN 1988, 105–11. See also relevant sections in the *Liber Pontificalis*.

25 See full discussion in CROKE and HARRIES 1982; MARKUS 1990; CAMERON 1999.

26 FROVA 1990, 195 indeed notes how the image for Rome proffered in the *Tabula Peutingeriana* is that of the Vatican church – *ad sanctum Petrum*. On post-Roman pilgrimage to the city: LLEWELLYN 1993, 173–98; BIRCH 1998.

27 Cf. MILANO 1990, 91–176.

28 RICKMAN 1980, 8–10. On wider issues of the nature of the changing population, see PURCELL 1999.

29 *Codex Theodosianus* 14.4.4; *Nov. Valent*. 34. Cf. HODGES and WHITEHOUSE 1983, 48–52; WHITEHOUSE 1988, 29–30; BARNISH 1987; DURLIAT 1990, 110f.

30 Particularly *Codex Theodosianus* 11.28.2 for AD 395, stating that "For the provincials of Campania we remit the taxes of 528,042 *iugera* (= 1332 sq. km) which appear to be located in deserted and unkempt districts of the said province, according to the report to us of the inspectors and records of the ancient documents."

31 CHRISTIE and RUSHWORTH 1988, 81–3.

32 E.g. *Nov. Valent*. 1.2, 5.1, 24, 33. On food shortages in general in the ancient world, see papers by GARNSEY 1990 and NEWMAN *et al.* 1990. Of immense note is the evidence for the 5th- and 6th-century decline of the port facilities, warehouses, etc. at Portus, implying reduced demands at Rome: COCCIA 1996, 297–99.

33 POTTER 1979, 139–46; BARKER 1989. Re-analysis of the South Etruria material is currently in progress at the British School at Rome – in conjunction with a major new project studying the Tiber valley; both projects hope to provide an enhanced image of the late Roman period and late antique-early medieval transition: PATTERSON and MILLETT 1998.

34 See MILANO 1990, 233–304.

35 See contribution by Mattingly and Aldrete in this volume. It is worth noting the documented presence in the 6th century and still in the 19th century of the floating mills on the Tiber, as well as the scattering of mills across the city, including on the Janiculum hill. On water mills see WIKANDER 1979; on late aqueducts and water see COATES STEPHENS 1998, 171–76; SQUATRITI 1998.

36 *Codex Theodosianus* 15.1.11–32; and 15.1.37 promulgated in AD 398; *Nov. Majorian* 4.1 of 458. Cf. WARD-PERKINS 1984, 45–6, 203–6.

37 See discussion in WARD-PERKINS 1999, and, more specifically on the laws, ALCHERMES 1994. There seems to have been little to worry about, however, in AD 357, according to Ammianus Marcellinus (16.10. 13), when Constantius II visited the city: "so then he entered Rome, the home of Empire and of every virtue, and when he had come to the Rostra, the most renowned ancient forum, he stood amazed; and on every side on which his eyes rested he was dazzled by the array of marvellous sights..."

38 Various volumes have appeared, but useful summaries are offered by MANACORDA 1990; 1993; MANACORDA and ZANINI 1989; *Lexicon* V, *s.v.* 'Theatrum Balbi', 30–1; *Lexicon* I, *s.v.* 'Crypta Balbi', 326–29; *Lexicon* V, 241. Most recent is the excellent guidebook CRYPTA BALBI 2000.

39 *CIL* 6.816; *Lexicon* IV, *s.v.* 'Porticus Minucia Vetus', 137–38.

40 *CIL* 6.29849a.

41 MANACORDA 1990, 79; CRYPTA BALBI 2000, 46. Lime kilns are a very common feature in early medieval contexts – in part surprising given that most domestic structures tend then to be timber-built, although we know too little of the reuse and thus maintenance of older Roman *insulae* and town houses, whose repair will have needed lime; alternatively the lime produced in various sites across Rome was chiefly for repairs to the innumerable churches, chapels and monasteries.

42 *Lexicon* III, *s.v.* 'S. Hadrianus', 8–9.

43 AUGENTI 1992, 393–99; 1996a; *Lexicon* I, *s.v.* 'Curia Iulia', 332–34.

44 MENEGHINI 1993, particularly 83–6; *Lexicon* II, *s.v.* 'Forum Traiani', 348–56. On the restricted archaeological data, see MENEGHINI 1989. Recent excavations in the Forum Piazza have found the paving to be surprisingly intact (BENSARD 2000, 42).

45 MENEGHINI 1993, 85–92; *Lexicon* II, *s.v.* 'Forum Traiani: Columna', 356–59. In a rental agreement of 1004 there is in fact reference to cultivated fig trees within the old Forum, and to adjoining properties in the possession of a stone merchant and a lime-burner – no doubt themselves both fully exploiting the ruins. The recent excavations on the Forum Nervae have, as noted, revealed well-preserved buildings (presumed to be private houses) of the 9th century, adding to this image of private colonization of old public space.

46 See, in general, GREENHALGH 1989.

47 GUIDOBALDI 1986; 1999 provide very full statements on late antique Roman elite buildings, while COATES-STEPHENS 1996 pieces together numerous strands of information to cover the post-Roman period, seeking to cover also non-elite housing. The latter notes the frequent partitioning up of *insulae* and other buildings with brick walling, further attesting a continued need for lime mortar (COATES-STEPHENS 1996, 252–53). See also the recent Palatine house excavations: HOSTETTER 1994.

48 For *Domus Ecclesiae* and *tituli* see *Lexicon* I, 37–8, 155, 206–7, 266–67, 278–79, 325, 338–39; II, 91–2, 166–67, 239–42, 371; III, 105–7, 178–79, 192–93, 210–14, 219–20, 342–44; IV, 62, 82–3, 161–63, 166–67, 177–78, 209, 221–23, 325–28, 330, 387–88; V, 232–33, 272, 272. Villas in northern Italy: MILANO 1990, 257–66. The shift of capital to Milan (284) and thence Ravenna (402), plus the creation of Constantinople (324) also provoked many elite transfers; the 5th-century disasters that befell Rome (see below) perhaps prompted an even more substantial exodus.

49 Milan: PERRING 1991. On Brescia see BROGIOLO 1989, particularly 156–59; 1999, 104–5, in which he notes the documented imposition of Gothic troops in Pavia, implying that billeting may well have been at the expense of such sizeable town houses. On housing in general see BROGIOLO 1994; on the 'town debate' – continuity or collapse – see WARD-PERKINS 1997.

50 WARD-PERKINS 1984, 92–118. The arrival of Christianity may have played a part in the closure of entertainment buildings, although the most vociferous orators (Salvian, Augustine) against mimes and blood-sports are from the later 4th century, with voices directed chiefly at the imperial *metropoleis*. Economic concerns more likely sealed the fate of theatres and amphitheatres elsewhere.

51 On pottery/trade: PANELLA 1986; WICKHAM 1989. On coinage: REECE 1982; WHITEHOUSE 1985, 173–74; SPAGNOLI 1993.

52 See note 32 above on declining activity and functional warehouses at Portus from the 5th century. The problem lies in determining whether the reduced numbers of imports = reduced population or reduced means (i.e. smaller market of purchasers, i.e. those able to buy, which need not equate with reduced numbers of actual people). Reduced goods = higher costs, meaning many people were squeezed out of the import market.

53 *Codex Theodosianus* 14.3–4, 14.7 for the 430s–450s; cf. Cassiodorus, *Selected Letters* 8.31–3, 11.39 and 12.12 for Ostrogothic period horse, cattle and pig-rearing in Lucania and Bruttium and wine production in Bruttium. PANELLA 1999 provides an up-to-date survey of supply.

54 WHITEHOUSE 1982; 1985; *Lexicon* IV, *s.v.* '"Schola Praeconum"', 254–55. For the Late Roman and later occupation of the Palatine see TAMM 1968, 153–58.

55 WHITEHOUSE 1982, 81–91.

56 WHITEHOUSE 1985, 181–89; although this decline could equally signify a decline in the personal wealth of the property owner rather than in Rome-wide market trends.

57 ARTHUR 1998, 174 argues that the subsequent Byzantine reconquest dramatically modified the nature of long-distance trade as it "reinforced an exchange system governed principally by exigencies dictated by the state and by the Church". Late antique and early medieval ceramic sequences are busy fields of research: see SAGUÌ 1998 with summaries of most recent projects.

58 SAGUÌ 1998.

59 LANCIANI 1897, 275–76.

60 WICKHAM 1981, 15–20; O'FLYNN 1983; FERRILL 1986, 83–7, 155–69; BARNWELL 1992.

61 See note 17 above for references.

62 A general summary is offered in MATTHEWS 1975, 284–306 and FERRILL 1986, 86–116 – but the account in GIBBON 1789–94 is far more exciting!

63 LANCIANI 1897, 290–92; KRAUTHEIMER 1980, 45–6; WARD-PERKINS 1984, 34–5; *Lexicon* I, *s.v.* 'Basilica Aemilia', 167–68. Cf. REECE 1982 on coin evidence from the Basilica Aemilia.

64 MANACORDA and ZANINI 1989, 29; MANACORDA 1990, 79;1993, 31–5; CRYPTA BALBI 2000, 20; cf. KRAUTHEIMER 1980, 64. Floods were, in fact, occurrences also in the earlier Roman centuries, but in the late and post-Roman period, the ability to cope and recover quickly seem to have diminished. Cf. CHRISTIE 1996, 272–74.

65 LANCIANI 1897, 291–93; FERRILL 1986, 136–55.

66 Of value is the reference in the *Liber Pontificalis* entry for Innocent I (401–417) detailing the bequest by the noblewoman Vestina and the foundation of the *titulus Vestinae* (now S. Vitale): DAVIS 1989, 28–9. For a recent review of 5th-century Rome see PANI ERMINI 1999.

67 See *Liber Pontificalis* for entries relating to church building and decoration: 5th century enterprises are summarized by KRAUTHEIMER 1980, 43–2; DAVIS 1989, 28–32. Santa Sabina: MILBURN 1988, 107–9; *Lexicon* IV, *s.v.* 'Santa Sabina, Basilica, Titulus', 221–23.

68 *Lexicon* II, *s.v.* 'Domus SS. Iohannis et Pauli', 117–18; *Lexicon* III, *s.v.* 'SS. Iohannus et Paulus', 105–7.

69 DAVIS 1989,30; MILBURN 1988, 109–10, 218–22; *Lexicon* III, *s.v.* 'S. Maria Maior, basilica', 217–18. As elsewhere in the *Liber Pontificalis*, the relevant entry barely mentions the form of the church, omits mention of mosaics, preferring to highlight the 'portable' wealth endowed – e.g. the three silver patens of 60lb, the 8lb silver handbasin, the 300lb altar of *finest* silver, the two gold service chalices of 1lb each – with weight and metal type the key indicators of vitality.

70 See DAVIS 1989, 33 regarding the provisioning of space and accommodation for pilgrims outside and around the main shrines under pope Symmachus (498–514). BIRCH 1998 offers an illuminating guide to pilgrimage, particularly to medieval Rome.

71 Olympiodorus fr.41.

72 AUGENTI 1996b, 959. On a maintained aristocratic presence, despite the outward, structural signs of decline, see MATTHEWS 1975, 360–62, 367–68, who also uses the poetry of Rutilius Namatianus to highlight a busy aristocratic countryside and coast north of Rome, with no obvious signs of abandonment on the part of their owners (352–54). See also the example of the Valerii *domus*: BRENK 1999.

73 AUGENTI 1996b, 962.

74 *CIL* 6.37128, 1718 and 31959; MATTHEWS 1975, 356 with notes 3 and 6, recording also how statues were transferred "from neglected parts of the city to more harmonious surroundings, evidently as part of an attempt to enhance streets and public places which must still, in many parts, have carried the scars of the sack of Rome". Noticeably, it is only the state officials who are undertaking such public works.

75 Best coverage is provided in the *Storia di Ravenna* volumes (SUSINI 1990; CARILE 1991), plus DEICHMANN 1989.

76 LLEWELLYN 1993, 21–32; MOORHEAD 1992, 32–65; BARNWELL 1992, 131–69.

77 See note 75, plus JOHNSON 1988.

78 See Cassiodorus, *Selected Letters* 1.21 and 25; 2.34 for funds and bricks for various repairs; and 7.5, 6, 15, 17 for the provision of a City Architect and ministers for overseeing various of the public works (notably the aqueducts). Later Procopius, *Gothic War* 4.22.5–6, admits the generally good state of repair of Rome's monuments in the 530s. But cf. WARD-PERKINS 1984, 46–7 and KRAUTHEIMER 1980, 65–6, claiming Rome overall was probably a place of 'utter shabbiness'.

79 MACPHERSON 1989, 99–102, quoting Cassiodorus' *Chronicle* entry for AD 500.

80 KRAUTHEIMER 1980, 69–87; RICHARDS 1980, 85–125; LLEWELLYN 1993, 78–108. Some of the relevant material is illustrated in CRYPTA BALBI 2000, 60–70.

81 KRAUTHEIMER 1980, 71; *Lexicon* I, *s.v.* 'SS. Cosmas et Damianus, basilica', 324–25.

82 An excellent summary of events between AD 530 and 590 is in LLEWELLYN 1993, 49–91.

83 OSBORNE 1985, 281–83; MENEGHINI and SANTANGELI VALENZANI 1993.

84 REA 1993a; *Lexicon* I, *s.v.* 'Amphitheatrum', 30–5.

85 REA 1993b, 71–3.

86 ARCHEOLOGIA 1989, 92–5 offers photographic illustrations of the level of soil build-up around the Colosseum before the major clearance operations of the 20th century. On the 5th-century role of the Colosseum, see ORLANDI 1999.

87 Cf. MARCELLI 1989 on Colle Oppio burials; more generally MENEGHINI and SANTANGELI VALENZANI 1993. Similarly, the Baths of Caracalla exhibit evidence of restoration up to the time of Theoderic but from the 6th century the outer precinct was being used for burials (DELAINE 1997, 39–40).

88 See BARNISH 1992, 37–53, introduction to his translation; cf. MACPHERSON 1989.

BIBLIOGRAPHY

Primary Sources

For a selection of 4th-century sources, particularly those pertaining to Pagan/Christian controversies, see CROKE and HARRIES 1982.

Ammianus Marcellinus, *History*. Translation by J. Rolfe, I–III, Loeb Classical Library, Heinemann, London, 1935. Penguin Classics selected translation (Books 14–21) by W. Hamilton, 1986.

Cassiodorus, *Variae*. In T. Mommsen (ed.), *Monumenta Germaniae Historica, Auctores Antiquissimi* 12, Berlin, 1893–1894. Translations by T. Hodgkin 1886: *The Letters of Cassiodorus (being a condensed version of the Variae Epistolae of Magnus Aurelius Cassiodorus Senator)*, Oxford University Press, 1886; selected translations by S.J.B. Barnish (Translated Texts for Historians 12), Liverpool University Press, Liverpool, 1992.

Claudius Claudianus, English translation by H. Isbell in *Last Poets of Imperial Rome*, Penguin Classics, London, 1971.

Codex Theodosianus, edited by T. Mommsen and P. Meyer, Berlin, 1905. Translation by C. Pharr, 1952: *The Theodosian Code and Novels and the Sirmondian Constitution*, Princeton University Press, Princeton, 1952 (repr. 1969).

Eusebius, *The Ecclesiastical History*. Translations by K. Lake, I; J. Oulton and H. Lawlor, II, Loeb Classical Library, Heinemann, London, 1926; 1932.

Liber Pontificalis, edited by L. Duchesne. Translation by R. Davis (Translated Texts for Historians 5, 13), Liverpool University Press, Liverpool, 1989; 1992.

Magister Gregorius, *Narracio de Mirabilibus Urbis Romae*. Translation by J. Osborne, 1987: *Master Gregorius The Marvels of Rome*, Toronto, 1987.

Notitia Dignitatum, edited by O. Seeck, Berlin, 1876.

Rutilius Claudius Namatianus, *De Reditu Suo.* English translation by H. Isbell in *Last Poets of Imperial Rome*, Penguin Classics, London, 1971.

Zosimus, *Nea Historia.* Translated by J. Buchanan and H. Davies, London, 1967; also by R. Ridley, (Byzantina Australiensa 2), Canberra, 1982.

Secondary Sources

ALCHERMES, J. 1994: 'Spolia in Roman cities of the late empire: legislative rationales and architectural reuse', *Dumbarton Oaks Papers* 48, 1994, 167–78.

ARCHEOLOGIA 1989: *Archeologia a Roma nelle Fotografie di Thomas Ashby, 1891–1930*, British School at Rome Archive 2, Napoli, 1989.

ARTHUR, P. 1998: 'Eastern Mediterranean amphorae between 500 and 700: a view from Italy', in SAGUÌ 1998, 157–83.

AUGENTI, A. 1994: 'Il Palatino nell'alto medioevo', in R. Francovich and G. Noyé (ed.), *La Storia dell'Alto Medioevo italiano (VI–X secolo) alla luce dell'archeologia*, Firenze, 1994, 659–91.

AUGENTI, A. 1996a: *Il Palatino nel Medioevo. Archeologia e topografia (secoli VI–XIII)*, BullCom Supplementi 4, Roma, 1996.

AUGENTI, A. 1996b: 'Roma. L'età tardoantica', *Enciclopedia dell'Arte Antica. Classica e orientale. Secondo supplemento, 1971–1994, IV: Nepal – Roma*, Roma, 1996, 957–81.

AUGENTI, A., MARLETTA, N. and RICCI, G. 1992: 'Roma – Scavo delle pendici Nord del Palatino. Relazione preliminare delle campagne di scavo 1990', *Archeologia Medievale* 19, 1992, 378–408.

BARKER, G. 1989: 'The Italian landscape in the first millennium AD: some archaeological approaches', in RANDSBORG 1989, 62–73.

BARNISH, S. 1987: 'Pigs, plebeians and potentes: Rome's economic hinterland, *c.* 350–600 AD', *PBSR* 55, 1987, 157–85.

BARNWELL, P. 1992: *Emperor, Prefects and Kings: The Roman West, 395–565*, London, 1992.

BAUER, F.A. 1999: 'Das Denkmal der Kaiser Gratian, Valentinian II und Theodosius am Forum Romanum', *RM* 106, 1999, 213–34.

BENSARD, E. 2000: 'Jubilé 2000. Les grands chantiers de Rome', *Archéologia* 368, 2000, 42–51.

BIRCH, D. 1998: *Pilgrimage to Rome in the Middle Ages. Continuity and Change*, Studies in the History of Medieval Religion 13, Woodbridge, 1998.

BONAMENTE, G. and NESTORI, A. (ed.) 1988: *I Cristiani e l'Impero nel IV secolo. Atti del Convegno, Macerata, 1987*, Macerata, 1988.

BRENK, B. 1999: 'La cristianizzazione della Domus dei Valerii sul Celio', in HARRIS 1999, 69–84.

BROGIOLO, G.P. 1989: 'Brescia: building transformations in a Lombard city', in RANDSBORG 1989, 156–65.

BROGIOLO, G.P. (ed.) 1994: *Edilizia residenziale tra V e VIII secolo, 4 seminario sul tardoantico e l'altomedieovo in Italia centrosettentrionale, Monte Barro-Galbiate, 1993*, Mantua, 1994.

BROGIOLO, G.P. 1999: 'Ideas of the town in Italy during the transition from Antiquity to the Middle Ages', in BROGIOLO and WARD-PERKINS 1999, 99–126.

BROGIOLO, G.P. and GELICHI, S. (ed.) 1996: 'Le ceramiche altomedievali (fine VI–X secolo)', in *Italia settentrionale: produzione e commerci*, Documenti di Archeologia 7, Mantua, 1996.

BROGIOLO, G.P. and WARD-PERKINS, B. (ed.) 1999: *The Idea and Ideal of the Town between Late Antiquity and the Early Middle Ages*, Transformation of the Roman World 4, Leiden, 1999.

CAMERON, Averil 1993: *The Mediterranean World in Late Antiquity, AD 395–600*, London, 1993.

CAMERON, Alan 1999: 'The last pagans of Rome', in HARRIS 1999, 109–21.

CANTINO WATAGHIN, G. 1996: 'Topografia della *civitas Christiana* tra IV e VI sec.', in G.P. Brogiolo (ed.), *Early Medieval Towns in the Western Mediterranean, Conference, Ravello, 1994*, Mantua, 1996, 17–41.

CARANDINI, A. 1993: 'L'ultima civiltà sepolta o del massimo oggetto desueto, secondo un archeologo', in A. Carandini, L.Cracco Ruggini and A. Giardina (ed.), *Storia di Roma 3.2: L'età tardoantica. I luoghi e le culture,* Torino, 1993, 11–38.

CARILE, A. (ed.) 1991: *Storia di Ravenna, II. Dall'età bizantina all'età ottoniana: territorio, economia, società*, Venezia, 1991.

CHRISTIE, N. 1992: 'Urban defence in later Roman Italy', *Papers of the Fourth Conference of Italian Archaeology, Part II: The Archaeology of Power*, London, 1992, 185–99.

CHRISTIE, N. 1996: 'Barren Fields? Landscapes and settlements in late and post-Roman Italy', in G. Shipley and J. Salmon (ed.), *Human Landscapes in Classical Antiquity. Environment and Culture*, London, 1996, 254–83.

CHRISTIE, N. and LOSEBY, S.T. (ed.) 1996: *Towns in Transition. Urban Evolution from Late Antiquity to the Early Middle Ages*, Aldershot, 1996.

CHRISTIE, N. and RUSHWORTH, A. 1988: 'Urban fortification and defensive strategy in fifth and sixth century Italy: the case of Terracina', *JRA* 1, 1988, 73–88.

CICATRIX, J. and ROWSON, M. 1995: *Imperial Exits*, London, 1995.

CLARIDGE, A. 1983: 'Roman methods of fluting corinthian columns and pilasters', in K. de Fine Licht (ed.), *Città e architettura nella Roma Inperiale*, Analecta Romana 10, Roma, 1983, 119–28.

COARELLI, F. 1999: 'L'edilizia pubblica a Roma in età tetrachica', in HARRIS 1999, 23–33.

COATES-STEPHENS, R. 1996: 'Housing in early medieval Rome, 500–1000 AD', *PBSR* 64, 1996, 239–59.

COATES-STEPHENS, R. 1997: 'Dark age architecture in Rome', *PBSR* 65, 1997, 177–232.

COATES-STEPHENS, R. 1998: 'The walls and aqueducts of Rome in the early Middle Ages. AD 500–1000', *JRS* 88, 1998, 166–78.

COCCIA, S. 1996: 'Il *portus Romae* alla fine dell'antichità nel quadro del sistema di approvigionamento della città di Roma', in GALLINA ZEVI and CLARIDGE 1996, 293–307.

COLLINS, R. 1991: *Early Medieval Europe, 300–1000*, London, 1991.

COZZA, L. 1987: 'Osservazioni sulle mura aureliane a Roma', *Analecta Romana Istituti Danici* 16, 1987, 25–53.

CROKE, B. and HARRIES, J. 1982: *Religious Conflict in Fourth-Century Rome. A Documentary Study*, Sydney, 1982.

CRYPTA BALBI 2000: *Museo Nazionale Romano. Crypta Balbi*, Milano, 2000.

DAVIS, R. 1989: *Liber Pontificalis*, Liverpool, 1989.

DEICHMANN, F.W. 1989: *Ravenna. Hauptstadt des spätantiken Abendlandes. Kommentar II.3. Geschichte, Topografie, Kunst und Kultur*, Stuttgart, 1989.

DEICHMANN, F.W. 1993: *Archeologia Cristiana*, Roma, 1993.

DELAINE, J. 1997: *The Baths of Caracalla. A study in the design, construction, and economics of large-scale building projects in imperial Rome*, JRA Supplementary Series 25, Portsmouth RI, 1997.

DURLIAT, J. 1990: *De la Ville Antique à la Ville Byzantine*, Roma, 1990.

FAGAN, G. 1996: 'The reliability of Roman building inscriptions', *PBSR* 64, 1996, 81–93.

FERRILL, A. 1986: *The Fall of the Roman Empire. The Military Explanation,* London, 1986.

FREND, W.H.C. 1984: *The Rise of Christianity*, London, 1984.

FROVA, A. 1990: 'Roma e la tetrarchia', in MILANO 1990, 193–95.

GALLINA ZEVI, A. and CLARIDGE, A. (ed.) 1996: *'Roman Ostia' Revisited: Archaeological and Historical Papers in Memory of Russell Meiggs*, London, 1996.

GARNSEY, P. 1990: 'Responses to Food Crisis in the Ancient Mediterranean World', in L.F. Newman (ed.), *Hunger in History. Food Shortage, Poverty and Deprivation*, Oxford, 1990, 126–46.

GAUTHIER, N. 1999: 'La topographie chretienne entre ideologie et pragmatisme', in BROGIOLO and WARD-PERKINS 1999, 195–209.

GIARDINA, A. (ed.) 1986: *Società Romana e Impero Tardoantico III: Le Merci, Gli Insediamenti*, Roma-Bari, 1986.

GIBBON, E. 1789–94: *The History of the Decline and Fall of the Roman Empire*, Oxford, 1789–94.

GREENHALGH, M. 1989: *The Survival of Roman Antiquities in the Middle Ages*, London, 1989.
GUIDOBALDI, F. 1986: 'L'edilizia abitativa unifamiliare nella Roma tardoantica', in GIARDINA 1986, 165–237.
GUIDOBALDI, F. 1999: 'Le *domus* tardoantiche di Roma come "sensori" delle trasformazioni culturali e sociali', in HARRIS 1999, 53–68.
HARRIS, W. V. (ed.) 1999: *The Transformations of* Vrbs Roma *in Late Antiquity*, JRA Supplementary Series 33, Portsmouth RI, 1999.
HODGES, R. and WHITEHOUSE, D.B. 1983: *Mohammed, Charlemagne and the Origins of Europe*, London, 1983.
HOSTETTER, E., HOWE, T., RASMUS BRANDT, J., ST. CLAIR, A., PENA, J., PARCA, M., GLEASON, K. and MILLER, N. 1994: 'A late Roman *domus* with apsidal hall on the north-east slope of the Palatine: 1989–1991 seasons', in FOLLETTE, L. la, PAVOLINI, C., TOMEI, M.A., HOSTETTER, E. *et al.* and BALL, L., *Rome Papers: the Baths of Trajan Decius, Iside e Serapide nel Palazzo, a late Domus on the Palatine, and Nero's Golden House*, JRA Supplementary Series 11, Ann Arbor, 1994, 131–81.
JOHNSON, M. 1988: 'Towards a history of Theoderic's building program', *Dumbarton Oaks Papers* 42, 1988, 73–96.
JOHNSON, S. 1983: *Late Roman Fortifications*, London, 1983.
KRAUTHEIMER, R. 1937–77: *Corpus Basilicarum Christianarum Romae* I–IV, Vatican City, 1937–77.
KRAUTHEIMER, R. 1980: *Rome. Profile of a City, 312–1308*, Princeton, 1980.
KRAUTHEIMER, R. 1983: *Three Christian Capitals. Topography and Politics*, Berkeley, 1983.
LANCIANI, R. 1897: *Ancient Rome in the Light of Recent Discoveries*, London, 1897.
LANCIANI, R. 1899: *The Destruction of Ancient Rome*, London, 1899.
LLEWELLYN, P. 1993: *Rome in the Dark Ages*, reprint of the 1971 ed., London, 1993.
LUSUARDI SIENA, S. 1984: 'Sulle tracce della presenza gota in Italia: il contributo delle fonti archeologiche', in *Magistra Barbaritas. I Barbari in Italia*, Milano, 1984, 509–58.
LUSUARDI SIENA, S. (ed.) 1994: *Ad Mensam. Manufatti d'uso da contesti archeologici fra tarda antichità e medioevo*, Udine, 1994.
MACPHERSON, R. 1989: *Rome in Involution. Cassiodorus' Variae in their Literary and Historical Setting*, Seria Filologia Klasyczna 14, Poznan, 1989.
MANACORDA, D. 1990: 'Excavations in the Crypta Balbi, Rome; a survey', *Accordia Research Papers* 1, 1990, 73–81.
MANACORDA, D. 1993: 'Trasformazioni dell'abitato nel Campo Marzio: l'area della "Porticus Minucia"', in PAROLI and DELOGU 1993, 31–52.
MANACORDA, D. and ZANINI, E. 1989: 'The first millennium A.D. in Rome: from the *Porticus Minucia* to the Via delle Botteghe Oscure', in RANDSBORG 1989, 25–32.
MARCELLI, M. 1989: 'Su alcune tombe tardo-antiche di Roma: nota preliminare', *Archeologia Medievale* 16, 1989, 525–40.
MARKUS, R. 1990: *The End of Ancient Christianity*, Cambridge, 1990.
MATTHEWS, J. 1975: *Western Aristocracies and Imperial Court, AD 364–425*, Oxford, 1975.
MENEGHINI, R. 1989: 'Roma. Ricerche nel Foro di Traiano – Basilica Ulpia: un esempio di sopravvivenza di strutture antiche in età medievale', *Archeologia Medievale* 16, 1989, 541–59.
MENEGHINI, R. 1993: 'Il foro ed i mercati di Traiano nel medioevo attraverso le fonti storiche e d'archivio', *Archeologia Medievale* 20, 1993, 79–120.
MENEGHINI, R. and SANTANGELI VALENZANI, R. 1993: 'Sepolture intramuranee e paesaggio urbano a Roma tra V e VII secolo', in PAROLI and DELOGU 1993, 89–112.
MILANO 1990: *Milano: capitale dell'impero romano 286–402 d.C. Palazzo Reale, Milano 24 gennaio – 22 aprile 1990*, Catalogo della mostra, Milano, 1990.
MILBURN, R. 1988: *Early Christian Art and Architecture*, Berkeley, 1988.
MOORHEAD, J. 1992: *Theoderic in Italy*, Oxford, 1992.
NEWMAN, L.F., BOEGEHOLD, A., HERLIHY, D., KATES, R.W. and RAAFLAUB, K. 1990: 'Agricultural Intensification, Urbanisation and Hierarchy', in L.F. Newman (ed.), *Hunger in History. Food Shortage, Poverty and Deprivation*, Oxford, 1990, 101–25.
O'FLYNN, J. 1983: *Generalissimos of the Western Roman Empire*, Edmonton, 1983.
ORLANDI, S. 1999: 'Il Colosseo nel V secolo', in HARRIS 1999, 249–63.
OSBORNE, J. 1985: 'The Roman catacombs in the Middle Ages', *PBSR* 53, 1985, 278–328.
PANELLA, C. 1986: 'Le merci: produzioni, itinerari e destini', in GIARDINA 1986, 431–59.
PANELLA, C. 1999: 'Rifornimenti urbani e cultura materiale tra Aureliano e Alarico', in HARRIS 1999, 183–215.
PANI ERMINI, L. 1999: 'Roma da Alarico a Teoderico', in HARRIS 1999, 35–52.
PAROLI, L. and DELOGU, P. (ed.) 1993: *La storia economica di Roma nell'alto medioevo alla luce dei recenti scavi archeologici. Atti del Seminario, Roma, 2–3 Aprile 1992*, Biblioteca di Archeologia Medievale 10, Firenze, 1993.

PATTERSON, H. and MILLETT, M. 1998: 'The Tiber Valley Project', *PBSR* 66, 1998, 1–20.
PAVAN, M. 1988: 'Cristianesimo e impero romano nel IV sec. d.C.', in BONAMENTI and NESTORI 1988, 1–16.
PAVOLINI, C. 1993: 'L'area del Celio fra l'antichità e il medioevo alla luce delle recenti indagini archeologiche', in PAROLI and DELOGU 1993, 53–70.
PAVOLINI, C. 1996: 'Mercato ostiense e mercato romano: alcuni contesti ceramici a confronto', in GALLINA ZEVI and CLARIDGE 1996, 223–42.
PENSABENE, P. and PANELLA, C. 1993–94: 'Reimpiego e progettazione architettonica nei monumenti tardoantichi di Roma', *RendPontAcc* 66, 1993–94, 112–283.
PERRING, D. 1991: 'Lo scavo di Piazza Duomo: età romana e altomedievale', in D. Caporusso (ed.), *Scavi MM3. Ricerche di archeologia urbana a Milano durante la costruzione della Linea 3 della Metropolitana, 1982–1990*, Milano, 1991, 105–61.
POTTER, T.W. 1979: *The Changing Landscape of South Etruria*, London, 1979.
POTTER, T.W. 1987: *Roman Italy*, London, 1987.
PURCELL, N. 1999: 'The populace of Rome in Late Antiquity: problems of classification and historical description', in HARRIS 1999, 135–61.
RANDSBORG, K. (ed.) 1989: *The Birth of Europe. Archaeology and Social Development in the First Millennium A.D.*, Analecta Romana Instituti Danici Supplementi 16, Roma, 1989.
REA, R. 1993a: 'Roma: l'uso funerario della valle del Colosseo tra tardo antico e alto medioevo', *Archeologia Medievale* 20, 1993, 645–58.
REA, R. 1993b: 'Il Colosseo e la valle da Teodorico ai Frangipane: note di studio', in PAROLI and DELOGU 1993, 71–88.
REECE, R. 1982: 'A collection of coins from the centre of Rome', *PBSR* 50, 1982, 116–45.
RICHARDS, J. 1980: *Consul of God. The Life and Times of Gregory the Great,* London, 1980.
RICHMOND, I. 1930: *The City Walls of Imperial Rome*, Oxford, 1930.
RICKMAN, G. 1980: *The Corn Supply of Ancient Rome*, Oxford, 1980.
SAGUÌ, L. 1998: 'Il deposito della Crypta Balbi: una testimonianza imprevidibile sulla Roma del VII secolo?' in SAGUÌ 1998, 305–34.
SAGUÌ, L. (ed.) 1998: *Ceramica in Italia: VI – VII secolo, Conference Proceedings, May 1995, Rome*, Firenze, 1998.
SPAGNOLI, E. 1993: 'Alcune riflessioni sulla circolazione monetaria in epoca tardoantica a Ostia (Pianabella) e a Porto: i rinvenimenti dagli scavi 1988–1991', in PAROLI and DELOGU 1993, 247–66.
SQUATRITI, P. 1998: *Water and Society in Early Medieval Italy, AD 400–1000*, Cambridge, 1998.
SUSINI, G. (ed.) 1990: *Storia di Ravenna, I: L'evo antico*, Venezia, 1990.
TAMM, B. 1968: 'Das Gebeit vor dem Reprasentationspalast des Domitians auf dem Palatin in forschungsgeschichtlicher Beleuchtung', *Opuscula Romana* 6, 1968, 145–91.
TODD, M. 1983: 'The Aurelianic wall of Rome and its analogues', in J. Maloney and B. Hobley (ed.), *Roman Urban Defences in the West*., CBA Research Report 51, London, 1983, 58–67.
VARAGNOLI, C. 1995: *Santa Croce in Gerusalemme*, Saggi di Opus 3, Roma, 1995.
WARD-PERKINS, B. 1984: *From Classical Antiquity to the Middle Ages. Urban Public Building in Northern and Central Italy, A.D. 300–850*, Oxford, 1984.
WARD-PERKINS, B. 1997: 'Continuists, catastrophists, and the towns of post-Roman northern Italy', *PBSR* 65, 1997, 157–76.
WARD-PERKINS, B. 1999: 'Reusing the architectural legacy of the past, entre ideologie et pragmatisme', in BROGIOLO and WARD-PERKINS 1999, 225–44.
WHITEHOUSE, D.B., BARKER, G., REECE, R. and REESE, D. 1982: 'The Schola Praeconum I', *PBSR* 50, 1982, 53–101.
WHITEHOUSE, D.B., COSTANTINI, L., GUIDOBALDI, F., PASSI, S., PENSABENE, P., PRATT, S., REECE, R. and REESE, D. 1985: 'The Schola Praeconum II', *PBSR* 53, 1985, 163–210.
WHITEHOUSE, D.B. 1988: 'Rome and Naples: survival and revival in central and southern Italy', in R. Hodges and B. Hobley (ed.), *The Rebirth of Towns in the West, A.D. 700–1050*, CBA Research Report 68, London, 1988, 28–31.
WICKHAM, C. 1981: *Early Medieval Italy. Central Power and Local Society, 400–1000*, London, 1981.
WICKHAM, C. 1989: 'Italy and the Early Middle Ages', in RANDSBORG 1989, 140–51.
WIKANDER, Ö. 1979: 'Water mills in ancient Rome', *Opuscula Romana* 12, 1979, 13–36.

13. Back to the Future: Archaeology and Innovation in the Building of *Roma Capitale*

Hugh Petter

Architects working in the Eternal City have, from the Renaissance onwards, drawn inspiration from Antiquity for the design of their buildings. This architectural tradition of taking both compositional devices and decorative details from Antique sources, breathing new life into them, and incorporating them into fresh designs can be appreciated readily by anyone visiting Rome today. Yet many of the buildings that one might admire on such a pilgrimage are the undervalued buildings of *Roma Capitale*, erected in the late 19th century by a forgotten generation of young Roman architects working to construct the new capital of a united monarchical Italy.[1]

The survival of this particularly Roman architectural tradition into the 20th century is remarkable, for the frantic transformation of the Eternal City into a modern European capital after 1870 brought with it a demand for a whole series of new building types, together with a bewildering palate of new materials and technology. These challenges were tackled by the architects of the day with the confidence which one can only expect from those who possess a profound grasp of their cultural traditions, and the results of their labours are worthy additions to the rich architectural heritage of Rome.

Before focusing upon specific architects and buildings, however, it is instructive to consider for a moment the physical state of Rome in 1870. The population of the city at this time numbered some two hundred and thirty thousand, seventy percent of whom were illiterate, and within the Aurelian walls only half of the area was occupied by the urban fabric: the rest was divided into secluded gardens for grand Renaissance villas and agricultural land.[2] Sheep and goats were a common sight in the streets and squares, and the Tiber regularly burst its banks, which it had done since Antiquity. This was the Rome so lovingly described by the guide books of Augustus Hare, the novels of Francis Marion Crawford,[3] the evocative watercolours of Ettore Roesler Franz,[4] and in the work of early photographers who were active in Rome from the late 1840s.[5]

The breach of the Aurelian Wall at Porta Pia by the royalist troops of the House of Savoy on 20th September 1870 was the crowning act of unification for the state of Italy.[6] Soon afterwards the capital of the nation formally moved from Florence to Rome, and with this shift of power came an urgent need for radical action to transform the picturesque but backward and decayed city into a modern capital of a suitable scale and grandeur to compete with Paris, Vienna and the other great European capitals.

Baron Haussmann, having recently completed his transformation of the French capital was consulted as to how Rome should be adapted to perform its new role. After some deliberation he concluded that the future development would lie on and about Monte Mario outside the fabric of the old city: but only more recently, however, has his prophecy been fulfilled. Similarly, the Piedmontese statesman Quintino Sella tried with limited success to

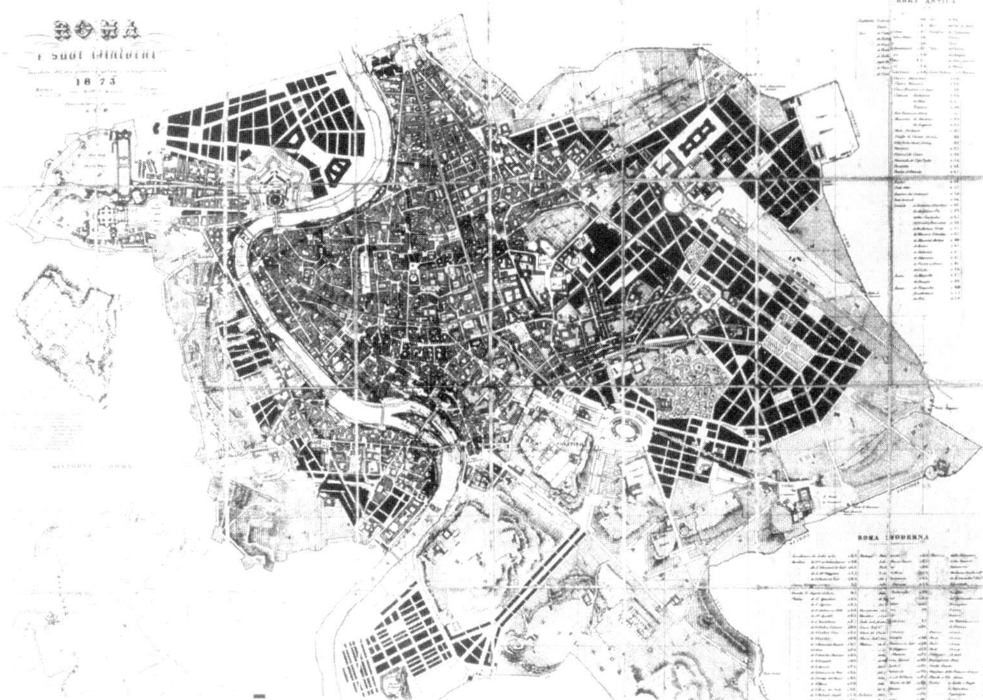

Fig. 13.1: 1873 Piano Regolatore of Rome. Planned new blocks in black (after Sanfilippo 1992).

create a new administrative core outside the historic city along the Via XX Settembre, and instead the historic fabric of Rome was altered and adapted by the new administration to enable it to function as the heart of the capital. The reasons for overlaying *Roma Capitale* on the historic fabric were both practical and ideological. On the one hand, the state simply did not possess the funds to devote to such a massive building enterprise, nor was there time to build a new city.[7] On the other hand, the whole reason for making Rome the capital of the nation was to forge a national identity with the cultural and historic splendours of the Eternal City. As Camillo Cavour, Prime Minister of Italy and architect of the Risorgimento, had said in 1860, "Our fate is to see to it that Rome, which in twenty five centuries has accumulated every kind of glory, becomes the splendid capital of the Italian Kingdom."

The central problem, therefore, was how to adapt the historic fabric and link it with the new quarters required for the rapidly expanding population,[8] whilst deritualizing Papal Rome which had for more than 1000 years been under the administration of St Peter, and establishing instead King Vittorio Emanuele II and the House of Savoy at the heart of the nation.

Within two weeks of the breach of the Aurelian wall, a Commission was set up to prepare a master plan (*Piano Regolatore*) for the "expansion and embellishment of the city".[9] After several abortive attempts, a master plan was finally approved by the city council in 1873 and, although never formally sanctioned by the state, this plan was used to control much of the urban activity during the early years of *Roma Capitale* (Fig. 13.1). Within the historic centre a number of existing streets were widened to open up the heart of the city. The Master Plan Commission pronounced that these new streets need not be straight or uniformly wide,[10] but could be irregular and discontinuous for the sake of sparing bits of extant construction.[11]

Pius IX, the last pope-king, had began to expand Rome to the eastern hills on the healthy high ground of the Esquiline and the Castro Pretorio, and the new railway station was erected on the Viminal by the Baths of Diocletian.[12] It was planned to link these new quarters to the historic centre by means of a new artery, the Via Nuova Pia, which soon after 1870 became the Via Nazionale.[13]

Pius IX's plans had only began to be realised before 1870 but, all the same, they were incorporated into the master plan of 1873 and the development of the eastern side of the city formed the first phase of the construction of the capital. The development of the Esquiline was laid out around the established routes of Pope Sixtus V's so-called star plan, centring on the Basilica of S. Maria Maggiore, to "avoid unnecessary destruction and to respect the valuable buildings," and to connect the area effectively with the rest of the urban fabric.[14]

The *Piano Regolatore* of 1873 also made provision for the embankment of Tiber and, after this work had been carried out, development began of the Prati di Castello to the North of the Borgo/Vatican[15] which had until then been an unhealthy marsh.[16]

In turning now to look in greater detail at the architectural activity of the period, it is clear that the advent of *Roma Capitale* caused a significant upheaval of the architectural establishment of the city. Before 1870, the majority of architectural commissions for those practitioners working in Rome were connected in some way with the Roman Catholic Church. However, the shifting of the capital to Rome, and the consequent divide between the 'black' and 'white' aristocracy, presented the established architects with a dilemma.[17] Should they, on the one hand, retain their allegiance to the Vatican and the black aristocracy or should they, on the other hand, align themselves with the white aristocracy and the new Royalist regime and vie for the many lucrative and exciting commissions that formed a part of the ambitious plans for the new capital? When faced with this situation, many of the established architects of the day remained '*nerissimo*' and, in so doing, effectively left the stage vacant for a rising generation of young architects to make their names in the building of *Roma Capitale*.

The architecture erected in the early years after 1870 can be broadly divided into two distinct categories. The 'Neo-High Renaissance,' or 'Neo-Cinquecento' style was used predominantly by those architects who worked on commissions controlled by the city council: the majority of the buildings erected in this period are designed in this manner. But a number of architects worked in a 'Neo-Antique' style, particularly those whose commissions came under the direct supervision of the state. Unlike the Neo-Cinquecento buildings, many of those in the Neo-Antique style incorporated cast iron elements, a building material which had only become widely available after Italy had established her own heavy industry for the development of her navy and the railways.

Neo-Cinquecentismo had been in vogue constantly in Rome since the High Renaissance, a fact which, in itself, is indicative of the pace of change in the city before 1870.[18] The majority of the architects working in this style had been trained at the notoriously reactionary and antiquated Accademia di San Luca in Rome. The curriculum of this Papal Academy, founded in 1577, had remained largely unchanged since its formation,[19] and was described by Camillo Boito[20] in an article on the teaching of architecture:

> "... the Genius can prove himself later when he has learned the elements ... The talented, when he has mastered these principles, does not pain himself by following in the footsteps of another, nor does he attach himself to the arm of anyone, but instead he develops his own technique. The teaching at the famous Accademia di San Luca follows precisely this principle.

> As soon as the young know how to copy from life, from paintings and from sculpture, they turn to that great museum that is Rome, learning, seeing, imitating ..."[21]

In another article on the hotly debated choice of an appropriate style for buildings in the new capital, Boito pronounced that,

> "In the city, where the Antique tradition has made itself so strongly felt ... to import a 'Foreign' or 'Italian' style to Rome out of the blue would be a bolt in it's history. In Rome, today's architects can, with the elements of Roman architecture, put together the modern style, creating a new organization and a new aesthetic. From the time of Bramante on, without leaving Rome or moving from ancient sources, an integral world of artistic concepts and ornamental forms is to be found. There is no need to call upon the 'charm' of modern foreign architecture, nor any of the 'beauty' of the medieval period, because the past of Rome and the creative fantasy of the artist are sufficient for everything."[22]

This article, so clearly putting the case for modern Roman architecture, caught the mood of the time and was often quoted by the architects of *Roma Capitale* in their own writings.[23]

The great architectural treatises of the High Renaissance, such as those by Serlio[24] and Vignola,[25] had been constantly in print in Italy from the time of their original publication. These texts formed a crucial part of the curriculum for the students at San Luca and were to be found on the shelves of the studios of all the architects working in *Roma Capitale*.[26] Serlio, as a young man, had worked with Peruzzi in Rome,[27] and his architectural treatise provided students with a rich diet of forms and details inspired by antique precedents. He took, for example, the *cyma reversa* bracket from the frieze of the crowning tier of the pilasters on the Colosseum and reworked it to form a bracketed version of the Doric triglyph which he showed in a plate for a door-case designed in the order.[28]

Vignola, another seminal architect of the High Renaissance, also drew heavily from Roman Antiquity for inspiration in his architectural treatise.[29] For example, he took the Doric order from the *fornix* of the Theatre of Marcellus, notable for its unusual dental cornice with a crowning *cavetto* moulding, added an idiosyncratic double *torus* base and published it in his treatise.[30] From the time of its publication, Vignola's treatise was unceasingly popular with Roman architects and consequently his Doric order is used widely in the city, even, as Krautheimer[31] has identified, in the baroque architecture of Bernini.[32]

At the Villa Giulia in Rome,[33] Vignola took Serlio's *cyma reversa* triglyph bracket and added a console bracket to support the crowning cornice, but instead of centring his bracket over the order in the conventional manner, he placed one on either side of the centre line of each pilaster. At the Palazzo Farnese at Caprarola,[34] completed shortly afterwards, Vignola modified the Villa Giulia entablature, this time centring the brackets over the pilasters. This latter design is illustrated in his treatise, and was subsequently reworked by Bernini for the crowning entablature of the Palazzo Odescalchi in Piazza di SS. Apostoli. Such an understanding of the evolution of architectural form from Antique sources in Rome formed a significant part of the curriculum at the Accademia di San Luca, and its graduates consequently emerged with a sound understanding of the architectural forms and architectural traditions of their city.

Turning now to consider how this education system affected the buildings of *Roma Capitale*, let us concentrate first upon the architects working in the Neo-Cinquecento style who drew heavily upon the treatises of the High Renaissance for their inspiration, rooted, as has been seen, in Antiquity.

Fig. 13.2: Piazza dell'Esedra, Rome, by Gaetano Koch (Photo: author).

Fig. 13.3: Detail of one end pavilion in Piazza dell'Esedra, Rome (Photo: author).

Fig. 13.4: Palazzo della Banca d'Italia, Rome, by Gaetano Koch (Photo: author).

By far the most skilful exponent of the Neo-Cinquecento style was Gaetano Koch[35] who, when he died prematurely in 1910, was acclaimed by his contemporaries as "without a doubt, the prince of contemporary Roman architects".[36] Upon graduating from the Accademia di San Luca, Koch quickly established himself in the young capital and within a few years was enjoying some of the most prestigious commissions of the day.

The project to design the arcaded palaces at the Piazza dell'Esedra at the head of the Via Nazionale provided Koch with a splendid opportunity to display his talents (Fig. 13.2). It was decided that the line of the exedra from the Baths of Diocletian should be retained with the building of two symmetrical crescents on the antique foundations, which would function as a grand gateway into the new capital from the railway station at the side of the Antique bath complex.[37] For the engaged columns of the arcade, Koch reworked Vignola's Doric order, but with Serlian *cyma reversa* triglyph brackets over the arches in the end pavilions. The majority of the remaining architectural details, however, take their cue from Vignola.

Antique victories bearing laurel wreathes are used as caryatids and replace the uppermost tier of pilasters on the pavilions at each end of the two crescents (Fig. 13.3). Above these figures, broken segmental pediments contain cartouches surrounded by allegoric groups, and the composition is dramatically completed with victory eagles standing on pedestals on each corner. It is clear from this composition that Koch processed a solid grasp of the symbolism of the decorative forms commonly found in Antiquity that he had undoubtedly gained whilst at San Luca, and the rich embellishment of these structures clearly indicates their perceived importance in the hierarchy of new buildings erected in the city.

Half way down the Via Nazionale on the left hand side is arguably Koch's finest public building, the Palazzo della Banca d'Italia, the seat of the new central bank of Italy (Fig. 13.4). The overall form of this long building, with two courtyards separated by a central staircase takes it's inspiration from Fuga's 18th century Palazzo Corsini in Trastevere which in turn draws inspiration from a design in Ammannati's[38] unpublished treatise from the High Renaissance, *La Città*.[39] The handling of the long elevation looks to Bernini's Palazzo Odescalchi, with unadorned walls at either end, framed by pilasters, and engaged columns across the central bays. The proportions of the main group of rooms on the *piano nobile*, as Meeks has identified, look to Palladio's work at the Palazzo Chiericati in Vicenza, which was inspired by the latter's detailed study of the Baths of Caracalla in Rome.[40]

Between the arched headed windows on the rusticated ground floor of the Banca d'Italia are a sequence of ships prows or *rostra* (Fig. 13.5), an architectural symbol of victory whose origins lie in the beaks of the ships captured after the battle of Antium in 338 BC which adorned the speakers rostrum in the Forum Romanum in Rome.[41] *Rostra* are to be found on many of the triumphal public buildings of *Roma Capitale*.

The crowning cornice of the Banca d'Italia presented Koch with a problem, since a conventional entablature of an appropriate size to cap this enormous structure would clearly have resulted in cantilevered stones of an unmanageable size. So instead Koch introduced acanthus leaf and scroll brackets into the frieze, and these support modillions in the cornice (Fig. 13.6). The resulting unification of these two parts of the entablature enabled Koch to reduce the overhang required to provide a satisfactory crown to the whole composition. For the design of the acanthus and scroll brackets in the frieze, it appears the Koch may have drawn inspiration from the *soffit* of the cornice of the Temple of Castor in the Roman Forum[42] and it is quite feasible that, especially in light of his training, Koch would have decided to draw inspiration for his innovative detail from an Antique source.

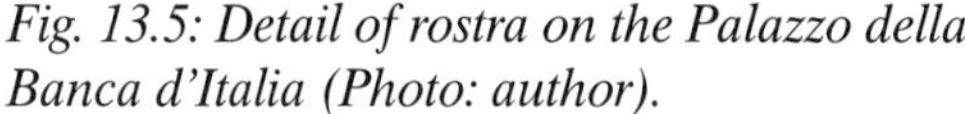

Fig. 13.5: Detail of rostra on the Palazzo della Banca d'Italia (Photo: author).

Fig. 13.6: Crowning entablature on the Palazzo della Banca d'Italia (Photo: author).

Koch gained great respect from his peers for his pioneering work in modifying the traditional Roman *palazzo* formula to provide simple apartment blocks for the large numbers of middle class bureaucrats pouring into the new administrative offices of the capital. The composition and decoration of these buildings, unsurprisingly, relies heavily upon the treatises of Serlio and Vignola,[43] giving his designs a peculiarly appropriate Roman flavour. One can appreciate, both from visual evidence and from contemporary accounts such as that supplied by Marcello Piacentini, that these sources from the High Renaissance were clearly used by the majority of architects working in *Roma Capitale*, albeit often with less grace and skill than Gaetano Koch.

Another architect of similar calibre was Pio Piacentini.[44] His Florentine design for the Banca d'Italia[45] was rejected in favour of Koch's more Roman design, but on the other side of the Via Nazionale, Piacentini was commissioned to design the Palazzo delle Esposizione, a grand new public building to provide a venue for the exhibition of the fine arts of the new nation (Fig. 13.7).

The blind walls of the galleries are articulated with Corinthian pilasters that, in the centre of the building, break forward to become free-standing columns framing the grand triumphal arch entrance (Fig. 13.8).[46] The forest of columns leading up the grand staircase form a subtle light filter to help the eye adjust from the intense light of the Roman summer to the more gentle light in the galleries.[47] The spandrels of the triumphal arch contain victories bearing Laurel wreathes and the central keystone supports a victorious eagle also with a wreath. Above the main cornice line, an attic over the entrance supports an allegorical group that crowns the whole composition. From such studies of the work of Piacentini, Koch and their contemporaries, it is clear that the architectural establishment at this time, together with other sectors of society, had a reasonable knowledge of the symbolic meaning of antique decorative forms. The majority of Piacentini's work is in the more sober Neo-Cinquecento style, but the commission for the Palazzo delle Esposizioni fell under the umbrella of the state administration, and this may account for the more Neo-Antique flavour of the design.

Fig. 13.7: Palazzo delle Esposizione in the Via Nazionale, Rome, by Pio Piacentini (Photo: author).

Fig. 13.8: Detail of the entrance arch of the Palazzo delle Esposizione (Photo: author).

Let us turn now to consider the second category of building which I identified earlier, namely those designed in a Neo-Antique style. Compared with the quantity of buildings designed in the Neo-Cinquecento style, the Neo-Antique buildings are far fewer in number, and all of them were erected by only a handful of architects working in the capital.

One such man was Ettore Bernich[48] who, in 1883, designed the aquarium[49] in the Piazza Mandredo Fanti near the centre of the new Esquiline Quarter of the city (Fig. 13.9). This building, intended as a place for public education, was one of a number encouraged by Quintino Sella, Piedmontese statesman and Comptian Positivist who, when asked what were his plans for Rome replied simply "knowledge".[50]

The Aquarium building consists of an elliptical hall, around the edge of which are grouped the tanks linked internally by a cast iron gallery[51] that allows the viewer to promenade and view

Fig. 13.9: Aquarium in Piazza Manfredo Fanti, Rome, by Ettore Bernich (Photo: author).

Fig. 13.10: Interior of Bernich's Aquarium (Photo: author).

Fig. 13.11: Detail of facade of Bernich's Aquarium (Photo: author).

Fig. 13.12: Doric aedicula from the façade of Bernich's Aquarium (Photo: author).

Fig. 13.13: Balcony on rostra in Bernich's Aquarium (Photo: author).

the fish (Figs. 13.10–13). Externally, a grand triumphal arch forms the entrance to the aquarium, with a large apsidal portico flanked by Doric *aediculae* (Figs. 13.11 & 12).[52]

The Doric order on either side of the entrance portico is of particular interest. The *soffit* of the brackets or *mutules* in the cornice contain little pegs called *guttae* as is commonly found with the Doric order, but Bernich added an additional row of *guttae* to the edge of these *mutules*. This idiosyncratic detail bears close resemblance to the antique 'Doric of Albano',[53] from a *nymphaeum* of Domitian's villa at Albano, designed by Rabirius in the late 1st century AD.[54] The related character of Rabirius's *nymphaeum* and Bernich's aquarium would provide a neat conceptual link which might explain the latter's use of this particular Antique order.

Below the curved *echinus* of the capital of the Doric order, an unadorned disc forms another distinctive feature. A similar detail may be found on the Doric order of the Basilica Iulia in the Forum, the excavation of which coincided with the erection of the aquarium.[55] It

Fig. 13.14: Palazzo facing the Colosseum, Rome, by Ettore Bernich (Photo: author).

Fig. 13.15: Detail from palazzo facing the Colosseum (Photo: author).

Fig. 13.16: Rinascente Department Store, Rome, by Giulio de Angelis (Photo: author).

is possible, therefore, that Bernich consciously used this detail from a great public building of Antiquity to adorn his own public building.

In the early 1880s Bernich had assisted the English archaeologist Parker in the excavation of the Baths of Agrippa behind the Pantheon, during the course of which the beautiful dolphin, trident and palmette frieze, visible today, were discovered.[56] Having already

Fig. 13.17: Monument to King Vittorio Emanuele II, Rome, by Giuseppe Sacconi et al. (Photo: author).

Fig. 13.18: Detail from the Monument to Vittorio Emanuele II (Photo: author).

Fig. 13.19: Interior of the Monument to Vittorio Emanuele II (Photo: author).

identified Bernich's predilection for drawing inspiration from appropriate antique sources, it comes as no surprise to see Agrippa's dolphin frieze reworked in the crowning entablature at the aquarium.

Cast iron was rarely used in buildings in Rome before 1870 as it had to be imported. But with the rapid programme of industrialization after unification of the nation, this material became more readily available, and for architects the arrival of cast iron provided a wealth of new structural and decorative possibilities.

In his book entitled *L'architettura domestica di svelte forme*,[57] the distinguished architect and archaeologist Luigi Canina encouraged those of his colleagues who were wrestling with the detailing of 'thin forms' in either wood or iron to look to the fantastical and theatrical architectural compositions in Second and Fourth Style wall paintings for inspiration. The

Fig. 13.20: Palazzo di Giustizia, Rome, by Guglielmo Calderini (Photo: author).

pages of Canina's book are full of exquisite engravings of such scenes from Antiquity, including those to be found at Nero's Domus Aurea, and other examples from Rome.

Bernich drew heavily from Canina's publication in the internal decoration at the aquarium, where many of the details have playful maritime references: for example, dolphins with curling tails take the place of conventional volutes on the capitals of some of the pilasters. This theme is continued with fish scale iron railings on the staircase, modelled on antique *transennae*, and with a balcony supported on large *rostra* on the first floor that displays the House of Savoy coat of arms. The remaining wall areas are covered with painted panels portraying a variety of well-known subjects from classical mythology and important scenes from the building of *Roma Capitale*.

Although the exterior fabric of the aquarium was relatively poorly constructed, its scholarly detail, it's innovative use of cast iron and its rich internal colour scheme make it one of the most interesting and imposing Neo-Antique buildings constructed in the early years of the capital.

Bernich's other buildings in Rome exhibit a similar delight in the reworking of Antique details. For example his *palazzo* facing the Colosseum fuses Vignola's Doric order from the Theatre of Marcellus with Rabirius's 'Doric of Albano' in the cornice crowning the rusticated ground and first floors (Figs. 13.14 & 15). The giant order which unites the *piano nobile* and second floor is Corinthian, with an eagle replacing the usual rosette under the abacus of the capital, similar to that found on the Corinthian order of the Portico of Octavia.[58] The overall form of this palazzo, however, with a rusticated base, a giant order and pavilions above the main cornice line, owes more to the High Renaissance and Serlio's idealized palace facades from his *Five Books of Architecture.*[59]

Giulio de Angelis[60] was one of the few architects working in *Roma Capitale* who, although Roman by birth, had received his architectural education at the Polytechnic of Milan. At that time, Milan was the most prosperous and industrialized city in the peninsula, and this fact, combined with the proximity to the rest of Europe, resulted in many of the early Italian cast iron buildings being erected there.[61] These revolutionary structures appear to have fired the imagination of the young De Angelis for, after graduating, he returned to his home city and produced many of the finest iron buildings in Rome over a short period in the early 1880s. His Rinascente department store on the Via del Corso was the first such building in the new capital (Fig. 13.16). De Angelis's composition has striking similarities with that of the Antique gates of Verona as illustrated in Serlio's treatise,[62] where a giant arcade is

Fig. 13.21: Victory statue facing towards the Vatican on the Vittorio Emanuele II Bridge, Rome (Photo: author).

Fig. 13.22: Victory Statue facing towards the city on the Vittorio Emanuele II Bridge, Rome (Photo: author).

surmounted by a two smaller arcaded galleries. The open façade proudly displays the iron structure, whilst also providing ample space for elaborate window displays. The interior of the building boasts a light cast iron structure with the various floors of the shop united by a central atrium, the detail of which draws inspiration from the plates of Canina's '*Svelte Forme*'. Externally the bronze *rostra* on the corner pilasters emphasize the triumphant air of the building sited on the corner of Piazza Colonna, the heart of the new administration.

Sadly, however, De Angelis' clients were all badly affected by the financial crash in the 1880s and he was forced to abandon architectural practice for a career in conservation, during which he restored a number of antique monuments.[63]

Arguably the best known and most criticized building in *Roma Capitale* is the monument to King Vittorio Emanuele II overlooking Piazza Venezia (Fig. 13.17). Much has been written about this pompous, self-conscious monument, although most of this criticism is, as David Watkin has correctly identified,[64] focused upon the position of the building rather than the architectural form and detail.

When Vittorio Emanuele II died in 1878, it was decided to host an international design competition to erect a suitable monument to the father of the Risorgimento. Competitors were free to locate their design wherever they pleased: the winning scheme by a young Frenchman, Henri-Paul Nénot, was to be sited in the Piazza dell'Esedra in front of the Baths of Diocletian. A central monumental column was to be surrounded by a D-shaped arcaded screen, at the middle of which a grand triumphal arch framed the entrance to the Via Nazionale. But Nénot's design was discovered to be related to his Grand Prix design of 1877 and this fact, combined with discontent that the competition for an Italian monument had been won by a Frenchman, led to the abandonment of Nénot's scheme.[65]

In 1882 a second competition was held, although this time the site was on the northern side of Capitoline Hill which, since antiquity, had been the seat of secular government of the city. In

Fig. 13.23: The fountain erected in the twilight of the Papal regime of Pope Pius IX in the Piazza dell'Esedra, Rome, to mark the head of the Aqua Marcia (after Sanfilippo 1992).

Fig. 13.24: Fontana delle Naiadi in Piazza dell'Esedra, Rome, erected by Rutelli in 1900, detail of Naiad (Photo: author).

Fig. 13.25: Satirical postcard caricaturing Rutelli's Fontana delle Naiadi, Rome (after Guidoni 1984).

this way, modern Rome took its place alongside Michelangelo's Campidoglio and the ancient Roman fora. But this was not the whole story. Erecting a monument on the Capitoline Hill involved the demolition of the tower of Paul III and of the convent of S. Maria in Aracoeli, thereby erasing Catholic connections with this important site and establishing in their place the House of Savoy. During the 1880s, Catholic subversion threatened the stability of the royalist regime and so the siting of the Vittorio Emanuele monument was highly political. As Domenico Farini, President of the Senate, recorded in his diary, "Italy had to do something big to show the Vatican".[66] Most would agree that she succeeded.

A little known architect, Giuseppe Sacconi,[67] won the second competition, and the project was to occupy him until his untimely death in 1905, after which, the completion of the monument was supervized by Koch, Piacentini and Manfredo Manfredi.[68]

Those who care to look beyond the obvious criticisms of Sacconi's creation are rewarded with an extremely articulate architectural design. Externally the decoration of the various terraces draws heavily upon ancient sources with, for example, *rostra*, victories, military trophies and garlands of oak leaves: the latter are without their acorns, which, in Antiquity, was a recognized funereal motif (Fig. 13.18). The labyrinthine interior contains an extraordinary sequence of vast exhibition halls, modelled upon ancient Roman bath buildings (Fig. 13.19). These are linked by a grand staircase which gently winds up through the various floors before arriving, finally, at the crowning colonnade from which one is rewarded with remarkable panoramic views of Rome. In front of the extraordinary theatrical backdrop a pedestal supports the huge bronze equestrian statue of Vittorio Emanuele, facing north across the Piazza Venezia towards the Via del Corso.[69]

The monument can be seen as one of the most brutal anti-papal acts of the new administration and it is significant that its siting, its decoration and the overall composition, which draws heavily on the ancient terraced sanctuary at Praeneste (Palestrina),[70] are deliberately connected with Antiquity. For it was the conscious forging of this link with the Antique which formed a key part of the new administration's attempts to loosen the grip of St. Peter on the new capital.

Apart from the monument to Vittorio Emanuele, the other well known and much maligned building of the early years of *Roma Capitale* is the vast Palazzo di Giustizia (1889–1911), on the Prati di Castello near the Vatican (Fig. 13.20). The palazzo is approached on axis via the Umberto I Bridge which, it had been suggested, emphasizes that it was the House of Savoy which had brought law and order to the capital.[71] The architect of the Palace of Justice, Guglielmo Calderini,[72] skilfully manipulates the orders to weave together this vast composition, the heavy rustication and ornamentation of which owes a good deal to Piranesi's fantastical engravings.[73]

Another new bridge, named after Vittorio Emanuele II, was erected to link the Vatican with the historic centre. At either end of this elegant stone structure, tall plinths bearing the House of Savoy's coat of arms support two pairs of antique victories: those facing the city proffer laurel wreathes, whilst those facing the Vatican hold swords, once again clearly demonstrating the manipulation of antique symbols for particular political effect (Figs. 13.21–22).[74]

Aside from the erection of such politically charged monuments the new administration decided that certain antique structures should be used for state occasions to assist in the forging of a national identity. To this end, it was decreed that the kings of united monarchical Italy should be buried in the Pantheon. Consequently, the tombs of Vittorio Emanuele II and Umberto I, each richly encrusted with Antique iconography, are to be found on either side of the great rotunda, together with that of Raphael, whose remains were moved there to accompany the fathers of modern Italy. Such was the importance of the ancient structure that in 1883 Bacelli, the Minister of Public Instruction, removed the two curious bell towers which had been added by Bernini in the 17th century to restore the monument to its ancient splendour.[75]

Similarly, the church of S. Maria degli Angeli, created by Michelangelo within the original structure of the Baths of Diocletian, was adopted for state occasions. Vanvitelli's undistinguished entrance façade, added in the 18th century when he altered the orientation of the church,[76] was removed in time for the international festival of the arts and archaeology in 1911 when *Roma Capitale* proudly showed herself to the rest of the world as a modern European capital.[77]

One of the final acts of the Papal administration of Pius IX had been to bless a sober new fountain marking the head of the ancient Aqua Marcia in Piazza dell'Esedra in front of the church of S. Maria degli Angeli. The prominent position of this fountain, together with the symbolic connection with Antiquity, ensured that the papal monument was soon replaced by the racy Fontana delle Naiadi ('Fountain of the Naiads') by Rutelli in 1900 (Fig. 13.23)[78], described in a contemporary guidebook as showing "naughty nymphs frolicking with sea creatures in positions one does not always want to show to children" (Fig. 13.24)! A satirical postcard of the time demonstrates that the erection of the new fountain was clearly seen as an anti-papal act (Fig. 13.25).

However, this self-conscious adoption of the Antique for particular political effect represents, as has been seen, only one aspect of the use of Antiquity as a source of inspiration by the architects of 19th century Rome.

The extraordinary development of Rome after 1870 is an enormous subject that has, for too long, remained in the shadows of the history of the Eternal City. The period is often only referred to in passing and under such derogatory titles as 'The Rape' or 'The Third Sack'.[79] But whilst the building of *Roma Capitale* is by no means the most distinguished period in the architectural history of the city, many of the architects of this frantic period of urban activity did manage to carry the long established architectural traditions of their city into the 20th century. It can only be lamented that in more recent times, Roman architects have self-consciously abandoned the traditions of their city, preferring instead to root their work in the barren soil of International Modernism.[80]

The results of this ingress of Modernist ideology into Rome is the ever thickening crust of concrete blocks which have neither the architectural nor the urban qualities of their 19th century ancestors. Yet, whilst the suburban sprawl of Rome today continues at an alarming rate, the centre of the city remains trapped in a time warp with the prohibition of any new development in the heart of the capital. Such paralysis, though widespread throughout the world, is clearly not healthy for the life of any town, and it is particularly tragic that even Rome, the Eternal City, has succumbed finally to this disease.

However, the rich architectural fabric of the centre of Rome clearly demonstrates that working within the spirit of the traditions of the city by no means stifles the creativity or imagination of the architect, whilst at the same time ensuring that the contribution of each generation respects the established architectural character of the extant buildings.

If only those responsible for the development of Rome today could be re-united with the threads of their rich architectural traditions, one could be sure that these would be woven in new and interesting ways, and that archaeology and innovation could be fused again in the development of the Eternal City.

ACKNOWLEDGEMENTS

I am enormously indebted to Dr Jon Coulston and Dr Hazel Dodge for the kind invitation to participate in their conference in Roman Archaeology in 1993 that planted the seed for my contribution to this book, and for their subsequent help and advice. Much of the material that I have drawn upon was gathered during my tenure of the Rome Scholarship in Architecture from 1990–92. I am most grateful to the Faculty of Fine Arts and Architecture of the British School at Rome for their support and to the staff of the British School at Rome: in particular Valerie Scott, Richard Hodges, Amanda Claridge and Maria Pia Malvezzi, whose wizardry in gaining access to obscure places and archives was invaluable. In addition, I should like to express my thanks to Emanuela Fabbricotti, whose generosity in allowing me to access to her family archives gave me a profound insight into the work of her great uncle Gaetano Koch; to ARCUK for their generous financial support in the form of the William Kretchmer Award; to Geoffrey Broadbent and Robert Adam who guided my programme of research and, with Peter Hodson, were constant sources of encouragement. I am greatly indebted to my fellow scholars Robin Williams, Terry Kirk, Francesco Garofalo who know far more about the political manipulation of the Antique than I ever shall and who drew my attention to many of the points made in the latter part of the essay, and all my other friends and family who have assisted me in the course of my labours. Finally, I should like to thank my long-suffering wife Chloë, for her endless patience and to whom I became engaged during the preparation of this chapter in Michelangelo's Piazza on the Capitoline Hill: what finer spot than the centre of the ancient world!

NOTES

1 On 20th September 1870, the Aurelian Wall was breeched at Porta Pia by troops of the House of Savoy. The capture of Rome was the crowning act of the Risorgimento that had preoccupied the Italian peninsular for much of the 19th century. In 1861 the state of Italy had been declared, but Pope Pius IX had retained control of Rome, protected by the French. In 1865 the capital of Italy was moved formally from Turin to Florence. Shortly afterwards, the French withdrew from Rome under the impression that moving the capital again, with all that that would entail, was unlikely. The Franco-Prussian War also played a part in this decision. As a result, Rome was captured after a token bombardment. This chapter focuses upon the architectural and urban activity that took place in Rome in the early years of the capital. The end of this frenzied period of activity was effectively 1911, when an ambitious exhibition was staged in the city to celebrate 50 years of the state of Italy (FRUTAZ 1962, Pl. 576; PIANTONI 1980). There was something of a priority in finishing major building projects in time for the 1911 festivities, much as there has been for the 2000 *Giubileo*. For the general historical background, see BARTOCCINI 1988; CARACCIOLO 1984; CLARK 1984, 12–178; CROCE 1929; CUCCIA 1991; FEO 1970; GLORNEY BOLTON 1970; HIBBERT 1985, 244–85; INSOLERA 1980, 359–410; KOSTOF 1973; MACK SMITH, 1989, 3–205; MEEKS 1966, 285–406; PERODI 1980; ROMA CAPITALE 1–13; ROME 1977, 7–30; SANFILIPPO 1992.

2 LANCIANI 1988, 171–74. For the progressive post-1870 erosion of the *disabitato* within the walls, see FRUTAZ 1962, Pls. 533–76.

3 Francis Marion Crawford was an Italian American author whose contemporary novels such as *Don Orsino* (1892) give a unique insight into the mood of the period in Rome. See ROME 1977, Nos. 8, 28, 59, 105, 107, 126, 131; HIBBERT 1985, Fig. 85.

4 Ettore Roesler Franz (1845–1907) painted some 120 views of Rome before the rude awakening of the city, after 1870. This collection, known affectionately as '*Roma Sparita*', is on view at the Museo di Roma (MASO and VENDITTI 1981).

5 BRIZZI 1975; ROME 1977, 39–51; EINAUDI 1978; BECCHETTI 1993.

6 See ROME 1977, Nos. 173–74, 193; MANACORDIA and TAMASSIA 1985, 95.

7 Many of the new ministries were initially housed in former monasteries or convents that, some have argued, was symbolic of the end of the Papal Regime. But this move was also an extremely practical solution to the problem of finding sizeable buildings to accommodate the new bureaucracies before the state could afford to erect new buildings. For example, the Domenican Monastery of the Minerva became first the Ministry of Finance, then that of Public Instruction; the Monastery of the Augustinians, the Naval Office; the Convent of the Virgins, the Treasury Department; the Monastery of the Filippines, the Law Courts, and the Monastery of San Silvestro was first the Home Office, then the Ministry of Public Works and finally the Post Office. See HIBBERT 1985, 277–78, 367–68; ROMA CAPITALE 13. Custom-built ministries came later, as for example the Ministeri delle Finanze e del Tesoro, di Difesa, and di Agricoltura (north, northwest and west of the Baths of Diocletian

respectively), and the Ministero d'Interno (west of SM. Maggiore). Another wave of such buildings was erected under Mussolini, principally along the Via Veneto, and out on the Via Flaminia (Ministero della Marina).

8 The population of Rome numbered more than 500,000 by 1900 (KOSTOF 1973, 6).

9 The Commission of eleven architects and engineers was led by Pietro Camporesi – see LAVORI 1870. For a full discussion of the early master plans, see CUCCIA 1991; INSOLERA 1959; 1980, 369–94; KOSTOF 1973, 41–50.

10 PIANO 1873, 6–7; FRUTAZ 1962, Pl. 536–37; KOSTOF 1973, 54–6.

11 The relatively sensitive approach to carving new arteries through the extant fabric of Rome contrasts strongly with that adopted in Paris where points were connected with straight lines and with little concern for what stood in the way of these new axial routes. For post-1870 archaeological excavation and conservation in Rome, see EINAUDI 1978, Nos. 19–21; LANCIANI 1988; MOATTI 1993, 120–29.

12 The original railway station at Termini was built by S. Bianchi (SGARBI 1991, 48) in 1864 (FRUTAZ 1962, Pl. 521; BRIZZI 1975, 85; ROME 1977, No. 57; ACCASTO 1970, 28).

13 The area surrounding the eastern end of the Via Nuova Pia was acquired in the late 1860s by the notorious Cardinale De Merode, the minister of arms in the Papal Regime, once it had been decided to erect the railway station by the Baths of Diocletian. De Merode began to develop his quarter in April 1867 on the gardens of the Villa Peretti, built by Sixtus V, having gained approval from the city council to develop the land between the exedra and the Via Quattro Fontane and to retain the semi-circular shape of the exedra. See PALERMO 1990; KOSTOF 1973, 52–3; ROMA CAPITALE 12, 295–325.

14 PIANO 1873. For the star plan see FRUTAZ 1962, Pl. 257, 259; INSOLERA 1980, 171.

15 The Prati district lies between the Borgo and Monte Mario (FRUTAZ 1962, Pl. 532, 546; BRIZZI 1975, 80–3; BECCHETTI 1993, No. 60). Plans to develop the Prati di Castello were also begun under the regime of Pius IX.

16 Hence the papal preference to residences in more healthy parts of the city: Palazzi S. Giovanni, S. Marco, Quirinale.

17 The 'Black' (*Nero*) aristocracy retained their allegiance to the Pope and refused to have anything to do with the administration. See CRAWFORD 1880; 1885; 1892; GLORNEY BOULTON 1970; HIBBERT 1985, 277–78.

18 I am indebted to Dr Janet Delaine for helping me to establish that the main sources for building materials (for example brick, travertine, pozzolana and pepperino) in the early years of *Roma Capitale* were the same as those that had been in constant use since Antiquity. See DELAINE 1995.

19 A common misconception is that the architectural training in Rome at this time was merely copying that at the Ecole des Beaux Arts in Paris. The reality, in fact, is that the reverse is true (EGBERT 1980, 19).

20 Camillo Boito (1836–1914) has been described as the 'Italian Ruskin'; see MEEKS 1966, 207–9 for a discussion on the man, his ideas on architecture and his influence. For some of his numerous articles, see CRIPPA 1988.

21 CRIPPA 1988, 147.

22 CRIPPA 1988, 63–66.

23 For example, see KOCH 1883, 40.

24 Sebastiano Serlio (1475–1554). SERLIO 1584. For a full discussion of the publications and influence of Serlio, see THOENES 1989.

25 Jacopo Barozzi da Vignola (1507–1573). See SGARBI 1991, 262–64. VIGNOLA 1585.

26 See PIACENTINI 1952, 72.

27 Serlio worked with Baldassare Peruzzi (1481–1536) from 1514 until the sack of Rome in 1527. Peruzzi was a considerable scholar of Antiquity, and his master's enthusiasm for the Antique clearly rubbed off on Serlio. His treatise was the first to codify the five Orders, together with information on how to construct them and examples of compositions from Antiquity, from the Renaissance and of his own designs.

28 SERLIO 1584, Book 4, Chapter 6, Fol. 23..

29 During the 1860s Vignola's treatise was published in special Roman editions including examples of the author's works in Rome and northern Lazio.

30 Anyone who has attempted a design in the Doric order will inevitably have encountered problems in spacing the triglyphs and metopes in the frieze. The triglyphs, which are half a diameter wide should be centred over the order and the metopes between these triglyphs. In the cornice, mutule brackets align over the triglyphs. In the abstract this sounds straight forward enough, but the problem becomes evident when one tries to integrate this rigid horizontal proportioning system with arches and other vertical elements, as at the Theatre of Marcellus – see FREART DE CHAMBRAY 1664, 16–7. The solution in this particular Antique example adopted by Vignola is brilliant in its simplicity. By using an essentially Ionic entablature with the Doric order and by suppressing the decorative detail in the frieze, the problem of the triglyph spacing disappears: as the cornice contains dentils rather than mutules, the horizontal proportioning become infinitely flexible to co-ordinate easily with other elements of the design. It is this neat solution to one of the most taxing problems facing architects working with the Doric order which has ensured that Vignola's version has remained so popular since its original publication. For the 'triglyph problem' in classical architecture, see COULTON 1977, 60–4.

31 See KRAUTHEIMER 1985, 37–47.

32 For example, the details from Bernini's Palazzo Odescalchi in Piazza SS. Apostoli are all taken directly from Vignola, as is the Doric order used in the famous Piazza S. Pietro, albeit in this latter example the order itself is stretched to an Ionic proportion.

33 The Villa Giulia was built between 1551–55 for Pope Julius III by Vignola, Vasari and Bartolomeo Ammannati with some help from Michelangelo.

34 Vignola worked on the Palazzo Farnese at Caprarola between 1552–73 after the pentagonal plan had been established by Sangallo the Younger and Peruzzi in the 1520s (PORTOGHESI 1996, 89–119, Pls. 25–9, 33–4).

35 Gaetano Koch (1849–1910). I should like to acknowledge my debt of gratitude to my friend Emanuela Fabbricotti, whose great uncle, Ottaviano, was Gaetano's brother. The two shared a studio and worked together.

36 Obituary in *La Tribuna*, 15 May 1910, 6.

37 CLARIDGE 1998, Fig. 174; *Lexicon* V, Fig. 34. Masonry of the exedra terrace wall is now visible in the underpass leading to the *Repubblica* Metropolitana station. 'Palimpsest' is when the buildings of one age take on a new significance or function in another age. This phenomenon is one of the characteristics of the architecture of Rome, where many of the surviving buildings from Antiquity have been reused in subsequent rebuildings of the city: obvious examples include the Pantheon and the Borsa (Hadrianeum: COZZA 1982, Fig. 49–57). One could argue that this phenomenon is also present in the decision to retain the line of the exedra with the new curved palaces that surround the Piazza dell'Esedra.

38 Bartolomeo Ammannati 1511–1592. See FOSSI 1970; SGARBI 1991, 27.

39 See FOSSI 1970, Fig. 148.

40 MEEKS 1966, 334.

41 CLARIDGE 1998, 81–3; *Lexicon* IV, *s.v.* 'Rostra (età repubblicana)', 212–14, Fig. 96.

42 The entablature of the Temple of Castor was published by Palladio in his *Four Books of Architecture* (1570), although the temple was not actually excavated fully until the early years of the 20th century (BRIZZI 1975, 159; ROME 1977, Nos. 30–2; BECCHETTI 1993, Nos. 10–1, 14, 22; *Lexicon* I, *s.v.* 'Castor, aedes, templum', 242–45).

43 We know from PIACENTINI 1952 that Koch and his contemporaries also had copies of Letarouilly's famous three volumes in their studios. In addition, Emanuela Fabbricotti recalls that Koch had a complete set of Piranesi's prints as a working copy in the studio. Consequently we can be reasonably sure that the libraries of these architects contained a reasonably comprehensive collection of the history of Roman architecture.

44 Pio Piacentini (1846–1928): see SGARBI 1991, 200–1.

45 Pio Piacentini's design for the Bank of Italy is illustrated in PIACENTINI 1952, 45.

46 For a full discussion of Piacentini's composition, refer to MEEKS 1966, 332. Meeks correctly points out that Piacentini's triumphal arch with the trabeated side openings is in fact a reworking of a Palladian motif, although of course its roots lie, ultimately, in the triumphal arches of Antiquity.

47 LAVAGNINO 1956, I, 609.

48 Ettore Bernich (1848?–1890): see SGARBI 1991, 43–4.

49 See FEO and STUCCHI 1983.

50 CROCE 1929.

51 The cast iron galleries of the aquarium are one of the earliest examples of the use of this material in *Roma Capitale*. The cast iron was manufactured at Castell Maggiore near Bologna.

52 Apsidal porticoes such as that on the aquarium are a common feature of Antique bath complexes (CLARIDGE 1998, Figs. 96, 138, 156, 174; *Lexicon* V, Figs. 26–7, 34, 39, 42). The related nature of these two types of buildings would form a neat conceptual reason for Bernich's use of the detail in this design.

53 I am indebted to Peter Hodson for drawing this point to my attention.

54 A fragment of this particular Doric order, found adjacent to the church of S. Maria della Rotunda in Albano. In Antiquity this building had been a *nymphaeum* of Domitian's Alban Villa before being converted into a Mediaeval church (ROMA E DINTORNI 1977, 724; COARELLI 1981, 88–90; MACADAM 1998, 393). The order had been drawn by the great High Renaissance architect Pirro Ligorio in the 16th century. A Frenchman, Roland Freart de Chambray, in the mid-17th century included the 'Doric of Albano' in his influential *Parallel of Orders*, translated into English in 1664 by John Evelyn, since when it has been used all over the world but is rarely found in Rome – see FREART DE CHAMBRAY 1664, 20–1. The Church was "restored" in 1937, as a result of which all traces of the order today have vanished from Albano, although I think that I have found one surviving *spolia* fragment fixed to the wall in the cloister of SS. Quattro Coronati in Rome.

55 BRIZZI 1975, 157; ROME 1977, Nos. 32, 39; BECCHETTI 1993, Nos. 8, 21; *Lexicon* I, *s.v.* 'Basilica Iulia', 177–79.

56 See LANCIANI 1988, 99; FINE LICHT 1966, 150, Fig. 165 (cf. Fig. 270); *Lexicon* I, *s.v.* 'Basilica Neptuni', 182–83.

57 See CANINA 1852.

58 NASH 1962, Pl. 1004–5; *Lexicon* IV, *s.v.* 'Porticus Octaviae', 141–45, Figs. 53–4.

59 SERLIO 1584, Book 4, Chapter 6, Fol. 30.

60 De Angelis (1845–1906): see SGARBI 1991, 86–7.

61 MEEKS 1966, 290.

62 SERLIO 1584, Book 3, Chapter 4, Fol. 66.

63 De Angelis went to restore many historic buildings in Lazio and the Abruzzo and directed the conservation works at the Baths of Caracalla (DELAINE 1997, 43).
64 WATKIN 1986, 430.
65 VITTORIANO 1988, I, 19; BRICE 1998, 123–36, Figs. 54–5.
66 FARINI 1961. See BRIZZI 1975, 56–7; ROME 1977, Nos. 24–5, 28; BECCHETTI 1993, Nos. 16, 79–80.
67 Giusseppe Sacconi (1854–1905): see SGARBI 1991, 227–29.
68 Manfredo Manfredi (1859–1927): see SGARBI 1991, 154.
69 For a detailed account of the competitions and design of the monument to Vittorio Emanuele II, see the two-volume catalogue VITTORIANO 1988, and now also BRICE 1998. Cf. FRUTAZ 1962, Pls. 556, 563–64; MANACORDA and TAMASSIA 1985, 128–35; BECCHETTI 1993, Nos. 128–29.
70 BOETHIUS 1978, 168–74; COARELLI 1982, 137–48. The upper sanctuary at Palestrina had recently been restored by Luigi Canina.
71 I am indebted to my fellow scholars Robin Williams and Terry Kirk for first drawing my attention to this juxtaposition. Cf. FRUTAZ 1962, Pl. 550.
72 Guglielmo Calderini (1837–1916): see SGARBI 1991, 6.
73 See MEEKS 1966, 354.
74 Other constructions may be seen in a similarly anti-papal light. The heresiarchs' monument (1889), on the site of papal executions in the Piazza Campo di Fiore, has Giordano Bruno's statue facing the Vatican (BECCHETTI 1993, No. 116). The *faro* (1911) flashed the colours of the national flag at the Vatican from the top of the Gianicolo. In the southern Prati, the Piazza Cola di Rienza (named for the 14th century secular leader during the papal 'Avignon Captivity') is connected by the Via Cola to Piazza Risorgimento, the latter lying directly below the pope's Belvedere appartments.
75 In AD 608–10 the Pantheon had been the first pagan temple in Rome to be converted directly into a church (S. Maria ad Martyres) when it was gifted by the eastern Roman usurper Phocas (FINE LICHT 1966, 238–40; KRAUTHEIMER 1980, 72; *Lexicon* III, *s.v.* 'S. Maria ad Martyres', 218). More recently, it was infamously stripped of its bronzework by Pope Urban VIII and Bernini's 'ass-ear' *campaniletti* were added (FINE LICHT 1966, 241; BECCHETTI 1993, No. 43. See also KRAUTHEIMER 1985, 104–9). For the 1878 royal funeral the Pantheon façade was 'restored' in temporary materials with classicising pedimental sculpture, statuary and a new inscription overlaying the Hadrianic 'Agrippan' text: VITTORIO EMANVELE II PADRE DELLA PATRIA. Thus the non-papal origins of the building were reasserted and emphasized (ROME 1977, Nos. 112–13).
76 Luigi Vanvitelli (1700–1773): see SGARBI 1991, 257–58; BECCHETTI 1993, No. 115.
77 ACCASTO 1971; PIANTONI 1980; PETTER 1992.
78 See MORTON 1966, 231–36. For the more simple predecessor decorated with four 'Egyptian' lions see BECCHETTI 1993, No. 115.
79 Many of the buildings in the Centro Storico date from this period of Rome's history: a fact that is either ignored or, more likely, not appreciated by many who write about the city. The Neo-cinquecento buildings of the post 1870 era, by and large, blend remarkably harmoniously with their older neighbours. It is staggering that, in view of the above and the contents of this chapter, few guide books even bother to mention the period. Much of what has been written is lamentably poor, and precious little on *Roma Capitale* has been published in English (GUTTRY 1989; REED 1950; HIBBERT 1985, 274–75, 280–83; SALVADORI 1990, 126–27).
80 *Roma Fascista* is beyond the ambit of this paper, but its combination of grandiloquent planning, ruthless clearance, and fast, unpublished, large-scale archaeological excavation contrast badly even with the post-1870 boom (CEDERNA 1980; BARROERO 1983; MANACORDIA and TAMASSIA 1985; HIBBERT 1985, 289–91; KOSTOF 1973; MOATTI 1993, 130–42). There is a worry that the *Giubileo* has dictated a similar pace of archaeological work in the city's monumental centre (see BENSARD 2000).

BIBLIOGRAPHY

ACCASTO, G., FRATICELLI, V. and NICOLINI, R. 1970: *L'Architettura di Roma Capitale 1870–1970*, Roma, 1970.

BARROERO, L., CONTI, A., RACHELI, A.M. and SERIO, M. 1983: *Via dei Fori Imperiale*, Venezia, 1983.

BARTOCINI, F. 1988: *Roma nell'ottocento*, Roma, 1988.

BECCHETTI, P. 1993: *Roma nelle fotografie della Fondazione Marco Besso, 1850–1920*, Roma, 1993.

BENSARD, E. 2000: 'Les grands chantiers de Rome', *Archéologia* 368, 2000, 43–51.

BOETHIUS, A. 1978: *Etruscan and Early Roman Architecture*, Harmondsworth, 1978.

BRICE, C. 1998: *Le Vittoriano. Monumentalité publique et politique à Rome*, Bibliothèque des écoles françaises d'Athènes et de Rome 301, Roma, 1998.

BRIZZI, B. 1975: *Roma cento anni fa nelle fotografie della raccolta Parker*, Roma, 1975.

CANINA, L. 1852: *Particolare genere di Architettura Domestica decorato con ornamenti di svelte forme*, Roma, 1852.
CARACCIOLO, A. 1984: *Roma Capitale*, Roma, 1984.
CEDERNA, A. 1980: *Mussolini urbanista*, Roma, 1980.
CLARIDGE, A. 1998: *Rome. An Oxford Archaeological Guide*, Oxford, 1998.
CLARK, M. 1984: *Modern Italy 1871–1982*, London, 1984.
COARELLI, F. 1981: *Dintorni di Roma*, Guide archeologiche Laterza, Roma-Bari, 1981.
COARELLI, F. 1982: *Lazio*, Guide archeologiche Laterza, Roma-Bari, 1982.
COULTON, J.J. 1977: *Greek Architects at Work. Problems of Structure and Design*, London, 1977.
COZZA, L. 1982: *Tempio di Adriano*, Roma, 1982.
CRAWFORD, F.M. 1880: *Sant Ilario*, London, 1880.
CRAWFORD, F.M. 1885: *Saracinesca*, London, 1885.
CRAWFORD, F.M. 1892: *Don Orsino*, London, 1892.
CRIPPA, M.A. (ed.) 1988: *Camillo Boito. II Nuovo e L'Antico in Architecture*, Milano, 1988.
CROCE, B. 1929: *A History of Italy, 1871–1915*, Oxford, 1929.
CUCCIA, G. 1991: *Urbanistica Edilizia Infrastrutture di Roma Capitale 1870–1990*, Roma-Bari, 1991.
DELAINE, J. 1995: 'The supply of building materials to the city of Rome', in N. Christie (ed.), *Settlement and Economy in Italy, 1500BC–1500AD*, Oxford, 1995, 555–62.
DELAINE, J. 1997: *The Baths of Caracalla. A study in the design, construction, and economics of large-scale building projects in imperial Rome*, JRA Supplementary Series 25, Portsmouth RI, 1997.
EGBERT, D.D. 1980: *The Beaux Arts Tradition in French Architecture*, New Jersey, 1980.
EINAUDI, K.B.S. 1978: *Fotografia Archeologica, 1865–1914*, Roma, 1978.
FARINI, D. 1961: *Diario di Fine Secolo*, Roma, 1961.
FEO, V. de 1969: *Roma 1870*, Milano, 1969.
FEO, V. de and STUCCHI, S. 1983: *L'Acquario Romano*, Roma, 1983.
FINE LICHT, K. de 1966: *The Rotunda in Rome. A Study in Hadrian's Pantheon*, Jutland Archaeological Society Publications 8, Aarhus, 1966.
FOSSI, M. (ed.) 1970: *Bartolomeo Ammanati. La Citta, appunti per un trattato*, Roma, 1970.
FREART DE CHAMBRAY, R. 1664: *A Parallel of the Ancient Architecture with the Modern*, London, 1664 (reprint 1970).
FRUTAZ, A.P. 1962: *Le Piante di Roma* I–III, Roma, 1966.
GLORNEY BOLTON, J.R. 1970: *Roman Century 1870–1970*, London, 1970.
GUIDONI, E. 1984: *Roma in Cartolina*, Roma, 1984.
GUTTRY, I. de 1989: *Guida di Roma Moderna dal 1870 ad oggi*, Roma, 1989.
HIBBERT, C. 1985: *Rome. The Biography of a City*, Harmondsworth, 1985.
INSOLERA, I. 1959: 'Storia del primo piano regolatore di Roma 1870–74', *Urbanistica* 27, 1959, 74–91.
INSOLERA, I. 1959: 'I piani regolatori dal 1880 alla secondo guerra mondiale', *Urbanistica* 28, 1959, 6–32.
INSOLERA, I. 1980: *Le città nella storia d'Italia: Roma; Immagini e realità dal X al XX secolo*, Roma-Bari, 1985.
KOCH, G. 1883: *Palazzo per La Banca Nazionale da costruisi in Roma. Relazione sul secondo progetto redatto dall'architetto Gaetano Koch*, Roma, 1883.
KOSTOF, S. 1973: *The Third Rome; Traffic and Glory 1870–1950*, Berkeley, 1973.
KRAUTHEIMER, R. 1980: *Rome. Profile of a City, 312–1308*, Princeton, 1980.
KRAUTHEIMER, R. 1985: *The Rome of Alexander VII, 1655–1667*, New Jersey, 1985.
LANCIANI, R. 1988: *Notes From Rome*, London, 1988.
LAVAGNINO, E. 1956: *L'Arte Moderne dai Neoclassici ai Contemporai*, Torino, 1956.
LAVORI 1870: *Dei lavori per l'ampliamento ed abbellimento di Roma proposte dalla commissione degli Architetti ed Ingegneri,* Roma, 1870.
MACADAM, A. 1998: *Rome*, Blue Guide, London, 1998.
MACK-SMITH, D. 1989: *Italy and its Monarchy,* New Haven, 1989.
MANACORDA, D. and TAMASSIA, R. 1985: *Il piccone del regime*, Roma, 1985.
MASO, L.B. dal and VENDITTI, A. 1981: *Rome the Picturesque*, Terni, 1981.
MEEKS, C.L.V. 1966: *Italian Architecture 1750–1914*, New Haven, 1966.
MOATTI, C. 1993: *In Search of Ancient Rome*, London, 1993.
MORTON, H.V. 1966: *The Waters of Rome*, London, 1966.
NASH, E. 1962: *Pictorial Dictionary of Ancient Rome* II, London, 1962.
PALERMO, I. 1990: *Roma, Via Nazionale: una strada per la città (1859–1876)*, in *Storia della Città,* Milano, 1990.
PERODI, E. 1980: *Roma Italiana 1870–1895*, Roma, 1980.

PETTER, H, 1992: *Lutyens in Italy: The Building of The British School at Rome*, Roma, 1992.
PIACENTINI, M. 1952: *Le Vicende Edilize di Roma dal 1870 ad oggi*, Roma, 1952.
PIANO 1873: *Sul Piano Regolatore di Roma: Relazione della Commissione Esaminatrice al Consiglio Comunale*, Roma, 1873.
PIANTONI, G. 1980: *Roma 1911*, Roma, 1980.
PORTOGHESE, P. (ed.) 1996: *Caprarola*, Roma, 1996.
REED, H.H. 1950: 'Rome: the Third Sack', *The Architectural Review* 107, 1950, 91–110.
ROMA CAPITALE 1: *Roma Capitale 1870–1911, 1, I Piaceri e i Giorni: la Moda*, Venezia, 1983.
ROMA CAPITALE 2: *Roma Capitale 1870–1911, 2, Frammenti di un scalotto. Giuseppi Primoli, i suoi kakemono e altro*, Venezia, 1984.
ROMA CAPITALE 3: *Roma Capitale 1870–1911, 3, Carozzi Libri e Corredi di Scuderia del Quirinale*, Venezia, 1984.
ROMA CAPITALE 4: *Roma Capitale 1870–1911, 4, Dalla mostra al museo. Dalla Mostra del 1911 al Museo della civiltà romana*, Venezia, 1984.
ROMA CAPITALE 5: *Roma Capitale 1870–1911, 5, La Biblioteca di un collezionista*, Venezia, 1984.
ROMA CAPITALE 6: *Roma Capitale 1870–1911, 6, Crepereia Tryphaena*, Venezia, 1984.
ROMA CAPITALE 7: *Roma Capitale 1870–1911, 7, L'Archeologia tra sterro e scavo*, Venezia, 1984.
ROMA CAPITALE 8: *Roma Capitale 1870–1911, 8, La nostra arca di noe*, Venezia, 1984.
ROMA CAPITALE 9: *Roma Capitale 1870–1911, 9, Una citta di pagina in pagina*, Venezia, 1984.
ROMA CAPITALE 10: *Roma Capitale 1870–1911, 10, La cultura scientifica a Roma*, Venezia, 1984.
ROMA CAPITALE 11: *Roma Capitale 1870–1911, 11, Dagli scavi al museo*, Venezia, 1984.
ROMA CAPITALE 12: *Roma Capitale 1870–1911, 12, Architettura e Urbanistica, Uso e transformazione della citta storica,* Venezia, 1984.
ROMA CAPITALE 13: *Roma Capitale 1870–1911, 13, I Ministeri di Roma Capitale*, Venezia, 1984.
ROMA E DINTORNI 1977: *Roma e Dintorni*, Milano, 1977.
ROME 1977: *Rome in Early Photographs. The Age of Pius IX. Photographs 1847–78 from Roman and Danish Collections*, Copenhagen, 1977.
SALVADORI, R. 1990: *Architects' Guide to Rome*, London, 1990.
SANFILIPPO, M. 1992: *La costruzione di una Capitale: Roma 1870–1911*, Milano, 1992.
SERLIO, S. 1584: *The Five Books of Architecture*, London, 1982.
SGARBI, V. 1991: *Dizionario dei Monumenti Italiani e dei Loro Autori*, Milano, 1991.
THOENES, C. (ed.) 1989: *Sebastiano Serlio*, Milano, 1989.
VIGNOLA, J.B. da 1585: *I Cinque Ordini di Architettura Civile*, Roma, 1585 (reprinted 1861).
VITTORIANO 1988: *Il Vittoriano* I–II, Roma 1988.
WATKIN, D. 1986: *A History of Western Architecture*, London, 1986.

Appendix: Sources for the Study of Ancient Rome

Jon Coulston and Hazel Dodge

Sources for the study of the ancient city of Rome are varied in both medium and usefulness. Several collections have been made to aid scholars' research, of which the most exhaustive is the monumental work of Giuseppe Lugli (LUGLI 1952–62; DUDLEY 1967; COULSTON, DODGE and SMITH forthcoming). A very useful overview is provided by Amanda Claridge (CLARIDGE 1998, 31–6), particularly a list of classical literary texts which touch upon the city's history and topography. This appendix takes the opportunity to expand on a number of important source areas and to provide bibliographical introduction.

REGIONARY CATALOGUES

Two surviving 4th century catalogues, entitled the *Notitia* (*c.* AD 354) and the *Curiosum* (*c.* AD 375), comprise lists of structures and topographic features listed first by *regio* (the 14 administrative sub-divisions of the city instituted by Augustus), then by type of feature.

The latter include local officials, wards, individual houses (*domus*) and apartment blocks (*insulae*), store-buildings (*horrea*), large and small baths (*thermae* and *balneae*), fountains and reservoirs, obelisks, bridges, hills, open spaces (*campi*), fora, basilicas, aqueducts, main roads, circuses, amphitheatres, colossal statues, honorific columns, markets, theatres, gladiatorial schools, *naumachiae*, large equestrian statues, *nymphaea*, gold and ivory gods, marble arches, gates, brothels, public lavatories, military formations and camps.

The texts are concerned to enumerate throughout, but this is not done accurately with the result that end-totals do not tally with individual listings. It is clear that accuracy was not important to the compilers and that the Catalogues were not designed to be used for the purposes of urban administration. Rather, they were a celebration of the scale and richness of the city, which may be compared with other ancient laudatory works (eg Zachariah of Mitylene, *Syriac Chronicle* 10.16; LUGLI 1952–62, I, 109–12), and they were thus the precursors of medieval guide-books and *mirabilia*. Thus, these figures have to be very cautiously applied, for example when matters of public facilities, housing and population are discussed (see HERMANSEN 1978). The most accessible texts of *Notitia* and *Curiosum* are those provided by NORDH 1949. A comparable work for Constantinople is available in SEECK 1962.

COINS

The representation of buildings on commemorative coins is a valuable, albeit small scale, pictorial source. Comparison may be made with surviving structures such as the Temple of Pius and Faustina in the Forum Romanum or the Colosseum. Information may be supplied for lost buildings such as the Temples of the Deified Augustus or Trajan. Details of missing features may also be supplied, such as statues in front of temples, adorning entertainment buildings or standing in open spaces (for example, the statue on Trajan's Column or the equestrian Statue of Domitian in the Forum Romanum). Considering the small size of coin representations, their artistry and accuracy, however stylised, is often remarkable (Fig. 4.2, 9.3, 9.10, 9.12, 9.19).

For collected reproductions of coins depicting buildings see NASH 1961–62; FRUTAZ 1962, Pl. 87; HILL 1989; STEINBY 1993–99.

INSCRIPTIONS

It has been very approximately estimated that some 300,000 inscriptions survive from the Roman world as a whole, of which over 50,000 have been found in Rome (these figures are ever-increasing, see KEPPIE 1991, 9; CLARIDGE 1998, 32). Every public building erected in the city bore an inscription advertising the identity of the builder and, where appropriate, the dedication. These contributed to republican élite competition and the advertisement of family (*gens*) success in war and public office. Emperors played this game on a massive scale, sometimes in competition with their predecessors, and the senate used epigraphy to honour the *princeps*. Individuals employed epigraphy to perpetuate after death their achievements in life. Predictably, the thousands of funerary inscriptions have been employed by scholars to study demographics and social structure, but there are well-recognized pitfalls, not least of which is the bias towards the wealthy who could afford the stone and masons' services.

Inscriptions from Rome are principally catalogued in *Corpus Inscriptionum Latinarum* (*CIL*), volume 6 and supplements, and *Inscriptiones Latinae Selectae* (*ILS*). New finds are published through the annual numbers of *L'Année Épigraphique* (*AE*). Specialised collections have also been published, for example inscriptions pertaining to gladiatorial games in Rome (SABBATINI TUMOLESI 1988). In general see KEPPIE 1991.

FORMA URBIS ROMAE

The '*Forma Urbis Romae*' (*FUR*, a modern title) was originally carved on the veneer panels (north-east facing wall) of the south corner room of the Templum Pacis (*regio* IV). It was carved *in situ* on 151 veneer slabs of Proconnesian marble attached to an 18 by 13 m wall, which still stands (Fig. 1). The first fragments were found in the 16th century, some of which have been subsequently lost, but survive as drawings. More pieces have been found in later excavations up to the present. Surviving fragments (1,163 pieces) and drawings make up 20% of the map area, but only 10% can be placed in identifiable positions. A numbering system for fragments was devised by Carettoni *et al* and this has been followed by later publications (CARETTONI 1960; RODRIGUEZ-ALMEIDA 1970–71; 1975–76; 1977; 1981; 1983; STACCIOLI 1962; TORTORICI 1988). The original locations of pieces may be identified by a number of methods:

- the carved detail of recognisable building plans, eg Largo Argentina temples;
- surviving ancient street lines, eg Clivus Suburanus/Via in Selce;
- building label inscriptions, eg 'Basilica Ulpia', 'Ludus Magnus';
- positions on individual veneer panels (ie edges, peg-holes);

Fig. 1: The wall of the Templum Pacis on which the Forma Urbis *was displayed. Brick-faced concrete with peg-holes for the attachment of marble veneer panels (Photo: editors).*

- the coloured banding of the marble and pink fire markings;
- breaks and joins (ie normal 'jigsaw' methods).

The scale is approximately 1:250. A broad date of AD 205–208 is given by the presence and absence of known buildings (eg the Severan Septizodium is present; the Basilica of Maxentius is absent). A narrower date bracket is provided by an inscription on the map labelling an Aventine building with the joint names of Severus and Caracalla (Fragment No. 42b, e: SEVERI ET ANTONINI AUGG NN). This Severan plan probably replaced and revised a Flavian predecessor.

Conventions: The carved details were originally painted. All the buildings, public and domestic, were represented in ground plan. Some public buildings are perhaps rendered in more careful detail at a slightly larger scale. This may be especially true of buildings restored after the Commodan fire by the Severi (eg Templum Pacis), and of new Severan edifices (eg the Septizodium with its massive label).

Specific conventions are used for:

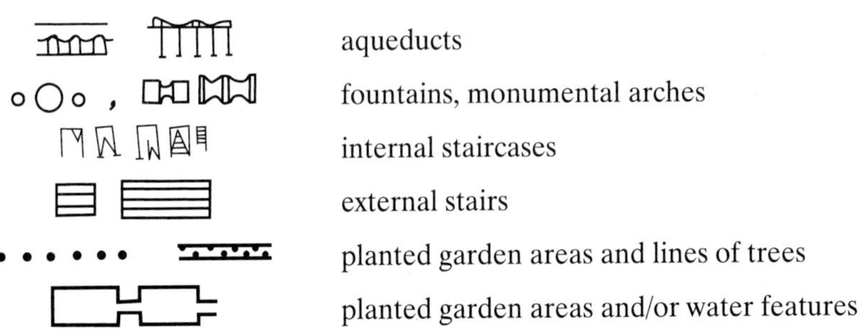

• • • • • ┐••┌ internal and external colonnades

□□□□ ⊢⊣ ⊢⊣ ⊢⊣ ⊢⊣ internal and external pier colonnades

Types of structure identified from ground plans and conventions include: temples, *quadraporticі*, *horrea*, streets, street colonnades, stepped streets, *piazze,* public fountains, atrium *domus*, residential *insulae*, *tabernae*, river frontages, *basilicae*, libraries, amphitheatres, theatres, *circenses*, baths, aqueducts, *horti*, *stagna*, *castra*. Comparisons may be made with classes of buildings listed in the Regionary Catalogues.

Identifiable individual buildings include: Amphitheatrum Flavium (*regio* III), Aqua Claudia (II), Arcus Minervae (IX), Armamentarium (III), Balneae Surae (XIII), Basilica Aemilia (VIII), Basilica Iulia (VIII), Basilica Ulpia (VIII), Castra Misenatium (III), Circus Flaminius (IX), Circus Maximus (XI), Diribitorium (IX), Forum Nervae (VIII), Forum Romanum (VIII), Horrea Galbana (XIII), Horrea Lolliana (XIII), Isola Tiberina, Largo Argentina temples (IX), Ludus Dacicus (III), Ludus Magnus (III), Porticus Aemilia (XIII), Porticus Divorum (IX), Porticus Liviae (III), Porticus Octaviae and temples (IX), Saepta Iulia (IX), Serapaeum and Iseum Campense (IX), Septizodium (X), Templum Castoris (VIII), Templum Divi Claudi (II), Templum Martis Ultoris (VIII), Templum Minervae (XIII), Templum Pacis (IV), Theatrum Balbi (IX), Theatrum Marcelli (IX), Theatrum Pompei (IX), Thermae Agrippae (IX), Thermae Traiani (III).

A recently established IT project at Stanford University has been scanning the surviving pieces for detailed recording with a view to positioning them more accurately. Further information may be obtained by searching 'Forma Urbis Romae' web-sites on the Internet.

The *Forma Urbis* has been a great boon to the topographic study of the ancient city, although with new research some pieces and buildings migrate to new reconstruction locations from time to time (eg Circus Flaminius, WARD-PERKINS 1962, Fig. 1–2). The combination of plans, standing or lost buildings, excavation plans, known road-lines and other evidence has built up palimpsest maps for the whole ancient city. The most notable and influential early attempt was that of Lanciani, and this research is forever being added to by new discoveries (see LANCIANI 1893–1901; FRUTAZ 1962, Pl. 1–11, 69, 84, 88–9, 91–9, 103–9, 118–22; SCAGNETTI and GRANDE 1979).

ANTIQUARIAN SOURCES AND PHOTOGRAPHY

The ancient buildings of Rome have always been of interest to the city's visitors, and from an early date guides and maps were produced with some form of pictorial content. Thus there is a long series of views (*vedute*) and maps (*piante*) which illustrate the changing urban topography (conveniently collected in FRUTAZ 1962). From the Renaissance period onwards artists and architects recorded individual buildings and their decorative details in a variety of media. Signal examples of these are Maarten van Heemskerck and Étienne du Pérac, working in the 1530s and 1570s respectively (FILIPPI 1990; PÉRAC 1575). Both recorded the city as it looked before major projects were inflicted during the pontificate of Sixtus V (1585–90). More floridly, Giovanni Battista Piranesi recorded buildings, views, sculpture and inscriptions in the city from his first visit until his death (1740–78). He was greatly influenced by collection together in papal ownership of the *Forma Urbis Romae* fragments in 1741 (PIRANESI 1756; FRUTAZ 1962, Pl. 69–79; WILTON-ELY 1978; FICACCI 2000).

The invention of photography enabled the recording of Rome from the late 1840s before the transformation of the city into the Italian capital (1870–71) with all the attendant replanning and destruction (See Research Bibliography, Section 2).

BIBLIOGRAPHY

CARETTONI, G. *et al.* 1960: *La Pianta marmorea di Roma: Forma Urbis Romae*, Roma, 1960.
CLARIDGE, A. 1998: *Rome: an Archaeological Guide*, Oxford, 1998.
COARELLI, F. 1992: 'Aedes Fortis Fortunae, Naumachia augusti, Castra Ravennatium. La via Campana-Portuensis e alcuni edifici adiacenti nella pianta marmorea severiana', *Ostraka* 1, 1992, 39–54.
COULSTON, J.C.N., DODGE, H. and SMITH, C.J. forthcoming: *The Ancient City of Rome: A Sourcebook*, Routledge, London.
DUDLEY, D.R. 1967: *Urbs Roma: a source book of Classical texts on the city and its monuments*, Aberdeen, 1967.
FICACCI, L. 2000: *Giovanni Battista Piranesi. The Complete Etchings*, Köln, 2000.
FILIPPI, E. 1990: *Maarten van Heemskerck. Inventio Urbis*, Milano, 1990.
FRUTAZ, A.P. (ed.) 1962: *Le Piante di Roma*, I–III, Roma, 1962.
HERMANSEN, G. 1978: 'The population of imperial Rome: the Regionaries', *Historia* 27, 1978, 129–68.
HILL, P.V. 1989: *The Monuments of Ancient Rome as Coin-Types*, London, 1989.
KEPPIE, L. 1991: *Understanding Roman Inscriptions*, London, 1991.
LANCIANI, R.A. 1893–1901: *Forma Urbis Romae*, Milano, 1893–1901; repr. 1989.
LLOYD, R.B. 1982: 'Three monumental gardens on the marble plan', *AJA* 86, 1982, 91–100.
LUGLI, G. 1952–62: *Fontes ad Topographiam veteris urbis Romae pertinentes* I–VIII, Roma, 1952–62.
NASH, E. 1961–62: *A Pictorial Dictionary of Ancient Rome*, I–II, Roma, 1961–62.
NORDH, A. 1949: *Libellus de regionibus urbis Romae*, Lund, 1949.
PÉRAC, E. du 1575: *Vestigi dell'antichità di Roma*, Roma, 1575.
PIRANESI, G.B. 1756: *Le Antichità Romane*, Roma, 1756.
RODRIGUEZ-ALMEIDA, E. 1970–71: 'Forma Urbis Marmorea: nuove integrazioni', *BullCom* 82, 1970–71, 105–35.
RODRIGUEZ-ALMEIDA, E. 1975–76: 'Aggiornamenta topografico dei colli Oppio, cispio e Viminale secondo la Forma Urbis Marmorea', *RendPontAcc* 48, 1975–76, 263–78.
RODRIGUEZ-ALMEIDA, E. 1977: 'Forma Urbis Marmorea: nuovi elementi di analisi e nuove ipotesi di lavoro', *MEFRA* 89, 1977, 219–57.
RODRIGUEZ-ALMEIDA, E. 1981: *Forma urbis marmorea: aggiornamento generale 1980*, Roma, 1981.
RODRIGUEZ-ALMEIDA, E. 1983: 'Un nuovo frammento della Forma Urbis Marmorea', in K. de Fine Licht (ed.), *Città e Architettura nella Roma Imperiale. Atti del seminario del 27 ottobre 1981*, Analecta Romana Instituti Danici Supplement 10, Odense, 1983, 87–92.
RODRIGUEZ-ALMEIDA, E. 1988: 'Un frammento di una nuova pianta marmorea di Roma', *JRA* 1, 1988, 120–31.
SABBATINI TUMOLESI, P. 1988: *Epigrafia Anfiteatrali dell'Occidente Romano* I, *Roma*, Roma, 1988.
SCAGNETTI, F. and GRANDE, G. 1979: *Roma Urbs Imperatorum Aetate*, Roma, 1979.
SEECK, O. 1962: *Notitia dignitatum: accedunt Notitia urbes Constantinopolitanae et Laterculi provinciarum*, Frankfurt am Main, 1962.
STACCIOLI, R. 1962: 'Tipi di "horrea" nella documentazione della "Forma Urbis"', in M. Renard (ed.), *Hommages à Albert Grenier*, Collection Latomus 63, Bruxelles, 1962, 1430–440.
STEINBY, E.M. (ed.) 1993–99: *Lexicon Topographicum Urbis Romae* I–V, Roma, 1993–99.
TORTORICI, E. 1988: 'Alcune osservazioni sulla tavola 8 della "Forma Urbis" del Lanciani', *Topografia romana: ricerche e discussioni*, Quaderni dell'Istituto della Università di Roma 10, Firenze, 1988, 7–15.
WARD-PERKINS, J.B. 1962: 'Recent Work in Rome', *Antiquity*, 36, 1962, 262–70.
WILTON-ELY, J. 1978: *The mind and art of Giovanni Battista Piranesi*, London, 1978.

Abbreviations

AA	Archäologischer Anzeiger
AJA	American Journal of Archaeology
AJAH	American Journal of Ancient History
AJP	American Journal of Philology
AL	Archeologia Laziale. Quaderni del Centro di studio per l'archeologia etrusco-italica
ANRW	Aufstieg und Niedergang der römischen Welt
ArchCl	Archeologia classica
BA	Bollettino di archeologia.
BAR	British Archaeological Reports
BdA	Bollettino d'Arte
BICS	Bulletin of the Institute of Classical Studies of the University of London
BullCom	Bullettino della Commissione archeologica comunale di Roma
CAH	Cambridge Ancient History
CIL	Corpus Inscriptionum Latinarum
CIMRM	Corpus Inscriptionum et Monumentorum Religionis Mithrae
CJ	Classical Journal
CP	Classical Philology
CQ	Classical Quarterly
CR	Classical Review
CRAI	Comptes rendus des séances de l'Académie des inscriptions et belles-lettres
DialArch	Dialoghi di Archeologia
IGUR	Inscriptiones Graecae Urbis Romae
ILS	Inscriptiones Latinae Selectae
JEcHist	Journal of Economic History
JRA	Journal of Roman Archaeology
JRS	Journal of Roman Studies
JSAH	Journal of the Society of Architectural Historians
Lexicon	STEINBY, E.M. (ed.) 1993–99: *Lexicon Topographicum Urbis Romae* I–V, Roma, 1993–99.
LSA	Lavori e Studi di Archeologia
MAAR	Memoirs of the American Academy in Rome
MEFRA	Mélanges d'archéologie et d'histoire de l'École française de Rome, Antiquité
MemLinc	Atti della Accademia Nazionale dei Lincei, Classe di scienze morali, storiche e filologiche. Memorie
MemPontAcc	Atti della Accademia Nazionale della Pontificia Accademia Romana di archeologia. Memorie
MonAnt	Monumenti Antichi
P&P	Past and Present
PBSR	Papers of the British School at Rome
RE	Pauly-Wissowa, *Real-encyclopädie der klassischen Alterumswissenschaft*
RendLinc	Atti dell'Accademia Nazionale dei Lincei. Rendiconti
RendPontAcc	Atti della Pontificia Accademia Romana di Archeologia. Rendiconti
RM	Mitteilungen des Deutschen Archäologischen Instituts, Römische Abteilung
TAPA	Transactions of the American Philological Association
ZPE	Zeitschrift für Papyrologie und Epigraphik

Research Bibliography for the City of Rome

It would be impossible in a volume of this size, and indeed in the lifetimes of the editors, to compile an exhaustive bibliography for the city of Rome. Everybody using this research bibliography will find 'favourite' references missing but, we hope, also hitherto unfamiliar works to pursue. Thus, what is presented here is a compilation of references which may serve as a research tool and as a window onto the city's past. Works not specific to the city of Rome have generally been omitted, but many may be found in the bibliographies in individual chapters. A starting point for any enquiry is STEINBY, E.M. (ed.) 1993–99: *Lexicon Topographicum Urbis Romae* I–V, Roma, 1993–99.

This Research Bibliography is organized both thematically and topographically in the following categories:

1. Guides
2. Antiquarian
3. General
4. History
5. Art, Architecture and construction
6. Urban Fabric & Administration
7. Religious & Social Life
   - *Religion*
   - *Life and Death*
   - *Entertainment, Leisure and the Games*
8. City Supply
   - *General*
   - *Food Supply*
   - *Water Supply*
9. Topography
   - *General Topography*
   - *Aventine*
   - *Caelian*
   - *Campus Martius (Campo Marzio)*
   - *Capitoline Hill (Campidoglio)*
   - *Esquiline Hill*
   - *Janiculum Hill (Gianicolo)*
   - *Lateran*
   - *Oppian Hill*
   - *Palatine Hill*
   - *Pincian Hill*
   - *Quirinal Hill*
   - *Tiber (Tevere)*
   - *Trastevere*
   - *Vatican*
   - *Velian Hill*
   - *Viminal Hill*
10. Individual Monuments:
    - *Baths*
    - *Commemorative Monuments*
    - *Defences*
    - *Entertainment buildings*
    - *Fora*
      - *General*
      - *Forum Romanum*
      - *Imperial Fora*
    - *Gardens*
    - *Imperial Residences*
    - *Obelisks*
    - *Temples and other religious structures*
    - *Tombs and catacombs*
11. *Roma Capitale*

1. Guides

CLARIDGE, A. 1998: *Rome: an Archaeological Guide*, Oxford, 1998.

COARELLI, F. 1972: *Guide di Monumenti* I, Roma, 1972.

COARELLI, F. 1974: *Guida archeologica di Roma*, Milano, 1974.

COARELLI, F. 1993: *Dintorni di Roma*, Guide archeologiche Laterza 7, Roma/Bari, 1993.

COARELLI, F. 1995: *Roma*, Guide archeologiche Laterza 6, Roma/Bari, 1995.

DELLI, S. 1975: *Le strade di Roma: una guida alfabetica alla storia, ai segreti, all'arte, al folklore*, Roma, 1975.

EVERYMAN GUIDE 1994: *Rome*, Everyman Guide, London, 1994.

MACADAM, A. 1998 : *Rome*, Blue Guides, London, 1998.

MCDONALD, F., RONAN, M. and STREIFFERT, A. (ed.) 1993: *Rome*, Eyewitness Travel Guides, London, 1993.

MOZZATI, L. 1995: *Roma*, Milano, 1995.

PAVIA, C. 1998: *Guida di Roma sotterranea*, Roma, 1998.

SALVADORI, R. 1990: *Architect's Guide to Rome*, London, 1990.

SCANO, G. (ed.) 1992: *Guide e descrizioni di Roma dal XVI al XX secolo nella biblioteca della Fondazione,* Roma, 1992.

STACCIOLI, R.A. 1994: *Guida di Roma Antica*, ed. 3, Milano, 1994.

STEFANO, A.M. di and SALVI, C. (ed.) 1991: *Le guide antiche di Roma nelle collezioni Communali, 1500–1850*, Roma, 1991.

2. Antiquarian

ANDREOTTI, G. ROLANDO, S. and VILLARI, L. 1990: *Roma. Un Capitale in Europa, 1870–1911*, Firenze, 1990.

ARCHEOLOGIA A ROMA 1989: *Archeologia a Roma nelle fotografie di Thomas Ashby, 1891–1930*, British School at Rome Archive 2, Napoli, 1989.

ASHBY, T. 1901: 'Recent excavations in Rome', *CR* 15, 1901, 136–42.

BARTOLI, A. 1915–22: *I monumenti antichi di Roma nei disegni degli Uffizi di Firenze* I–VI, Roma, 1915–22.

BARTOLI, A. 1911: *Cento Vedute di Roma Antica*, Firenze, 1911.

BECCHETTI, P. 1983: *La fotografia a Roma nel origini al 1915*, Roma, 1983.

BECCHETTI, P. 1993: *Roma nelle fotografie della Fondazione Marco Besso 1850–1920*, Roma, 1993.

BECCHETTI, P. and PIETRANGELI, C. (ed.) 1982: *Tevere e Agro Romano dalle fotografie di Guiseppe Primoli*, Roma, 1982.

BECCHETTI, P. and PIETRANGELI, C. 1987: *Un inglese fotografo a Roma: Robert MacPherson*, Roma, 1987.

BLASCO, L. and OSTI, S. (ed.) 1991: *Indice delle immagini fotografiche a soggetto antropologico conservate negli archivi fotografici Romani*, Roma, 1991.

BRIZZI, B. 1975: *Roma cento anni fa nelle fotografie della raccoltà Parker*, Roma, 1975.

BRIZZI, B. 1978: *Roma fine secolo nelle fotografie di Ettore Roesler Franz*, Roma, 1978.

BRIZZI, B. (ed.) 1980: *Album di Roma*, Roma, 1980.

BULL-SIMONSEN EINAUDI, K. (ed.) 1978: *Fotografia archeologica 1865–1914*, Roma, 1978.

BUONOCORE, M. 1997: *Appunti di topografia Romana nei codici Lanciani nella Biblioteca Apostolica Vaticana*, Roma, 1997.

CAMPAGNA 1986: *Thomas Ashby. Un archeologo fotografa la Campagna romana tra ' 800 e '900*, British School at Rome Archive 1, Roma, 1986.

CASAMASSIMA, E. and RUBINSTEIN, R. 1993: *Antiquarian Drawings from Dosio's Roman Workshop. Biblioteca Nazionale Centrale di Firenze, N.A.1159*, Milano, 1993.

CAVAZZI, L., MARGIOTTA, A. and TOZZI, S. (ed.) 1987: *Pittori fotografici a Roma 1845–1870. Immagini della raccoltà fotografica communale*, Roma, 1987.

CIANFARANI, V. 1976: *Immagini Romane*, Roma, 1976.

COEN, P. 1996: *Le magnificenze di Roma nelle incisioni di Giuseppe Vasi: un affascinante viaggio settecentesco dalle Mura Aureliane fino alle maestose ville patrizie, attraverso le antiche rovine, le basiliche e le più belle piazze della Città Eterna*, Roma, 1996.

COLINI, A.M. 1929: *Antiquarium. Descrizione delle collezioni dell'Antiquarium communale ampliato e riordinato*, Roma,1929.

CUBBERLEY, T. and HERRMANN, L. 1992: *Twilight of the Grand Tour. A catalogue of the drawings by James Hakewill in the British School at Rome Library*, Roma, 1992.

D'ONOFRIO, C. 1982: *Roma dal cielo. Itinerari antichi nella città moderna. Laterano-Borgo-Vaticano*, Roma, 1982.

D'ONOFRIO, C. 1988: *Visitiamo Roma mille anni fa: la città dei Mirabilia*, Roma, 1988.

D'ONOFRIO, C. 1989: *Visitiamo Roma nel quattrocento: la città degli Umanisti*, Roma, 1989.

EGGER, H. 1906: *Codex Escurialensis. Ein Skizzenbuch aus der Werkstatt Domenico Grirlanaios*, Wien, 1906.

FICACCI, L. 2000: *Giovanni Battista Piranesi. The Complete Etchings*, Köln, 2000.
FILIPPI, E. 1990: *Maarten van Heemskerck. Inventio Urbis*, Milano, 1990.
FRUTAZ, A.P. (ed.) 1962: *Le Piante di Roma*, I–III, Roma, 1962.
GAUNT, W. 1926: *Rome: Past and Present*, London, 1926.
GRELLE, A. 1987: *Vestigi delle antichità di Roma...et altri luoghi: momenti dell'elaborazione di un'imagine*, Roma, 1987.
HECK, A. van 1977: *Breviarium Urbis Romae antique*, Leiden, 1977.
IACOPI, I. 1974: *L'Antiquarium Forense*, Roma, 1974.
INSOLEVA, I. 1980: *Roma. Immagini e realtà dal X al XX secolo*, Bari, 1980.
KEAVENEY, R. 1988: *Views of Rome from the Thomas Ashby Collection in the Vatican Library*, London, 1988.
KELLER, J. and BREISCH, K.A. (ed.) 1980: *A Victorian View of Ancient Rome. The Parker Collection of Historical Photographs in the Kelsey Museum of Archaeology*, Michigan, 1980.
LANCIANI, R. 1897: *Ancient Rome in the Light of Recent Discoveries*, London, 1897.
LANCIANI, R. 1902–94: *Storia degli scavi di Roma*, I–V, Roma, 1902–94.
MANDOWSKY, E. and MITCHELL, C. (ed.) 1963: *Pirro Ligorio's Roman Antiquities. The drawings in MS XIII.B.7 in the National Library in Naples*, London, 1963.
MOATTI, C. 1993: *The Search for Ancient Rome*, London, 1993.
MUNSTERBERG, M. 1986: 'A Biographical Sketch of Robert Macpherson', *The Art Bulletin* 68, 1986, 142–153.
NEGRO, S. 1965: *Nuovo Album Romano. Fotografie di un secolo*, Vicenza, 1965.
NESSELRATH, A. 1993: *Das Fossombroner Skizzenbuch*, London, 1993.
NEUMAISTER, C. 1991: *Das Antike Rom. Ein literarische Stadtfürer*, München, 1991.
NIBBY, A. 1848–49: *Analisi storico topografico-antiquaria della carta dei dintorni di Roma* I–III, ed. 2, Roma, 1848–49.
NIBBY, A. 1839: *Delle antichità di Roma*, Roma, 1839.
NICHOLS, F.M. 1877: *The Roman Forum: a topographical study*, London, 1877.
NICHOLS, F.M. 1885: *Notizie dei Rostri del Foro Romano e dei monumenti contigui*, Roma, 1885.
OLSEN, H.P. 1985: *Roma com'era nei dipinti degli artisti danesi dell' Ottocento*, Roma, 1985.
OSBOURNE, J. 1987: *Master Gregorius. The Marvels of Rome*, Ontario, 1987.
PÉRAC, E. du 1575: *Vestigi dell'antichità di Roma*, Roma, 1575.
PIRANESI, G.B. 1756: *Le Antichità Romane*, Roma, 1756.
PORTOGHESI, P. 1981: *Roma: un'altra città. Eccezionali fotografie d'epoca rivelamo immagini segrete di luoghi, monumenti e ambienti di una vita urbana sparita*, Roma, 1981.
RIDLEY, R.T. 1992: *The Eagle and the Spade. The Archaeology of Rome during the Napoleonic Era 1809–1814*, Cambridge, 1992.
ROME 1977: *Rome in Early Photographs. The Age of Pius IX. Photographs 1847–78 from Roman and Danish Collections*, København, 1977.
ROSA, P.A. de and TRASTULLI, P.E. 1991: *Roma d'una volta*, Roma, 1991.
ROSSI, G.B. de 1857–58: *Inscriptiones christianae urbis Romae: septimo saeculo antiquiores* I–II, Roma, 1857–58.
ROSSI, G.B. de 1879: *Piante iconografiche e prospettiche di Roma anteriori al secolo XVI*, Roma, 1879.
RUSHFORTH, G. 1919: '"Magister Gregorius de Mirabilibus urbis Romae": a new description of Rome in the Twelfth Century', *JRS* 9, 1919, 14–58.
SETA, M. della and JANNATTONI, L. (ed.) 1978: *Vecchie Istantane al Portico d'Ottavia: fotografie del conte Guiseppe Primoli – Old Pictures of the Roman Ghetto*, Roma, 1978.
TELLINI SANTONI, B., MANABONI, A., CAPODIFERRO, A. and PIRANOMONTE, M. 1998: *Archeologia in Posa. Dal Colosseo a Cecilia Metella nell'antica documentazione fotografica*, Milano, 1998.
UGINET, F.-C. (ed.) 1985: *Roma Antiqua. Envois des architectes français (1788–1924). Forum, Colisee, Palatin*, Roma.
WILTON-ELY, J. 1978: *The mind and art of Giovanni Battista Piranesi*, London, 1978.

3. General

ASHBY, T. 1923: 'Rome', *Town Planning Review* 10, 1923, 43–52.
BENEVOLO, L. 1985: *Roma. Studio per la sistemazione dell'area archeologica centrale*, LSA 7, Roma 1985.
BENEVOLO, L. and SCOPPOLA, F. (ed.) 1988: *L'Area Archeologia Centrale e la Città Moderna*, LSA 10, Roma, 1988.
BUZZETTI, C., IOPPOLO, G. and PISANI SARTORIO, G. (ed.) 1998: *Appunti degli scavi di Roma* I, Roma, 1998.
CASTAGNOLI, F. 1978: *Roma Antica. Profilo urbanistico*, Roma, 1978.
COARELLI, F. 1971: *Roma: i grandi monumenti*, Verona, 1971.
CONNOLLY, P. and DODGE, H. 1998: *The Ancient City*, Oxford, 1998.

CORNELL, T.J. 1994: 'Rome: the history of an anachronism', in A. Molho, K. Raaflaub and J. Emlen (ed.), *City-states in classical antiquity and medieval Italy: Athens and Rome, Florence and Venice*, Ann Arbor, 1994, 53–70.
DUDLEY, D.R. 1967: *Urbs Roma: a source book of classical texts on the city and its monuments*, Aberdeen, 1967.
DURET, L. and NERAUDEAU, J.-P. 1983: *Urbanisme et métamorphoses de la Rome antique*, Paris, 1983.
EDWARDS, C. 1996: *Writing Rome: textual approaches to the city*, Cambridge, 1996.
FAGIOLO, M. 1991: *Roma antica*, Lecce, 1991.
FORI 1981: *Roma: continuità dell'antico. I Fori Imperiali nel progetto della città*, Roma, 1981.
FRUTAZ, A.P. (ed.)1962: *Le piante di Roma*, I–III, Roma, 1962.
GREENHALGH, M. 1989: *The Survival of Roman Antiquities in the Middle Ages*, London, 1989.
GUARDUCCI, M. 1969: *Pietro ritrovato: i martiri, la tomba, le reliquie*, Verona, 1969.
HIBBERT, C. 1985: *Rome: the biography of a city*, London, 1985.
HILL, P.V. 1989: *The Monuments of Ancient Rome as Coin Types*, London, 1989.
JORDAN, H. and HÜLSEN, C. 1878–1907: *Topographie der Stadt Rom im Althertum*, I.1–3, Berlin, 1878–1907.
KRAUTHEIMER, R. *et al.* 1937–77: *Corpus Basilicarum Christianarum Romae* I–V, Città di Vaticano, 1937–77.
KRAUTHEIMER, R. 1980: *Rome: Profile of a City, 312–1308*, Princeton, 1980.
KRAUTHEIMER, R. 1983: *Three Christian Capitals. Topography and Politics*, Berkeley, 1983.
LANCIANI, R.A. 1888: *Ancient Rome in the Light of Recent Discoveries*, London, 1888.
LANCIANI, R.A. 1896: *The Ruins and Excavations of Ancient Rome*, Boston, 1896.
LANCIANI, R.A. 1899: *The Destruction of Ancient Rome, London, 1899.*
LANCIANI, R.A. 1902–12: *Storia degli scavi di Roma* I–IV, Roma, 1902–12.
LANCIANI, R.A. 1970: *L'antica Roma*, Roma, 1970.
LANCIANI, R.A. 1971: *La distruzione di Roma antica*, Milano, 1971.
LANCIANI, R.A. 1986: *La distruzione di Roma antica*, Roma, 1986.
LANCIANI, R.A. 1988: *Notes from Rome*, edited by A.L. Cubberley, London, 1988.
LA ROME IMPÉRIALE 1997: *La Rome Impériale: démographie et logistique. Actes de la Table ronde, Rome 25 mars 1994*, Collection de l'École française de Rome 230, Roma, 1997.
LUGLI, G. 1931–40: *I monumenti antichi di Roma e suburbio* I–III, Roma, 1931–40.
LUGLI, G. 1946: *Roma antica: il centro monumentale*, Roma, 1946.
LUGLI, G. 1950: *Roma nei suoi monumenti*, Roma, 1950.
LUGLI, G. 1952–62: *Fontes ad Topographiam veteris urbis Romae pertinentes* I–VIII, Roma, 1952–62.
LUGLI, G. 1970: *Itinerario di Roma antica*, Milano, 1970.
MIDDLETON, J.H. 1892: *The Remains of Ancient Rome*, London, 1892.
MÜLLER KARPE, H. 1959: *Vom Anfang Roms*, Heidelberg, 1959.
MÜLLER KARPE, H. 1962: *Zur Stadtwerdung Roms*, Heidelberg, 1962.
NARDUCCI, P. 1889: *Sulla fognatura della città di Roma*, Roma, 1889.
NASH, E. 1961–62: *A Pictorial Dictionary of Ancient Rome*, 2 vols, Roma, 1961–62.
NORDH, A. 1949: *Libellus de regionibus urbis Romae*, Lund, 1949.
PALUZZI, C.G. 1926–28: *Bibliografia Romana – Bullettino metodico critico delle pubblicazioni Italiane e straniere riguardanti Roma* I–II, Roma, 1926–28.
PANELLA, R. 1989: *Roma Città e Foro. Questioni di progettazione del centro archeologico monumentale della capitale*, Roma, 1989.
PATTERSON, J.R. 1992: 'The City of Rome: from Republic to Empire', *JRS* 82, 1992, 186–215.
PATTERSON, H. and MILLETT, M. 1998: 'The Tiber Valley Project', *PBSR* 66, 1998, 1–20.
PICCIONI, E. (ed.) 1989: *Roma bibliografia. Trent'anni di bibliografia romana, 1959–1988*, Roma, 1989.
PLATNER, S.B. and ASHBY, T. 1929: *A Topographical Dictionary of Rome*, Oxford, 1929.
PRESSOUYRE, S. 1973: *Rome au fil du temps: atlas historique d'urbanisme et d'architecture*, Boulogne 1973.
PROGETTO 1983: *Roma Archeologia e Progetto*, Roma, 1983.
QUILICI, L. 1974: 'La campagna romana come suburbio di Roma antica', *La Parola del Passato* 29, 1974, 410–38.
REECE, R. 1982: 'A collection of coins from the centre of Rome', *PBSR* 50, 1982, 116–45.
RICHARDSON, L. 1992: *A New Topographical Dictionary of Ancient Rome*, Baltimore, 1992.
ROBERTIS, F.M. de 1935: *Lavoro e lavoratori nel mondo romano*, Bari, 1935.
ROBINSON, O.F. 1992: *Ancient Rome: City Planning and Administration*, London, 1992.
ROMA 1993: *Roma*, Guida d'Italia del Touring Club Italiano, ed. 8, Milano, 1993.
ROME EN PÉRIL 1984: *Rome en Péril*, Les Dossiers Histoire et Archéologie 82, 1984.
STAMBAUGH, J.E. 1988: *The Ancient Roman City*, Baltimore, 1988.
STEINBY, E.M. (ed.) 1993–99: *Lexicon Topographicum Urbis Romae* I–V, Roma, 1993–99.

THOMPSON, D. 1971: *The Idea of Rome from Antiquity to the Renaissance*, Albuquerque, 1971.
VENTRIGLIA, U. 1971: *La geologia della città di Roma*, Roma, 1971.
WARD-PERKINS, J.B. 1962: 'Recent Work in Rome', *Antiquity*, 36, 1962, 262–70.
WHITEHOUSE, D. 1983: 'The future of Ancient Rome', *Antiquity* 57, 1983, 38–44.
WISEMAN, T.P. 1987: *Roman Studies: Literary and Historical*, Liverpool, 1987.

4. History

ALFÖLDI, A. 1963: *Early Rome and the Latins*, Ann Arbor, 1963.
ALFÖLDI, G. 1992: *Studi sull' augustea e tiberiana di Roma*, Roma, 1992.
AMPOLO, C. 1980–82: 'Le origini di Roma e la "Cité Antique"', *MEFRA* 92, 1980, 567–76.
AMPOLO, C. 1981: 'I gruppi etnici in Roma arcaica: posizione del problema e fonti,' in *Gli Etruschi in Roma. Atti dell'Incontro di studio in onore di M. Pallotino, Roma 11–13 dicembre 1979*, Roma, 1981, 45–70.
AMPOLO, C. 1983: 'La storiografia su Roma arcaica e i documenti', in E. Gabba (ed.), *Tria Corda: Scritti in onore di Arnaldo Momigliano*, Como, 1983, 9–26.
AMPOLO, C. 1988: 'La "grande Roma dei Tarquini" revisitata', in E. Campanile (ed.), *Alle origini di Roma*, Pisa, 1988, 77–87.
ANZIDEI, A.P., BIETTI-SESTIERI, A.M., and SANTIS, A. de 1985: *Roma e il Lazio dall'età della pietra alla formazione della città*, Rome, 1985.
BENARIO, H.W. 1958: 'Rome of the Severi', *Latomus* 17, 1958, 712–22.
BIETTI SESTIERI, A.M. and SANTIS, A. de 2000: *Protostoria dei Popoli Latini. Museo Nazionale Romano, Terme di Diocleziano*, Milano, 2000.
BIRCH , D.J. 1998: *Pilgrimage to Rome in the Middle Ages*, Woodbridge, 1998.
BLOCH, R. 1960: *The Origins of Rome*, London, 1960.
BOATWRIGHT, M.T. 1987: *Hadrian and the city of Rome*, Princeton, 1987.
BRENTANO, R. 1990: *Rome Before Avignon*, London, 1990.
CANTER, H.V. 1932: 'Conflagrations in Ancient Rome', *CJ* 27, 1932, 270–88.
CARANDINI, A. and CAPPELLI, R. (ed.) 2000: *Roma, Romolo, Remo e la fondazione della città*, Milano, 2000.
CEDERNA, A. 1980: *Mussolini urbanista. Lo sventramento di Roma negli anni del consenso*, Roma, 1980.
COARELLI, F. 1987: 'La situazione edilizia di Roma sotto Severo Alessandro', in C. Pietri (ed.) 1987, *L'Urbs. Espace urbain et histoire*, Collection de l'École Française de Rome 98, Roma, 1987, 429–56.
COARELLI, F. *et al.* 1987: *Roma repubblicana dal 270 a.C. all'età augustea*, Roma, 1987.
COLONNA, G. 1974: 'Preistoria e protostoria di Roma e del Lazio', *Popoli e Civiltà dell'Italia Antica* 2, 1974, 283–346.
COLONNA, G. 1981: 'Quali Etruschi a Roma', in *Gli Etruschi in Roma: Incontro di studio in onore di M. Pallotino, Roma 11–13 dicembre 1979*, Roma, 1981, 159–72.
CORNELL, T.J. 1978: 'The Foundation of Rome in the Ancient Literary Tradition', in H. Blake, T.W.Potter and D.B. Whitehouse (ed.), *Papers in Italian Archaeology* I, BAR, Oxford, 1978, 131–39.
CORNELL, T.J. 1995: *The Beginnings of Rome: Italy and Rome from the Bronze Age to the Punic Wars (c. 1000–264 BC)*, London, 1995.
CRISTOFANI, M. (ed.) 1990: *La grande Roma dei Tarquini: Roma, Palazzo delle Esposizioni, 12 giugno–30 settembre 1990*, Catalogo della mostra, Roma, 1990.
CULHAM, P. 1989: 'Archives and alternatives in Republican Rome', *CP* 84, 1989, 100–15.
CURRAN, J. 2000: *Pagan City and Christian Capital. Rome in the 4th Century*, Oxford, 2000.
DARWALL-SMITH, M. 1996: *Emperors and Architecture: A Study of Flavian Rome*, Collection Latomus 231, Bruxelles, 1996.
DONDERO, I. and PENSABENE, P. (ed.) 1982: *Roma Repubblicana fra il 509 e il 270 a.C.*, Roma, 1982.
EDER, W. (ed.) 1990: *Staat und Staatlichkeit in der frühen römischen Republik*, Stuttgart, 1990.
FAVRO, D. 1991: '*Pater urbis*: Augustus as City Father of Rome', *JSAH* 51, 1991, 61–84.
FAVRO, D. 1996: *The Urban Image of Augustus*, Cambridge, 1996.
GORRIE, C.L. 1997: *The Building Programme of Septimius Severus in the City of Rome*, Ph.D. dissertation, University of British Columbia, 1997.
GROSS, H. 1990: *Rome in the Age of Enlightenment*, Cambridge, 1990.
GUICCIARDINI, L. 1993: *The Sack of Rome*, translated by J.H. McGregor, New York, 1993.
GJERSTAD, 1953–73: *Early Rome* I–VI. Acta Instituti Romani Regni Sueciae 17.6, Lund, 1953–73.
GRANDAZZI, A. 1991: *La fondation de Rome. Reflexion sur l'histoire*, Paris, 1991.
GRANDAZZI, A. 1993: 'La *Roma Quadrata*: Mythe ou Réalité?', *MEFRA* 105.2, 1993, 493–545.
GRANDAZZI, A. 1997: *The Foundation of Rome: Myth and History*, Cornell, 1997.

HARRIS, W.V. (ed.) 1999: *The Transformations of Urbs Roma in Late Antiquity*, JRA Supplementary Series 33, Portsmouth RI, 1999.
HÖFTER, M. *et al.* (ed.) 1988: *Kaiser Augustus und die verloren Republik: eine Ausstellung im Martin-Gropius-Bau, Berlin, 7. Juni-14, August 1988*, Ausstellung und Katalog, Mainz, 1988.
HOLLOWAY, R.R. 1994: *The Archaeology of Early Rome and Latium*, London, 1994.
HOPE, V. 2000: 'The city of Rome: capital and symbol', in J. Huskinson (ed.), *Experiencing Rome: Culture, Identity and Power in the Roman Empire*, London, 2000, 63–93.
HUBERT, E. 1990: Espace urbain et habitat à Rome du Xe siècle à la fin du XIIIe siècle, Roma, 1990.
HÜLSEN, C. 1897: 'Der Umfang der Stadt Rom zur Zeit des Plinius', *RM* 12, 1897, 148–60.
KIENAST, D. 1980: 'Zur Baupolitik Hadrians in Rom', *Chiron* 10, 1980, 391–412.
KRAUTHEIMER, R. 1980: *Rome: Profile of a City, 312–1308*, Princeton, 1980.
KRAUTHEIMER, R. 1983: *Three Christian Capitals: topography and politics*, Berkeley, 1983.
KRAUTHEIMER, R. 1985: *The Rome of Alexander VII: 1655–1667*, Princeton, 1985.
KÜNZL, E. 1988: *Der römische Triumph. Siegesfeiern im antiken Rom*, München, 1988.
LAZIO ARCAICO 1977: *Lazio arcaico e mondo greco*, La Parola del Passato 32, 1977.
LAZIO PRIMITIVO 1971: *Civiltà del Lazio primitivo, Palazzo delle Esposizioni*, Catalogo della mostra, Roma, 1971.
LLEWELYN, P. 1971: *Rome in the Dark Ages*, repr. 1993, London, 1971.
MAGDELAIN, A. 1977: 'L'inauguration de l'*urbs et imperium*', *MEFRA* 89, 1977, 11–29.
MANACORDA, D. and TAMASSIA, R. 1985: *Il piccone del Regime*, Roma, 1985.
MEDIO REPUBBLICANA 1973: *Roma Medio Repubblicana: aspetti culturali di Roma e del Lazio nei secoli IV e III a.C.*, Catalogo della mostra, Roma, 1973.
MEYER, J.C. 1983: *Pre-Republican Rome: an analysis of cultural and chronological relations*, Odense, 1983.
MILLAR, F. 1983: 'Empire to City, Augustus to Julian: obligations, excuses and status', *JRS* 73, 1983, 76–96.
MOATTI, C. 1993: *The Search for Ancient Rome*, London, 1993.
MOCCHEGIANI CARPENO, C. 1984: 'Le cloache dell'antica Roma', in *Roma Sotterranea,* Roma, 1984, 164–78.
MOMIGLIANO, A. 1963: 'An interim report on the origins of Rome', *JRS* 53, 1993, 95–121.
MORSELLI, C. 1985: 'Ricostruzione delle principali vicende urbanistiche fino allo suentramento di Via dei Fori Imperiali', in *Roma: archeologia nel centro I; l'area archeologica centrale*, Roma, 1985, 250–57.
PALMER, R.E.A. 1970: *The Archaic Community of the Romans*, Cambridge, 1970.
PATTERSON, J.R. 2000: *Political Life in the City of Rome*, London, 2000.
PARTRIDGE, L. 1996: *The Renaissance in Rome*, London, 1996.
PURCELL, N. 1996: 'Rome and its development under Augustus and his succesors', *CAH* 10, 1996, 782–811.
RICHARDSON, L.1991: 'Urban Development in Ancient Rome and the Impact of Empire', in M. Molho, K. Raaflaub and J. Emlen (ed.), *City States in Classical Antiquity and Medieval Italy*, Ann Arbor, 1991, 381–402.
ROLLINS, A. 1991: *Rome in the Fourth Century A.D.: an annotated bibliography with historical overview*, Jefferson/ London, 1991.
SCOTT-RYBERG, I. 1940: *An Archaeological Record of Rome from the 7th to the 2nd centuries BC*, London, 1940.
SMITH, C.J. 1996: *Early Rome and Latium. Economy and Society c.1000–500 BC*, Oxford, 1996.
STINGER, C.L. 1985: *The Renaissance in Rome*, Bloomington, 1985.
THORNTON, M.K. 1986: 'Julio-Claudian building programs: eat, drink and be merry', *Historia* 35,1986, 28–44.
THORNTON, M.K. and THORNTON, R.L. 1989: *Julio-Claudian Building Programs: a quantitative study in political management*, Wauconda, 1989.
TORTORICI, E. 1990: 'L'attività edilizia di Agrippa a Roma', in *Il bimillenario di Agrippa. Atti delle 17e giornate filologiche genovesi, 20 e 21 febbraio 1989*, Genova, 1990, 19–55.
VERZAR, M. 1976–77; 'L'Umbilicus urbis. Il Mundus in età tardo-repubblicana', *DialArch* 9–10, 1976–77, 378–98.
WALLACE-HADRILL, A. 1993: *Augustan Rome*, Bristol, 1993.
WESTFALL, C.W. 1974: *In This Most Perfect Paradise. Alberti, Nicholas V, and the Invention of Conscious Urban Planning in Rome, 1447–55,* University Park Pennsylvania, 1974.
WISEMAN, T.P. 1979: 'Topography and Rhetoric: the trial of Manlius', *Historia* 28, 1979, 32–50.
WISEMAN, T.P. 1991: *Flavius Josephus. Death of an Emperor*, Exeter Studies in History 30, Exeter, 1991.
WISEMAN, T.P 1995: *Remus. A Roman Myth*, Cambridge, 1995.
WISEMAN, T.P 1996: 'What do we know about early Rome?', *JRA* 9, 1996, 310–15.
ZANKER, P. 1988: *The Power of Images in the Age of Augustus*, Ann Arbor, 1988.

5. Art, Architecture and Construction

ABERSON, M. 1994: *Temples votifs et butin de guerre dans la Rome républicaine*, Roma, 1994.

ALBERTSON, F.C. 1990: 'The Basilica Aemilia Frieze: religion and politics in Late Republican Rome', *Latomus* 49, 1990, 801–15.

AMELUNG, W. 1903–8: *Die Sculpturen des Vaticanischen Museums* I–II, Berlin/New York, 1903–8.

AMPOLO, C. 1981: 'Il gruppo acroteriale di S. Omobono', *La Parola del Passato* 36, 1981, 32–35.

ANDERSON, J.C. 1997: *Roman Architecture and Society*, Baltimore, 1997.

ANDERSON, W.J., SPIERS, R.P. and ASHBY, T. (ed.) 1927: *The Architecture of Ancient Rome*, London, 1927.

ANDREAE, B. 1977: *The Art of Rome*, London, 1977.

BANDINELLI, R.B. 1969: *Roma: L'arte romana nel centro del potere*, Milano, 1969.

BANDINELLI, R.B. 1970: *Roma: La fine dell'arte antica. L'arte dell'impero romano da Settimio Severo a Teodosio I*, Milano, 1970.

BANDINELLI, R.B. 1971: *Rome. The Late Empire*, London, 1971.

BECATTI, G. 1960: *La Colonna coclide istoriata. Problemi storici, iconografici, stilistici*, Roma, 1960.

BLAKE, M.E. 1930: 'The Pavements of the Roman Buildings of the Republic and Early Empire I', *MAAR* 8, 1930, 7–160.

BLAKE, M.E. 1940: 'Mosaics of the Late Empire in Rome and Vicinity', *MAAR* 17, 1940, 81–130.

BLAKE, M.E. 1947: *Ancient Roman Construction in Italy from the Prehistoric Period to Augustus*, Washington, 1947.

BLAKE, M.E. 1959: *Roman Construction in Italy from Tiberius through the Flavians*, Washington, 1959.

BLAKE, M.E. 1973: *Roman Construction in Italy from Nerva through the Antonines*, Philadelphia, 1973.

BLANCKENHAGEN, P.H. von 1940: *Flavische Architektur und ihre Dekoration*, Berlin, 1940.

BLOCH, H. 1968: *I bolli laterizi e la storia edilizia romana: contributi all'archeologia e alla storia romana*, ed. 3, Roma, 1968.

BOËTHIUS, A. 1934: 'Remarks on the development of domestic architecture in Rome', *AJA* 38, 1934, 158–70.

BOËTHIUS, A. 1978: *Etruscan and early Roman architecture*, Harmondsworth, 1978.

BOËTHIUS, A. and WARD-PERKINS, J.B. 1970: *Etruscan and Roman Architecture*, Harmondsworth, 1970.

BONANNO, A. 1976: *Portraits and other heads on Roman historical reliefs up to the Age of Septimius Severus*, BAR, Oxford, 1976.

BORGHINI, G. (ed.) 1989: *Marmi Antichi*, Roma, 1989.

BOURNE, F.C. 1946: *The public works of the Julio-Claudians and Flavians*, Princeton, 1946.

BRILLIANT, R. 1963: *Gesture and Rank in Roman Art: the use of gesture to denote status in Roman sculpture and coinage*, New Haven, 1963.

BRILLIANT, R. 1986: *Visual Narratives: storytelling in Etruscan and Roman art*, ed. 2, London, 1986.

BRUNT, P.A. 1980: 'Free labour and public works at Rome', *JRS* 70, 1980, 81–100.

BRUUN, C. 1997: 'A City of Temples and Squares, Emperors, Horses and Houses', *JRA* 10, 1997, 394–98.

BUSAGLI, M. (ed.) 1999: *Rome. Art and Architecture*, Köln, 1999.

CARETTONI, G. 1983: 'Le anterides di Vitruvio: un esempio di applicazione pratica', in K. de Fine Licht (ed.), *Città e Architettura nella Roma Imperiale. Atti del seminario del 27 ottobre 1981*, Analecta Romana Instituti Danici Supplement 10, Odense, 1983, 15–20.

COARELLI, F. 1973: 'Frammento di affresco dall'Esquilino con scena storica', in *Roma medio-repubblicana: aspetti culturali di Roma e del Lazio nei secoli IV e III a.C*, Catalogo della mostra, Roma, 1973, 200–8.

COARELLI, F. 1977: 'Public building in Rome between the Second Punic War and Sulla', *PBSR* 45, 1977, 1–23.

COARELLI, F. 1983: 'Architettura sacra e architettura privata nella tarda Repubblica', in *Architecture et société: de l'archaisme grec à la fin de la Republique romain. Actes du colloque international, Rome 2–4 decembre 1980*, Collection de l'École Française de Rome 66, Roma, 1983, 191–217.

COARELLI, F. 1987: 'La situazione edilizia di Roma sotto Severo Alessandro', in C. Pietri (ed.) 1987, *L'Urbs. Espace urbain et histoire*, Collection de l'École Française de Rome 98, Roma, 1987, 429–56.

COARELLI, F. 1998: 'The Odyssey Frescoes of the Via Graziosa: a proposed context', *PBSR* 66, 1998, 21–37.

COARELLI, F. 1999: 'L'edilizia pubblica a Roma in età tetrarchica', in W.V. Harris (ed.), *The Transformations of* Urbs Roma *in Late Antiquity*, JRA Supplementary Series 33, Portsmouth RI, 1999, 23–34.

COATES-STEPHENS, R. 1997: 'Dark Age Architecture in Rome', *PBSR* 65, 1997, 177–232.

COZZA, G. 1928: *Ingegneria romana: maestranze romane, strutture preromane, strutture romane, le costruzioni dell'anfiteatro Flavio, del Pantheon, dell'emissario del Fucino*, Roma, 1928.

DACOS, R. 1962: 'Les stucs du Colisée. Vestiges archéologiques et dessius de la Renaissance', *Latomus* 21, 1962, 334–55.

DARWALL-SMITH, M. 1996: *Emperors and Architecture: A Study of Flavian Rome*, Collection Latomus 231, Bruxelles, 1996.

DELAINE, J. 1995: 'The Supply of Building Materials to the City of Rome', in N. Christie (ed.), *Settlement and Economy in Italy 1500 BC–AD 1500. Papers of the Fifth Conference of Italian Archaeology*, Oxford, 1995, 555–62.

DELBRÜCK, R. 1907–12: *Hellenistische Bauten in Latium*, Strasbourg, 1907–12.

DESNIER, J.-L. 1993: 'Omina et Realia: naissance de *l'urbs sacra* Sévérienne', *MEFRA* 105.2, 1993, 547–620.

DODGE, H. and WARD-PERKINS B. 1992: *Marble in Antiquity, Collected Papers and lectures of J.B. Ward-Perkins*, British School at Rome Archaeological Monograph 6, London, 1992.

DUNN, F.S. 1914–15: 'Rome, the unfinished and unkempt', *CJ* 10, 1914–15, 312–22.

ELSNER, J. 1994: 'Constructing decadence; the representation of Nero as imperial builder', in J. Elsner and J. Masters (ed.), *Reflections of Nero: culture, history, and representation*, London, 1994, 112–27.

FAVRO, D. 1994: 'The Street Triumphant: the urban impact of Roman triumphal parades', in Z. Çelik, D. Favro and R. Ingersoll (ed.), *Streets of the World: Critical Perspectives on Public Space*, Berkeley, 1994, 151–64.

FINE LICHT, K. de (ed.) 1983: *Città e Architettura nella Roma Imperiale. Atti del seminario del 27 ottobre 1981*, Analecta Romana Instituti Danici Supplement 10, Odense, 1983.

FRANK, T. 1924: *Roman Buildings of the Republic: an attempt to date them from their materials*, Roma, 1924.

FUCHS, G. 1969: *Architekturdarstellungen auf römischen Münzen der Republik und der frühen Kaiserzeit*, Berlin, 1969.

GALLOTTINI, A. 1998: *Le Sculture della Collezione Giustiniani*, I. *Documenti*, Xenia Antiqua 5, Roma, 1998.

GIGLIOLI, G.Q. (ed.) 1976: *Museo Nazionale di Villa Giulia in Roma*, Roma, 1976.

GIULIANO, A. 1979– : *Museo Nazionale Romano. Le Sculture*, Roma, 1979– .

GNOLI, R. 1988: *Marmora Romana*, ed. 2, Roma, 1988.

GORRIE, C.L. 1997: *The Building Programme of Septimius Severus in the City of Rome*, Ph.D. dissertation, University of British Columbia, 1997.

GOWERS, E. 1995: 'The anatomy of Rome from Capitol to Cloaca', *JRS* 85, 1995, 23–32.

GROS, P. 1976: 'Les premières generations d'architectes hellenistiques à Rome', *Mélanges offerts à Jacques Heurgon* I. *L'Italie préromaine et la Rome républicaine*, Roma, 1976, 387–409.

GROS, P. 1978: *Architecture et Société à Rome et en Italie centro-meridionale aux deux derniers siècle de la République*, Collection Latomus 156, Bruxelles, 1978.

GUIDOBALDI, F. and SALVATORI, A. 1988: 'The introduction of polychrome marbles in late Republican Rome: the evidence from mosaic pavements with marble insertions', in N. Herz and M. Waelkens (ed.), *Classical Marble: Geochemistry, Technology, Trade*, Dordrecht/London, 1988, 171–75.

HELBIG, W. 1899–1972: *Führer durch die öffentlichen Sammlungen klassicher Altertümer in Rom.* II, Tübingen, 1899–1972.

HELEN, T. 1975: *Organisation of Roman Brick Production*, Helsinki, 1975.

HERES, T.L. 1982: *Paries. A Proposal for a Dating System of Late-antique Masonry Structures in Rome and Ostia*, Amsterdam, 1982.

KELLUM, B.A. 1990: *The City Adorned: Programmatic Display at the Aedes Concordiae Augustae, between Republic and Empire*, Berkeley, 1990.

KÜTHMANN, H. *et al.* 1973: *Bauten Roms auf Münzen und Medaillen*, München, 1973.

LANCASTER, L.C. 1991: *The vaulting at Trajan's Markets and its place in the development of Roman concrete construction*, Unpublished M.Phil Dissertation, Oxford, 1991.

LEHMANN-HARTLEBEN, K. 1938: *'Maenianum* and *basilica', AJP* 59, 280–96.

MACDONALD, W.L. 1982: *The Architecture of the Roman Empire* I, New Haven/London, 1982.

MAISCHBERGER, M. 1997: *Marmor in Rom*, Wiesbaden, 1997.

MÂLE, E. 1960: *The Early Churches of Rome*, London 1960.

MARIA, S. de 1988: *Gli archi onorari di Roma e dell'Italia romana*, Roma, 1988.

MARK, M. and HUTCHINSON, P. 1986: 'On the structure of the Roman Pantheon', *The Art Bulletin* 68, 1986, 24–34.

MARTIN, H.G. 1987: *Römische Tempelkultbilder: eine archäologischer Untersuchung zur späten Republik*, Roma, 1987.

MARVIN, M. 1983: 'Freestanding sculptures from the Baths of Caracalla', *AJA* 87, 1983, 347–84.

MASTROCINQUE, A. 1998: 'Roma Quadrata', *MEFRA* 110.2, 1998, 681–97.

MINO, M.R. di and BERTINETTI, M. (ed.) 1990: *Archeologia a Roma: la materia e la tecnica nell'arte antica*, Catalogo della mostra: Terme di Diocleziano, Roma aprile–dicembre 1990, Roma, 1990.

MORRICONE MATINI, M.L. 1968: *Mosaici antichi in Italia: Roma, Regio X: Palatium*, Roma, 1968.

PICARD, G.C. 1962: 'Origines et sens des reliefs sacrificiels de l'Arc des Argentiers', in M. Renard (ed.), *Hommages à Albert Grenier*, Collection Latomus 63, Bruxelles, 1962, 1254–260.

PICARD, M.T. 1960: 'La Frise du Forum de Nerva à Rome et l'iconographie latine des Parques', in *Hommages à Léon Herrmann*, Collection Latomus 44, Bruxelles, 1960, 607–16.

PINOT DE VILLECHENON, M.N. 1998: *Domus Aurea. La decorazione pittorica del palazzo neroniano nell'album delle 'Terme di Tito' conservato al Louvre*, Milano, 1998.

POLLITT, J.J. 1983: *The Art of Rome, c. 753 B.C.– A.D. 337*, Cambridge, 1983.

RAKOB, F. 1983: 'Opus caementicium und die Folgen', *RM* 90, 1983, 359–72.
RICH, J.W. 1998: 'Augustus' Parthian Honours, the Temple of Mars Ultor and the Arch in the Forum Romanum', *PBSR* 66, 1998, 71–128.
RIZZO, G.E. 1936: *Roma: Monumenti della pittura antica scoperti in Italia. Sezione Terza: La pittura ellenistico-romano*, 3 vols. Roma, 1936.
ROUILLET, A: 1972: *The Egyptianizing Monuments of Imperial Rome*, Leiden, 1972.
RUGGIERO, E. de 1925: *Lo stato et le opere pubbliche in Roma antica*, Torino, 1925.
SANZI DI MINO, M.R. 1998: *La Villa Farnesina in Palazzo Massimo alle Terme*, Milano, 1998.
SCHÄFER, T. 1979: 'Zum Schlachtsarkophag Borghese', *MEFRA* 91, 355–82.
SCHNEIDER, R. 1986: *Bunte Barbaren*, Worms, 1986.
SETÄLÄ, P. 1977: *Private Domini in Roman brick stamps of the Empire: a historical and prosoprographical study of landowners in the district of Rome*, Helsinki, 1977.
SHIPLEY, F.W. 1931: 'Chronology of the building operations in Rome from the death of Julius Caesar to the death of Augustus', *MAAR* 9, 1931, 7–60.
SHIPLEY, F.W. 1933: *Agrippa's building activities in Rome*, Washington, 1933.
SKYDSGAARD, J.E. 1983: 'Public building and society', in K. de Fine Licht (ed.), *Città e Architettura nella Roma Imperiale. Atti del seminario del 27 ottobre 1981*, Analecta Romana Instituti Danici Supplement 10, Odense, 1983, 223–27.
SINN, F. 1991: *Museo Gregoriano Profano ex Lateranense, Katalog der Skulpturen*, I.1, *Die Grabdenkmäler* 1, *Reliefs Altäre Urnen*, Mainz, 1991.
SINN, F. and FREIBERGER, K.S. 1996: *Vatikanische Museen. Museo Gregoriano Profano ex Lateranense. Katalog der Skulpturen I.2, Die Grabdenkmäler 2, Die Ausstattung des Hateriergrabes*, Mainz, 1996.
STEINBY, M. 1974–75: 'La cronologia delle "figlinae" doliari urbane dalla fine dell'età repubblicana fino all'inizio del III secolo', *BullCom* 84, 1974–75, 7–132.
STEINBY, M. 1978: 'Ziegelstempel v. Rom und Umgebung', *RE* 15, 1978, 1489–531.
STEINBY, M. 1986: 'L'industria laterizia di Roma nel tardo impero', in A. Giardina (ed.), *Roma: politica economia paessaggio urbano*, Società romana e impero tardoantico II, Roma/Bari, 1986, 99–164.
STIERLIN, H. 1984: *Hadrien et l'architecture romaine*, Freiburg, 1984.
STRONG, D.E. 1953: 'Late Hadrianic Architectural Ornament in Rome', *PBSR* 21, 1953, 118–51.
STRONG, D.E. 1968: 'The Administration of Public Building in Rome during the Late Republic and Early Empire', *BICS* 15, 1968, 97–109.
STUART JONES, H. (ed.) 1912: *A Catalogue of the Ancient Sculptures preserved in the Municipal Collections of Rome. The Sculptures of the Museo Capitolino*, Oxford, 1912.
TAMM, B. 1963: *Auditorium and Palatium: a study on assembly-rooms in Roman palaces during the 1st century B.C. and the 1st century A.D.*, Lund, 1963.
TAMM. B. 1970: *Neros Gymnasium in Rom*, Stockholm, 1970.
THORNTON, M.K. 1986: 'Julio-Claudian building programs: eat, drink and be merry', *Historia* 35, 28–44.
THORNTON, M.K. and THORNTON, R.L. 1983: 'Manpower needs for the public works program of the Julio-Claudian emperors', *Journal of Economic History* 43, 1983, 373–78.
THORNTON, M.K. and THORNTON, R.L. 1989: *Julio-Claudian Building Programs: a quantitative study in political management*, Wauconda, 1989.
TORELLI, M. 1981: 'Innovazioni nelle tecniche edilizie romane tra il I sec. a.C. e il I sec. d.C.', in *Tecnologia, economia e società nel mondo romano. Atti del Convegno di Como, 27–29 settembre 1979*, Como, 1981, 139–161.
TORTORICI, E. 1990: 'L'attività edilizia di Agrippa a Roma', in *Il bimillenario di Agrippa. Atti delle 17e giornate filologiche genovesi, 20 e 21 febbraio 1989*, Genova, 1990, 19–55.
WARD-PERKINS, J.B. 1981: *Roman Imperial Architecture*, ed. 2, Harmonsdworth, 1981; repr. New Haven/ London, 1994.
WARD-PERKINS, B. 1984: *From Classical Antiquity to the Middle Ages*, Oxford, 1984.
WILPERT, G. 1917: *Die römischen Mosaiken und Malereien der kirchlichen Bauten vom IV bis XIII. Jahrhundert* I–IV, Freiburg, 1917.
ZANKER, P. 1988: *The Power of Images in the Age of Augustus*, Ann Arbor, 1988.
ZEVI, F. 1993: 'Transformazioni monumentali a Roma in età tardo-repubblicana', in *La ciutat en el món romà. Actes XIV Congres Internacional d'Arqueologia Classica*, Tarragona, 1993, 395–98.

6. Urban Fabric & Administration

ABSIL, M. 1997: *Les préfets du prétoire d'Auguste à Commode, 2 avant Jésus-Christ – 192 après Jésus-Christ*, Paris, 1997.

ALFÖLDI, A. 1974: 'Les *Praefecti Urbi* de César', *Mélanges d'histoire ancienne offerts à W. Seston*, Paris, 1974, 1–14.
BAILLIE REYNOLDS, P.K. 1923: 'Troops quartered in the Castra Peregrinorum', *JRS* 13, 1923, 168–89.
BAILLIE REYNOLDS, P.K. and ASHBY, T. 1923: 'The Castra Peregrinorum', *JRS* 13, 1923, 152–67.
BAILLIE REYNOLDS, P.K. 1926: *The Vigiles of Imperial Rome*, Oxford, 1926.
BELLEN, H. 1981: *Die Liebwache der römischen Kaiser des julisch-claudischen Hauses*, Wiesbaden, 1981.
BOATWRIGHT, M.T. 1984–85: 'Tacitus on Claudius and the *pomerium*'', *CJ* 80, 1984–85, 36–44.
BOATWRIGHT, M.T. 1986: 'The pomerial extension of Augustus', *Historia 35, 1986, 13–27.*
BRANCHER, M. 1909: *La jiridiction civile du praefectus urbi*, Paris, 1909.
BROUGHTON, T.R.S. 1951–68: *The Magistrates of the Roman Republic* I–III, New York, 1951–68.
CAGNAT, R. 1919: 'Urbanae Cohortes', in C. Daremburg and E. Saglio (ed.), *Dictionnaire des Antiquités Grecques et Romaines* V, Paris, 1919, 602–04.
CAGNAT, R. 1919: 'Vigiles', in C. Daremburg and E. Saglio (ed.) *Dictionnaire des Antiquités Grecques et Romaines* V, Paris, 1919, 867–89.
CECILIA, L. 1986: 'Castra Praetoria', *BullCom* 91, 1986, 366–68.
CHASTAGNOL, A. 1966: *Le senat romain sous le regne d'Odoacre. Recherches sur l'Épigrahie du Colisée au Ve Siècle*, Bonn, 1966.
DURRY, M. 1938: *Les cohortes prétoriennes*, Paris, 1938.
DURRY, M. 1954: *'Praetoriae cohortes'*, *RE* XXII.2, 1954, 1607–34.
ECHOLS, E.J. 1958: 'The Roman City police: origin and development', *CJ* 53, 1958, 377–85.
ERTMAN, P.C. 1980: *Curatores viarum: a study of the superintendents of highways in ancient Rome*, Ann Arbor, 1980.
FRANK, T. 1930: 'Roman census statistics from 508 to 225 BC', *AJP* 51, 1930, 313–24.
FREDERIKSEN, M.W. 1965: 'The Republican municipal laws: errors and drafts', *JRS* 55, 1965, 183–98.
FREIS, H. 1965: *'Urbanae cohortes'*, *RE* 10, 1965, 1125–140.
FREIS, H. 1967: *Die cohortes urbanae*, Köln, 1967.
GERKAN, A. von 1949: 'Grenzen und Grössen der 14 Regionem Roms', *Bonner Jahrbücher 149, 1949, 5–65.*
GRAFFUNDER, P. 1914: *'Regiones*', *RE* 1A.1, 1914, 480–86
GROS, P. and TORELLI, M. 1988: *Storia dell'urbanistica: Il mondo Romano*, Roma/Bari, 1988.
GROSSO, F. 1966: 'Equites singulares Augusti', *Latomus* 25, 1966, 900–9.
GUILHEMBET, J.-P. 1996: 'La densité des *domus* et des *insulae* dans les XIV régions de Rome selon les Régionnaires: représentations cartographique', *MEFRA* 108.1, 1996, 7–26.
HOWE, L.L. 1942: *The Praetorian Prefect from Commodus to Diocletian*, Chicago, 1942.
JONES, A.H.M. 1972: *The Criminal Courts of the Roman Republic and Principate*, Oxford, 1972.
KENNEDY, D.L. 1978: 'Some observations on the Praetorian Guard', *Ancient Society* 9, 1978, 275–301.
KEPPIE, L. 1996: 'The Praetorian Guard before Sejanus', *Athenaeum* 84, 1996, 101–24.
KNAPP, C. 1925: 'The care of city streets in ancient Rome', *Classical World* 19, 1925, 82, 98, 114, 159.
LABROUSSE, M. 1937: 'Le *Pomerium* de la Rome impériale', *MEFRA* 54, 1937, 165–99.
LE GALL, J. 1939: 'Notes sur les prisons de Rome á l'époque républicaine', *MEFRA* 56, 1939, 60–80.
LIEB, H. 1986: 'Die constitutiones für die stadtrömischen Truppen', in W. Eck and H. Wolff (ed.), *Heer und Integrationspolitik. Die römischen Militärdiplome als historische Quelle*, Köln, 1986, 322–46.
LIÉNARD, E. 1939: 'Les dégâts matériels causés par l'incendie de 64', *Latomus* 3, 1939, 52–57.
LIOU-GILLE, B. 1993: 'Le Pomerium', *Museum Helveticum* 50, 1993, 94–106.
MURATORI, S. 1963: *Operante Storia Urbana di Roma*, Roma, 1963.
NASH, E. 1976: 'Secretarium Senatus', in L. Bonfante and H. von Heintze (ed.), *Essays in Archaeology and the Humanities: in memoriam O.J. Brendel*, Mainz, 1976, 191–204.
NIPPEL, W. 1984: 'Policing Rome', *JRS* 74, 1984, 20–29.
NIPPEL, W. 1995: *Public Order in Ancient Rome*, Cambridge, 1995.
OLIVER, J.H. 1932: 'The Augustan *pomerium', MAAR* 10, 1932, 145–82.
PAILLER, J.-M. 1985: 'Rome au cinq régions?', *MEFRA* 97, 1985, 785–97.
PALMER, R.E.A. 1974–75: 'The *excusiato magisteri* and the administration of Rome under Commodus', *Athenaeum* 52, 1974, 268–88; 53, 1975, 57–87.
PASSERINI, A. 1969: *Le coorti pretorie*, ed. 2, Roma, 1969.
RAINBIRD, J.S. 1976: *The Vigiles of Rome*, Unpublished Dissertation, Durham, 1976.
RAINBIRD, J.S. 1986: 'The Fire Stations of Imperial Rome', *PBSR* 54, 1986, 147–69.
RANKOV, B. 1994: *The Praetorian Guard*, London, 1994.
ROBERTIS, F.M. de 1935: 'La *cura regionum urbis* nel periodo imperiale', *Athenaeum* 13, 1935, 171–86.
ROBERTIS, F.M. de 1936: *L'espropriazione per pubblica utilità*, Bari, 1936.

ROBERTIS, F.M. de 1937: *La repressione penale nella circoscrizione dell'urbe*, Bari, 1937.
ROBERTIS, F.M. de 1938: *Diritto associativo romano*, Bari, 1938.
ROBINSON, O.F. 1968: 'Private Prisons', *Revue Internationale des Droits de l'Antiquité* 15, 1968, 389–98.
ROBINSON, O.F. 1977: 'Fire prevention at Rome', *Revue Internationale des Droits de l'Antiquité* 24, 1977, 377–88.
ROBINSON, O.F. 1992: *Ancient Rome: City Planning and Administration*, London, 1992.
RUGGIERO, F. de 1925: *Lo stato e le opere pubbliche in Roma antica*, Roma, 1925.
SABLAYROLLES, R. 1996: *Libertinus Miles. Les cohortes de vigiles*, Collection de l'École Française de Rome 224, Roma, 1996.
SACHERS, E. 1954: *'Praefectus Urbi'*, *RE* 22.2, 1954, 2513–532.
SCHILLER, A.A. 1949: 'The jurists and the Prefects of Rome', *Revue Internationale des Droits de l'Antiquité* 31, 1949, 319–59.
SINNIGEN, W.G. 1959: 'The *vicarius urbis Romae* and the Urban Prefecture', *Historia* 8, 1959, 97–112.
SPEIDEL, M. 1965: *Die equites singulares Augusti*, Bonn, 1965.
SPEIDEL, M.P. 1988: 'Les prétoriens de Maxence. Les cohortes palatines romaines', *MEFRA* 100, 1988, 183–86.
SPEIDEL, M. 1994: *Riding for Caesar: the Roman Emperors' horse guards*, London, 1994.
STRONG, D.E. 1968: 'The administration of public building in Rome during the Late Republic and Early Empire', *BICS* 15, 97–109.
TALBERT, R.J.A. 1984: *The Senate of Imperial Rome*, Princeton, 1984.
TURPIN, W. 1991: 'Imperial subscriptions and the administration of justice', *JRS* 81, 1991, 101–18.
VIGANÒ, R. 1969: 'Sull' *edictum de fluminibus retandis*', *Labeo* 15, 1969, 168–77.
VIGANÒ, R. 1972: 'Appunti sulla *cua riparum et alvei Tiberis*: gestione diretta o indiretta', *Studi in onore di G. Scherillo* 2, Milan, 1972, 803–8.
VIGNEAUX, P.E. 1896: *Essai sur l'histoire de la préfectura urbis à Rome*, Paris, 1896.
VITUCCI, G. 1956: *Ricerche sulla praefectura urbi in età imperiale*, Roma, 1956.
WATSON, A. 1992: *The State, Law and Religion in Pagan Rome*, Athens, 1992.
YAVETZ, Z. 1969: *Plebs and Princeps*, Oxford, 1969.

7. Religious & Social Life

Religion

AMPOLO, C. 1981: 'La città arcaica e le sue feste: due ricerche sul Septimontium e sull'Equus October', *AL* 4, 1981, 233–40.
BEARD, M. 1980: 'The sexual status of the Vestal Virgins', *JRS* 70, 1980, 12–27.
BEARD, M. 1994: 'The Roman and the foreign: the cult of the "Great Mother" in imperial Rome', in N. Thomas and C. Humphrey (ed.), *Shamanism, History and the State*, Ann Arbor, 1994, 164–90.
BEARD, M., NORTH, J. and PRICE, S. (ed.) 1998: *Religions of Rome: a sourcebook* I–II, Cambridge, 1998.
BEAUJEU, J. 1960: *L'incendie de Rome en 64 et les chrétiens*, Collection Latomus 49, Bruxelles, 1960.
BELLELLI, G.M. 1997: 'Les sanctuaires de Iuppiter Dolichenus à Rome', in G.M. Bellelli and U. Bianchi. (ed.), *Orientalia Sacra Urbis Romae: Dolichena et Heliopolitana. Recueil d'études archéologiques et historico-religieuses sur les cultes cosmopolites d'origine commagénienne et syrienne*, Roma, 1997, 305–28.
BELLELLI, G.M. and BIANCHI, U. (ed.), *Orientalia Sacra Urbis Romae: Dolichena et Heliopolitana. Recueil d'études archéologiques et historico-religieuses sur les cultes cosmopolites d'origine commagénienne et syrienne*, Roma, 1997.
BROISE, H. and SCHIED, J. 1993: 'Étude d'un cas: Le *lucus Deae Diaea* á Rome,' in O. le Cazanove and J. Scheid (ed.), *Les Bois Sacrés*, Napoli, 1993, 145–57.
CARETTONI, G. 1978–80: 'La Domus virginium vestalium e la domus pubblicana del periodo repubblicano', *RendPontAcc* 51–2, 1978–80, 325–55.
CASTAGNOLI, F. 1946: 'Atrium Libertatis', *RendLinc* 8.1, 1946, 276–91.
COLINI, A.M. 1935: 'La scoperta del santuario di Giove Dolicheno', *BullCom* 63, 1935, 145–59.
DUBOURDIEU, A. 1989: *Les origines et la developement du culte des Penates à Rome*, Roma, 1989.
DUMÉZIL, G. 1970: *Archaic Roman Religion: with an appendix on the religion of the Etruscans* I–II, Chicago/London, 1970.
FRASCHETTI, A. 1981: 'L'atrium Minervae in epoca tardoantica', *Opuscula Instituti Romani Finlandiae* 1, 1981, 25–40.
GASPARRI, C. 1979: *Aedes Concordiae Augustae*, Roma, 1979.
GOODNIK WESTENHOLZ, J. 1995: *The Jewish Presence in Ancient Rome*, Jerusalem, 1995.
GUARDUCCI, M. 1971: 'Enea e Vesta', *RM* 78, 1971, 73–118.
KÜNZL, E. 1988: *Der römische Triumph. Siegesfeiern im antiken Rom*, München, 1988.

LAURENCE, R. 1993: 'Emperors, Nature and the City: Rome's ritual landscape', *Accordia Research Papers* 4, 1993, 79–87.
LAURENCE, R. and SMITH, C. 1995–96: 'Ritual, time and power in ancient Rome', *Accordia Research Papers* 6, 1995–96, 133–51.
LEMBKE, K. 1994: *Das Iseum Campense in Rom. Studie über den Isiskult unter Domitian*, Heidelberg, 1994.
MÂLE, E. 1960: *The Early Churches of Rome*, London 1960.
MANCINELLI, F. 1981: *Catacombs and basilicas. The Early Christians in Rome,* Firenze, 1981.
MORGAN, M.G. 1973: 'Villa Pubblica and Magna Mater', *Klio* 54, 1973, 215–45.
NORTH, J. 1986: 'Religion and politics from Republic to Principate', *JRS* 86, 1986, 251–58.
OGILVIE, R.M. 1986: *The Romans and their Gods*, London, 1986.
PAVIA, C. 1986: *Roma Mitraica*, Udine, 1986.
QUINTO, R. and MANZANO, P. di 1984: 'Area di S. Balbina', *BullCom* 89, 1984, 68–81.
ROMANELLI, P. 1964: '*Magna Mater* e *Attis* sul Palatino', in M. Renard and R. Schilling (ed.), *Hommages à Jean Bayet*, Collection Latomus 70, Bruxelles, 1964, 619–26.
ROUILLET, A: 1972: *The Egyptianizing Monuments of Imperial Rome*, Leiden, 1972.
RUTGERS, L.V. 1995: *The Jews in Late Ancient Rome*, Leiden, 1995.
SCULLARD, H. 1981: *Festivals and Ceremonies of the Roman Republic*, London, 1981.
TORELLI, M. 1987: 'Culto imperiale e spazi urbani in età flavia. Dai rilievi Hartwig all'arco di Tito', in C. Pietri (ed.), *L'Urbs: Espace urbain et histoire*, Collection de l'École Française de Rome 98, Roma, 1987, 563–82.
VERMASEREN, M.J. and ESSEN, C. C. van 1965: *The Excavations in the Mithraeum of the Church of Santa Prisca in Rome*, Leiden, 1965.
VERSNEL, H.S. 1970: *Triumphus. An Inquiry into the Origin, Development and Meaning of the Roman Triumph*, Leiden, 1970.
VIVER QUOTIDIANA 1989: *Il Viver Quotidiano in Roma arcaica: materiali dagli scavi del tempio arcaico nell'area sacra di S. Omobono*, Roma, 1989.
VOS, M. de 1994: 'Aegyptiaca Romana', *La Parola del Passato* 49, 1994, 130–59.
WISSOWA, G. 1912: *Religion und Kultus der Römer* I–II, München, 1912.

Life and Death

ALBENTIIS, E. de 1990: *La Casa dei Romani*, Milano, 1990.
AMULREE, L. 1973: 'Hygienic conditions in ancient Rome', *Medical History* 17, 1973, 244–55.
ANDRÉ, J. 1980: 'La notion de *Pestilentia* à Rome', *Latomus* 39, 1980, 3–16.
ANDRÉ, J. 1987: *Etre médecin à Rome*, Paris, 1987.
ARCE, X. 1988: *Funus Imperatorium: los funerales de los imperadores romanos,* Madrid, 1988.
BARTOLONI, G. 1987: 'Esibizione di richezza a Roma nel VI e V secolo: Doni votivi e corredi funerari', *Scienze dell'antichità: storia archeologia antropologia* 1, 1987, 143–59.
BEAUJEU, J. 1960: 'L'incendie de Rome en 64 et les chrétiens', *Latomus* 19, 1960, 65–80.
BERCHEM, D. van 1939: *Les distributions de blé et de l'argent à la plèbe romaine sous l'empire*, Geneva, 1939.
BOËTHIUS, A. 1956: 'L'insula romano secondo Léon Homo', *L'Erma*, 1956, 1–12.
BOLLMANN, B. 1997: 'La distribuzione delle *scholae* delle corporazioni a Roma', in C. Virlouvet (ed.), *La Rome impériale: démographie et logistique*, Collection de l'École Française de Rome 230, Roma, 1997, 209–25.
BOOTH, A.D. 1979: 'The schooling of slaves in first century Rome', *TAPA* 109, 1979, 11–19.
BONNER, S.F. 1977: *Education in Ancient Rome*, Berkeley, 1977.
BOYD, C.E. 1916: *Public Libraries and Literary Culture in Ancient Rome*, Chicago, 1916.
BRADSHAW, H.C. 1923: 'A note on housing conditions in ancient Rome', *Town Planning Review* 10, 1923, 53–55.
BURN, A.R. 1953: '*Hic breve vivitur*: a study of the expectation of life in the Roman empire', *P&P* 4, 1953, 2–31.
CALZA, G. 1914: 'La preminenza dell' "insula" nella edilizia romana', *MonAnt* 23, 1914, 541–608.
CALZA, G. and LUGLI, G. 1941: 'La popolazione di Roma antica', *BullCom* 69, 1941, 142–65.
CARANDINI, A., RICCI, G., D'ALESSIO, M.T., DE DAVIDE, C. and TERRENATO, N. 1997: 'La villa dell'auditorium dell'età arcaica all'età imperiale', *RM* 104, 1997, 117–48.
CARDINI, M. 1909: *L'igiene pubblica di Roma antica*, Prato, 1909.
CARCOPINO, J. 1956: *Daily Life in Ancient Rome*, repr. 1964, London, 1956.
COATES-STEPHENS, R. 1996: 'Housing in early Medieval Rome', *PBSR* 64, 1996, 239–59.
CORBETT, P.E. 1930: *The Roman Law of Marriage*, Oxford, 1930.
D'ARMS, J.H. 1981: *Commerce and Social Standing in Ancient Rome*, Cambridge Mass., 1981.
DRUMMOND, A. 1989: 'Rome in the fifth century: I: The social and economic framework', in *CAH*^{2} 7.2, 1989, 113–71.

ECK, W. 1997: '*Cum dignitate otium*. Senatorial *domus* in Imperial Rome', *Scripta Classica Israelica* 16, 1997, 162–90.

EDWARDS, C. 1993: *The Politics of Immorality in Ancient Rome*, Cambridge, 1993.

EVANS, J.K. 1991: *War, Women and Children in Ancient Rome*, London, 1991.

FLAMBARD, J.-M. 1980: 'Clodius, les collèges, la plèbe et les esclaves', *MEFRA* 89, 1980, 115–56.

FOWLER, W.W. 1908: *Social Life at Rome in the Age of Cicero*, London, 1908.

FRIER, B. 1977: 'The rental market in early imperial Rome', *JRS* 67, 1977, 27–37.

FRIER, B. 1980: *Landlords and Tenants in Imperial Rome*, Princeton, 1980.

FRIER, B. 1982: 'Roman life expectancy: Ulpian's evidence', *Harvard Studies in Classical Philology* 86, 1982, 213–51.

GARNSEY, P.D.A. 1976: 'Urban property investment', in M.I. Finley (ed.), *Studies in Roman Property*, Cambridge, 1976, 123–36.

GIARDINA, A. (ed.) 1986: *Roma: politica economia paesaggio urbano*, Società romana e impero tardoantico II, Roma/Bari, 1986.

GIARDINA, A. and SCHIAVONE, A. (ed.) 1981: *Società Romana e produzione schiavistica* I–III, Roma/Bari, 1981.

GILLIAM, J.F. 1961: 'The plague under Marcus Aurelius', *AJP* 82, 1961, 225–51.

GIOVANNI, A. 1985: 'Le sel et la fortune de Rome', *Athenaeum* 63, 1985, 373–86.

GUIDOBALDI, F. 1986: 'L'edilizia abitativa unifamiliare nella Roma tardoantica', in A. Giardina (ed.), *Roma: politica economia paessaggio urbano*, Società romana e impero tardoantico II, Roma/Bari, 1986, 165–238.

HERMANSEN, G. 1970: 'The *medianum* and the Roman apartment', *Phoenix* 24, 1970, 342–47.

HERMANSEN, G. 1978: 'The population of imperial Rome: the Regionaries', *Historia* 27, 1978, 129–68.

HOPKINS, K. 1965: 'The age of Roman girls at marriage', *Population Studies* 18, 1965, 309–27.

HOSTETTER, E., HOWE, T.N., BRANDT, J.R., ST. CLAIRE, A., PEÑA, J.T., PARCA, M., GLEASON, K. and MILLER, N.F. 1994: 'A Late-Roman Domus with apsidal hall on the NE slope of the Palatine: 1989–1991 seasons', in L. La Follette *et al.*, *Rome Papers*, JRA Supplementary Series 11, Ann Arbor, 1994, 131–82.

HÜLSEN, C. 1897: 'The burning of Rome under Nero', *AJA* 13, 1909, 45–48.

IACOPI, I. 1985: 'Esempi di stratificazione pittorica dalla domus sotto le terme', in *Roma: archeologia nel centro II; La 'Città Murata'*, Roma, 1985, 605–22.

LENDON, J.E. 1997: 'Social control at Rome', *CJ* 93, 1997, 83–92.

LINTOTT, A.W. 1968: *Violence in Republican Rome*, Oxford, 1968.

LITTMAN, R.J. and LITTMAN, M.L. 1973: 'Galen and the Antonine Plague', *AJP* 94, 243–55.

LO CASCIO, E. 1997: 'Le procedure di *recensus* dalla tarda repubblica al tardoantico e il calcolo della populazione di Roma', in *La Rome impériale. Démographie et logistique. Actes de la table ronde (Rome, 25 mars 1994)*, Roma, 1997, 3–76.

LUGLI, G. 1947: 'La "vecchia città" incendiata da Nerone', *Capitolium* 22, 1947, 41–50.

MACMULLEN, R. 1970: 'Market days in the Roman Empire', *Phoenix* 24, 1970, 333–41.

MARQUARDT, J. 1886: *Das Privatleben der Römer*, ed. 2, Leipzig, 1886.

NEEDLEMAN, L. and NEEDLEMAN D. 1985: 'Lead poisoning and the decline of the Roman aristocracy', *Echos du Monde Classique* 29, 1985, 63–94.

NEWBOLD, R.F. 1974: 'Some Social and Economic Consequences of the A.D. 64 Fire at Rome', *Latomus* 33, 1974, 858–69.

NICOLET, C. 1980: *The World of the Citizen in Republican Rome*, London, 1980.

NOY, D. 2000: *Foreigners at Rome. Citizens and Strangers*, London, 2000.

NRIAGU, N.J. 1983: *Lead and Lead-Poisoning in Antiquity*, New York, 1983.

OATES, W.J. 1934: 'The Population of Rome', *CP* 29, 1934, 101–16.

OOTEGHEM, J. van 1960: 'Les Incendies à Rome', *Les Études Classiques* 28, 1960, 305–12.

PACKER, J.E. 1967: 'Housing and Population in imperial Ostia and Rome', *JRS* 57, 1967, 80–95.

PACKER, J. 1968–69: 'La casa di Via Giulio Romano', *BullCom* 81, 1968–69, 127–48.

PANCIERA, S. 1993: 'Soldati e civili a Roma nei primi tre secoli dell'impero', in W. Eck (ed.), *Prosopographie und Sozialgeschichte*, Köln, 1993, 261–76.

PAOLI, U.E. 1963: *Rome: its People, Life and Customs*, New York, 1963.

PENSO, G. 1984: *La médecine romaine*, Paris, 1984.

PURCELL, N. 1994: 'The city of Rome and the *plebs urbana* in the late Republic', *CAH*[2] 9, 1994, 644–88.

PURCELL, N. 1999: 'The populace of Rome in Late Antiquity: problems of classification and historical description', in W.V. Harris (ed.), *The Transformations of* Urbs Roma *in Late Antiquity*, JRA Supplementary Series 33, 1999, 135–62.

RAAFLAUB, K.A. (ed.) 1986: *Social Struggles in Archaic Rome: New Perspectives on the Struggle of the Orders*, California, 1986.
RAMAGE, E. 1983: 'Urban problems in Ancient Rome', in M. Marchese (ed.), *Aspects of Graeco-Roman Urbanism: Essays on the Classical City*, BAR, Oxford, 1983, 61–92.
ROBINSON, O.F. 1975: 'The Roman law on burials and burial grounds', *The Irish Jurist* 10, 1975, 175–86.
RODGER, A. 1972: *Owners and Neighbours in Roman Law*, Oxford, 1972.
SALLER, R.P. 1994: *Patriarchy, Property and Death in the Roman Family*, Cambridge, 1994.
SCARBOROUGH, J. 1969: *Roman Medicine*, London, 1969.
SCOBIE, A. 1986: 'Slums, sanitation and mortality in the Roman world', *Klio* 68, 1986, 399–433.
SHAW, B.D. 1996: 'Seasons of death: Aspects of mortality in Imperial Rome', *JRS* 86, 1996, 100–138.
TOYNBEE, J.M.C. 1971: *Death and Burial in the Roman World*, London, 1971.
TREGGIARI, S.M. 1973: 'Domestic staff at Rome in the Julio-Claudian period, 27 B.C. to A.D. 68', *Histoire Sociale/Social History* 6, 1973, 241–55.
TREGGIARI, S.M. 1980: 'Urban Labour in Rome: Mercennarii and Tabernarii', in P. Garnsey (ed.), *Non-Slave Labour in the Greco-Roman World*, Cambridge, 1980, 48–64.
VIRLOUVET, C. 1985: *Famines et émeutes à Rome des origines de la République à la mort de Néron*, Roma, 1985.
WATSON, A. 1970: 'Drunkenness in Roman Law', in W.G. Becker and L.S. von Carolsfield (ed.), *Sein und Werden im Recht: Festgabe für U. von Lübtow*, Berlin, 1970, 381–87.
WERNER, P. 1906: *De incendiis urbis Romae*, Leipzig, 1906.
YAVETZ, Z. 1958: 'The Living Conditions of the Urban Plebs in Ancient Rome', *Latomus* 17, 1958, 500–17.

Entertainment, Leisure and the Games

AUGUET, R. 1972: *Cruelty and Civilization: the Roman games*, London, 1972.
BEACHAM, R.C. 1999: *Spectacle Entertainments of Early Imperial Rome*, Yale, 1999.
BERNSTEIN, F. 1998: *Ludi publici. Untersuchungen zur Entstehung und Entwicklung der öffentlichen Spiele im republikanischen Rom*, Stuttgart, 1998.
BALSDON, J.P.V.D. 1969: *Life and Leisure in Ancient Rome*, London, 1969.
COLEMAN, K.M. 1990: 'Fatal charades: Roman executions staged as mythological enactments', *JRS* 80, 1990, 44–73.
COLEMAN, K.M. 1993: 'Launching into history: aquatic displays in the early Empire', *JRS* 83, 1993, 48–74.
COULSTON, J.C.N. forthcoming: 'Gladiators and soldiers: personnel and equipment in *ludus* and *castra*', *Journal of Roman Military Equipment Studies* 9, forthcoming.
CROWTHER, N.B. 1983: 'Greek Games in Republican Rome', *Antiquité Classique* 52, 1983, 268–73.
DODGE, H. 1999: 'Amusing the Masses: Buildings for Entertainment and Leisure in the Roman World', in D.S. Potter and D.J. Mattingly (ed.), *Life, Death and Entertainment in the Roman Empire*, Ann Arbor, 1999, 205–55.
EDMONDSON, J.C. 1996: 'Dynamic Arenas: Gladiatorial presentations in the City of Rome and the Construction of Roman Society in the early Empire', in W.J. Slater (ed.), *Roman Theater and Society*, Ann Arbor, 1996, 69–112.
FACCHINI, S. 1990: *I luoghi dello sport nella Roma antica e moderna*, Roma, 1990.
GALSTERER, H. 1981: 'Spiele und "Spiele": Die Organisation der *ludi juvenales* in der Kaiserzeit', *Athenaeum* 59, 1981, 410–38.
GOLDBERG, S.M. 1998: 'Plautus on the Palatine', *JRS* 88, 1998, 1–20.
GUARINO, A. 1985: 'Il *leasing* dei gladiatori', *Index* 13, 1985, 461–65.
ISIDORI FRASCA, R. 1980: *Ludi nell'antica Roma*, Bologna, 1980.
JENNISON, G. 1937: *Animals for Show and Pleasure in Ancient Rome*, Manchester, 1937.
JORY, E.J. 1970: 'Associations of actors in Rome', *Hermes* 98, 1970, 224–53.
LIM, R. 1999: 'People as power: games, munificence and contested topography', in W.V. Harris (ed.), *The Transformations of* Urbs Roma *in Late Antiquity*, JRA Supplementary Series 33, Portsmouth RI, 1999, 265–82.
PLASS, P. 1997: *The Game of Death in Ancient Rome. Arena Sports and Political Suicide*, Madison, 1997.
POE, J.P. 1984: 'The secular games, the Aventine, and the Pomerium in the Campus Martius', *Californian Studies in Classical Antiquity* 3, 1984, 57–81.
RAWSON, E. 1981: 'Chariot Racing in the Roman Republic', *PBSR* 49, 1981, 1–16.
RAWSON, E. 1985: 'Theatrical life in Republican Rome and Italy', *PBSR* 53, 1985, 97–113.
RAWSON, E. 1987: '*Discrimina ordinum:* the *lex Julia theatralis*', *PBSR* 55, 1987, 83–114.
SABBATINI TUMOLESI, P. 1988: *Epigrafia Anfiteatrali dell'Occidente Romano* I, *Roma*, Roma, 1988.
SALETTA, V. 1967: *Ludi circensi*, Roma, 1967.
SCOBIE, A. 1988: 'Spectator security and comfort at gladitorial games', *Nikephoros* I, 1988, 191–243.

THUILLIER, J.P. 1982: 'Le programme athlétique des ludi circenses dans la Rome républicaine', *Latomus* 60, 1982, 105–22.
WIEDEMANN, T. 1992: *Emperors and Gladiators*, London-New York, 1992.

8. City Supply
General

ANDRÉ, J. 1961: *L'alimentation et la cuisine à Rome*, Paris, 1961.
BLAZQUEZ, J.M. 1990: *El monte Testaccio: archivo del commercio de Roma*, Belem, 1990.
BLAZQUEZ, J.M. 1995: *El programa Testaccio*, Roma, 1995.
BRUNT, P.A. 1971: *Italian Manpower, 225 BC – AD 14*, Oxford, 1971.
BRUNT, P.A. 1981: 'The Revenues of Rome', *JRS* 71, 1981, 161–72.
CAPRARIIS, F. de 1999: 'I porti di Roma nel IV secolo', in W.V. Harris (ed.), *The Transformations of* Urbs Roma *in Late Antiquity*, JRA Supplementary Series 33, Portsmouth RI, 1999, 216–34.
CARUSO, L. 1986: *Testaccio*, Roma, 1986.
CASCIO, E. lo 1999: '*Canon frumentarius, suarius, vinarius*: stato e privati nell'approvionamento dell'*Urbs*', in W.V. Harris (ed.), *The Transformations of* Urbs Roma *in Late Antiquity*, JRA Supplementary Series 33, Portsmouth RI, 1999, 163–83.
CASSON, L. 1965: 'Harbour and river boats of ancient Rome', *JRS* 55, 1965, 31–39.
CASTAGNOLI, F. 1980: 'Installazioni portuali a Roma', in D'ARMS and KOPFF 1980, 35–42.
COLINI, A.M. 1980: 'Il porto fluviale del foro boario a Roma', in D'ARMS and KOPFF 1980, 43–53.
D'ARMS, J.H. and KOPFF, E.C. (ed.) 1980: *The Seaborne Commerce of Ancient Rome*: *Studies in Archaeology and History*, MAAR 36, Roma, 1980.
DELAINE, J. 1995: 'The supply of building materials to the city of Rome. Some economic implications', in N. Christie (ed.), *Settlement and Economy in Italy 1500 BC to AD 1500. Papers of the Fifth Conference of Italian Archaeology*, Oxbow Monograph 41, Oxford, 1995, 555–62.
DRESSEL, H. 1878: *Ricerche sul monte Testaccio*, Roma, 1878.
ÉTIENNE, R. 1949: 'Les amphores du Testaccio au III siècle', *MEFRA* 61, 1949, 151–81.
FRANK, T. (ed.) 1933–40: *Economic Survey of Ancient Rome* I–V, Baltimore, 1933–40.
INCITTI, M., MENEGHINI, R. and MOCCHEGIANI CARPANO, C. 1986: 'Lungotevere Testaccio', *BullCom* 91, 1986, 560–95.
LO CASCIO, E. 1999: *Canon frumentarius, suarius, vinarius*: stato e privati nell'approvigionamento dell'*Vrbs'*, in W.V. Harris (ed.), *The Transformations of* Urbs Roma *in Late Antiquity*, JRA Supplementary Series 33, Portsmouth RI, 1999, 163–182.
LUGLI, G. and FILIBECK, G. 1935: *Il porto di Roma imperiale e l'agro romano*, Roma, 1935.
MEIGGS, R. 1973: *Roman Ostia*, ed. 2, Oxford, 1973.
MEIGGS, R. 1980: 'Sea-borne timber supplies to Rome', in D'ARMS and KOPFF 1980, 185–96.
MOCCHEGIANI CARPANO, C. and MENEGHINI, R. 1985: 'Lungotevere Testaccio', *BullCom* 90, 1985, 864–95.
MORLEY, N. 1996: *Metropolis and Hinterland: The city of Rome and the Italian economy, 200 BC – AD 200*, Cambridge, 1996.
PALMER, R.E.A. 1980: 'Customs on market goods imported into the city of Rome' in D'ARMS and KOPFF 1980, 217–33.
PANELLA, C. 1986: 'Le merci: produzioni, itinerari e destini', in A. Giardina (ed.), *Società Romana e impero tardo antico* III, Roma/Bari, 1986, 431–59.
PAROLI, L. and DELOGU, P. (ed.) 1993: *La storia economica di Roma nell'alto medioevo alla luce dei recenti scavi archeologici. Atti del seminario, 2–3 aprile 1992*, Biblioteca di Archeologia Medioevale 10, Firenze, 1993.
RODRIGUEZ-ALMEIDA, R. 1980: 'Vicissitudini nella gestione del commercio dell' olio betico da Vespasiano a Severo Alessandro', in D'ARMS and KOPFF 1980, 277–90.
ROSTOVTZEFF, M. 1957: *The Social and Economic History of the Roman Empire*, ed. 2, Oxford, 1957.
TESTAGUZZA, O. 1964: 'The port of Rome', *Archaeology* 17.3, 1964, 173–79.

Food Supply

ALDRETE, G.S. and MATTINGLY, D.J. 1999: 'Feeding the City: the organization, operation and scale of the supply system for Rome', in D.S. Potter and D.J. Mattingly (ed.), *Life, Death and Entertainment in the Roman Empire*, Ann Arbor, 1999, 171–204.
ASTOLFI, F., GUIDOBALDI, F. and PRONTI, A. 1978: 'Horrea Agrippiana', *ArchCl* 30, 1978, 31–106.

BABLED, H. 1892: *De la cura annonae chez les romains*, Paris, 1892.
BARNISH, S. 1987: 'Pigs, plebeians and potentes: Rome's economic hinterland, *c.*350–600 A.D.', *PBSR* 55, 1987, 157–85.
BELL, M. 1994: 'An Imperial Flour Mill on the Janiculum', in *Le ravitaillement en blé de Rome et des centres urbains des débuts de la République jusqu'au Haut Empire*, Roma, 1994, 73–89.
CASSON, L. 1980: 'The role of the state in Rome's grain trade', in J.H. D'Arms and E.C. Kopff (ed.), *The Seaborne Commerce of Ancient Rome: Studies in Archaeology and History*, MAAR 36, Roma, 1980, 21–33.
GARNSEY, P.D.A. 1983: 'Famine in Rome', in P.D.A. Garnsey and C.R. Whittaker (ed.), *Trade and Famine in Classical Antiquity*, Cambridge Philological Society Supplementary Volume 8, Cambridge, 1983, 56–65.
GARNSEY, P.D.A. 1983: 'Grain for Rome', in P.D.A. Garnsey, K. Hopkins and C.R. Whittaker (ed.), *Trade in the Ancient Economy*, London, 1983, 118–30.
GARNSEY, P.D.A. (ed.) 1988: *Famine and Food Supply in the Graeco-Roman World: responses to risk and crisis*, Cambridge, 1988.
GARNSEY, P.D.A. and RATHBONE, D. 1985: 'The background to the grain law of C. Gracchus', *JRS* 75, 1985, 20–5.
HERMANSEN, G. 1978: 'The bread line through Ostia to Rome', *Proceedings of the African Classical Association* 14, 1978, 21–26.
MARTINORI, E. 1931: *Via Salaria (antica e moderna): Via Claudia nova. Studio storico-topografico di Edoardo Martinori*, Roma, 1931.
MORITZ, L. 1958: *Grain Mills and Flour in Classical Antiquity*, Oxford, 1958.
PALOMBI, D. 1990: 'Gli horrea della Via Sacra: dagli appunti di G. Boni ad una ipotesi su Nerone', *DialArch* III.8, 1990, 53–72.
PAVIS D'ESCURAC, H. 1976: *La préfecture de l'annone, service administratif impériale d'Auguste à Constantin*, Roma, 1976.
RICKMAN, G. 1971: *Roman Granaries and Store Buildings*, Cambridge, 1971.
RICKMAN, G. 1980: *The Corn Supply of Ancient Rome*, Oxford, 1980.
RODRIGUEZ-ALMEIDA, E. 1978–79: 'Cohortes tres Horreorum Galbianorum', *RendPontAcc* 50, 1978–79, 9–26.
RODRIGUEZ-ALMEIDA, R. 1984: *Il Monte Testaccio: ambiente, storia, materiali*, Roma, 1984.
SINNIGEN, W. 1962: 'The origins of the *frumentarii*', *MAAR* 27, 1962, 211–24.
SIRKS, A.J.B. 1984: *Qui annonae urbis serviunt*, Amsterdam, 1984.
SIRKS, A.J.B. 1991: 'The size of the grain distributions in imperial Rome and Constantinople', *Athenaeum* 69, 1991, 215–38.
SIRKS, A.J.B. 1991: *Food for Rome: the legal structure of the transportation and processing of supplies for the imperial distributions in Rome and Constantinople*, Amsterdam, 1991.
STACCIOLI, R. 1962: 'Tipi di "horrea" nella documentazione della "Forma Urbis"', in M. Renard (ed.), *Hommages à Albert Grenier*, Collection Latomus 63, Bruxelles, 1962, 1430–440.
TCHERNIA, A. 1986: *Le vin d'Italie romaine: essai d'histoire economique d'aprés les amphores*, Roma, 1986.
TENGSTRÖM, E. 1974: *Bread for the People: studies of the corn-supply of Rome during the late Empire*, Stockholm, 1974.
VEYNE, P. 1990: *Bread and Circuses: the historical sociology of a political pluralism*, translation B. Pearse, London, 1990.
VIRLOUVET, C. 1987: 'La topographie des distributions frumentaires avant la création de la Porticus Minucia', in C. Pietri (ed.), *L'Urbs: Espace urbain et histoire*, Collection de l'École Française de Rome 98, Roma, 1987, 175–89.
VIRLOUVET, C. 1995: *Tessara frumentaria*, Roma, 1995.
ZEVI, F. 1993: 'Per l'identificazione della Porticus Minucia Frumentaria', *MEFRA* 105.2, 1993, 661–708.

Water Supply

AICHER, P.J. 1993: 'Terminal Display Fountains (*Mostre*) and the Aqueducts of Ancient Rome', *Phoenix* 47.4, 1993, 339–352.
AICHER, P.J. 1995: *Guide to the Aqueducts of Ancient Rome*, Chicago, 1995.
ASHBY, T. 1935: *The Aqueducts of Ancient Rome*, Oxford, 1935.
ASHBY, T. 1991: *Gli acquedotti dell'antica Roma*, Roma, 1991.
ASTIN, A.E. 1961: 'Water to the Capitol: a note on Frontinus *De Aquis* 1.7.5', *Latomus* 20, 1961, 541–48.
BAILLIE REYNOLDS, P.K. and BAILEY, T.A. 1966: 'The aqueduct in the grounds of the British Embassy in Rome', *Archaeologia* 100, 1966, 81–104.
BAUER, H. 1989: 'Die Cloaca Maxima in Rom', *Mitteilungen des Leichtweiss-Institutes für Wasserbau der Technischen Universität Braunschweig* 103, 1989, 45–67.

BIZZARRI VIVARELLI, D. 1976: 'Un ninfeo sotto il parco di Traiano', *MEFRA* 88, 1976, 719–53.

BLACKMAN, D.R. 1978: 'The volume of water delivered by the four great aqueducts of Rome', *PBSR* 46, 1978, 52–72.

BLACKMAN, D.R. 1979: 'The length of the four great aqueducts of Rome', *PBSR* 47, 1979, 12–18.

BLOCH, H. 1944: 'Aqua Traiana', *AJA* 48, 1944, 337–41.

BONFANTE, P. 1922: 'Il regime delle acque dal diritto romano al diritto odierno', *Annales de géographique* 34, 1922, 3–16.

BRUUN, C. 1987: 'Water for the Castra Praetoria', *Arctos* 21, 1987, 7–18.

BRUUN, C. 1989: 'Statio Aquarum', in M. Steinby (ed.), *Lacus Iuturnae* I, Roma, 1989, 127–47.

BRUUN, C. 1991: *The water supply of ancient Rome: a study of Roman Imperial administration*, Commentationes Humanarum Litterarum 93, Helsinki, 1991.

BRUUN, C. 1997: 'Acquedotti e condizioni sociali di Roma Imperiale: immagini e realtà', in *La Rome Impériale: démographie et logistique. Actes de la Table ronde, Rome 25 mars 1994*, Collection de l'École Française de Rome 230, Roma, 1997, 123–55.

BUREN, A.W. van 1955: 'Wasserleitungen', *RE* 8.A.1, 1955, 453–85.

BUREN, A.W. van and STEVENS, G.P. 1917: 'The Aqua Traiana and the mills on the Janiculum', *MAAR* 1, 1917, 59–62.

BUREN, A.W. van and STEVENS, G.P. 1927: 'The Aqua Alsietina on the Janiculum', *MAAR* 6, 1927, 137–46.

BUREN, A.W. van 1941–41: 'Come fu condotta l'acqua al Monte Capitolino', *RendPontAcc* 18, 1941–42, 65–70.

CARUSO, G. and GIUSBERTI, P. 1993: 'Acquedotto Alessandrino. Restauro del tratto tra via del Fossa di Centocelle e Via dei Pioppi', *BullCom* 95.2, 1993, 116–121.

CHINI, P. 1993: 'Latrina romana in Via Garibaldi', *BullCom* 95.2, 1993, 211–15.

COATES-STEPHENS, R. 1998: 'The Walls and Aqueducts of Rome in the Early Middle Ages, A.D. 500–1000', *JRS* 88, 1998, 166–178.

COZZA, L. 1974–75: 'I recenti scavi delle Sette Sale', *RendPontAcc* 47, 1974–75, 79–101.

COSTA, E. 1919: *Le acque nel diritto romano*, Bologna, 1919.

D'AMATO, C. 1986: 'L'amministrazione delle acque in età romana', in G. Pisano Sartorio and A. Liberati Silverio (ed.), *Il trionfo dell'acqua: acque e acquedotti a Roma, IV sec. a.C. – XX sec., Museo della civiltà 31 ottobre 1986–15 gennaio 1987,* Catalogo della mostra, Roma, 1986, 176–87.

FINE LICHT, K. de 1983: 'Scavi alle Sette Sale', in K. de Fine Licht (ed.), *Città e Architettura nella Roma Imperiale. Atti del seminario del 27 ottobre 1981*, Analecta Romana Instituti Danici Supplement 10, Odense, 1983, 187–202.

DEMAN, E.B. van 1934: *The Building of the Roman Aqueducts*, Washington, 1934.

DIFENIZIO , C. 1916: 'Sulla portata degli acqua dotti romani e determinazione della *quinaria*', *Giornale del Genio Civile* 14, 1916, 226–331.

D'ONOFRIO, C. 1986: *Le fontane di Roma*, Roma, 1986.

ECK, W. 1982: 'Die *fistulae aquariae* der Stadt Rom. Zum Einfluss des sozialen Status auf administratives Handeln', *Tituli* 4, 1982, 197–225.

EVANS, H.B. 1982: 'Agrippa's water plan', *AJA* 86, 1982, 193–204.

EVANS, H.B. 1983: 'Nero's *Arcus Caelimontani*', *AJA* 87, 1983, 392–399.

EVANS, H.B. 1991: 'Water distribution in Ancient Rome: *Quorsum et Cui Bono?*', in A.T. Hodge (ed.), *Future Currents in Aqueduct Studies*, Leeds, 1991, 21–7.

EVANS, H.B. 1993: '*In Tiburtium Usum*: special arrangements in the Roman water system (Frontinus, Aq. 65)', *AJA* 97.3, 1993, 447–55.

EVANS, H.B. 1994: *Water distribution in ancient Rome: the evidence of Frontinus*, Ann Arbor, 1994.

FABRETTI, R. 1788: *De aquis et aquaeductibus veteris Romae dissertationes tres*, repr. 1972, Roma, 1788.

FRONTINUS-GESELLSCHAFT, 1982: *Wasserversorgung im Antiken Rom: Sextus Iulius Frontinus, curator aquarum*, München/Wien, 1982.

FRONTINUS-GESELLSCHAFT 1983–87: *Geschichte der Wasserversorgung* I: München/Wien, 1983; II: Mainz, 1987; III: Mainz 1988.

GARBRECHT, G. 1982: 'Wasserversorgungstechnik in römischer zeit', in *Wasserversorgung im antiken Rom*, München, 1982, 9–43.

GARBRECHT, G. and MANDERSCHEID, H. 1992: '*Etiam fonte novo Antoniniano*. L'acquedotto Antoniniano alle Terme di Caracalla', *Archeologia Classica* 44, 1992, 193–234.

GARBRECHT, G. and MANDERSCHEID, H. 1995: 'Die Wasserversorgung der Caracallathermen durch die Aqua Antoniniana', *Antike Welt* 26, 1995, 195–202.

GATTI, E. 1912: 'Avanzi di acquedotti romani scoperti presso Porta Maggiore', *BullCom* 40, 1912, 228–36.

GRIMAL, P. (ed.) 1961: *Frontinus*, Paris, 1961.
HAINZMANN, M. 1975: *Untersuchungen zur Geschichte und Verwaltung der stradrömischen Wasserleitungen*, Wien, 1975.
HERSCHEL, C. 1913: *The Two Books on the Water Supply of Sextus Julius Frontinus*, ed. 2, London, 1913.
HODGE, A.T. 1983: 'Siphons in Roman aqueducts', *PBSR* 51, 1983, 174–221.
HODGE, A.T. 1988: 'How did Frontinus measure the quinaria?', *AJA* 88.2, 1988, 205–16.
HODGE, A.T. 1989: 'Aqueducts', in I.M. Barton (ed.), *Roman Public Buildings*, Exeter, 1989, 127–49.
HODGE, A.T. 1992: *Roman Aqueducts and Water Supply*, London, 1992.
LANCIANI, R. 1881: 'Topografia di Roma antica. I comentarii di Frontino intorno le acque e gli acquedotti. Silloge epigrafica aquaria', *MemLinc* 3.4, 1881, 215–616. Repr. 1975: *Le acque e gli acquedotti di Roma antica*, Roma, 1975.
LAVAGNE, H. 1970: 'Le nymphée au Polypheme de la Domus Aurea', *MEFRA* 82, 1970, 673–721.
LLOYD, R.B. 1979: 'The Aqua Virgo, Euripus and pons Agrippae', *AJA* 83, 1979, 193–204.
LONGO, G. 1934: 'Sull'uso delle acque pubbliche in diritto romano', in E. Albertario (ed.), *Studi in memoria di U. Ratti*, Milano, 1934, 55–93.
MORGAN, M.H. 1902: 'Remarks on the Water Supply', *TAPA* 33, 1902, 30–37.
MORGAN, M.G. 1978: 'The Introduction of the Aqua Marcia into Rome, 144–140 B.C.', *Phililogus* 122, 1978, 25–58.
MORTON. H.V. 1966: *The Waters of Rome*, London, 1966.
NICOLET, C. 1976: 'Le Temple des Nymphes et les distributions frumentaires à Rome', *CRAI*, 1976, 29–51.
PACE, P. 1983: *Gli acquedotti di Roma e il "de aquaeductu" di Frontino*, Roma, 1983.
PALMA, A. 1987: 'Le derivazioni di acqua *ex castello*', *Index* 15, 1987, 439–57.
PANELLA, C. 1996: *Meta Sudans* I: *Un'area sacra in Palatino e le valle del Colosseo primo e dopo Nerone*, Roma, 1996.
PANIMOLLE, G. 1984: *Gli acquedotti di Roma antica*, Roma, 1984.
PARKER, J.H. 1876: *The Archaeology of Rome: the aqueducts*, Oxford/London, 1876.
PINTO, J.A. 1986: *The Trevi Fountain*, New Haven, 1986.
PISANO SARTORIO, G. and LIBERATI SILVERIO, A. (ed.) 1986: *Il trionfo dell'acqua: acque e acquedotti a Roma, IV sec. a.C. – XX sec., Museo della civiltà 31 ottobre 1986–15 gennaio 1987,* Catalogo della mostra, Roma, 1986.
PISANO SARTORIO, G. and LIBERATI SILVERIO, A. (ed.) 1992: *Il trionfo dell'acqua. Atti del convegno "Gli antichi acquedotti di Roma: problemi di conoscenza, conservazione e tutela", Roma 29–30 ottobre 1987*, Roma, 1992.
QUILICI, L. 1989: 'Gli acquedotti di Roma', *Archeo: attualità del passato* 53, 1989, 51–97.
ROBINSON, O.F. 1980: 'The water supply of ancient Rome', *Studia et Documenta Historiae et Iuris* 46, 1980, 44–86.
RODGERS, R.H. 1982: '*Curatores Aquarum*', *Harvard Studies in Classical Philology* 86, 1982, 171–80.
RODGERS, R.H. 1986: '*Copia Aquarum*: Frontinus' Measurements and the Perspective of Capacity', *TAPA* 116, 1986, 353–60.
SCHIØLER, T. and WIKANDER, Ö 1983: 'A Roman water-mill in the baths of Caracalla', *Opuscula Romana* 14, 1983, 47–64.
TAYLOR, R. 1995: '*A citeriore ripa aquae*: Aqueduct River Crossings in the Ancient City of Rome', *PBSR* 63, 1995, 75–103.
TAYLOR, R. 1997: 'Torrent or Trickle? The Aqua Alsietina, the Naumachia Augusti, and the Transtiberim', *AJA* 101, 1997, 465–92.
TEDESCHI GRISTANTI, G.I. 1977: *I 'trofei' di Mario: il ninfeo dell'Acqua Giulia sull'Esquilino*, Roma, 1977.
TORTORICI, E. 1993: 'La "Terrazza domizianea", *l'aqua Marcia* ed il taglio della sella tra Campidoglio e Quirinale', *BullComm* 95.2, 1993, 7–24.
ÜRLICH, R.B. 1986: 'The Appiades Fountain of the Forum Iulium', *RM* 93, 1986, 405–23.
VOLPE, R. 1996: *Aqua Marcia: lo scavo di un tratto urbano*, Firenze, 1996.
WERNER, D. 1986: *Wasser für das antike Rom*, Berlin, 1986.
WENTWORTH RINNE, K. 1996: 'Aquae Urbis Romae: an historical overview of water in the public life of Rome', in N. De Haan and G.C.M. Jansen, *Cura Aquarum in Campania*, Roma, 1996, 145–51.
WIKANDER, 1979: 'Water-Mills in ancient Rome', *Opuscula Romana* 12, 1979, 13–36.

9. Topography

General Topography

ARCHEOLOGIA NEL CENTRO 1985: *Roma: archeologia nel centro I, l'area archeologica centrale*; *II, La 'Città Murata'*, LSA 6, Roma, 1985.
ANDERSON, J.C. 1983: 'A topographical tradition in the fourth century chronicles', *Historia: revue d'histoire ancienne* 32, 1983, 93–105.
BURANELLI, LE PERA, S. and D'ELIA, L. 1986: '*Sacra via*. Note topografiche', *BullCom* 91, 1986, 241–62.

BUONOCORE, M. 1997: *Appunti di Topografia Romana nei Codici Lanciani della Biblioteca Apostolica Vaticana* I–II, Città di Vaticano, 1997.
CAPODIFERRO, A., CONFORTO, M. L., PAVOLINI, C. and PIRANOMONTE, M. 1985: *Forma la città antica e il suo avvenire*, Roma, 1985.
CAPRARIIS, F. de 1991–92: 'Due note di topografia romana', *Rivista dell'Istituto nazionale d'archeologia e storia dell'arte* 14–15, 1991–92, 153–91.
CARETTONI, G. 1960: 'Excavations and discoveries in the Forum Romanum and on the Palatine during the past 50 years', *JRS* 50, 1960, 197–203.
CARETTONI, G. 1960: *La pianta marmorea di Roma antica*, Roma, 1960.
CARETTONI, G. *et al.* 1966: *La Pianta marmorea di Roma: Forma Urbis Romae*, Roma, 1966.
CAROLIS, M. de (ed.) 1986: *Area archeologica centrale e città*, Roma, 1986.
CASSATELLA, A. 1985: 'Il tratto orientale della Via Sacra', in *Roma: archeologia nel centro I; L'area archeologica centrale*, Roma, 1985, 99–105.
CASTAGNOLI, F. 1969: *Topografia e urbanistica di Roma antica*, Bologna, 1969.
CASTAGNOLI, F. 1980: *Topografia e urbanistica di Roma antica*, ed. 3, Torino, 1980.
CASTAGNOLI, F. 1985: 'Un nuovo documento per la topografia di Roma antica', *Studi Romani* 33, 1985, 205–11.
CASTAGNOLI, F. 1988: 'Itam forte Via Sacra', *Topografia romana: ricerche e discussioni*, Quaderni dell'Istituto della Università di Roma 10, Firenze, 1988, 99–114.
CASTAGNOLI, F., CECCHELLI, C., GIOVANNONI, G. and ZOCCZ, M. 1958: *Topografia e urbanistica di Roma*, ed. 2, Bologna, 1958.
CARTA ARCHEOLOGICA 1962–77: *Carta archeologica di Roma*, Firenze, 1962–77.
CENTRO STORICO 1985–88: *Carta del centro storico di Roma*, Roma, 1985–88.
CHAMPLIN, E. 1982: 'The *suburbium* of Rome', *AJAH* 7, 1982, 97–117.
COARELLI, F. 1986: 'L'urbs e il suburbio', in A. Giardina (ed.), *Roma: politica economia paessaggio urbano*, Società romana e impero tardoantico II, Roma/Bari, 1986, 1–58.
COARELLI, F. 1992: 'Aedes Fortis Fortunae, Naumachia augusti, Castra Ravennatium. La via Campana-Portuensis e alcuni edifici adiacenti nella pianta marmorea severiana', *Ostraka* 1, 1992, 39–54.
COLINI, A.M., SARTORIO, G.P., BUZZETTI, C., SANTI, M.N. and VIRGILI, P. 1985: 'Notizario di scavi e scoperte in Roma e Suburbio, 1946–60', *BullCom* 90, 1985, 307–440.
DEMAN, E.B. van 1922: 'The *sacra via* of Nero', *MAAR* 5, 1925, 115–26.
DEMAN, E.B. van 1923: 'The Neronian *sacra via*', *AJA* 27, 383–424.
DONDIN PAYRE, M. 1987: 'Topographie et propagande gentilice. Le "compitum Acilium" et l'origine des Acilii Glabriones', in C. Pietri (ed.), *L'Urbs: Espace urbain et histoire*, Collection de l'École Française de Rome 98, Roma, 1987, 87–109.
DUDLEY, D. 1967: *Urbs Roma: A Sourcebook of Classical Texts on the City and its Monuments*, London, 1967.
FRUTAZ, A.P. (ed.) 1962: *Le Piante di Roma*, I–III, Roma, 1962.
GATTI, J. 1989: *Topografia ed edilizia di Roma antica*, Roma, 1989.
GELSOMINO, R. 1975: *Varrone e i sette colli di Roma*, Roma, 1975.
GIGHI, L. (ed.) 1990: *Strade, piazze e monumentali nelle G.R. di Roma*, Roma, 1990.
HARRIS, W.V. (ed.) 1999: *The Transformations of Urbs Roma in Late Antiquity*, JRA Supplementary Series 33, Portsmouth RI, 1999.
KIEPERT, H. and HÜLSEN, C. 1896: *Formae Urbis Romae Antiquae*, Berlin, 1896.
KÜNZL, E. 1988: *Der römische Triumph. Siegesfeiern im antiken Rom*, München, 1988.
LABROUSSE, M. 1937: 'Le pomerium de la Rome impériale: notes de topographie romaine', *MEFRA* 54, 1937, 165–99.
LANCIANI, R.A. 1893–1901: *Forma Urbis Romae*, Milano, 1893–1901; repr. 1989.
LISSI CARONNA, E. 1985: 'Un complesso edilizio tra via in Arcione, via dei Maroniti e vicolo dei Maroniti', in *Roma: archeologia nel centro II, La 'Città Murata'*, Roma, 1985, 360–65.
LUCIANI, R. (ed.) 1984: *Roma sotteranea: Porta San Sebastiano, 15 ottobre–14 gennaio 1985*, Catalogo della mostra, Roma, 1984.
MANACORDA, D. and ZANINI, E. 1989: 'The first millennium A.D. in Rome: from the *Porticus Minucia* to the Via delle Botteghe Oscure', in K. Randsborg (ed.), *The Birth of Europe: archaeology and social development in the first millennium A.D.*, Analecta Romana Instituti Danici Supplement 12, Roma, 1989, 25–32.
NASH, E. 1961–62: *A Pictorial Dictionary of Ancient Rome*, Roma, 1961–62.
NORDH, A. 1949: *Libellus de regionibus urbis Romae*, Lund, 1949.

PALOMBI, D. 1988: 'Contributo alla topografia della Via Sacra, dagli appunti inediti di Giacomo Boni', *Topografia romana: ricerche e discussioni*, Quaderni dell'Istituto della Università di Roma 10, Firenze, 1988, 77–97.

PALOMBI, D. 1997: *Tra Palatino ed Esquilino: Velia, Carinae, Fagutal. Storia urbana di tre quartieri di Roma antica*, Roma, 1997.

PANELLA, C. 1990: 'La valle del Colosseo nell' antichità', *BA* 1–2, 1990, 35–88.

PLATNER, S.B. 1911: *The Topography and Monuments of Ancient Rome*, Boston, 1911.

PLATNER, S.B. and ASHBY, T. 1929: *A Topographical Dictionary of Rome*, Oxford, 1929.

PORTELLA, I. della 2000: *Subterranean Rome*, Roma, 2000.

RICHARDSON, L. Jr. 1992: *A New Topographical Dictionary of Ancient Rome*, Baltimore, 1992.

RICHTER, O. 1901: *Topographie der Stadt Rome*, ed. 2, München, 1901.

RODRIGUEZ-ALMEIDA, E. 1970–71: 'Forma Urbis Marmorea: nuove integrazioni', *BullCom* 82, 1970–71, 105–35.

RODRIGUEZ-ALMEIDA, E. 1975–76: 'Aggiornamenta topografico dei colli Oppio, Cispio e Viminale secondo la Forma Urbis Marmorea', *RendPontAcc* 48, 1975–76, 263–78.

RODRIGUEZ-ALMEIDA, E. 1977: 'Forma Urbis Marmorea: nuovi elementi di analisi e nuove ipotesi di lavoro', *MEFRA* 89, 1977, 219–57.

RODRIGUEZ-ALMEIDA, E. 1981: *Forma urbis marmorea: aggiornamento generale 1980*, Roma, 1981.

RODRIGUEZ-ALMEIDA, E. 1983: 'Un nuovo frammento della Forma Urbis Marmorea', in K. de Fine Licht (ed.), *Città e Architettura nella Roma Imperiale. Atti del seminario del 27 ottobre 1981*, Analecta Romana Instituti Danici Supplement 10, Odense, 1983, 87–92.

RODRIGUEZ-ALMEIDA, E. 1988: 'Un frammento di una nuova pianta marmorea di Roma', *JRA* 1, 1988, 120–31.

SANTANGELI VALENZIANI, R. and VOLPE, R. 1989–90: 'Nova Via', *BullCom* 93, 1989–90, 23–31.

SCAGNETTI, F. and GRANDE, G. 1979: *Roma Urbs Imperatorum Aetate*, Roma, 1979.

STEINBY, E.M. (ed.) 1993–99: *Lexicon Topographicum Urbis Romae* I–V, Roma, 1993–99.

TORELLI, M. 1992: 'Topografia e iconologia: Arco di Portogallo, Ara Pacis, Ara Providentiae, Templum Solis', *Ostraka* 1, 1992, 105–31.

TORTORICI, E. 1988: 'Alcune osservazioni sulla tavola 8 della "Forma Urbis" del Lanciani', *Topografia romana: ricerche e discussioni*, Quaderni dell'Istituto della Università di Roma 10, Firenze, 1988, 7–15.

TORTORICI, E. 1991: *Argiletum: commercio, speculazione edilizia e lotta politica dall'analisi topografica di un quartiere di Roma di età repubblicana*, Roma, 1991.

VALENTINI, R. and ZUCCHETTI, G. 1940–53: *Codice topografico della città di Roma* I–IV, Roma, 1940–53.

VERSNEL, H.S. 1970: *Triumphus. An Inquiry into the Origin, Development and Meaning of the Roman Triumph*, Leiden, 1970.

Aventine Hill

CASSATELLA, A. and VENDITELLI, L. 1985: 'Santuario di Diana sull'Aventino: il problema della localizzazione', in *Roma: archeologia nel centro II; La 'Città Murata'*, Roma, 1985, 442–51.

CHINI, P. 1997: 'Le Dolochenum de l'Aventin: interprétation des structures', in G.M. Bellelli and U. Bianchi. (ed.), *Orientalia Sacra Urbis Romae: Dolichena et Heliopolitana. Recueil d'études archéologiques et historico-religieuses sur les cultes cosmopolites d'origine commagénienne et syrienne*, Roma, 1997, 329–47.

DARSY, F.M.D. 1968: *Recherches archéologiques à Saint Sabine sur l'Aventin*, Città di Vaticano, 1968.

MERLIN, A. 1906: *L'Aventin dans l'antiquité*, Paris, 1906.

VENDITELLI, L. 1987: 'Aventino: la localizzazione del tempio di Diana: Saggi di scavo nell'area tra v. S. Alberto Magno e Largo Arrigo VII', *AL* 8, 1987, 33–8.

VENDITELLI, L. 1988: 'Prosecuzione delle indagini topografiche sull'Aventino: la localizzazione del Tempio di Diana', *AL* 9, 1988, 105–10.

Caelian Hill (Celio)

BRENK, B. 1999: 'La cristianizzazione della Domus dei Valerii sul Celio', in W.V. Harris (ed.), *The Transformations of* Urbs Roma *in Late Antiquity*, JRA Supplementary Series 33, Portsmouth RI, 1999, 69–84.

CARIGNANI, A. *et al.* 1990: 'Nuovi dati sulla topografia del Celio: le ricerche nell'area dell'ospedale militare', *AL* 10, 1990, 72–80.

COLINI, A.M. 1944: *Storia e topografia del Celio nell'antichità*, MemPontAcc 3.7, Roma, 1944.

COLINI, A.M. 1973: *Via Appia*, Rome, 1973.

GIULIANI, E. and PAVOLINI, C. 1999: 'La "Biblioteca di Agapito" e la Basilica di Sant'Agnese', in W.V. Harris (ed.), *The Transformations of* Urbs Roma *in Late Antiquity*, JRA Supplementary Series 33, Portsmouth RI, 1999, 85–108.
LISSI CARONNA, E. 1982: 'Scoperte sotto S. Stefano Rotundo', *MemPontAcc* 15, 1982, 175–83.
PAVOLINI, C. 1987: 'Lo scavo di Piazza Celimontana. Un'indagine nel *Caput Africae', in C. Pietri (ed.), L'Urbs: Espace urbain et histoire*, Collection de l'École Française de Rome 98, Roma, 1987, 653–85.
PAVOLINI, C. 1988: 'Indagini archeologiche a Piazza Celimontana (1984–87)', *AL* 10, 1988, 97–104.
PAVOLINI, C. 1990: 'Celio: ospedale militare. La Basilica Hilariana', *BA* 1–2, 1990, 171–76.
PAVOLINI, C. 1993: 'L'area del Celio fra l'antichità e il medioevo alla luce delle recenti indagini archeologiche', in L. Paroli and P. Delogu (ed.), *La storia economica di Roma nell'alto medioeve alla luce dei recenti scavi archeologici. Atti del seminario, 2–3 aprile 1992*, Biblioteca di Archeologia Medioevale 10, Firenze, 1993, 53–70.
PAVOLINI, C. *et al.* 1993: 'La topografia antica della sommità del Celio', *RM* 100, 1993, 443–505.
PAVOLINI, C. 1993: Caput Africae: *indagini archeologiche a Piazza Celimontana (1984–1988)* I–II, Roma, 1993.
QUILICI GIGLI, S. 1990: *La Via Appia: decimo incontro di studio del Comitato per l'archeologia laziale*, AL 18, Roma, 1990.

Campus Martius (Campo Marzio)
BIANCHI, P. and TUCCI, P.L. 1996: 'Alcuni esempi di riuso dell'antico nell'area del Circo Flaminio', *MEFRA* 108.1, 1996, 27–82.
BOYD, M.J. 1953: 'The Porticoes of Metellus and Octavia and their two temples', *PBSR* 21, 1953, 152–59.
BUCHNER, E. 1976: 'Solarium Augusti und Ara Pacis', *RM* 83, 1976, 319–65.
BUCHNER, E. 1980–82: 'L'orologio solare di Augusto', *RendPontAcc* 53–54, 1980–82, 331–45.
BUZZETTI, C. 1984: 'Ustrini imperiali a Montecitorio', *BullCom* 89, 1984, 27–28.
CASTAGNOLI, F. 1946: 'Il Campo Marzio nell'antichità', *MemLinc* 7.1, 1946, 93–193.
CASTAGNOLI, F. 1983: 'Porticus Philippi', in K. de Fine Licht (ed.), *Città e Architettura nella Roma Imperiale. Atti del seminario del 27 ottobre 1981*, Analecta Romana Instituti Danici Supplement 10, Odense, 1983, 93–104.
CIANFA, T., CUSANNO, A.M., LABIANCA, L., PAPARATTI, E. and PETSECCA, M. 1985: 'Area Archeologica del Teatro di Marcello e del Portico d'Ottavia', in *Roma: archeologia nel centro II, La 'Città Murata'*, Roma, 1985, 533–45.
COARELLI, F. 1971–72: 'Il Complesso pompeiano del Campo Marzio e la sua decorazione scultorea', *RendPontAcc* 44, 1971–72, 99–122.
COARELLI, F. 1977: 'Il Campo Marzio occidentale: storia e topografia', *MEFRA* 89, 1977, 807–46.
COARELLI, F. 1997: *Il Campo Marzio: dalle origini alla fine della Repubblica*, Roma, 1997.
GHINI, G. 1988: 'Le Terme Alessandrine nel Campo Marzio', *MonAnt* 3:4, 1988, 121–67.
GIANFRONTTA, P.A. 1985: 'Indagini nell'area della Porticus Philippi', in *Roma: archeologia nel centro* II, *La 'Città Murata'*, Roma, 1985, 376–84.
JOLIVET, V. 1988: 'Les cendres d'Auguste: note sur la topographie monumentale du Champ de Mars septentrional', *AL* 9, 1988, 89–96.
LA ROCCA, E. 1984: *La riva a mezzaluna: culti, agoni, monumenti funerari presso il Tevere nel Campo Marzio occidentale*, Roma, 1984.
LAUTER, H. 1980–81: 'Porticus Metelli: die baulichen Reste', *BullCom* 87, 1980–81, 37–46.
LEMBKE, K. 1994: *Das Iseum Campense in Rom. Studie über den Isiskult unter Domitian*, Heidelberg, 1994.
MANACORDA, D. 1982: *Archeologia urbana a Roma: il progetto della Crypta Balbi*, Firenze, 1982.
MANACORDA, D. 1987: 'Scavi alla Crypta Balbi: problemi di topografia antica', in C. Pietri (ed.), *L'Urbs: Espace urbain et histoire*, Collection de l'École Française de Rome 98, Roma, 1987, 597–610.
MANACORDA, D. 1990: 'Excavations in the Crypta Balbi, Rome: a survey', *Accordia Research Papers* 1, 1990, 73–81.
MANACORDA, D. 1993: 'Trasformazioni dell'abitato nel Campo Marzio: l'area della "*Porticus Minuciae*"', in L. Paroli and P. Delogu (ed.), *La storia economica di Roma nell'alto medioeve alla luce dei recenti scavi archeologici. Atti del seminario, 2–3 Aprile 1992*, Biblioteca di Archeologia Medioevale 10, Firenze, 1993, 31–52.
MANACORDA, D. *et al* 2000: *Crypta Balbi*, Milano, 2000.
MATTERN, T. 1999: 'Ammerkungen zur Bebauung des nördlichen Marsfeldes in Rom', *RM* 106, 1999, 277–87.
MORGAN, M.G. 1971: 'The Porticus of Metellus: a reconsideration', *Hermes* 99, 1971, 480–505.
MUZZIOLI, M.P. 1992: 'Fonti per la topografia della IX regione di Roma: alcune osservazioni', *PBSR* 60, 1992, 179–211.
OLINDER, B. 1974: *Porticus Octavia in Circo Flaminio: topographical studies in the Campus region of Rome*, Stockholm, 1974.
PALMER, R.E.A. 1990: *Studies of the Northern Campus Martius in Ancient Rome*, Transactions of the American Philosophical Society 80.2, 1990.

QUILICI, L. 1983: 'Il Campo Marzio occidentale', in K. de Fine Licht (ed.), *Città e Architettura nella Roma Imperiale. Atti del seminario del 27 ottobre 1981*, Analecta Romana Instituti Danici Supplement 10, Odense, 1983, 59–86.
QUILICI GIGLI, S. 1983: 'Estremo Campo Marzio: alcune osservazioni sulla topografia', in K. de Fine Licht (ed.), *Città e Architettura nella Roma Imperiale. Atti del seminario del 27 ottobre 1981*, Analecta Romana Instituti Danici Supplement 10, Odense, 1983, 47–58.
RAKOB, F. 1987: 'Die Urbanisierung des nordlichen Marsfeld', in C. Pietri (ed.), *L'Urbs: Espace urbain et histoire*, Collection de l'École Française de Rome 98, Roma, 1987, 687–712.
RICKMAN, G. 1983: 'Porticus Minucia', in K. de Fine Licht (ed.), *Città e Architettura nella Roma Imperiale. Atti del seminario del 27 ottobre 1981*, Analecta Romana Instituti Danici Supplement 10, Odense, 1983, 105–08.
RODRIGUEZ, C. 1992: 'The *Porticus Vipsania* and contemporary poetry', *Latomus* 51, 1992, 79–93.
SAGUÌ, L. 1998: 'Il deposito della Crypta Balbi: una testimonianza imprevidibile sulla Roma del VII secolo?' in L. Saguì (ed.), *Ceramica in Italia: VI – VII secolo, Conference Proceedings, May 1995, Rome*, Firenze 1998, 305–34.
SAURON, G. 1987: 'Le complexe pompeien du Champ de Mars', in C. Pietri (ed.), *L'Urbs: Espace urbain et histoire*, Collection de l'École Française de Rome 98, Roma, 1987, 457–73.
SEDIARI, M. 1997: 'La topografia della Regia IX in età severiana', *BullCom* 98, 1997, 215–48.
WALL, B. 1932: 'Porticus Minuciae', *Acta Instituti Romani Regni Sueciae* 2, 1932, 31–54.
WISEMAN, T.P. 1979: 'Strabo on the Campus Martius: 5.3.8, C235', *Liverpool Classical Monthly* 4.7 (July), 1979, 129–34.

Capitoline Hill (Campidoglio)

BONNEFOND, M. 1987: 'Transferts de functions et mutation idéologique: le Capitole et le Forum d'Auguste', in C. Pietri (ed.), *L'Urbs: Espace urbain et histoire*, Collection de l'École Française de Rome 98, Roma, 1987, 251–78.
CAMPIDOGLIO 1984: *Il Campidoglio all'epoca di Raffaello*, Roma 1984.
COARELLI, F. 1984: 'Iside Capitolina, Clodia e i mercanti di schiavi', in N. Bonacasa and A.D. Vita (ed.), *Alessandria e il mondo ellenistico-romano. Studi in onore di A. Adriani* III, Roma, 1984, 461–75.
COLINI, A.M. 1942: 'Aedes Veiovis inter Arcem et Capitolium', *BullCom* 70, 1942, 5–55.
COLINI, A.M. 1965: 'Il Campidoglio nell'antichità', *Capitolium* 4, 1965, 175–85.
CORBIER, M. 1984: 'L'aerarium militare sur le Capitole', *Cahiers Armées Romaines* 3, 1984, 147–60.
DEGRASSI, A. 1945–46: 'L'edificio dei Fasti Capitolini', *RendPontAcc* 21, 1945–46, 57–104.
FRASCHETTI, A. 1986: 'Costantino e l'abbandono del Campidoglio', in A. Giardina (ed.), *Roma: politica economia paessaggio urbano*, Società romana e impero tardoantico II, Roma/Bari, 1986, 59–98.
KLEINER, F.S. 1992: 'The Trajanic Gateway to the Capitoline sanctuary of Jupiter Optimus Maximus', *Jahrbuch des Deutschen Archäologischen Instituts* 107, 1992, 149–74.
LINTOTT, A.W. 1978: 'The Capitoline Dedications to Jupiter and the Roman People', *ZPE* 30, 1978, 137–44.
MELLOR, R. 1978: 'The Dedications on Capitoline Hill', *Chiron* 8, 319–30.
MUNOZ, A. and COLINI, A.M. 1930: *Campidoglio*, Rome, 1930.
MURA SOMMELLA, A. 1984: 'L'esplorazione per il restauro del Tabularium', *AL* 6, 1984, 159–63.
REUSSER, C. 1983: *Der Fidestempel auf dem Kapitol in Rom und seine Ausstattung*, Roma, 1983.
SOMELLA MURA, A. 1978: 'Roma: Campidoglio e Esquilino', *AL* 1, 1978, 28–9.
TORTORICI, E. 1993: 'La "Terrazza domizianea", *l'aqua Marcia* ed il taglio della sella tra Campidoglio e Quirinale', *BullComm* 95.2, 1993, 7–24.
WISEMAN, T.P. 1978: 'Flavians on the Capitol', *AJAH* 3, 1978, 163–75.

Esquiline Hill

ALBERTONI, M. 1983: 'La necropoli esquilina arcaica e repubblicana', *in Roma Capitale 1870–1911: l'archeologia in Roma tra sterro e scavo*, Roma, 1983, 140–55.
BARBERA, M. and PARIS, R. 1996: *Antiche Stanze: un quartiere di Roma imperiale nella zona di Termini, Roma dicembre 1996–giugno 1997*, Catalogo della mostra, Roma, 1996.
BAUER, H. 1983: 'Porticus Absidata', *RM* 90, 1983, 111–84.
BUZZETTI, C. and COLINI, A.M. 1963–64: 'Il Fagutal e le sue adiacenze nell'epoca antica', *RendPontAcc* 36, 1963–64, 75–91.
COLINI, A.M. 1966: *Ricerche intorno a S. Pietro in Vincole*, MemPontAcc 9.2, 1966.
ERKELL, H. 1990: 'From the Esquiliae to the Esquiline', *Eranos* 88, 1990, 125–37.
FRIDH, A. 1990: 'Esquiliae, Fagutal, and Subura once again', *Eranos* 88, 1990, 139–62.
GUIDOBALDI, F. 1978: *Il complesso archeologico di San Clemente: risultati degli scavi più recenti e riesame dei resti architettonici*, Roma, 1978.
GUIDOBALDI, F. 1992: *San Clemente: gli edifici romani, la basilica paleocristiana e le fasi altomedioevali*, Roma, 1992.

LA ROCCA, E. 1974–75: 'Due tombe dell'Esquilino: alcune novità sul commercio euboica in Italia centrale nell'VIII secolo a.C.', *DialArch* 8, 1974–75, 86–103.
MAGI, F. 1972: *Il calendario dipinto sotto Santa Maria Maggiore*, MemPontAcc 11.1, 1972.
RODRIGUEZ-ALMEIDA, E. 1987: 'Qualche osservazione sulle Esquiline patrizie e il Lacus Orphei', in C. Pietri (ed.), *L'Urbs: Espace urbain et histoire*, Collection de l'École Française de Rome 98, Roma, 1987, 415–28.
THYLANDER, H. 1938: 'Le pretendu Auditorium Maecenatis', *Acta Archaeologica* 9, 1938, 101–126.

Janiculum Hill (Gianicolo)
BELL, M. 1993: 'Mulini ad acqua sul Gianicolo', *AL* 11, 1993, 65–72.
BELL, M. 1994: 'An Imperial Flour Mill on the Janiculum', in *Le ravitaillement en blé de Rome et des centres urbains des débuts de la République jusqu'au Haut Empire*, Roma, 1994, 73–89.
BUREN, A.W. van and STEVENS, G.P. 1933: 'Antiquities of the Janiculum', *MAAR* 11, 1933, 67–79.
CALZINI GYSENS, J. and DUTHOY, F. 1992: 'Nuovi elementi per una cronologia del santuario siriaco del Gianiciolo', *Ostraka* 1, 1992, 133–35.
GAUCKLER, P. 1912: *Le Sanctuaire syrien du Janicule*, Paris, 1912.
GOODHUE, N. 1975: *The Lucus Furrinae and the Syrian Sanctuary on the Janiculum*, Amsterdam, 1975.
STEINBY, E.M. 1996: *Ianiculum-Gianicolo: storia, topografia, monumenti, leggende dall'antichità al rinascimento*, Roma, 1996.

Lateran
CONSALVI, F. 1997: 'Problemi di topografia lateranense', *BullCom* 98, 1997, 111–28.
LIVERANI, P. 1988: 'Le proprietà private nell'area lateranense fino all'età di Constantino', *MEFRA* 100, 1988, 891–915.
LIVERANI, P. 1993: 'Note di topografia lateranense: le strutture di via Amba Aradam', *BullCom* 95, 1993, 143–52.
LIVERANI, P. (ed.) 1998: *Laterano* I. *Scavi sotto la Basilica di S. Giovanni*, Città di Vaticano, 1998.
PELLICCIONI, G. 1973: *Le nuove scoperte sulle origini del Battistero Lateranense*, Roma, 1973.
SANTA MARIA SCRINARI, V. 1983: 'Il Laterano e le fornaci di epoca imperiale', in K. de Fine Licht (ed.), *Città e Architettura nella Roma Imperiale. Atti del seminario del 27 ottobre 1981*, Analecta Romana Instituti Danici Supplement 10, Odense, 1983, 203–18.
SANTA MARIA SCRINARI, V. 1991–97: *Il Laterano Imperiale* I–III, Città di Vaticano, 1991–97.

Oppian Hill
CORDISCHI, L. 1993: 'Nuove acquisizioni su un'area di culto al Colle Oppio', *AL* 11.2, 1993, 39–44.
PANELLA, S. 1987: 'L'organizzazione degli spazi sulle pendici settentrionali del Colle Oppio tra Augusto e i Severi', in C. Pietri (ed.), *L'Urbs: Espace urbain et histoire,* Collection de l'École Française de Rome 98, Roma, 1987, 611–51.

Palatine Hill
AUGENTI, A., MARLETTA, N. and RICCI, G. 1992: 'Roma – Scavo delle pendici Nord del Palatino. Relazione preliminare delle campagne di scavo 1990', *Archeologia Medievale* 19, 1992, 378–408.
AUGENTI, A. 1994: 'Il Palatino nell'alto medioevo', in R. Francovich and G. Noyé (ed.), *La Storia dell'Alto Medioevo italiano (VI–X secolo) alla luce dell'archeologia*, Firenze, 1994, 659–91.
AUGENTI, A. 1996: *Il Palatino nel Medioevo: archeologia e topografia (secoli VI – XIII)*, BullCom Supplementi 4, Roma, 1996.
BALLAND, A. 1984: 'La casa Romuli au Palatin et au Capitole', *Revue des études latines* 62, 1984, 57–80.
BASANOFF, V. 1939: *Pomerium Palatinum*, MemLinc 6.9.1, Roma, 1939.
CAPPELLI, R. 1990: 'Augusto e il culto di Vesta sul Palatino', *BA* 1–2, 1990, 29–33.
CARANDINI, A. 1986: 'Domus e insulae sulla pendice settentrionale del Palatino', *BullCom* 91, 1986, 263–78.
CARANDINI, A. 1990: 'Domus aristocratiche sopra le mura e il pomerio del Palatino', in M. Cristofani (ed.), *La grande Roma dei Tarquini. Palazzo delle esposizioni, Roma 12 giugno–30 settembre 1990*, Catalogo della mostra, Roma, 1990.
CARANDINI, A. 1990: 'Palatino: Campagne di scavo delle pendice settentrionali', *BA* 1–2, 1990, 159–65.
CARANDINI, A. 1992: 'La Mura del Palatino: nuove fonte sulla Roma di età regia', *BA* 16–18, 1992, 1–18.
CARETTONI, G. 1966–67: 'I problemi della zona Augustea del Palatino', *RendPontAcc* 34, 1966–67, 55–75.
CARETTONI, G. 1978: 'Le costruzioni di Augusto e il Tempio di Apollo sul Palatino', *AL* 1, 1978, 72–74.
CASTREN, P. and LILIUS, H. 1970: *Graffiti del Palatino, II: Domus Tiberiana*, Acta Instituti Romani Finlandiae 4, Helsinki, 1970.

CERUTTI, S.M. 1997: 'The location of the houses of Cicero and Clodius and the *Porticus Catuli* on the Palatine Hill in Rome', *AJP* 118, 1997, 417–26.
CORBIER, M. 1992: 'De la Maison d'Hortensius à la *Curia* sur le Palatin', *MEFRA* 104.2, 1992, 871–916.
EVANS, H.B. 1980: 'The Romulean gates of the Palatine', *AJA* 84, 1980, 93–96.
FLORY, M. 1984: '*Sic exempla parantur*: Livia's shrine to *concordia* and the Porticus Liviae', *Historia* 33, 1984, 309–330.
GOLDBERG, S.M. 1998: 'Plautus on the Palatine', *JRS* 88, 1998, 1–20.
HURST, H. 1988: 'Nuovi scavi nell'area di Santa Maria Antiqua', *AL* 9, 1988, 13–17.
IACOPI, I. 1997: *Gli Scavi sul Colle Palatino. Testimonianze e Documenti*, Roma, 1997.
IACOPI, I. 1997: *La decorazione pittorica dell'Aula Isiaca*, Milano, 1997.
IACOPI, I. and TEDONE, G. 1990: 'Palatino: il settizodio severiano', *BA* 1–2, 1990, 149–55.
MICHELS, A.K. 1953: 'The Topography and Interpretation of the Lupercalia', *TAPA* 84, 1953, 35–59.
PENSABENE, P. 1978: 'Roma: saggi di scavo sul tempio della Magna Mater del Palatino', *AL* 1, 1978, 67–71.
PENSABENE, P. 1979: '"Aug" e il tempio della Magna Mater', *AL* 2, 1979, 67–74.
PENSABENE, P. 1980: 'La zona sud-occidentale del Palatino', *AL* 3, 1980, 65–81.
PENSABENE, P. 1981: 'Nuove acquisizione nella zona sud-occidentale del Palatino', *AL* 4, 1981, 101–18.
PENSABENE, P. 1983: 'Quinta campagna di scavo nell'area sud-ovest del Palatino', *AL* 5, 1983, 65–75.
PENSABENE, P. 1984: 'Sesta e settima campagna di scavo nell'area sud-ovest del Palatino', *AL* 6, 1984, 149–58.
PENSABENE, P. 1985: 'Ottava campagna di scavo nell'area sud-ovest del Palatino', *AL* 7, 1985, 149–55.
PENSABENE, P. 1988: 'Scavi nell'area del tempio della Vittoria e del santuario della Magna Mater sul Palatino', *AL* 9, 1988, 54–68.
PENSABENE, P. 1990–91: 'Casa Romuli sul Palatino', *RendPontAcc* 63, 1990–91, 155–62.
PENSABENE, P. COLAZINGARI, O., BORRELLO, L., BATISTELLI, P. and FALZONE, S. 1995: 'L'area sud occidentale del palatino dai primi insediamenti all'età media repubblicana', in N. Christie (ed.), *Settlement and Economy in Italy 1500 BC – AD 1500,* Papers of the Fifth Conference of Italian Archaeology, Oxford, 1995, 455–64.
PISANI SARTORIO, G., CHINI, P. and MANCIOLI, D. 1987: 'Indagini archeologiche nell'area del Settizodio Severiano', *AL* 8, 1987, 57–69.
PUGLISI, S.M. 1951: 'Gli abitatori primitivi del Palatino attraverso le testimonianze archeologiche e le nuove indagini stratigrafiche sul Germalo', *MonAnt* 41, 1951, 1–98 and 101–46.
ROMANELLI, P. 1976: *The Palatine*, Roma, 1976.
ROMANELLI, P. 1963: 'Lo scavo al tempio della Magna Mater sul Palatino e nelle sue adiacenze', *MonAnt* 46, 1963, 201–330.
ROYO, M. 1986: 'Topographie ancienne at fouilles sur la Vigna Barberini', *MEFRA* 98, 1986, 707–66.
ROYO, M. 1987: 'Le quartier republicain du Palatin. Nouvelles hypotheses de localisation', *Revue des études latines* 65, 1987, 89–113.
SENGELIN, T. 1983: *Apollo Palatinus. Die apollinische Prasenz auf dem Palatin in augusteischer Zeit*, Wien, 1983.
SOLIN, H. and ITKONEN-KALIA, M. 1966: *Graffiti del Palatino,* 1. *Paedogogium*, Acta Instituti Romani Finlandiae 3, Helsinki, 1966.
VERBOGEN, J. 1982: 'Contribution à l'étude du *Septizonium*', *Acta Archeologia Lovanensia* 21, 1982, 127–40.
WISEMAN, T.P. 1981: 'The Temple of Victory on the Palatine', *Antiquaries Journal* 61, 1981, 35–52.
WISEMAN, T.P. 1987: 'Josephus on the Palatine', in *Roman Studies Literary and Historical*, Liverpool, 1987, 167–75.
ZANKER, P. 1983: 'Der Apollotempel auf dem Palatin: ausstattung und politische Sinnbezüge nach der Schlacht von Actium', in K. de Fine Licht (ed.), *Città e Architettura nella Roma Imperiale. Atti del seminario del 27 ottobre 1981*, Analecta Romana Instituti Danici Supplement 10, Odense, 1983, 21–40.
ZIEGLER, K. (1949): 'Palatium', *RE* 18.2, 1949, 5–81.

Pincian Hill

HOFFMANN, P. 1967: *Il Monte Pincio e la casina Veladier*, Roma, 1967.
RIEMANN, H. 1950: 'Pincius Mons', *RE* 20, 1950, 1483–1603.

Quirinal Hill

COARELLI, F. 1981: 'La doppia tradizione sulla morte di Romolo e gli auguracula dell'Arx e del Quirinale', in *Gli Etruschi in Roma. Atti dell' incontro di studio in onore di M. Pallottino, Roma 11–13 dicembre 1979*, Roma, 1981, 173–88.
FERDINANDI, S. 1990: 'Ambienti romani presso Piazza della Pilotta', *AL* 10, 1990, 88–94.

MORES, G. Manca di 1982–83: 'Terrecotte architettoniche e problematica topografica. Contributo all'identificazione del tempio di Quirino sul Colle Quirinale', *Annali della Facoltà di lettere e filosofia, Università degli studi di Perugia* 20, 1982–83, 323sgg.

RODRIGUEZ-ALMEIDA, E. 1986: 'Alcune notule topografiche sul Quirinale di epoca domizianea', *BullCom* 91, 1986, 49–60.

SANTANGELO, M. 1941: 'Il Quirinal nell'antichità classica', *MemPontAcc* 3.5, 1941, 77–217.

SANTANGELI VALENZIANI, P. 1991–92: 'Osservazione sul tempio di piazza del Quirinale', *BullCom* 94, 1991–92, 7–16.

TORTORICI, E. 1993: 'La "Terrazza domizianea", *l'aqua Marcia* ed il taglio della sella tra Campidoglio e Quirinale', *BullComm* 95.2, 1993, 7–24.

Tiber (Tevere)

BESNIER, M. 1901: *L'îsle Tibérine dans l'antiquité*, Paris, 1901.

BRUCIA, M.A. 1991: *Tiber Island in Medieval Rome*, Ann Arbor, 1991.

BUREN, A.W. van 1952: 'Pons...Pontes', *RE* 21.2, 1952, 2428–437, 2450–484.

CALDI, A. 1845: *La navigazione del Tevere*, Roma, 1845.

CHINI, P. 1993: 'Latrina romana in Via Garibaldi', *BullCom* 95.2, 1993, 211–15.

COLINI, A.M. 1986: 'Portus Tiberinus', in S. Quilici Gigli (ed.), *Il Tevere e le altri vie d'acque nel Lazio antico: settimo incontro di studio del comitato per l'archeologia laziale*, AL 12, Roma, 1986, 157–97.

COLINI, A.M. and BUZZETTI, C. 1986: 'Aedes Portuni in Portu Tiberino', *BullCom* 91, 1986, 7–30.

DEGRASSI, D. 1987: 'Interventi edilizi sull'Isola Tiberina nel I secolo a.C.', *Athenaeum* 65, 1987, 521–27.

D'ONOFRIO, C. 1970: *Il Tevere e Roma*, Roma, 1970.

D'ONOFRIO, C. 1980: *Il Tevere: l'isola Tiberina, le inondazioni, i molini, i porti, le rive, i muraglioni, i ponti di Roma*, Roma, 1980.

GUARDUCCI, M. 1971: 'L'Isola Tiberina e la sua tradizione ospitaliera', *RendLinc* 26, 1971, 267–81.

LE GALL, I. 1953: *Le Tibre, fleuve de Rome dans l'antiquité*, Paris, 1953.

LE GALL, I. 1953: *Recherches sur le culte du Tibre*, Paris, 1953.

MONTANI, C. 1931: 'L'Isola Sacra', *Capitolium* 7, 1931, 95–104.

QUILICI GIGLI, S. 1986: *Il Tevere e le altri vie d'acque nel Lazio antico: settimo incontro di studio del comitato per l'archeologia laziale*, AL 12, Roma, 1986.

SMITH, S.A. 1877: *The Tiber and its Tributaries*, London, 1877.

Trastevere

PALMER, R.E.A. 1981: 'The topography and social history of Rome's Trastevere: southern sector', *TAPA* 25, 1981, 368–97.

PARMEGIANI, N. and PRONTI, A. 1990: 'Il complesso archeologico sotto la basilica di S. Cecilia in Trastevere', *AL* 10, 1990, 105–11.

SAVAGE, S.M. 1940: 'The Cults of Ancient Trastavere', *MAAR* 17, 1940, 26–56.

Vatican

ALFÖLDI, G. 1990: *Der Obelisk auf dem Petersplatz in Rom*, Heidelberg, 1990.

BUZZETTI, C. 1968: 'Nota sulla Topografia dell'Ager Vaticanus', *Quaderni dell'Istituto della Università di Roma* 5, 1968, 105–11.

CASTAGNOLI, F. 1959–60: 'Il Circo di Nerone in Vaticano', *RendPontAcc* 32, 1959–60, 97–121.

CASTAGNOLI, F. 1992: *Il Vaticano nell'antichità classica*, Roma, 1992.

D'ONOFRIO, C. 1978: *Castel Sant'Angelo e Borgo tra Roma e papato*, Roma, 1978.

D'ONOFRIO, C. 1984: *Castel Sant'Angelo: immagine e storia*, Roma, 1984.

MAGI, F. 1972–73: 'Il Circo Vaticano in base alle più recenti scoperte, il suo obelisco e i suoi "carceres"', *RendPontAcc* 45, 1972–73, 37–73.

Velian Hill

BUZZETTI, C. 1985: 'Velia', *BullCom* 90, 1985, 314–20.

COARELLI, F. 1989: 'L'area tra Velia e Carinae: un Tentativo di ricostruzione topografica', in R. Panella (ed.), *Roma città e foro: questioni di progettazione del centro archeologico monumentale della capitale*, Roma, 1989, 341–47.

COLINI, A.M. 1983: 'Considerazioni su la Velia da Nerone in poi', in K. de Fine Licht (ed.), *Città e Architettura nella Roma Imperiale. Atti del seminario del 27 ottobre 1981*, Analecta Romana Instituti Danici Supplement 10, Odense, 1983, 129–46.

PALOMBI, D. 1997: 'Aedes Deum Penatium in Velia', *RM* 104, 1997, 435–63.

PISANI SARTORIO, G. 1983: 'Una domus sotto il giardino del Pio Istituto Rivaldi sulla Velia', in K. de Fine Licht (ed.), *Città e Architettura nella Roma Imperiale. Atti del seminario del 27 ottobre 1981*, Analecta Romana Instituti Danici Supplement 10, Odense, 1983, 147–68.

TERRENATO, N. 1992: 'Velia and Carinae: some observations on an area of archaic Rome', *Papers of the Fourth Conference of Italian Archaeology*, 3–4, London, 1992, 31–47.

Viminal Hill

BARBERA, M. and PARIS, R. 1996: *Antiche Stanze: un quartiere di Roma imperiale nella zona di Termini, Roma dicembre 1996–giugno 1997*, Catalogo della mostra, Roma, 1996.

CAPRARIIS, F. de 1987–88: 'Topografia archeologica dell'area del Palazzo del Viminale', *BullCom* 92, 1987–88, 109–126.

CAPRARIIS, F. de 1988: 'Le Pendici settentrionali del Viminale ed il settore sud-ovest del Quirinal', *Topografia romana: ricerche e discussioni*, Quaderni dell'Istituto della Università di Roma 10, Firenze, 1988, 17–29.

RAMIERI, A.M. 1980: 'Roma: Regio VI. Via Cimarra: resti di edifici monumentali del I sec. a.C. sulle pendici del Viminale', *Notizie degli scavi*, 1980, 25–49.

10. Individual Monuments

Baths

ANDERSON, J.C. 1985: 'The date of the *thermae Traiani* and the topography of the *Oppius Mons*', *AJA* 89, 1985, 499–509.

ANGELIS D'OSSAT, G. de 1943: *Tecnica costruttiva e impianti delle terme*, Roma, 1943.

AURIGEMMA, S. 1974: *Le Terme di Diocleziano e il Museo Nazionale Romano*, Roma, 1974.

BRÖDNER, E. 1983: *Die römischen Thermen und das antike Badewesen*, Darmstadt, 1983.

BRÖDNER, E. 1989: *Untersuchungen an den Caracallathermen*, Berlin, 1989.

BROISE, H. and SCHEID, J. 1987: *Le balneum des frères arvales. Recherches archeologiques a la Magliana*, Roma, 1987.

BRUNDRETT, N.G.R. and SIMPSON, C.J. 1997: 'Innovation and the Baths of Agrippa', *Athenaeum* 85, 1997, 220–27.

BRUUN, C. 1999: 'Ownership of Baths in Rome: the evidence from lead-pipe installations', in D.E. Johnston and J. Delaine (ed.), *Roman Baths and Bathing*, JRA Supplementary Series 37, Portsmouth RI, 1999, 75–85.

CARETTONI, G. 1972: 'Terme di Settimio Severo e Terme di Massenzio in Palatio', *ArchCl* 24, 1972, 96–104.

CARUSO, G. and CECCHERELLI, A. 1987–88: 'Terme di Tito', *BullCom* 92, 1987–88, 317–23.

CARUSO, L., CECCHERELLI, A., GIUSBERTI, P., MAESTRI, L. and VANNICOLA, C. 1990: 'Scavi alle Terme di Tito', *AL* 10, 1990, 58–67.

CASSATELLA, A. and IACOPI, I. 1991: 'Il balneum presso le Scalae Caci sul Palatino', in M. Lenoir (ed.), *Les thermes romains: Actes de la table ronde organiseé par l'École française de Rome, 11–12 novembre 1988*, Collection de l'École Française de Rome 142, Roma, 1991, 129–38.

CATTALINI, D. and TEDESCHI GRISANTI, G. 1986: 'Trofei di Mario', *BullCom* 91, 1986, 343–49.

DELAINE, J. 1987: 'The "Cella Solearis" of the Baths of Caracalla: a reappraisal', *PBSR* 55, 1987, 147–56.

DELAINE, J. 1988: 'Recent research on Roman baths', *JRA* 1, 1988, 11–31.

DELAINE, J. 1990: 'The *Balneum* of the Arval Brethren', *JRA* 3, 1990, 321–24.

DELAINE, J. 1997: *The Baths of Caracalla: a study in the design, construction, and economics of large-scale building projects in imperial Rome*, JRA Supplementary Series 25, Portsmouth RI, 1997.

FAGAN, G.G. 1999: *Bathing in Public in the Roman World*, Ann Arbor, 1999, (with extensive analysis of the epigraphic evidence, and Appendix 'The Distribution of Non-Imperial Baths in Rome').

FINE LICHT, K. de 1974: *Untersuchungen an den Trajansthermen zu Rom*, Analecta Romana Instituti Danici Supplement 7, København, 1974.

FINE LICHT, K. de *et al.* 1990: *Untersuchungen an den Trajansthermen zu Rom.* II: *Sette Sale*, Roma, 1990.

FOLLETTE, L. La 1985: 'Le Terme Deciane sull'Aventin', *AL* 7, 1985, 139–44.

FOLLETTE, L. La 1994: 'The Baths of Trajan Decius on the Aventine', in L. La Follette *et al.*, *Rome Papers*, JRA Supplementary Series 11, Ann Arbor, 1994, 6–88.

GHINI, G. 1988: 'Le Terme Alessandrine nel Campo Marzio', *MonAnt* 4, 1988, 121–177.

GROS, R. 1987: 'Les thermes dans la Rome antique', *Histoires des Sciences Médicales* 21, 1987, 45–50.

HEINZ, W. 1983: *Römische Thermen: Badewesen und Badeluxus in Römischen Reich*, München, 1983.

HERMANN, J.J. Jr. 1976: 'Observations on the Baths of Maxentius in the Palace', *RM* 8, 1976, 403–24.
HÜLSEN, C. 1910: *Die Thermen des Agrippa in Rom: ein beitrag zur topographie des Marsfeldes in Rom*, Roma, 1910.
LOMBARDI, L. and CORAZZA, A. 1995: *Le Terme di Caracalla*, Roma, 1995.
MANDERSCHEID, H. 1988: '*Quantum aquarum per gradus cum fragore labentium*. Überlegungen zu Wasserversogung und Wasernutzung der Caracallathermen', *Archäologisches Korrespondenzblatt*, 13.3, 1988, 291–99.
MANDERSCHEID, H. 1991: 'La gestione idrica delle terme di Caracalla: alcuni osservazioni', in *Les Thermes Romains. Actes de la table ronde organisée par l'École Française de Rome, 11–12 novembre 1988*, Collection de l'École Française de Rome 142, Roma, 1991, 49–60.
NIELSEN, I. 1990: *Thermae et Balnea: the architecture and cultural history of Roman public baths*, Aarhus, 1990.
PARIBENI, E. 1932: *Le Terme di Diocleziano e il Museo Nazionale Romano*, Roma, 1932.
PETRASSI, L. 1985: 'Terme di Caracalla. Indagini geotecniche', *Lavori e studi di archeologia* 6.2, Roma, 1985, 601–4.
STACCIOLI, R.A. 1961: 'Terme minori e balnea nella documentazione della 'Forma Urbis'', *ArchCl* 13, 1961, 92–102.
TORTORICI, E. 1993: 'Terme Severiane, Terme "Severiane" e Terme Septimianae', *BullCom* 95, 1993, 161–72.
VILUCCHI, S. 1986: 'Le Terme di Costantino sul Quirinale e gli edifici privati di età precedente', *BullCom* 91, 1986, 350–55.

Commemorative Monuments

ADRIANO 2000: *Adriano. Architettura e Progetto*, Milano, 2000.
ARCE, J., MAR, R. and SANCHEZ-PALENCIA, F.-J. 1990: 'Monumento presso l'arco di Tito nel Foro Romano: campagna 1989', *AL* 10, 1990, 43–51.
BAUMER, L.E., HÖLSCHER, T. & WINKLER, L. 1991 'Narrative Systematik und politisches Konzept in den Reliefs der Trajanssäule. Drei Fallstudien', *Jahrbuch des deutschen archäologischen Instituts* 106, 1991, 261–95.
BRILLIANT, R. 1967: *The Arch of Septimius Severus in the Roman Forum*, MAAR 29, Roma, 1967.
CAPRINO, C., COLINI, A.M., GATTI, G., PALLOTTINO, M. and ROMANELLI, P. 1955: *La Colonna di Marco Aurelio*, Roma, 1955.
CASTAGNOLI, F. 1984: 'L'arco di Germanico', *ArchCl* 36, 1984, 329–32.
CICHORIUS, C. 1896–1900: *Die Traianssäule*, Berlin, I–III, Berlin, 1896–1900.
CLARIDGE, A. 1993: 'Hadrian's Column of Trajan', *JRA* 6, 1993, 5–22.
CLARIDGE, A. and COZZA, L. 1985: 'Arco di Settimio Severo', in *Roma: archeologia nel centro I, L'area archeologica centrale*, Roma, 1985, 34–39.
COARELLI, F. 1968: 'La Porta Trionfale e la Via dei Trionfi', *DialArch* 2, 1968, 55–103.
COARELLI, F. 2000: *The Column of Trajan*, Roma, 2000.
COLONNA 1988: *La Colonna Traiana e gli artisti francesi da Luigi XIV a Napoleone I*, Roma, 1988.
COULSTON, J.C.N. 1990: 'Three New Books on Trajan's Column', *JRA* 3, 1990, 290–309.
COULSTON, J.C.N. 1989: 'The value of Trajan's Column as a source for Roman military equipment', in C. van Driel-Murray (ed.), *Roman Military Equipment: the Sources of Evidence. Proceedings of the Fifth Roman Military Equipment Conference*, BAR International Series 476, Oxford, 1989, 31–44.
COULSTON, J.C.N. 1990: 'The architecture and construction scenes on Trajan's Column', in M. Henig, (ed.), *Architecture and Architectural Sculpture in the Roman Empire*, Oxford, 1990, 39–50.
COULSTON, J.C.N. forthcoming: 'Emperor and army on Trajan's Column: a study in composition and propaganda', in A.M. Liberati (ed.), *Traiano. Optimus Princeps*, Roma, forthcoming.
DAVIES, P. 1997: 'The Politics of Perpetuation: Trajan's Column and the art of commemoration', *AJA* 101, 1997, 41–65.
FARINELLA, V. 1981 'La Colonna Traiana: un esempio di lettura verticale', *Prospettiva* 26, 1981, 2–9.
FISCHER, B. 1982–83: 'Monumenta et ara honoris virtutisque causa: evidence of memorials for Roman civic heroes', *BullCom* 88, 1982–83, 51–86.
FLORESCU, F.B. 1969: *Die Traianssäule*, Bucarest & Bonn, 1969.
FROEHNER, W. 1865: *La colonne Trajane*, ed. 2, Paris, 1865.
GAGÉ, J. 1977: '*Fornix Ratumen(sus)*: L'entrée étrusque et la "porta triumphalis" de Rome', in J. Gagé (ed.), *Enquêtes sur les structures sociales et religieuses de la Rome primitive*, Collection Latomus 152, Bruxelles, 1977, 69–90.
GATTI, G. 1945–46: 'La riconstruzione dell'Arco di Augusto al Foro Romano', *RendPontAcc* 21, 1945–46, 105–122.
GAUER, W. 1977: *Untersuchungen zur Trajanssaule, 1: Darstellungsprogramm und kunstlerischen Entwurf*, Berlin, 1977.
GAZDA, E.K. and HAECKL, A.E. 1996: *Images of Empire. Flavian Fragments in Rome and Ann Arbor Rejoined*, Ann Arbor, 1996.
GIULIANO, A. 1955: *Arco di Costantino*, Milano, 1955.
GHEDINI, F. 1986: 'Riflessi della politica domizianea nel rilievi flavi di Palazzo della Cancelleria', *BullCom* 91, 1986, 291–309.

HAMBERG, P.G. 1945: *Studies in Roman Imperial Art, with Special Reference to the State Reliefs of the 2nd Century*, København, 1945.

HANNESTAD, N. 1986: *Roman Art and Imperial Policy*, Aarhus, 1986.

HAYNES, D.E.L. and HIRST, P.E.D. 1939: *Porta Argentariorum*, London, 1939.

KÄHLER, H. 1964: *Das Fünfsaulendenkmal für die Tetrarchen auf dem Forum Romanum*, Berlin, 1964.

KLEINER, F.S. 1988: 'The arch in honour of C. Octavius and the Fathers of Augustus', *Historia* 37.3, 1988, 347–57.

KLEINER, F.S. 1985: *The Arch of Nero in Rome: a study of the Roman honorary arch before and under Nero*, Roma, 1985.

KOEPPEL, G. 1982: 'The Grand Pictorial Tradition of Roman Historical Representation during the Early Empire', *ANRW* II, *Kunste* 12.1, 1982, 507–35.

KOEPPEL, G. 1982: 'Official State Reliefs of the City of Rome in the Imperial Age. A Bibliography', *ANRW* II, *Kunste* 12.1, 1982, 477–506.

KOEPPEL, G.M. 1983: 'Two reliefs from the Arch of Claudius in Rome', *RM* 90, 1983, 103–9.

KOEPPEL, G.M. 1984: 'Die historisches Reliefs der römischen Kaiserzeit II, Stadtrömischer Denkmäler unbekannter Bauzugehörigkeit aus flavischer Zeit', *Bonner Jahrbücher* 184, 1984, 1–65.

KOEPPEL, G.M. 1985: 'Die historisches Reliefs der römischen Kaiserzeit III, Stadtrömischer Denkmäler unbekannter Bauzugehörigkeit aus trajanischer Zeit', *Bonner Jahrbücher* 185, 1985, 143–213.

KOEPPEL, G.M. 1986: 'Die historisches Reliefs der römischen Kaiserzeit IV, Stadtrömischer Denkmäler unbekannter Bauzugehörigkeit aus hadrianischer bis konstantinischer Zeit', *Bonner Jahrbücher* 186, 1986, 1–90.

KOEPPEL, G.M. 1989: 'Die historisches Reliefs der römischen Kaiserzeit VI. Reliefs von bekannten Bauten der augusteischen bis antoninischen Zeit', *Bonner Jahrbücher* 189, 1989, 17–71.

KOEPPEL, G.M. 1990: 'Die historisches Reliefs der römischen Kaiserzeit VII. Der Bogen des Septimius Severus, die Decennalienbasis und der Konstantinsbogen', *Bonner Jahrbücher* 190, 1990, 1–64.

KOEPPEL, G.M. 1991: 'Die historisches Reliefs der römischen Kaiserzeit IX. Der Fries der Trajanssäule in Rom. Teil 1: Der Erste Dakische Krieg, Szenen I–LXXVIII', *Bonner Jahrbücher* 191, 1991, 135–98.

KOEPPEL, G.M. 1992: 'Die historisches Reliefs der römischen Kaiserzeit IX. Der Fries der Trajanssäule in Rom. Teil 2: Der Zweite Dakische Krieg, Szenen LXXIX–CLV', *Bonner Jahrbücher* 192, 1992, 61–122.

LANCASTER, L. 1999: 'Building Trajan's Column', *AJA*, 103, 1999, 419–39.

LA ROCCA, E. 1974: 'Un frammento dell'Arco di Tito al Circo Massimo', *Bollettino dei Musei Comunali di Roma* 21, 1974, 1–5.

LA ROCCA, E. 1987: 'L'adesione senatoriale al "consensus": i modi della propaganda augustea e tiberiana nei monumenti "in circo Flaminio"', in C. Pietri (ed.), *L'Urbs: Espace urbain et histoire,* Collection de l'École Française de Rome 98, Roma, 1987, 397–72.

LA ROCCA, E. 1992: 'Disiecta membra neroniana. L'arco partico di Nerone sul Campidoglio', in T.H. von Heide Froning, T. Hölscher and H. Mielsch (ed.), *Kotinos: Festschrift für E. Simon*, Mainz, 1992, 400–414.

LA ROCCA, E. 1993: 'L'arco di Germanico in Circo Flaminio', *BullCom* 95, 1993, 83–92.

LAUBSCHER, B. 1976: 'Arcus Novus und Arcus Claudii', *Nachrichten von der Akademia der Wissenschaften in Göttingen*, 1976, 64–108.

LEANDER TOUATI, A.M. 1987: *The Great Trajanic Frieze. The Study of a Monument and of the Mechanisms of Message Transmission in Roman Art*, Stockholm, 1987.

LEGA, C. 1989–90: 'Il Colosso di Nerone', *BullCom* 93, 1989–90, 339–378.

LEHMANN HARTLEBEN, K. 1934: 'L'Arco di Tito', *BullCom* 62, 1934, 89–122.

LEHMANN HARTLEBEN, K. 1926: *Die Trajanssaule: ein römisches Kunstwerk zu Beginn der Spätantike* I–II, Berlin/Leipzig, 1926.

LEPPER, F. and FRERE, S. 1988: *Trajan's Column*, Gloucester, 1988.

L'ORANGE, H.P. and GERKAN, A. von 1939: *Der spätantike Bildschmuck des Konstantinsbogen*, Berlin, 1939.

MAGI, F. 1945: *I rilievi Flavi del palazzo della Cancelleria*, Roma, 1945.

MARIA, S. de 1988: *Gli archi onorari di Roma e dell'Italia romana*, Roma, 1988.

MELUCCI VACCARO, A. and MURA SOMMELLA, A. (ed.) 1989: *Marco Aurelio. Storia di un monumento e del suo restauro*, Milano, 1989.

MONTE, M. del, AUSSET, P. & Lefevre, R.A. 1998 'Traces of the colours on Trajan's Column', *Archaeometry* 40, 1998, 403–12.

MORRIS, J. 1952: 'The dating of the column of Marcus Aurelius', *Journal of the Warburg and Courtauld Institute* 15, 1952, 33s–48.

NARDI, R. 1985: 'Arco di Settimio Severo: analisi archeologica e conservativa', in *Roma: archeologia nel centro I; L'area archeologica centrale*, Roma, 1985, 41–55.

NEDERGAARD, E. 1988: 'Nuove indagini sull'Arco di Augusto nel Foro Romano', *AL* 9, 1988, 37–43.

NEDERGAARD, E. 1994–95: 'La collocazione originaria dei *Fasti Captitolini* e gli archi di Augusto nel Foro Romano', *BullCom* 96, 1994–95, 33–70.
PALLOTTINO, W. 1938: 'Il grande fregio di Traiano', *BullCom* 66, 1938, 17–56.
PALLOTTINO, M. 1946: *L'Arco degli Argentarii*, Roma, 1946.
PETERSEN, E., DOMASZEWSKI, A. von and CALDERINI, G. 1896: *Die Marcus-Säule auf der Piazza Colonna in Rom*, Monaco, 1896.
PFANNER, M. 1983: *Der Titusbogen*, Mainz, 1983.
PICARD, G.C. 1957: *Les Trophées Romains. Contribution à l'histoire de l'art triomphal de Rome*, Paris, 1957.
PIETILÄ-CASTRÉN, L. 1987: *Magnificentia Publica. The Victory Monuments of the Roman Generals in the Era of the Punic Wars*, Commentationes Humanarum Litterarum 84, Helsinki, 1987.
RICH, J.W. 1998: 'Augustus' Parthian Honours, the Temple of Mars Ultor and the Arch in the Forum Romanum', *PBSR* 66, 1998, 71–128.
ROCKWELL, P. 1981–83: 'Preliminary study of the carving techniques on the Column of Trajan', *Marmi Antichi*, Studi Miscellenei 26, 1981–83, 101–11.
ROSSI, L. 1971: *Trajan's Column and the Dacian Wars*, London, 1971.
RYBERG, I.S. 1967: *The Panel Reliefs of Marcus Aurelius*, New York, 1967.
SCHEIPER, R. 1982: *Bildpropaganda der römischen Kaiser unter besonderer Berücksichtigung der Traianssäule in Rom und korrespondierender Münzen*, Bonn, 1982.
SETTIS, S., REGINA, A. la and AGOSTI FARINELLA, V. 1988: *La Colonna Traiana*, Turin, 1988.
TARDEM, L. 1991: *The Spoils of Jerusalem on the Arch of Titus: a re-investigation*, Stockholm, 1991.
VOGEL, L. 1973: *The Column of Antoninus Pius*, Cambridge Mass., 1973.
WILSON-JONES, M. 1993: 'One hundred feet and a spiral stair: the problem of designing Trajan's Column', *JRA* 6, 1993, 23–38.
WREDE, H. 1981: 'Der genius populi Romani und das Fünfsaulendenkmal der Tetrarchen auf dem Forum Romanum', *Bonner Jahrb 181, 1981, 111–42.*

Defences

CAMBEDDA, A. and CECCHERELLI, A. 1990: *Le Mura di Aureliano dalla Porta Appia al Bastione Ardeatina*, Roma, 1990.
COATES-STEVENS, R. 1998: 'The walls and aqueducts of Rome in the Early Middle Ages, A.D. 500–1000', *JRS* 88, 1998, 166–178.
COZZA, L. 1986–88: 'Mura Aureliane', *BullCom* 91–92, 1986–88, 137–74.
COZZA, L. 1987: 'Osservazioni sulle Mura Aureliane a Roma', *Analecta Romana Instituti Danici* 16, 1987, 25–53.
COZZA, L. 1989: 'Le Mura Aureliane dalla Porta Flaminia al Tevere', *PBSR* 57, 1989, 1–5.
COZZA, L. 1992: 'Le Mura di Roma, dalla Porta Flaminia alla Pinciana', *Analecta Romana Instituti Danici* 20, 1992, 93–138.
COZZA, L. 1993: 'Le Mura di Roma, dalla Porta Pinciana alla Salaria', *Analecta Romana Instituti Danici* 21, 1993, 81–139.
COZZA, L. 1994: 'Le Mura di Roma dalla Porta Salaria alla Nomentana', *Analecta Romana Instituti Danici* 22, 1994, 61–95.
GJERSTAD, E. 1954: 'The fortifications of early Rome', *Opuscula Romana* 1, 1954, 50–65.
LUGLI, G. 1933: 'Le mura di Servio Tullio e le cosidette mura seviane', *Historia* 7, 3–45.
QUERCIOLI, M. 1982: *Le mura e le porte di Roma*, Roma, 1982.
RICHMOND, I.A. 1927: 'The relation of the Praetorian Camp to Aurelian's Wall of Rome', *PBSR* 10, 1927, 12–22.
RICHMOND, I. 1930: *The City Walls of Imperial Rome*, Oxford, 1930.
SÄFLUND, G. 1932: *Le mura di Roma repubblicana*, Acta Instituti Romani Regni Sueciae I, Lund, 1932.
STACCIOLI, R.A. and LIVERANI, P.G. 1974: *Le Mura Aureliane*, Roma, 1974.
TODD, M. 1978: *The Walls of Rome*, London, 1978.
TODD, M. 1983: 'The Aurelianic wall of Rome and its analogues', in J. Maloney and B. Hobley (ed.), *Roman Urban Defences in the West*, CBA Research Report 51, London, 1983, 58–67.
WISEMAN, T.P. 1998: 'A walk along the rampart', in *Horti Romani*, Bullettino della Commissione Archeologica Comunale di Roma, Supplementi 6, Roma, 1998, 13–22.

Entertainment Buildings

ALFÖLDY, G. 1995 'Eine Bauinschrift aus dem Colosseum', *Zeitschrift für Papyrologie und Epigraphik* 109, 1995, 195–226.

BESTE, H.J. 1999: 'Neue Forschungsergebnisse zu einen Aufzugssystem im Unter geschoss des Kolosseums', *RM* 106, 1999, 249–76.
BIEBER, M. 1961: *The History of the Greek and Roman Theatre*, Princeton, 1961.
BOMGARDNER, D.L. 2000: *The Story of the Roman Amphitheatre*, London, 2000.
BUZZETTI, C. 1989: 'Odeon di Domiziano: nota su alcune vecchie scoperte', *Bollettino della Storia del'Arte* 32, 1989, 27–30.
CARETTONI, G. 1956–58: 'Le gallerie Ipogee del foro romano e i ludi gladiatori forensi', *BullCom* 76, 1956–58, 23–44.
CIANCIO ROSSETTO, P. 1987: 'Circo Massimo: il circo cesariano e l'arco di Tito', *AL* 8, 39–46.
COLAGROSSI, P. 1913: *L'Anfiteatro Flavio*, Firenze, 1913.
COLINI, A.M. 1943: *Stadium Domitiani: ristampa anastatica con aggiornamenti*, Roma, 1943.
COLINI, A.M. and CIANCIO ROSSETTO, P. 1979: 'Il circo Massimo', *AL* 2, 1979, 77–81.
COLINI, A.M. and COZZA, L. 1962: *Ludus Magnus*, Roma, 1962.
COLLI, D. 1997: 'Le campagne de scavo nell'anfiteatro castrense a Roma: nuovi acquisizioni', *BullCom* 98, 1997, 242–82.
COZZO, G. 1971: *The Colosseum, the Flavian Amphitheatre*, Roma, 1971.
FIDENZONI, P. 1970: *Il teatro di Marcello*, Roma, 1970.
FRÉZOULS, E. 1982: 'Histoire architecturale du théâtre romain', *ANRW* 12.1 Künste, Berlin/New York, 1982, 343–441.
FRÉZOULS, E. 1983: 'La Construction du *theatrum lapideum* et son contexte politique', in *Théâtre et spectacles dans l'antiquite. Actes du colloque de Strasbourg 1981*, Leiden, 1983, 193–214.
FUCHS, M. 1982: 'Eine Musengruppe aus dem Pompeius-Theater', *RM* 89, 1982, 69–80.
FUCHS, M. 1987: *Untersuchungen zur Ausstattung römischer Theater*, Mainz, 1987.
GABUCCI, A. (ed.) 1999: *Il Colosseo*, Milano, 1999.
GATTI, G. 1960: 'Dove erano situati il Teatro di Balbo e il Circo Flaminio?', *Capitolium* 35.7, 1960, 3–12.
GOLDBERG, S.M. 1998: 'Plautus on the Palatine', *JRS* 88, 1998, 1–20.
GOLVIN, J.-C. 1988: *L'amphithéâtre romain* I–II, Paris, 1988.
GROS, P. 1987: 'La Fonction symbolique des édifices théâtraux dans le paysage urbain de la Rome augustéenne', in C. Pietri (ed.), *L'Urbs: Espace urbain et histoire*, Collection de l'École Française de Rome 98, Roma, 1987, 319–46.
HÖNLE, A. and HENZE, A. 1981: *Römische Amphitheater und Stadien: Gladiatorenkampfe und Circusspiele*, Feldmeilen, 1981.
HUMPHREY, J.H. 1986: *Roman Circuses: arenas for chariot-racing*, London, 1986. (Review by R.J.A Wilson, *JRS* 77, 1987, 206–10).
LABIANCA, L. and PETRECCA, M. 1986: 'Teatro di Marcello', *BullCom* 91, 1986, 389–94.
ORLANDI, S. 1999: 'Il Colosseo nel V secolo', in W.V. Harris (ed.), *The Transformations of* Urbs Roma *in Late Antiquity*, JRA Supplementary Series 33, Portsmouth RI, 1999, 249–64.
PATERNA, S. 1996: 'Il Circo Vaticano a Roma', *MEFRA* 108.2, 1996, 817–53.
PEARSON, J. 1975: *Il Colosseo*, Milano, 1975.
PRIUILI, S. 1985: 'Epigrafi dell'Anfiteatro Flavio', in *Roma: archeologia nel centro I; L'area archeologica centrale*, Roma, 1985, 138–46.
QUINN-SCHOFIELD, W.K. 1969: 'Sol in the Circus Maximus', in J. Bibauw (ed.), *Hommages à Marcel Renard* II, Collection Latomus 102, Bruxelles, 639–49.
REA, R. 1987–88: 'Anfiteatro Flavio', *BullCom* 92, 1987–88, 323–28.
REA, R. 1996: *Anfiteatro Flavio*, Roma, 1996.
REA, R., GARELLO, F. and OTTAVIANI, L. 1991: 'Gli ipogei dell'Anfiteatro Flavio nell'analisi delle strutture murariae', *Mededelingen van het Nederlands Historisch Instituut te Rome* 50, 1991, 167–72.
REA, R. 1993: 'Il Colosseo e la valle da Teodorico ai Frangipane: note di studio', in L. Paroli and P. Delogu (ed.), *La storia economica di Roma nell'alto medioeve alla luce dei recenti scavi archeologici. Atti del seminario, 2–3 aprile 1992*, Biblioteca di Archeologia Medioevale 10, Firenze, 1993, 71–88.
REGGIANI, A.M. (ed.) 1988: *Anfiteatro Flavio: immagini, testimonianze, spettacoli*, Roma, 1988.
RICHARDSON, L. Jr. 1987: 'A Note on the Architecture of the *Theatrum Pompei* in Rome', *AJA* 91, 1987, 123–26.
ROSETTO, P.C. 1984: 'Le maschere del teatro di Marcello', *BullCom* 88, 1984, 7–50.
SEAR, F.B. 1993: 'The *Scaenae Frons* of the Theatre of Pompey', *AJA* 97, 1993, 687–701.
THUILLIER, J.P. 1987: 'Les cirques romaines', *Echos du Monde Classique* 6, 1987, 93–111.
WELCH, K. 1991: 'Roman amphitheatres revived', *JRA* 4, 1991, 272–81.
WISEMAN, T.P. 1974: 'Circus Flaminius', *PBSR* 42, 1974, 3–26.

Fora

General

COARELLI, F. 1988: *Il Foro Boario: dalle origini alla fine della Repubblica*, Roma, 1988.

CROZZOLYAITE, L. 1981: 'I tre templi del Foro Olitorio', *MemPontAcc* 13, 1981, 3–136.

GROS, P. and ADAM, J.-P. 1986: 'Temple ionique du Forum Boarium. Sondage Sud-est', *BullCom* 91, 1986, 31–34.

LYNGBY, H. 1954: *Beiträge zur Topographie des Forum Boarium Gebietes in Rom*, Acta Instituti Romani Regni Sueciae 8, Lund, 1954.

RUGGIERO, I. 1990: 'La cinta muraria presso il Foro Boario in età arcaica e medio Repubblicana', *AL* 10, 1990, 23–30.

Forum Romanum

AMMERMAN, C. 1965: 'On the origins of the Forum Romanum', *AJA* 94, 1965, 627–45.

AMMERMAN, A.J. 1996: 'The Comitium in Rome from the Beginning', *AJA* 100, 1996, 121–36.

BARTOLI, A. 1963: *Curia Senatus: lo scavo e il restauro*, Roma, 1963.

BAUER, F.A. 1999: 'Das Denkmal der Kaiser Gratian, Valentinian II und Theodosius am Forum Romanum', *RM* 106, 1999, 213–34.

BAUER, H. 1988: 'Basilica Aemilia', in M. Höfter *et al.* (ed.) *Kaiser Augustus und die verlorene Republik. Eine Ausstellung und Katalog im Martin-Gropius-Bau, Berlin 7 Juni-14 August 1988*, Ausstellung und Katalog, Mainz, 1988, 200–12.

BROWN, F.E. 1935: 'The Regia', *MAAR* 12, 1935, 67–88.

BROWN, F.E. 1967: 'New Soundings in the Regia: the evidence for the early Republic', in *Les Origines de la République Romaine,* Fondation Hardt Entretiens sur l'Antiquité Classique 13, Geneva 167, 45–64.

BROWN, F.E. 1974–75: 'La protostoria della Regia', *RendPontAcc* 47, 1974–75, 15–36.

CARAFA, P. 1998: *Comizio di Roma dalle origini all'età di Augusto*, BullCom Supplementi 5, Roma, 1998.

CARANDINI, A. and TERRENATO, N. 1994: 'The Forum of Rome', *Current Archaeology* 139, June/August 1994, 261–65.

CARETTONI, G. 1956–58: 'Le gallerie Ipogee del foro romano e i ludi gladiatori forensi', *BullCom* 76, 1956–58, 23–44.

CARETTONI, G. 1961: 'Il fegio figurato della Basilica Emilia', *Rivista dell'Istituto nazionale d'archeologia e storia dell'arte* 19, 1961, 53–60.

CARETTONI, G. and FABBRINI, L. 1961: 'Esplorazioni sotto la Basilica Giulia al Foro Romano', *RendLinc* 16, 1961, 53–60.

CARNABUCI, E. 1991: 'L'angolo sud-orientale del Foro Romano nel manoscritto inedito di Giacomo Boni', *MemLinc* 9.1.4, 1991, 251–365.

CHIOFFI, L. 1986: *Gli Elogia Augustei del Foro Romano. Aspetti epigrafici e topografici*, Roma, 1986.

COARELLI, F. 1976–77: 'Ara Saturni, Mundus, Senaculum. La parte occidentale del foro in età arcaica', *DialArch* 9–10, 1976–77, 346–77.

COARELLI, F. 1977: 'Comizio dalle origini alla fine della Repubblica', in *Lazio arcaico e mondo greco*, La Parola del Passato 32, 1977, 346–77.

COARELLI, F. 1983: *Il Foro Romano: periodo arcaico*, Roma, 1983.

COARELLI, F. 1985: *Il Foro romano: periodo repubblicano e augusteo*, Roma, 1985.

DEMAN, E.B. van 1922: 'The Sullan Forum', *JRS* 12, 1922, 1–31.

FASELLA, G. 1990: 'Il cosidetto tempio di Giove Statore al Foro Romano: studio preliminare', *Italica* 8, 1990, 135–53.

FLACCOMIO, G., TALAMO, E. and LUPI, L. 1981: *Il "Tempio di Romolo" al Foro Romano*, Roma, 1981.

FUCHS, G. 1956: 'Zur Baugerschichte der Basilica Aemilia in republikanischer Zeit', *RM* 63, 1956, 14–25.

GAGGIOTTI, M. 1985: 'Atrium Regium, Basilica (Aemilia): una insospettata continuità storica e una chiave ideologica per la soluzione del problema dell'origine della basilica', *Analecta Romana Instituti Danici* 14, 1985, 53–80.

GIULIANI, C.F. 1987: 'Il foro romano in età augustea', in F. Coarelli *et al.*, *Roma repubblicana dal 270 a.C. all'età augustea*, Roma, 1987, 23–28.

GIULIANI, C.F. and VERDUCHI, P. 1980: *Foro Romano: l'area centrale*, Firenze, 1980.

GIULIANI, C.F. and VERDUCHI, P. 1987: *L'area centrale del Foro Romano*, 2 vols, Firenze, 1987.

GRANT, M. 1970: *The Roman Forum*, Verona, 1970.

HAFNER, G. 1984: 'Aedes Concordiae et Basilica Opimia', *AA* 1984, 591–96.

HÜLSEN, C. 1905: *Das Forum Romanum: seine Geschichte und seine Denkmaler*, ed. 2, Roma, 1905.

HURST, H. 1988: 'Nuovi scavi nell'area di Santa Maria Antiqua', *AL* 9, 1988, 13–17.

KRAUSE, C. 1976: 'Zur baulischen Gestalt des republikanischen Comitiums', *RM* 83, 1976, 31–69.

LUGLI, G. 1947: *I monumenti minori del Foro Romano*, Roma, 1947.
LUGLI, G. 1970: *The Roman Forum and the Palatine*, Roma, 1970.
MAETZKE, G. 1986: 'Area nord-occidentale del Foro Romano', *BullCom* 91, 1986, 372–80.
MAETZKE, G. 1991: 'La struttura stratigrafica dell'area nord-occidentale del Foro Romano come appare dai recenti interventi di scavo', *Archeologia Medievale* 18, 1991, 43–200.
NICHOLS, F.M. 1877: *The Roman Forum: a topographical study*, London, 1877.
NICHOLS, F.M. 1885: *Notizie dei Rostri del Foro Romano e dei monumenti contigui*, Roma, 1885.
PURCELL, N. 1989: 'Rediscovering the Roman forum', *JRA* 2, 1989, 156–66.
ROHDE, P.P 1971: *Forum Romanum*, København, 1971.
ROMANELLI, P. 1984: 'Ricerche intorno ai monumenti del Niger Lapis al Foro Romano', *MemLinc* 52, 1984, 1–37.
RUGGIERO, E. de 1913: *Il Foro Romano*, Roma, 1913.
SCOTT, R.T. 1988: 'Regia Vesta', *AL* 9, 1988, 18–26.
STEINBY, E.M. 1987: 'Il lato orientale del Foro Romano. Proposte di lettura', *Arctos* 21, 1987, 139–84.
STEINBY, E.M. 1988: 'Il lato orientale del Foro', *AL* 9, 1988, 32–36.
STEINBY, E.M. 1989: *Lacus Iuturnae* I, Roma, 1989.
STRONG, D.E. and WARD-PERKINS, J.B. 1962: 'The Temple of Castor in the Forum Romanum', *PBSR* 30, 1962, 1–30.
WELIN, E. 1953: *Studien zur Topographie des Forum Romanum*, Lund, 1953.
WISEMAN, T.P. 1990: 'The central area of the Roman forum', *JRA* 3, 1990, 245–46.
ZANKER, P. 1972: *Forum Romanum: die Neugestalung durch Augustus*, Tübingen, 1972.
ZANKER, P. 1972: *Il Foro Romano: la sistemazione da Augusto alla tarda antichità*, Roma, 1972.
ZEVI, F. 1991: 'L'atrium regium', *ArchCl* 43, 1991, 475–87.

Imperial Fora

AMICI, C.M. 1991: *Il Foro di Cesare*, Firenze, 1991.
AMICI, C.M. 1982: *Foro di Traiano: Basilica Ulpia e Biblioteche*, Roman, 1982.
ANDERSON, J.C. 1984: *The Historical Topography of the Roman Imperial Fora*, Bruxelles, 1984.
BARROERO, L., CONTI, A., RACHELI, A.M. and SERIO, M. 1983: *Via dei Fori Imperiali: la zona archeologica di Roma*, Roma/Venezia, 1983.
BAUER, H. 1976–77: 'Il Foro Transitorio e il Tempio di Giano', *RendPontAcc* 49, 1976–77, 117–50.
BAUER, H. 1987: 'Nuove ricerche sul Foro di Augusteo', in C. Pietri (ed.), *L'Urbs: Espace urbain et histoire*, Collection de l'École Française de Rome 98, Roma, 1987, 763–70.
BAUER, H. 1988: 'Der Urplan des Forum Transitorium', in H. von Buesing and F. Hiller (ed.), *Bathron: Beitrage zur Architektur und Verwandten Künsten für H. Drerup*, Saarbrucken, 1988, 41–57.
BERTOLDI, M.E. 1962: *Ricerche sulla decorazione architettonica del Foro Traiano*, Roma, 1962.
CASTAGNOLI, F. and COZZA, L. 1956–58: 'L'angolo meridionale del Foro della Pace', *BullCom* 76, 1956–58, 119–42.
COLINI, A.M. 1937: 'Forum Pacis', *BullCom* 65, 1937, 7–40.
CONSENSO IMPERIALE 1995: *I luoghi del consenso imperiale: il Foro di Augusto, il Foro di Traiano* I–II, Roma, 1995.
D'AMBRA, E. 1993: *Private lives, Imperial virtues: the frieze of the Forum Transitorium in Rome*, Princeton, 1993.
FIORANI, G. 1968: 'Problemi architettonici del Foro di Cesare', *Quaderni dell'Istituto della Università di Roma* 5, 1968, 91–103.
FRAZER, A. 1993: 'The Imperial Fora. Their dimensional link', in *Studies F. E. Brown*, 1993, 410–19.
GJERSTAD, E. 1944: 'Die Ursprungsgeschichte der römischen Kaiserfora', *Acta Instituti Romani Regni Sueciae* 10, 1944, 40–71.
HASTRUP, T. 1962: 'Forum Iulium as a manifestation of power', *Analecta Romana Instituti Danici* 2, 1962, 45–61.
LA ROCCA, E. 1998: 'Il Foro di Traiano ed i fori tripartiti', *RM* 105, 1998, 149–73.
LA ROCCA, E., UNGARO, L. & MENEGHINI, R. 1993: *I luoghi del consenso imperiale. Il Foro di Augusto. Il Foro di Traiano,* I–II, Roma, 1993.
MENEGHINI, R. 1989: 'Roma: ricerche nel Foro di Traiano – Basilica Ulpia: un esempio di sopravvivenza di strutture antiche in età medioevale', *Archeologia Medievale* 16, 1989, 541–559.
MENEGHINI, R. 1991: *Il Foro di Nerva*, Roma, 1991.
MENEGHINI, R. 1995: *Il Foro e Mercato di Traiano*, Roma, 1995.
MENEGHINI, R. 1998 'L'architettura del Foro di Traiano attraverso i ritrovamenti archeologici piu' recenti', *RM* 105, 1998, 127–48.

MENEGHINI, R., MESSA, L. and UNGARO, L. 1990: *Il Foro di Traiano*, Roma, 1990.
MENEGHINI, R. 1993: 'Il foro ed i mercati di Traiano nel medioevo attraverso le fonti storiche e d'archivio', *Archeologia Medievale* 20, 1993, 79–120.
MENEGHINI, R. 1998: 'L'architettura del Foro Traiano attraverso i ritrovamenti archeologici più recenti', *RM* 105, 1998, 127–48.
MORSELLI, C. and TORTORICI, E. (ed.) 1989: *Curia Forum Iulium. Forum Transitorium* I–II, Roma, 1989.
PACKER, J.E. 1983: 'A new excavation in Trajan's Forum', *AJA* 87, 1983, 165–72.
PACKER, J.E. 1992: 'Trajan's Forum in 1989', *AJA* 96, 1992, 151–62.
PACKER, J.E. 1994: 'Trajan's Forum again: the Column and the Temple of Trajan in the master plan attributed to Apollodorus(?)', *JRA* 7, 1994, 163–82.
PACKER, J.E. 1997: *The Forum of Trajan: a study of the monuments* I–II, Berkeley, 1997.
PACKER, J.E. 1997: 'Report from Rome: the Imperial Fora, a retrospective', *AJA* 101, 1997, 307–30.
PURCELL, N. 1993: 'Atrium Libertatis', *PBSR* 61, 1993, 125–55.
STUCCI, S. 1989: '*TANTIS VIRIBVS*. L'area della colonna nella concezione generale del Foro di Traiano', *Archeologia Classica* 41, 237–92.
UNGARO, L. & MESSA, L. 1989 'Panelli con rilievi d'armi dal Foro di Traiano: nota preliminare', *Archeologia Classica* 41, 215–36.
URLICH, R.B. 1993: 'Julius Caesar and the creation of the Forum Iulium', *AJA* 97, 1993, 49–80.
VISCIGLIOSI, A. 2000: *I Fori Imerpiali nei disegni d'architettura del primo cinquecento. Richerche sull'architettura e l'urbanista di Roma*, Roma, 2000.
WESTALL, R. 1996: 'The Forum Iulium as representation of Imperator Caesar', *RM* 103, 1996, 83–118.
ZANKER, P. 1970: 'Das Trajansforum als Monument imperialer Selbstdastellung', *AA*, 1970, 499–544.
ZANKER, P. 1972: *Forum Augustum: das Bildprogramm*, Tübingen, 1972.

Gardens

BIANCHI, L. 1993: '*Palatiolum* e *palatium Neronis*: topografia antica del Monte di Santo Spiritu in Roma', *BullCom* 95.2, 1993, 25–46.
BROISE, H. and JOLIVET, V. 1987: 'Recherches sur les jardins de Lucullus', in C. Pietri (ed.), *L'Urbs: Espace urbain et histoire*, Collection de l'École Française de Rome 98, Roma, 1987, 747–61.
BROISE, H. and JOLIVET, V. 1998: 'Il giardino e l'acqua: l'esempio degli horti Lucullani', in M. Cima and E. La Rocca (ed.), *Horti Romani: atti del convegno internazionale, Roma, 4–6 maggio 1995*, Roma, 1998, 189–202.
CASTELLI, M. 1988: 'Venus Heruciona e Venus hortorum Sallustianorum', *BdA* 49, 1988, 53–62.
CIMA, M. and LA ROCCA, E. 1998: *Horti Romani: atti del convegno internazionale, Roma, 4–6 maggio 1995*, Roma, 1998.
CIPRIANI, G. 1982: *Horti Sallustiani*, Roma, 1982.
COLINI, A.M. 1955: 'Horti Spei Veteris, Palatium Sessorianum', *MemPontAcc* 3.8, 1955, 137–77.
GREGORI, G.L. 1987–88: '*Horti sepulchrales* e *cepotaphia* nelle iscrizioni urbane', *BullCom* 92, 1987–88, 175–188.
GRIMAL, P. 1984: *Les jardins romains*, ed. 3, Paris, 1984.
HAUBER, R.C. 1990: 'Zur Topographie der Horti Maecenatis und der Horti Lamiani auf dem Esquilin in Rom', *Kölner Jahrbuch für Vor- und Frühgeschichte* 23, 1990, 11–107.
HAUBER, R.C. 1991: *Horti Romani: Die Horti Maecenatis und die Horti Lamiani auf dem Esquilin*, Köln, 1991.
KASTER, G. 1974: *"Die Garten des Lucullus": Entwicklung und Bedeutung der Bebauung des Pincio-Hugels in Rom*, Dissertation, Technische Universität München, Monaco, 1974.
LLOYD, R.B. 1982: 'Three monumental gardens on the marble plan', *AJA* 86, 1982, 91–100.
TALAMO, E. 1998: 'Gli orti di Sallustio a Porta Collina', in M. Cima and E. La Rocca (ed.), *Horti Romani: atti del convegno internazionale, Roma, 4–6 maggio 1995*, Roma, 1998, 113–69.
TOMEI, M.A. 1992: 'Nota sui giardini antichi del Palatino', *MEFRA* 104.2, 1992, 917–51.
WISEMAN, T.P. 1998: 'A walk along the rampart', in *Horti Romani*, Bullettino della Commissione Archeologica Comunale di Roma, Supplementi 6, Roma, 1998, 13–22.

Imperial Residences

BALL, L.F. 1994: 'A Reappraisal of Nero's *Domus Aurea*', in L. La Follette *et al.*, *Rome Papers*, JRA Supplementary Series 11, Ann Arbor, 1994, 183–254.
BASTET, F.L. 1971: 'Domus Transitoria I', *Bulletin Antieke Beschaving* 46, 1971, 144–71.
BELLWALD, U., CASSATELLI, A., GLUTZ, R., HUGI, H., KRAUSE, C., LOCHER, R., MÖRSCH, G., MONACO, E., SIGEL, B. and STUDER, E. 1985: *Domus Tiberiana. Nuove richerche, studi di restauro*, Zürich, 1985.

BOETHIUS, A. 1960: *The Golden House of Nero: some aspects of Roman architecture*, Ann Arbor, 1960.

CARETTONI, G. F. 1983: *Das Haus des Augustus auf dem Palatin*, Mainz, 1983.

CARETTONI, G. 1988: 'Die Bauten des Augustus auf dem Palatin', in M. Höfter *et al.* (ed.) *Kaiser Augustus und die verlorene Republik. Eine Ausstellung und Katalog im Martin-Gropius-Bau, Berlin 7 Juni–14 August 1988*, Ausstellung und Katalog, Mainz, 1988, 263–72.

CIMA, M. and LA ROCCA, E. (ed.) 1986: *Le tranquille dimore degli dei: la residenza imperiale degli horti Lamiani*, Catalogo della mostra, Roma, 1986.

COLLI, D. 1996: 'Il Palazzo Sessoriano nell'area archeologica di S. Croce in Gerusalemme: ultima sede imperiale a Roma?', *MEFRA* 108.2, 1996, 771–815.

COLLI, D. 1997: 'Le campagne de scavo nell'anfiteatro castrense a Roma: nuovi acquisizioni', *BullCom* 98, 1997, 242–82.

D'ELIA, L. and PERA BURANELLI, S. le 1985: 'Rilievo del peristilio inferiore della Domus Augustea', in *Roma: archeologia nel centro I; L'area archeologica centrale*, Roma, 1985, 176–78.

ESSEN, C.C. van 1954: *La topographie de la Domus Aurea Neronis*, Amsterdam, 1954.

FABBRINI, L. 1982: '*Domus Aurea*: il piano superiore del quartiere orientale', *MemPontAcc* 14, 1982, 5–24.

FABBRINI, L. 1983: '*Domus Aurea*: una nuova lettura planimetrica del palazzo sul colle Oppio', in K. de Fine Licht (ed.), *Città e Architettura nella Roma Imperiale. Atti del seminario del 27 ottobre 1981*, Analecta Romana Instituti Danici Supplement 10, Odense, 1983, 169–86.

FABBRINI, L. 1985–86: 'I corpi edilizi che condizionarono l'attuazione del progetto del palazzo esquilino di Nerone', *RendPontAcc* 58, 1985–86, 129–79.

FINSEN, H. 1962: *Domus Flavia sur le Palatin*, Analecta Romana Instituti Danici Supplement 2, Hafniae, 1962.

FINSEN, H. 1969: *La résidence de Domitien sur le Palatin*, Analecta Romana Instituti Danici Supplement 5, Odense, 1969.

GIBSON, S., DELAINE, J. and CLARIDGE, A. 1994: 'The Triclinium of the Domus Flavia: a new reconstruction', *PBSR* 62, 1994, 67–97.

GIULIANI, C.F. 1977: '*Domus Flavia*: una nuova lettura', *RM* 84, 1977, 91–106.

GIULIANI, C.F. 1982: 'Note sull'architettura delle residenze imperiali dal I al III sec. d.C.', *ANRW* 2.12.1, Berlin/New York, 1982, 233–58.

HEMSOLL, D. 1990: 'The Architecture of Nero's Golden House', in M. Henig (ed.), *Architecture and Architectural Sculpture in the Roman Empire*, Oxford, 1990, 10–38.

HERMANSEN, G. 1975: 'Nero's Porticus', *Grazer Beiträge* 3, 1975, 159–76.

IACOPI, I. 1997: *Gli Scavi sul Colle Palatino. Testimonianze e Documenti*, Roma, 1997.

IACOPI, I., TOMEI, M.A. and MEOGROSSI, P. 1986: 'Complesso Severiano', *BullCom* 91, 1986, 486–98.

IACOPI, I. and TOMEI, M.A. 1988: 'Indagini al complesso Severiano sul Palatino', *AL* 9, 1988, 69–76.

KRAUSE, C. and MÖRSCH, G. 1994: *Domus Tiberiana I: gli scavi*, BA 25–27, Zürich, 1994.

KRAUSE, C. 1985: 'Domus Tiberiana: progetto di studio e di restauro', in *Roma: archeologia nel centro I; L'area archeologica centrale*, Roma, 1985, 158–69.

KRAUSE, C. 1987: 'La Domus Tiberiana e il suo contesto urbano', in C. Pietri (ed.), *L'Urbs: Espace urbain et histoire*, Collection de l'École Française de Rome 98, Roma, 1987, 781–98.

LEHMANN HARTLEBEN, K. and LINDROS, J. 1935: 'Il palazzo degli Orti Sallustiani', *Opuscula Romana* 1, 1935, 197–227.

LEONE, E. 1985: 'Domus Aurea e Meta Sudans', in *Roma: archeologia nel centro I; L'area archeologica centrale*, Roma, 1985, 113–19.

LUCIANI, R. and SPEDUTI, L. 1993: *Domus Aurea Neronis*, Roma, 1993.

LUGLI, G. 1968: *Nero's Golden House and the Trajan Baths*, Roma, 1968.

PAVOLINI, C. and TOMEI, M.A. 1994: 'Iside e Serapide nel Palazzo. Lucerne isiache dalle Domus Tiberiana', in L. La Follette *et al.*, *Rome Papers*, JRA Supplementary Series 11, Ann Arbor, 1994, 89–130.

PENSABENE, P. 1997: 'Elementi architettonici dalla Casa di Augusto sul Palatino', RM 104, 1997, 149–92.

PERRIN, Y. 1987: *La Domus Aurea et l'idéologie neronienne. Le système palatial en orient, en Grece et a Rome*, Leiden, 1987.

PINOT DE VILLECHENON, M.N. 1998: *Domus Aurea. La decorazione pittorica del palazzo neroniano nell'album delle 'Terme di Tito' conservato al Louvre*, Milano, 1998.

PRUCKER, A. and STORZ, S. 1974: 'Beobachtungen im Oktogon der Domus Aurea', *RM* 81, 1974, 323–39.

RESIDENZA DI MASSENZIO 1980: *La Residenza Imperiale di Massenzio: Villa, Circo, Mausoleo*, Roma, 1980.

RICCI, A. (ed.) 1998: *La Villa dei Quintili. Fontiscritti e fonte figurate*, Roma, 1998.

ROYO, M. 1999: *Domus Imperatoriae: topographie, formation et imaginaire des palais imperiaux du Palatin (IIe siècle av. J.-C. – Ier siècle ap. J.-C.)*, Roma, 1999.

SANZIANI MINO, M.R. (ed.) 1998: *La Villa della Farnesina in Palazzo Massimo alle Terme*, Roma, 1998.

SEGALA, E. and SCIORTINO, I. 1999: *Domus Aurea*, Milano, 1999.

TAMM, B. 1968: 'Das Gebiet vor dem Repräsentationspalast des Domitian auf dem Palatin in forschungsgeschichtlicher Beleuchtung', *Opuscula Romana* 6, 1968, 145–91.

TOMEI, M.A. 1986: 'Domus Tiberiana', *BullCom* 91, 1986, 438–70.

VOISIN, J.L. 1987: '"Exoriente sole" (Suétone, *Nér.* 6). D'Alexandrie à la Domus Aurea', in C. Pietri (ed.), *L'Urbs: Espace urbain et histoire*, Collection de l'École Française de Rome 98, Roma, 1987, 509–43.

WARD-PERKINS, J.B. 1956: 'Nero's Golden House', *Antiquity* 30, 1956, 209–19.

WATAGHIN CANTINO, G. 1966: *La Domus Augustana*, Torino, 1966.

WISEMAN, T.P. 1987: 'Josephus on the Palatine', in *Roman Studies Literary and Historical*, Liverpool, 1987, 167–75.

Obelisks

ALFÖLDI, G. 1990: *Der Obelisk auf dem Petersplatz in Rom*, Heidelberg, 1990.

D'ONOFRIO, C. 1965: *Gli obelischi di Roma*, Roma, 1965.

GRATWICK, A.S. forthcoming: 'Pliny, The Obelisk, and Novius Facundus', *JRS*, forthcoming.

GRIMM, A., KESSLER, D. and MEYER, H. 1994: *Der Obelisk des Antinöos*, München, 1994.

IVERSON, E. 1968: *Obelisks in Exile* I: *The obelisks of Rome*, København, 1968.

Temples and Other Religious Structures

ABERSON, M. 1994: *Temples votifs et butin de guerre dans la Rome républicaine*, Roma, 1994.

ADAM, J.-P. 1994: *Le temple de Portunus à Rome*, Roma, 1994.

ANDERSON, J.C. 1982: 'Domitian, the Argiletum and the Temple of Peace', *AJA* 86, 1982, 101–10.

ANGELIS, S. de 1992: *Templum Divi Vespasiani*, Roma, 1992.

BARATTOLO A. 1973: 'Nuove Ricerche sull'architettura del Tempio di Venere e Roma in età adrianea', *RM* 80, 1973, 243–69.

CARCOPINO, J. 1944: *La basilique pythagoricienne de la Porte Majeure*, Paris, 1944.

CASSOLA, F. 1970: 'Livio, il tempio di Giove Feretrio e l'inaccessibilità dei santuari in Roma', *Rivista storica italiana* 82, 1970, 5–31.

CASSOLA, F. 1981: 'I templi di Marte Ultore e i Ludi Martiales', in *Scritti sul mondo antico in memoria di F. Grosso*, Roma, 1981, 99–118.

CASTAGNOLI, F. 1978–80: 'Due disegni inediti di Pirro Ligorio e il tempio del Sole', *RendPontAcc* 51–52, 1978–80, 371–87.

CASTRIOTA, D. 1995: *The Ara Pacis Augustae and the Imagery of Abundance in later Greek and early Roman Imperial Art*, Princeton, 1995.

COARELLI, F. 1965–67: 'Il Tempio di Bellona', *BullCom* 80, 1965–67, 37–72.

COARELLI, F. 1983: 'Il Pantheon, l'apoteosi di Augusto e l'apoteosi di Romolo', in K. de Fine Licht (ed.), *Città e Architettura nella Roma Imperiale. Atti del seminario del 27 ottobre 1981*, Analecta Romana Instituti Danici Supplement 10, Odense, 1983, 41–46.

COARELLI, F., KAJANTO, I. and NYBERG, U. 1981: *L'area sacra di Largo Argentina* I: *topografia e storia*, Roma, 1981.

COLINI, A.M. 1941: *Il Tempio di Apollo*, Roma, 1941.

COLINI, A.M. 1943: *Il Tempio di Veiove: aedes veiovis inter arcem et capitolium*, ed. 2, Roma, 1943.

COLINI, A.M. and BUZZETTI, C. 1986: 'Aedes Portuni in Porto Tiberino', *BullCom* 91, 1986, 7–30.

COLONNA, G. 1981: 'Tarquinio Prisco e il tempio di Giove Capitolino', *La Parola del Passato* 36, 1981, 41–59.

CONTICELLO DE' SPAGNOLIS, M. 1984: *Il Tempio dei Dioscuri nel Circo Flaminio*, Roma, 1984.

CONTICELLO DE' SPAGNOLIS, M. 1986: 'Nuove osservazioni sull'area del Tempio dei Dioscuri in Circo Flaminio', *BullCom* 91, 1986, 91–96.

COZZA, L. (ed.) 1982: *Tempio di Adriano*, Roma, 1982.

CREMA, L. 1962: 'Il pronao del Pantheon', in M. Renard (ed.), *Hommages à Albert Grenier*, Collection Latomus 58, Bruxelles, 1962, 457–61.

DAVIES, P, HEMSOLL, D. and WILSON-JONES, M. 1987: 'The Pantheon: triumph of Rome or triumph of compromise', *Art History* 10.2, 1987, 133–53.

DEMAN, E.B. van 1909: *The Atrium Vestae*, Washington DC, 1909.

ELSNER, J. 1991: 'Cult and Sculpture: sacrifice in the Ara Pacis Augustae', *JRS* 81, 1991, 50–61.
FISHWICK, D. 1992: 'On the temple of Divus Augustus', *Phoenix* 46, 1992, 232–55.
FIECHTER, E.R. 1906: 'Der ionische Tempel am Ponte Rotto', *RM* 21, 1906, 220–79.
FINE LICHT, K. de 1968: *The Rotunda in Rome: a study of Hadrian's Pantheon*, København, 1968.
GIANELLI, G. 1980–81: 'Il tempio di Giunone Moneta e la casa di Marco Manlio Capitolino', *BullCom* 87, 1980–81, 7–36.
GJERSTAD, E. 1962: 'The temple of Saturn in Rome', in M. Renard (ed.), *Hommages à Albert Grenier*, Collection Latomus 63, Bruxelles, 1962, 757–62.
GRAS, M. 1987: 'Le temple de Diane sur l'Aventin', *Revue des études anciennes* 89, 1987, 47–61.
GRONNE, C. 1987: 'Ultime indagini al tempio dei Castori', *AL* 8, 1987, 83–87.
GROS, P. 1976: *Aurea Templa: recherches sur l'architecture religieuse de Rome à l'époque d'Auguste*, Roma, 1976.
GRUBEN, D. and G. 1997: 'Die Türe des Pantheon', *RM* 104, 1997, 3–74.
GRUMMOND, N.T. de 1990: 'Pax Augusta and the Horae on the Ara Pacis Augustae', *AJA* 94, 1990, 663–77.
HOLLIDAY, P. 1990: 'Time, history and ritual on the Ara Pacis Augustae', *Art Bulletin* 72.4 (December), 1990, 542–57.
KAHLER, H. 1937: 'Zum Sonnentempels Aurelians', *RM* 52, 1937, 94–105.
KELLUM, B.A. 1985: 'Sculptural Programs and Propaganda in Augustan Rome. The Temple of Apollo on the Palatine', in R. Winkes (ed.), *The Age of Augustus. Interdisciplinary Conference held at Brown University, April 30–May 2 1982*, Providence, 1985, 169–76.
KLEINER, D.E. 1978: 'The Great Friezes of the Ara Pacis Augustae: Greek sources, Roman derivatives, and Augustan social policy', *MEFRA* 90, 1978, 753–85.
KOCKEL, V. 1983: 'Beobachtungen zum tempel des Mars Ultor und zum Forum des Augustus', *RM* 90, 1983, 421–48.
KOEPPEL, G. 1987: 'Die historischen Reliefs der römischen Kaiserzeit. Ara Pacis Augustae: Teil 1, *Bonner Jahrbücher* 187, 1987, 101–157.
KOEPPEL, G. 1988: 'Die historischen Reliefs der römischen Kaiserzeit. Ara Pacis Augustae: Teil 2, *Bonner Jahrbücher* 188, 1988, 97–106.
KRAUS, T. 1953: *Die Ranken der Ara Pacis*, Berlin, 1953.
LA ROCCA, E. 1983: *Ara Pacis Augustae: in occasione del restauro della fronte orientale*, Roma, 1983.
LA ROCCA, E. 1985: *Amazonomachia: le sculture frontonali del tempio di Apollo Sosiano*, Roma, 1985.
LEFEVRE, E. 1989: *Das Bildprogram des Apollo-Tempels auf dem Palatin*, Constance, 1989.
LISSI CARONNA, E. 1986: *Il Mitreo dei Castra Peregrinorum*, Leiden, 1986.
LUGLI, G. 1950: 'Le temple d'Apollon et les édifices d'Auguste sur le Palatin', *CRAI* 1950, 276–85.
LUSCHI, L. 1984: 'L'iconografia dell'edificio rotondo nella monetazione massenziana e il "tempio del divo Romolo"', *BullCom* 89, 1984, 41–54.
MANACORDA, D. 1990: 'Il tempio di Vulcano in Campo Martio', *DialArch* 3.8, 1990, 35–51.
MARCHETTI-LONGHI, G. 1960: *L'area sacra del Largo Argentina*, Roma, 1960.
MARK, M. and HUTCHINSON, P. 1986: 'On the structure of the Roman Pantheon', *The Art Bulletin* 68, 1986. 24–34.
MARTIN, H.G. 1987: *Römische Tempelkultbilder*, Roma, 1987.
MARTINA, M. 1981: 'Aedes Herculis Musaru', *DialArch* 3, 1981, 49–68.
MARTINEZ-PINNA, J. 1981: 'Evidenza di un tempio di Giove Capitolino a Roma all'inizio del 6 sec. a. C.', *AL* 4, 1981, 249–52
MCDONALD, W.L. 1976: *The Pantheon: Design, Meaning and Progeny*, London, 1976.
MONETI, A. 1990: 'Posizione e aspetti del tempio del Sole di Aureliano a Roma', *Palladio* 6, 1990, 9–23.
MONTAGNA PASQUINUCCI, M. 1973: 'La decorazione architettonica del Tempio del Divo Giulio nel Foro Romano', *MonAnt* 48, 1973, 257–82.
MORETTI, G. 1946: *Ara Pacis Augustae*, Rome, 1946.
MORRICONE MATINI, M.L. 1987: 'Edificio sotto il tempio di Venere e Roma', in *Studi per Laura Breglia* III, Bollettino di Numismatica Supplementi 4, Roma, 1987, 69–83.
MUNOZ, A. 1925: *Il restauro del tempio della Fortuna Virile*, Roma, 1925.
NIEDDU, G. 1986: 'Il portico degli dei Consenti', *BdA* 71, 1986, 37–52.
NIELSEN, I. and ZAHLE, J. 1987: 'The Temple of Castor and Pollux on the Forum Romanum: a preliminary report on the Scandinavian excavations 1983–85, I', *Acta Archaeologica* 56, 1987, 1–29.
NIELSEN, I. and POULSEN, B. 1992: *The Temple of Castor and Pollux* I, Roma, 1992.
PAIS, A.M. 1979: *Il "podium" del Tempio del Divo Adriano in piazzo di Pietra*, Roma, 1979.
PALMER, R.E.A. 1990: 'Cults of Hercules, Apollo Caelispex and Apollo Fortuna in and around the Roman cattle market', *JRA* 3, 1990, 234–44.

PANELLA, S. 1985: 'Scavo nella platea del tempio di Venere e Roma', in *Roma: archeologia nel centro* I; *L'area archeologica centrale*, Roma, 1985, 106–12.
PAVIA, C. 1986: *Roma Mitraica*, Udine, 1986.
PAVIA, C. 1999: *Guida dei Mitrei di Roma Antica*, Roma, 1999.
PEÑA, M.J. 1981: 'La dedicacion y el dedicante del tempio de Jupiter Capitolino', *Faventia* 3.2, 1981, 149–70.
PENSABENE, P. 1984: *Tempio di Saturno: architettura e decorazione*, Roma, 1984.
PENSABENE, P. 1991: 'Il tempio della Vittoria sul Palatino', *BA* 11–12, 1991, 11–54.
PIETRANGELI, C. 1940: 'Il Mitreo del Palazzo dei Musei di Roma,' *BullCom* 68, 1940, 143–73.
RAKOB, F. and HEILMEYER, W.D. 1973: *Der Rundtempel am Tiber in Rom*, Mainz, 1973.
REUSSER, C. 1983: *Der Fidemstempel auf dem Kapitol in Rom und seine Austattung*, Roma, 1983.
ROCKWELL, P. 1989: 'Carving instructions on the Temple of Vespasian', *RendPontAcc* 60, 1989, 53–70.
SIMON, E. 1967: *Ara Pacis Augustae*, Tübingen, 1967.
SIMPSON, C.J. 1991: 'Livia and the Constitution of the Aedes Concordiae', *Historia* 40, 1991, 449–55.
STRONG, D.E. and WARD-PERKINS, J.B. 1962: 'The Temple of Castor in the Forum Romanum', *PBSR* 30, 1962, 1–30.
THOMAS, E. 1997: 'The architectural history of the Pantheon in Rome from Agrippa to Septimius Severus via Hadrian', *Hephaistos* 15, 1997, 163–86.
TOMEI, M.A. 1993: 'Sul Tempio di Giove Statore al Palatino', *MEFRA* 105.2, 1993, 621–59.
TORELLI, M. 1987: 'Culto imperiale e spazi urbani in età flavia', in C. Pietri (ed.), *L'Urbs: Espace urbain et histoire*, Collection de l'École Française de Rome 98, Roma, 1987, 563–82.
TORTORICI, E. 1988: 'Il tempio presso S. Salvatore in Campo, V. Vespignani ed Ermodoro di Salamina', *Topografia romana: ricerche e discussioni*, Quaderni dell'Istituto della Università di Roma 10, Firenze, 1988, 59–75.
VERMASEREN, M.J. and ESSEN, C.C. van 1965: *The Excavations in the Mithraeum of the Church of Santa Prisca in Rome*, Leiden, 1965.
WEINSTOCK, S. 1960: '*Pax* and the "ara Pacis"', *JRS* 50, 1960, 44–58.
WISEMAN, T.P. 1981: 'The Temple of Victory on the Palatine', *Antiquaries Journal* 61, 1981, 35–52.
ZANKER, P. 1983: 'Der Apollotempel auf dem Palatin: ausstattung und politische Sinnbezüge nach der Schlacht von Actium', in K. de Fine Licht (ed.), *Città e Architettura nella Roma Imperiale. Atti del seminario del 27 ottobre 1981*, Analecta Romana Instituti Danici Supplement 10, Odense, 1983, 21–40.
ZEVI, F. 1976: 'L'identificazione del Tempio di Marte', in *Mélanges offerts à Jacques Heurgon. L'Italie préromaine et la Rome républicaine* II, Roma, 1976, 1047–1064.
ZEVI, F. 1997: 'Il tempio dei Lari Permarini, La Roma degli Emilii e il Mondo Greco', *RM* 104, 1997, 81–115.
ZIOLKOWSKI, A. 1986: 'Les temples A et C du Largo Argentina', *MEFRA* 98, 1986, 623–41.
ZIOLKOWSKI, A. 1988: 'Mummius' temple of Hercules Victor and the round temple on the Tiber', *Phoenix* 42, 1988, 309–33.
ZIOLKOWSKI, A. 1989: 'The *Sacra Via* and the Temple of Juppiter Stator', *Opuscula Romana* 17, 1989, 225–39.
ZIOLKOWSKI, A. 1992: *The Temples of Mid-Republican Rome and their Historical and Topographical Context*, Roma, 1992.

Tombs and Catacombs

BEDINI, A. 1988–89: 'Tor de' Cenci (Roma) – Tombe protostoriche', *Notizie degli scavi* 42–43, 1988–89, 221–82.
BETELLI, M. 1997: *Roma, la città prima della città: i tempi di una nascita. La cronologia delle sepolture ad inumazione di Roma e del Lazio nella prima et del ferro*, Studia archeologia 86, Roma, 1997.
BOATWRIGHT, M.T. 1985: 'The "Ara Ditis-Ustrinum of Hadrian" in the Western Campus Martius and other problematic Roman ustrina', *AJA* 89, 1985, 485–97.
BRANDT, O. 1993: 'Recent research on the tomb of Eurysaces', *Opuscula Romana* 19, 1993, 13–7.
BRUTO, M.L., MESSINEO, G. and FRIGGERI, R. 1987–88: 'Tor di Quinto', *BullCom* 92, 1987–88, 477–89.
CANCIANI, F. and HASE, F.-W. von 1979: *La Tomba Bernardini di Palestrina*, Roma, 1979.
CIANCIO ROSSETTO, P. 1973: *Il sepolcro del fornaio M. Virgilio Eurisace a Porta Maggiore*, Roma, 1973.
COARELLI, F. 1968: 'L'Ara di Domizio Enobarbo e la cultura artistica in Roma nel II secolo a.C.', *DialArch* 2, 1968, 302–68.
COARELLI, F. 1972: 'Il sepolcro degli Scipioni', *DialArch* 6, 1972, 36–106.
COARELLI, F. 1984: *Roma sepolta*, Roma, 1984.
EISNER, M. 1979: 'Zur typologie der Mausoleen des Augustus und des Hadrian', *RM* 86, 1979, 319–24.
EISNER, M. 1986: *Zur Typologie der Grabbauten im Suburbium Roms*, RM Supplement 26, Mainz, 1986.
ESBERG, H. von and PANCIERA, S. 1994: *Das Mausoleum des Augustus*, München, 1994.

FERRUA, A. 1991: *The Unknown Catacomb: a unique discovery of early Christain art*, New Lanark, 1991.
GREGORI, G.L. 1987–88: '*Horti sepulchrales* e *cepotaphia* nelle iscrizioni urbane', *BullCom* 92, 1987–88, 175–188.
GRENIER, J. and COARELLI, F. 1986: 'La tombe d'Antinous a Rome', *MEFRA* 98, 1986, 217–53.
HESBERG, H. von and PANCIERA, S. 1994: *Das Mausoleum des Augustus: der Bau und seine Inschriften*, München, 1994.
HIMMELMANN, N. 1975: *Das Hypogaum der Aurelier am Viale Manzoni*, Mainz, 1975.
HOLLOWAY, R.R. 1966: 'The Tomb of Augustus and the Princes of Troy', *AJA* 79, 1966, 171–73.
KRAFT, K. 1967: 'Der Sinn des Mausoleums des Augustus', *Historia* 16, 1967, 189–206.
LA ROCCA, E. 1974–75: 'Due tombe dell'Esquilino: alcune novità sul commercio euboica in Italia centrale nell'VIII secolo a.C.', *DialArch* 8, 1974–75, 86–103.
MANCINELLI, F. 1981: *Catacombs and Basilicas. The Early Christians in Rome,* Firenze, 1981.
MARCELLI, M. 1989: 'Su alcune tombe tardo-antiche di Roma: nota preliminare', *Archeologia Medievale* 16, 1989, 525–40.
MARUCCHI, O. 1933: *Le catacombe romane: opera postuma*, Roma, 1933.
MENEGHINI, R. and SANTANGELI VALENZANI, R. 1993: 'Sepolture intramuranee e paesaggio urbano a Roma tra V e VII secolo', in L. Paroli and P. Delogu (ed.), *La storia economica di Roma nell'alto medioeve alla luce dei recenti scavi archeologici. Atti del seminario, 2–3 Aprile 1992*, Biblioteca di Archeologia Medioevale 10, Firenze, 1993, 89–112.
NESTORI, A. 1993: *Repertorio topografico delle pitture delle catacombe di Roma*, ed. 2, Città del Vaticano, 1993.
OSBORNE, J. 1985: 'The Roman catacombs in the Middle Ages', *PBSR* 53, 1985, 278–328.
PARIS, R. (ed.) 2000: *Via Appia. Il Mausoleo di Cecilia Metella e il Castrum Caetani*, Milano, 2000.
PAVIA, C. 1985: *Roma sotterranea e segreta*, Roma, 1985.
PAVIA, C. 1998: *Guida di Roma sotterranea*, Roma, 1998.
PAVIA, C. 2000: *Guida delle catacombe romane*, Roma, 2000.
PERGOLA, P. 1986: 'Le catacombe romane: miti e realtà (a proposito del cimitero di Domitilla)', in A. Giardina (ed.), *Roma: politica economia paessaggio urbano*, Società romana e impero tardoantico II, Roma/Bari, 1986, 333–50.
PERGOLA, P. 1989: *Guide with Reconstructions of the Roman Catacombs and the Vatican Necropolis*, Roma, 1989.
PIERCE, S.R. 1925: 'The Mausoleum of Hadrian', *JRS* 15, 1925, 75–103.
QUILICI, L. 1989: *Via Appia da Porta Capena ai Colli Albani*, Roma, 1989.
RASCH, J.J. 1998: *Das Mausoleum der Kaiserin Helena in Rom und der 'Tempio della Tosse' in Tivoli*, Spätantike Zentralbauten in Rom und Latium 3, Mainz, 1998.
REA, R. 1993: 'Roma: l'uso funerario della valle del Colosseo tra tardo antico e alto medioevo', *Archeologia Medievale* 20, 1993, 645–58.
REBILLARD, E. 1997: 'L'Église de Rome et le développement des catacombs: a propos de l'origine des cimitières chrétiens', *MEFRA* 109.2, 1997, 741–63.
RICHARD, J.C. 1980: 'Les funérailles des empereurs romains aux premiers siècles de notre ère', *Klio* 62, 1980, 461–71.
STEVENSON, J. 1978: *The Catacombs. Rediscovered Monuments of Early Christianity*, London, 1978.
TESTINI, P. 1966: *Le catacombe e gli antichi cimiteri cristiani in Roma*, Bologna, 1966.
VISMARA, C. 1986: 'I cimiteri ebraici di Roma', in A. Giardina (ed.), *Roma: politica economia paessaggio urbano*, Società romana e impero tardoantico II, Roma/Bari, 1986, 351–92.
WILPERT, G. 1903: *Roma sotterranea: Le pitture delle catacombe romane* I–III, Roma, 1903.

11. *Roma Capitale*

ABOUT, E. 1861: *Roma Contemporanea*, Roma, 1861.
ACCIARESI, P. 1911: *Giuseppe Sacconi e l'opera sua massima*, Roma, 1911.
ANDREOTTI, G., ROLANDO, S. and VILLARI, L. 1990: *Roma. Un Capitale in Europa, 1870–1911*, Firenze, 1990.
ARNAUD, J. 1886: *L'Accademie de San Luc a Rome*, Roma, 1886.
BANCA D'ITALIA 1971: *I cento edifici della Banca D'Italia*, 1971.
BARBIERE 1927: *Per La Grande Roma*, Roma, 1927.
BARUCCI, C. 1984: *Strumente e Cultura del Progetto: Manualistica e letturatura tecnica in Italia 1860–1920*, Roma, 1984.
BASILE, E. 1984: 'Per il mio progetto di Palazzo di Giustizia e per l'arte', in *L'Ingegnieria Civile le Arti Industriale*, 1884.
BELTRAMI, L. 1902: *Per la Difesa di Roma: Il Tevere*, Milano, 1902.
BERNICH, E.: *Didascalia al progetto per l'Aquario a via Nazionale*, Roma.
BIANCHI, V.E. 1897: *Guida di Roma e Dintorni*, Torino, 1897.

BIRINDELLI, M. 1978: *Roma Italiana come fare una capitale e disfare una citta*, Roma, 1978.

BOITO, C. 1893: 'Il monumento nazionale a Vittorio Emanuele', in *Questioni Practiche di Belle Arti*, Milano, 1893.

BOLDI, M.A. 1900: 'La Sistemazione del centro cittadino di Roma', in *Annuale della Societa Ingegneri e Architetti Italiani*, 1900.

BONETTI, A.M. 1896: *Venticinque anni di Roma Capitale d'Italia e suoi precedente*, Roma, 1896.

BOTTAZZI, U. 1931: 'L'architettura del Secolo XIX in Roma', in *Capitolium* III–IV, Roma, 1931.

BUSIRI-VICI, A. 1907: *Roma sparice*, Roma, 1907.

CACCHIATELLI, P. and CLETER, C. 1865: *Le Scienze e le Arti sotto il Pontificato di Pio IX*, Roma, 1865.

CALDERINI, G. 1875: *Michelangelo Buonarroti e l'architettura moderna*, Perugia, 1875.

CALDERINI, G. 1887: *Relazione esplicativa del progetto per il Palazzo di Giustizia in Roma*, Perugia, 1887.

CALDERINI, G. 1890: *Il Palazzo della Giustizia in Roma*, Roma, 1890.

CALDERINI, G. 1892: *Compendio delle lezioni di architettura tecnica date nella regia scuola di applicazione per gli ingegneri di Roma*, Roma, 1892.

CALDERINI, G. 1902: *Progetto per la sistemazione di Piazza Colonna*, Roma, 1902.

CALVO, M. 1882: *Osservazioni intorno alle costruzione ai Prati di Castello*, Roma, 1882.

CALZA, A. 1911: *Roma Moderna 1911*, Milano, 1911.

CALZA, A. 1923: *La Nouva Edilizia di Roma*, Roma, 1923.

CANEVARI, R. 1875: *Studi per la sistemazione del Tevere nel tronco entro Roma*, Roma, 1875.

CAPUTO, R. (ed.) 1980: *La via XX Settembre e le sue transformazioni urbanistiche e l'architettura dei ministri*, Roma, 1980.

CARACCIOLO, A. 1984: *Roma Capitale*, Roma, 1984.

CARBONE, D. 1883: *Piano per lo sviluppo di Roma al Mare*, Roma, 1883.

CARNEVALE, P. 1884: *I progetti per il Palazzo del Parliamento*, Roma, 1884.

CARNEVALE, P. 1885: *La vecchia e la nuova Roma*, Roma, 1885.

CARTOCCI, S. 1982: *Roma Sparita*, Roma, 1982.

CASTAGNOLI, F., CECCHELLI, C., GIOVANNONI, G. and ZOCCA, M. 1958: *Storia di Roma 20: Topografica urbanistica di Roma*, Bologna, 1958.

CATTANI, L. 1954: *Urbanistica Romana, una battaglia liberale in Campidoglio*, Roma, 1954.

CESARE, R. de 1907: *Roma e lo Stato del Papa dal ritorno di Pio IX al XX Settembre*, Roma, 1907.

COLONNA, G.B. 1927: *Roma Neoclassica*, Firenze, 1927.

COMMISSIONE ESAMININATRICE AL CONSIGLIO COMUNALE 1873: *Sul Piano Regolatore di Roma*, Rome, 1873.

COMUNE DI ROMA 1990: *Il Palazzo delle Esposizione*, Catalogo della mostra, Roma, 1990.

CONTI, O.P. 1876: *Sistemazione del Tevere*, Roma, 1876.

CRAWFORD, F.M. 1899: *Ave Roma Immortalis*, London, 1899.

CRISPI, F. 1862: *Roma Capitale d'Italia*, 1862.

CRISPI, F. 1863: *Roma Italiana*, 1863.

CRISPI, F. 1864: *Transferemento della Capitale*, 1864.

CRISPI, F. 1867: *Roma Capitale d'Italia*, 1867.

CRISPI, F. 1870: *Questione di Roma*, 1870.

CUCCIA, G. 1991: *Urbanistica Edilizia Infrastrutture di Roma Capitale 1870–1990*, Roma-Bari, 1991.

DAL MASO, L.B. and VENDITTI, A. 1981: *Rome the picturesque*, Terni, 1981.

D'IDEVILLE, H. 1874: *Les Piedmontois a Rome*, Paris, 1874.

DEMORE, G. 1882: *Il piano Regolatore di Roma e le antichita classiche. Observazione e proposte*, Roma, 1882.

DOSSI, C. 1884: *I Mattoidi al primo concorso per il monumento a Vittorio Emanuele*, Roma, 1884.

FELICE, C. 1904: *Roma Contemporanea*, Roma, 1904.

FEO, V. de 1969: *Roma 1870*, Milano, 1969.

FLERES, U. 1911: *Roma nell 1911*, Roma, 1911.

FLORIDO, G.B. 1931: *Raccolta completa di regolamenti edilizi e di norme di edilita riguardanti la citta di Roma, dal 1864 ad oggi*, Roma, 1931.

FRANCESCANGELI, L (ed.) 1980*: Il risorgimento e l'idealita di Roma Capitale*. I *ministeri e l'arte amministrativa*, Roma, 1980.

FRATICELLI, V. 1982: *Roma 1914–1929*, Roma, 1982.

FREMIOTTI, P. 1928: *Nuovi edifici pubblici nella capitale*, 1928.

FRUTAZ, A.P. (ed.) 1962: *Le Piante di Roma*, I–III, Roma, 1962.

GARLANDA, F. 1902: *La Terza Roma. Lettere di uno Yankee*, Roma, 1902.

GAUNT, W. 1926: *Rome, past and present*, London, 1926.
GIOVENALE, G.B. 1884: *Il Palazzo de Giustizia*, Roma, 1884.
GIOVANNONI, G. 1936: 'Roma Capitale', in *Enciclopedia Italiana* XXIX, Roma, 1936.
GRIMALDI, F. 1887: *Rome après 1870*, Roma, 1887.
GRIMM, H. 1886: *La distruzione di Roma*, Firenze, 1886.
GUEZ, R and PAPA, A. 1970: *Roma Capitale*, Roma, 1970.
GUIDONI, E. 1990: *L'Urbanistica di Roma tra uniti e progetti*, Roma, 1990.
GUTTRY, I. de 1989: *Guida di Roma Moderna dal 1870 ad oggi*, Roma, 1989.
INSOLERA, I. 1962: *Roma moderna, un secolo di storia urbanistica*, Roma, 1962, (revised 1971).
Il progetto fontana per la sistemazione delle strade fra l'Esquilino e il Viminale, Roma, 1872.
JOLLY, H. 1894: *La Rome d'aujourd'hui*, Paris, 1894.
KOSTOF, S. 1973: *The Third Rome; Traffic and Glory 1870–1950*, Berkeley, 1973.
LETAROUILLY, P.M. 1860: *Edifices de Rome Moderne*, Paris, 1860.
LETI, G. 1911: *Roma e lo Stato Pontifico dal 1849–1870*, Piceno, 1911.
LUCCHINI, F. 1987: *L'auditorium e i teatri per Roma (1789–1953)*, Roma, 1987.
LUPANO, M. 1991: *Marcello Piacentini*, Roma, 1991.
MANACORDA, D. and TAMASSIA, R. 1985: *Il piccone del Regime*, Roma, 1985.
MANASSEI, A. 1906: *Il Palazzo delle Assicurazione Generali in Roma e il Leone di San Marco della Facciata*, Roma, 1906.
MARTINELLI, A. 1871: *Roma nuova nell'iconografia delle grande strade e nei prospetti di vari grandi monumenti*, Roma, 1871.
MARTINELLI, A. 1880: *Le strade di Roma e la grande viabilita per concorso governativo*, Roma, 1880.
MASSOTTI, C. 1881: *Monographia della citta di Roma e della campagna romana*, Roma, 1881.
MAZZANTI, F. 1880: *La Roma degli Italiani*, Roma, 1880.
MENGONI, G. 1873: *Piano di sistemazione e ampliamento della citta di Roma*, Roma, 1873.
MISURACA, G. 1899: 'Il Nuovo Palazzo della Banca D'Italia in Roma', in *L'Edilizia Moderna, Anno VIII*, 1899.
MONTET, C.E. 1914: *Les Deux Rome*, Paris, 1914.
MOROLLI, G. 1980: *Arte a Roma dalla capitale all'eta umbertina*, Roma, 1980.
MOROSINI, L. 1928: *Giuseppe Sacconi. La vita e l'opera*, Roma, 1928.
NARCUCCI 1881: *Progetto di una nouva via centrale da collegarsi con la Via Nazionale*, Roma, 1881.
NATOLI, A. 1954: *Il sacco di Roma. La speculazione edilizia in Campidoglio*, Roma, 1954.
NEGRI, E. 1929: 'La scuola Romana degli architetti e l'opera della associazione Artistica fra i cultori di Architettura in Roma', in *Atti del Congresso Nazionale di Studi Romani*, Roma, 1929.
NEGRO, S. 1943: *Seconda Roma (1850–1870)*, Milano, 1943.
NEGRO, S. 1964: *Nuovo album Romano, Fotografia di un secolo*, Vicenza, 1964.
NISCO, A. 1878: *Roma prima e dopo il 1870*, Roma, 1878.
OJETTI, U. 1907: *Il monumento a Vittorio Emanuele in Roma e le sue Avventure,* Roma, 1907.
PALERMO, I. 1990: *Roma, Via Nazionale: una strada per la città (1859–1876)*, in *Storia della Città,* Milano, 1990.
PAOLIS, S. de and RAVAGLIOLI, A. (ed.) 1971: *La Terza Roma*, Roma, 1971.
PERODI, E. 1980: *Roma Italiana 1870 – 1895*, Roma, 1980.
PESCI, U. 1907: *I Primi Anni Di Roma Capitale (1870–1878)*, Firenze, 1907.
PIACENTINI, M. 1908: *Concorso per il progetto del palazzo dell'Esposizione per le feste del 1911 in Roma*, Roma, 1908.
PIACENTINI, M. 1930: *L'Architettura d'oggi*, Roma, 1930.
PIACENTINI, M. 1952: *Le Vicende Edilize di Roma dal 1870 ad oggi*, Roma, 1952.
PIACENTINI, P. 1916: *Piazza Venezia e via Cavour*, Roma, 1916.
PIANCIANI, L. 1873: *Discorso sul Piano Regolatore del 1873*, Roma, 1873.
PIANTONI, G. 1980: *Roma 1911*, Roma, 1980.
PIETRANGELI, F. and NEGRO, S. 1953: *Mostra della fotografia a Roma dal 1840 al 1915*, Roma, 1953.
POLLA, E. 1977: 'La Via XX Settembre a Roma', in *Quaderni dell'Istituto di Storia dell'Architettura*, 1977.
POLLA, E. 1979: *Il Palazzo delle Finanze di Roma Capitale*, Roma, 1979.
QUAGLIA, P. 1882: *100 schizzi dei projetti per il monumento a Vittorio Emanuele*, Roma, 1882.
QUAGLIA, P. 1884: *Il primo concorso del Palazzo di Giustizia*, Napoli, 1884.
RACHELI, A.M. 1979: *Sintesi delle vicende urbanistiche di Roma dal 1870–1911*, Roma, 1979.
RAVAGLIOLI, A. 1981: *Vecchia Roma I, 1850–1900*, Aosta, 1981.
ROMA CAPITALE 1: *Roma Capitale 1870–1911, 1, I Piaceri e i Giorni: la Moda*, Venezia, 1983.

ROMA CAPITALE 2: *Roma Capitale 1870–1911, 2, Frammenti di un scalotto. Giuseppi Primoli, i suoi kakemono e altro*, Venezia, 1984.
ROMA CAPITALE 3: *Roma Capitale 1870–1911, 3, Carozzi Libri e Corredi di Scuderia del Quirinale*, Venezia, 1984.
ROMA CAPITALE 4: *Roma Capitale 1870–1911, 4, Dalla mostra al museo. Dalla Mostra del 1911 al Museo della civiltà romana*, Venezia, 1984.
ROMA CAPITALE 5: *Roma Capitale 1870–1911, 5, La Biblioteca di un collezionista*, Venezia, 1984.
ROMA CAPITALE 6: *Roma Capitale 1870–1911, 6, Crepereia Tryphaena*, Venezia, 1984.
ROMA CAPITALE 7: *Roma Capitale 1870–1911, 7, L'Archeologia tra sterro e scavo*, Venezia, 1984.
ROMA CAPITALE 8: *Roma Capitale 1870–1911, 8, La nostra arca di noe*, Venezia, 1984.
ROMA CAPITALE 9: *Roma Capitale 1870–1911, 9, Una citta di pagina in pagina*, Venezia, 1984.
ROMA CAPITALE 10: *Roma Capitale 1870–1911, 10, La cultura scientifica a Roma*, Venezia, 1984.
ROMA CAPITALE 11: *Roma Capitale 1870–1911, 11, Dagli scavi al museo*, Venezia, 1984.
ROMA CAPITALE 12: *Roma Capitale 1870–1911, 12, Architettura e Urbanistica, Uso e transformazione della citta storica,* Venezia, 1984.
ROMA CAPITALE 13: *Roma Capitale 1870–1911, 13, I Ministeri di Roma Capitale*, Venezia, 1984.
ROSSI, R. 1908: *Palazzo di Guistizia*, Roma, 1908.
SACHERI, G. 1901: *La sistemazione del Tevere Urbano*, Turino, 1901.
SANJUST DI TEULADA, E. 1908: *Piano regulatore della citta di Roma*, Roma, 1908.
SANFILIPPO, M. 1992: *La costruzione di una Capitale: Roma 1870–1911*, Milano, 1992.
SAPORI, F. 1953: *L'architettura di Roma 1901–1950*, Roma, 1953.
SCHIAVO, A. 1981: *Villa Ludovisi e Palazzo Margherita*, Roma, 1981.
SETTA, P. and R. della 1988: *I Suoli di Roma*, Roma, 1988.
SIMONI, L. de 1975: *Roma Capitale. I Primi Anni di Vita*, Roma, 1975.
SPAGNESI, G. 1974: *Edilizia romana nella seconda meta del XIX secolo (1848–1905)*, Roma, 1974.
SPAGNESI, G. 1978: *L'architettura a Roma al tempo di Pio IX*, Roma, 1978.
SPERA, G. 1907: *Roma nel 1911 e i festeggiamenti per il anniversario della sua proclamazione a capitale d'Italia*, Roma, 1907.
SPIELMANN, I. (ed.) 1913: *International Fine Arts Exhibition in Rome 1911. Souvenir of the British section*, London, 1913.
STRAPPA, G. 1989: Tradizione e innovazione nell'architettura di Roma capitale (1870–1930), Roma, 1989.
TORRE, P. della 1946: *L'Opera riformazione e amministrativa di Pio IX tra il 1850 ed il 1870*, Rome 1946.
TOSCHI, L. 1983: *Edilizia e populare nello sviluppo urbanistico di Roma moderna (1870–1903)*, Roma, 1983.
TUPPATI, C. 1970: *Roma Capitale, Documenti* II, Roma, 1970.
VESCOVALI, A. 1875: *Piano d'esecuzione pei lavori di sistemazione del tronco urbano del Tevere*, Roma, 1875.
VIGNOLA, G.B. 1861: I *Cinque Ordini di Architettura Civile (secundo edizione Romano)*, Roma, 1861.
VITTORIANO 1988: *Il Vittoriano* I–II, Roma 1988.
ZOLA, E. 1896: *Roma*, Paris, 1896.

Index